The Student Writer

EDITOR AND CRITIC

EIGHTH EDITION

BARBARA FINE CLOUSE

Boston Burr Ridge, IL Dubuque, IA New York San Francisco St. Louis
Bangkok Bogotá Caracas Kuala Lumpur Lisbon London Madrid Mexico City
Milan Montreal New Delhi Santiago Seoul Singapore Sydney Taipei Toronto

Published by McGraw-Hill, an imprint of The McGraw-Hill Companies, Inc., 1221 Avenue of the Americas, New York, NY 10020.

This book is printed on acid-free paper.

4 5 6 7 8 9 0 DOC/DOC 1 5 4 3 2 1

ISBN: 978-0-07-338380-4
MHID: 0-07-338380-5

Editor in Chief: *Michael Ryan*
Publisher: *David Patterson*
Sponsoring Editor: *Christopher Bennem*
Marketing Manager: *Allison Jones*
Director of Development: *Dawn Groundwater*
Production Editor: *Regina Ernst*
Manuscript Editor: *Thomas Briggs*
Design Manager: *Ashley Bedell*
Photo Researcher: *Toni Michaels, PhotoFind, LLC*
Production Supervisor: *Louis Swaim*
Composition: *10/12 Palatino by Aptara®, Inc.*
Printing: *45# New Era Matt Plus, R. R. Donnelley & Sons/Crawfordsville, IN*

Cover: 2006 Getty

Credits: The credits section for this book begins on page 675 and is considered an extension of the copyright page.

Library of Congress Cataloging-in-Publication Data

Clouse, Barbara Fine.
The student writer : editor and critic / Barbara Fine Clouse.—8th ed.
p. cm.
Includes bibliographical references and indexes.
ISBN-13: 978-0-07-338380-4 (alk. paper)
ISBN-10: 0-07-338380-5 (alk. paper)
1. English language—Rhetoric. 2. Report writing. 3. Criticism. 4. Editing. I. Title.
PE1408.C537 2009
808′.042—dc22 2009021190

The Internet addresses listed in the text were accurate at the time of publication. The inclusion of a Web site does not indicate an endorsement by the authors or McGraw-Hill, and McGraw-Hill does not guarantee the accuracy of the information presented at these sites.

www.mhhe.com

For Greg, Karen, Violet, Jeffrey, and Crysta Clouse
and
In loving memory of Faye Thomas Clouse

BRIEF CONTENTS

CONTENTS

PART 2 PATTERNS OF DEVELOPMENT 141

CHAPTER 11

Cause-and-Effect Analysis 303

CHAPTER 12

Definition 333

PART 4 A BRIEF GUIDE TO SENTENCE ERRORS 561

THEMATIC TABLE OF CONTENTS

Education

Family Life

Human Nature

*Student Essay
**Student Essay with Research

Interpersonal Relationships

Multicultural Experiences

Places

Political Issues

Popular Culture

Memorable Experiences

Science and Health

Sports

Stages of Life

Work

PREFACE

This eighth edition of *The Student Writer: Editor and Critic* strengthens the text's commitment to helping students become better writers by helping them develop their own successful writing processes and become reliable critics and editors of their own texts. It also maintains the text's commitment to demonstrating the importance of writing across the curriculum, in the workplace, and in students' private lives.

FEATURES

A number of features distinguish *The Student Writer: Editor and Critic* and help it fulfill its goals. Many of these features have been suggested by students and teachers who have used the text in its previous seven editions.

An Emphasis on the Connection between Reading and Writing

- Chapter 1 explains and illustrates strategies for reading analytically.
- To help students succeed in all their college classes, Chapter 1 teaches strategies for writing in response to reading, including writing personal reactions, summarizing, and evaluating ideas.
- Throughout the text, students have many opportunities to write in response to essays.

An Integrated Focus on the Student's Writing Process

- Process guidelines offer extensive support at every stage of the writing process. Students learn a variety of strategies—including strategies for writing at the computer—for selecting topics, identifying audience and purpose, generating ideas, and rewriting. They are encouraged to sample some or all of them as they work to improve their writing processes. Additionally, the process guidelines include suggestions for securing feedback from reliable readers.
- In Part 1, a student essay in progress—presented with commentary—illustrates the writing process.

- "Being a Responsible Writer" sections discuss ethical concerns associated with writing in the patterns of development. Many of these sections include help in avoiding plagiarism.

An Emphasis on Revision

- "Think like a Critic; Work like an Editor" sections teach strategies for evaluating drafts (to help students think like a critic) and for making changes (to help students work like an editor). These sections help students understand the importance of revision, and they offer specific tools for revising.
- Some of the "Think like a Critic; Work like an Editor" sections provide a close-up look at how student writers whose essays appear in the book critically evaluated sections of their drafts and acted as editors to revise in response to their evaluations.
- To help students evaluate their drafts (that is, to help them become reliable critics) and to help them revise accordingly, "Process Guidelines" offer a variety of revising strategies.
- Guidelines for giving and receiving reliable feedback on their drafts help students build reader response into their revision processes. In addition, the "Process Guidelines" accompanying writing assignments include suggestions for securing peer response.

An Emphasis on Writing Purposes

- Writing is presented as a purposeful activity that helps people share feelings and experiences, inform, and persuade; the patterns of development are discussed as strategies that can be used individually and in combination to help writers fulfill their purposes for writing.
- "Occasions for Writing" sections help students see how they can use writing to achieve a variety of purposes in and out of the classroom. These sections also demonstrate how the rhetorical patterns can be used across the disciplines, in the workplace, and in students' personal lives.
- "Beyond the Writing Classroom" assignments help students see the purpose of writing outside of the composition class.

An Emphasis on Combining the Patterns of Development

- In each chapter devoted to a pattern, students learn how to combine the pattern with other patterns to help them achieve their purposes for writing.
- In each chapter devoted to a pattern, one or more professional essays illustrate how to combine patterns.
- Chapter 14, "Combining Patterns of Development," explains strategies for combining patterns and offers student and professional essays as examples of combining patterns to achieve a range of purposes.

A Focus on Visual Material

- Chapter 1 helps students become critical readers of visual texts. The chapter explains the components of images and shows students how to analyze and evaluate images.
- "Looking Ahead" images with related writing prompts help preview chapter contents.
- Each chapter discussing a pattern of development includes a graph, photograph, cartoon, or advertisement that incorporates the pattern. Study questions help students understand what the patterns of development contribute to the image and encourage students to consider the image critically.
- Graphic representations of the patterns, found in sections titled "Visualizing a [Name of Pattern] Essay," enhance text discussions of the patterns of development and provide important support for visual learners.
- A full-color casebook of advertisements, news photographs, cartoons, and diagrams helps students learn about visual argument.
- A smart, attractive design includes images throughout that enhance and reinforce the material.

A Rich Variety of Opportunities for Reading and Writing

- More than 60 student and professional essays—most at about the length instructors require of their students—offer models for writing and ideas for essays. One-fourth of the essays are new.
- *The Student Writer* has more student essays than most similar rhetorics. Reviewers consistently praised the student essays, calling them "empowering" because they are high-quality examples that represent attainable goals.
- One student essay in each pattern-of-development chapter is annotated as a study aid. The other student essays and all the professional essays are accompanied by study questions.
- In addition to the student research paper, three other student essays draw on sources.
- Many of the professional essays demonstrate how to combine patterns to achieve various purposes for writing.
- Each chapter on a pattern of development includes a generous number of writing topics, including:
  - Several topics that require students to write in the pattern
  - Several topics that require students to respond to a theme evident in the readings
  - One topic that requires a response to visual material
  - One topic that is either cross-disciplinary or otherwise related to concerns outside the writing classroom
- Each professional essay is followed by a topic that students can discuss in class or write about in their journals.

Substantial Coverage of Argument

- A focus on issues and claims helps students write sound thesis statements for argumentation.
- A detailed discussion of kinds of persuasive purposes helps students establish reasonable goals for their argument papers.
- A detailed discussion of kinds of audiences helps students gear their supporting details to the level of resistance their claim is likely to meet.
- Explanations of logical, emotional, and ethical appeals and combining patterns of development help students address their audiences and argue their claims effectively.
- A full-color casebook of images—advertisements, news photographs, cartoons, and diagrams—teaches how arguments can be made in visual form.
- Three student essays, one that includes source material, illustrate effective argumentation.
- Process guidelines help students move from idea generation through proofreading.

Substantial Coverage of Research

- A new "Using Sources for a Purpose" feature in each rhetorical pattern chapter illustrates how students can quote, paraphrase, and summarize material from readings in *The Student Writer* to support ideas in their own essays. These features include "Myths about Sources" sections that address common misconceptions about using source material and "Avoiding Plagiarism" sections that help students avoid common pitfalls.
- Research writing is covered in two chapters: Chapter 16, "Conducting Research," and Chapter 17, "Writing with Sources and Using Proper Documentation." These chapters feature:
  - Coverage of MLA style—that reflects the updated guidelines—and coverage of APA style
  - Coverage of using the Internet to conduct research and of evaluating Internet sources
  - Full-color annotated screenshots showing examples of library computer catalogs, periodical databases, and online search engines
  - Comprehensive coverage of plagiarism, including online plagiarism
  - Full-color annotated MLA works-cited entry models with accompanying images of source material, showing students where to find citation information in a source
  - Color-coded models accompanying every MLA and APA citation entry
  - Discussion of using sources in a brief essay to support the student's ideas and of using sources as the primary detail in a traditional research paper
  - A thorough explanation of the research process
  - Information on field research
  - A discussion of how to read sources strategically
  - An annotated student research paper on genetically modified food

Coverage of Portfolios, Essay Examinations, and Writing about Literature

- Chapter 18 explains the purposes of and requirements for a writing portfolio, including the self-reflection essay.
- Chapter 18 includes process guidelines for writing essay examination answers, strategies for reducing anxiety about test-taking, and a sample answer for study.
- Chapter 19 explains how to write about literature. It includes instruction in reading and writing about literature, an annotated student essay in response to a poem, and a short story and poem with accompanying writing topics.

A Focus on Improving Style and Correcting Sentence-Level Errors

- "Style Notes" and other special notes point out features of style, organization, punctuation, and diction evident in the readings.
- Part 4, "A Brief Guide to Sentence Errors," is a ready reference for correcting sentence-level errors. It includes succinct explanations, exercises, and "ESL Notes" for students who use English as a second language.
- An appendix on the parts of speech supplements the explanations of grammar and usage in "A Brief Guide to Sentence Errors."

New to the Eighth Edition

- New, more analytic student and professional essays on high-interest topics, including video games, torture warrants, e-mail communication between students and professors, and public displays of anger, energize this edition.
- Several new, interesting images increase the visual appeal and offer a new focus for writing topics.
- Expanded discussions of audience, purpose, thesis development, order of details, introductions, conclusions, and body paragraphs are even more helpful to students.
- "Using Sources for a Purpose" sections in each pattern-of-development chapter demonstrate how students can paraphrase, quote, and summarize from the readings in the book to support ideas in their own essays.
- "Avoiding Plagiarism" sections in each pattern-of-development chapter explain how to avoid unintentional plagiarism.
- "Myths about Sources" in each pattern-of-development chapter dispel common misconceptions students have about using sources.
- Thoroughly revised coverage of research conforms to new MLA guidelines and gives special attention to electronic research and online citations.
- Tighter prose and screened displays to highlight material provide more focused presentation of material.
- Coverage of agreement with plural indefinite pronouns has been added.

Supplements

- An Instructor's Manual provides strong support for instructors, including chapter goals, classroom activities, suggestions for using the computer in the classroom, journal prompts, and an answer key.
- A comprehensive website <www.mhhe.com/tsw> features all the resources of Catalyst 2.0, McGraw-Hill's state-of-the-art online writing and research tool. Catalyst 2.0 offers course management and peer review tools, interactive tutorials, diagnostic tests, and thousands of electronic grammar exercises and activities. Boxes in the margins of *The Student Writer* direct students to these online resources.

ACKNOWLEDGMENTS

I am indebted to the English team at McGraw-Hill, an exceptionally smart, energetic group dedicated to developing the highest-quality textbooks. I am particularly grateful to Christopher Bennem, the immensely capable sponsoring editor of *The Student Writer,* whose faith in the book made the expanded, four-color edition possible. In the previous edition, development editor Joshua Feldman contributed immeasurably; in this edition, director of development Dawn Groundwater took over to keep everything moving on a very tight schedule. I also thank Regina Ernst, the project manager who steered the manuscript through all the twists and turns of production and copyeditor Thomas Briggs. To Meg Botteon, I extend my gratitude and sincere admiration for the exceptional contributions to the instructor's manual and for her other contributions. Laura Olson and Carol Newell are responsible for much in the excellent new research chapters. Their work and knowledge are exceptional.

I am also indebted to the following reviewers, whose sound counsel informs this revision. I very much appreciate the gift of their time and expertise:

Craig Albin, *Southwest Missouri State University–West Plains*
Michael S. Allen, *North Central State College*
Gwen Barclay-Toy, *Durham Technical Community College*
Dana Barnett, *Midwestern State University*
Winfred Bridges, *Arkansas State University*
Ludger Brinker, *Macomb Community College*
N. Ann Chenoweth, *University of Texas–Pan American*
Bill Church, *Missouri Western State College*
Doris M. Colter, *Henry Ford Community College*
James Cornish, *McLennan Community College*
Steve Crow, *St. Cloud State University*
Frederic Giacobazzi, *Kirtland Community College*
Sherry Gott, *Danville Community College*
Anita G. Gorman, *Slippery Rock University*
Kathy Henning, *Gateway Technical College*
Vicki M. Houser, *Northeast State Technical College*
Kevan B. Jenner, *Mississippi Gulf Coast Community College*

Lori Kanitz, *Oral Roberts University*
Bonni Miller, *University of Maryland Eastern Shore*
Jason Murray, *Bacone College*
Mary Anne Nagler, *Oakland Community College–Southfield*
Sally Nielsen, *Florida Community College*
Mary Alice Palm, *Schoolcraft College*
Drue Parker, *Collin County Community College*
Edwin Sapp, *Prince George's Community College*
Carsten Schmidtke, *Oklahoma State University–Okmulgee*
James Schwartz, *Wright State University*
Cathryn Smith, *Monroe Community College*
Samantha Streamer Veneruso, *Montgomery College*
Barbara Vielma, *University of Texas–Pan American*
Kate Waites, *Nova Southeastern University*
Cynthia Walker, *Faulkner University*

As always, I owe profound gratitude to my husband, Dennis, for his abiding support, patience, and understanding.

Barbara Fine Clouse

GUIDED TOUR

Part 1 of *The Student Writer* introduces you to strategies for critical reading and to the stages of the writing process. **Part 2** provides chapters on the patterns of development, and **Part 3** shows you how to use the patterns in argument, in research papers, in literary analyses, and more. **Part 4** is a guide to correcting errors in grammar, punctuation, and mechanics.

BRIEF CONTENTS

v

LOOKING AHEAD

Earlier chapters of this book focus on *what* you say—on the ideas you include in your essays, on how you discover those ideas, on how you develop them, and on how you arrange them. However, it's not just what you say that matters. *How* you say it is also important, so this chapter focuses on the expression of ideas. To look ahead and consider the importance of the way we express ourselves, consider the campaign poster here. The poster aims to convey the idea that Barack Obama offers something different from the politics of the past and that the change offered was the kind that people could trust to be an improvement. But the poster does not say, "Barack Obama offers a break from the politics of the past in order to bring change people can trust to be an improvement." Instead, it expresses the ideas more effectively by saying simply, "Change we can believe in." Politicians understand that it is not just what you say that counts; it's how you say it. Advertisers understand that fact as well. So do good writers.

To consider the importance of effective expression, list 10 or so phrases, sentences, or expressions from advertisements, political speeches (such as the Gettysburg Address), and important documents (such as the Declaration of Independence) that have staying power because they are so well expressed.

Looking Ahead sections begin every chapter in Parts 1, 2, and 3. These images with accompanying questions will help stimulate your thinking as you begin the new chapter and give you an opportunity to practice your visual analysis skills.

The sun was a bright red ball that rolled along the horizon as we turned to head back. It gave an orange glow to the hazy horizon, and orange tinted fog drifted below a light violet sky. It was a display that could only be witnessed from the air. The earth slowly rotated, and the great fireball lowered beneath the land. 8

Gene gave the signal that we were on our final approach for landing. I watched the ground as it rose to our level. As the craft leveled after its shallow dive, my stomach dropped. The effect of that small G-force was my last taste of flight. We were back on solid ground. 9

I have flown many times since then, and I always get the same rush of freedom and thrill from the perspective that being airborne provides. Flying intrigued me before I ever left the ground. Once I did, I was hooked. 10

EXERCISE Considering "My First Flight"

1. What is Jerry Silberman describing, and what is his dominant impression?
2. Cite one paragraph that includes objective description, one that includes subjective description, and one that includes both.
3. Cite two concrete sensory details that you find effective. What makes them effective?
4. What is Jerry Silberman's purpose for writing? How does the description help him achieve that purpose? How does the narration help him achieve that purpose? ■

THINK LIKE A CRITIC; WORK LIKE AN EDITOR:
The Student Writer at Work

Writing description often involves a series of revisions to get the images just right. Here, for example, is the first draft of one of Jerry Silberman's more descriptive paragraphs, followed by his first two revisions. The changes are noted in color, with underlining to mark additions, and strikeovers to mark deletions. Notice that with this revision, Jerry added descriptive details and used more specific word choice.

158 **Part 2** Patterns of Development

Written with the kind of supportive tone often found in a writing workshop, *The Student Writer* puts you in control of your own writing process. Each chapter in Part 2 ends with **"Process Guidelines"** that will help you at every stage of the writing process. **"Think like a Critic; Work like an Editor"** sections help you to look critically at your own drafts and revise them effectively.

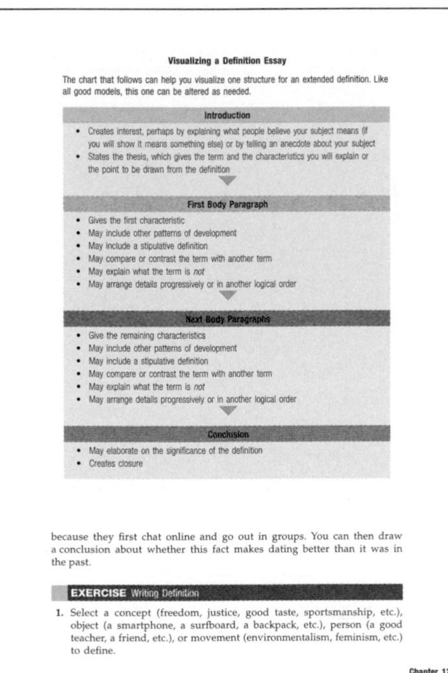

Visualizing a Definition Essay

The chart that follows can help you visualize one structure for an extended definition. Like all good models, this one can be altered as needed.

Introduction
- Creates interest, perhaps by explaining what people believe your subject means (if you will show it means something else) or by telling an anecdote about your subject
- States the thesis, which gives the term and the characteristics you will explain or the point to be drawn from the definition

First Body Paragraph
- Gives the first characteristic
- May include other patterns of development
- May include a stipulative definition
- May compare or contrast the term with another term
- May explain what the term is *not*
- May arrange details progressively or in another logical order

Next Body Paragraphs
- Give the remaining characteristics
- May include other patterns of development
- May include a stipulative definition
- May compare or contrast the term with another term
- May explain what the term is *not*
- May arrange details progressively or in another logical order

Conclusion
- May elaborate on the significance of the definition
- Creates closure

because they first chat online and go out in groups. You can then draw a conclusion about whether this fact makes dating better than it was in the past.

EXERCISE Writing Definition

1. Select a concept (freedom, justice, good taste, sportsmanship, etc.), object (a smartphone, a surfboard, a backpack, etc.), person (a good teacher, a friend, etc.), or movement (environmentalism, feminism, etc.) to define.

Chapter 12 Definition 341

Diagrams of the patterns of development reinforce the text discussion of each pattern by helping you visualize how the pattern works in an essay.

Each chapter on a pattern in Part 2 also includes a **photograph, diagram, cartoon,** or **advertisement** that makes use of the pattern, and study questions that help you read the visual critically.

SUGGESTIONS FOR WRITING

Writing Description

1. Describe a crowded or hectic spot (e.g., a subway station at rush hour, the campus green at noon, your dining hall at the busiest time of day, the freeway at 5:00).
2. Describe one of the following:
   a. A favorite campus spot
   b. A favorite night spot

Occasions for Writing boxes in each chapter of Part 2 explore the pattern discussed in a variety of contexts and demonstrate how it can be used to achieve a range of writing aims.

To inform (of the lack of respect we have for the elderly)	Examples of incidents when the elderly have been treated with disrespect
To persuade (to convince the reader to vote against allowing casino gambling)	Examples of the negative effects of casino gambling in communities that have allowed it

Exemplification across the Disciplines and Beyond

Exemplification in the Classroom

Exemplification is critical in all your classes because your examinations and papers will often require you to cite examples to show you understand concepts. In a biology class, you might define and give examples of *natural selection*. In an art history class, you might use exemplification to show ways wood carving was important to colonial Americans. In an education class, you might explain and give examples of different learning styles. *As you read your textbooks and listen to lectures in your other classes, notice how often examples are used. Would the material be more difficult to understand or less interesting without the examples? How many of those examples will you be expected to know and include in papers and exams?*

Exemplification in Daily Life

Exemplification is likely to be a common component of writing you do in your personal life. E-mail to friends and family about your life will include examples of what you have been doing. A condolence letter might include examples of fond memories you have of the deceased. A letter to your residence life director about problems in your residence hall will include examples to illustrate the problems. *Make a list of the writing you do on a regular basis outside the classroom and workplace. How can examples help you achieve your purposes for that writing?*

Exemplification on the Job

Exemplification is an important component of workplace writing. For example, physical and occupational therapists write instructions for patients with examples of activities to engage in and to avoid. Safety officers and trade union officials write documents with examples of unsafe workplace conditions. Teachers write instructions that include examples of what is required to complete assignments. Stockbrokers send letters to clients with examples of different financial instruments available for investment. *How do you think you would use examples in a résumé? How would you use them in a recommendation letter for a friend or colleague? Select three of the following and indicate how you think they use examples: architects, police officers, nutritionists, child care workers, accountants, marketing directors.*

OCCASIONS FOR WRITING

Elements of an MLA Works-Cited Entry: Newspaper Article. To find the citation information for a newspaper article, look on both the page or pages the article appears on and the front page of the newspaper (where you will find, for example, the edition of the newspaper).

Elliott, Andrea. "Tending to Muslim Hearts and Islam's Future." *New York Times* 7 Mar. 2006, natl. ed.: A1+. Print.

514 Part 3 Using the Patterns of Development

Research coverage in Chapters 16 and 17 provides a comprehensive overview of the research process, including extensive coverage of electronic research tools, updated MLA and APA citation, drafting and editing essays with sources, and more.

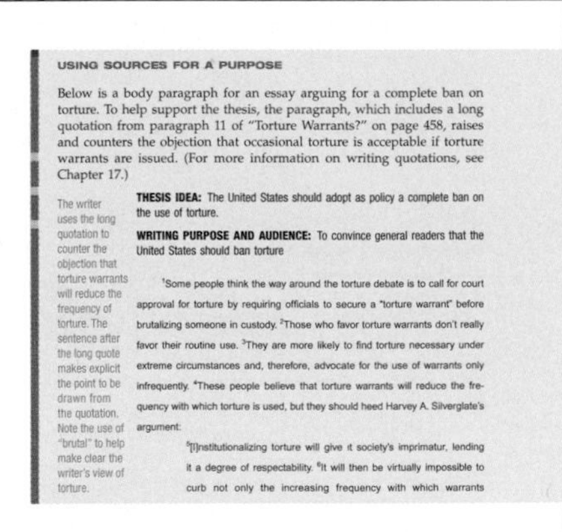

USING SOURCES FOR A PURPOSE

Below is a body paragraph for an essay arguing for a complete ban on torture. To help support the thesis, the paragraph, which includes a long quotation from paragraph 11 of "Torture Warrants?" on page 458, raises and counters the objection that occasional torture is acceptable if torture warrants are issued. (For more information on writing quotations, see Chapter 17.)

The writer uses the long quotation to counter the objection that torture warrants will reduce the frequency of torture. The sentence after the long quote makes explicit the point to be drawn from the quotation. Note the use of "brutal" to help make clear the writer's view of torture.

THESIS IDEA: The United States should adopt as policy a complete ban on the use of torture.

WRITING PURPOSE AND AUDIENCE: To convince general readers that the United States should ban torture

[1]Some people think the way around the torture debate is to call for court approval for torture by requiring officials to secure a "torture warrant" before brutalizing someone in custody. [2]Those who favor torture warrants don't really favor their routine use. [3]They are more likely to find torture necessary under extreme circumstances and, therefore, advocate for the use of warrants only infrequently. [4]These people believe that torture warrants will reduce the frequency with which torture is used, but they should heed Harvey A. Silverglate's argument:

> [5][I]nstitutionalizing torture will give it society's imprimatur, lending it a degree of respectability. [6]It will then be virtually impossible to curb not only the increasing frequency with which warrants

An argument essay often will draw on multiple patterns of development. For example, to convince people to vote for Chris Politician, you might give examples of problems Politician has solved creatively, contrast his qualifications with those of his opponent, and explain the effects of his connections in state government.

BEING A RESPONSIBLE WRITER

Responsible writers use emotional appeals fairly and with restraint. They do not play on a reader's vulnerabilities to manipulate emotions in order to achieve their purpose. Thus, as a responsible writer, you can call upon the reader's patriotism to earn support for defense spending, but you should not whip up emotions by saying that anyone who does not support the spending is un-American and supports terrorists. To do so is unfair, untrue, and inflammatory. It also preys on the reader's fear of undermining the country's safety.

438 Part 3 Using the Patterns of Development

A new **"Using Sources for a Purpose"** feature shows you how to use material from the readings to support your own ideas. Expanded coverage of avoiding plagiarism in both print and electronic contexts will help you maintain a high ethical standard for your writing.

Strategies for Reading and Writing

PART 1

LOOKING AHEAD

- Reading is an important part of all your classes, including the writing class you are currently taking. This chapter discusses the importance of reading for college students, explains how reading and writing are connected, and describes procedures you can follow when you must read important material. As you look ahead to that information, consider the answers to these questions:
- Why is reading so important to your college studies?
- What point about reading does the above *Calvin and Hobbes* cartoon make?
- How is the importance of reading reflected in the cartoon?

The Reading–Writing Connection

The connection between reading and writing is a strong and important one. For one thing, writing in response to reading is the most important way scholars, including student scholars, communicate with one another. Teachers, students, and researchers write about their findings, debate important issues, and discuss matters of interest in scholarly journals, newsletters, listservs, books, student newspapers, and research papers. Other teachers, students, and researchers read these materials and write their responses, and so the conversation continues.

As college students, you will read material and then write in response to what you read because you are part of this community of writers who read and react in writing in order to share ideas, report on developments, and argue points of view. In addition, writing in response to reading helps you grapple with ideas and determine your reaction to them. In short, writing in response to reading helps you learn.

Finally, the more you read, the more aware you will become of readers' needs, so you can use words and details that best address your particular readers. You will also become a more sensitive reader of your own drafts. This sensitivity will help you judge what changes you should make. In other words, you will become a more reliable critic and a better editor of your own writing.

READING ANALYTICALLY

Your college reading must be **analytical reading.** To read analytically, pay close attention to ideas, evaluate their merit, and consider how they relate to other ideas you have encountered, both in and out of the classroom. Question assumptions, draw conclusions, form opinions, test ideas, weigh things, judge the significance of points, reconsider, and perhaps change your mind.

Step 1: Preview the Material

Before reading, preview the material in the ways described below. Previewing is helpful because it gives you a sense of what the reading is about, it piques your interest in the material, and it improves your reading comprehension.

1. **Consider the title and author, for they may hint at what you can expect.** Some titles will be a good indication of content, and some will not. You may have heard of the author or read something else by him or her. Together or separately, the author and title may suggest how important the piece is, whether it will be humorous or serious, and whether it aims to inform or persuade.
2. **Read headings, captions, and bold and italicized type.** Look at photos, figures, charts, and lists. These offer clues to content and may suggest how the piece is organized.
3. **Read the first paragraph and the first sentence of the other paragraphs.** This preview can tell you the selection's main points. It can also tell you how challenging the material is, what your level of interest in the subject is, and whether you are already familiar with some of the ideas.

On the basis of your preview, reflect on your expectations for this reading. What questions do you think it will answer? What information do you think it will provide? What do you hope it will tell you? As you consider your expectations, keep an open mind and allow for the possibility that the author will go in a different direction and not meet those expectations.

Step 2: Read Thoughtfully

Analytical reading is thoughtful reading that often requires you to read a selection more than once; a particularly challenging piece may need several readings. Specifically, you should do the following:

1. Determine the author's thesis.
2. Consider the intended audience and purpose.
3. Distinguish between facts and opinions.
4. Draw inferences.
5. Make connections.

6. Assess the quality of the material.
7. Draw conclusions.
8. Mark the text.

Determine the Author's Thesis

The **thesis** is the main idea the author wants to convey. Sometimes the thesis is specifically stated near the beginning or at the end of an essay in one or more sentences. Sometimes it is implied rather than stated, and you must determine the main point from the evidence in the text. Either way, to be an analytical reader, you must identify the main point of what you are reading.

Consider the Intended Audience and Purpose

Who is the author writing for, and why? Was the piece written for readers of a metropolitan newspaper, specialists who subscribe to a professional journal, parents of teenagers, or college students? Does the author want to convey information, share an experience, convince the reader to think a certain way, or call the reader to action? Consider how the author addresses the needs of the intended audience and works to achieve his or her purpose for writing. For example, you can consider the strategies the writer uses to engage the reader's interest, look for ideas that are particularly relevant to the audience, and notice the language the author uses to fulfill his or her purpose.

Distinguish between Facts and Opinions

A **fact** has already been proven or it can be proven: It is a *fact* that genetic testing can tell people whether they will contract certain diseases. An **opinion,** on the other hand, is a belief or judgment, so it cannot be proven: It is my *opinion* that people are better off not knowing whether they are going to get certain diseases. Writing is often a blend of fact and opinion, and the analytical reader is careful to distinguish between the two. A skillful writer can make an opinion seem like fact, so do not be misled. For example, consider this statement:

> It is a fact that campaign finance reform, which is favored by most of the electorate, is necessary to restore faith in our two-party system.

Is it really a fact that campaign finance reform is favored by most of the electorate? Maybe it is, and you can find this out with a bit of research. Is it a fact that the reform is necessary to restore faith in the two-party system? No, this is an opinion—even though it is presented as a fact.

Many people think that facts are better than opinions, but both facts and opinions are important. If you are trying to decide whom to vote for, you can gather facts about the candidates and read editorial opinions about who is likely to do the best job. Together, the facts and opinions can help you decide. Also, a reasoned, well-supported opinion is valuable, particularly because so much in life cannot be proven. For example, is cloning a good idea? No facts say yes or no, but thoughtful essays offering opinions on the implications of cloning can help you decide.

Facts also form the basis for well-reasoned opinions. However, facts can be misleading. Statistics seem compelling—but they can steer a reader in the wrong direction if they are not current. Results of research studies seem like solid evidence—but they can be incomplete or outdated, or from a study that scientists find faulty.

Thus, to be an analytical reader, you must identify the facts and the opinions, and you must determine how reliable the facts are and how well reasoned and supported the opinions are.

Draw Inferences

When you draw an **inference,** you read between the lines. That is, you think beyond what is overtly *stated* to draw conclusions about what is *suggested.* Suppose you read this passage in a newspaper article about your state legislature's most recent session:

> Last week the state legislature voted overwhelmingly for a bill outlawing physician-assisted suicide. The importance of the legislation is primarily symbolic, as no prior law had legalized physician-assisted suicide. By passing a law outlawing the practice, lawmakers sent a message to those who would try to pass enabling legislation.

You can read between the lines to infer that legislators either feared or expected that someone would try to pass a law permitting physician-assisted suicide. The passage does not explicitly say so, but the clue is there: The lawmakers were trying to send a message, and the logical recipients of that message are people who favor physician-assisted suicide.

To be an analytical reader, draw inferences, but draw ones supported by the text. For example, you cannot reasonably infer from the above passage that the lawmakers are religious fanatics. Nothing in the passage supports that notion.

Make Connections

Analytical readers relate facts and opinions to their own experience and knowledge. For example, when the author of "School Is Bad for Children" on page 8 says that in school a child learns to feel "worthless [and] untrustworthy," you might be reminded of a time you lost your self-confidence when an essay you were proud of earned a low grade. In this case, your experience bears out what the author says. You may also be able to relate what the author says to something you have learned. A fact or concept you learned in an educational psychology class may relate to an idea in "School Is Bad for Children," perhaps by exemplifying it, lending it credence, or refuting it.

When you connect readings to your knowledge and experience, you remember the information better because you relate it to what you already know or have experienced. The reading ceases to be an isolated text and becomes an integral part of your understanding. Such connections can also provide topics for your own writing.

Assess the Quality of the Material

People often believe that anything in print or online is reliable. However, much published material is untrustworthy, so to be an analytical reader, you must not believe everything you read. Evaluate the quality of the material by asking questions like these:

- Are there enough convincing details to explain or prove the thesis?
- Is the author stating opinions as facts? Are statistics and other information current? Are opinions backed up with evidence?
- Is the treatment of controversial issues fair and balanced, or does the author ignore opposing viewpoints?
- What is the source of details? Is the author writing from personal experience, from observations, or from research findings? Are the sources of the author's details reliable?

Draw Conclusions

Draw conclusions by asking questions. Do you agree or disagree with the author? What is the significance of the material? How can the ideas be applied? For example, when you read "School Is Bad for Children," you might decide that you share the author's belief that students should work collaboratively but disagree with his notion that students should evaluate their own work. You might also decide that the essay's significance lies in the important implications it has for education reform.

Mark the Text

Your thoughtful reading should be done with a pen or pencil in hand, so you can mark the text as you go. Marking a text will stimulate your thinking about it, provide a record of your observations so they are available for class discussions and written responses, and highlight main points as a study aid. The following strategies can help you mark a text productively. In addition, an example of a marked text appears on page 8.

1. **Underline or highlight the thesis and major points.** Avoid marking too much; the goal is to emphasize the most important ideas.
2. **If you are reading for a specific purpose, underline, highlight, bracket, or checkmark the points that will help you achieve that purpose.** For example, if you are reading an essay you must write a paper about, note ideas that can be paper topics.
3. **Jot down your responses—such as conclusions, areas of agreement and disagreement, personal associations and connections, and questions—in the margins.** If you particularly like or dislike the way something is expressed, note that too—perhaps with an exclamation point or the word "nice." If you do not understand something, write a question to ask in class.

Step 3: Review and Write for Retention

You will need to remember textbook material and other assigned readings. A good way to review is to return to the text and follow these guidelines:

1. **Reread the material you underlined or highlighted.** Think about each point. Do you understand it? Do you know its significance? Do you recall how the author supported or explained it? If you cannot answer these questions, reread the relevant paragraphs.
2. **Review and reflect upon your marginal notes.** Are there any questions that remain unanswered? If so, ask those questions in class.
3. **Write a summary of the selection, following the guidelines on page 13.** Doing so "sets" information so you remember it. You can also write an outline of the piece that includes the most important ideas, or write test questions for the selection and turn around and answer them.

A SAMPLE MARKED TEXT

The following example gives you an idea of how analytic readers can mark a text. Notice that main ideas are underlined and that reactions, questions, and personal connections are recorded in the margins.

LEARNING FROM OTHER WRITERS: Professional Essay

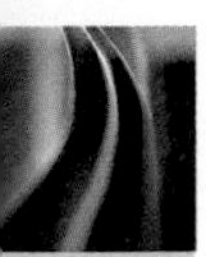

School Is Bad for Children

JOHN HOLT

John Holt (1923–1985) was a teacher and writer who gained notoriety in the 1960s and 1970s for advocating that children control their own learning. His most famous book is How Children Fail *(1964). The essay reprinted here first appeared in 1969 in the* Saturday Evening Post. *Are Holt's ideas still relevant today?*

Almost every child, on the first day he sets foot in a school building, is smarter, more curious, less afraid of what he doesn't know, better at finding and figuring things out, more confident, resourceful, persistent and independent than he will ever be again in his schooling—or, unless he is very unusual and very lucky, for the rest of his life. Already, by paying close attention to and interacting with the world and people around him, and without any school-type formal instruction, he has done a task far more difficult, complicated, and abstract than anything he will be asked to do in school, or than any of his teachers has done for years. He has solved the mystery of language. He has discovered it—babies don't even know that language exists—and he has found out how it works and learned to use it. He has done it by exploring, by experimenting, by developing his own model of the grammar of language, by trying it out and seeing whether it works, by gradually changing it and refining it until it does work. And while he has been doing this, he has been learning other things as well, including many of the "concepts" that the schools 1 think only they can teach him, and many that are more complicated than the ones they do try to teach him.

In he comes, this curious, patient, determined, energetic, skillful learner. We sit him down at a desk, and what do we teach him? Many things. First, that learning is separate from living. "You come to school to learn," we tell him, as if the child hadn't been learning before, as if living were out there and learning were in here, and there were no connection between the two. Secondly, that he cannot be trusted to learn and is no good at it. Everything we teach about reading, a task far simpler than many that the child has already mastered, says to him, "If we don't make you read, you won't, and if you don't do it exactly the way we tell you, you can't." In short, he comes to feel that learning is a passive process, something that someone else does to you, instead of something you do for yourself. 2

Sexist: What about females?

In a great many other ways, he learns that he is worthless, untrustworthy, fit only to take other people's orders, a blank sheet for other people to write on. Oh, we make a lot of nice noises in school about respect for the child and individual differences, and the like. But our acts, as opposed to our talk, say to the child, "Your experience, your concerns, your curiosities, your needs, what you know, what you want, what you wonder about, what you hope for, what you fear, what you like and dislike, what you are good at or not so good at—all this is of not the slightest importance, it counts for nothing. What counts here, and the only thing that counts, is what we know, what we think is important, what we want you to do, think, and be." The child soon learns not to ask questions—the teacher isn't there to satisfy his curiosity. Having learned to hide his curiosity, he later learns to be ashamed of it. Given no chance to find out who he is—and to develop that person, whoever it is—he soon comes to accept the adults' evaluation of him. 3

Yes! I've seen this happen many times.

School becomes a game.

He learns many other things. He learns that to be wrong, uncertain, confused, is a crime. Right Answers are what the school wants, and he learns countless strategies for prying these answers out of the teacher, for conning her into thinking he knows what he doesn't know. He learns to dodge, bluff, fake, cheat. He learns to be lazy. Before he came to school, he would work for hours on end, on his own, with no thought of reward, at the business of making sense of the world and gaining competence in it. In school he learns, like every buck private, how to goldbrick, how not to work when the sergeant isn't looking, how to know when he is looking, how to make him think you are working even when he is looking. He learns that in real life you don't do anything unless you are bribed, bullied, or conned into doing it, that nothing is worth doing for its own sake, or that if it is, you can't do it in school. He learns to be bored, to work with a small part of his mind, to escape from the reality around him into daydreams and fantasies—but not like the fantasies of his preschool years, in which he played a very active part. 4

Yes, just do the minimum to get by.

This guy really hates teachers.

The child comes to school curious about other people, particularly other children, and the school teaches him to be indifferent. The most interesting thing in the classroom—often the only interesting thing in it—is the other children, but he has to act as if these other children, all about him, only a few feet away, are not really there. He cannot interact with them, talk with them, smile at them. In many schools he can't talk to other children in the halls between classes; in more than a few, and some of these in stylish suburbs, he can't even talk to them at lunch. Splendid training for a world in which, when you're not studying the other person to figure out how to do him in, you pay no attention to him. 5

In fact, he learns how to live without paying attention to anything going on around him. You 6
might say that school is a long lesson in how to turn yourself off, which may be one reason why so many young people, seeking the awareness of the world and responsiveness to it they had when they were little, think they can only find it in drugs. Aside from being boring, the school is almost always ugly, cold, inhuman—even the most stylish, glass-windowed, $20-a-square-foot schools.

Nice sarcasm.

I disagree here.

And so, in this dull and ugly place, where nobody ever says anything very truthful, where 7
everybody is playing a kind of role, as in a charade, where the teachers are no more free to respond honestly to the students than the students are free to respond to the teachers or each other, where the air practically vibrates with suspicion and anxiety, the child learns to live in a daze, saving his energies for those small parts of his life that are too trivial for the adults to bother with, and thus remain his. It is a rare child who can come through his schooling with much left of his curiosity, his independence, or his sense of his own dignity, competence, and worth.

No! Lots of kids thrive in this environment.

So much for criticism. What do we need to do? Many things. Some are easy—we can do 8
them right away. Some are hard, and may take some time. Take a hard one first. We should abolish compulsory school attendance. At the very least we should modify it, perhaps by giving children every year a large number of authorized absences. Our compulsory school-attendance laws once served a humane and useful purpose. They protected children's right to some schooling, against those adults who would otherwise have denied it to them in order to exploit their labor, in farm, store, mine, or factory. Today the laws help nobody, not the schools, not the teachers, not the children. To keep kids in school who would rather not be there costs the schools an enormous amount of time and trouble—to say nothing of what it costs to repair the damage that these angry and resentful prisoners do every time they get a chance. Every teacher knows that any kid in class who, for whatever reason, would rather not be there not only doesn't learn anything himself but makes it a great deal tougher for anyone else. As for protecting the children from exploitation, the chief and indeed only exploiters of children these days *are* the schools. Kids caught in the college rush more often than not work 70 hours or more a week, most of it on paper busywork. For kids who aren't going to college, school is just a useless time waster, preventing them from earning some money or doing some useful work, or even doing some true learning.

No way!

Kids still need protection.

Objections. "If kids didn't have to go to school, they'd all be out in the streets." No, they 9
wouldn't. In the first place, even if schools stayed just the way they are, children would spend at least some time there because that's where they'd be likely to find friends; it's a natural meeting place for children. In the second place, schools wouldn't stay the way they are, they'd get better, because we would have to start making them what they ought to be right now—places where children would *want* to be. In the third place, those children who did not want to go to school could find, particularly if we stirred up our brains and gave them a little help, other things to do—the things many children now do during their summers and holidays.

Jobs aren't that plentiful.

Get real!

There's something easier we could do. We need to get kids out of the school buildings, give 10
them a chance to learn about the world at first hand. It is a very recent idea, and a crazy one, that the way to teach our young people about the world they live in is to take them out of it and shut them up in brick boxes. Fortunately, educators are beginning to realize this. In Philadelphia and Portland, Oregon, to pick only two places I happen

I agree.

to have heard about, plans are being drawn up for public schools that won't have any school buildings at all, that will take the students out into the city and help them to use it and its people as a learning resource. In other words, students, perhaps in groups, perhaps independently, will go to libraries, museums, exhibits, courtrooms, legislatures, radio and TV stations, meetings, businesses, and laboratories to learn about their world and society at first hand. A small private school in Washington is already doing this. It makes sense. We need more of it.

We did something like this in 8th grade & it was great.

11 As we help children get out into the world, to do their learning there, we can get more of the world into the schools. Aside from their parents, most children never have any close contact with any adults except people whose sole business is children. No wonder they have no idea what adult life or work is like. We need to bring a lot more people who are *not* full-time teachers into the schools, and into contact with the children. In New York City, under the Teachers and Writers Collaborative, real writers, working writers—novelists, poets, playwrights—come into the schools, read their work, and talk to the children about the problems of their craft. The children eat it up. In another school I know of, a practicing attorney from a nearby city comes in every month or so and talks to several classes about the law. Not the law as it is in books but as he sees it and encounters it in his cases, his problems, his work. And the children love it. [It is real, grown-up, true, not *My Weekly Reader,*] not "social studies," not lies and baloney.

A good way for high school kids to learn about careers.

Nice!

12 Something easier yet. Let children work together, help each other, learn from each other and each other's mistakes. We now know, from the experience of many schools, both rich-suburban and poor-city, that children are often the best teachers of other children. What is more important, we know that when a fifth- or sixth-grader who has been having trouble with reading starts helping a first-grader, his own reading sharply improves. A number of schools are beginning to use what some call Paired Learning. This means that you let children form partnerships with other children, do their work, even including their tests, together, and share whatever marks or results this work gets—just like grown-ups in the real world. It seems to work.

I hate group work. Someone always takes over.

Take tests together? Is this fair?

13 Let the children learn to judge their own work. A child learning to talk does not learn by being corrected all the time—if corrected too much, he will stop talking. He compares, a thousand times a day, the difference between language as he uses it and as those around him use it. Bit by bit, he makes the necessary changes to make his language like other people's. In the same way, kids learning to do all the other things they learn without adult teachers—to walk, run, climb, whistle, ride a bike, skate, play games, jump rope—compare their own performance with what more skilled people do, and slowly make the needed changes. But in school we never give a child a chance to detect his mistakes, let alone correct them. We do it all for him. We act as if we thought he would never notice a mistake unless it was pointed out to him, or correct it unless he was made to. Soon he becomes dependent on the expert. We should let him do it himself. Let him figure out, with the help of other children if he wants it, what this word says, what is the answer to that problem, whether this is a good way of saying or doing this or that. If right answers are involved, as in some math or science, give him the answer book, let him correct his own papers. Why should we teachers waste time on such donkey work? Our job should be to help the kid when he tells us that he can't find a way to get the right answer. Let's get rid of all this nonsense of grades, exams, marks. We don't know now, and we never will know, how to measure what another person knows or understands. We certainly can't find out by asking him questions. All we find out is what he doesn't know—which is what most tests are for, anyway. Throw it all out, and

let the child learn what every educated person must someday learn, how to measure his own understanding, how to know what he knows or does not know.

Yes! Yes! Yes! In college too.

14 We could also abolish the fixed, required curriculum. People remember only what is interesting and useful to them, what helps them make sense of the world, or helps them get along in it. All else they quickly forget, if they ever learn it at all. The idea of a "body of knowledge," to be picked up in school and used for the rest of one's life, is nonsense in a world as complicated and rapidly changing as ours. Anyway, the most important questions and problems of our time are not *in* the curriculum, not even in the hotshot universities, let alone the schools.

15 Children want, more than they want anything else, and even after years of miseducation, to make sense of the world, themselves, and other human beings. Let them get at this job, with our help if they ask for it, in the way that makes most sense to them.

WRITING IN RESPONSE TO READING

Your instructors may ask you to summarize an author's main points to be sure you have read and comprehended important material, or they may ask you to analyze an author's position and assess its worth. At times, you will be asked to express your reactions to a reading. Although you are writing as a student for a teacher, make no mistake—you are part of the exchange of views and information that is at the heart of the academic community.

When you write in response to reading, you will draw on the patterns of development you will study in this book. For example, suppose you respond to "School Is Bad for Children" by explaining the advantages of collaborative learning. You might *define* collaborative learning, *describe* collaborative learning procedures, *include examples* of successful collaborative learning activities, and then *explain the effects* of collaborative learning.

In addition to using patterns of development, you may want to paraphrase and quote from the reading you are responding to. (Paraphrasing and quoting are discussed in Chapter 17.) For example, consider again a response to "School Is Bad for Children." This time, assume that you wish to disagree with the author and argue that we should not abolish compulsory school attendance laws. To do this, you can bring up the author's points by paraphrasing and quoting them and then go on to counter those points with your own ideas.

Detail for your essay can come from your own experience and observation, as well as from material you have learned in your classes and from books and articles in the library. If you borrow material from books and articles, remember to document these borrowings according to the conventions described in Chapter 17.

Writing a Summary

To summarize, restate an author's most important ideas in your own words and writing style. Do not add your own thinking in any way, and do not comment on the ideas, interpret them, evaluate them, or include anything that does not appear in the original selection. Teachers often ask students to summarize material to check their comprehension. Sometimes teachers ask students first to summarize reading material and then to respond to it in some way. However, unless specifically directed to do so, do not add your own ideas.

The following suggestions can help you write summaries:

1. Underline or list the most important ideas in the selection. Do not note supporting details, as they will not appear in the summary.
2. Write an opening sentence that includes the author's name, the title of the reading selection, and the thesis (statement of what the essay is about). Here is an example from the summary below:

   In "School Is Bad for Children," John Holt notes the failure of modern education.

3. After the first use of the author's full name, refer to the author with his or her last name or with a pronoun.

   In "School Is Bad for Children," John Holt notes the failure of modern education. He claims that most children are brighter and more intellectually inclined on the first day of school than at any other time during the education process. Holt identifies the reason . . .

4. As the above examples illustrate, use a present-tense verb with the author's name.
5. Draft the body of the summary by writing in your own words and style the main ideas you underlined or listed. If some of the ideas are difficult to express in your own words, quote them, but use quotation sparingly.
6. Revise to be sure you have not included ideas that did not appear in the original and that you have not altered the meaning of the original.

The following summarizes the first six paragraphs of "School Is Bad for Children."

Summary of the First Six Paragraphs of "School Is Bad for Children"

Howard Rohan

In "School Is Bad for Children," John Holt notes the failure of modern education. He claims that most children are brighter and more intellectually inclined on the first day of school than at any other time during the educational process. Holt maintains the reason for this phenomenon is that we teach children some unfortunate things, including the notions that "learning is separate from living" and that children do not know how to learn on their own. He says that American education

casts children in the role of passive learners, whose questions, experiences, and concerns are of no interest. Once children learn these unfortunate things, Holt explains that they cease asking questions and recognize that "to be wrong, uncertain, confused, is a crime." Then students become lazy, maneuvering to get the right answers out of the teacher rather than discovering them on their own. They work to create the illusion that they are knowledgeable when they are not. Holt further explains that once their curiosity is extinguished, students become indifferent to other children and turned off in general, a fact Holt believes explains drug use among young people.

Sharing Personal Reactions and Associations

The following student essay is an example of a piece that shares personal reactions and associations. After reading "School Is Bad for Children," the student was moved to draw on her own school experiences to bear out Holt's point that in school a child "learns that he is worthless, untrustworthy, fit only to take other people's orders." To make her point, the student combines exemplification, narration, and cause-and-effect analysis.

School Was Bad for Me

Susan Schantz

I share John Holt's view that school harms children. My own negative experiences in elementary school have haunted me over the years and affected the way I present myself to my college professors. In fact, it has taken two years of college life for me to really feel comfortable talking to my instructors, largely because of my early school experiences with teachers. 1

Holt says that a child in school "learns that he is worthless, untrustworthy, fit only to take other people's orders," and I couldn't agree more. I can remember walking into Crestview Elementary School on the first day of first grade, anxious, nervous, and very shy. The first thing the teacher did was go over all the rules and procedures for the class: We were not allowed to speak without raising our hands; we could only get a drink when we went to the lav and we 2 could only go to the lav once in the morning and once in the afternoon; both of our feet had to be on the floor at all times; and we had to respect the rights of others (that was a big one, but I was never sure what it meant). Of course, the teacher was careful to point out that any infraction of the class rules would be swiftly and severely punished. From that moment, I was terrified that I would break a rule. To be sure that I didn't, I didn't do anything. I didn't speak, I didn't ask questions, and I didn't participate in any way. From the start, I knew that she was the general and I was the soldier trying to get through basic training without getting into any trouble. I was so intimidated that when any child broke a rule, I shook in sympathy. When Tommy's spelling words weren't written neatly enough and he had to do them over, my stomach ached. When Erica's math paper had messy erasure smudges and she was accused of having a messy mind, I smarted with humiliation. I was always sure I would be the next to break a rule.

I made it through first grade by keeping my mouth shut, but second grade proved more troublesome. My coping strategy failed me almost at once. Soon into the year, the teacher asked a question, but rather than call on someone whose hand was waving wildly in the air, she called on me. I instantly panicked. The words stuck in my throat and my lips froze. I couldn't utter a sound. "What's the matter; has the cat got your tongue?" the teacher cleverly asked. I've never forgotten the humiliation of that moment. 3

Although I have had positive experiences with teachers over the years, that initial put-down made me hesitant to speak out in class by voicing an opinion or asking a question. Even in college, I could not at first participate in class or ask a question when I did not understand. Yes, as Holt points out, I felt worthless and fit only to take orders. That's what I learned in school. 4

Evaluating an Author's Ideas

The following student essay responds to reading by evaluating an author's ideas. The student argues that Holt is wrong—abolishing compulsory education would be a mistake. To make his point, he cites ideas in Holt's essay and refutes them, and he also draws on examples from his personal experience.

Compulsory School Attendance Laws Make Sense

Thomas Hickman

In "School Is Bad for Children," John Holt says, "We should abolish 1
compulsory school attendance." He believes that only those who want to go to school should attend and that children should be allowed unauthorized absences. I disagree with Holt completely. School is not bad for children. On the contrary, children need to be educated, and for that to happen, children need to be in school. Compulsory attendance laws, therefore, should not be abolished.

Holt claims that at one time mandatory attendance laws made sense 2
because children needed to be protected from adults who would keep them out of school and send them to work. Sad to say, children still need the protection the laws afford, for exploitive and abusive adults still exist and children still need protection from them. Without the law, plenty of parents would force their children into the workforce and worse. For children born into poverty and abusive homes, education may be the only way to a better life. If compulsory attendance laws did not exist, then these children would lose their tickets out of difficult situations.

Even if children do not need protection from adults, they must be re- 3
quired to attend school to improve their situations. Holt says that "for kids who aren't going to college, school is just a useless time waster, preventing them from earning some money." Sure, they can earn money doing minimum wage jobs that do not require a diploma. But how can people support themselves as well as a family earning a little more than five dollars an hour? An education is more important than a low-paying job at an early age because a person must have a chance at a better job in the future. I know of one person who dropped out of school, and today he is on welfare trying to support three children. He is twenty-six and has little to look forward to. Furthermore, his children are already at a disadvantage because their needs cannot be met, and they cannot enjoy the benefits that many of us had when

we were young. Fortunately, these children will be required to go to school, so they may find a way out of their poverty.

Holt also blames compulsory attendance for the problems that exist in 4 schools today. Those who don't want to be in school, says Holt, make things difficult for those who do. Perhaps, but the solution is not to let young people leave school. Instead, the solution is to find ways to make these people want to be in school. We need to do whatever it takes to attract the most talented people into teaching so all students can be motivated to stay in school and learn.

Some might think that Holt's suggestion that students be given unautho- 5 rized absences makes sense. But here too I see problems. How is a teacher supposed to maintain continuity with a steady stream of students coming and going? The teacher would spend more time repeating lessons to bring students up to date than teaching necessary material.

Mandatory attendance should not be abolished. Students need to be in 6 school to receive the education they need to make a satisfactory life for themselves. Doing away with compulsory attendance laws would do more harm than any Holt sees with the existing laws.

AN ESSAY FOR READING AND RESPONSE

The next reading offers you an opportunity to practice your analytical reading skills and strategies. Follow the guidelines to preview, mark, and read thoughtfully as explained in this chapter. Then answer the questions that follow the reading.

The Environmental Issue from Hell BILL MCKIBBEN

In this 2001 article from These Times, *Bill McKibben says that global warming is really a moral crisis and that how we deal with that crisis will affect future generations. As you read, decide what you think about the action McKibben recommends in the face of that crisis.*

When global warming first emerged as a potential crisis in the late 1980s, one academic analyst called it "the public policy problem from hell." The years since have only proven him more astute: Fifteen years into our understanding of climate change, we have yet to figure out how we're going to tackle it. And environmentalists are just as clueless as anyone else: Do we need to work on lifestyle or on lobbying, on photovoltaics[1] or on politics? And is there a difference? How well we handle global warming will determine what kind of century we inhabit—and indeed what kind of planet we leave behind. The issue cuts close to home and also floats off easily into the abstract. So far it has been the ultimate "can't get there from here" problem, but the time has come to draw a road map—one that may help us deal with the handful of other issues on the list of real, world-shattering problems. 1

Typically, when you're mounting a campaign, you look for self-interest, you scare people by saying what will happen to us if we don't do something: All the birds will die, the canyon will disappear beneath a reservoir, we will choke to death on smog. But in the case of global warming, that doesn't exactly do the trick, at least in the time frame we're discussing. In temperate latitudes, climate change will creep up on us. Severe storms already have grown more frequent and more damaging. The progression of seasons is less steady. Some agriculture is less reliable. But face it: Our economy is so enormous that it takes those changes in stride. Economists who work on this stuff talk about how it will shave a percentage or two off the GNP[2] over the next few decades. And most of us live lives so divorced from the natural world that we hardly notice the changes anyway. Hotter? Turn up the air-conditioning. Stormier? Well, an enormous percentage of Americans commute from remote-controlled garage to office parking space—it may have been some time since they got good and wet in a rainstorm. By the time the magnitude of the change is truly in our faces, it will be too late to do much about it: There's such a lag time to increased levels of carbon dioxide in the atmosphere that we need to be making the switch to solar and wind and hydrogen power right now to prevent disaster decades away. Yesterday, in fact. 2

So maybe we should think of global warming in a different way—as the great moral crisis of our time, the equivalent of the civil rights movement of the 1960s. 3

Why a moral question? In the first place, no one's ever figured out a more effective way to screw the marginalized and poor of this planet than climate change. Having taken their dignity, their resources, and their freedom under a variety of other schemes, we now are taking the very physical stability on which their already difficult lives depend. 4

Our economy can absorb these changes for a while, but consider Bangladesh for a moment. In 1998 the sea level in the Bay of Bengal was higher than normal, just the sort of thing we can expect to become more frequent and severe. The waters sweeping down the Ganges and the Brahmaputra rivers from the Himalayas could not drain easily into the ocean—they backed up across the country, forcing most of its inhabitants to spend three months in thigh-deep water. The fall rice crop didn't get planted. We've seen this same kind of disaster over the past few years in Mozambique and Honduras and Venezuela and other places. 5

And global warming is a moral crisis, too, if you place any value on the rest of creation. Coral reef researchers indicate that these spectacularly intricate ecosystems are also spectacularly vulnerable. Rising water temperatures are likely to bleach them to extinction by mid-century. In the Arctic, polar bears are 20 percent scrawnier than they were a decade ago: As pack ice melts, so does the opportunity for hunting seals. All in all, the 21st century seems poised to see extinctions at a rate not observed since the last big asteroid slammed into the planet. But this time the asteroid is us. 6

[1]Photovoltaics is technology that produces power from sunlight.

[2]GNP is the gross national product.

It's a moral question, finally, if you think we owe any debt to the future. No one ever has figured out a more thoroughgoing way to strip-mine the present and degrade what comes after—all the people who will ever be related to you. Ever. No generation yet to come will ever forget us—we are the ones present at the moment when the temperature starts to spike, and so far we have not reacted. If it had been done to us, we would loathe the generation that did it, precisely as we will one day be loathed. 7

But trying to launch a moral campaign is no easy task. In most moral crises, there is a villain—some person or class or institution that must be overcome. Once the villain is identified, the battle can commence. But you can't really get angry at carbon dioxide, and the people responsible for its production are, well, us. So perhaps we need some symbols to get us started, some places to sharpen the debate and rally ourselves to action. There are plenty to choose from: our taste for ever bigger houses and the heating and cooling bills that come with them, our penchant for jumping on airplanes at the drop of a hat. But if you wanted one glaring example of our lack of balance, you could do worse than point the finger at sport utility vehicles. 8

SUVs are more than mere symbols. They are a major part of the problem—we emit so much more carbon dioxide now than we did a decade ago in part because our fleet of cars and trucks actually has gotten steadily less fuel efficient for the past 10 years. If you switched today from the average American car to a big SUV, and drove it for just one year, the difference in carbon dioxide that you produced would be the equivalent of opening your refrigerator door and then forgetting to close it for six years. SUVs essentially are machines for burning fossil fuel that just happen to also move you and your stuff around. 9

But what makes them such a perfect symbol is the brute fact that they are simply unnecessary. Go to the parking lot of the newest suburban supermarket and look around: The only conclusion you can draw is that to reach the grocery, people must drive through three or four raging rivers and up the side of a canyon. These are semi-military machines, armored trucks on a slight diet. While they do not keep their occupants appreciably safer, they do wreck whatever they plow into, making them the perfect metaphor for a heedless, supersized society. 10

That's why we need a much broader politics than the Washington lobbying that's occupied the big environmental groups for the past decade. We need to take all the brilliant and energetic strategies of local grassroots groups fighting dumps and cleaning up rivers and apply those tactics in the national and international arenas. That's why some pastors are starting to talk with their congregations about what cars to buy, and why some college seniors are passing around petitions pledging to stay away from the Ford Explorers and Excursions, and why some auto dealers have begun to notice informational picketers outside their showrooms on Saturday mornings urging customers to think about gas mileage when they look at cars. 11

The point is not that such actions by themselves—any individual actions—will make any real dent in the levels of carbon dioxide pouring into our atmosphere. Even if you get 10 percent of Americans really committed to changing their energy use, their solar homes wouldn't make much of a difference in our national totals. But 10 percent would be enough to change the politics around the issue, enough to pressure politicians to pass laws that would cause us all to shift our habits. And so we need to begin to take an issue that is now the province of technicians and turn it into a political issue, just as bus boycotts began to make public the issue of race, forcing the system to respond. That response is likely to be ugly—there are huge companies with a lot to lose, and many people so tied in to their current ways of life that advocating change smacks of subversion. But this has to become a political issue—and fast. The only way that may happen, short of a hideous drought or monster flood, is if it becomes a personal issue first. 12

EXERCISE Reading "The Environmental Issue from Hell" Analytically

1. When you previewed the essay, you formed expectations for its content. Were your expectations accurate? Explain.
2. When you read the essay thoughtfully, you should have drawn some conclusions about it. Give two of them.
3. Did you have any trouble distinguishing facts from opinions? Why or why not? State one fact that is in the essay. State one opinion that is in the essay.
4. What is your assessment of the quality of the essay? Why?
5. To review and write for retention, write and answer two test questions on the essay's content.
6. Review your markings in the essay. If you were asked to evaluate the author's ideas in an essay, which of your markings would help you generate ideas? ■

WRITING ASSIGNMENT

www.mhhe.com/tsw
For further help with visual content, go to Catalyst 2.0 > Writing > Visual Rhetoric Tutorial

In two or three pages, summarize and write a response to "The Environmental Issue from Hell" that either connects the essay to your own experience or agrees or disagrees with it.

ANALYZING VISUAL CONTENT

On television, in movies, on billboards, in store windows, in grocery store aisles, on the sides of buses, on cereal boxes, in magazines and newspapers, in your textbooks, on the Internet—visual content is everywhere. Like the written word, pictures, maps, drawings, photographs, and charts convey meaning and are constructed for a purpose. To consider visual content thoughtfully, you can apply much of what you have learned about *reading* words analytically to *viewing* images analytically. In the next sections, you will read about how to analyze advertisements, photographs, and charts and graphs by answering the questions in this box.

Questions for Analyzing Images

- What is the *topic* of the image?
- Who is the *intended audience*?
- What is the *purpose* of the image?
- What are the *components* of the image? How do they help the image achieve its purpose?
- What can you *infer* from the image?
- What is the importance of any *text* that accompanies the image?
- Is the information conveyed in the image and text *accurate or misleading*?

Analyzing Advertisements

Because advertisements routinely try to influence your thinking and behavior, knowing how to analyze them is important. If you do not consider advertisements thoughtfully, you can fall victim to their persuasive strategies. Consider, for example, the advertisement for Organics shampoo on page 22, and then study the answers to the analysis questions.

What is the topic of the image? The topic is Organics shampoo.

Who is the intended audience? The audience is females who want their hair to look good.

What is the purpose of the image? The purpose is to convince women to use Organics shampoo.

What are the components of the image? How do they help the image achieve its purpose? The image includes attractive young women who are so happy they are disregarding the "Do not touch" sign, and they have taken off their shoes and are jumping on a bed in a furniture store. The product that put them in such a good mood appears in the lower right corner in green. Other than the green that highlights the product and screens the text, colors are muted, making the green highlighting the product more prominent. The components create the sense that using Organics shampoo will lead to a good day, and it will create happiness, spontaneity, and good-natured fun. It will also help the user look more like the women in the ad.

What can you infer from the image? You can infer three messages that the makers of this ad want you to come away with: Beautiful hair makes women happy; Organics shampoo can make women happy because it gives them beautiful hair; and young, attractive, fun-loving women use Organics shampoo.

What is the importance of any text that accompanies the image? The text is very important because it makes explicit the notion that Organics shampoo makes women both look good and feel good. It also states that the oils are the component in the shampoo responsible for these effects.

Is the information conveyed in the image and text accurate or misleading? The information is somewhat misleading. Although the shampoo with its essential oils can possibly contribute to attractive hair, it will not guarantee a good day.

Once you have analyzed the advertisement by answering the questions, you can see that the ad has an emotional appeal that works to persuade young females that they can have good days filled with fun, friendship, and happiness if they use Organics shampoo. Since presumably most women seek fun, friendship, and happiness, the ad can be very persuasive.

Analyzing Photographs

Whether candid or posed, photographs convey information to achieve a particular purpose. In your textbooks, photographs convey meaning about the subject under study. For example, a photograph of Grant and Lee at Appomattox can help history students visualize the circumstances of General Lee's surrender to end the Civil War. Photographs in newspapers and magazines

Very Dire Straits

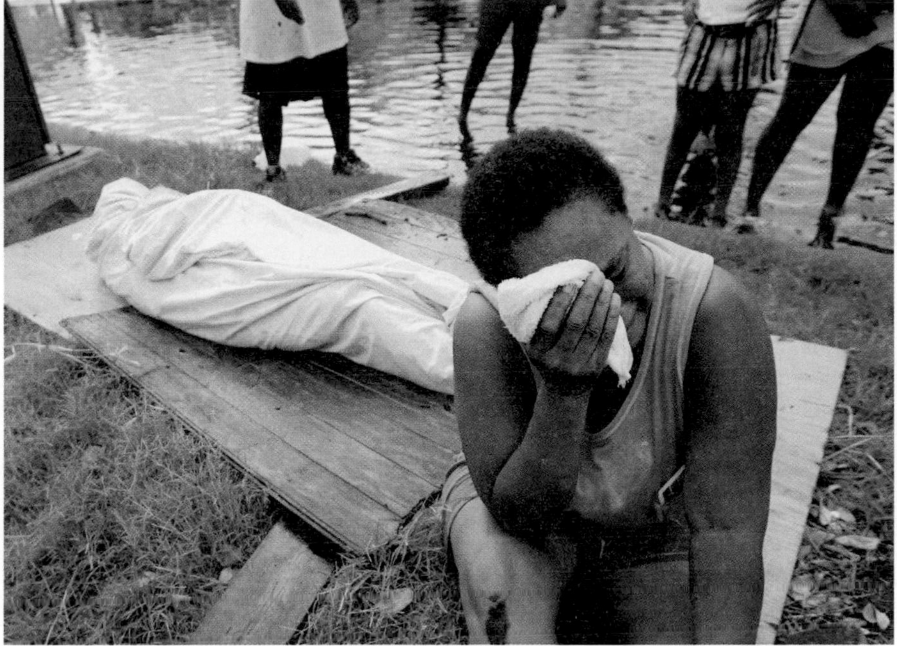

As rising flood waters took lives in New Orleans, residents struggled to find dry land, food and drinking water. Search and rescue teams continued to look for survivors across the region on Aug. 31, two days after Hurricane Katrina came bearing down on the Gulf Coast. Residents of several cities report that bodies still have not been collected. Many in need of medical attention remain stranded by water or impassable roads. From Texas to Alabama, hundreds of thousands of refugees simply tried to make do. Many have lost their homes. There's no electricity or running water in many areas, and in most cases no communication. It will be some time before any sense of normalcy returns to this part of the world.

can stir emotions and incite us to act. For example, a magazine article about famine in Africa may include photos of starving children. These photos can move readers to send contributions to a famine relief agency.

To practice analyzing photographs, consider the above photograph of Hurricane Katrina victims, and then study the answers to the analysis questions.

What is the topic of the image? The topic is the victims of Hurricane Katrina in New Orleans.

Who is the intended audience? Since the photograph appeared in *Newsweek* and on MSNBC's website, the audience is the people who read such material. This generally means middle-class individuals with at least a high school diploma.

What is the purpose of the image? The image informs readers of the death, pain, and devastation associated with Hurricane Katrina. The purpose may also be to arouse emotions and elicit sympathy for the hurricane victims.

What are the components of the image? How do they help the image achieve its purpose? The components include a weeping woman with a cut knee, a shrouded corpse, partial images of onlookers, and floodwater. The image may convey the photograph's message with more power than words because of its poignancy and starkness.

What can you infer from the image? You can infer that the woman may be mourning the loss of the person who has died, although that cannot be known for sure from the photo. Also, since her leg wound is not bandaged, you can infer that medical care has not been administered to her. Finally, since the corpse remains on the ground, you can infer that procedures for removing the dead are going slowly.

What is the importance of any text that accompanies the image? The caption accompanying the photograph is very important because it confirms and expands upon the content of the photograph. The caption explains that the image is representative of a very big problem: In the wake of Katrina, bodies remain in the street; people are without shelter, electricity, running water, and communication; medical attention is not forthcoming; and the situation is not likely to improve significantly very soon. The title of the photograph, "Very Dire Straits," summarizes the situation.

Is the information conveyed in the image and text accurate or misleading? The information is accurate and conveys a true sense of post-Katrina suffering. Not all news reporting is entirely accurate, but you can trust major news sources to do their best to offer the truth.

Photographs can incite people to action. After Hurricane Katrina, photographs like the one in this chapter appeared in newspapers and magazines and on websites. The powerful images were partly responsible for the outpouring of private contributions and other aid that went to the Gulf Coast region after the hurricane.

Analyzing Charts and Graphs

Charts and graphs convey a great deal of information succinctly, and they often show how individual pieces of information relate to each other. You will encounter charts, line graphs, and bar graphs often in your textbooks, where they can either summarize information in the text or convey new information. Charts and graphs are also common in newspapers and magazines and on the Internet, where they often give a visual representation of the information in articles and essays.

To practice analyzing charts and graphs, consider the bar graph on page 25 from a political science textbook, and then study the answers to the analysis questions.

What is the topic of the image? The topic of the bar graph is the opinions about taxing and spending that people have.

Opinions on Taxing and Spending
People's opinions are sometimes contradictory. Americans say, for example, that taxes are too high and yet also say government is spending too little in areas such as health, education, and the environment.

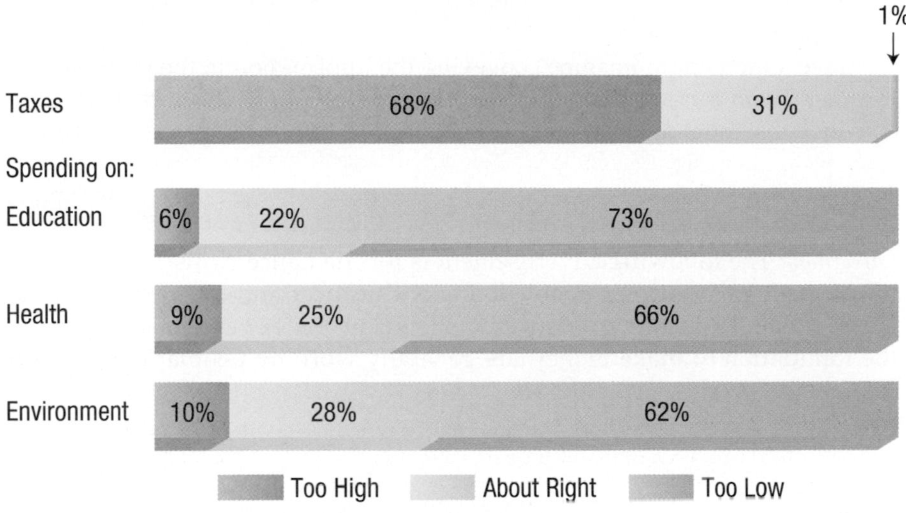

Used by permission of National Opinion Research Center, University of Chicago.

Who is the intended audience? The audience is college students in a political science class.

What is the purpose of the image? The purpose is to inform students through graphics and statistics that the opinions people have on taxing and spending can be contradictory.

What are the components of the image? How do they help the image achieve its purpose? The graph is composed of four bars of three colors that designate the percentage of people who hold opinions about taxing generally and spending for education, health, and the environment in particular. The graph also has a title, a caption, and a source note. The title and caption give the overriding conclusion of the graph and one example of that conclusion. The components convey a great deal of information about people's opinions in an easily grasped visual depiction.

What can you infer from the image? You can conclude that people want more money spent on education, health, and the environment, but they do not want the money to come from them. You can infer, therefore, that people are unrealistic about how services are paid for. You can also conclude that people think education is more underfunded than health and the environment.

What is the importance of any text that accompanies the image? The title is important for interpreting the graph, but the caption is a summary of information the reader could figure out. It is, therefore, helpful but not vital.

Is the information conveyed in the image and text accurate or misleading? The source is the University of Chicago, a highly respected institution, so there is no reason to consider the information misleading or unreliable. However, without knowing when the data were compiled, you cannot know how current the information is.

Take a moment to imagine conveying the information in the graph in text form, and you can see that an important function of graphs and charts is to convey substantial amounts of information in a brief, easily grasped form.

EXERCISE Analyzing Visual Content

Directions: The following advertisement is for the Lance Armstrong Foundation, a support group for people living with cancer and for those who care about them. The yellow wristbands shown in the advertisement, sold by the foundation to make money, are generally worn by people who support

the foundation's goals. Study the advertisement, and answer the following questions.

1. What is the purpose of the advertisement? Who is the targeted audience?
2. The advertisement includes both picture and text. What is the role of each? How does each help the ad achieve its purpose?
3. Does the advertisement appeal more to the reader's emotions or intellect? Explain.
4. What assumptions does the ad make? ■

LOOKING AHEAD

Sometimes writers get lucky and the lightbulb of inspiration burns brightly. Unfortunately, inspiration is overrated; it just can't be counted on to show up when you need it. Therefore, you need strategies for discovering ideas in the absence of inspiration, and that is what much of this chapter is about. Before you learn about those strategies, take some time to consider how you come up with ideas by answering these questions:

- How do you usually discover ideas for your writing?
- Have you ever experienced writer's block? If so, what did you do about it?

Getting Started

Maybe you think that writers are born, not made. If so, you may see no need for a writing class. After all, either you were born a writer or you were not—and no amount of instruction will change that fact.

Certainly, some people are born writers, but the rest of us can learn to *become* excellent writers. Here is what it takes:

1. **Use your resources, including your instructor, the writing center staff, and your classmates.** Follow your instructor's advice, and ask questions when you are uncertain. Visit your writing center if you need extra help or want a sensitive reader to respond to your drafts (but not to correct your work; that's *your* job). Work collaboratively with your classmates by brainstorming for ideas and reacting to each other's work in progress. And remember one of your most important resources: your mistakes! When you make errors, learn from them. If you do not understand why something is a problem, ask your instructor for clarification.
2. **Remember that writing is a *process*.** Expect to start and stop, write and rewrite, go forward and double back. Expect to write multiple drafts, change approaches, revise wording, and rearrange ideas. Sometimes you will start over. You will have brainstorms and experience writer's block. In short, you cannot write a polished piece quickly any more than you can plan a big event—such as a wedding—quickly.
3. **Think of yourself as a critic and an editor.** You are not expected to produce your best work in a first draft. First drafts are rough until they are polished. Thus, you should think of yourself as a *critic,* as someone

who will assess your early drafts to determine their strengths and weaknesses. You should also think of yourself as an *editor,* as someone who can make the changes in a draft that your critical assessment calls for.

4. **Respect your learning style.** Understand your preferences and use them to your advantage. If you prefer group work over individual work, form a writers' group and meet regularly to brainstorm for ideas and share drafts. If you prefer listening to lectures over reading textbooks, have someone read your draft out loud so you can listen for its strengths and weaknesses. If you favor pictures and diagrams over words, use mapping (page 37) rather than freewriting (page 32) to generate writing ideas. If you are a methodical planner, outline in detail before drafting; if you prefer to plunge right in, draft first and then outline to order the chaos.

THE PROCESS OF WRITING

Ask 20 successful writers what they do when they write, and you could get 20 different answers, because different people approach their writing in different ways. Ask one successful writer what happened when he or she wrote 20 different pieces, and once again, you could get 20 different answers, because the same person does not always use the same strategies. Thus, we can make two important points about the process of writing. First, there is no *one* process, and different approaches can work equally well. Second, the same person does not always use the same procedures—an individual may adjust the process for a number of valid reasons.

What if I told you it is possible to identify steps in the writing process? "Ah," you might say. "I just learn the steps and perform them in order, right?" Actually, no. Writers often step back before going forward. Suppose you have shaped a topic and generated ideas, so you begin to consider ways to arrange your ideas. However, while you are arranging, you discover a relationship between your ideas that had not occurred to you before. This discovery prompts you to go back and shape your topic a bit differently. You have stepped back before going forward. In short, writing is not linear (advancing in a straight line through a series of steps) but **recursive** (advancing with some doubling back and more advancing—perhaps in a new direction).

Developing an Effective Writing Process

Even though writers do different things when they write, most successful writers focus on these six areas:

1. Generating ideas, establishing purpose, and identifying audience (Chapter 2)
2. Ordering ideas (Chapter 3)
3. Writing the first draft (Chapter 3)
4. Revising (improving content, organization, and the expression of ideas) (Chapters 4 and 5)

5. Correcting errors (in grammar, spelling, capitalization, and punctuation) (Chapters 20–27)
6. Proofreading (making corrections in the final copy)

To develop your own successful writing process, you must discover procedures for working effectively and efficiently through each of the six areas of writing. This book will help you do that by describing a variety of writing techniques for you to sample until you find the ones that work best for you.

CHOOSING A WRITING TOPIC

www.mhhe.com/tsw

For further help selecting a topic, go to Catalyst 2.0 > Writing > Paragraph/Essay Development > Prewriting

Sometimes your writing topic is determined for you by an instructor, boss, or situation. Your music appreciation instructor might tell you to write an essay about the origins of jazz; your boss might tell you to write a report summarizing ways to cut the budget by 10 percent; an incorrect bill might prompt you to write a letter to a company's billing department. When your writing topic is not determined for you, and a suitable topic does not strike you right away, try the strategies explained next.

Notice the World around You

Notice events swirling around you, and you will become aware of many writing topics.

1. **Pay attention to the media.** The events, issues, controversies, and concerns reported in your campus and local newspapers—such as tax hikes, curriculum changes, pending legislation, and actions of officials or citizens or students—can make good writing topics. Similarly, what you hear on the radio or view on television can suggest ideas. Did you watch a reality program and decide that the reality trend has finally gone too far? Then you can write an essay about the cruelty in reality TV. You can also get ideas for writing topics at news websites, including the *New York Times* (www.nyt.com), the *Washington Post* (www.washingtonpost.com), the *Los Angeles Times* (www.latimes.com), and CNN (cnn.com). Remember, you are just looking for topics; if you use words and ideas from these sites, you must document using the conventions explained in Chapter 17.
2. **Consider what you have learned in your other classes.** Perhaps you just heard a lecture on business ethics in your business management class. That lecture might prompt an essay on truth in advertising. Or perhaps you read a chapter in your American history book about Ellis Island. That material might prompt you to write about the advantages of keeping our borders open.
3. **Listen to people around you.** If you hear your roommate complain about her high credit card bills, you might be prompted to write about the ethics of marketing credit cards to college students. If a sign in a campus parking lot reminds you to lock your car, you might be prompted to write about crime on campus.

Freewrite

To **freewrite,** write nonstop for 5 or 10 minutes. Record *everything* that comes to mind, even if it seems silly or irrelevant. DO NOT STOP WRITING FOR ANY REASON. If you run out of ideas, then write names of your family members; or write, "I don't know what to say"; or write the alphabet—anything. You will not share your freewriting with a reader, so you can say what you want and disregard spelling, grammar, neatness, and form. Just jot your ideas down any way you can. After 5 or 10 minutes, read over your freewriting—you will likely find at least one idea for a writing topic. Here is an example that yields several broad topics:

> *I have to find a writing subject. Let's see, there's politics and school, but politics is boring and school is done to death (and it's going to kill me, hah). What else? Television, there ought to be a lot there. The shows, the commercials, the sex and violence. I could do something with arguing about the violence. Pop culture is possible too, especially MTV. I haven't watched it for awhile but it used to be really racy. What about soaps? Let's see, what else? A B C D E F G H What else? My friends, my family. I could write about Dad—he'd be a book, not an essay. Especially if I write about his drinking—no, better not. I could write about Janet's accident and the courage she showed or I could write about courage in general. That could be hard. I don't know, what else? Teachers roommates studying grades? Stress? I should have enough now.*

The freewriting suggests a number of writing topics, including these:

- Violence on television
- Whether MTV is too racy
- Soap operas
- The writer's father and his alcoholism
- Janet's accident and courage
- Teachers
- Roommates
- Stress

Certainly, each of these topics must be refined, but each makes an excellent starting point.

If you like to compose at the computer, freewrite "blindfolded" by turning down the brightness on your monitor until you cannot see what you write. You will have many typographical errors, but your inability to see your writing will deter you from censoring yourself and allow your thoughts to flow freely.

Fill in the Blanks

You can discover a topic by filling in the blanks in key sentences like these:

1. Although many people say __________, I think __________.
2. I agree with people who say __________, but I would add __________.
3. Is there anything more frustrating (interesting/exciting) than __________?
4. This world can certainly do without __________.

5. What the world needs is _________.
6. After _________, I changed my mind about _________.
7. _________ is better (or worse) than _________.
8. The main cause (or effect) of _________ is _________.
9. Many people do not understand the real meaning of _________.
10. The best way to do _________ is _________.

NARROWING A BROAD TOPIC

To keep your topic manageable, you may have to narrow it to something suitable for the required or desired length of your essay. For example, whole books are written on advertising, so "advertising" is not narrow enough for an essay. "Truth in advertising" is narrower, but it still takes in a great deal of territory. "Truth in advertising to children" is narrower still, but consider how much more manageable this topic is:

truth in television advertising of children's toys

To shape a manageable topic, you may need to narrow in steps. Suppose you must write about peer pressure. To begin shaping the topic into something manageable, you might first narrow to the causes or the effects of peer pressure. Both of those are still very broad, so next you might narrow to the effects of peer pressure on students. But do you want to write about all age groups? That could be a very long essay, so you might decide to narrow again, perhaps to the effects of peer pressure on middle school students. Still have too much to say in one essay of a reasonable length? You might narrow again, this time to get the effects of peer pressure on middle school boys, a topic that might work. Still, if you want to narrow even more, you might focus on how peer pressure can lead middle school boys to become bullies.

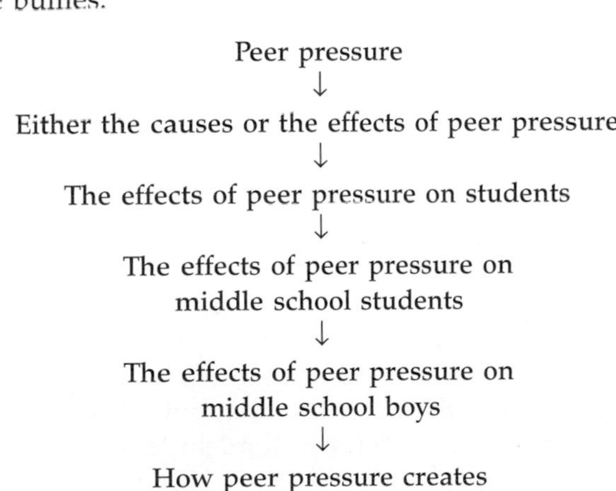

The procedures explained in the next sections can help you narrow a topic.

Freewrite

Freewrite for 10–15 minutes on your broad topic, and a narrow topic may surface. Here is a sample freewriting on soap operas, one of the broad topics discovered in the freewriting on page 32.

> *Soap operas have been around a long time. They are hugely popular. They're on day and night. Lots of different kinds of people watch them. Even very bright, professional people who you would think have better things to do. What now? ABCDE. Let's see. Soaps are interesting to some people and entertaining to others, but why I don't know because I think they are pretty stupid. Have you ever really listened to these things? Must be a reason people like them. Maybe several reasons. Entertainment? People are bored? Lots of famous actors started on soaps. I can't think of who, though. At 1:00 half my residence hall meets to watch All My Children. Some people even schedule their classes around their favorite soaps. Good grief. My mother used to call them her "stories."*

This freewriting could lead to several narrow topics:

- Why soap operas are popular
- The people who watch soap operas
- The steps people will take to ensure they do not miss their soap operas

Write a List

Write your broad topic at the top of a page, and below it list every aspect of the topic you can think of. Do not evaluate the worth of the items; just list everything that occurs to you. A list for the broad topic "stress" might look like this:

Stress
effects on health
stress management
fear of failure
exam anxiety
school stress
job stress
stress in children
stress in athletes
peer pressure

Sometimes one list is enough. For example, you might look at it and decide to write about "exam anxiety," perhaps focusing on ways students can cope with this anxiety. Other times, you may need a second list to narrow your topic further. For example, you could look at the first list and narrow to "school stress." That is a step in the right direction, but "school stress" is still quite broad. You could try a second list, which might look something like this:

School Stress
exam anxiety
coping with a roommate
picking a major

dealing with stress
effects on studies
fear of flunking out
trying to fit in

Your second list could lead you to one of several narrow topics. For example, studying this list could lead you to write about ways a college student can deal with stress.

Consider the Patterns of Development and Their Uses

Part 2 of this book explains **patterns of development,** which are ways to think about your topic and develop an essay. A good way to narrow a topic is to consider how these patterns can be used to think about your broad topic. Do so by asking the questions in the following chart. (You may not be able to answer every question for every topic.)

Considering the Patterns of Development to Narrow a Topic

Description (Chapter 6). Can I describe my topic? What does my topic look, sound, feel, taste, or smell like? What are the main characteristics of my topic?

Narration (Chapter 7). Can I tell a story about my topic? What is the significance of the story?

Exemplification (Chapter 8). What examples illustrate my topic? What do the examples say about the topic?

Process Analysis (Chapter 9). Can I explain how my topic works or how it is made or done?

Comparison-Contrast (Chapter 10). What can I compare or contrast my topic with? What do the similarities and differences say about the topic?

Cause-and-Effect Analysis (Chapter 11). What are the significant causes or effects of my topic? Should the causes be encouraged? Are the effects positive or negative? Who is affected?

Calvin and Hobbes by Bill Watterson

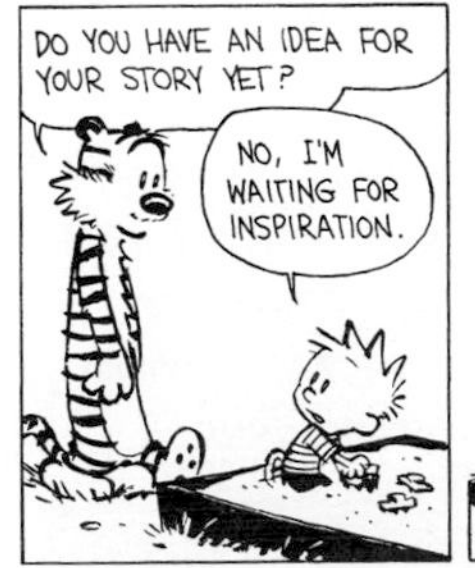

Definition (Chapter 12). Can I explain what my topic means? Does everyone agree about the meaning?

Classification and Division (Chapter 13). Can my topic be broken down into categories or parts? What do they say about the topic?

Argumentation (Chapter 15). What controversies or arguments surround my topic? What do people disagree about?

Here is an example of how considering the patterns of development can help you narrow a topic. Assume your broad topic is "athletic scholarships."

- Can I describe my topic?

  I can describe the terms of common athletic scholarships, including mine. I can also describe the way people see the typical student athlete on a scholarship.

- Can I tell a story about my topic? What is the significance of the story?

  I can tell the story of how I got my athletic scholarship. The significance is what the scholarship has meant to me.

- What examples illustrate my topic? What do the examples say about the topic?

  I can give the examples of my teammates who have athletic scholarships and the players I graduated with who did not get them. The examples will show that the scholarships provide opportunities.

- Can I explain how my topic works or how it is made or done?

  I can explain how an athlete gets and keeps a scholarship. I can also explain how schools get the money for scholarships and how they decide who gets the money.

- What can I compare or contrast my topic with? What do the similarities and differences say about the topic?

  I can compare and contrast the terms of athletic scholarships and academic scholarships. The similarities show that both kinds of scholarships reward talent.

- What are the significant causes or effects of my topic? Should the causes be encouraged? Are the effects positive or negative? Who is affected?

  I can explain the reasons schools give athletic scholarships and how they benefit from them, including the money the athletes bring to the schools and the good public relations. I can also explain how athletes benefit from the scholarships. There are also some negative effects of the scholarships on schools and students that I could explain, including illegal recruiting and giving students false expectations.

- Can I explain what my topic means? Does everyone agree about the meaning?

  I can explain the meaning of a scholarship and of an athletic scholarship. People agree on the meaning. I can also define the typical student athlete on a scholarship. People disagree on that.

- Can my topic be broken down into categories or parts? What do they say about the topic?

  I can examine the different kinds of athletic scholarships or the different kinds of scholarships and financial aid in general.

- What controversies or arguments surround my topic?

  People who misunderstand athletic scholarships and the good they do, especially people who think student athletes are dumb jocks who have no business being in school, could learn something.

The answers suggest many narrow topics, including these:

- A comparison of athletic and academic scholarships
- The benefits of athletic scholarships for schools and students
- The problems with athletic scholarships for schools and students
- The image of student athletes on scholarships
- An argument for or against giving athletic scholarships

Map Your Broad Topic

To map a broad topic, write it in the center of a page and circle it, like this:

drinking

Next, let your thoughts flow freely, and record all the associations that occur to you; circle and connect these associations to the core circle, like this:

As ideas continue to strike you, write them down and connect them to the appropriate circles:

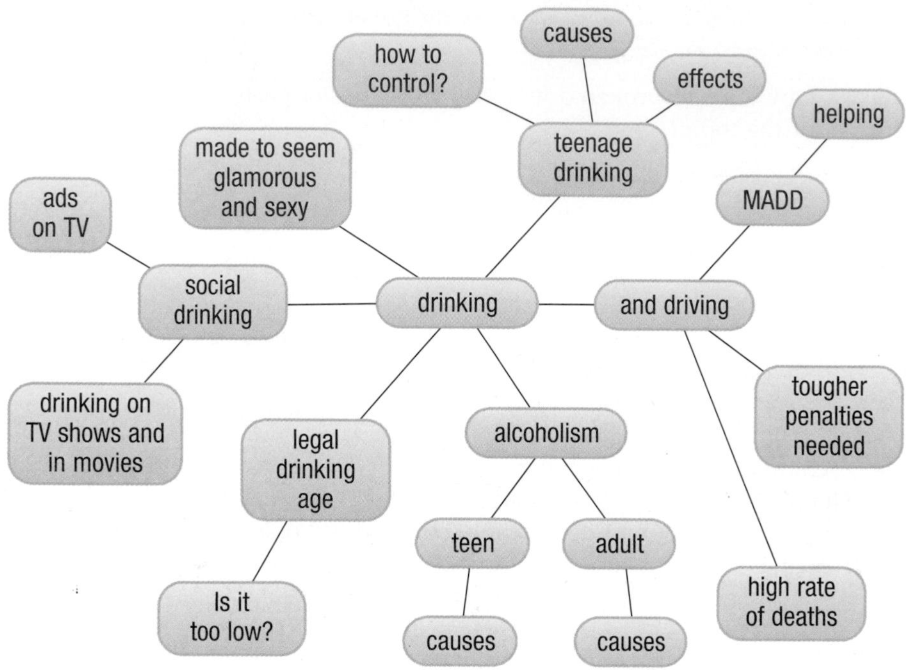

This mapping reveals several narrow topics:

- The causes of teenage drinking
- The effects of teenage drinking
- How to control teenage drinking
- How MADD (Mothers Against Drunk Driving) is working to end drunk driving
- The need for tougher penalties for drunk driving
- The causes of teenage alcoholism
- The causes of adult alcoholism
- What the legal drinking age should be
- How drinking is made to seem glamorous and sexy on television and in the movies

EXERCISE Choosing and Narrowing a Writing Topic

1. Identify five broad topics you could write an essay about. If you cannot arrive at five after some thought, try one or more of the techniques described in this chapter.
2. Using three of your responses to number 1, shape three narrow essay topics. If necessary, use one or more of the techniques described in this chapter.

3. Below are five broad writing topics. Select two of them and write one narrow topic for each. Use any of the techniques described in this chapter.
   a. Studying for exams
   b. Team sports
   c. Technology
   d. Difficult decisions
   e. Interesting (or unusual) people ■

ANTHONY'S ESSAY IN PROGRESS: Discovering a Writing Topic

Throughout this chapter and the next, you will have the opportunity to see how student writer Anthony Torres handled a specific writing task for his first-year writing class. His assignment was to tell about an experience he had that makes an important point.

Anthony's initial thinking. Anthony first considered the world around him and realized that his job as an emergency medical technician (EMT) could provide him with ideas for a topic because it gave him so many stories to tell.

Anthony's freewriting. Anthony did the following freewriting about his job as an EMT to see what would surface.

> *As an EMT I'm used to life and death situations all the time so I feel I'm more in touch with the gritty side of life and whats important. There should be lots of stuff in there to tell and lots of lessons to be learned too. Mostly there not very positive lessons because people are so damn stupid that their doing things all the time to get hurt. Like they never learn not to drink and drive. I can't even say how many accident scenes I've gone to where the driver killed or maimed some innocent person because he was drinking and driving. I could also tell stories about people who die young. Lots of people, esp. men who have heart attacks and die leaving little kids and widows behind. The lesson in that is that you never know what the future holds so live each day like its your last one. The saddest stuff is the little kids who die. Crib deaths rip you up but theres lots of deaths from accidents like drowning and car accidents. I don't know what the lesson in that is unless its that people should have to have lisenses before they become parents. Too many idiots don't watch their kids right and then they die needlessly. To tell the truth, I'm pretty bitter. These lessons are obvious I need something better. Bike accidents are bad. I could write about how everyone who rides should have to wear a helmet. I've seen nasty stuff and people don't realize. There was a little kid who is paralyzed because a hit and run driver hit her and she didn't have a helmet on and cracked her head bad on the road. I could write about how EMTs burn out because they see so much of this junk. Is that on the topic? I could ask. What about the abandoned babies. That's the worst. People leave helpless babies out in the cold and we have*

to try to save them after hours and hours of exposure and it makes you hate people. I could write about the baby I worked on who was in the parking lot in an abandoned car and how we should have one of those drop off programs at the hospitals for people who don't want their kids.

Anthony's topic selection. After reading over his freewriting, Anthony decided to write about the time he was called to the scene of an accident victim, a little girl on a bicycle who had been hit by a car. The point of the story would be that bicyclists should be required by law to wear helmets.

ESTABLISHING YOUR PURPOSE

In addition to narrowing your topic, to get started on a writing project, you must ask yourself *why* you are writing a particular piece. The answer will help you establish your **purpose,** your reason for writing. Your reason for writing will typically be one or a combination of these purposes:

- To **entertain** your reader
- To **share** your feelings or experiences with your reader
- To **inform** your reader of something
- To **persuade** your reader to think or act a particular way

Sometimes your writing purpose is established for you. For example, your political science instructor may ask you to write an informational paper about the origins of the two-party system, or you may need to write a letter of complaint to persuade a customer service representative to refund your money for a faulty product. Other times, it will fall to you to establish your purpose, and when it does, asking the questions in the following box may help you.

Questions for Establishing Purpose

- Can I entertain my reader? Why do I want to entertain? How do I want my reader to respond?
- What feelings or experiences can I share with my reader? Why do I want to share these feelings or experiences? How do I want my reader to react to these feelings or experiences?
- Of what can I inform my reader? Why do I want to inform my reader? How do I want my reader to react to the information?
- What do I want to convince my reader to think or do? Why do I want to convince my reader to think or act this way?

You must be clear about your writing purpose, because your purpose helps determine what you say and how you say it. Suppose you are writing about the difficulties you encountered during your first term in college. If your purpose is to share your feelings and experiences, you might include accounts of what went wrong for you, along with descriptions of your emotional reactions to these events. However, if your purpose is to inform your reader that college is harder than many people realize, you might write an explanation of the problems you encountered without a discussion of your reactions. Further, if your purpose is to convince your reader that a better orientation program is needed on your campus, you might write about only those difficult experiences that could have been avoided if a better orientation program existed.

Now suppose that your writing topic is that college students spend too much time online. Here are some examples of how answering the questions for establishing purpose can lead to very different essays on that topic.

- Can I entertain my reader? Why do I want to entertain? How do I want my reader to respond?

  I want to make my reader laugh with funny stories about students in my dorm whose lives are spent almost entirely online.

- What feelings or experiences can I share with my reader? Why do I want to share these feelings or experiences? How do I want my reader to react to these feelings or experiences?

  I can share what happened when I became addicted to a chat room so my reader understands how easily a person can become addicted to being online.

- Of what can I inform my reader? Why do I want to inform my reader? How do I want my reader to react to the information?

  I want to inform my reader about the dangers of spending too much time online, so he or she will avoid becoming addicted.

- What do I want to convince my reader to think or do? Why do I want to convince my reader to think or act this way?

  I want to convince my reader to limit the amount of time spent on the Internet for non-school-related activities to three hours a day, so he or she will not become addicted.

IDENTIFYING AND ASSESSING YOUR AUDIENCE

In addition to narrowing your topic and establishing your purpose for writing, you must identify who will read your essay—that is, your **audience.** Readers are not necessarily like you, and they are not like each other. Readers have different backgrounds, circumstances, beliefs, and needs. You must take those differences into consideration in order to achieve your purpose for writing. For example, if you are writing to convince your budget-minded school administration to improve the orientation program, you might show that your ideas are affordable. However, if you are writing to convince the student council to run the program, you might emphasize that running the program could increase student support for council-sponsored activities.

Perhaps you are thinking that because you are in a writing class, your audience is your instructor—and of course, you are right. However, writing teachers understand that you need experience writing for a variety of audiences, so they are willing to assume the identities of different readers. Thus, you can try writing for different readers, or you can identify your audience as "the average, general reader." Think of the average, general reader as the typical reader of a metropolitan daily newspaper.

Many times, your assignment will specify a reader. Other times—as when you write a report for work, for example—you know who your reader is. When your reader is not built into your writing task, you should think of an audience and have that reader in mind as you write. The questions in the following box can help you both identify the reader and assess that audience's characteristics and needs.

Questions for Identifying and Assessing Audience

To identify a suitable audience, ask these questions:

- **Who would enjoy reading about my topic?** You might use this audience if your purpose is to entertain, share, and/or inform.
- **Who shares an interest in my topic?** You might use this reader if your purpose is to share and/or entertain.
- **Who would find my topic important?** You might use this audience if your purpose is to inform and/or persuade.
- **Who could learn something from my writing? Who needs to hear what I have to say?** You might use this audience if your purpose is to inform.
- **Who could be influenced to think or act in a particular way?** You might use this audience if your purpose is to persuade.

To assess your audience, ask these questions:

- **What does my reader already know about my topic?** You do not want to bore your reader with unnecessary information.
- **What information does my reader need to understand and appreciate my ideas?** You should provide that information.
- **What strong attitudes, beliefs, or biases does my reader have?** You will have to take those feelings into consideration. For example, if you are writing in favor of using animals to test new drugs and your reader is a vegetarian, you may need to address strong animal rights sentiments.
- **What is my audience's age, gender, income, job, and education?** One or more of these factors may influence what you say to achieve your writing purpose. For example, it will be more difficult to convince a reader with a low income to eat organic food (because it is more expensive) than it will be to convince someone with a high-paying job.

ANTHONY'S ESSAY IN PROGRESS:
Establishing Purpose and Identifying and Assessing Audience

On page 39, you saw how student writer Anthony Torres narrowed his topic to write about requiring bicyclists to wear helmets.

Anthony's determination of purpose. Anthony knew immediately that his purpose was to convince his audience that bicyclists should be required to wear helmets. When he asked himself why he wanted to persuade his readers, he realized that he believed that helmets would reduce the number of head injuries.

Anthony's identification of audience. At first, Anthony thought his audience would be state or federal legislators, but he decided that he had a better chance of convincing parents. He figured that if he convinced parents, they might write legislators and pressure them to pass a law.

Anthony's assessment of audience. To assess his audience, Anthony looked over the audience assessment questions on page 42 and developed this list of audience characteristics:

protective
loving
possibly unaware of how badly children on bikes can be hurt
receptive to the message and easily persuaded

While considering purpose and audience, Anthony decided to narrow his topic further. Rather than write that all bicyclists should be required to wear helmets, he decided to limit his focus to bicyclists under age 18.

DISCOVERING IDEAS TO DEVELOP YOUR TOPIC

Many people believe that ideas come in a blinding flash of inspiration, in some magic moment of discovery that propels the writer forward and causes word upon wonderful word to spill onto the page. Yes, such moments occur from time to time, but they are the exception rather than the rule. More typically, writers cannot depend on inspiration, because it does not make scheduled appearances. Often it does not arrive at all.

So, what should you do in the absence of inspiration? Fortunately, there are strategies to start the flow of ideas. These strategies are called **idea generation techniques,** and they are discussed next.

Freewrite

You know about freewriting to find and narrow a topic. (See page 34.) You can also freewrite to discover ideas to develop your narrow topic. For 10 minutes, write down everything that occurs to you about your narrow topic without censoring yourself. You can shift direction and pursue an idea as far as it will take you; you can be flip, serious, or angry. Just go with the flow of your thoughts.

Next, read your work. It will be rough, but you will notice at least one or two ideas that can be polished and developed in your essay. Underline these ideas. They may be enough to get you started. If not, you can freewrite again, this time focusing on the ideas you underlined.

Here is a freewriting passage used to discover ideas for an essay on why people watch soap operas, a narrow topic discovered in the freewriting on page 34. Notice that usable ideas are underlined.

> Why do people watch soap operas? I guess some people find them entertaining, but they must like pretty mindless stuff. Probably the sick and elderly get hooked on them. After awhile the people on soaps probably seem like family. I don't know what to say now. cow how sow plow Let me think. Well, sometimes people want entertainment that doesn't require them to think too much. Mindless entertainment can be very relaxing. Also, today's soaps can be very steamy. And people love to watch sex. Anything else? They deal with important social issues, like Aids. Are people who watch lonely? Not always. Lots of people I know watch them and I'm sure they're not all lonely. Some people started watching as kids & just stayed with it. Soaps are campy and fun. That may be why college students like them. ABCDEFGHIJKL I can't think of anything else right now. Maybe the storylines are good. I'll have to watch some more and see.

Write a List

In addition to helping you narrow a topic, listing can help you generate ideas to develop that topic. Begin by listing every idea that occurs to you about your narrow topic. Don't stop to evaluate the ideas; just press on until you can't think of anything else. Then review your list, and cross out any ideas you do not want to include. If other ideas occur to you, add them to the list.

Here is a list one student wrote to find ideas for an essay about the trauma he experienced when his family moved to a new town, and he had to change schools:

> loved old school
> comfortable with friends—knew them 12 years
> at new school I was outsider
> everyone belonged to a clique
> sleepless nights for weeks before the move
> asked if I could live with my aunt so I wouldn't have to move
> ~~my parents tried to reassure me~~
> I knew I would never see my old friends again
> scared to leave familiar for unknown
> new school was ugly
> ~~I resented my parents for transplanting me~~

~~I became argumentative with my parents~~
I was behind in my schoolwork at new school
I didn't get on basketball team at new school

Some of the ideas in the list are crossed out because the writer decided he did not want to work with these ideas after all, probably because they focused on his relationship with his parents. Rather, he wanted to concentrate on his adjustment to the school and his relationship with his classmates.

After the writer eliminated ideas unsuited to his purpose, he reviewed his list and added new ideas he thought of. After this step, the list looked like this:

loved old school
comfortable with friends—knew them 12 years
at new school I was an outsider
everyone belonged to a clique
sleepless nights for weeks before the move
asked if I could live with my aunt so I wouldn't have to move
~~my parents tried to reassure me~~
I knew I would never see my old friends again
scared to leave familiar for unknown
new school was ugly
~~I resented my parents for transplanting me~~
~~I became argumentative with my parents~~
I was behind in my schoolwork at new school
I didn't get on basketball team at new school
~~new math teacher tried to help me adjust~~
at new school I was stared at like a freak
I would skip lunch because I didn't know anyone to sit with
I was popular & respected at old school—at new I was a nobody
new school was old, needed repair—describe ugly classrooms
math & science classes were way ahead of my old ones & my grades suffered
I was center on basketball team before—at new school I didn't make team
I couldn't go to games & cheer for a team I wasn't playing on & felt no loyalty toward

You will not necessarily include all of the points, examples, and details in your list in the essay. Instead, your list can provide a starting point.

Some writers like to turn their idea generation list into a **scratch outline** to guide their writing of a first draft. A scratch outline organizes idea generation material by grouping related ideas together, like this:

Before Move
loved old school
comfortable with friends—knew them 12 years
sleepless nights for weeks before the move
I knew I would never see my old friends again
asked if I could live with my aunt
scared to leave familiar for unknown

After Move
Classmates
I was outsider
everyone belonged to clique
stared at like a freak
skipped lunch cause had no one to sit with
I was a nobody instead of popular & respected
Basketball
didn't make team—was center before
couldn't go to games & cheer for a team I wasn't playing on & felt no loyalty toward
Surroundings
new school was ugly
new school was old & needed repairs
describe classrooms
Schoolwork
I was behind
math & science classes way ahead of me & my grades suffered

Answer Questions

Answering questions about your topic is another way to develop ideas. Some of the most useful questions are the standard journalist's questions: Who? What? When? Where? Why? How? You can shape these questions to suit your topic. The next box gives you some examples. If you like to compose at the computer, create a file with the questions in the box. You can call up that file whenever you want to use these questions for generating ideas.

Questions for Generating Ideas

1. Who is involved?
2. Who is affected?
3. Who is for (or against) it?
4. Who is interested in it?
5. What happened?
6. What does it mean?
7. What causes it?
8. What are its effects?
9. What is it like (or different from)?
10. What are its strengths (weaknesses)?
11. What are its parts?
12. When does it happen?
13. When will it end (or begin)?
14. When is it important?
15. Why does it happen?
16. Why is it important?
17. Why is it interesting?
18. Why is it true?
19. Where does it happen?
20. How does it happen?
21. How does it make people feel?
22. How does it change things?
23. How often does it happen?
24. How is it made?
25. How should people react to it?

Here are some questions a student asked herself for an essay about government regulation of the food supplement industry. Notice that she shaped questions to suit her narrow topic.

- What happened?

  My friend became seriously ill with kidney failure after taking a supplement for weight loss from a health food store. She almost died.

- Why did it happen?

  The product interacted with medication she was on. There are no warnings on these products about drug interactions.

- Who else could this happen to?

  Many people could become seriously ill from food supplements if they are taking medication or have medical conditions—like polycystic kidney disease—that they don't realize they have.

- What should be done about it?

  The Food and Drug Administration should determine the safety of food supplements. They should require warning labels when drug interactions or adverse effects can occur.

- Why is it important?

  People can die. My friend is permanently disabled. Recent reports say kava can cause liver damage.

- What else could happen?

  Sometimes people pay money for supplements that don't work because claims are made that aren't proven. Reports now say that St. John's Wort, which people take for depression, is not helpful.

- Who is affected?

  People who take food supplements or use weight loss products and who take prescription drugs or have medical conditions they may be unaware of.

Create a Map

Mapping can help you narrow a topic. (See page 37.) It can also help you discover ideas to develop that topic. Just write your narrow topic in the center of a page and circle it. Below is one of the narrow topics discovered in the map shown on page 38:

how to control teenage drinking

Next, let your thoughts flow freely and record all the ideas that occur to you, circling and connecting the ideas as appropriate. Do not pause to evaluate ideas; just go with the flow of your thoughts. Here is a map to generate ideas for an essay about how to control teenage drinking:

Write a Letter

Sometimes writers have trouble generating ideas because they do not relax enough to allow a free flow of thought. If this happens to you, write a "letter" to someone you feel comfortable with and can open up to easily. The subject of your letter is your narrow topic. Use this letter as an opportunity to explore ideas about your topic. Since you are writing to someone you are comfortable with, you will not hold anything back.

To discover ideas for developing her topic—the roles of women—a student wrote the letter that follows. The letter explores some difficulties the writer faces meeting the demands of her various roles.

Dear Liz,

I guess I'm what you'd call a modern woman, but I'm not sure I like it very much. I know this is what I asked for, but it's a lot rougher than I expected and frankly less exciting.

The kids are 10 and 13 now, so they are fairly independent, but they still make a lot of demands on my time. Katie's adolescence has her turned inside out, and half the time she's crying and the other half she's mad at me for something. She's really on my mind a lot. Jenny is pretty together, but her gymnastics, Camp Fire activities, and swim meets really keep me on the fly. She makes a big demand on my time.

Then there's the job. I know it's only part-time, but those 20 hours really eat up my week. I can't keep up with the cleaning or the kids. And poor Jim really gets shortchanged. Actually, I feel pretty guilty that he works all day and then has to come home and help with laundry, dinner, and things. He doesn't mind, but I do. I feel like he's always picking up my slack and I'm not pulling my weight.

To top it off, now I'm in school. I must be crazy to make my work load even heavier than it already is. Still, I want my degree badly. I don't know, maybe I'm just in a slump, but I feel like I'm not doing anything well. Being liberated is not all I thought it would be. It's really very hard. I think I'm paying a big price for being a modern woman.

Love,

Marge

Investigate Sources

Use your campus library or the Internet to locate facts, expert opinions, statistics, and studies to spur ideas. When you use source material, be sure to handle it responsibly by following the conventions explained in Chapter 17.

Interviewing people is another way to discover ideas to include in your writing. For example, if you are writing an essay about the difficulties of being a student athlete, you might interview several athletes on your campus to learn what challenges they face. When you use material, quotations, and ideas from interviews, be sure to document the material according to the guidelines in Chapter 17.

Keep a Journal

A journal is not a diary that records the events of your day; a journal is a place to respond to those events, to write on how you feel about them and to reflect on your thoughts and feelings. You can explore strong emotions and perhaps deal with them. You can also be creative and experiment with writing styles. When you write in your journal, you are writing for yourself, so you need not worry about grammar, spelling, and other matters of form.

Journals can be handwritten in a notebook or composed in a computer file. Either way, date and begin each entry on a new page. Write each day or two, and soon journal writing will become a rewarding habit. Then, when you need ideas for writing topics or details to develop a topic, scan your journal for ideas.

Your instructor may give you topics from time to time, but most often, you can write about whatever you wish.

"Go do something, honey. Then you can write in your journal."

Topics for Journal Writing

If you need ideas for journal entries, try one of these prompts:

1. Write about someone you admire.
2. Explore your feelings about college.
3. Consider where you see yourself five years from now.
4. React to a book you recently read or a movie you recently saw.
5. Write about a problem you have and explore possible solutions.
6. Record a vivid childhood memory.
7. Write about an event of the day that prompted a strong emotion.
8. Write about your family relationships or about a friendship.

To practice writing in the patterns, try one of these prompts:

9. Describe a painting, an advertisement, or a valued possession.
10. Narrate an account of a time you learned a valuable lesson.
11. Use examples to illustrate a personality trait of someone you care about.
12. Explain how to do something that you do well (process analysis).

13. Compare or contrast the person you are now and the person you would like to be (or the person you used to be).
14. Explain the effects of an important decision you made.
15. Explain the different kinds of friends (classification), and tell what kind of friend you are.
16. Write a definition of education, and explain what kind of education you want.
17. Identify one change that would make your school a better place, and argue for that change.

Work Collaboratively

Sometimes two heads really are better than one, because one person's ideas can stimulate another person's thinking. To work collaboratively, you can adapt many of the idea generation techniques for use with a partner. For example, pair up with another writer, and have that person ask you the questions on page 46 that relate to your topic. Then return the favor and ask your partner questions about his or her topic. (Be sure to write down the ideas that surface.) To list with a partner, designate one person to record the ideas that the two of you come up with to develop one topic. Then repeat the process for the other person's topic. Similarly, to map with a partner, have one person write the map as the two of you come up with thoughts and decide where to connect them on the map. Another way to work collaboratively is to use e-mail or instant messaging to discuss writing topics, kick around ideas, and ask each other questions.

Breaking through Writer's Block

All writers experience writer's block from time to time, so if it happens to you, first recognize that you are not alone. Then take action.

- **Take a break.** Go for a walk, listen to music, call a friend—relax, and when you return to your writing, the block may be gone.
- **Force yourself to write.** Writing stimulates thinking. If necessary, write a poem, draw a picture, or write the reasons you are having trouble writing. Fill a page or the computer screen with nonsense if you must, but keep writing. Ideas may surface.
- **Allow time for ideas to surface.** If you expect too much too soon, the pressure can cause a block.
- **Accept rough ideas.** Nothing is polished in the early stages of writing, so look for the *possibilities* your rough ideas offer up.
- **Try a different idea generation technique.** Freewriting may usually work for you, but this time, mapping may be more productive. Try a technique

you have never used before. Or combine techniques. Follow listing with answering questions and see what happens.
- **Consider what people who disagree with you might say.** You can use their ideas as a departure point.
- **Write about what you know.** You may have trouble coming up with ideas because you do not know enough about your topic.

EXERCISE Establishing Purpose, Identifying Audience, and Discovering Ideas

1. For an essay about campus life, do the following:
   a. First, develop a narrow topic about campus life, using one or more of the techniques described in this chapter. Then establish a purpose for an essay on this topic by answering the questions on page 40.
   b. Establish the audience by answering the questions on page 42.
   c. Determine the nature of the audience by answering the questions on page 42.
   d. Using any two techniques described in this chapter, generate at least five ideas that could be included in an essay with the topic from item a.
2. When you responded to number 2 and number 3 of the exercise on pages 38–39, you shaped five essay topics. (If you did not complete this exercise, do so now.) For each of these topics, discover at least four ideas worthy of inclusion in an essay. Try at least two different idea generation techniques.
3. Which idea generation technique(s) worked best for you? Which are you likely to use in the future? ■

DEVELOPING A PRELIMINARY THESIS

www.mhhe.com/tsw
For more information on writing a thesis, go to Catalyst 2.0 > Writing > Paragraph/Essay Development > Thesis/Central Idea

Your **thesis** is the sentence or two that states what your essay is about. Often appearing early in the essay, your thesis lets your reader know your writing topic and the central point you will make about that topic. Here is an example:

> The current television rating system does little to help parents make wise programming choices for their children.
>
> **Topic:** The current television rating system
>
> **Central point:** It does little to help parents decide what their children should watch.

Another kind of thesis previews your essay by indicating the main ideas you will cover, along with your topic and central point. Here is an example:

> Working mothers have changed the character of the American family by contributing a second paycheck, by popularizing day care, and by creating a new division of labor in the home.

Topic:	Working mothers
Central point:	Working mothers have changed the American family.
Main ideas to be discussed:	the contribution of a second paycheck, the popularization of day care, a new division of labor in the home

Your thesis is important because it focuses your essay: Everything you write must help explain the thesis or prove that it is true. Therefore, your reader develops expectations according to what your thesis promises your essay will be about.

Because the thesis is so important, you should not begin a first draft without one. However, first drafts are tentative, so thesis statements in first drafts can be equally tentative. In fact, the early version of your thesis—the one that guides and focuses your first draft—is often a **preliminary thesis** because, like everything else in a first draft, it is subject to change.

The Qualities of an Effective Thesis

To write a strong thesis, keep the following points in mind.

1. **State your topic and your central point about the topic.** Here is an example:

Thesis:	More and more high school students are working while they attend school, but this trend is unhealthy.
Topic:	High school students who work
Central point:	It is unhealthy for high school students to work.

2. **State your central point clearly.** Rather than merely indicate that you *have* a central point, state what it is.

Unclear central point:	Although there are pros and cons on both sides of the issue, I have decided how I feel about affirmative action.
Better:	Although there are pros and cons on both sides of the issue, I am convinced that affirmative action laws do more harm than good.

3. **Limit your thesis to one topic and one central point.** In a standard college essay, a thesis with two topics or two central points will force you to write too much.

Two topics:	The violence on television has an adverse effect on children, as does the blatant sexuality on MTV.
Better:	The violence on television has an adverse effect on children.
Better:	The blatant sexuality on MTV has an adverse effect on children.
Two central points:	Divorce would be less traumatic if custody laws were revised and if attorneys counseled their clients more carefully.

Better: Divorce would be less traumatic if custody laws were revised.

Better: Divorce would be less traumatic if attorneys counseled their clients more carefully.

4. **Avoid broad statements.** A thesis that is too broad will force you into a vague, superficial discussion that lacks substance.

   Too broad: The role of women has changed dramatically in the last 60 years.

   Better: The leadership role of women in national politics has changed dramatically in the last 60 years.

   Explanation: To discuss all the changes in 60 years would require more pages than a typical college essay runs. If the essay were a more manageable length, you could do little more than skim the surface.

5. **Express your central point in specific words.** You want your reader to have a clear understanding of your central point.

   Vague: It is interesting to consider the various meanings of *love.*

   Better: We apply the word *love* to a broad spectrum of emotions.

6. **Avoid factual statements.** They leave you with nothing to say.

   Factual statement: The city is considering tax breaks for new businesses.

   Better: Offering tax breaks for new businesses will encourage economic growth in our city.

7. **Avoid writing a formal announcement.** A formal announcement begins with words such as "This paper will show," "As I will prove," or "The following essay will explain." In some disciplines, particularly some of the sciences and social sciences, an announcement is acceptable; however, in English classes and many of the humanities, the announcement is considered poor style.

   Announcement: I will explain why the state board of education should consider establishing magnet schools.

   Better: The state board of education should consider establishing magnet schools.

8. **Avoid expressions such as "In my opinion," "I believe," "It seems to me," and "I think."** *You* are writing the thesis, so it is obvious that you are expressing what you think. Such expressions make you seem uncertain.

   Uncertain: In my opinion, the Women's Center performs a valuable service and deserves a budget renewal.

   Better: The Women's Center performs a valuable service and deserves a budget renewal.

9. **Preview the main ideas in your essay if doing so is helpful.** Previewing your ideas is not required, but if knowing them in advance will help you organize your essay, achieve your writing purpose, or assist your reader, you may include them in your thesis, in the order they will appear in your essay. Here is an example, using a revision of the thesis in number 1 above. The main ideas that will appear in the essay are underlined as a study aid.

   Preview of main ideas: More and more high school students are working while they attend school, but this trend is unhealthy because students are distracted from their studies, unable to participate in normal teenage activities, and jeopardizing their health.

EXERCISE The Thesis

1. In the following preliminary thesis statements, identify the topic and the central point.

How to Draft Your Preliminary Thesis

PROCESS GUIDELINES

- Study your idea generation material, looking for ideas that seem related to each other, an idea that seems the most important, or an idea you most want to write about. From one of these, identify a narrow topic and central point.
- If you cannot identify both a narrow topic and a central point, return to idea generation.
- Write out your preliminary thesis as best you can. You can revise it later to be sure it has all the qualities of an effective thesis.
- Remember the recursive nature of writing. Drafting your preliminary thesis may prompt you to reconsider your narrow topic, your audience, and/or your purpose. And those reconsiderations may prompt you to reconsider your preliminary thesis.

   a. No experience is more exasperating than taking preschool children to the grocery store on a Saturday to do a week's worth of shopping.
   b. My brother, Jerry, taught me the meaning of courage.
   c. Television news does not adequately inform the U.S. public.
   d. No one is more skilled at diplomacy than people who make their living selling clothes.
   e. Many people believe a little white lie can be better than the truth, but even these seemingly harmless fibs can cause trouble.

2. In the following preliminary thesis statements, identify the topic, the central point, and the main ideas to be developed in the essay.
   a. Socrates Pappas would make an excellent mayor because he is an experienced manager, he is fiscally conservative, and he is well connected in the state capital.
   b. Different communication styles and different agendas make it difficult for men and women to communicate effectively.
   c. Her eccentricity, her courage, and her unusual lifestyle would make Juliette Gordon Low, the founder of the Girl Scouts, the subject of an entertaining movie.
   d. The speed limits on our highways should be 55 mph to save lives and reduce the cost of automobile insurance.
   e. The student production of *Macbeth* is a big hit because of its excellent production values and daring direction.
3. Decide whether each of the following thesis statements is acceptable or unacceptable. If the thesis is unacceptable, explain what the problem is.
   a. There are many game shows on television.
   b. Schools should not be funded by property taxes.
   c. I would like to explain why I am an avid reader.
   d. Higher education is in need of reform.
   e. College students can learn to handle stress if they follow my advice.
   f. My Christmas cruise to the Bahamas was nice.
   g. The Nontraditional Student Center and the International Student Union are two university organizations that serve students well.
   h. My parents own a beach house.
   i. This essay will explain the best way to choose a major.
   j. I do not think that reality shows deserve their bad reputation.
   k. For today's young people, the shopping mall offers a variety of entertainment options.
   l. The wise woman learns how to manage her own finances, and she learns how to take care of her car.
4. Rewrite the unacceptable preliminary thesis statements from number 3 to make them acceptable.
5. Below are four broad topics. Select two of them and narrow them so that you are treating a topic manageable in 500–700 words. Write a preliminary thesis for an essay about each.

   Example: Saturday morning cartoons: If parents took the time to watch Saturday morning cartoons with their children, they would be surprised by how violent these programs really are.

a. Sports
b. Large parties
c. A childhood memory
d. Grades

6. When you completed number 1 in the exercise on page 52, you shaped a topic about campus life, established a purpose, identified an audience, and generated some ideas. Now review that material and develop a preliminary thesis that is compatible with it. Do you need to revise your topic, audience, or purpose? Do you need to eliminate some of the ideas you generated or generate additional ideas? Explain. ■

ANTHONY'S ESSAY IN PROGRESS: Discovering Ideas and Developing a Preliminary Thesis

You have been following along as student writer Anthony Torres decided on a writing topic, established a purpose, and identified and assessed his audience. Now observe what he did to generate ideas to develop his essay about requiring bicyclists to wear helmets.

Anthony's idea generation. Because he was telling a story, Anthony knew that much of his essay would explain what happened. Although he felt he had those details firmly in mind, he listed the main points and some ideas about how the story illustrates the importance of bicycle helmets. Notice that Anthony made notes to himself in parentheses and that he placed a question mark next to a point he was uncertain he should cover.

Lou and I get call.
We travel to scene.
We find young girl (Kelly) in bad shape from a hit-and-run driver (describe injuries).
We transport her.
Tell about arrival at the hospital?
Kelly ends up paralyzed.
Explain how helmet would have helped.
—protect head
—probably prevent paralysis
—injuries would have been less extensive

Kelly illustrates the importance of helmets. (Get statistics and information on how much helmets help?)

Anthony's preliminary thesis. Anthony knew what his preliminary thesis was likely to be after he settled on his topic, purpose, and audience. To guide his draft, he wrote it this way:

Requiring everyone under 18 to wear bicycle helmets would reduce the number of tragic injuries.

WRITING ASSIGNMENT

When you completed the chapter exercises, you shaped an essay topic about campus life, determined a purpose for this essay, identified and assessed audience, discovered at least five ideas, and wrote a preliminary thesis. Now you can develop this material into an essay. As you do, keep the following points in mind:

1. Remember that any or all of the material you have already developed can be changed. You can even start over with a new topic.
2. As needed, discover additional ideas to include in your essay.
3. To plan your draft, list your ideas in the order you think they should appear.
4. Write a rough draft from this list of ideas. Do not be concerned about the quality of this draft; simply jot your ideas down without worrying about anything.
5. Leave your rough draft for at least a day. Then go over it and make necessary changes. To decide what changes to make, be sure that
   a. Each idea is clearly explained.
   b. Each idea is backed up with examples and/or explanation.
   c. All ideas are related to the thesis.
   d. Ideas appear in a logical order.
6. After making changes in your draft, recopy it and ask two classmates to read it and make suggestions.
7. Check your work for correct grammar, spelling, and punctuation.

LOOKING AHEAD

The workers in the photograph are completing the framework that will define the structure of a drilling platform. Good structure is necessary in architecture because without it buildings, bridges, platforms, towers, and other constructions would collapse. Structure is important in writing, too, as this chapter will help you see. Think of other times when structure is important, and list them. Think of instances when structure is not very important, and list those as well.

Organizing and Drafting

Once you have a preliminary thesis, some ideas to develop that thesis, and a sense of your audience and purpose, you are ready to begin drafting your essay. The strategies in this chapter can help you.

ORDERING YOUR IDEAS

To achieve your writing purpose, you must arrange your ideas in an easy-to-follow order. The next sections explain three common strategies for doing so.

Chronological Order

Chronological order is time order. You begin with what happened first, move to the second event, on to the third, and so on. Chronological order is often used to tell a story by presenting events in the order they occurred or to give the steps in a process in the order they are performed. Suppose you are writing an explanation of the best way to shop in an outlet store. Here is how you can arrange your ideas in chronological order.

Chronological Order

Preliminary thesis:	To save money shopping in an outlet store, plan ahead and proceed with caution.
	↓
First event or step in time:	Do your homework. Find out what the items you are looking for cost at full price.
	↓
Second event or step in time:	Write a shopping list so you buy only what you intend to buy and so you avoid impulse shopping. Include the amount of money you are willing to pay, so you do not overspend.
	↓
Third event or step in time:	Gather information. Walk around the store to assess the quality of the merchandise. Look at price tags of items on your list to determine whether the price is right. Ask a salesclerk whether the items are imperfect or top quality. Learn the return policy.
	↓
Fourth event or step in time:	Perform a final check by trying on all clothing and looking over items for defects.

Spatial Order

With **spatial order,** you move across space in some specific way, such as from top to bottom, outside to inside, near to far, or left to right. Spatial order is often used when you want to describe something. Suppose you want to describe your dorm room for a friend considering living on campus. Here is how you can arrange your ideas in a spatial order that moves around the room in clockwise direction.

Spatial Order

Preliminary thesis:	A dormitory room has *none* of the comforts of home.
	↓
Standing at the door and looking to the left:	Describe the bunk beds: institutional, dilapidated, uncomfortable.
	↓
To the right of the beds:	Describe the window: graying curtains; filmy, depressing view of power plant.
	↓

To the right of the window:	Describe the two dressers: too small, scratched, broken drawer, old-fashioned.
	↓
To the right of the dressers:	Describe the two study desks: facing each other, gooseneck lamps, hard wood chairs, too small for computers, no bookshelves, uneven legs.
	↓
To the right of the desks:	Describe the closet: room for hanging clothes for a three-year-old, no shelves, funhouse mirror on the door.

Progressive Order

With **progressive order,** you move from the *least* compelling idea to the *most* compelling one according to how important, surprising, convincing, representative, interesting, or unusual the ideas are. With your most compelling points at the end, you leave your reader with a strong final impression. Or you can arrange your ideas from the most to the least compelling, for the strongest possible opening. A third variation is to open *and* close with your strongest points. Of course, how compelling an idea is will often vary from audience to audience. For example, the idea that an increase in the state sales tax will benefit schools may not be a compelling reason for a senior citizen on a fixed income to vote for the tax, but it is likely to be a compelling reason for parents of young children. Progressive order is most often used when you want to persuade your reader to think or act in a particular way. Suppose you are writing to convince parents of young children that schools should offer classes in conflict resolution. Here is how you could arrange your ideas in a progressive order.

Progressive Order

Preliminary thesis:	Beginning in first grade, schools should offer conflict resolution classes.
	↓
Least compelling idea:	The courses are inexpensive to run.
	↓
Somewhat more compelling idea:	The courses will help students resolve their own disputes and free teachers from this distraction.
	↓
Even more compelling idea:	Students will learn skills that will eventually aid them in their personal lives and in the workplace.
	↓
Most compelling idea:	Studies show that the classes are likely to reduce the amount of lethal and nonlethal violence in schools.

EXERCISE Ordering Ideas

Directions: For each preliminary thesis, decide whether chronological, spatial, or progressive order would be suitable. Be prepared to explain your choice. (In some cases, more than one arrangement can be effective.)

1. The events that network news programs do *not* report are often more important than the stories they *do* report.
2. The new office tower downtown is not designed with the architecture of surrounding buildings in mind.
3. Since the attacks on the World Trade Center and Pentagon on September 11, 2001, I have a better sense of what is important in life.
4. The first vacation I took with my husband was a comedy of errors.
5. The housing development on the edge of town is perfect for families with young children.
6. Police officers and firefighters should not be permitted to strike.
7. Now that it has been restored, the lobby of Bicksford Inn has an inviting Victorian charm.
8. With the right tools and materials, anyone can build a sturdy bookcase.
9. There are three effective ways to deal with a bully.
10. After my three-year-old twins' birthday party, my backyard looked like the site of a natural disaster. ■

Outlining

Once you have a sense of the best ordering strategy for your ideas, you can arrange your ideas using that order with the help of an outline. Many student writers resist outlining because they see it as time-consuming, difficult, and unnecessary. Yet outlining does not deserve this reputation. Because it helps you organize your ideas before drafting, outlining can ensure the success of an essay and make drafting easier. If you do not order and group your ideas with some kind of outline, prior to drafting, you will have to order and group your ideas as you draft, which complicates the drafting process.

Outlines can be detailed or sketchy, formal or informal. Long, complex essays often call for formal, detailed outlines, while briefer pieces can be planned with less detailed, more informal outlines.

The Formal Outline

The **formal outline,** which is the most detailed, structured outline, allows you to plot all your main ideas and major supporting details. This is the outline that uses roman numerals, letters, and arabic numbers. Main ideas are designated with roman numerals; supporting details to develop a main idea are designated with capital letters; points to further develop supporting details are designated with arabic numbers. The format looks like some variation of this:

Preliminary Thesis

I. Main idea
  A. Supporting detail
  B. Supporting detail
  C. Supporting detail
II. Main idea
  A. Supporting detail
    1. Further development
    2. Further development
  B. Supporting detail

Here is an example of a formal outline written for an essay about the attitudes of children toward food. Note that each main idea and supporting detail is stated in a complete sentence. Also note that the ordering strategy is progressive.

Thesis: Children can be taught to have healthy attitudes about food.

I. Parents should make mealtimes pleasant.
  A. Keep conversation enjoyable.
    1. Avoid discussing problems.
    2. Avoid arguments about food.
  B. Serve balanced meals and let children choose quantities.
  C. Avoid eating in front of the television.
II. Parents should not forbid children to eat certain foods.
  A. Children will want what they cannot have.
  B. Reasonable amounts of sugar and fat are not harmful.
III. Parents should stress health and fitness.
  A. Teach nutrition.
  B. Serve healthy foods.
  C. Exercise with children.
  D. Set an example.
IV. Parents should praise children for their behavior, not their appearance.
  A. Children should take pride in what they do, not in how thin they are.
  B. Those with a tendency toward carrying more weight need to like themselves.

www.mhhe.com/tsw

For more help with outlining, go to Catalyst 2.0 > Writing > Outlining Tutor

You may prefer writing a formal outline with phrases rather than with sentences, as in this excerpt of a phrase outline for an essay on the causes of eating disorders.

I. Poor self-image
  A. Caused by media emphasis on thinness
  B. Caused by self-hatred

Outline Cards

To outline using cards, you need several large index cards (or you can use sheets of paper). Use one card to plan each paragraph. On each of your cards, list your ideas in the order they will appear in the paragraph the card represents.

One advantage of cards is flexibility: You can shuffle paragraph cards into different sequences to examine alternative arrangements.

The Outline Worksheet

The outline worksheet, like outline cards, allows you to plot organization in as great or as little detail as you require. While it is not as easy to rework parts of the outline when the worksheet is used (this is the advantage of cards), it is easy to get a clear overview of your organization (this is one advantage of the formal outline).

Below is a sample outline worksheet. To use it, fill in the blanks with the amount of detail that works for you.

Sample Outline Worksheet

Introduction

Detail to generate reader interest ______________________________

____

____

Preliminary thesis ______________________________

____

Paragraph

Main idea ______________________________

Supporting details ______________________________

____

____

Paragraph

Main idea ______________________________

____

Supporting details ______________________________

____

____

____

(*Note:* The number of paragraph sections will correspond to the number of paragraphs planned for the first draft.)

Conclusion

Detail to provide closure ______________________________

____

____

Here is a sample outline worksheet for an essay about the attitudes of children toward food.

Sample Outline Worksheet

Introduction

Detail to generate reader interest *Give statistics on number of overweight children in the United States.*

Preliminary thesis *Children can be taught to have healthy attitudes about food.*

Paragraph

Main idea *Parents should stress health and fitness.*

Supporting details *Teach nutrition, serve healthy foods, exercise with children, set example.*

Paragraph

Main idea *Parents should make mealtime pleasant.*

Supporting details *Keep conversation enjoyable, serve balanced meals, let children choose quantities, avoid eating in front of television.*

Paragraph

Main idea *Parents should not forbid children to eat certain foods.*

Supporting details *Children will want what they can't have. Reasonable amounts of sugar and fat are not harmful.*

Paragraph

Main idea *Parents should praise children for their behavior, not appearance.*

Supporting details *Children should be proud of what they do, not how thin they are. Heavier-set children need to like themselves.*

Conclusion

Detail to provide closure *Explain how important it is for children to have healthy attitudes about food.*

The Outline Tree

An outline tree helps you visualize the relationships among ideas. It also helps you determine where more ideas are needed. The following example uses ideas discovered in the mapping on page 48.

To develop an outline tree, first write your preliminary thesis. Then place the first branches of the tree, using your main ideas.

There are a number of ways to control teenage drinking.

start a "Just Say No" campaign like for drugs

eliminate TV ads

run antidrinking ads on TV and radio

have antidrinking programs in school

Each of the first branches will be the main idea of one or more paragraphs. Next, build the tree by adding additional branches.

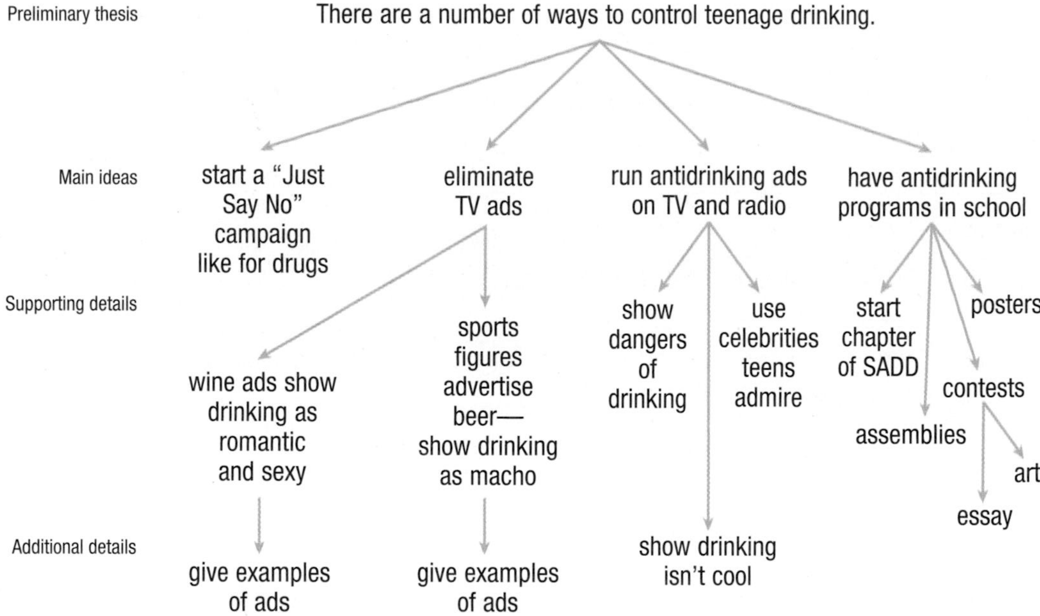

Notice that this tree grows down rather than up. The first level of branches gives the main ideas. The branches after the first level represent supporting details to develop main ideas. You can study your outline tree to determine where detail is needed. For example, studying the above outline tree reveals that supporting details are needed to develop the main idea that a "Just Say No" campaign could be started. If detail cannot be developed for this idea, then it should be eliminated or combined with "have antidrinking programs in school." Further study shows that examples of wine ads and sports figures must be generated.

The Scratch Outline

You learned about the scratch outline when you read about idea generation on page 45. This outline is for writers who prefer to come to the first draft knowing only the main ideas that will be discussed and maybe the order they will be presented in. The outline does not usually include much of the detail that will develop the main ideas, so writers who use it must have in mind how their ideas will be supported, or they must be capable of developing the ideas as they draft.

An example of a scratch outline appears on pages 45–46. It shows how to turn an idea generation list into a scratch outline that groups related ideas. Some scratch outlines offer even less organizational guidance. The following scratch outline for an essay on why schools should ban cell phones is such an outline. This outline lists ideas; the numbers give the order in which the ideas will be written in the draft. The ordering strategy seems to be progressive.

③ *students leave class to place calls*
② *ring in class*
⑤ *have games on them played in class*
⑥ *used to cheat—instant messaging, store answers*
④ *one kid used the phone to order pizza in study hall*
① *distracting*
⑦ *used to get in trouble (drug dealing)*

PROCESS GUIDELINES

Outlining

- If you have trouble developing your outline, return to idea generation.
- As you outline, be prepared to rethink your preliminary thesis, add or delete ideas, reconsider your audience, or change your purpose as you make discoveries.
- In general, recognize that more detailed outlines make for smoother drafting.
- If your computer has an outline program, try it out to see if you like it.

ANTHONY'S ESSAY IN PROGRESS: Outlining

In Chapter 2, you observed student writer Anthony Torres as he decided on a writing topic; determined his purpose, audience, and preliminary thesis; and developed ideas for his essay about requiring bicyclists to wear helmets. Now observe how Anthony outlined.

Anthony's idea generation and preliminary thesis. Anthony studied his idea generation list and preliminary thesis, which are reproduced here.

Preliminary thesis: Requiring everyone under 18 to wear bicycle helmets would reduce the number of tragic injuries.

Lou and I get call.
We travel to scene.
We find young girl (Kelly) in bad shape from a hit-and-run driver (describe injuries).
We transport her.
Tell about arrival at the hospital?
Kelly ends up paralyzed.
Explain how helmet would have helped.
—protect head
—probably prevent paralysis
—injuries would have been less extensive
Kelly illustrates the importance of helmets. (Get statistics and information on how much helmets help?)

When he studied this material, Anthony decided that he knew what his main ideas would be. However, he was unsure how he would develop those ideas, and he could not visualize how his essay would come together.

Anthony's outline worksheet. Anthony decided to write an outline worksheet to see how his ideas would fit into paragraphs. Notice that sometimes Anthony indicated specific details, and sometimes he merely noted the general sense of what he wanted to say. He also generated some additional ideas.

Sample Outline Worksheet

Introduction

Detail to generate reader interest *Lou and I are in crew quarters taking inventory and call comes in. What I saw on the call made me realize how dangerous bikes are.*

Preliminary thesis *Requiring everyone under 18 to wear bicycle helmets would reduce the number of tragic injuries.*

Paragraph

Main idea *We travel to the scene.*

Supporting details *Tell what we saw—Kelly in bad shape: multiple lacerations, fractured leg, collapsed lung, internal bleeding.*

Paragraph

Main idea *Kelly's heart stops.*

Supporting details *Explain what we did.*

Paragraph

Main idea *We transport Kelly.*

Supporting details *At the hospital medical team works on her and she has surgery. Kelly paralyzed.*

Paragraph

Main idea *How helmet would have helped*

Supporting details *Protect head, prevent paralysis, injuries would have been less extensive (give stats?).*

Conclusion

Detail to provide closure *Kelly illustrates importance of helmets—if only she had been wearing one.*

EXERCISE Your Essay in Progress

Directions: After completing this exercise, save your responses. They will be used again in this chapter and later as you work toward a completed essay.

1. Assume you have won a writer's contest. As the winner, you may write a four-page, typed article that will be published in the magazine of your choice. You may write on any topic. What topic will you write about? (Use the idea generation techniques described in Chapter 2 if you have trouble choosing a topic.)
2. For what purpose will you write this article? (If necessary, determine your purpose by answering the questions on page 40.)
3. What magazine will you publish your article in?
4. What are the typical readers of this magazine like? (If necessary, answer the audience assessment questions on page 42.)
5. Generate as many ideas as you can to include in this article. Try using at least two of the idea generation techniques described in Chapter 2.
6. What ordering strategy do your ideas suggest? Select the outlining technique that most appeals to you, and outline your ideas.
7. Now select a different outlining technique, and outline your ideas a second time.
8. Do you like one of the outlining techniques better than another? If so, which one, and why? ■

DRAFTING AND STRUCTURING YOUR ESSAY

A first draft, often called a **rough draft,** is an initial effort to transform your ideas and outline into an essay. This early effort is tentative, subject to changes of every kind. It will have errors and rough spots, but it provides material to shape into a finished piece. By the time the final essay *is* complete, you may have made so many changes that it bears little resemblance to the original draft.

As you draft, remember that most essays have three parts: an introduction, body paragraphs, and a conclusion.

The opening paragraph or paragraphs of an essay are the **introduction.** Your introduction should create interest in your essay so your reader wants to read on. The introduction often includes your thesis, to let your reader know your topic, as well as the central point you will make about that topic.

The middle of your essay is composed of **body paragraphs.** These are the heart of your essay because they explain or prove your thesis. In other words, this is where you include ideas to *develop* your thesis. A body paragraph often has a **topic sentence** that states the main idea of the paragraph.

The final paragraph or paragraphs are the **conclusion.** The conclusion brings your essay to a satisfying finish.

LEARNING FROM OTHER WRITERS: Student Essay

The next draft of a student essay illustrates essay structure. The marginal notes call your attention to the structural features discussed throughout the rest of this chapter.

Paragraph 1
This is the introduction. It aims to spark reader interest, and it presents the thesis, which is the last sentence. The thesis gives the topic as banning alcohol on campus property and at campus events; the central point is that the alcohol should be banned.

Banning Alcohol on College Campuses

Marcie Katz

When you think of the Massachusetts Institute of Technology (MIT to most of us), does your mind call up images of computer nerds and engineering geeks who spend every waking hour of every day bent over their textbooks or glued to their computer monitors? Do you think of super-intellectuals on their way to the library in pants a few inches too short, revealing white socks and an inch or so of skin at the ankle? Even if these are not the images the school conjures up for you, I doubt you think of wild fraternity parties and nonstop drinking. After all, those are the images of a party school, and MIT is certainly not that—or is it? Scott Krueger, a fraternity pledge at MIT, did what far too many college students do. He drank himself to death. And so did Benjamin Wynne at Louisiana State, Matthew Farofalo at the University of Iowa, Samantha Spady at Colorado State University, and Blake Adam Hammontree at the University of Oklahoma. These are not isolated cases. Drinking on college campuses is legendary, but it must stop because students are dying. Colleges must ban all alcohol consumption on college property and at all campus events. 1

Colleges know they have a responsibility to protect students, but they are not living up to that responsibility. Many schools sponsor alcohol awareness programs and responsible drinking seminars in an effort to fulfill their responsibility to educate and protect students, but these measures have not worked, and students are dying as a result. During my first-year orientation, the dean of students lectured us about drinking, but most of us just laughed the lecture off. No one took the talk seriously. Many students respond to the lecture by saying that the dangers of drinking are overrated, that they are adults who can drink in moderation. However, most first and second year students are *not* adults; they are under 21, which is the legal drinking age. Further, many of these students are not drinking in moderation. They are binge drinking and dying as a result, so a measure more effective than lectures and programs is called for, and that measure is banning alcohol completely. 2

Paragraph 2
This is a body paragraph. The first sentence is the topic sentence, which gives the main idea of the paragraph as colleges failing to live up to their responsibility to protect students. The rest of the paragraph develops and explains the topic sentence idea and restates the need to ban alcohol.

Of course, when schools ban alcohol, the ban cannot be for students alone. There can be no drinking anywhere on campus for any function, even if students are not in attendance. That means no drinking in the president's box of the football stadium, no drinking at faculty mixers on college property, no drinking at tailgate parties, and so on. The statement must be made from the top down: Drinking is dangerous and cannot be allowed. Certainly, many faculty, staff, and alumni will object to attending functions where no alcohol is served, but that grousing will be temporary. I am confident that after some time, people will adjust and enjoy themselves while remaining sober, and they will recognize that they are setting a good example for students. And even if they don't adjust, we have to ask what is more important—appeasing some who can't live without a drink or protecting students. 3

Paragraph 3
This is a body paragraph. The topic sentence, which is formed by the first two sentences, gives the main idea as banning alcohol for everyone on campus, not just students. The rest of the paragraph explains why that is necessary and what the possible outcome will be.

By itself, banning alcohol is not enough because many students will ignore the ban. Some students are compelled to test authority. Other students think drinking is part of the privilege of going to college, and they think they cannot enjoy themselves unless they drink. However, strong punishment attached to the ban would be a deterrent. I recommend a single warning followed by suspension. Most students threatened with suspension are not likely to risk drinking. And if 4

Paragraph 4
This is a body paragraph. The fourth sentence is the topic sentence, which gives the main idea that strong punishment should be attached to the ban. The rest of the paragraph explains how that punishment would work.

some students are suspended, the university will be better off with them gone because they were bad examples. Of course, once the ban against alcohol is published and becomes widely known, students will make their peace with not drinking on campus property. They—like everyone else—can still drink off campus, when they can do so legally, so the ban I propose is not a universal prohibition. However, to help guard against life-threatening drinking, colleges should use the single-warning-followed-by-suspension punishment for any student who is drunk on campus, who is found to be drinking underage, or who is arrested by local police for intoxication. Off-campus drinking cannot be stopped, but it can be deterred enough to save some lives.

Paragraph 5
This is the conclusion. It brings the essay to a satisfying end by restating the thesis and the related idea that colleges are responsible for alcohol-related deaths if they do not ban drinking.

Binge drinking and alcoholism are serious problems in this country and 5
on our campuses. When colleges allow drinking, they are contributing to the problem—and the deaths that result. No longer can schools stand by, content that "safe drinking" lectures fulfill their obligation to protect students. They need to take bold action. They need to ban drinking altogether.

www.mhhe.com/tsw
For online exercises and information on introductions, go to Catalyst 2.0 > Writing > Paragraph/Essay Development > Introductions

THE INTRODUCTION

The introduction to your essay shapes your reader's first impression, and first impressions count. Have you ever dropped a course after attending just one class session or selected a restaurant based on its name? If so, you know the importance of first impressions.

To make a good first impression and keep your audience reading, craft your introduction to engage your reader's interest and set the tone of your essay, marking it as serious, satirical, angry, concerned, and so on. Finally, you can note what your essay is about by including the thesis in your introduction.

To create interest in your essay, suit your introduction to your audience and purpose. For example, if your purpose is to inform your reader about dangerous spam e-mail, you should not begin with a humorous anecdote about a piece of unsolicited pornographic e-mail you received. However, your introduction might tell about a time pornographic spam reached a child. If you are writing to the editor of your local newspaper, you should not open with a graphic description of a pornographic spam e-mail, but you might do so for the customer service representative of your Internet provider.

Finally, do not refer to your title as if it were part of your introduction. For example, if your title is "The Impact of the Internet," avoid beginning with "It has changed the way we work and live."

Below are some strategies for creating interest in your essay, along with sample introductions to illustrate each technique. Each thesis is underlined as a study aid. Notice that often, the thesis is the last sentence of the introduction, but it can also come first or fall in the middle.

The strategies given here are possibilities; you are not limited to them. As you draft, you may find a different, more suitable strategy.

Provide Background Information

Rick was always taking crazy chances. Even in elementary school, he was the one to lock himself in the teacher's supply closet or lick a metal pole in the dead of a subzero winter. By high school, Rick had moved on to wilder things, but his drinking was the biggest concern. I guess that is why no one was really surprised when he drove off the road and killed himself the day after his 18th birthday.

Tell a Pertinent Story

Last winter while home alone, I tripped on the garden hose and fell in my garage when the door was down. The pain was excruciating, and I could not move. I lay there for two hours, sobbing, until my son came home. I am not an old woman; I am just 45. However, that experience made me feel fearful of growing old and living alone.

Explain Why Your Topic Is Important

The recent tuition hike proposed by the Board of Trustees has serious implications for everyone on this campus—students, faculty, and staff alike.If tuition goes up 45 percent as expected, fewer students will be able to attend school, which will mean fewer faculty and staff will be employed. Once the cost of school becomes prohibitive for all but the wealthy, then this university will begin a downward spiral that will eventually compromise its quality. There is only one way to solve our economic woes. We must embark on an austerity program that makes the tuition hike unnecessary.

Present Some Interesting Images or Use Description

It was a cool, crisp October morning. Sunrise was complete, the countryside awake and responding to another day. As I turned and slowly made my way into the woods, I had no idea what lay ahead on the path I was to follow that day.

Present an Intriguing Problem or Raise a Provocative Question

Are you a Dr. Jekyll who transforms into Mr. Hyde the minute you get behind the wheel of a car? Are you a kind little old lady who becomes Mario Andretti's pace car driver the instant you hit the freeway? Are you an Eagle Scout by day and a marauding motorist by night? The chances are good that you are because people's personalities change the moment they strap on that seat belt and head out on the highway.

Present an Opposing Viewpoint

People opposed to putting warning labels on CDs with sexually explicit or otherwise offensive lyrics have their reasons. They cite free speech, and they say teens will be encouraged to buy the CDs with the advisory labels. Even so, I favor warning labels on certain kinds of CDs.

Establish Yourself as Someone Knowledgeable about the Topic

Believe me, racial prejudice is still a fact of American life, no matter what you hear to the contrary. You see, I am what is known as an "army brat." My dad is a career army man who gets moved from post to post. Since he takes his family along with him, I have lived in eight cities over the course of my 19 years. I have known small towns and large, northern cities and southern, rural environments and urban centers. And no matter where I have lived, as an African-American, I have encountered prejudice.

Note: Avoid apologizing. Statements like "I really don't know much about this topic" or "I doubt that anyone can understand this issue" will cause your reader to lose confidence in what you have to say.

Open with an Attention-Grabbing Statement

What your family doctor does not know may surprise you—or it may kill you. We assume our doctors are smart and caring, that they will do whatever it takes to keep us well. We put our trust in them and never question their advice or decisions. Unfortunately, such trust is often misplaced. For the best health care, we need to learn to question our doctors carefully.

Explain Your Purpose

All students should contact the Dean of Academic Affairs to protest the cancellation of the artist-in-residence program. If enough students express their unhappiness, the dean will be forced to reinstate the program.

Find Some Common Ground to Establish a Bond with Your Reader

None of us goes through life without doing something that we later regret. In fact, we often have many regrets. Fortunately, we are often given second chances and we redeem ourselves. It should not be any different for people released from prison after serving their sentences. These people should not be denied their second chances. Convicted felons who have served their sentences should be allowed to vote.

Provide an Interesting Quotation

Mark Twain said, "Man is the only animal who blushes—or needs to." I take comfort in that statement when I recall the most embarrassing night of my life.

Note: Your quotation should not be a **cliché** (overused expression), such as "It's always darkest before the dawn" or "Fools rush in where angels fear to tread." Clichés are boring and will not spark interest in your essay.

Define Something

A good teacher is someone who sees what students can do, rather than what they cannot do. A good teacher shares knowledge, helps students achieve their potential, and fosters self-esteem. Without a doubt, Dr. Sorenson is a good teacher.

Note: Avoid using a dictionary definition because it can be dull or overused.

Give Relevant Examples

Sometimes telling a lie is better than telling the truth. When a friend asks you what you think of the hideous glasses he just paid a great deal of money for, when your grandmother asks you what you think of the rubber chicken she lovingly prepared for your birthday, when your girlfriend asks if her dress makes her look fat—it is best to lie.

PROCESS GUIDELINES

Drafting Introductions

If you have trouble drafting your introduction, try the following:

- Skip it and come back to it after drafting the rest of your essay, but jot down your preliminary thesis to guide and focus your draft.
- Keep it simple, even just one or two sentences to create interest, and then state your thesis.

EXERCISE The Introduction

1. Read the introductions of three articles in newsmagazines or newspapers. Do they engage your interest? Explain why or why not.
2. Below are three introductions written by students, each in need of revision. Select one and revise it so that it stimulates interest and has a suitable thesis.

   a. It was snowing when I boarded the plane. But I was terrified. I have always been afraid of air travel, and hopefully I will someday overcome this fear.

   Some suggestions for revision: Create some images. Describe the weather in more detail. Specify the kind of airplane and explain more carefully the feeling of terror. Also, does the thesis present one or two opinions? It should present only one.

   b. I set the alarm two hours earlier than usual and spent the morning cleaning like crazy. At 11:00 I went to the grocery store and bought all the necessary food. All afternoon I cooked; by 5:00 I was dressed and ready; but still the first meal I cooked for my in-laws was bad.

   Some suggestions for revision: Be more specific. What time did the alarm go off? Give an example or two of the cleaning you did. What food did you buy? Was it expensive? What did you cook? How bad was it? Can you find a word or words more specific than *bad*?

c. Does crime pay? Does justice win out? Do the police always get their man? The day I shoplifted a box of candy I learned the answers to these questions.

Some suggestions for revision: Substitute more interesting questions for these trite, rather boring ones—perhaps some questions that focus on the writer's feelings, such as "Have you ever wondered what a criminal feels when he or she gets caught?" Create some interest by naming the brand or type of candy and giving its price and by giving the name of the store.

3. Select one of the preliminary thesis statements you shaped when you responded to question 5 on page 56. Establish an audience and purpose, and write an introduction for an essay that might use that thesis. Feel free to alter the original thesis. ■

BODY PARAGRAPHS

Body paragraphs, which explain or prove your thesis, are the core of your essay. They can be written using a variety of patterns of development, such as description, narration, exemplification, and cause-and-effect analysis, all of which are explained in Part 2.

A typical body paragraph has two parts: the topic sentence and the supporting details. The **topic sentence** states the focus of the paragraph, the main idea the paragraph will discuss. The **supporting details** are all the information that explains or proves the topic sentence.

Qualities of an Effective Topic Sentence

An effective **topic sentence** has these characteristics:

- It accurately and clearly states the main idea of the body paragraph.
- It states only one main idea.
- It states an idea related to the thesis.

First, a topic sentence should accurately and clearly state the main idea of the body paragraph. If your topic sentence indicates one main idea for the paragraph, but your supporting details go in a different direction, your reader will be confused. To state the main idea precisely, be specific.

Vague: Colleges know they should behave responsibly when it comes to their students. [What is proper behavior?]

Specific: Colleges must ban all alcohol consumption on college property and at all campus events. [The specific behavior is given.]

Second, a topic sentence should state one main idea. A topic sentence that presents more than one main idea splits your focus and gives you too much to do in a single paragraph.

Split focus: Online shopping offers convenience and affordability.

One main idea: Online shopping offers convenience.

One main idea: Online shopping offers affordability.

Third, a topic sentence should state a main idea related to the thesis. The topic sentence idea must be related to both the topic and the central point of the thesis, or your essay will wander off course.

Thesis: Oprah Winfrey has had an impact on literary culture.

Unrelated sentence: When Oprah endorses a movie, ticket sales soar. [This topic sentence does not focus on the central point—that Oprah has affected *literary* culture.]

Related topic: Thanks to Oprah's book club, more Americans are buying and reading books. [This topic sentence focuses on both the thesis topic—Oprah Winfrey—and the central point—she has affected American literary culture.]

Placement of the Topic Sentence

The topic sentence most often appears first, announcing the paragraph's focus. When the topic sentence comes first, the supporting details that follow explain or prove the topic sentence, as the following example from "Banning Alcohol on Campus" illustrates. The topic sentence is underlined as a study aid.

Thesis: Colleges must ban all alcohol consumption on college property and at all campus events.

Colleges know they have a responsibility to protect students, but they are not living up to that responsibility. Many schools sponsor alcohol awareness programs and responsible drinking seminars in an effort to fulfill their responsibility to educate and protect students, but these measures have not worked, and students are dying as a result. During my first-year orientation, the dean of students lectured us about drinking, but most of us just laughed the lecture off. No one took the talk seriously. Many students respond to the lecture by saying that the dangers of drinking are overrated, that they are adults who can drink in moderation. However, most first and second year students are *not* adults; they are under 21, which is the legal drinking age. Further, many of these students are not drinking in moderation. They are binge drinking and dying as a result, so a measure more effective than lectures and programs is called for, and that measure is banning alcohol completely.

Your topic sentence can also come *near* but not *at* the beginning of the paragraph, especially when you want to open the paragraph with a sentence or two that links it to the one before, to achieve *coherence* (discussed in the next chapter). To illustrate, here is paragraph 3 from "Banning Alcohol on College Campuses." The bracketed sentence links the paragraph to paragraph 2 (the first illustration paragraph above). The topic sentence is underlined.

> [Of course, when schools ban alcohol, the ban cannot be for students alone.] <u>There can be no drinking anywhere on campus for any function, even if students are not in attendance.</u> That means no drinking in the president's box of the football stadium, no drinking at faculty mixers on college property, no drinking at tailgate parties, and so on. The statement must be made from the top down: Drinking is dangerous and cannot be allowed. Certainly, many faculty, staff, and alumni will object to attending functions where no alcohol is served, but that grousing will be temporary. I am confident that after some time, people will adjust and enjoy themselves while remaining sober, and they will recognize that they are setting a good example for students. And even if they don't adjust, we have to ask what is more important—appeasing some who can't live without a drink or protecting students.

At times, placing your topic sentence at the end of the paragraph will be effective. In this case, it draws a conclusion from the supporting details. Here is another example from "Banning Alcohol on College Campuses." Again, the topic sentence is underlined.

> By itself, banning alcohol is not enough because many students will ignore the ban. Some students are compelled to test authority. Other students think drinking is part of the privilege of going to college, and they think they cannot enjoy themselves unless they drink. However, strong punishment attached to the ban would be a deterrent. I recommend a single warning followed by suspension. Most students threatened with suspension are not likely to risk drinking. And if some students are suspended, the university will be better off with them gone because they were bad examples. Of course, once the ban against alcohol is published and becomes widely known, students will make their peace with not drinking on campus property. They—

like everyone else—can still drink off campus, when they can do so legally, so the ban I propose is not a universal prohibition. However, to help guard against life-threatening drinking, colleges should use the single-warning-followed-by-suspension punishment for any student who is drunk on campus, who is found to be drinking underage, or who is arrested by local police for intoxication. Off-campus drinking cannot be stopped, but it can be deterred enough to save some lives.

The Implied Topic Sentence

When a topic sentence is implied rather than stated, the details in the paragraph clearly suggest the main idea. Here is an example from "That Street Called Cordova" on page 90. The thesis is that something was always happening on Cordova, the street where the writer grew up.

Two hours later, I was back outside, looking for all the kids, and I ran into Ms. Berry. "What are you doing outside, Boy?" she asked. "Haven't you had enough drama today to last you a lifetime?" I had a quick flashback to this morning. "Haven't you had enough of boyfriends to last you two lifetimes?" I replied. Her mouth dropped as she raised her hand. I don't know what I was thinking. I could do nothing but brace myself for the impact. SLAP! "Don't you ever disrespect your elders again. Now go tell your mama that I smacked your mouth, and then tell her why." My mother and Ms. Berry were like sisters, and my mother had given Ms. Berry permission to whoop us kids if she ever caught us getting out of line when she wasn't around. I felt like crying, but Ms. Berry would have slapped me again. So I ran. I ended up at the candy lady's house for something to take my mind off the sting. Some Now & Laters did it.

The Qualities of Effective Supporting Details

Supporting details demonstrate the truth of the topic sentence. Effective supporting details have these characteristics:

- They are adequate (there must be enough of them).
- They are relevant to the topic sentence.

First, supporting details should be adequate. Supporting details are *adequate* when there are enough of them to prove or explain the topic sentence idea. The best way to provide adequate detail is to *show* as well as *tell.* For example, read the following body paragraph from an early draft of "Banning Alcohol on College Campuses":

> By itself, banning alcohol is not enough because many students will ignore the ban. However, strong punishment would be a deterrent. I recommend a single warning followed by suspension. And if some students are suspended, the university will be better off with them gone because they were bad examples. Of course, once the ban against alcohol is published and becomes widely known, students will make their peace with not drinking on campus property. And although schools cannot ban off-campus drinking, they can still punish those who drink off campus.

The supporting details in this early draft are not adequate because they *tell* that some students will ignore the ban, they *tell* that strong punishment will be a deterrent to drinking, and they *tell* that schools can punish those who drink off campus—but they do not *show* by explaining or proving any of these points. If you compare this paragraph to the final version, which follows, you will see that the writer added the underlined points. Do you think they are enough to make the detail adequate?

> By itself, banning alcohol is not enough because many students will ignore the ban. Some students are compelled to test authority. Other students think drinking is part of the privilege of going to college, and they think they cannot enjoy themselves unless they drink. However, strong punishment attached to the ban would be a deterrent. I recommend a single warning followed by suspension. Most students threatened with suspension are not likely to risk drinking. And if some students are suspended, the university will be better off with them gone because they were bad examples. Of course, once the ban against alcohol is published and becomes widely known, students will make their peace with not drinking on campus property. They—like everyone else—can still drink off campus, when they can do so legally, so the ban I propose is not a universal prohibition. However, to help guard against life-threatening drinking, colleges should use the single-warning-followed-by-suspension punishment for any student who is drunk on campus, who is found to be drinking underage, or who is arrested by local police for intoxication. Off-campus drinking

cannot be stopped, but it can be deterred enough to save some lives.

Second, in addition to being adequate, supporting details must be *relevant,* or clearly and directly related to the main idea expressed in the topic sentence. Consider this paragraph from an early draft of an essay about the determination of the writer's brother, Hugh, who had only one arm:

> Hugh's inability to swim was yet another problem that he had to overcome. For years, he thought that he could not swim with one arm, so he never tried. It was not until I was drowning in Lake Erie that Hugh decided he would learn to swim. Much to his own surprise, he found that he could stay afloat. It was his determination to overcome fear that gave him the confidence to jump in the water and save my life that day. Of course, once he realized that he wouldn't drown, Hugh went on to practice his swimming techniques with the same determination he brings to every challenge. Now he swims farther and faster than I do. Hugh can also beat me in any short distance race, which is a further indication that his disability does not stand in his way.

Did you notice the irrelevant sentence? The last sentence does not belong in the paragraph because it is about running—and the topic sentence focuses on swimming.

PROCESS GUIDELINES

Drafting Body Paragraphs

- Keep your audience and purpose in mind, and think about how your supporting details are helping you achieve your purpose with your particular reader.
- Be receptive to new ideas and discoveries. Be prepared to go back and alter decisions you made before drafting. Remember, your outline and idea generation material are flexible.
- Do not expect your body paragraphs to be richly detailed, beautifully expressed, or perfectly organized. Just do the best you can. Remember, revision comes next.
- If you have trouble drafting:
  - If you like to compose at the computer, keep in mind that when you have trouble with a paragraph, you can paste in the relevant portion of your outline as a placeholder and a reminder of what goes in that spot.

- Write your draft as you would explain your ideas to a close friend, or write the draft as a letter to a friend.
- Stop and generate more ideas with one or more of the idea generation techniques; you may not have enough material yet to begin a draft.
- Revise your topic to something easier to write about.
- Leave your work for a while. Your ideas may need an incubation period. Obviously, you must start your writing early, so you have time for an incubation period, something Sally fails to understand in the *Peanuts* comic strip.

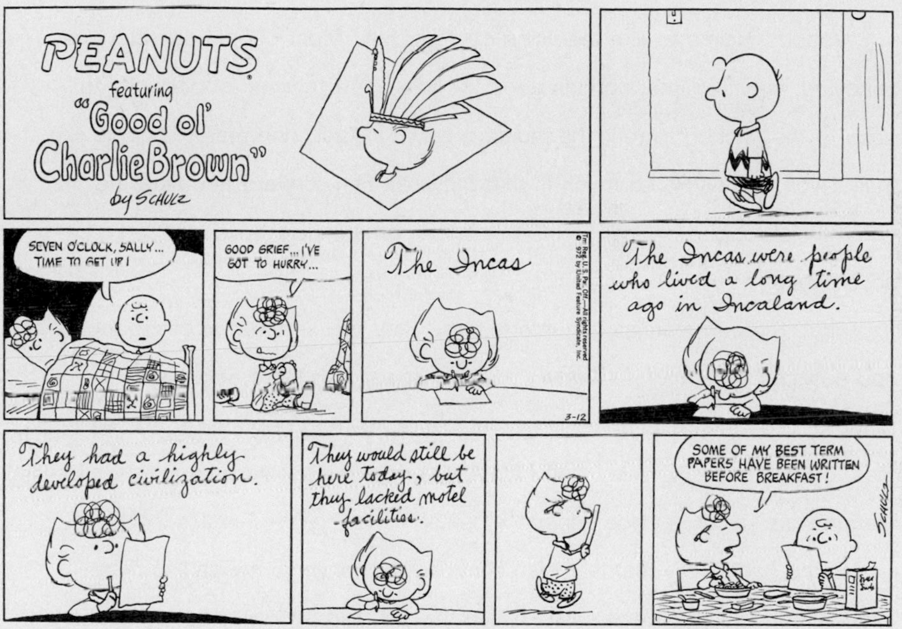

Peanuts reprinted by permission of United Feature Syndicate, Inc.

When to Begin a New Paragraph

The following can help you determine when to begin a new body paragraph:

1. Begin a new paragraph each time you begin discussing a new point to explain or prove your thesis.
2. If the supporting details make for a very long paragraph, break up the discussion into two or more paragraphs.
3. If you want to give an idea special emphasis, place it in its own paragraph. Do not overuse this strategy, however, or it will have the opposite of the intended effect.

EXERCISE Body Paragraphs

1. Read the following first draft of an essay. For each body paragraph (paragraphs 2–5), list the revisions you would recommend to the writer. Your suggestions might include comments such as "Delete the third sentence because it is repetitious" and "Add examples of informative commercials to show and not just tell."

Let's Hear It for Commercials

Nobody claims to like television commercials. Most people say they are annoying, insulting interruptions good for little more than an opportunity to dash to the kitchen to refill the munchie bowl. In fact, one reason people like their TiVos and DVRs so much is that they can fast forward and skip the commercials. Nonetheless, I think television commercials have decided advantages. 1

First, the commercials are informative. They advise viewers of products and services they may not know about. A viewer can learn about a wide range of products, everything from medication to treat depression and allergies to shampoos for shiny, soft hair. A viewer can also learn important information from public service announcements. 2

Some people say that television commercials are more misleading than informative. However, viewers who watch the ads with a clear head will not be misled or manipulated. Instead, they will gain useful information. They will learn about products and not have an exaggerated sense of what the product can do. 3

In addition to informing viewers, television commercials often entertain them. In fact, some commercials are more clever and entertaining than the programs they interrupt. The series of ads currently running for Macintosh computers is a good example. The nerdy man who represents "the PC" is cast as a loser next to the cool guy who represents "the Mac" computer. These ads are very clever and entertaining. Entertaining commercials can be so well done that people can watch them repeatedly without getting bored. 4

More than anything, television commercials are valuable because they pay for the programs we view. The ads may be an interruption, but without them there would be no shows on commercial television to interrupt. Without the revenue from commercials, networks and local stations would have to charge viewers, the way cable channels currently do. People who could not afford to pay would be forced to live without television. 5

Television commercials are underappreciated. They inform and entertain, and they pay for the programs we watch. And let's not forget that by encouraging us to buy, the commercials stimulate the economy. 6

2. Pick one of the body paragraphs and rewrite it to make it better. What changes did you make? Why? ■

THE CONCLUSION

Have you ever seen a movie that starts out strong and then fizzles at the end? As you walked out of the theater, you probably talked about the disappointing ending, not the strong beginning or middle. Writing works the same way. Even if it has a strong introduction and body, an essay with a weak conclusion will leave the reader feeling let down.

When you draft your conclusion, be sure to consider your body paragraphs, audience, and purpose. Should you summarize your main points? If you made many points, your reader may find a summary helpful. But if you made only a few, your reader may find a summary unnecessary and even patronizing. Should you end by asking your reader to take a specific action? That may depend on your purpose. If your goal is to convince your reader to do something, such as start a recycling program on campus, a call to action is appropriate.

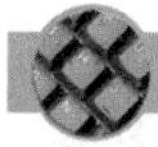

www.mhhe.com/tsw
For online exercises and information on conclusions, go to Catalyst 2.0 > Writing > Paragraph/Essay Development > Conclusions

The length of your conclusion will vary from essay to essay. Sometimes a single sentence ties everything up perfectly. Other times, you need a paragraph of several sentences. A long essay or research paper may require a conclusion of more than one paragraph. No matter what the length, keep your conclusion in proportion to the rest of your essay. Short essays have short conclusions, and longer essays can have longer conclusions.

Regardless of the length of your conclusion, you should generally avoid these expressions: "In conclusion," "In summary," "To conclude,"

Luann

"To summarize," and "In closing." They are overused and can be flat and lifeless.

If a suitable conclusion does not immediately occur to you, try one or more of the following approaches.

Restate Your Thesis and/or Your Main Points

Restating your thesis can provide emphasis, but it can also seem uninspired, so use this strategy cautiously. If you do restate your thesis, do so using different language. Restating your main points can also emphasize them, but only if the technique does not seem inappropriately repetitious. Here is an example of restating the thesis and main points for an essay with the thesis "Ability grouping is harmful to many students."

> Clearly, ability grouping causes many students to feel unsuccessful, and it damages their self-esteem. That fact, alone, should be enough to prompt educators to discontinue this harmful practice.

Introduce a Related Idea

You can mention an idea you have not mentioned before—an observation, conclusion, or impression drawn from your essay, perhaps. Be sure the idea is clearly related to the ideas in your essay, so your reader is not caught off guard by an idea that seems to spring from nowhere. Here is an example for an essay with the thesis "Everyone should take a self-defense class."

> Learning how to defend yourself does more than help keep you safe. It gives you a sense of confidence and power that carries over into your personal and professional life.

Look to the Future

Here is an example for an essay with the thesis "The United States should not torture suspected terrorists unless a federal court issues a special torture warrant."

> We live in frightening times, and the temptation is great to do whatever it takes to stay safe. However, routine torture should not be an option. A society is judged by how it treats its prisoners. If we allow torture to be a routine part of our political incarcerations, history will judge us harshly.

Explain the Significance of Your Topic

This approach is particularly effective when your essay tells a story and you want to note why that story is important. Here is an example from an essay that tells the story of the time the author's house burned down:

> Although young people generally think they are immortal, as a result of that fire, I no longer take my safety for granted. Wherever I live, I plan an escape route in the event of fire. I have two smoke detectors, and I keep a chain ladder by my second-story bedroom window.

Make a Recommendation or Call Your Reader to Action

This approach is often appropriate for essays with a persuasive purpose. Here is an example for an essay with the thesis "Because there are too few organs for all the patients needing transplants, federal laws should govern how the limited number of organs are allocated":

> It is time that we began a letter-writing campaign to urge our representatives and senators to support organ allocation legislation. If enough people write, we can have equitable distribution of organs.

Explain the Consequences of Ignoring Your View

This approach also works well for essays with a persuasive purpose. Here is an example for the thesis used in the previous example:

> If we do not legislate the allocation of transplant organs, then we cannot be sure that the sickest patients will be first on the list. Instead, the wealthy and the famous will use their influence to get organs that more appropriately belong to others.

Combine Approaches

You can also combine two or more strategies. For example, you can restate the thesis and then summarize. Or you can make a determination and then give an overall reaction. A related idea can appear with a restatement. Any combination of approaches is possible.

PROCESS GUIDELINES

Drafting Conclusions

If you have trouble drafting your conclusion, try the following:

- Keep it short. Effective conclusions do not have to be long.
- Use your introduction as a conclusion, and rewrite your introduction.
- Give your draft to a reliable reader, and ask that person to suggest an approach to your introduction.

EXERCISE The Conclusion

1. Locate two essays with formal conclusions. You might check the library for books of essays, weekly newsmagazines, and newspaper editorial pages. Read the essays and answer the following questions:
   a. Does the conclusion bring the essay to a satisfying close? Explain.
   b. What approach is used for the conclusion? Is it one described in this chapter?
   c. Does the conclusion leave you with a positive final impression? Why or why not?
2. The following essay lacks a conclusion, so write your own. In class, take turns reading your conclusions and note the variety of approaches. You will find it interesting to see how many different ways the conclusion can be handled. ■

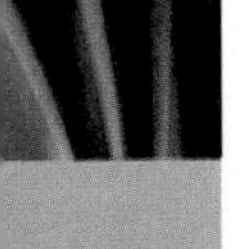

That Street Called Cordova

Robert Howard

I was awakened by Ms. Berry yelling, as she threw out her boyfriend again. I hurried down from the bunk bed to join my older brothers and older sister as they watched the whole thing from the bedroom window. We laughed as she chased him down the pavement in her housecoat with rollers in her hair. "You dirty, no good, two-timing dog!" she yelled as she continued 1 her chase. This incident was a typical start to a typical day on Cordova, where something was always happening.

My parents did not allow us to go off of the street, so we made up our own games with neighborhood kids. This day we played Bat on the Bounce. It was like stickball, except we used a metal bat with a tennis ball. We played it on a big dirt field in the middle of the projects. One day while I was standing off to the side watching the game, the ball I was holding rolled out of my hands and into play. I did not want the batter to trip over the ball, so I hurried to pick it up before he swung the bat. BUNNG! The bat smashed me so hard on my head that my neck snapped back. I felt my knees buckle as I fell in slow motion to the ground. My ears were ringing a thousand bells at once. I started crying, and my brothers took off after the batter, who had dropped the bat and tried to run home. They caught him at his front door and beat him up. My sister helped me to my feet. I knew that it was not that guy's fault because I walked out in front of him. But he still came to my house and apologized, and my mother made me give him a hug. 2

Two hours later, I was back outside, looking for all the kids, and I ran into Ms. Berry. "What are you doing outside, Boy?" she asked. "Haven't you had enough drama today to last you a lifetime?" I had a quick flashback to this morning. "Haven't you had enough of boyfriends to last you two lifetimes?" I replied. Her mouth dropped as she raised her hand. I don't know what I was thinking. I could do nothing but brace myself for the impact. SLAP! "Don't you ever disrespect your elders again. Now go tell your mama that I smacked your mouth, and then tell her why." My mother and Ms. Berry were like sisters, and my mother had given Ms. Berry permission to whoop us kids if she ever caught us getting out of line when she wasn't around. I felt like crying, but Ms. Berry would have slapped me again. So I ran. I ended up at the candy lady's house for something to take my mind off the sting. Some Now & Laters did it. 3

I met up with my brothers just as it was getting dark. It was time to play Kissy Catchers. This game was played at sunset. All the girls hid, while the 4 boys tried to find them. If found, the girl had to kiss the guy. I didn't like the game much because I always found the same ugly girl who lived two doors down from me. At the time, I didn't think she knew how to play very well because she always told me where she was going to hide.

DRAFTING THE TITLE OF YOUR ESSAY

A good title can intrigue your reader and draw that person in. Sometimes the perfect title strikes you early, perhaps during idea generation or while you are drafting. Other times, a good title does not occur to you until you are revising.

When you draft your title, consider the content of your essay, your audience, and your purpose. If you are writing a serious piece about changing immigration laws, a humorous title will undermine your purpose. However, a humorous title might work well for an essay about everything that went wrong the first time you met your future in-laws. If your audience is your computer science instructor, you will indicate the contents of your writing with a title like "Project Management in Networked Environments," because your reader will expect a title that previews the writing's focus.

Finally, when you draft your title, remember the following points:

1. **Be specific.** Specific titles give your reader a sense of what your essay is about. For this reason, "Understanding E-mail Etiquette in Business" is a much better title than "E-mail."
2. **Do not restate your thesis.** If your thesis is "Trying juveniles as adults is not justice," your title should not be "Trying Juveniles as Adults Is Not Justice." You could, however, use "Juveniles in Adult Courts: An Alarming Miscarriage of Justice."
3. **Do not write a title that tricks or misleads your reader.** If you title your essay "Making a Fortune from Home," and then write that the joys of being a stay-at-home parent are worth a fortune, your reader will feel betrayed.

ANTHONY'S ESSAY IN PROGRESS: The First Draft

Using the outline and preliminary thesis he developed, which is reproduced on pages 69–71, Anthony wrote the following first draft. (You may want to refer to the outline as you study the draft.) The marginal notes call your attention to some important features of the draft and Anthony's writing process.

The Importance of Using Bicycle Helmets

1 My partner Lou and I were doing inventory on our ambulance when suddenly we got a call. We'd already been on a number of calls that day, and we were hoping to finish the inventory that we had started at 8:00 A.M. Suddenly, beckoning through the silence of our station was the dual-pitched tone alert, and we were off on another call. Little did I know at the time that this was going to be one of the most heart breaking experiences I had ever encountered. From it, I learned the importance of bicycle helmets and now believe we should require them of everyone under 18.

2 We powerfully made our way through the congested rush-hour traffic becoming annoyed at the unconcerned drivers who refused to pull to the side of the road. As we approached the scene of the accident, we saw people and police cruisers. The ambulance halted to a stop and almost immediately, the passenger door was pulled open. A police officer grabbed me by the arm and cried, "Hurry! There's a little girl in the street. She was on a bike and . . ." Lou and I hurried around to the side door of the ambulance to get our airway kit, drug box, and cardiac monitor. We shoved our way through the panic-stricken crowd to find a pathetic, lifeless-appearing, 8–10 year old girl lying in a pool of blood. She couldn't have weighed more than 50 pounds. She was in very bad shape. We put her on oxygen and assessed her vital signs only to find her respirations shallow at a rate of 40/min and her pulse was 150/min—very weak. I then yelled to Lou, "I need some I.V.'s set up. She needs fluids. She's bleeding internally." She had a collapsed lung and a badly broken leg. I stuck I.V. needles into one arm and we straightened her leg and applied a Hare-traction splint to save it from amputation. As we finally became prepared to load her into the ambulance, I looked down at the cardiac monitor. Her heart was beating rapidly but had no significant abnormalities. Suddenly, within seconds, her cardiac rhythm deteriorated—her heart stopped! Immediately, I reached for the defibrillator paddles, charged them up

The Title
Although it appears first, Anthony wrote the title after he finished drafting.

Paragraph 1
Anthony altered his preliminary thesis somewhat. Writers often do that at this stage.

Paragraph 2
Anthony added the point about Kelly's heart stopping; this point is not in the outline. Writers often add and delete ideas at this stage.

with 300 joules of energy and shouted, "All clear!" Within a few seconds her heart started beating again, but the EKG was far from normal. With this additional crisis, we began our desperate journey to South Side Hospital.

Paragraph 3
Anthony added a note to himself in brackets. He knew he needed more detail, but he wasn't sure what to write. To avoid bogging down, he wrote the note and pushed on.

3 As we pulled into the hospital, we saw the trauma team anxiously waiting our arrival at the entrance of the emergency room. We quickly unloaded the girl from the ambulance and made our way into Trauma Room I. As I gave my verbal report of the accident details, to the resident in charge the medical team, he laboriously made every effort to further stabilize the girl and prepare her for surgery. Within minutes, she was in surgery to repair her injuries. [add more]

Paragraph 4
In response to the note in his outline, Anthony added a statistic he researched on the Internet.

4 Kelly is still alive today, two years after her hit-and-run accident. Being a quadriplegic confined to a wheel chair, she will never be able to go for another bicycle ride. Her damaged brain only permits her to utter a few incomprehensible words. Kelly is one of the many innocent victims who suffered drastically from a hit-and-run trauma accident. Unfortunately, her assailant still remains unidentified and unpunished. But it didn't have to be this way because if Kelly had been wearing a bicycle helmet the odds are good that her injuries would not have been as devastating. Her helmet would have protected her head and prevented her paralysis. According to the Consumer Product Safety Commission, "Wearing a bike helmet can reduce the risk of head injury by 85 percent." For this reason, everyone under 18 should wear a helmet, for the same reason we wear seat belts. It's a matter of safety.

5 It is too late for Kelly, but not for the rest of us. If you ride a bike, wear a helmet. If you have children, be sure they wear their helmets.

EXERCISE Your Essay in Progress

Directions: After completing this exercise, save your draft. You will use it in the next chapter as you work toward your completed essay.

1. Using one of the outlines you wrote when you completed the exercise on page 71, write a first draft. Do not worry about getting everything down in perfect form; just write your ideas as best you can. Skip any troublesome sections.

2. Study your draft. Does it suggest that you should return to an earlier stage in the process? If so, which one(s), and why? Return to those stages now and do what is necessary.
3. Ask yourself if you were comfortable writing your first draft. If not, what will you do differently the next time you draft? Why? ■

WRITING ASSIGNMENT

In an essay, explain how you feel about writing and about taking a writing course. Also explain why you feel the way you do—perhaps an early school experience or particular response to your writing helped shape your attitude. Your audience is your writing instructor, and your purpose is to help that person learn more about you.

You can use the strategies discussed in Chapter 2 and this chapter to generate ideas, outline, and draft. When you complete your draft, make whatever changes you think are needed. Then ask two classmates to read the draft and answer the following questions:

- What do you like best about the draft?
- Does the introduction engage your interest? Why or why not?
- What is the thesis?
- Do any ideas need more development? If so, underline them.
- Are any ideas irrelevant? If so, bracket them.
- Is anything unclear? If so, place a question mark next to unclear ideas.
- Does the conclusion create a positive final impression? Explain why or why not.

LOOKING AHEAD

The finished product we admire is rarely born fully formed. For example, an orchestra rehearses many hours before a performance, changing the tempo, the balance of instruments, and the order of selections; a tennis player masters a serve only after many hours of practice to alter how high to throw the ball, where to put the feet, and how much spin to give the ball; a department store window display is perfected only after different layouts, concepts, and color schemes are tried. Consider, too, the potter in the photograph. This artisan gradually and repeatedly shapes the clay until it takes on the desired form. Good writing is also the result of successive changes over time, as this chapter and the next explain. What else is well done only after a series of changes? List as many of these endeavors as you can think of.

Revising for Content and Organization

No matter how rough it is, your first draft gives you raw material you can refine into a strong essay through the process of reworking that is **revision.** Inexperienced writers often misunderstand revision in one of two ways. Sometimes they read over their first draft, fail to notice problems and just correct a few spellings, add a few commas, retype, and consider the job done. Other times, they read over their first draft, feel overwhelmed by how rough it is, slip into denial, ignore the problems, retype, and hope for the best.

Revision (re-vision) means "seeing again." The revision process involves looking again at your writing, but seeing it from your reader's point of view, so you avoid the kind of miscommunication illustrated in the *Non Sequitur* cartoon on page 98 and achieve your writing purpose.

THINK LIKE A CRITIC; WORK LIKE AN EDITOR: REVISING CONTENT

A *critic* is a judge of both the strong and the weak qualities of something. For example, movie critics review films and write their assessments of the strong and the weak aspects in reviews. When you revise, you must think like a critic to assess your draft and decide what is strong and what is weak. Doing so helps you to determine what changes you need to make.

An *editor* makes changes in writing. For example, publishing companies employ editors to make changes to improve the content, organization, and expression of ideas in manuscripts. When you revise, you must function like

Non Sequitur

an editor and make the needed changes in your draft that you identified in your role of critic.

You may think that editors focus on correcting sentence structure and mistakes with grammar, punctuation, and capitalization. However, being an editor means revising for content, organization, and expression of ideas as well. Editing for sentence structure, grammar, spelling, and punctuation should come later, when you are finished making changes to improve your content, organization, and expression of ideas. Why check the correctness of words and sentences that you may change during revision?

In Chapters 2 and 3, you learned about the qualities of an effective thesis, introduction, body paragraphs, and conclusion. When you revise for content, keep these qualities, along with your purpose and audience, firmly in mind. In addition, the following will help you think like a critic and work like an editor as your revise.

Evaluate and Revise Your Thesis

Carefully reconsider your thesis. Revise, if necessary, to be sure your thesis meets the criteria in the following box.

Evaluating and Revising Your Thesis

Your thesis should:

- Be suited to your audience and purpose
- Include only one topic and one central point
- Express the central point in specific language

Your thesis should *not:*

- Be a statement of fact or an announcement
- Include an overused expression such as "in my opinion"

If your thesis previews the main points in your essay, state those points in the same order as they are discussed in the body paragraphs.

Evaluate and Revise Your Body Paragraphs

When you consider your body paragraphs, remember that your ultimate goal is to meet the needs of your audience and to achieve your purpose for writing. Revise, if necessary, to be sure your body paragraphs meet the criteria in the following box.

Evaluating and Revising Your Body Paragraphs

Your topic sentences should:

- Indicate accurately the main idea of the body paragraph
- State only one main idea
- Be relevant to the thesis

Your supporting details should:

- Be adequate by showing as well as telling
- Avoid saying the same thing in different ways
- Be relevant to the topic sentence (and, therefore, the thesis)

If your detail is not adequate, try adding examples or brief stories to show and not just tell. If you still need details, return to idea generation, perhaps trying a different technique this time. If idea generation does not produce what you need, you may need to change your thesis or topic to something you have more ideas about.

If you have a relevance problem, try to slant the detail to make it relevant. If that does not work, alter your thesis or topic sentence to accommodate the detail, but be sure the change does not create a relevance problem elsewhere. If these strategies do not help, eliminate the irrelevant detail.

Evaluate and Revise your Introduction, Conclusion, and Title

Your introduction, conclusion, and title are important because they influence your reader's initial and final impressions. Consider these elements of your draft, and revise, if necessary, to be sure they meet the criteria in the following box.

Evaluating and Revising Your Introduction, Conclusion, and Title

Your introduction should:

- Create interest in your essay
- Be suited to your audience and purpose

Your conclusion should:

- Leave you reader with a positive final impression
- Be suited to your audience and purpose
- Avoid expressions such as "in conclusion" and "to summarize"

Your title should:

- Be suited to your content, audience, and purpose
- Avoid misleading your reader or restating the thesis
- Be specific

THINK LIKE A CRITIC; WORK LIKE AN EDITOR: REVISING ORGANIZATION

When you evaluate and revise your organization, keep your audience and purpose in mind, and consider the criteria in the following box.

Evaluating and Revising Your Organization

Your ideas should:

- Be arranged in a chronological, spatial, progressive, or other logical order
- Follow logically one to the next
- Have coherence (explained in the next section)
- Have appropriate paragraphing

A good way to check the arrangement of your ideas is to outline your draft *after* you have written it—even if you outlined before. A close look at the outline can reveal problems with your organization. If you need to change the order of ideas and you work on a computer, the cut/paste function will expedite the process. If you have written out your draft on one side of the page only, you can use scissors and tape to cut and rearrange sentences and paragraphs.

Achieving Coherence

To meet the needs of your reader and achieve your purpose for writing, you must do more than simply arrange ideas logically and effectively. You must also connect ideas smoothly and show how they relate to each other. When you connect ideas smoothly and demonstrate their relationship to each other, you achieve **coherence.** Two ways to achieve coherence are with transitions and repetition.

Use Transitions to Achieve Coherence

Transitions are connective words and phrases that show the relationship between ideas. Consider, for example, the following sentences:

```
Advertisements often present luxuries as necessities.
People want what they don't truly need.
```

The relationship between the ideas in the two sentences is not immediately clear, so the sentences are confusing. Look what happens, however, when a transitional phrase is added:

```
Advertisements often present luxuries as necessities.
As a result, people want what they don't truly
need.
```

The transitional phrase *as a result* signals that the ideas in the first sentence function as a cause, and the ideas in the second sentence function as the effect of that cause. By demonstrating this cause-and-effect relationship, the transition smooths the flow of ideas and helps the reader understand how the writer is connecting the two thoughts.

In addition to connecting ideas in different sentences, transitions can clarify the relationship between ideas in the same sentence:

```
In her campaign speech, the senator claimed she
favored economic aid to the unemployed and the
elderly; however, her voting record demonstrates
otherwise.
```

The transitional word *however* signals to the reader that what comes after it is in contrast to what comes before it.

Transitional words and phrases can signal a variety of relationships. The following chart presents these relationships and some common transitions used to signal them.

Transitions

To Show	Common Transitions	Example
Addition	also, and, and then, too, in addition, furthermore, moreover, equally important, another, first (second, third, etc.)	The mayor expects city council to approve her salary recommendations. In addition, she expects to gain support for her road repair program.
Time sequence	now, then, before, after, afterward, earlier, later, immediately, soon, next, meanwhile,	Before an agreement can be reached between the striking workers and

www.mhhe.com/tsw

For online exercises and information on coherence, go to Catalyst 2.0 > Writing > Paragraph/Essay Development > Coherence

To Show	Common Transitions	Example
	gradually, suddenly, finally, previously, before, next, often	management, both sides must soften their stands.
Spatial arrangement	near, nearly, far, far from, beside, in front of, beyond, above, below, to the right, around, on one side, outside, across, opposite to	As you leave the fair grounds, turn right on Route 76. Just beyond the junction sign is the turnoff you need.
Comparison	in the same way, similarly, just like, just as, in like manner, likewise	The current administration must not abandon the poor. Similarly, it must not forget the elderly.
Contrast	but, still, however, on the other hand, yet, on the contrary, nevertheless, despite, in spite of	In spite of the currently depressed housing market, money can still be made in real estate.
Cause and effect	because, since, so, consequently, hence, as a result, therefore, thus	Because of this year's frost, most of the fruit crop was lost.
Purpose	for this purpose, so that this may occur, in order to	In order to pass the tax levy, we must show that more money is needed.
Emphasis	indeed, in fact, surely, undoubtedly, without a doubt, certainly, truly, to be sure, I am certain	Adolescence is not a carefree time. In fact, it can be a very unsettled period.
Illustration	for example, for instance, as an illustration, specifically, to be specific, in particular	The parents complained that the schools were too easy. They said, for example, that their children received no homework.
Summary or clarification	in summary, in conclusion, as I have shown, in brief, in short, in other words, all in all, that is	The used car I bought needed brakes, shocks, and tires. In brief, it was in bad shape.
Conceding a point	although, while this may be the case, granted, even though, whereas	Whereas too many Americans cannot read and write, this country's literacy rate is high.

Use Repetition to Achieve Coherence

You can achieve coherence by repeating key words to demonstrate the relationship between ideas. Consider these sentences:

> Exam anxiety is more prevalent among students than many instructors realize. Many students who understand the material are prevented from demonstrating their knowledge.

These sentences have a relationship to each other (cause and effect), but that relationship is not revealed as clearly as it could be. In the revised version, strategic repetition solves the problem:

> Exam anxiety is more prevalent among students than many instructors realize. Such anxiety prevents many students who understand the material from demonstrating their knowledge.

The repetition of *anxiety* at the beginning of the second sentence clarifies the relationship between ideas. In addition, this repetition smooths the flow from the first sentence to the second.

You can also achieve coherence by repeating a key idea rather than a key word. Consider the following sentences:

> Mr. Ferguson, driving at close to 60 miles per hour, took his eyes off the road for only a second to light a cigarette. A three-car pileup put two people in the hospital.

The relationship between these two sentences is not as clear as it should be. The repetition of a key idea can solve the problem:

> Mr. Ferguson, driving at close to 60 miles per hour, took his eyes off the road for only a second to light a cigarette. This momentary lapse caused a three-car pileup that put two people in the hospital.

At the beginning of the second sentence, the phrase *this momentary lapse* refers to the action described in the first sentence. It repeats that idea to achieve coherence.

One other way to achieve coherence is to use synonyms to repeat an idea. Consider these sentences:

> Jenny has been in bed with strep throat for a week. Her illness may force her to drop her courses this term.

Notice that the second sentence begins with *her illness.* The word *illness* is a synonym for *strep throat,* which appears in the first sentence. This synonym repeats a key idea to achieve coherence.

Use Transitions and Repetition to Achieve Coherence between Paragraphs

You can use transitions and repetition to link the end of one paragraph and the beginning of the next. Used this way, transitions and repetition tighten organization by demonstrating how ideas in different paragraphs are related. They also improve the flow of these paragraphs.

Achieving Coherence between Paragraphs

Use a Transition

End of one paragraph:	The students believe that the proposed library will not meet their needs.
Beginning of next paragraph:	In addition, students oppose construction of the library for economic reasons.

Repeat Key Words

End of one paragraph:	Clearly, teacher burnout is a serious problem.
Beginning of next paragraph:	Unfortunately, teacher burnout is not the only serious problem facing our schools.

Repeat a Key Idea

End of one paragraph:	For the first time in years, the American divorce rate is beginning to drop.
Beginning of next paragraph:	The reasons for this new trend deserve our attention.

Use a Synonym

End of one paragraph:	All signs indicate that the safety forces strike will continue for at least another week.
Beginning of next paragraph:	If the work stoppage does last seven more days, the effects will be devastating.

EXERCISE Coherence

1. Write sentences and supply transitions according to the directions given. The first one is done as an example.
   a. Write two sentences about the way women are portrayed in television commercials. Link the sentences with a transitional word or phrase signaling contrast.

      Example: Television ads do not depict women realistically. *However,* today's commercials are an improvement over those of 10 years ago.

   b. Write one sentence about exams that has a transitional word or phrase of addition to link two ideas.

c. Write two sentences about a television show, movie, or book. Link the sentences with a transitional word or phrase signaling emphasis.

d. Write one sentence about a holiday. Include a transitional word or phrase of contrast.

e. Write two sentences that describe the location of items in your bedroom. Link the sentences with a transitional word or phrase to signal spatial arrangement.

f. Write one sentence about a campus issue. Include a transitional word or phrase for admitting a point.

g. Write two sentences about someone you enjoy being with. Link the sentences with a transitional word or phrase of illustration.

h. Write two sentences, each about a different family member. Link the sentences with a transitional word or phrase of either comparison or contrast.

i. Write two sentences about what you do upon waking in the morning. Link the sentences with a transitional word or phrase to show time sequence.

j. Write two sentences about your favorite teacher. Link the sentences with a transitional word or phrase of clarification.

2. In the following sentences, fill in the blanks with one or more words according to the directions given. The first one is done as an example.

   a. *Repeat key word:* I am uncomfortable with the principle behind life insurance. Basically, such insurance means I am betting some giant corporation that I will die before my time.

   b. *Repeat key word:* Over the years, graduation requirements have become increasingly complex, causing students to become confused and frustrated. These __________ are now being studied by campus administrators in an effort to streamline procedures.

   c. *Use a synonym for* additional week: Because so many students found it impossible to complete their term papers by Friday, Dr. Rodriguez was willing to give an additional week to work on them. __________ helped everyone feel more comfortable with the assignment.

   d. *Repeat key idea:* The Altmans returned from their weekend trip to discover that their house had been broken into and ransacked. __________ was so extensive, it took them two full days to get everything back in order.

   e. *Repeat key idea:* According to the current charter, the club's president can serve for only one term. __________ was meant to ensure that there would be frequent change in leadership. ■

REVISING WITH READER RESPONSE

Nothing helps a writer make revision decisions more than the thoughtful responses of a reliable reader. Even professional writers make changes based on the responses of reliable readers such as editors and reviewers.

Procedures for Getting Reader Response

To get reader response to your draft as part of your revision process, you can follow one of the following procedures or use one your instructor recommends. No matter what procedure you use, give your reader a clean, typed copy of a draft that has progressed past the rough-draft stage. (For an example of reader response, see page 108.)

Procedure 1

Give your reader a copy of your draft, and ask him or her to indicate the chief strengths and weaknesses in a summary comment at the end. Ask your reader to be specific, using language like this: "Good intro—it gets my interest; I don't understand the point you are making in paragraph 2—an example would help; paragraph 3 reads well, but I'm not sure how it relates to your thesis; the description at the end is vivid and interesting."

Procedure 2

Give your reader a copy of your draft, and ask him or her to write comments directly on the draft and in the margin the way an instructor might. Ask your reader to note strengths and weaknesses, and to use the same kind of specific language explained for procedure 1.

Procedure 3

Ask your reader to write specific answers to the following questions on a separate sheet of paper:

- What is the thesis of the essay?
- Is there anything that does not relate to the thesis?
- Are any points unclear?
- Do any points need more explanation?
- Is there any place where the relationship between ideas is unclear?
- Does the introduction engage interest?
- Does the conclusion provide a satisfying finish?
- What is the best part of the essay?
- What is the weakest part of the essay?

Procedure 4

Give your reader a list of questions that reflect the concerns you have about the draft, such as "Does the introduction arouse interest?" "Is the example in paragraph 2 detailed enough?" and "Is there a better approach to the conclusion?"

When You Are the Writer

As a writer seeking reader response, remember the following:

1. **Choose objective readers willing to offer constructive criticism.** A parent who likes everything you do is not a good choice, nor is a roommate who always tries to please people and never offers criticism.

2. **Choose readers who know the qualities of effective writing.** Students in your writing class, students who have already taken composition and done well, and writing center staff are good choices.
3. **Use more than one reader.** Multiple readers give you multiple perspectives. Look for agreement, but if your readers disagree and you are unsure who is right, talk to your instructor or a writing center staff member.
4. **Form a group with several classmates.** You can meet regularly to exchange and comment on drafts.
5. **Evaluate responses.** Avoid automatic acceptance of every comment. Instead, assess the responses and accept or reject them thoughtfully.

When You Are the Reader

As a reader offering response to a draft, remember the following:

1. **Before commenting, read through the entire draft.** You may be tempted to write as you begin reading, but reading through to get an overview will help you decide what the most important issues are.
2. **State reasons for your reactions.** Instead of saying, "Your introduction wasn't very interesting," say, "Your introduction wasn't interesting because I have heard the opening story many times before."
3. **Avoid overwhelming the writer with too many reactions.** Focus on the most important points.
4. **Strike the right balance of comments on strengths and weaknesses.** Too much criticism is demoralizing, so concentrate on the most important weaknesses; too much praise is not helpful because it does not help the writer revise.
5. **Avoid commenting on grammar, spelling, punctuation, and capitalization.** These concerns will be dealt with later.

Revising

- Take a break for a day. The time away will help restore your objectivity so you can better assess your draft from your reader's perspective.
- To keep your audience firmly in mind, answer the audience assessment questions on page 42.
- Revise in stages, taking breaks as you need them. You can make the easier changes and move on to the harder ones, or move paragraph by paragraph from the top down, or revise content and then organization.
- Ask someone to read your draft to you. Listen like your reader, and you may hear problems that you overlooked in print.
- Trust your instincts. If you sense a problem, the odds are good that one exists, even if you cannot name it. Speak to your instructor or a writing center staff member if you cannot determine the nature of the problem.

- Revise typed copy, but remember that word-processed pages can be deceiving. Their neat, professional appearance can make you think your writing is in better shape than it really is.
- Avoid dwelling on grammar, spelling, and punctuation. You can consider these later, when you edit.
- Revise more than once. Professional writers do, so why shouldn't you?
- If you revise at the computer, try these strategies:
  - If you use Microsoft Word, use "Track Changes" to highlight your changes while preserving the original. Your revisions do not become permanent until you make them so.
  - Send your draft as an attachment to a reader for response. If both you and your reader have word-processing programs that allow you to insert comments, use that function. Otherwise, comments can be inserted in a second color.
  - To check coherence, copy and paste the last sentences of each body paragraph and the first sentences of the next body paragraph into a new file. Is the connection between ideas apparent?

ANTHONY'S ESSAY IN PROGRESS: Revising the First Draft

Anthony Torres was pleased with his first draft (which appears on page 93). He knew it needed work, but he felt he had a compelling thesis and strong details. Observe how Anthony approached his revision.

Anthony's first reaction. Anthony put his draft away for a day and didn't think much about it. When he reread it, he felt confident that he could revise successfully, but he had a nagging feeling about his focus. As mentioned earlier, he wasn't sure whether his emphasis was on Kelly or on helmet laws. It seemed to be split. He wasn't sure what to do, so he decided to ask a reliable reader. He chose a writing center staff member.

A reader's response to Anthony's draft. After writing the draft that appears on page 93, Anthony asked his reliable reader (the writing center staff member) the questions from procedure 3 on page 106. He also added a question of his own about his essay's split focus. Here are his reader's answers with marginal notes to point out important features. In addition, notice how gentle yet specific the reader is.

1. What is the thesis of the essay?

Reader explains *why* he reacts as he does and addresses the writer's concern. Note the detailed response.

Here is why you think your focus is split. You seem to have two thesis statements. The last sentence of paragraph 1 seems to be your thesis at first. So I approached the essay assuming you would focus on the idea that everyone under 18 should have to wear bike helmets. But then an interesting thing happened. Almost all of your essay is the story of what happened to Kelly, so the second-

to-the-last sentence of paragraph 1 could be the thesis. I'd say you are right to be concerned. Your focus is split.

2. Is there anything that does not relate to the thesis?

Everything relates to one possible thesis or the other. Relevance is not an issue.

3. Are any points not clear?

The only thing I wasn't sure about was what you meant in paragraph 2 by "powerfully made our way through." Depending on your audience, you might want to define medical terms like Hare-traction and quadriplegic. Other than that, all your points are very understandable. You write clearly.

4. Do any points need more explanation?

I think you need to turn your attention to paragraph 4. Three things are going on in it, and none is developed very much. Your discussion of Kelly's injuries is pretty good, but you also mention that the driver of the car wasn't caught and do nothing with that point. Is it relevant? Do you want to do more with it and show its relevance? Third, you mention the need to use helmets. The statistic is persuasive. More evidence like that would really be persuasive.

Reader suggests a revision. Reader explains why he reacts as he does. Notice how detailed and specific the answer is.

5. Is there any place where the relationship between ideas is unclear?

Again, paragraph 4 has three main thrusts, and you need to connect them better. I'm thinking that you might put each focus in its own paragraph and develop it more fully. Then you could use transitions to connect the paragraphs.

A revision strategy is offered.

6. Does the introduction engage interest?

I think your introduction is excellent. It engaged my interest immediately, partly because I'm curious about the work of paramedics. They seem like heroes. There is a real sense of drama that I think you can capitalize on in your revision. More description of the call coming in maybe?

7. Does the conclusion provide a satisfying finish?

There's definitely a sense of closure, but the conclusion is not as strong as the introduction. Is there a way to make the conclusion as dramatic as the body of the essay? Maybe with some questions like "Imagine what happened to Kelly happening to your child. Does that motivate you to make sure your child wears a bike helmet?"

Reader explains the reason for his response and suggests a possible revision. Notice the specific suggestion.

Reader gives specific examples.

8. What is the best part of the essay?

I'm impressed with much of your description and specific word choice: "congested rush-hour traffic," "cardiac rhythm deteriorated," "desperate journey," for example. I also like the narrative flow and the way you make me care about Kelly. Your essay has dramatic impact that I think you should develop even more in your revision.

A revision strategy is suggested.

9. What is the weakest part of the essay?

The area I would concentrate most on during revision is eliminating the split focus. If you decide to do more with helmet laws, you should add more persuasive detail, perhaps more statistics.

10. Is the focus of the essay split between what happened to Kelly and helmet laws?

Reader offers further assistance.

I've dealt with this issue above. While your focus is split, I think you can find a way to merge the two aspects of your essay coherently. Try it, and if you want me to look at your revision, stop by or e-mail me a copy.

Anthony's solution. Anthony read his reader's responses with mixed feelings. He was pleased that the reader liked so much of the draft and that his own instinct about a split focus was a good one, but the split focus presented a difficult problem. He was worried, so he took a walk to think about the problem. On the walk, Anthony realized that he meant the story about Kelly to prove that children should wear helmets. He would try to make that fact clearer in the essay. Here is Anthony's revision, with the changes in color.

Paragraph 1
Anthony added details about earlier calls to create interest. As his reader suggested, he added description on the call coming in and revised his thesis.

Paragraph 2
At his reader's suggestion, Anthony eliminated the problem with "powerfully" and added detail for dramatic effect.

The Importance of Using Bicycle Helmets

1 My partner Lou and I were doing inventory on our ambulance when suddenly we got a call. We'd already been on a number of calls that day including a motorcycle accident, a stroke patient, an overdose victim, and a woman in labor. ~~and we~~ We were hoping to finish the inventory that we had started at 8:00 A.M. Suddenly, beckoning through the silence of our station was the dual-pitched tone alert. After a tense 3-second pause, we heard the sound of the dispatcher's voice. "Unit 200, respond code 1, signal 6, auto-bicycle accident at Midlothian and Glenwood." ~~and we~~ We were off on another call. Little did I know at the time that this was going to be one of the most heartbreaking experiences I had ever encountered—heartbreaking and unnecessary because a simple, inexpensive bicycle helmet could have prevented the tragedy. ~~From it, I learned the importance of bicycle helmets and now believe we should require them of everyone under 18.~~

2 With light flashing and siren wailing, we ~~powerfully made~~ forced our way through the congested rush-hour traffic becoming ~~annoyed~~ angry at the

unconcerned drivers who refused to pull to the side of the road. As we approached the scene of the accident, we saw people and police cruisers. The ambulance halted to a stop and almost immediately, the passenger door was pulled open by a ~~A~~ police officer who grabbed me by the arm and cried, "Hurry! There's a little girl in the street. She was on a bike and . . ." Tears were welling up in this cops eyes, so we knew the little girl was in bad shape. Lou and I hurried around to the side door of the ambulance to get our airway kit, drug box, and cardiac monitor. We shoved our way through the panic-stricken crowd to find a pathetic, lifeless-appearing, 8–10 year old girl lying in a pool of blood. The remains of her bicycle were 30 feet aside. Her long blonde hair had tints of red throughout. She had multiple lacerations over her whole body. Her left leg was obviously fractured. The bone of her upper leg had pierced through her thigh. No air exchange could be heard with a sththoscope over her left lung—it was collapsed. She couldn't have weighed more than 50 pounds. She was in very bad shape. "Place her on a high flow of ~~We put her on~~ oxygen," I shouted. Lou checked her pupils and found them to be pinpoint in size. He replied, "I think she has a massive head injury." Meanwhile, I ~~and~~ assessed her vital signs only to find her respirations shallow at a rate of 40/min and her pulse was 150/min—very weak. I then yelled to Lou, "I need some I.V.'s set up. She needs fluids. She's bleeding internally." I stuck I.V. needles into one arm and into the uninjured leg and pumped in 3 liters of fluid. She had a collapsed lung and a badly broken leg. ~~I stuck I.V. needles into one arm and~~ We straightened her leg and applied a Hare-traction splint to save it from amputation. As we finally became prepared to load her into the ambulance, I looked down at the cardiac monitor. Her heart was beating rapidly but had no significant abnormalities. Suddenly, within seconds, her cardiac rhythm deteriorated—her heart stopped! Immediately, I reached for the defibrillator paddles, charged them up with 300 joules of energy and shouted, "All clear!" Within a few seconds her heart started beating again, but the EKG was far from normal. With this additional crisis, we began our desperate journey to South Side Hospital.

Paragraph 3
Responding to a note to himself on the first draft, Anthony added detail.

3 As we pulled into the hospital, we saw the trauma team anxiously waiting our arrival at the entrance of the emergency room. We quickly unloaded the girl from the ambulance and made our way into Trauma Room 1. As I gave my verbal report of the accident details to the resident in charge, the medical team~~, he~~ laboriously made every effort to further stabilize the girl and prepare her for surgery. They transfused a large amount of blood into her jugular vein, then placed a chest tube into her left lung to reinflate it. A needle was punctured through her abdomen to determine the extent of internal hemorrhage. One doctor replied, "She has lost a large amount of blood into the peritoneum. Let's get her upstairs." Within minutes, she was in surgery to repair her injuries.

Paragraph 4
Anthony decided not to discuss the driver and followed his reader's advice to give the paragraph a single focus.

4 Kelly is still alive today, two years after her hit-and-run accident. Being a quadriplegic confined to a wheel chair, she will never be able to go for another bicycle ride. Her damaged brain only permits her to utter a few incomprehensible words. The future does not look good for Kelly because there is little hope she will regain the function she lost that tragic day. ~~Kelly is one of the many innocent victims who suffered drastically from a hit and run trauma accident. Unfortunately, her assailant still remains unidentified and unpunished.~~

Paragraph 5
This is a new paragraph that focuses on wearing helmets. Anthony added another statistic, as his reader suggested, to make his point more persuasive.

5 One of the most tragic elements of Kelly's fate is that ~~But~~ it didn't have to be this way. ~~because if~~ If ~~Kelly~~ she had been wearing a bicycle helmet the odds are good that her injuries would not have been as devastating. Her helmet would have protected her head and prevented her paralysis. According to the Consumer Product Safety Commission, "Wearing a bike helmet can reduce the risk of head injuries by 85 percent." Yet the Insurance Institute for Highway Safety says that an incredible 90 percent of people killed in bicycle accidents in 2000 were not wearing helmets. Helmets can save lives and reduce the risk of head injuries—yet we are not wearing them. Let's at least protect our children and require ~~For this reason,~~

everyone under 18 ~~should~~ to wear a helmet, for the same reason we wear seat belts. It's a matter of safety.

It is too late for Kelly, but not for the rest of us. If you ride a bike, wear a helmet. If you have children, be sure they wear their helmets. Just stop and think for a moment about how you would feel if what happened to Kelly happened to your child. 6

Paragraph 6
Anthony revised the conclusion to be more dramatic.

EXERCISE Evaluating a Draft

Directions: Read the following draft and list three of its strengths. Then list three important revisions that you would recommend to the writer, and explain why these revisions are needed. Exchange lists with another classmate, and identify your areas of agreement and disagreement. Work together to come up with lists that you can agree on. ■

Me

From birth until I was ten, I lived in seven different places, from the slums of Squirrel Hill to the woods of Conneaut Lake, from urban North Lauderdale to suburban Cleveland. I attended five different elementary schools, which was very difficult for me. Being tossed around from school to school was very hard. 1

I was ridiculed and talked about because I was different from everybody else. To make matters worse, the teacher would sometimes give me special attention to help me feel comfortable. This would cause the other kids to call me the teacher's pet. It always seemed that once I did feel comfortable in my new school, we would be packing and moving again. 2

I wanted so badly to fit in at my new schools, but I never did. Moving from the city to the country, from the North to the South, meant that my 3 clothes and other things about me were not quite right. I stood out for lots of reasons, so I was constantly laughed at. I was never with the rest of my class in my studies. I was either ahead or behind, labeled "Miss Brain" or "dimwit." No matter how hard I tried, I never fit in. I suppose, though, that all the rejection made me stronger.

Being a new kid in school is no fun at all. As a result of all the years of moving around and trying to fit in, I still feel insecure and unaccepted. I will never start a family until I am sure I am firmly rooted in one place. 4

EXERCISE Your Essay in Progress

Directions: After completing this exercise, save your revision. You will use it in the next chapter as you work toward your completed essay.

1. Review the chapter and make a list of the revising techniques you would like to try—the ones that seem like they might work for you.
2. Use the techniques in your list to revise the draft you wrote in response to the exercise on page 94.
3. Did your revision activities prompt you to return to any earlier stages of the process? If so, which ones?
4. Were the revision procedures you followed helpful? If not, what will you do differently the next time you revise? Why? ■

LOOKING AHEAD

Earlier chapters of this book focus on *what* you say—on the ideas you include in your essays, on how you discover those ideas, on how you develop them, and on how you arrange them. However, it's not just *what* you say that matters. *How* you say it is also important, so this chapter focuses on the expression of ideas. To look ahead and consider the importance of the way we express ourselves, consider the campaign poster here. The poster aims to convey the idea that Barack Obama offers something different from the politics of the past and that the change offered was the kind that people could trust to be an improvement. But the poster does not say, "Barack Obama offers a break from the politics of the past in order to bring change people can trust to be an improvement." Instead, it expresses the ideas more effectively by saying simply, "Change we can believe in." Politicians understand that it is not just what you say that counts; it's how you say it. Advertisers understand that fact as well. So do good writers.

To consider the importance of effective expression, list 10 or so phrases, sentences, or expressions from advertisements, political speeches (such as the Gettysburg Address), and important documents (such as the Declaration of Independence) that have staying power because they are so well expressed.

Revising for Effective Expression

Good ideas are not enough to keep your reader's interest. You must also express those ideas well. Thus, an important part of revising is assessing your sentences and words, and making changes to express your ideas as effectively as possible.

THINK LIKE A CRITIC; WORK LIKE AN EDITOR: REVISING SENTENCES

When you revise for effective expression, your goal is to achieve a pleasing style that keeps your reader interested in what you have to say. The next sections will explain how to achieve this pleasing style.

Use Active Voice

In the **active voice,** the subject of the sentence *acts.* In the **passive voice,** the subject of the sentence is *acted upon.*

Active: The optometrist examined the child's eyes. [The subject, *optometrist,* performs the action of the verb, *examined.*]

Passive: The child's eyes were examined by the optometrist. [The subject, *child's eyes,* is acted upon.]

Most often, you should use the active voice rather than the passive voice because it is more vigorous and less wordy, as the following examples illustrate.

Passive: The ball was thrown into the end zone by the quarterback.

Active: The quarterback threw the ball into the end zone.

Another reason to favor the active voice is that the passive may not indicate who or what performed the action.

Passive: The workers were criticized for their high absentee rate. [Who did the criticizing?]

Active: The new corporate vice president criticized the workers for their high absentee rate. [Now we know who did the criticizing.]

Usually, you should choose the active over the passive voice. However, sometimes the passive voice is more appropriate, particularly when the performer of the action is either unknown or unimportant, as is often the case for business, legal, and technical writing.

Appropriate passive voice: After germination, the plants are thinned so they are spaced 6 inches apart. [Who thins the plants is not important.]

Appropriate passive voice: The chicken was baked until it was tough and tasteless. [The person who baked the chicken is unknown.]

Be wary when a writer or speaker uses the passive voice to hide information.

Passive voice used to conceal: I have been told that someone is stealing from the cash register. [The writer or speaker does not want to reveal who did the telling.]

Use Coordination

www.mhhe.com/tsw

For online exercises and information on coordination and subordination, go to Catalyst 2.0 > Editing > Coordination and Subordination

A word group that has both a subject and a verb is a **clause.** If the clause can stand alone as a sentence, it is an **independent clause.**

Independent clause: this year's citrus crop was damaged by frost

Subject: this year's citrus crop

Verb: was damaged

Sentence: This year's citrus crop was damaged by frost.

For **coordination,** join two independent clauses in the same sentence with a comma and one of the following **coordinating conjunctions:**

and	or
but	so
for	yet
nor	

Independent clause: the storm caused a power failure

Independent clause:	we lit the candles
Sentence with coordination:	The storm caused a power failure, so we lit the candles.

The coordinating conjunction does more than join the independent clauses; it also indicates the relationship between the ideas in the clauses, as the following chart explains.

Coordinating Conjunctions

Coordinating Conjunctions	Relationship
and	The idea in the second independent clause functions as an addition to the idea in the first independent clause.

Example: The mayor urged a 14 percent budget cut, and she suggested a freeze on hiring.

but/yet	The idea in the second independent clause contrasts with the idea in the first independent clause.

Example: The temperatures have been warm for December, but [yet] we may have snow for Christmas.

for	The idea in the second independent clause tells why the idea in the first independent clause happened or should happen.

Example: Television talk shows are popular, for viewers never tire of watching celebrities talk about themselves.

nor	The idea in the second independent clause is a negative idea functioning in addition to the negative idea in the first independent clause.

Example: The school board cannot raise teacher salaries, nor can it renovate the high school buildings.

or	The idea in the second independent clause is an alternative to the idea in the first independent clause.

Example: Your research paper must be handed in on time, or you will be penalized.

so	The idea in the second independent clause functions as a result of the idea in the first independent clause.

Example: Dr. Wesson was ill last week, so our midterm exam is postponed until Thursday.

When you join ideas with coordination, be sure the relationship between the ideas is clear.

Unclear: My advisor is coming at noon today, and I have a doctor's appointment this morning.

Clear: My advisor is coming at noon today, but I will miss her because of my doctor's appointment this morning.

Use Subordination

A **dependent clause** has a subject and a verb, but it cannot stand alone as a sentence. It must be joined to an independent clause.

Dependent clause:	because this year's citrus crop was damaged by the frost
Subject:	this year's citrus crop
Verb:	was damaged
Independent clause:	orange juice will cost more
Sentence:	Because this year's citrus crop was damaged by the frost, orange juice will cost more.

For **subordination,** join an independent clause and a dependent clause in the same sentence with one of the following **subordinating conjunctions.**

Subordinating Conjunctions

Subordinating Conjunctions	**Relationship**
because, in order that, since	To show why the idea in the independent clause occurs or occurred

Example: Because the traffic signal on Darborn Street is out, cars are backed up for two blocks.

after, as, before, when, whenever, while	To show when the idea in the independent clause occurs or occurred

Example: Before the city council considers tax incentives, we must be sure the city can afford them.

where, wherever	To show where the idea in the independent clause occurs or occurred

Example: Janine attracts attention wherever she goes.

as if, as though	To show how the idea in the independent clause occurs or occurred

Example: The mayor was speaking as if she were not facing a no-confidence vote.

if, once, provided, unless	To show under what condition the idea in the independent clause occurs or occurred

Example: Unless the additional computers are purchased, we cannot compete with more wired campuses.

although, even though, though	To concede a point

Example: Although the executive apologized, the board of directors still fired him.

When you use subordination, place the idea you want to emphasize in the independent clause. Notice that different ideas are emphasized in these two sentences.

Sluggish economy emphasized:	Although unemployment is lower than last year, the economy is sluggish.
Lower unemployment emphasized:	Although the economy is sluggish, unemployment is lower than last year.

Punctuation note: As the previous examples show, a dependent clause at the beginning of a sentence is followed by a comma.

Achieve Sentence Variety

For a pleasing rhythm, strive for **sentence variety** by using different sentence structures. When you vary your sentences, you avoid the monotonous rhythm that comes from too many sentences with the same pattern. For example, the following paragraph lacks sentence variety. As you read it, notice how you react.

> My son is in third grade. He told me yesterday that he was one of 12 students selected to take French. Greg is delighted about it. I am annoyed. I feel this way for several reasons. The French classes will be held three days a week. The students will have French instead of their usual reading class. I believe at the third-grade level, reading is more important than French. I do not want my son to miss his reading class. The teacher says Greg reads well enough for his age. I maintain that there is still room for improvement. Some people might say that learning French at an early age is a wonderful opportunity. They say students will be exposed to another language and culture. This will broaden their awareness. This may be so. I do not think students should be forced into French for this. They should have a choice of languages to study, the way they do in high school.

The paragraph has an unsatisfactory rhythm because all the sentences begin the same way—with the subject. To achieve sentence variety and improve your style, include a mix of sentence structures by following the suggestions below.

1. **Use coordination to combine some of your sentences.**

   Examples: Gregory is delighted to be learning French, but I am annoyed about it.

   Third graders are not ready for a foreign language, and I doubt they will profit much from it.

2. **Begin some sentences with dependent clauses.**

   Examples: While I believe the study of French can be beneficial, I do not feel it should be taught to third graders at the expense of reading instruction.

   If my son is to learn another language, I prefer that he choose the one he wishes to study.

3. **Begin some sentences with one or two *-ly* words (adverbs).** When you use two *-ly* words to begin a sentence, these words may be separated in one of four ways: with *but* or *yet*, with *and*, or with a comma.

   Examples: Excitedly, Greg told me of his opportunity to take French.

   Patiently but [yet] firmly, I told Greg I did not want him to take French.

   Loudly and angrily, I told Greg's teacher I did not want Greg to take French.

   Slowly, thoroughly, Greg's teacher explained why Greg should take French.

   Punctuation note: As the above examples illustrate, two *-ly* words are separated by a comma when *and, but,* or *yet* is not used. Also, an introductory *-ly* word or a pair of introductory *-ly* words is followed by a comma.

   Examples: Wearily, I explained to Greg for the fifth time why he would not be taking French.

   Loudly and irritably, I argued with the principal about the wisdom of teaching French to third graders.

4. **Begin some sentences with a participle or an infinitive.** The *-ing* form of a verb is the **present participle.** The *-ed, -en, -n,* or *-t* forms of the verb are the **past participle.** The base form of the verb used with *to* is the **infinitive.** These forms can appear alone, in pairs, or in phrases.

   Examples: Sobbing, Greg explained that all his friends were taking French and he wanted to also.

   Frustrated and defeated, I finally allowed Greg to take the French class.

   To understand my reaction, you must realize that I value reading above all other subjects.

Punctuation note: As the above examples illustrate, introductory participles are followed by a comma. Introductory infinitives are followed by a comma only if the infinitive is followed by an independent clause.

Examples: To study French in third grade, Greg would miss his reading class.

To study French in third grade seems foolish.

Caution: When you begin a sentence with a participle or infinitive—whether it appears alone, in a pair, or with a phrase—follow the participle or infinitive with a sentence subject that the participle or infinitive can sensibly refer to. Otherwise, you will have a dangling modifier, which creates an illogical or silly sentence.

Dangling modifier: Still having trouble with reading English, it is not time for Greg to learn French. ["Still having trouble with reading English" refers to "it," which is illogical.]

Correction: Still having trouble with reading English, Greg is not ready to learn French. ["Still having trouble with reading English" refers to "Greg."]

Dangling modifier: To study French, a book must be purchased. [Is a book studying French?]

Correction: To study French, Greg purchased a book.

5. **Begin some sentences with a prepositional phrase.** A **preposition** is a word that signals direction, placement, or connection. Common prepositions include the following:

about	among	between	from	of	over	under
above	around	by	in	off	through	with
across	before	during	inside	on	to	within
along	behind	for	into	out	toward	without

A **prepositional phrase** is a preposition plus the words that are functioning with it. Here are some examples:

across the bay	of the United States
before the rush hour	to me
at the new shopping mall	without the slightest doubt

To achieve sentence variety, you can begin some of your sentences with one or more prepositional phrases.

Examples: For a number of reasons, I oppose French instruction at the third-grade level.

By my standards, reading is more important than French for third graders.

Punctuation note: As the above examples illustrate, introductory prepositional phrases are followed by a comma.

6. **Vary the placement of transitions.** Many transitions can function at the beginning, in the middle, or at the end of a sentence. To achieve sentence

variety, vary the placement of transitions. (See page 101 for a chart of transitions.)

Examples: *Indeed,* Greg was disappointed that I would not allow him to take French.

He was so disappointed, *in fact,* that I felt compelled to give in.

This does not mean my belief has changed, *however.*

Punctuation note: As the above examples illustrate, transitions are set off with commas.

7. **Begin some sentences with the subject.** Sentence variety refers to mixing sentence structures to avoid monotony, so begin some sentences with the subject.

8. **Balance long and short sentences.** Follow a long sentence with a shorter one, or a short sentence with a longer one. While you need not follow this pattern throughout an essay, on occasion it can enhance rhythm and flow.

Examples: Although I explained to Greg why I believed he was better off taking reading rather than French, he never understood my view. Instead, he was heartbroken.

I did my best. I reasoned with him, bribed him, and became angry with him, but still I could not convince Greg that he would be better off to wait a few years before studying a foreign language.

Use Parallel Structure

www.mhhe.com/tsw

For online exercises and information on parallelism, go to Catalyst 2.0 > Editing > Parallelism

For **parallel structure,** use the same grammatical form for sentence elements of equal importance serving the same function. The following sentence has parallel structure:

Mrs. Chen found the novel outrageous, offbeat, and shocking.

The underlined words have the same function (to describe *novel*), and they all have the same degree of importance in the sentence. To emphasize this relationship, then, the words all take the same grammatical form—they are adjectives.

If sentence elements that have the same function and importance are not parallel, the result is an awkward sentence, as in the following example.

Nonparallel: I have always liked hiking and to swim.

Because *hiking* and *to swim* have the same function (as the object of the verb *have liked*), and because they are of equal importance, they should both have the same grammatical form.

Parallel: I have always liked hiking and swimming.

Parallel: I have always liked to hike and to swim.

1. **Be sure sentence elements forming a series or pair have the same grammatical form.**

Nonparallel: You can get to Toronto by car, bus, or fly.

Parallel: You can get to Toronto by car, bus, or plane.

Nonparallel: Before my first date, Mother told me to be in by midnight, and she said I was to be a gentleman.

Parallel: Before my first date, Mother told me to be in by midnight and to be a gentleman.

2. **Be sure items compared or contrasted in a sentence have the same grammatical form.**

Nonparallel: I love a day at the beach more than to spend a day in the country.

The contrasted elements are not parallel because the noun phrase *a day at the beach* is contrasted to the verb phrase *to spend a day in the country.* To be parallel, the contrast should be expressed in one of the following ways.

Parallel: I love a day at the beach more than a day in the country.

Parallel: I love spending a day at the beach more than spending a day in the country.

Sometimes parallelism problems crop up because the writer fails to mention the second item being compared or contrasted, as in the following sentence:

Nonparallel: I like small, intimate restaurants better.

This sentence does not indicate what *small, intimate restaurants* is contrasted with. To solve the problem, add the missing contrast:

Parallel: I like small, intimate restaurants better than crowded, noisy cafeterias.

3. **Use correlative conjunctions correctly. Correlative conjunctions** are conjunctions used in pairs. The following are correlative conjunctions:

either . . . or	both . . . and
neither . . . nor	not only . . . but [also]

To achieve parallelism with correlative conjunctions, be sure that the same grammatical structure follows both conjunctions.

Nonparallel: I want either to spend my vacation in New York City or in Bermuda.

Parallel: I want to spend my vacation either in New York City or in Bermuda.

Nonparallel: The ballet was both brilliantly performed and had lavish sets.

Parallel: The ballet had both brilliant performances and lavish sets.

EXERCISE Revising Sentences

1. Five of the following sentences are in the active voice; five are in the passive voice. Rewrite those in the passive voice so they are in the active voice.
   - **a.** The elaborate sand castle was built by Tina, Jerry, and their father.
   - **b.** By noon, the high tide had washed away most of their creation.
   - **c.** While I was shopping in the mall, my purse was snatched by a teenager dressed in torn blue jeans and a green sweatshirt.
   - **d.** The police reported that someone matching that description had stolen three other purses the same day.
   - **e.** The antique necklace I wear so often was given to me by my favorite aunt.
   - **f.** Aunt Sadie collected antique jewelry and gave me a piece every year for my birthday.
   - **g.** A surprise birthday party was thrown for Rhoda by three of her closest friends.
   - **h.** Unfortunately, Rhoda did not arrive when she was expected, so she ruined the surprise.
   - **i.** I asked my academic advisor how to improve my calculus grade.
   - **j.** I was told by my advisor to spend two hours a week in the math lab.
2. For each general subject, write one sentence with coordination and one with subordination to demonstrate the specific relationships indicated. Try to place some of your dependent clauses before the independent clauses and some of them after. The first one is done for you as an example.
   - **a.** *Exams:* (A) coordinate to show contrast; (B) subordinate to concede a point
     - (A) I have three exams today, but I have time for lunch.
     - (B) Although Dr. Manolio is known for giving difficult tests, her exams are always fair.
   - **b.** *Spring:* (A) coordinate to show addition; (B) subordinate to show when
   - **c.** *Your best friend:* (A) coordinate to show contrast; (B) subordinate to concede a point
   - **d.** *Your favorite restaurant:* (A) coordinate to show an alternative; (B) subordinate to show why
   - **e.** *Your first day of college:* (A) coordinate to show a result; (B) subordinate to show when
   - **f.** *A miserable cold:* (A) coordinate to continue a negative idea; (B) subordinate to show under what condition
   - **g.** *The first day of summer vacation:* (A) coordinate to show why; (B) subordinate to show when

h. *A party:* (A) coordinate to show addition; (B) subordinate to show where

i. *Your favorite teacher:* (A) coordinate to show why; (B) subordinate to show how

j. *A movie you have seen:* (A) coordinate to show result; (B) subordinate to concede a point

k. *A holiday celebration:* (A) coordinate to show contrast; (B) subordinate to show why

3. Rewrite the paragraph on page 121 to give it sentence variety. You may alter the existing wording, and you may add words (transitions, for example). Many revisions are possible.

4. Rewrite the following sentences to achieve parallel structure.

   a. The boutique is known for its variety of styles, for its haughty salesclerks, and daring new designs.

   b. The police car sped up the street, its lights flashing, its siren wailing, and racing its engine.

   c. I find playing tennis to be better exercise than volleyball.

   d. Kim not only has bought a CD player but also an MP3 player.

   e. Susan is beautiful, arrogant, and has been spoiled by her parents.

   f. My neighbor wants either to resurface his driveway or be painting his house.

   g. Carlos plans to attend the university, study biology, and being accepted into medical school.

   h. Neither is the newspaper column timely nor interesting.

   i. Lisa enjoys working for a large corporation for its many chances for advancement, for its excitement, and because of its many fringe benefits.

   j. The research paper was not acceptable because it was late, it was too short, and needed typing. ■

THINK LIKE A CRITIC; WORK LIKE AN EDITOR: REVISING DICTION

Diction is word choice. Because they convey your meaning and contribute to your style, the words you choose are very important.

Use an Appropriate Level of Diction

Levels of diction can be formal, popular, or informal, and should be suited to your audience.

A *formal* level of diction is appropriate when you write for specialists. If you were writing a government report, an article for a scholarly journal, a master's degree thesis, or an annual report for a corporation, you would use a formal level of diction. Typically, formal diction requires strict adherence to all the rules of grammar. It includes technical language and long sentences and avoids the personal pronouns *I* and *you,* and contractions such as *don't* and *aren't.* The tone is impersonal, humorless, and unemotional.

A *popular* level of diction is common in many magazines, newspapers, and books. If you are using popular diction, you should adhere to grammar rules, but you can usually use contractions and the personal pronouns *I* and *you.* You can also express emotion and humor. Your tone will usually be relaxed, and you can let your personality show through. A popular level of diction is suitable for most college essays written in your English class.

An *informal* level of diction is very much like the way you speak to your friends. Informal diction does not include specialized terms, sentences are short, and slang expressions may appear. Readers do not expect strict adherence to the rules of grammar. Informal diction is not acceptable for college papers (unless you are reproducing someone's exact words), but it is often suitable for friendly letters, e-mail, and personal journals.

When you revise your essays, eliminate any informal diction.

Use Words with the Appropriate Connotation

Words have both denotations and connotations. A word's **denotation** is its literal dictionary definition; a word's **connotation** is the emotions and ideas associated with it. For example, the denotations of *excited* and *agitated* are similar, but their connotations are different. Readers associate *agitated* with a negative nervousness, and they associate *excited* with a positive enthusiasm. If you use words with the wrong connotations, you can mislead your reader and fail to achieve your purpose. For example, notice the different meanings conveyed in these sentences with verbs that have similar denotations but different connotations:

Lee *chewed* the steak.
Lee *gnawed* the steak.

When you revise your essays, pay attention to the connotations of your words.

Avoid Colloquial Language

Colloquial language is informal. It includes abbreviated forms ("b-school" for "business school"), ungrammatical usages ("It's me"), informal phrases ("tough break"), and slang ("Dilberted" for "exploited by the boss"). Colloquial language is used among friends, with family, and in speech. Generally, colloquial language is not suitable for college essays. The following examples of colloquial language will give you an idea of the kinds of expressions to avoid:

cool	awesome	feeling lousy	sweet (very good)
off the wall	bummed out	having a cow	chill out

When you revise your essays, eliminate colloquial language.

Use Specific Diction

General words present a broad (and often vague) sense of your ideas, whereas **specific words** present a more precise sense.

General Words	Specific Words
shoe	dress pumps
hat	baseball cap
woman	Mrs. Hernandez
went	stormed out
nice	colorful

Most often, you should use specific words because they give your reader a more precise understanding. Consider the following sentence:

I walked across campus, feeling good about the test I just took.

The word *walked* is general and vague. Here are more specific alternatives that can be used with *feeling good:*

strolled	strutted	bounced
sauntered	trotted	lilted

Substituting the more specific *strutted* for *walked* gives us this sentence:

I strutted across campus, feeling good about the test I just took.

Now we have a more accurate sense of how the writer moved across campus, but to improve the sentence further, replace *good* with one of these more specific alternatives:

positive	elated	at ease	delighted	jubilant
pleased	satisfied	exhilarated	cheerful	optimistic

To work with *strutted,* the word needs to convey lots of good feeling because people strut when they are feeling very happy. For example, if we select *exhilarated,* we get this sentence:

I strutted across campus, exhilarated by the test I just took.

This sentence is more interesting and effective than the one we started out with because it is more specific and vivid.

When you revise, work to make your sentences more specific by focusing on nouns and verbs. Instead of general nouns like *magazine, hat,* and *dog,* use the more specific *Newsweek, stocking cap,* and *collie.* Instead of general verbs like *said, moved,* and *drank,* use the more specific *blurted out, bolted,* and *sipped.*

Adding specific modifiers can also make a sentence more precise. For example, instead of "Cans and candy wrappers are on the floor," you can revise to get "Smashed Coke cans and crumpled Milky Way wrappers are scattered across the floor."

Of course, you must be careful not to overdo it, because too much specific word choice, especially description, can create a bulky, overwhelming sentence, like this:

Dozens of smashed, twisted, red-and-white Coke cans, lying bent on their distorted sides, and at least 40 crumpled, brown, wadded-up, misshapen

Milky Way wrappers representing two weeks of my traditional midnight sugar intake are scattered in heaps everywhere across the green, plush-carpeted floor of my small, third-floor bedroom with its green walls and white ceiling.

Use Simple Diction

Some writers believe that effective, sophisticated sentences include obscure words with many syllables. They use *pusillanimous* when *cowardly* would do as well—even better, actually. If these writers do not have words like *egregious* or *inveigle* in their vocabularies, they pull them out of a dictionary or thesaurus and plunk them into their writing. Such writers are guilty of using **inflated language,** which is overblown usage that makes the writer seem self-important. Inflated language is wordy and full of important-sounding substitutes for common expressions, like the following:

Inflated: It would appear that the functionality of the new generation of personal computers can be demonstrated most readily by a cursory exhibition.

Better: A quick demonstration reveals the functions of the new generation of computers.

A sentence cannot be effective if your reader cannot understand it. Remember, you can be specific and accurate by using the wealth of simple, clear words you have at your disposal. Consider the following sentences taken from student essays:

The impetuous drive of youth mellows into the steady pull of maturity.
The car vibrated to a halt.
Unnoticed, light filters in beneath the blinds.

"O.K. What part of 'malignant regression and pathogenic reintrojection as a defense against psychic decompensation' don't you understand?"

These sentences are interesting and clear because of the specific word choice. Although specific, words like *filters, mellows, impetuous, drive, pull, vibrated,* and *halt* are also simple and are part of our natural, everyday vocabularies, demonstrating that you need not hunt for high-flown words. Specific yet simple words create an appealing style.

In addition to avoiding inflated language, you can keep your words simple and your meaning clear by avoiding jargon. **Jargon** is the technical language of a particular profession. It is the language of insiders and should be used only when you are addressing an audience of specialists. Thus, you can use terms like *mitochondria* and *endoplasmic reticulum* when you are addressing cellular biologists, but for other audiences, you need more easily understood substitutes, or you need to supply definitions—something that the psychiatrist in the cartoon failed to remember.

Use Gender-Neutral, Inoffensive Language

To avoid offending members of your audience, use inclusive language and revise to eliminate offensive language in the following ways:

1. **Avoid masculine pronouns that inappropriately exclude females.**

   No: Each student should bring his catalog to orientation.

   Yes: Each student should bring his or her catalog to orientation.

   Yes: Each student should bring a catalog to orientation.

   Yes: All students should bring their catalogs to orientation.

2. **Use gender-neutral titles.**

No	Yes
policeman	police officer
fireman	firefighter
waitress	table server
mailman	mail carrier
chairman	chair/chairperson

   No: The committee will elect its own chairman.

   Yes: The committee will elect its own chairperson.

3. **Avoid assigning roles to a single gender.**

   No: Mothers worry when their children leave home.

   Yes: Parents worry when their children leave home.

4. **Avoid using terms that demean a gender.**

   No: The company promoted three girls to district manager.

   Yes: The company promoted three women to district manager.

5. **Avoid referring to women with the *-ess* suffix.**

   No: Emily is a promising young poetess.

   Yes: Emily is a promising young poet.

6. **Avoid stereotypes.** A **stereotype** is a generalization that ascribes certain characteristics to all members of a group. Because stereotypes like the following are illogical and offensive, you should avoid them.

   Democrats are bleeding-heart liberals.
   People on welfare don't really want to work.
   Blondes have more fun.
   Men won't talk about their feelings.

   When you revise, rewrite any statements that are based on stereotypes.

   No: I am opposed to bilingual education because immigrants are too lazy to learn English.

   Yes: Rather than bilingual education, I favor more classes to teach English as a second language.

7. **Use the designations that people prefer.** For example, use *Asian* rather than *Oriental* and *disabled* rather than *handicapped.*

Eliminate Wordiness

www.mhhe.com/tsw

For online exercises and information on wordiness, go to Catalyst 2.0 > Editing > Wordiness

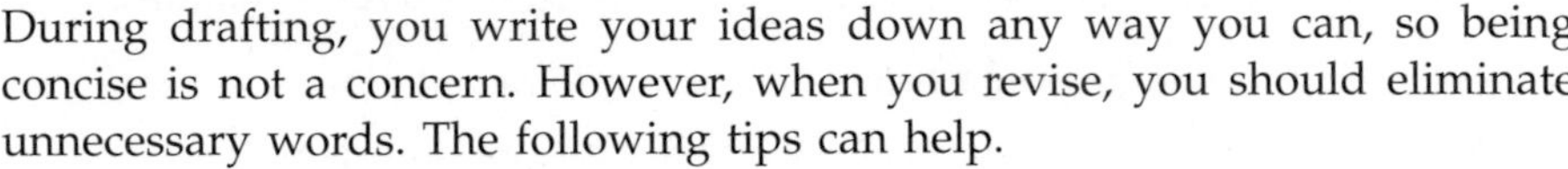

During drafting, you write your ideas down any way you can, so being concise is not a concern. However, when you revise, you should eliminate unnecessary words. The following tips can help.

1. **Reduce empty phrases to a single word.**

Phrase	Revision
at this point in time	now
in this day and age	now
due to the fact that	because
on a frequent basis	often/frequently
has the ability to	can
being that	since
at that time	then
in the event that	if
for the purpose of	so
in society today	today

   Wordy: The mayor has the ability to alter that policy.

   Revision: The mayor can alter that policy.

2. **Eliminate redundancy.** A **redundancy** is a phrase that says the same thing more than once.

Redundancy	Revision
the color yellow	yellow
circle around	circle
mix together	mix
reverted back	reverted

the reason why	the reason
the final conclusion	the conclusion
true fact	true

Wordy: The Joint Chiefs of Staff felt an increased military budget would be the final outcome.

Revision: The Joint Chiefs of Staff felt an increased military budget would be the outcome.

3. **Eliminate deadwood.** Words that add no meaning are **deadwood,** and they should be deleted.

Wordy: Joyce is a clever type of person.

Revision: Joyce is a clever person. [Joyce is clever.]

Wordy: A multiple choice kind of question is difficult to answer.

Revision: A multiple choice question is difficult to answer.

4. **Eliminate repetition.**

Wordy: The first car in the accident was smashed and destroyed.

Revision: The first car in the accident was destroyed.

Wordy: I think and believe the way you do.

Revision: I think [believe] the way you do.

5. **Avoid opening with *there* when possible.**

Wordy: There are many things we can do to help.

Revision: We can do many things to help.

Wordy: There was an interesting mix of people attending the party.

Revision: An interesting mix of people attended the party.

6. **Reduce the number of prepositional phrases.**

Wordy: The increase of violence in this country suggests a decline in moral values.

Revision: This country's increasing violence suggests moral decline.

7. **Reduce the number of *that* clauses.**

Wordy: The students asked the instructor to repeat the explanation that she gave earlier.

Revision: The students asked the instructor to repeat her earlier explanation.

Wordy: The book that is on the table is yours.

Revision: The book on the table is yours.

Note: Sometimes writers leave in words that could be cut so a sentence works better with the ones before and after it. You should eliminate unpleasant wordiness while achieving a readable style with sentences that flow well together. Thus, whether a writer uses "Most people notice right off that Kim is a sarcastic person" or "Most notice immediately that Kim is sarcastic" will depend on which version reads better with the sentences before and after.

Avoid Clichés

www.mhhe.com/tsw

For online exercises and information on clichés, go to Catalyst 2.0 > Editing > Clichés, Slang, Jargon

A **cliché** is an overworked expression. At one time, a cliché was an interesting way to say something, but as a result of overuse, it has become dull. Below is a list of some clichés you may have heard:

black as night	free as a bird
bright-eyed and bushy-tailed	hard as nails
clear as a bell	the last straw
cold as ice	over the hill
crawl out from under	the quick and the dead
cried like a baby	sadder but wiser
drank like a sailor	scarce as hen's teeth
first and foremost	tried but true

Avoid clichés by finding more interesting ways to express your ideas. Consider this student sentence:

> When my father accepted a job in Ohio, my heart sank.

The cliché *my heart sank* creates two problems. First, it is vague. Just how bad did the writer feel? Was the writer depressed, scared, or what? Second, the sentence is not interesting because the cliché is dull. Consider this revision:

> When my father accepted a job in Ohio, I lost sleep worrying about whether I could make new friends.

The revised sentence shows both the nature and the extent of the writer's negative feeling.

EXERCISE Revising Diction

1. Revise the sentences by substituting specific words for the general ones. In some cases, you may want to substitute several words for one general word and add additional detail, as in the following example.

   Example: The happy boy ran down the street.

   Revision: The paper boy sprinted down Ford Avenue, excited that he had finished his route an hour early.

   a. The room was a mess.
   b. By afternoon, the child was feeling terrible.
   c. The food tasted awful.
   d. The way that person was driving his car almost caused an accident.
   e. The sound of that baby's cry really bothered me.
   f. The movie was very good.
   g. Carlotta watched the ballplayers practice.

2. Write the following ideas in sentences with specific diction. (You may need to revise a number of times before you are satisfied.)

   Example: the pleasant ringing of church bells

   Sentence: The melodious ring of St. John's bells announced the start of morning worship.

   a. A squirrel running back and forth across a branch
   b. The smell of brownies baking in the oven
   c. The sound of rain on a roof
   d. A woman wearing too much floral-scented perfume
   e. Walking barefoot and stepping on a sharp stone

3. Revise the sentences to eliminate wordiness.

   Example: The most frightening experience that I think I ever had occurred when I was 15.

   Revision: The most frightening experience I had occurred when I was 15. [My most frightening experience occurred when I was 15.]

   a. The only audible sound to be heard was the blower of the heater motor as it worked to produce a soft, low hum.
   b. The reason I feel our nation is so great is that both men and women of the species have opportunities to excel.
   c. Until that day I did not realize or consider that people such as Corey are the most dangerous of all because they are so extremely selfish.
   d. In my opinion, it seems that a physical education requirement for college students is a complete waste of time.
   e. This particular kind of sport is ideal for the person who desires exercise but is not in the best physical condition in the world.
   f. There are many reasons why beer commercials should be banned from television.
   g. The explanation of my son for why he was home late was the same explanation that he gave me last Saturday night.
   h. The tiny little package that Jimmy gave Conchetta for her birthday held the ring that was for her engagement.
   i. In the event that I am unable to join you, please start and begin to eat without my presence.
   j. There were six dogs that were roaming the neighborhood that the dog warden found it necessary to take to the city pound.

4. Revise the sentences to eliminate the italicized clichés. Feel free to add any detail you wish.

   Example: My sixth-grade teacher was *mad as a hatter.*

   Revision: My sixth-grade teacher was so eccentric that she wore the same faded green dress from September until Christmas break.

a. Cassandra is never bored because she is always *busy as a beaver.*

b. *It's a crying shame* that rainy weather spoiled your vacation.

c. Anyone who can sit through Professor James's lectures deserves a medal, because the man has a *voice that would shatter glass.*

d. Juan is *happy as a clam* because he got an A in calculus.

e. Poor Godfrey is so clumsy he is *like a bull in a china shop.*

5. Revise the sentences to eliminate problems with connotation, colloquialisms, and offensive language.

   a. Skinny and muscled, the bride was lovely in her designer gown.

   b. I am having trouble finding the doctor I want as a general practitioner. He must include both alternative medicine and herbal remedies in his practice.

   c. Because of the road construction on the interstate, we journeyed a mere five miles in 30 minutes.

   d. Ralph has problems keeping a job because he is a mental case.

   e. To sell cars, a salesman must be patient and knowledgeable about his product. ■

PROCESS GUIDELINES

Revising for Effective Expression

- Read your draft aloud. If anything sounds choppy or singsongy, you may need to improve your sentence variety.
- Know that you cannot always substitute one word for another. You may need to replace a word with a phrase or even a sentence.
- If you have trouble expressing an idea, imagine yourself explaining what you mean to a friend, and then write the passage the way you would speak it. If necessary, you can revise to improve the sentences.
- Use your natural style. If you try to impress your reader by sounding overly sophisticated or intellectual, you will end up sounding pretentious.
- Use the dictionary and thesaurus—either online or in paper—carefully. Be sure you understand both the denotations and the connotations of words you take from these sources, so you do not lapse into a pretentious style or use the words inappropriately.
- If you revise at the computer, consider these strategies:
  - Use the "Find" function to locate general words you habitually use, such as *good, great, bad, nice,* and *awful*. Then evaluate the appropriateness of these words, and revise as necessary.
  - Use the style checker cautiously. It can help you in some ways—by flagging passive voice, for example—but it can also make mistakes.

ANTHONY'S ESSAY IN PROGRESS: The Final Draft

Anthony Torres revised the draft that appears on page 110 and corrected errors. The final draft appears here with underlining to show additions and strikeovers to show deletions. Each change is marked with a letter that corresponds to an explanatory marginal note.

Ⓐ **Learning from Tragedy: The Importance of Using Bicycle Helmets**

1 My partner Lou and I were doing inventory on our ambulance when suddenly we got a call. We'd already been on a number of calls that day, including a motorcycle accident, a stroke patient, an overdose victim, and a woman in labor. We were hoping to finish the inventory that we had started at 8:00 A.M. Suddenly, beckoning through the silence of our station was the dual-pitched

Ⓐ Revised title links the narration and the point to be drawn from it.

Paragraph 1
The introduction engages interest by beginning the narration. The last sentence is the thesis.

tone alert. After a tense 3-second pause, we heard the sound of the dispatcher's voice. "Unit 200, respond code 1, signal 6, auto-bicycle accident at Midlothian and Glenwood." We were off on another call. Little did I know at the time that this was going to be one of the most heartbreaking experiences I had ever encountered—heartbreaking and unnecessary because a simple, inexpensive bicycle helmet could have prevented the tragedy.

Paragraph 2
The narration continues. Notice the specific, simple verbs like "wailing" and "welling up."

- (B) Corrected error.
- (C) More specific word choice.
- (D) Deadwood eliminated.

With lights[B] flashing and siren wailing, we forced our way through the congested rush-hour traffic,[B] becoming [C] ~~angry~~ furious at the unconcerned drivers who refused to pull to the side of the road. As we approached the scene of the accident, we saw people and police cruisers. The ambulance halted, [D] ~~to a stop~~ and almost immediately the passenger door was pulled open by a police officer who grabbed me by the arm and cried, "Hurry! There's a little girl in the street. She was on a bike and . . ." Tears were welling up in this cop's[B] eyes, so we knew the little girl was in bad shape. Lou and I hurried around to the side door of the ambulance to get our airway kit, drug box, and cardiac monitor. 2

(E) Paragraph 3
The narration continues. Notice the specific, simple modifiers like "panic-stricken" and "twisted." The details about how badly Kelly was hurt help move the reader's emotions.

- (F) Improved diction.
- (G) Detail added for clarity.
- (H) Semicolon used to show close relationship of main clauses.
- (I) Specific detail added.

(E) We shoved our way through the panic-stricken crowd to find [F] an unconscious ~~pathetic, lifeless appearing,~~ 8–10 year old girl lying in a pool of blood. The [G] twisted remains of her bicycle were 30 feet aside. Her long blonde hair [F] was streaked with the red of her blood. ~~had tints of red throughout.~~ She had multiple lacerations over her whole body. Her left leg was obviously fractured[G], as it was twisted under her buttocks. The bone of her [G] right upper leg had pierced through her thigh. No air exchange could be heard with a [B] stethoscope over her left lung—it was collapsed. [G] The poor little thing ~~She~~ couldn't have weighed more than 50 pounds. She was in very bad shape. "Place her on a high flow of oxygen," I shouted. Lou checked her pupils and found them to be pinpoints [F] ~~in size~~. He replied, "I think she has a massive head injury." Meanwhile, I assessed her vital signs only to find her respirations shallow at a rate of 40/[B] per minute ~~min~~[H]; ~~and~~ her pulse was 150 [B] beats per minute ~~/min~~—very weak. I then yelled to Lou, "I need some I.V.'s set up. She needs fluids. She's bleeding internally." I stuck I.V. needles into one arm and into the uninjured 3 leg and pumped in 3 liters of fluid. She had a collapsed lung and a badly broken leg. We straightened her <u>left</u> leg and applied a Hare-traction splint to save it from amputation. As we finally became prepared to load her into the ambulance, I looked down at the cardiac monitor. Her heart was beating rapidly but had no significant abnormalities. Suddenly, within seconds, her cardiac rhythm deteriorated—her heart stopped! Immediately, I reached for the defibrillator paddles, charged them up with 300 joules of energy and shouted, "All clear!" <u>Watching her pale, innocent body jump from the jolt of electricity that passed through it brought tears to everyone's eyes. I had to fight back mine in the name of professionalism.</u> Within a few seconds her heart started beating again, but the EKG was far from normal. With this additional crisis, we began our desperate journey to South Side Hospital.

As we pulled into the hospital <u>at 5:45 P.M.</u>, we saw the trauma team 4
anxiously waiting our arrival at the entrance of the emergency room. We quickly unloaded the girl from the ambulance and made our way into Trauma Room I. As I gave my verbal report of the accident details to the resident in charge, the medical team <u>worked furiously</u>~~laboriously made every effort~~ to further stabilize the girl and prepare her for surgery. They transfused a large amount of blood into her jugular vein, then placed a chest tube into her left lung to reinflate it. A needle was punctured through her abdomen to determine the extent of internal hemorrhage. One doctor ~~replied~~<u>announced,</u> "She has lost a large amount of blood into the peritoneum. Let's get her upstairs." Within minutes, she was in surgery to repair her injuries.

Kelly is still alive today, two years after her hit-and-run accident. Being a 5
quadriplegic confined to a wheel chair, she will never be able to go for another bicycle ride. Her damaged brain only permits her to utter a few incomprehensible words. The future does not look good for Kelly because there is little hope she will regain the function she lost that tragic day.

One of the most tragic elements of Kelly's fate is that it didn't have to 6
be this way. If she had been wearing a bicycle helmet the odds are good

Paragraph 4
Repetition of "hospital" provides coherence. The narration continues. The topic sentence (the first sentence) states that the paragraph's focus is on what happened at the hospital.

J Sentence smoothed out.

Paragraph 5
The paragraph is transitional, connecting the narration to the point to be drawn from the story.

Paragraph 6
The first sentence is the topic sentence. The word "fate" helps achieve coherence by referring to ideas in the previous paragraph. Read the paragraph aloud to hear how well the paragraph flows because of sentence variety.

that her injuries would not have been as devastating. Her helmet would have protected her head and prevented her paralysis. According to the Consumer Product Safety Commission, "Wearing a bike helmet can reduce the risk of a head injury by 85 percent" (qtd. in Bicycle Helmet Safety Institute). Yet the Insurance Institute for Highway Safety says that an incredible 86 percent of people killed in bicycle accidents in 2005 were not wearing helmets (Bicycle Helmet Safety Institute). Helmets can save lives and reduce the risk of head injuries—yet we are not wearing them. Let's at least protect our children and require everyone under 18 to wear a helmet, for the same reason we wear seat belts. It's a matter of safety.

Paragraph 7
The conclusion achieves closure by calling the reader to action. This paragraph and paragraph 6 explain the significance of the narration.

It is too late for Kelly, but not for the rest of us. If you ride a bike, wear a helmet. If you have children, be sure they wear their helmets. Just stop and think for a moment about how you would feel if what happened to Kelly happened to your child. 7

Source is documented.

Work Cited

"Helmet Related Statistics from Many Sources." *Bicycle Helmet Safety Institute.* Bicycle Helmet Safety Institute, April 2008. Web. 18 Aug. 2008.

EXERCISE Your Essay in Progress

1. Continue revising the draft you worked on for the exercise on page 114, paying particular attention to your sentences and words. Then put the essay aside for a day or so.
2. When you return to your essay, make your final revisions. Then print out the essay or type it into its final form. Proofread and submit it if your instructor asks you to.
3. If you completed all the "Your Essay in Progress" exercises, you sampled a number of writing strategies. Which of them worked well for you? ■

Patterns of Development

PART 2

LOOKING AHEAD

The descriptions on a menu have both an informational and a persuasive purpose. First, the descriptions let diners know what the various dishes are like—that's the informational purpose. Second, the descriptions are written in a way to entice diners to order food they might not otherwise bother with—that's the persuasive purpose. In this chapter, you will learn more about descriptive writing and its purposes. As you look ahead to that information, think of the other times when you encounter written description. Do you ever order extra food or other goods just because of an appealing description? How are you persuaded?

Description

In "Postcard: Brazil," an essay for a regular *Time* magazine column about people and places around the world, Andrew Downie writes about the motorbike medics who race to accidents in São Paulo, Brazil—accidents that larger first-responder vehicles can't get to because of streets clogged with traffic. Downie's first paragraph includes this description:

> From the way they handle their bikes I can tell [the motorbike medics] are used to weaving through the nose-to-tail traffic. I, on the other hand, feel as if I am in a deadly video game. . . . Everywhere we turn, obstacles rush at as. As we approach the city's cathedral, striking postal workers spill onto the road and force us to swerve into the middle lane. Just around the corner, a boxy Fiat cuts us off and sends us veering into the gutter.

Downie describes downtown streets to evoke an image in his readers' minds and, thereby, set the scene. As they read about the job the motorcycle medics perform in order to save lives, Downie wants readers to understand how treacherous and frightening the traffic is that these medics must negotiate before they ever see their patients. And that's what description does—it creates images, establishes context, evokes a mood, and aids understanding.

WHY IS DESCRIPTION IMPORTANT?

Description moves our emotions and expands our experience. When we read descriptions of beautiful places and scenes, we are uplifted; when we read newspaper accounts of the devastation of wars and natural disasters, we are saddened. Description expands our experience by taking us to places we might not otherwise know much about, which explains the popularity of descriptive travel essays in magazines and newspapers. Description can also give us a fresh appreciation for the familiar. For example, a description of a neighborhood park can help someone who passes it every day rediscover its beauty.

As social beings, we want to share our experience, so we write to others to describe things such as vacations, childhood homes, and people we encounter. We even use description to persuade others to think or act in particular ways: Advertisers describe products to persuade us to buy them; travel agents describe locales to entice us to visit them; and real estate agents describe properties to stimulate a desire to see them. As the examples in the following chart show, description enables us to entertain, share feelings and experiences, inform, and persuade.

Purposes for Description

Purpose	Sample Description
To entertain	An amusing description of a teenager's bedroom
To share feelings and experiences	A description of your childhood home so your reader understands the poverty you grew up in and why you found excuses not to go home after school
To inform (for a reader unfamiliar with the subject)	A description of a newborn calf for a reader who has never seen one
To inform (to create a fresh appreciation for the familiar)	A description of an apple to help the reader rediscover the joys of this simple fruit
To persuade (to convince the reader that some music videos degrade women)	A description of a degrading music video

OCCASIONS FOR WRITING

Description across the Disciplines and Beyond

Description in the Classroom

You may be surprised by how important description is across the disciplines. For example, in a paper for an advertising class, you might describe the persuasive visuals in print advertisements. For a history class, you might describe the conditions in a 1920s sweatshop. For an art exam, you might describe the technique of a particular artist. *Think about three classes you are taking this term or expect to take soon. How might description be part of the reading and writing for those classes? What would be lost if the descriptive component were eliminated from the classes?*

Description in Daily Life

Description is important to the writing you do in your personal life. Your diary and journal entries might include descriptions of people and scenes. Your vacation letters and e-mails to friends and family will describe places you visit. And if you have to write a toast for a friend's award banquet, you might describe that person's best trait. *If you were involved in an auto accident and had to complete an accident report for your insurance company, how might you use description? Which of the purposes of writing would the description fulfill?*

Description on the Job

Description is often used on the job. Engineers and architects, for example, write descriptions of building sites. Campus admissions officials write promotional materials that describe the campus. Police officers describe crime scenes and suspects in their reports. *How do you think travel agents use description? What about newspaper reporters? What job do you hope to pursue after finishing school? How would description be useful in this job?*

COMBINING DESCRIPTION WITH OTHER PATTERNS

Because description adds interest and helps your reader form mental images, you will often use it with other patterns of development. For example, if you narrate a story, you might describe a person or setting to add vividness; if you compare and contrast two restaurants, you might include a description of their decors; if you explain the effects of not having zoning laws, you might describe what an area without zoning laws looks like; if you classify kinds of jazz, you might include a description of what the different kinds of jazz rhythms sound like; if you write a definition of *tacky*, you might illustrate with descriptions of tacky items. Thus, description is a good way to provide specific detail; it can often help you show and not just tell.

Because description can create interest in a topic, you may use it often in your introductions, regardless of the dominant pattern of development in the essay. Here is an example:

> It was a cool, crisp October morning. Sunrise was complete, the countryside awake and responding to another day. As I turned and slowly made my way into the woods, I had no idea what would happen on the path I was to follow that day.

SELECTING DETAIL

When you write description, you will have many decisions to make about the best details to include. The following discussion explains these decisions.

Focus Your Description with a Dominant Impression

Because you can't describe everything about your subject in a single essay, you should settle on one *dominant impression* (notable quality) and describe only those features that contribute to that impression. Suppose the attic of your grandmother's house has intrigued you since you were a small child, and so you decide to write a descriptive essay about it. Or suppose your grandmother herself has always interested you, and so you decide to describe *her* in an essay. Either way, you cannot describe *everything* about your subject. If you tried to include every detail about your grandmother or her attic, the result would be an unwieldy essay. However, you can write the reasons you are intrigued: Perhaps your grandmother's attic is eerie, full of reminders of the past, and unusual. Pick one of these three impressions to form the dominant impression and thereby supply the central point of your description. Then describe only those features of the attic that convey the impression you have settled on. Similarly, if your grandmother is interesting because she is enthusiastic, eccentric, and young at heart, decide which of these three qualities will be your central point, and then describe only features that convey that dominant impression.

To see how description can convey one impression (in this case, "gloomy"), read the following paragraph written by a student:

> It was late last night as I reluctantly took the steps down to the gloomy fruit cellar. Its dark, dusty shelves are located behind the crumbling basement walls. I fumbled in the dark for the lifeless screw-in light bulb and managed to twist it to a faint glow. With that the musty room was dimly lit, and long dark shadows lurked on the ceiling, outlining enlarged, misshapen jars of fruit. Water condensed and dripped from the ceiling, shattering the eerie silence. Cobwebs suspended in every corner hid their makers in a gray crisscross of lines. Hesitantly I took a step, my sneakers soaking up the black water lying 2 inches deep on the floor. A rat darted through a hole in the wall, and jars of fruit peered at me with their glassy eyes. The rotting shelves looked as if at any moment they would fall to the floor. The cold, gray walls reminded me of an Egyptian tomb forgotten long ago. Yet mummies don't decay, and I distinctly smelled the odor of something rotting.

Determine Your Need for Objective and Subjective Description

Descriptive details can be objective or subjective. **Objective description** includes observable, factual details expressed in unemotional language. For example, a real estate appraiser would write an objective description of a house to determine its fair market value. A teacher writing a grant proposal to buy playground equipment would write an objective description of that equipment.

Subjective description includes expressive, emotional language to convey the writer's feelings about what is being described or to move the reader's emotions. For example, a history teacher might include subjective description in a lecture describing the conditions on slave ships. To convince your classmates to volunteer for the municipal cleanup campaign, you might write subjective details in a letter to the editor of your campus newspaper describing the deplorable state of the littered streets near campus.

Writers combine objective and subjective description. For example, a food columnist might use objective description to tell readers what a dessert looks like and go on to use subjective description to explain what the dessert tastes like.

Notice the difference between the factual language of objective description and the expressive language of subjective description in these two examples, taken from selections in this chapter.

Objective description: An ultralight is the most basic aircraft made. It is almost a hang glider, except that it has an engine. Its structure is made entirely of aluminum tubing, dacron fabric, and stainless steel cables. The engine is fifty horsepower, two cycle, two cylinder, 503. This is the same size as the average snowmobile engine. The cockpit is open, meaning that one sits right out in the open—there are no walls, floor or windshield. ("My First Flight")

Subjective description: The rich, sweet smell of the barns fills the air—especially on hot days—and is noticeable even at the far end of the fairgrounds. A combination of hay and warm animal skins (with the undeniable tang of livestock manure), the smell sends city slickers racing from the barns with handkerchiefs covering their noses. However, even after seven years away from the countryside, I prefer the smell to the hot asphalt and thick exhaust fumes of a city summer. ("A Day at the Fair")

Use Concrete Sensory Detail

To create vivid mental images, use **concrete sensory detail,** which consists of specific words that appeal to the senses (sight, sound, taste, smell, touch). Look back at the paragraph describing the fruit cellar, and notice the strong mental images created with concrete sensory detail. Take, for example, the sentence "Cobwebs suspended in every corner hid their makers in a gray crisscross of lines." The detail here is *sensory* because it appeals to the sense of sight. It is *concrete* (specific) because of specific words like *suspended* and *crisscross of lines.* This specific detail that appeals to the sense of sight creates a mental picture for the reader much more vivid than one that would be formed from a more matter-of-fact statement like "cobwebs were in every corner, hiding spiders."

Notice, too, that the writer appeals to more than just the sense of sight. He also includes sound (water "shattering the eerie silence"), smell ("the odor of something rotting"), and touch ("my sneakers soaking up the black water"). While descriptions typically rely more on one sense than the others, writers convey impressions most clearly when they bring in as many senses as are pertinent. Be careful, though. Too much concrete sensory detail overwhelms your reader with mental images, as in this sentence:

> The small, fluffy, gray terrier danced and jumped with excitement and pleasure as her master took the hard, crunchy, brown dog biscuit from the large red-and-white sack.

As this overblown sentence shows, you must recognize when enough is enough. This principle of restraint holds true in paragraphs as well. Often when you have a complex, highly descriptive sentence in a paragraph, you should precede or follow it with a simpler, less descriptive one. Consider the following two sentences from "Prairie Vertigo" on page 160:

> One family on a farm outside Clara City had put a life-size Santa Claus on a telephone pole, arms and legs wrapped round it as though Santa were hanging on to keep the prevailing wind from blowing him away like so much topsoil. It was no exaggeration.

The first, very descriptive sentence appears next to a shorter, simpler one to create balance and prevent the reader from feeling overwhelmed.

Note: Concrete sensory detail is best achieved with specific, simple diction, which is explained on pages 129–31.

Use Similes and Metaphors

Similes and metaphors are forms of figurative language that can help you create vivid descriptions. A **simile** uses the words *like* or *as* to compare two things that are not usually seen as similar. For example, people are not typically compared to warehouse items, but they are in this simile from "Anguished Cries in a Place of Silence," which appears later in this chapter:

> People were stacked like goods in a warehouse.

A **metaphor** also compares two things not usually seen as similar, but it does so without using the words *like* or *as.* For example, an excavation site is not usually compared to a "bowl of light" but in "Where Nothing Says Everything" (page 165), the author writes this metaphor:

> Ground Zero is a great bowl of light, an emptiness that seems weirdly spacious and grand.

Consider Your Purpose and Audience

Your purpose will influence the details you select. Suppose you wish to describe your car and you want your reader to understand that the car is a reflection of your outgoing personality. You might describe the flashy colors, custom dash, unusual hood ornament, elaborate sound system, and so forth. Now suppose you want your reader to come to a fresh appreciation of the familiar. In this case, you might describe the features of your car that show it to be a marvel of engineering. If, however, you want to convince your reader to view the car as something that does more harm than good, you might describe the features that contribute to air and noise pollution, that contribute to laziness, and that can kill.

Your audience, like your purpose, also affects detail selection. How much your reader knows about your subject, how your reader feels about your subject, how interested your reader is in your subject—these factors influence your choice of details. For example, suppose you plan to describe the beauty of a local park in winter. If your reader is from a warm climate and has never seen snow, you will have to provide more details to create mental images than you would if your reader were familiar with snow. If your reader hates winter, you will have to work harder to help him or her appreciate the park's beauty than you would if your reader enjoyed winter.

BEING A RESPONSIBLE WRITER

Omitting important descriptions can give your reader a false impression. If you are describing a Tiffany lamp to sell on eBay, you will certainly want to describe the colors and pattern of the glass—but to omit the fact that the lamp needs to be rewired would be deceptive. If you write a classified ad for the local newspaper in order to sell your car, you will certainly want to describe its condition—but do so accurately. If the leather upholstery is badly torn and the tires are bald, you cannot say that the car is in pristine condition.

In addition, use descriptive words the way your reader does. If you are renting your house for the summer and call it "deluxe," your reader will expect accommodations well above average. If your house is small, lacks air conditioning, and is in need of paint, your renter will feel deceived because such a house is not typically considered "deluxe."

USING SOURCES FOR A PURPOSE

The paragraph below is a body paragraph for an essay about the need to teach Holocaust studies in high school. It illustrates one way to use sources from this book in your writing. The paragraph includes a summary of some of the material in paragraphs 5, 6, 8, 10, and 11 of "Anguished Cries in a Place of Silence" on page 161. (For information on how to write a summary, see page 12.)

The summary helps establish that resources for teaching about the Holocaust exist. It counters the objection that teaching about the Holocaust is difficult because of lack of materials. The writer needs to counter the objection to help make the case that the Holocaust should be taught in all high school history classes.

THESIS IDEA: All high school history classes should include a week or more of Holocaust studies.

WRITING PURPOSE AND AUDIENCE: To convince state school board members and curriculum directors to require Holocaust studies in high school history classes.

[1]In the past, many teachers have taught about the Holocaust by inviting a survivor to their classrooms to speak to students, but now that the generation of first-hand witnesses is dying off, some teachers have stopped teaching about this important historical event. [2]However, many other resources are available for teaching about the Holocaust. [3]As Lynn Sherr notes in "Anguished Cries in a Place of Silence," considerable historical data and artifacts exist for teachers to draw on. [4]When Sherr visited two concentration camps, she saw the "barracks, barbed wire, watch towers and a crematorium, all still menacing despite decades of abandonment." [5]She also saw other evidence, including primitive sinks and toilets, displays of tattoos that branded the prisoners, German records of who was imprisoned and for what offenses (such as the crime of offering assistance to Jews), and more

To be a responsible writer when you describe, ask yourself these questions:

- Is the description accurate?
- Am I omitting any important features?
- Am I using descriptive words to mean what my reader will understand them to mean?

ORGANIZING DESCRIPTION

Your thesis can note what you are describing and your dominant impression about your subject, like this:

than 2,000 pounds of prisoners' hair meant for manufacture into cloth. [6]Most disturbing to Sherr was the pile of suitcases of the victims, all identified with the names of their owners, including those of children (162–63). [7]Teachers can use accounts such as Sherr's, along with instructional materials that any Holocaust museum will provide. [8]Even a quick Google search of "Holocaust teaching materials" yields a wealth of useful items. [9]In truth, teachers should have no problem putting together valuable lesson plans on the Holocaust.

Avoiding Plagiarism

The paragraph illustrates some points about avoiding plagiarism. (For more on using source material, see Chapter 17.)

- **Introduce your summary with the source and reintroduce as necessary.** As sentence 3 illustrates, identify the author and title of the source you are summarizing and use a *present-tense* verb. As sentences 4–6 illustrate, repeat the author's name or use a pronoun as necessary to make clear that you are still working with source material.
- **Place key words and phrases in quotation marks.** You should summarize using your own words and style, but as sentence 4 shows, you can include some of the source's exact wording if you place it in quotation marks.

Myths about Sources

MYTH: A summary stands on its own and need not be synthesized with other ideas in the essay.

FACT: You must show how the summary supports or develops your thesis, topic sentence, or a supporting point. Notice the synthesis in the sample paragraph:

- Sentence 3 indicates that the source supports the topic sentence idea that resources for teaching the Holocaust exist: Lynn Sherr has seen some of the data and artifacts that can serve as resources.
- Sentences 4–6 support the topic sentence by noting specifically what some of the data and artifacts are.

As a child, and now as an adult, I have always been drawn to Grandma's attic because it is filled with reminders of the past.

The thesis indicates that you will describe Grandma's attic and that the impression you will convey is that it is filled with reminders of the past.

When you form your thesis, express your impression in specific language. Impressions expressed in words like *nice, great, wonderful, awful, terrible,* and *bad* are too vague to tell the reader much. However, words like *relaxing, scenic, cheerful, depressing, congested,* and *unnerving* are specific and give your reader a clear understanding of your impression.

As an alternative, your thesis can tell your reader what you are describing *without* specifying your impression. Instead, your reader gathers the impression from the details in the body. The thesis for such a paper might look like this:

> As a child, and now as an adult, I have always been drawn to Grandma's attic.

You can arrange descriptive details in several ways. If you are describing a place, you can use **spatial order** and move from left to right, top to bottom, near to far, center to periphery, or inside to outside. Sometimes a **progressive order** is effective. You can arrange your details so that they build to the features that most clearly or strikingly convey your impression. A **chronological order** can be effective when you are describing what you see as you move through a place or how something has changed over time. For more on these ways to order details, see Chapter 3.

Sometimes the best way to organize a description is by sensory impressions. For example, if you are describing a ballpark during a game, you could first describe the sights, then the sounds, next the smells, and so forth.

EXERCISE Writing Description

1. Write two different dominant impressions you could use for two different descriptions of each of the following places.
   a. Your bedroom
   b. A store where you shop
   c. A campus dining hall
   d. An area outside a campus building
2. Select one of the places you used for number 1 and one of the dominant impressions you had of the place. Then mention three elements you could describe to convey that dominant impression.
3. Write one descriptive sentence for each of the items in your list from number 2. Be sure to keep your dominant impression in mind.
4. Write a simile or metaphor for each of the following:
   a. A stubborn child
   b. The sound of a lawn mower
   c. The smell of burning food
   d. The feel of cat fur
5. Write a one-sentence objective description of an item of clothing you are wearing. Then rewrite that sentence to make the description subjective.
6. Write a one-paragraph *objective* description of some part of your writing classroom. Then, on a separate sheet, write a one-paragraph *subjective* description of the same aspect. ■

Visualizing a Descriptive Essay

The chart that follows can help you visualize one structure for a descriptive essay. Like all good models, this one can be altered as needed.

Introduction

- Creates interest in what you are describing
- Can state the thesis, which can indicate what you are describing and your dominant impression

First Body Paragraph

- Includes objective or subjective description or both to convey your dominant impression
- Includes concrete sensory details
- May include similes and metaphors
- Arrange details in spatial, progressive, chronological, or other logical order, such as according to sensory impressions

Next Body Paragraphs

- Continue the description by conveying the dominant impression
- Include concrete sensory details
- May include similes and metaphors
- Arrange details in spatial, progressive, chronological, or other logical order, such as according to sensory impressions

Conclusion

- Provides closure
- Leaves your reader with a strong final impression

LEARNING FROM OTHER WRITERS: Student Essays

The first student essay, "A Day at the Fair," includes marginal notes that point out many of the essay's key features. As you read, notice the writer's careful attention to providing vivid, concrete sensory details.

In the second student essay, "My First Flight," the author combines description with narration to convey what it was like when he flew in his brother's ultralight plane. Notice that the author uses both objective and subjective description; consider whether he uses each appropriately.

Paragraph 1
The introduction engages interest with background information. The thesis is the last sentence. It notes that the animal barns will be described and that the dominant impression is that they are fascinating.

Paragraph 2
The topic sentence, which gives the focus of the paragraph as the 4-H barns, is the first sentence. Notice the specific words, such as "tang," "racing," and "thick exhaust fume." Much of the concrete sensory detail appeals to smell.

Paragraph 3
The focus is on the animals in the barn. Notice the concrete sensory details that appeal to the senses of sight and sound. The details are both expressive and objective, and include specific words such as "bits of hay dance" and "shufflings, slurpings, munchings."

A Day at the Fair

Adell Lindsey

For the last seven years, I have lived in Minneapolis. I seem to spend my life in my car, commuting from work to school and back to my apartment again. Although I enjoy the bustle and convenience of city life, every summer I find myself becoming nostalgic for the country, particularly the farm animals. A few years ago, I rediscovered one of the great summer pleasures of my childhood—the Crow Wing County agricultural fair. Now, in the second week of each August I make the two-hour drive north to the fairgrounds of the community where I grew up, just to see the fascinating animal barns. 1

I spend most of my time at the fairgrounds in the 4-H animal barns. (The 4-H organization provides educational and recreational opportunities for young people in rural communities.) The rich, sweet smell of the barns fills the air—especially on hot days—and is noticeable even at the far end of the fairgrounds. A combination of hay and warm animal skins (with the undeniable tang of livestock manure), the smell sends city slickers racing from the barns with handkerchiefs covering their noses. However, even after seven years away from the countryside, I prefer the smell to the hot asphalt and thick exhaust fumes of a city summer. 2

Entering the barns, I always need to stop and blink for a few moments to adjust to the dimmer light. To keep the animals cool, the barns are lofty and shady. Dust motes and bits of hay dance in the few rays of light that slide through gaps in the roof. Soon, I see aisles of clean, low stalls, each stacked with bales of hay. Depending on the day of the fair, the stalls hold goats, pigs, or heifers—as well as the occasional llama, a newer category in 4-H livestock competitions. Their shufflings, slurpings, munchings, and grunts make a low-key accompaniment to the distant bells and tinny music of the midway attractions. 3

The animals are not alone in their stalls. Brushing the animals, mucking out their stalls, napping on hay bales, or changing water dishes, children 4 and young teenagers from 4-H spend all day with and around their animals. For them, I think, the ribbons and certificates awarded to the "best" specimens are not as important as the bonds developed with their animals. I'll always remember one little boy, probably seven or eight years old, fast asleep on a hay bale with one of his arms thrown around the neck of his black-and-white-spotted goat, who seemed to lie watchfully and protectively beside him.

Near the animal barns is the competition ring where 4-H participants 5
show off their calves and heifers to judges. The ring smells sweetly of sawdust—mostly because one little boy, in a cowboy hat that seems far too large for his head, scoots into the ring with a big shovel to clean up any messes the nervous animals might leave. The announcer is a very large gentleman, his face hidden behind mirrored sunglasses, who always seems to find something nice to say about the animals as well as their young handlers. "Let's have a big round of applause for the little lady!" he'll bellow after a tiny girl has finished leading an enormous cow around the ring.

On the drive back to the city, when I'm full of corn dogs and blueberry 6
milkshakes, I wonder about the turn my life could have taken. What if my parents had signed me up for 4-H instead of soccer? What if, instead of an aloof cat, a 300-pound pig was waiting back in my apartment for its dinner? Back at home, I scrape the mud and hay fragments from my boots and look in the fridge for dinner. Hamburger? Pork chops? I decide to make a salad instead, and vow to start growing herbs in my windowbox.

Paragraph 4
The first sentence provides transition, and the second is the topic sentence, giving the focus on 4-H members. The writer's purpose seems to be to share an experience and express feelings—and perhaps create appreciation for the animal barns and 4-H experience.

Paragraph 5
The first sentence—the topic sentence—moves the essay to the competition ring. Transition is achieved and spatial order is indicated with "Near the animal barns." Readers may disagree about the relevance of this paragraph to the thesis. Notice the expressive detail. The concrete sensory details appeal to sight and sound, and include specific words such as "smells sweetly of sawdust" and "bellow."

Paragraph 6
The conclusion provides closure by returning the author home and adding a touch of humor. What does this paragraph suggest about the intended audience for the essay? Did you notice the combination of spatial and chronological order in the essay?

My First Flight

Jerry Silberman

The one consistent love I have had throughout my life is flying. Dreams, books, and the experiences of pilots I knew made me long to fly before I ever experienced my first flight. It was, in fact, all I talked about. Then my brother Gene bought a two-seat ultralight. For nineteen years, my feet had not left the ground. Now it was time to fly, and the experience did not disappoint. 1

An ultralight is the most basic aircraft made. It is almost a hang glider, except that it has an engine. Its structure is made entirely of aluminum tubing, dacron fabric, and stainless steel cables. The engine is fifty horsepower, two cycle, two cylinder, 503. This is the same size as the average snowmobile engine. The cockpit is open, meaning that one sits right out in the open—there are no walls, floor, or windshield. In front of the pilot are two pedals to control the rudder and a control stick for the throttle, spoilerens, and elevators. The gauges consist of a tachometer, wind speed indicator, and altimeter. That is all there is to the craft. It isn't much, but, oh, the thrill it provides! 2

On the day of my first flight, I was dressed in old jeans, a flight jacket, goggles, and a helmet. I felt more like a World War I flying ace than a modern aviator. "Clear prop" were the last words I heard until landing. Because of the engine noise, everything communicated in the air would be in sign language or by facial expression. Gene pull-started the engine. We taxied to the end of our runway and turned to face the wind. I gave Gene thumbs up to let him know I was ready. Boy, was I ready! He nodded, twisted the throttle, and we bounced over the rough field. We were airborne. 3

The only way to pinpoint exactly where one leaves the ground is by noting the extreme smoothness of air after the choppiness of the grassy field. I felt suspended. The ground dropped silently away as we climbed to 4 clear the maples at the end of the runway. Gene's hand gripped tightly on the control stick as we skimmed thirty feet above the leaves. It felt less like we were rising above the earth, than that the earth was falling away from us. Gene banked to the right and we headed north, climbing higher and higher.

Suddenly, I was scared. In an instant, the reality of my situation had 5
hit me, and there wasn't a thing I could do about it. Gene was in control, and all I could do was breathe deeply to keep from throwing up. Fortunately, as soon as we swept over another group of trees, the trauma of takeoff passed, and a rush of excitement replaced it. My brain could not work fast enough to take it all in. My eyes darted left and right, trying to see everything at once, and my brain worked to process the fact that I was sitting out in the open hundreds of feet above the ground. Then I felt the most powerful rush of all: freedom! That is what flying is all about for me. I never felt more free. There were no restrictions on me as we soared high above the land.

Going thirty miles an hour at one thousand feet, which felt practically like 6
hovering, we crossed empty fields, large wooded areas, and some sparsely populated streets. I could see people out in their yards and imagined them watching in awe those crazy people in their kitelike craft.

The day was mostly clear with just a few scattered clouds to remind 7
us of our altitude. Lack of oxygen prevented us from climbing above the clouds, but we were close to the same level as a few of the lower ones. Clouds look different from up close and from the side. They seem more substantial, more cottony. Viewed from the air, clouds have a three-dimensional reality instead of the two-dimensional sense we get when we view them from the ground. The rays of the setting sun were diffused through the undersides, giving the clouds between us and the sun a luminescent silver base that seemed to support the puffy white foam that billowed upward from the silver.

The sun was a bright red ball that rolled along the horizon as we turned to head back. It gave an orange glow to the hazy horizon, and orange tinted fog drifted below a light violet sky. It was a display that could only be witnessed from the air. The earth slowly rotated, and the great fireball lowered beneath the land. 8

Gene gave the signal that we were on our final approach for landing. I watched the ground as it rose to our level. As the craft leveled after its shallow dive, my stomach dropped. The effect of that small G-force was my last taste of flight. We were back on solid ground. 9

I have flown many times since then, and I always get the same rush of freedom and thrill from the perspective that being airborne provides. Flying intrigued me before I ever left the ground. Once I did, I was hooked. 10

EXERCISE Considering "My First Flight"

1. What is Jerry Silberman describing, and what is his dominant impression?
2. Cite one paragraph that includes objective description, one that includes subjective description, and one that includes both.
3. Cite two concrete sensory details that you find effective. What makes them effective?
4. What is Jerry Silberman's purpose for writing? How does the description help him achieve that purpose? How does the narration help him achieve that purpose? ■

THINK LIKE A CRITIC; WORK LIKE AN EDITOR: The Student Writer at Work

Writing description often involves a series of revisions to get the images just right. Here, for example, is the first draft of one of Jerry Silberman's more descriptive paragraphs, followed by his first two revisions. The changes are noted in color, with underlining to mark additions, and strikeovers to mark deletions. Notice that with this revision, Jerry added descriptive details and used more specific word choice.

First draft

It was a clear day, but the few clouds made us realize how high we were. Lack of oxygen prevented us from going above the clouds, but we were close to the same level as a few of the lower ones. Clouds look different from up close and from the side. The rays of the setting sun reflected off the bottoms and gave the clouds a silver glow from within. The clouds billowed upward, giving them a three dimensional image instead of the sense of paintings we get from the ground.

First revision

It was a clear day, but the fewscattered clouds made us realize how high we were. Lack of oxygen prevented us from ~~going~~ climbing above the clouds, but we were close to the same level as a few of the lower ones. Clouds look different from up close and from the side. They seem more fragile and less like thick cotton. The rays of the setting sun reflected off the bottoms and gave the clouds a silver tinge.~~glow from within.~~ The clouds billowed upward, giving them a three-dimensional image instead of the sense of paintings we get from the ground.

Second revision

It was a clear day, but the few scattered clouds reminded ~~made~~ us of~~realize~~ how high we were. Lack of oxygen prevented us from climbing above the clouds, but we were close to the same level as a few of the lower ones. Clouds look different from up close and from the side. They seem more fragile and less like thick cotton. The rays of the setting sun were diffused through~~reflected off~~ their undersides~~bottoms~~ and gave the clouds between us and the sun a silver tinge. The clouds billowed upward, giving them a three-dimensional reality~~image~~ instead of the two-dimensional sense of paintings we get from the ground.

In this second revision, Jerry shaped the description a bit more. However, this is still not the final version you read in the essay. After studying Jerry's revisions and final version, how would you describe his revision process?

Prairie Vertigo

VERLYN KLINKENBORG

"Prairie Vertigo" appeared in the New York Times *in 2000, on the paper's editorial page, as part of the author's regular "The Rural Life" series. In the piece, which includes both objective and subjective description, the author does not explicitly state a thesis with his subject and his dominant impression. As you read, consider what his thesis might be.*

Up past Pipestone, Minn., Highway 23 angles away to the north-northeast, through Lyon, Yellow Medicine and Chippewa Counties, and through the heart of what for 12 years in the mid-19th century was the Dakota Reservation and before that the Dakota homeland. It had snowed a couple of days earlier, and the highway was a patchwork of dry pavement and hard, rutted ice, where drifting snow had blown across the asphalt in a warm southern wind and frozen overnight. But now the wind was changing. Second by second, the balance of brightness shifted back and forth between the overcast sky and the snow-glazed earth, like flakes of mica[1] mirroring each other. 1

I had flown over this country two days earlier and nothing seemed to be moving below me, nothing large enough to leave a track through new-fallen snow. The landscape was nearly as still from the highway. Snowmobiles had run along the ditches, and steers had in some places been turned out into the cornfields, but those were the only signs of movement. 2

Except for the wind. One family on a farm outside Clara City had put a life-size Santa Claus on a telephone pole, arms and legs wrapped around it as though Santa were hanging on to keep the prevailing wind from blowing him away like so much topsoil. It was no exaggeration. On the farm I had come to visit, we walked between the house and the sow barn with all the haste we could muster, heads bowed, talking only in the lee.[2] The temperature had already fallen 20 degrees that day, and it was still going down, dropping as fast, it seemed, as the second hand on its way toward 6. 3

I was supposed to return to that farm for supper. I left the motel in the early darkness and headed west out of Willmar, in Kandiyohi County. The wind had risen even higher and was now on its hind legs, a steady gale out of the northwest, and with the rising wind the snow rose too. Sometimes I could see the sulfur glow of lights on a turkey barn or the double halo of approaching headlights. Then the snow thickened and the highway disappeared again and again into the nullifying glare of my own headlights. Six miles outside of town, in an unbroken whiteout, I turned around. 4

It was the first time I ever felt the vertigo that settlers often felt when they first came to the prairie. There are many descriptions of it, but here's what I understood. When the wind blows from the northwest in western Minnesota, it blows from infinity. Northwest is the one direction that goes on forever there, without any barriers, beyond the indiscernible horizon and away to the arctic. Most of the fence lines are gone in that cash-grain country, and there is no such thing as a tree line, no rimrock or buttes to hold in the landscape. There is only the sound of the wind skirling down with its endless driven snows upon you. 5

[1]Mica is a group of minerals that can be silvery and easily separated into thin leaves.
[2]The lee is the direction toward which the wind is blowing.

Considering Ideas

1. Klinkenborg does not include a thesis sentence that states what he is describing and his dominant impression. What do you think he is describing, and what is his dominant impression?
2. "Prairie Vertigo" originally appeared in the *New York Times.* For what purpose do you think the author wrote the piece? How likely do you think it is that he achieved his purpose with this particular audience?
3. In paragraph 1, Klinkenborg mentions that the section of prairie he was on was home to the Dakota Indians. Why do you think he includes that information? How does it help him achieve his writing purpose?
4. In paragraph 5, the author says that the wind "blows from infinity." What does he mean?
5. In your own words, explain what "prairie vertigo" is.

Considering Technique

1. Vertigo is not specifically mentioned until the last paragraph. What purpose do the first four paragraphs serve?
2. Two similes appear in paragraph 3. What are they? What metaphor appears in paragraph 4?
3. Cite two examples of simple, specific verbs; two of simple, specific nouns; and two of simple, specific modifiers. How do these word choices help the author achieve his writing purpose?
4. What approach does the author take to the conclusion of "Prairie Vertigo"? What do you think of the ending?

For Group Discussion or Journal Writing

How does Klinkenborg feel about what he experienced on the prairie? How do you know?

Anguished Cries in a Place of Silence

LYNN SHERR

In this 2002 essay that first appeared in the travel section of the New York Times, *Lynn Sherr describes what she witnessed when she visited two Nazi concentration camps. The description is powerful, yet most of it is objective rather than subjective. As you read, think about why the objective details convey so much emotion.*

It was smaller than I'd imagined, a black iron portal of human dimensions rather than the monstrous symbol of terror it has become. But the cynical words arching overhead, "ARBEIT MACHT FREI," or "Work Makes You Free," transported me directly into the footsteps of those who had once shuffled into Auschwitz with no hope of leaving alive. Our guide pointed to the handmade sign: "Look at the 'B' in "ARBEIT," he said. "It's upside down. A prisoner's rebellion—a sign of resistance." It was one of the only moments of triumph for the next five and a half hours. 1

I had come to Auschwitz to pay my respects, to touch the

horror I had been spared only because my grandparents left Poland when the tyrant was the Czar, not Hitler. I went home convinced that everyone ought to visit. To feel. To bear witness. To preserve the lesson. 2

The death camp known during World War II as Konzentrationslager Auschwitz I is today Auschwitz-Birkenau State Museum, a sprawling monument to Nazi depravity and global neglect in southern Poland. This complex was the largest of the lagers, ultimately encompassing a chain of subcamps, and was responsible for the systematic murders of nearly 1.5 million people, almost all Jews, from the day it opened in June 1940 until the Soviet liberation in January 1945. Now it is less a tourist spot than a pilgrimage site for an estimated half a million visitors a year. Poles, Americans and Germans are the most numerous; many visitors are Jews, looking for traces of lost relatives or, like me, for a moment to mourn. Groups of German schoolchildren also come, to help maintain the museum by cutting the grass and doing other odd jobs as volunteers. "It is very hard for the German kids," the museum's Polish deputy director, Krystyna Olesky, told me in an interview before my tour. 3

I started my trip in Krakow, where my companions hired a car and driver for the 45-minute drive southwest, mostly on the well-maintained A-4 toll road through gentle hills and past small brick houses. The ordinariness was jarring: taking a taxi to a concentration camp on a gorgeous, warm day last August. But when we passed the first set of railroad tracks, my blood ran cold. That was how prisoners arrived 60 years ago. In fact, the camp was built here precisely because of the conjunction of major railroad lines in the town of Oswiecim, which the Third Reich renamed Auschwitz after occupying Poland in 1939. 4

My first impression of the camp itself was vastness—nearly 50 acres of barracks, barbed wire, watch towers and a crematorium, all still menacing despite decades of abandonment. I fell uncharacteristically silent. And I wasn't the only one. There were several large groups there when I visited—Japanese tourists and French boy scouts among them. Few were laughing or posing. 5

Instead, we proceeded along the neat rows of barracks, or blocks, with their exhibits on camp life. And death. The blocks themselves are red brick, two-story buildings, each designed to house 700 prisoners. In reality, each held up to 2,000, crammed so tight on concrete floors that at night, according to our guide, "when one turned, all had to turn." The toilets were lidless and doorless; the sinks, long troughs. This was where the lucky ones lived, or rather existed, while they worked in the fields or factories nearby. 6

I thought of the words of Primo Levi, the Italian chemist and writer who spent nearly a year here: "It is not possible to sink lower than this; no human condition is more miserable than this, nor could it conceivably be so." 7

One display shows the variety of tattoos[1] used at Auschwitz, the only camp to use them; another, the train tickets the Nazis sold (yes, sold) to prisoners for their trip to the camp. An immense array of prison cards (häftlingskarten) listed not only a person's name and usual statistics, but also the shape of his or her face (including eyes, nose, ears, teeth and lips) and the reason for the arrest. One poor soul's offense was "helping Jews"; another's, "listening to foreign radio station." 8

The Nazi compulsion to document atrocities is stunning, the deceit infuriating. Death records for Russian prisoners of war—exterminated for being soldiers, not Jews—are recorded in black ink with a steady hand, noting precisely the time of execution: 8 p.m., 8:05, 8:10, 8:45. One book records the names of 22,000 Gypsy victims, including their children born at Auschwitz. A postcard to the Red Cross from a Czech Jew—forced to write in German—reads: "I am in good health, I feel good." 9

And then there is the hair. On the second floor of Block 4, in a case some 20 yards long, are layer after layer of braids and tresses and curls, all gone gray now but once blond and brown and black and auburn. The hair weighs more than two tons, less than a third of what the Allied troops originally found. Hair was sold to be woven into textiles; gold fillings from teeth went to the German treasury. 10

Each display was more dreadful than the last, but the one that hit me hardest was the suitcases: a room-length mound of leather and cardboard valises one packed with the illusion that the owners were headed for a place where they could use their belongings. Names and statistics were carefully lettered outside with what looked like white shoe polish: "L. Bermann, 26.12.1886, Hamburg." As if poor Mr. Bermann ever would see his bag, or his world, again. "Sometimes visitors say, 'That's my father,' our guide told me. I scanned the mass of lost hopes and stopped short at a brown leather valise, with the name "Petr Eisler, KIND," meaning child. Petr's birth date was two days from my own. 11

As we were led from building to building along the wide, deceptively tranquil roads of the camp on this gloriously sunny day, I recognized the incongruities. The lawn was too lush ("If there had been grass, the starving prisoners would have eaten it," our guide said) and it was peaceful. The crematorium, with its tracks for the smooth delivery of bodies to ovens, has been restored. There is no shortage of grisly reminders, like Block 11 with its one-foot-square "standing cell" and its suffocating starvation cell, torturous punishment for disobedient prison laborers. A placard points out that Jakob Rosenzweig spent five nights here because he was "talking during work." Still, it's tidy—put in order—after all, a museum. "Auschwitz has a certain progression," explained one of my companions, a rabbi based in Warsaw, ushering me back into the taxi after three hours for the next part of our visit. "But Birkenau gets right away to the bones." 12

Birkenau is shorthand for KL Auschwitz II, built as an expansion to the main camp in 1941 in the nearby village of Brzezinka, a quick, two-mile drive. 13

Birkenau is where it all began and ended; where you stepped out of your boxcar and faced a lineup of storm troopers and snarling dogs and where one man would decide whether you lived temporarily or died immediately. It was called the Selection. You've no doubt seen the photographs—the ones with the Nazi officer pointing to the right (forced labor) or left (gas chamber), taking lives and splitting families. It's where

[1]The tattoos were prisoner identification numbers tattooed on the arms of Auschwitz prisoners.

Sophie had to make her unbearable choice.[2] 14

I walked down the tracks in utter silence. This camp, nearly 10 times the size of Auschwitz, has largely been left as it was, an eerie ghost town spread across an immense field with the remains of four gas chambers and crematoriums, and a sickeningly efficient reception area called the sauna, where prisoners chosen for forced labor were shaved, stripped and hosed down. 15

There are also rows of squalid barracks—one-story structures originally designed as stables, with 52 rings for horses still on the wall. They housed up to 1,000 humans each. Here the toilets were buckets, the beds triple-tiered shelves where the people were stacked like goods in a warehouse. Finally I understood the photographs of the liberation: this is where the men, or women, lay staring out at their rescuers, human cordwood too feeble to move. 16

The ovens they'd escaped are not intact. Unlike the restoration at Auschwitz, some are in clumps, ruins left by the SS when they blew them up in an attempt to destroy all evidence before retreating. Another was partly destroyed by Jewish prisoners, who somehow managed to marshal the strength of the powerless during a 1944 revolt. An enlarged photograph by the rubble puts it back together. 17

Even the ground at Birkenau is authentic—so thoroughly saturated with the remains of the prisoners' bodies, I was warned to be careful where I walked. "The ashes were dumped in the pond," I was told, "but in fact the ashes are all around here." I heard about visitors who found bits of bones in the soil sticking up near the footpaths. 18

Finally, at the far end of the grounds, we reached the memorial—a line of plaques unveiled in 1967 with the same message in 19 languages. It reads in part: "Forever let this place be a cry of despair and a warning to humanity." That thought was echoed in my introductory conversation with Krystyna Olesky, the deputy director who has worked there for 20 years. Yes, she told me, it is difficult "but someone has to do it." Why? "Because of all those who died here." 19

She described the staff efforts to catalog prison records into a new database, to shore up the crumbling buildings, to repair the damage from acid rain, paid for mostly by international contributions organized by the Ronald S. Lauder Foundation. 20

"This is an extraordinary cemetery, the scene of a crime," she told me. "We could flatten everything, let the grass grow, and we would have in some sense fulfilled that need to commemorate. But history teaches us. The maintenance of historical knowledge is our obligation. This must never happen again." 21

I left feeling drained and shaken but curiously satisfied. I had wanted to see Auschwitz with my own eyes, not because I doubted its existence or expected to make sense of it, but to make it part of my life. "No one who has not experienced the event will ever be able to understand it," wrote Elie Wiesel, the Nobelist who survived Auschwitz. Primo Levi described winter in Auschwitz, when an icicle he'd broken off was snatched away. 22

Why?" he asked his tormentor, who replied, "There is no why here." 23

[2]In the William Styron novel *Sophie's Choice* (1979), a sadistic doctor in Auschwitz forces Sophie to choose in mere seconds which of her two children will live, her 4-year-old daughter or her 10-year-old son.

Considering Ideas

1. Lynn Sherr calls the words over the Auschwitz gate ("Arbeit Macht Frei" or "Work makes you free") cynical. Why does she think so? Do you agree? Why or why not?
2. In paragraph 3, Sherr notes, "It is very hard for the German kids" who volunteer at the museum. Why do you think it is hard for these children?

3. For what purpose do you think Sherr wrote "Anguished Cries in a Place of Silence"? Where is her purpose best stated?
4. Explain the meaning of the title. Is the title a good one for this essay?
5. The essay contains a number of contrasting ideas. In the title, for example, cries are heard although the place is silent. What other contrasts do you notice in the essay? How do these contrasts help the author achieve her purpose for writing?

Considering Technique

1. Ordinarily, subjective description rather than objective description moves a reader's emotions. The description in this essay is primarily objective, yet the essay is very powerful. How do you explain the fact that so much emotion and power are conveyed by objective details rather than subjective ones?
2. Cite two examples of concrete sensory details that create clear mental images.
3. Cite one example each of a specific yet simple noun, verb, and modifier.
4. Paragraph 16 includes one simile and one metaphor. What are they? How do they add to the description?
5. In what order are the details arranged? How can you tell?

For Group Discussion or Journal Writing

In paragraph 2, Sherr notes that a particular lesson needs to be preserved. What is that lesson? Do you agree that it should be preserved? Why or why not? What other lesson from history do you think should be preserved? Why?

Combining Patterns of Development

Where Nothing Says Everything

Suzanne Berne

After the terrorist attack on the World Trade Center, people from around the world were compelled to visit the site. Novelist Suzanne Berne uses description, narration, and contrast to tell about her own visit six months after the towers collapsed. As you read this essay that first appeared in the New York Times *in 2002, consider the meaning of the title.*

On a cold, damp March morning, I visited Manhattan's financial district, a place I'd never been, to pay my respects at what used to be the World Trade Center. Many other people had chosen to do the same that day, despite the raw wind and spits of rain, and so the first thing I noticed when I arrived on the corner of Vesey and Church Streets was a crowd. 1

Standing on the sidewalk, pressed against aluminum police barricades, wearing scarves that flapped into their faces and woolen hats pulled over their ears, were people apparently from everywhere. Germans, Italians, Japanese. An elegant-looking Norwegian family in matching shearling coats. People from Ohio and California and Maine. Children, middle-age couples, older people. Many of them were clutching cameras and video

recorders, and they were all craning to see across the street, where there was nothing to see. 2

At least, nothing is what it first looked like, the space that is now ground zero. But once your eyes adjust to what you are looking at, "nothing" becomes something much more potent, which is absence. 3

But to the out-of-towner, ground zero looks at first simply like a construction site. All the familiar details are there: the wooden scaffolding; the cranes, the bulldozers and forklifts; the trailers and construction workers in hard hats; even the dust. There is the pound of jackhammers, the steady beep-beep-beep of trucks backing up, the roar of heavy machinery. 4

So much busyness is reassuring, and it is possible to stand looking at the cranes and trucks and feel that mild curiosity and hopefulness so often inspired by construction sites. 5

Then gradually your eyes do adjust, exactly as if you have stepped from a dark theater into a bright afternoon, because what becomes most striking about this scene is the light itself. 6

Ground zero is a great bowl of light, an emptiness that seems weirdly spacious and grand, like a vast plaza amid the dense tangle of streets in lower Manhattan. Light reflecting off the Hudson River vaults into the site, soaking everything—especially on an overcast morning—with a watery glow. This is the moment when absence begins to assume a material form, when what is not there becomes visible. 7

Suddenly you notice the periphery, the skyscraper shrouded in black plastic, the boarded windows, the steel skeleton of the shattered Winter Garden. Suddenly there are the broken steps and cracked masonry in front of Brooks Brothers. Suddenly there are the firefighters, the waiting ambulance on the other side of the pit, the police on every corner. Suddenly there is the enormous cross made of two rusted girders. 8

And suddenly, very suddenly, there is the little cemetery attached to St. Paul's Chapel, with tulips coming up, the chapel and grounds miraculously undamaged except for a few plastic-sheathed gravestones. The iron fence is almost invisible beneath a welter of dried pine wreaths, banners, ribbons, laminated poems and prayers and photographs, swags of paper cranes, withered flowers, baseball hats, rosary beads, teddy bears. And flags, flags everywhere, little American flags fluttering in the breeze, flags on posters drawn by Brownie troops, flags on T-shirts, flags on hats, flags streaming by, tied to the handles of baby strollers. 9

It takes quite a while to see all of this; it takes even longer to come up with something to say about it. 10

An elderly man standing next to me had been staring fixedly across the street for some time. Finally he touched his son's elbow and said: "I watched those towers being built. I saw this place when they weren't there." Then he stopped, clearly struggling with, what for him, was a double negative, recalling an absence before there was an absence. His son, waiting patiently, took a few photographs. "Let's get out of here," the man said at last. 11

Again and again I heard people say, "It's unbelievable." And then they would turn to each other, dissatisfied. They wanted to say something more expressive, more meaningful. But it is unbelievable, to stare at so much devastation, and know it for devastation, and yet recognize that it does not look like the devastation one has imagined. 12

Like me, perhaps, the people around me had in mind images from television and newspaper pictures: the collapsing buildings, the running office workers, the black plume of smoke against a bright blue sky. Like me, they were probably trying to superimpose those terrible images onto the industrious emptiness right in front of them. The difficulty of this kind of mental revision is measured, I believe, by the brisk trade in World Trade Center photograph booklets at tables set up on street corners. 13

Determined to understand better what I was looking at, I decided to get a ticket for the viewing platform beside St. Paul's. This proved no easy task, as no one seemed to be able to direct me to South Street Seaport, where the tickets are distributed.

Various police officers whom I asked for directions, waved me vaguely toward the East River, differing degrees of boredom and resignation on their faces. Or perhaps it was a kind of incredulousness. Somewhere around the American Stock Exchange, I asked a security guard for help and he frowned at me, saying, "You want tickets to the disaster?" 14

Finally I found myself in line at a cheerfully painted kiosk, watching a young juggler try to entertain the crowd. He kept dropping the four red balls he was attempting to juggle, and having to chase after them. It was noon; the next available viewing was at 4 P.M. 15

Back I walked, up Fulton Street, the smell of fish in the air, to wander again around St. Paul's. A deli on Vesey Street advertised a view of the World Trade Center from its second-floor dining area. I went in and ordered a pastrami sandwich, uncomfortably aware that many people before me had come to that same deli for pastrami sandwiches who would never come there again. But I was here to see what I could, so I carried my sandwich upstairs and sat down beside one of the big plate-glass windows. 16

And there, at last, I got my ticket to the disaster. 17

I could see not just into the pit now, but also its access ramp, which trucks had been traveling up and down since I had arrived that morning. Gathered along the ramp were firefighters in their black helmets and black coats. Slowly they lined up, and it became clear that this was an honor guard, and that someone's remains were being carried up the ramp toward the open door of an ambulance. 18

Everyone in the dining room stopped eating. Several people stood up, whether out of respect or to see better, I don't know. For a moment, everything paused. 19

Then the day flowed back into itself. Soon I was outside once more, joining the tide of people washing around the site. Later, as I huddled with a little crowd on the viewing platform, watching people scrawl their names or write "God Bless America" on the plywood walls, it occurred to me that a form of repopulation was taking effect, with so many visitors to this place, thousands of visitors, all of us coming to see the wide emptiness where so many were lost. And by the act of our visiting—whether we are motivated by curiosity or horror or reverence or grief, or by something confusing that combines them all—that space fills up again. 20

Considering Ideas

1. Berne says that there was nothing more than a construction site where the World Trade Center once stood. Why, then, did so many people visit the site?
2. What do you think accounts for the "brisk trade in World Trade Center photograph booklets" (paragraph 13)?
3. For Berne, what does the light reflecting off the Hudson River bring to the World Trade Center site?
4. Explain the meaning of Berne's title.

Considering Technique

1. What does the description in paragraphs 1 and 2 contribute to the essay?
2. Which paragraphs include objective description? Why does Berne use objective description rather than subjective description in these paragraphs?
3. What contrast does Berne highlight in paragraph 9? What is the significance of that contrast?

4. What narration does Berne include in "Where Nothing Says Everything"?
5. What metaphor appears in paragraph 20? Is the metaphor effective? Explain.

For Group Discussion or Journal Writing

In paragraph 3, Berne says that absence is more than nothingness. Explain what she means, and give an example to illustrate that meaning.

ORGANIZATION NOTE

Short Paragraphs

You probably noticed that the paragraphs in "Prairie Vertigo" and "Where Nothing Says Everything" are often short, sometimes just one, two, or three sentences. Both of these selections originally appeared in newspapers, so they are written in a journalistic style—a style that often incorporates short paragraphs. Because newspaper articles are printed in narrow columns, even a brief paragraph can appear long, so frequent paragraphing gives the reader's eyes a rest.

In addition, in all writing, brief paragraphs can provide transition. For example, this paragraph from "Where Nothing Says Everything" is a transition from the paragraphs about *viewing* the World Trade Center site to the ones on *talking* about it:

> It takes quite a while to see all of this; it takes even longer to come up with something to say about it.

Short paragraphs can also provide emphasis. For example, this one-sentence paragraph from "Where Everything Says Nothing" emphasizes the strangeness of life going on after such devastation:

> And there, at last, I got my ticket to the disaster.

DESCRIPTION IN AN IMAGE

The advertisement that follows promotes the state of Colorado.

Considering the Image

1. What audience does the advertisement hope to reach?
2. How does the picture help persuade this audience to vacation in Colorado? How do the words help persuade this audience?
3. What dominant impression is conveyed by the picture? By the words?
4. Explain the irony of the quotation marks and the slogan "Let's talk Colorado."

SUGGESTIONS FOR WRITING

Writing Description

1. Describe a crowded or hectic spot (e.g., a subway station at rush hour, the campus green at noon, your dining hall at the busiest time of day, the freeway at 5:00).
2. Describe one of the following:
    a. A favorite campus spot
    b. A favorite night spot

c. A schoolyard at recess
d. A room after a big party or celebration
e. A place you go for solitude

3. Describe an ugly building, room, or painting, being sure to convey why it is so unappealing.
4. Describe a place during a holiday celebration.

Reading Then Writing Description

1. Like Klinkenborg in "Prairie Vertigo" (page 160), write a description of a weather event, such as a gathering storm, the calm after a storm, a morning frost, an ice storm, or a nor'easter.
2. Like Klinkenborg in paragraph 2 of "Prairie Vertigo," describe a landscape.
3. Like Sherr in "Anguished Cries in a Place of Silence" (page 161) and Berne in "Where Nothing Says Everything" (page 165), describe a place that evokes strong emotion. The emotion can be your dominant impression.
4. Like Sherr and Berne, write an objective description of a place that teaches a lesson, such as a monument, a gravesite, or a historical site.
5. If you have visited the World Trade Center site, write a description of what you witnessed and experienced.

Description beyond the Writing Classroom

Assume you want to sell one of your possessions. It could be your car, guitar, sofa, CD collection, or anything else. Design a poster to place around campus or around town to advertise the item. You may include a picture if you want, but you must include text that accurately describes the item and creates interest in it among the members of your target audience.

Responding to Theme

1. In "Prairie Vertigo," Klinkenborg mentions the effect of the whiteout he was driving in—he was forced to turn back, and he felt vertigo. Write about how you were affected by some weather event, such as a heavy snowfall when you were a child, a flooding after a heavy rainstorm, a heatwave, or a drought.
2. Using the information in "Anguished Cries in a Place of Silence," along with your own experience and observation, explain the importance of museums and historical sites that help preserve the past for future generations.
3. Suzanne Berne tells about her reaction when she visited the site of the World Trade Center (page 165). Tell how you have been affected by the attacks of September 11, 2001. Alternatively, tell how you were affected by another event reported in your local or campus newspaper.

4. Survey the advertisements in your favorite magazine, and write an essay that discusses how description is used to persuade consumers.
5. *Connecting the readings:* "Anguished Cries in a Place of Silence" and "Where Nothing Says Everything" speak to the human need to visit the sites of tragedy and commemorate them. Select either the Holocaust or the terrorist attacks of September 11, 2001, and explain how you think these events should be commemorated.

Writing Description

These strategies are not meant to replace your own tried-and-true procedures; they are here to sample as you develop your own effective writing process.

www.mhhe.com/tsw

For further help with writing description, go to Catalyst 2.0 > Writing > Writing Tutors > Description

PROCESS GUIDELINES

Think like a Writer: Generating Ideas, Considering Audience and Purpose, and Ordering Ideas

- Describe a subject that you can observe or that is vivid in your memory.
- To establish your audience, answer the questions on page 42. In particular, these questions are especially relevant:
  - With whom would I like to share my perceptions?
  - Who could come to appreciate my subject by reading my essay?
- Use these questions to help you assess your reader's needs:
  - How much experience has my reader had with my subject?
  - What does my reader need to know about my subject?
  - How much interest does my reader have in my subject?
- Use these questions to help you determine your purpose:
  - Can I help a reader understand why I perceive my subject a particular way or understand the effect my perception has on me?
  - Can I help my reader appreciate something he or she has not experienced before, or achieve a fresh appreciation for something familiar?
  - Can I convince my reader to view something as I do?
- To generate ideas, observe your subject and list key details, ones that relate to your dominant impression. A list for an essay about your intimidating grandmother might read, in part, like this:

  gnarled hands
  wrinkled, scary face
  powerful voice
  won't take no for an answer
  pinches my shoulder when angry
  fearsome eyes

- Study your list. Do the details suggest a chronological, spatial, or progressive order?

Think like a Writer: Drafting

- Think about your dominant impression, your purpose, and your reader as you draft.
- Remember that description requires successive revisions, so do not worry about getting your sensory language "just right" the first time.

Think like a Critic; Work like an Editor: Revising

- Be sure your dominant impression is expressed in specific language.
- Because writing description involves multiple revisions, take breaks as you need them.
- Read your draft aloud. If some description seems overdone, follow highly descriptive sentences with simpler ones.
- Use a thesaurus and dictionary if you need help with word choice, but be certain you understand the connotations of any words that you take from these sources.
- To secure reader response, see page 105. In addition, ask your reader to circle words and concrete sensory details that should be reconsidered and to place a check mark next to words and concrete sensory details that are particularly effective.

Think like a Critic; Work like an Editor: Correcting Errors

- Review Chapter 25, "Modifiers." Because description includes so many modifiers, this chapter is particularly relevant.
- Refer to page 634 on using commas between coordinate modifiers and to page 658 on using a hyphen between words to form modifiers.

Remember

- Be aware that a description—even an objective description—must be more than a list. Avoid cataloguing like this: "To the left is my CD player, and sitting next to it are my softball trophies. Immediately to the right of the trophies is a stack of unread magazines."
- Avoid shifting your vantage point. If you are describing the view from your classroom window, do not mention the ants marching along the sidewalk across the street, as you cannot see them from where you are positioned.

LOOKING AHEAD

In this chapter, you will learn about narration—about storytelling. How important were stories in your childhood? Like the children in the cartoon, did you expect each day to end with a good story? Did you frequently hear stories of the experiences of grandparents or other relatives? Was supper a time for family members to share stories of their day? In a brief paragraph, tell to what extent stories were a part of your childhood. How were you affected by the stories—or lack of them?

Narration

Deborah Hautzig sent this story to the *New York Times,* where it appeared in the newspaper's "Metropolitan Diary" column in 2002:

> While shopping at Fairway, I came across a distraught-looking mother pushing a large shopping cart. She had two children in tow, about 3 and 5 years old, both of whom were whining ceaselessly. They yanked at her clothes and pleaded for candy, and her attempts to soothe them failed utterly.
>
> Finally, when the older child—for at least the 20th time—screamed, "Mom-EEEEE," the mother looked straight ahead and said, "There is no one here by that name."

Why did Hautzig send this story to the *Times,* and why did the newspaper run it as a human interest feature? Hautzig wrote it, and the *Times* printed it, because stories convey so much. For example, the story of the harried mother amuses, illustrates one behavior of young children, sheds light on the frustrations of parenting, and offers an example of how to handle a difficult situation with humor—and it does all that in just four sentences!

Another name for a story is a **narration.** A short narration—like the one here—is an **anecdote.** A long narration—one that is essay or even book length—is an **extended narration.** In this chapter, you will learn about essay-length, extended narrations.

WHY IS NARRATION IMPORTANT?

Stories can entertain, instruct, clarify, and persuade. They can show us how the world works, how people behave, and how events unfold. In short, stories help us understand and cope with the world. Think about it—a history textbook tells the story of our past so we can better understand our present. We tell our children stories with morals to help them learn important lessons. If you keep a diary, you write out the events of your life to examine and record them. You e-mail family and friends about events that happen to you in order to share your life with them. Narration can even have a therapeutic value. Psychologists often have patients write about events to understand and cope with them. For example, a patient who fears water may be asked to write about a childhood boating accident to examine the event as a cause of the fear. In short, narration can fulfill any of the purposes for writing, as the following chart illustrates.

Purposes for Narration

Purpose	**Sample Narration**
To entertain	An account of your first meeting with your father-in-law, when you mistook him for an annoying insurance salesman
To share feelings and experiences	An account of what happened when your best friend betrayed you
To inform (to explain what happens when a person is arrested)	An account of the time you were wrongly arrested for shoplifting
To inform (to teach a lesson)	An account of a time you got in trouble for cheating
To persuade (to convince the reader that community service should be required in high school)	An account of the community service you performed as a high school senior

COMBINING NARRATION WITH OTHER PATTERNS

Memorable narrations often include specific, descriptive details to make the story vivid. Important details of scene are described, as are key people and events. To appreciate the importance of description, compare these two versions of a narration:

```
The child drove his tricycle down the driveway
into the path of an oncoming car. Fortunately,
```

Narration across the Disciplines and Beyond

Narration in the Classroom

Narration is important in many kinds of classes. For instance, in a paper for a political science class, you might narrate the sequence of events leading to the failure of the League of Nations. In an education class, you might narrate an event you observed during student teaching. *Think about your own courses, and times when you have needed to use narration to complete an assignment. What was the assignment and how did narration help you do it? Why do you think narration is so useful in so many courses?*

Narration in Daily Life

Narration may be the most common form of writing you use in your personal life. Diaries, blogs, and journal entries include narrative accounts of the events in your life. Letters and e-mails to friends and family include stories of events that happened to you. And if you have to deliver a speech or give a toast, you will likely include one or more anecdotes. *Describe a recent situation in which you used narration. What were the circumstances? Which of the purposes of writing did your narration fulfill?*

Narration on the Job

Many professions require narrative writing. Police officers write arrest reports with narrative accounts of crimes. Safety workers write accident reports that narrate the causes of injuries. Social workers write narrative accounts of events in their clients' lives. *Think of other careers in which narration would be a common component. Is there a particular job you hope to pursue after finishing school? How would narration be useful in this job?*

> the driver, who was speeding, was able to swerve in time to avoid a collision.
>
> Four-year-old Ishmael hopped on his racing red tricycle and began pedaling furiously down his driveway. By the time he reached the end, he had gathered too much speed to stop. With fear in his eyes, he screamed mightily as his out-of-control trike headed into the path of a speeding Chevy Lumina. The teenage driver, startled into action, swerved just in time to avert disaster.

Did you find the second version more interesting because of the description?

Because narration can help explain, illustrate, or support a point, it often appears in essays developed primarily with other patterns. For example, if you are writing a definition of *friendship,* and you identify loyalty as one of its characteristics, you could narrate an account of the time your best friend refused to believe rumors about you. The story could explain and illustrate what you mean by *loyalty*. If you are classifying types of teachers and you establish one type as "authoritarian," you can tell the story of an encounter you had with an authoritarian teacher to show what that type is like. Similarly, if you are explaining the effects of divorce on children, you can illustrate one of the effects by narrating what happened when your father was not around when you needed him. No matter what your dominant pattern of development is, narration may help you achieve your purpose.

SELECTING DETAIL

Storytelling comes naturally to us, in part because we speak, hear, read, and write stories so often. Nonetheless, when you write narration, you must choose your details thoughtfully.

Answer the Journalist's Questions

To choose details, answer the standard journalist's questions: *Who? What? When? Where? Why? How?* In most cases, a reader will want to know what happened, when it happened, where it happened, why it happened, how it happened, and who was involved. If you answer each of these questions, you are likely to include all the significant information.

However, do not get carried away and include ideas not pertinent to the who, what, when, where, why, and how of your narration. We have all seen movies that drag because of unnecessary detail, action, explanation, or dialogue. Such movies are boring. To avoid boring your reader, maintain a brisk pace by including only the significant details.

You must also determine which of these significant details require emphasis. For some narrations, the who and where may deserve extended treatment, while the why, when, and how merit less development. Other narrations may require detailed discussion of the why. Your purpose and audience will help you determine which details to emphasize.

Write Dialogue

Including what people said can move a story forward by adding information or by lending insight into people's character. When you write dialogue, you generally do not repeat everything the characters said word for word. Instead, choose significant conversations or parts of conversations—ones that serve a purpose such as advancing the story line, revealing character, or adding vitality.

Typically, sentences that contain dialogue have two parts: a part that notes what was said, and a part that indicates who did the speaking. How you punctuate depends on where these parts appear.

When the spoken words come before the statement of who spoke:

"Get out of here while you can," the stranger warned.
"What chance do I have?" Joyce wondered.

- Spoken words are enclosed in quotation marks.
- Spoken words are followed by a comma, which appears before the closing quotation mark. If a question is asked, then a question mark is used.
- The first word after the closing quotation mark begins with a lowercase letter unless it is a proper noun (like *Joyce*) or a word always capitalized (like *I*).

When the statement of who spoke comes before the words spoken:

Alex responded quietly, "My sister is the one to blame."

- The statement of who spoke is followed by a comma.
- The spoken words appear in quotation marks.
- The first spoken word is capitalized.
- The spoken words are followed by a period, which appears before the closing quotation mark.

When the spoken words come both before and after the statement of who spoke:

"I wish I knew," Paulette sighed, "why I always end up doing most of the work."

"Please be here by 8:00," Dad cautioned. "We don't want to get a late start."

- The first and second groups of spoken words appear inside separate sets of quotation marks.
- The first group of spoken words is followed by a comma.
- If the first group of spoken words is not a sentence, a comma appears after the statement of who spoke, and the second group of spoken words does not begin with a capital letter.
- If the first group of spoken words forms a sentence, the statement of who spoke is followed by a period, and the second group of spoken words begins with a capital letter.
- The second group of spoken words is followed by a period, which appears inside the final quotation marks.

When the spoken words form a question:

Malcolm asked, "Where did you park my van?"
"When is the last day of the book sale?" Carla questioned.
"Can we go now," Sis asked, "or do we still have to wait for Joe?"

- In each case, the question mark replaces the period or comma because the spoken words form a question.
- The question mark appears inside the quotation marks.

When the entire sentence, rather than just the spoken words, forms the question:

> Can you believe that Professor Golden said, "If you want, we will postpone the test until Monday"?

- The question mark is outside the quotation marks because the entire sentence, not the spoken words, forms the question.

When you are writing someone's thoughts, they are punctuated the same way as spoken words:

> Joshua thought to himself, "I'm sure I can win this event if I get a fast start."

Note: To be more precise and to increase the vitality of your writing, do not overuse *said* and *asked*. Try synonyms like these:

announced	questioned	snapped
blurted out	replied	whimpered
cried	responded	whispered
explained	shouted	wondered
inquired		

Note: When you use quotation marks to signal the use of dialogue, be careful that you really do have spoken words. Notice the two sentences below:

> Maria announced that she was quitting her job to attend school full-time.
> Maria announced, "I'm quitting my job to attend school full-time."

- Although it is tempting to use quotation marks in the first sentence, no spoken words appear there.
- Since the second sentence does have spoken words, quotation marks are necessary.

Describe a Person, Place, or Scene

Use description to help your reader form a mental picture of a person, place, or scene. Description can also give your narration energy and create interest. For example, in "The Boys" on page 194, Maya Angelou uses description to help the reader "see" the sunlight in the store:

> The light would come in softly (we faced north), easing itself over the shelves of mackerel, salmon, tobacco, thread. It fell flat on the big vat of lard and by noontime during the summer the grease had softened to a thick soup.

She also uses descriptive language to help the reader "hear" the sheriff:

> His twang jogged in the brittle air.

Tell Your Story for a Reason

Tell your story for a specific purpose. Perhaps it is entertaining, or points to an important truth, or teaches a lesson. Maybe it illustrates a fact of life or offers an observation. If you do not think that the point of your story is strongly implied in the details, you can state the point in the thesis or in the conclusion. For example, the student author of "The Sudden Storm" on page 187 narrates an account of the time he was riding his bike and narrowly escaped a tornado. The author explains the significance of the event—a lesson he learned—in the thesis:

> However, one afternoon, when I was thirteen, my enjoyment of these storms turned to fear and respect.

Consider Your Purpose and Audience

How do you know which of the journalist's questions to answer and which to emphasize? How do you decide whether to include dialogue or description or whether to state or imply the point of your narration? To decide, consider your purpose and audience.

Suppose you tell the story about the time you felt that your psychology teacher was unfair to you. If your purpose is to express your anger, you might focus on yourself and your feelings. If your purpose is to convince your reader that students need a grievance procedure, you might focus more on what happened. If your purpose is to inform your reader that even the best professors have their bad moments, you might emphasize what happened, why it happened, and who the instructor was. For this purpose, you might also describe the instructor as typically fair, which is something you would not do for the first two purposes.

Like your purpose, your audience will influence what details you include and what you emphasize. Let's return to the story of the unfair psychology professor. If your reader knows little about the workings of a college classroom, you might include more explanatory detail than if your reader is currently attending the university. If your audience is a classmate who witnessed the incident, you might emphasize what happened less than if your audience is someone who did not witness the event.

BEING A RESPONSIBLE WRITER

Because good stories can be irresistible, people tend to repeat them. However, if you use a story you heard or read somewhere else, give credit to the source, so you are not guilty of plagiarism. If you are unsure how to credit the author of a story you take from a published work, check Chapter 17.

To be a responsible writer, do not make up stories and pass them off as actual events. If your untrue story damages a person's reputation, you can be guilty of libel. You *can* make up an anecdote as a hypothetical example, but be sure your reader will recognize that the story is hypothetical. (For more on hypothetical examples, see page 213.)

USING SOURCES FOR A PURPOSE

The paragraph below, which is the introduction to an essay that defines *progress,* illustrates one way to use sources from this book in your writing. This paragraph includes paraphrase and quotation of some of the material in paragraphs 2, 6, 24, and 25 of "The Telephone" on page 197. (For more information on writing quotations and paraphrases, see Chapter 17.)

THESIS IDEA: How, then, do we define progress?

WRITING PURPOSE AND AUDIENCE: To inform general readers about the meaning of progress and to help them understand that what we currently call progress can create hardship.

The quotations and paraphrases in sentences 4–7 help the author make the point that sometimes progress comes at a price.

[1]In the United States, we worship at the altar of progress and strive to do things better and faster. [2]Rarely satisfied with the status quo, we covet the latest technology and buy products that are new and improved, no matter how similar they are to the older models we currently have. [3]In short, we assume that progress is inherently good—but is it? [4]Consider "The Telephone," Anwar Accawi's account of progress in a Lebanese village: Before the village's only telephone was installed, life was so simple that time was marked by catastrophic events "that Allah himself set down." [5]For example, when asked when something occurred, an old woman replied, "'Oh, about the time we had the big earthquake that cracked the wall in the east room'" (197). [6]However, once a single telephone arrived, Accawi explains, most of the inhabitants left the village for the outside world the telephone made them aware of. [7]Accawi says that when the villagers left for more modern places, the simple village became a virtual ghost town, and those who

Finally, be careful about telling unflattering stories or breaking confidences. If you are delivering a speech at a retirement dinner for your boss, think twice before narrating an account of the time she called in sick and was seen playing golf. If you promised your best friend never to reveal that he dyes his hair, do not tell the story of the time he left the dye on too long.

To be a responsible writer, ask yourself these questions:

- Do I need to credit the source of my story?
- Is the story true? Are all the facts accurate?
- If the story is hypothetical, will my reader recognize it as such?
- Will my story embarrass or otherwise hurt anyone?
- Do any parts of my story violate a confidence?

departed didn't find a life as good as the one they previously had (201). [8]In this case, progress was not inherently good. [9]How, then, do we define progress?

Avoiding Plagiarism

The paragraph illustrates some points about using sources and avoiding plagiarism.

- **Introduce the source of quotations and paraphrases correctly.** As in sentences 4, 6, and 7, introduce the author and title of your source with a present-tense verb. As sentence 4 shows, when the introduction is a formal, compete sentence, follow it with a colon, but when the introduction is a more standard "she says," "the author explains," or "as one researcher believes," use a comma.
- **Use quotation marks correctly.** As illustrated in sentences 4 and 5, use double quotation marks to signal where a quotation begins and ends. Use single quotation marks when a quotation appears within a quotation.

Myths about Sources

MYTH: A sentence can have only one paraphrase or one quotation.

FACT: You can combine paraphrase and quotation, as long as you document according to the conventions in Chapter 17. To illustrate, sentences 4 and 5 are reprinted below, with the quotations underscored once and the paraphrase underscored twice.

Consider "The Telephone," Anwar Accawi's account of progress in a Lebanese village: Before the village's only telephone was installed, life was so simple that time was marked by catastrophic events "that Allah himself set down." For example, when asked when something occurred, an old woman replied, "'Oh, about the time we had the big earthquake that cracked the wall in the east room'" (197).

ORGANIZING NARRATION

Narrative details are arranged in **chronological** (time) order. Usually, you start with what happened first, move to what happened next, and so forth. However, you can also begin at the end and then flash back to the first event and proceed in chronological order from there. Or you can begin somewhere in the middle of a story and then flash back to the beginning.

Suppose you want to narrate an account of preparing for and taking a final exam. If you want to use flashback, you could begin in the middle:

> The alarm jarred me from a fitful three hours' sleep, and I knew the time for preparation was

gone. In just two hours I would be sweating over my statistics exam. "Well, girl," I tried to reassure myself, "you certainly studied hard enough." Yes, I put in some kind of night preparing for the test.

From here, you could flash back to narrate the night of study, return to the time you woke up, and move through the events leading up to and including the exam.

Or you could start at the end:

As I left the classroom, I knew I would be lucky to get a C- on my stat exam. Anything higher would call for divine intervention. Yet, it wasn't like I hadn't prepared for the test.

From this point, you could flash back to the night of study and detail the events chronologically up to and including the exam.

To signal your chronological order and help your reader follow along, transitions like these are important:

at first	later
by noon	next
earlier	soon
in the evening	suddenly
in the meantime	that evening

Because narration has a logical chronology easily recognized by your reader, topic sentences are not always necessary. Once your reader grasps the time sequence at work, he or she understands how ideas are grouped and presented.

Similarly, you may decide to omit the introductory or concluding paragraph, particularly when the first or last event in the narration is dramatic, and you want to use it for an attention-grabbing opening or an arresting finish. However, should you decide to state the point your narration makes, you may want to do that in an opening thesis or concluding remark. Or if your reader needs background information in order to appreciate the narration and its significance, you can provide it in the introduction, the way the student author of "The Sudden Storm" does. Before narrating the events of the storm, he provides background information on the typical nature of these storms:

Where I grew up, in a suburb of Tulsa, Oklahoma, late summer afternoons were frequently interrupted by violent thunderstorms. Even if the sun was shining, the air would become very hot and humid, and the western horizon would have a dark smudge of storm that moved toward us as the day progressed. These storms always seemed to break around rush hour with a downpour of rain, an

```
eerie green light that meant hail, and wind gusts
that bent the trees to the ground. The radio and
television would crackle with alerts and warnings,
and sometimes the sirens would wail. Strangely
enough, I always loved these storms. They cooled
the air quickly and were beautiful in an awe-
inspiring way. However, one afternoon when I was
thirteen, my enjoyment of these storms turned to
fear and respect.
```

EXERCISE Writing Narration

1. Think back over your experiences, and identify two narrations you could tell about your family and two that you could tell about college life.
2. For each of the narrations you identified for number 1, establish a purpose and identify a suitable audience.
3. Select one of the experiences you identified for number 1, and write an interesting dialogue that was part of that experience. Then go over what you have written and check it for correct punctuation.
4. Description can enhance a narration with details that help readers form vivid mental images. In the cartoon below, however, Snoopy is having trouble adding strong description to his narration. Help him out by writing two or three sentences that answer the question "How spooky was he?"

PEANUTS reprinted by permission of UFS, Inc.

5. Select one event from a recent writing class session that you can narrate in a paragraph. For example, you can use a portion of a workshop, the handing back of papers, a pop quiz, or a discussion of a reading. Write two drafts that narrate the event, but each should emphasize a different journalist's question. For example, one draft might emphasize who was involved; the other might emphasize where the event took place. Compare the results and discuss how the drafts differ according to what is emphasized. ■

Visualizing a Narrative Essay

The chart that follows can help you visualize one structure for a narrative essay. Like all good models, this one can be altered as needed.

Introduction

- May provide background information
- May set the scene
- May state the thesis or give the point your narration makes
- May begin the story

▼

First Body Paragraph

- May begin the story (or continue it if the story was begun in the opening paragraph)
- May include description
- May include dialogue
- Includes answers to one or more of the journalist's questions
- Arranges details in chronological order, perhaps with flashback

▼

Next Body Paragraphs

- Continue the narration
- May include description
- May include dialogue
- Include answers to one or more of the journalist's questions
- Arrange details in chronological order, perhaps with flashback

▼

Conclusion

- May narrate the last event
- May explain the significance of the event or the point of the narration

LEARNING FROM OTHER WRITERS: Student Essays

The first student essay, "The Sudden Storm," includes marginal notes that point out many of the essay's key features. As you read, notice the specific word choices and descriptive details.

The second student essay, "The Great Buffalo Hunt," is a longer narration about a childhood adventure—or misadventure. Notice that the writer tells the story from a child's perspective and uses effective description. Think about how the perspective affects the detail the writer has selected and the words he has chosen.

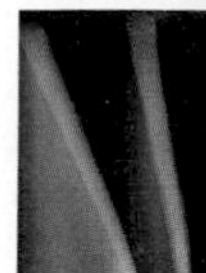

The Sudden Storm

Ben Kreuger

Where I grew up, in a suburb of Tulsa, Oklahoma, late summer afternoons were frequently interrupted by violent thunderstorms. Even if the sun was shining, the air would become very hot and humid, and the western horizon would have a dark smudge of storm that moved toward us as the day progressed. These storms always seemed to break around rush hour with a downpour of rain, an eerie green light that meant hail, and wind gusts that bent the trees to the ground. The radio and television would crackle with alerts and warnings, and sometimes the sirens would wail. Strangely enough, I always loved these storms. They cooled the air quickly and were beautiful in an awe-inspiring way. However, one afternoon, when I was thirteen, my enjoyment of these storms turned to fear and respect. 1

Paragraph 1
This is the introduction. Notice the description that adds vividness. The thesis is the last sentence. The paragraph answers the question "When did it happen?"

I was out riding bikes with my friends Jim and Brian. It was very hot, probably 90 degrees, and we wanted to go to the swimming pool, but for some reason we decided to go to the woods instead. These weren't really wild woods—just a park near the pool that was surrounded by houses. On the way, we stopped at a 7-Eleven for drinks. Behind the cash register the radio was playing, and an announcer broke in with a warning about approaching storms. 2

Paragraph 2
This paragraph answers the questions "Who was involved?" and "Where did it happen?"

We did not take the warning seriously, but by the time we got to the park the weather had changed. The sky was getting black, and even though it was not raining, the air smelled like rain and electricity. Brian's house was closest, so we decided to race our bikes there to wait out the storm. 3

Paragraph 3
This paragraph and all the others answer the question "What happened?"

As we pedaled away from the park, the rain started to fall. It was hard, heavy, cold rain, heavier than any rain I had ever seen in my life. I prayed it would not start to hail. "Come on!" hollered Brian. We were riding as fast as we could down the middle of the street. There was no traffic at that point—everyone had pulled over. Just then, the tornado sirens went off. I had never been scared by that sound before, but I was terrified then. 4

Paragraph 4
Notice the opening transition of time, "as," and the dialogue.

Paragraph 5
Notice the opening transition of time, "when," and the dialogue. Also notice the brisk pacing of the narration throughout.

When we passed the library, Jim swerved his bike up the sidewalk. "Stop here!" he yelled. We just dropped our bikes and ran inside the library. The librarian was taking people down a staircase into the building's basement. As we started down, the lights went off. As I descended the stairs on shaking legs, I remember thinking, stupidly, about my bike. I had not locked it or even tied it to anything. I was worried that it would get blown away and that my dad would be mad at me for losing it. 5

Paragraph 6
Notice that here and throughout, the details are in chronological order.

The librarian had a radio, and we listened to the news for the next half-hour. A funnel cloud had touched down on the east side and skipped across the town, causing power outages and considerable property damage. Amazingly, no one was killed. We did not hear that train sound people who have survived tornados describe, but when we came out of the basement, we saw that several trees around the library had been blown down and part of the roof was off the building. Sure enough, my bike was gone. 6

Paragraph 7
Notice the dialogue. The last event provides closure.

I ran home. My dad was standing in the kitchen, crying. I had never seen him cry before. I thought something horrible had happened to my mom. But she was safe at work. Dad was crying because he did not know what had happened to me. I tried to tell him about the bike, but he just hugged me for the longest time. 7

The Great Buffalo Hunt

Brian DeWolf

My friend Joey and I finally managed to escape the internment camp cleverly disguised as Defiance Public Schools midway through the June of 1990. One large school housed children in grades from kindergarten to high school, a prison for the little people in this quaint farm town. Joey and I thought we were free for good, lucky escapees of an evil system, but an older kid warned us that come August we would be dragged back, kicking 1 and screaming into something called the first grade. We were not sure what this first grade was, we just knew that we would not fall prey to this dastardly scheme.

Among our picture books were several old western stories, tattered books with pictures of mountain men who lived off the land and never bathed or went to school. The lifestyle greatly appealed to our young sensibilities, so after we learned of this impending first grade we immediately decided to set off for the mountains. Throwing clothes, food, and of course our trusty slingshots into packs the size of adolescent whales, we trudged off into the wilderness without compass or map. The lack of these navigation aids was fairly irrelevant since neither of us had a truly firm grasp on counting and reading. 2

Four hours into our trek, we were deep in the treacherous back country, also known as the Marshalls' cow pasture, when Joey shouted, "Look!" and pointed at some prints in the wet mud, "Buffalo tracks!" 3

"Let's follow them and we can have buffalo for supper, and warm blankets, and buffalo chips for our fire," I said. 4

We both agreed and set off in search of the massive beasts, slingshots in hand. Joey stayed glued to the tracks, with me sneaking right behind him. Yet no matter how long we trailed the buffalo, we always ran into a few of the Marshalls' cows looking dumbly at us, and the trail would end. Finally we gave up and settled for a bag of cookies Joey had sneaked away from the cupboard the night before. 5

"You know," Joey said between chomps of cookie, "this is probably better than any stupid old buffalo. Besides that, I didn't know what part of the buffalo the chips come from anyway." 6

As night settled in, we began to seriously question our trip. Darkness had crept up on us and was beginning to tighten its grip, with a little help from another enemy of ours, the cold, chilling us to the bone. To make matters worse, an eerie howl cut through the night, turning our bones into ice. Like any intelligent children we knew that under the cover of darkness, 7 herds of sasquatch wandered through the nearby woods; after all the older kids wouldn't say it if it was not true. Luckily we were able to channel our panic into speed and make it to a nearby hay shed. Scurrying up the side we slipped into the loft and curled up for a safe, soft night's sleep, both of us wisely avoiding a discussion about whether or not sasquatch could scurry up things.

The second day of the Great Buffalo Hunt had the mighty hunters trailing off in search of their prey. By the afternoon we had consumed another bag of stale chocolate cookies as well as two quarts of lukewarm milk fresh from the Marshalls' storage tanks. We had also decided to give up on our search for buffalo, as they had somehow managed to get the neighbors' cows to help in their evasion. Still the sight of two pack-laden youths popping out of the bushes, arms extended, totally focused on holding their slingshots back did put a few cows into motion although most of them came to a halt after a few yards. 8

Since we could no longer hunt the mighty buffalo, we decided to make a break for Canada since we thought we were heading north anyway. The woods had grown thicker, darker and creepier, although we felt the spookiness was worth the absence of cow pastures and their familiar odor. The mud squished through our toes, despite our shoes, the soles of which had disintegrated eons ago. 9

We walked along, whistling merrily and occasionally bolting through the trees at the snap of a nearby twig. Most of the time we passed over the ground in mid-air as we careened off logs and boulders, hotly pursued by something ferocious. We never knew what it was that pursued us. The cracking twigs were proof enough for us that it was something big. To allay our fears the third night, we slept back to back, and somehow we managed to doze with our slingshots armed and ready for use. 10

The fourth afternoon brought rain, lots of rain. It pelted us brutally, as if attacking our plans and insulting us for daring to venture out into the wilds unattended. We laughed it off after seeking cover under a large pine tree and donning our thickest, warmest jackets. We planned to spend the afternoon 11 under our tree and protected from the torrential rain until the first explosion of thunder sat us up, ramrod straight. After the thunder rumbled off, we heard a strange muffled cry, and pulled each other close.

"Joey! Brian! Boys can you hear me? It's okay to come out now," a voice called. 12

Another chimed in, "Hurry up you fools, this storm's getting bad!" 13

Immediately I recognized the second caller, mainly because he was standing about five feet from me. "Hi, Dad!" I yelled, my call punctuated by a crash of thunder. 14

He leapt higher than anyone I've ever seen and then pulled a radio out of his pocket, mumbled something into it, and added, "They are alive, for the moment at least." 15

Obviously we were alive, what did they think? We had both left our parents notes, telling them where we were going. Of course neither of us had much talent for writing so the mix-up was fairly understandable. 16

The sentencing process for these two fugitives was fairly short, two weeks without any contact with unsavory characters, namely each other. That sentence being served, we were given a second punishment, a return to school and the first grade. Only years later would we understand the extent of our crimes and the search and rescue mission; oddly enough, that was about the same time either of us could sit down without a pillow handy. To this day it eludes me, as well as the authorities, how two plucky six-year-olds trekked over twenty miles without even a clue as to where they were going. 17

EXERCISE Considering "The Great Buffalo Hunt"

1. For what purpose do you think Brian DeWolf wrote "The Great Buffalo Hunt"?
2. The essay offers insight into the thinking of the writer and his friend when they were six years old. For example, in paragraph 1, DeWolf says that he and Joey saw school as a prison and that they feared first grade and were not planning to go. Cite another example of the thinking of the children. How does this detail help the writer achieve his purpose for writing?

3. Cite three examples of description in the essay. How does the description help the writer achieve his purpose?
4. How does the writer use transitions to achieve coherence in the opening of paragraphs 3, 7, 8, and 11?
5. What purpose does the dialogue in paragraphs 12–15 serve? How would the essay be different without it? ■

THINK LIKE A CRITIC; WORK LIKE AN EDITOR: The Student Writer at Work

In an early draft of "The Sudden Storm," Ben Kreuger thought he would state the lesson he learned from his experience in his conclusion. Here is what that conclusion looked like (with the lesson underlined as a study aid).

> I ran home. My dad was in the kitchen, and he was crying, which is something I had never seen him do before. I thought something had happened to my mom. But she was safe. Dad was crying because he thought something had happened to me. I tried to tell him I lost my bike, but he just hugged me and told me never to go out in a storm like that again. As a result of that day, I learned to fear and respect violent thunderstorms.

After a series of revisions, Ben decided that ending the essay with his father hugging him provided a dramatic element and closure for the essay, so he decided to move his statement of the lesson he learned to the introduction. The final introduction and conclusion appear in the essay on page 187. Do you think Ben did the right thing? Why or why not?

LEARNING FROM OTHER WRITERS: Professional Essays

In Line at the Post Office

Steven Doloff

You are in a long line at a post office window, and someone who has lost a quarter in the stamp machine walks to the front of the line to ask the teller for a refund. What do you think? How do you act? Consider the answers to these questions as you read this essay from The Epoch Times *(2007), a weekly paper published around the world.*

It's not quite the same as the Stockholm syndrome—where hostages come to identify with their captors. It's more like what happens in the 1992 Tom Cruise movie "A Few Good Men," where a substandard marine is punished by his fellow leathernecks for being perceived as a hindrance to their mission. 1

I was sixth in a line of 25 people in my local post office in the East Village, Manhattan. There were six designated full service windows and one teller on duty—no unusual thing in that location, regardless of the line length. Service was averaging about one customer every four or five minutes. I checked the clock on the wall (a lot). 2

A woman, maybe 45, with straggly hair and some missing front teeth approached the teller from outside the line and asked what she could do about having just lost 25 cents in the stamp vending machine. When the lone teller instructed the woman to go to the end of the line and wait her turn, the woman understandably began to protest, saying (many times) that it was "abusive" to be made to wait so long for 25 cents. The quarter was obviously important to her. But the requirement to get in the line really got her ticked. 3

When the female teller decided to take the "abuse" charge personally and started shouting back through the two-inch thick bulletproof glass protecting her that the woman's indignant "tone" was "abusive" to her, the teller, the people in the line began seriously to pay attention—but not in the way I expected. 4

Many of the line people, and especially those at the front ahead of me, were plainly angry with the woman who was distracting the teller over 25 cents and holding up the line! Three of them, with undisguised disdain, held out quarters to the lady just to get her away from the teller's window. Obviously feeling insulted by the teller and her fellow customers, she took one of the offered quarters and left, yet again pronouncing the post office "abusive." 5

Five minutes later (now I was fifth from the window) two burly New York City police officers stalked into the post office and very aggressively eyeballed the line. Then they went over to the teller and asked loudly enough to be heard by half the people in the building where the troublemaker was who was causing a reported disturbance. I couldn't believe it, somebody had ratted on the quarter lady. 6

I remember reading somewhere that class distinction in America is most frequently revealed by how long people personally have to wait in lines for things. The post office, I guess, is a pretty good example of this kind of economic taxonomy. 7

Standing in line at the post office for 50 minutes, staring at five out of six empty teller windows, may certainly indicate something about the current problems of the U.S. postal system, but what it mostly reminds me of is that I'm just too poor to pay someone else to do it for me (or use FedEx for everything). 8

Of course, I have learned to live with this burden, and know that life has many worse indignities I have gratefully been spared. It's just that when I see someone for whom 25 cents and personal dignity are "on the line" stand up for herself, it is depressing to realize how so many people virtually in the same situation (and I'm sure with not that many more quarters than she had) could so quickly see her as making their lives miserable, and not the malaise of the federal bureaucracy undermining all those who must wait in lines. Why didn't they identify with her and rail against the post office—at least until the police showed up? 9

P.S. I wrote this while waiting in line at the post office. 10

Considering Ideas

1. In paragraph 3, Doloff says, "The quarter was obviously important to her. But the requirement to get in the line really got her ticked." Why did the necessity to get in line bother the woman so much? Do you agree that the requirement was abusive?
2. In paragraph 4, Doloff says that the response to the woman who lost the quarter was not what he expected. What do you think he expected? Why?
3. Do you think the behavior of the teller and the people in line was appropriate and justified? Explain.

4. What point does the narration make? Is that point stated or implied?
5. What does the essay say about the way people identify with groups?

Considering Technique

1. Which of the journalist's questions does Doloff emphasize the most?
2. What do you judge to be Doloff's writing purpose, and who is his intended audience?
3. *Combining patterns:* What elements of description appear in the essay? What element of comparison-contrast? What element of cause-and-effect analysis? How do each of those patterns help the author achieve his purpose with his particular audience?
4. How does Doloff introduce his narration? How does he conclude it? Are the introduction and conclusion effective? Why or why not?
5. Do you think Doloff should have included dialogue that repeats what the teller and woman said to each other? Explain.

For Group Discussion or Journal Writing

Doloff poses a question in paragraph 9, but he does not answer it. Answer it for him.

The Boys

Maya Angelou

In a powerful narrative taken from her autobiography I Know Why the Caged Bird Sings *(1969), poet, actor, and civil rights activist Maya Angelou shares a childhood reminiscence of a dark period of American history. The narration does not begin immediately. Try to determine why.*

Weighing the half-pounds of flour, excluding the scoop, and depositing them dust-free into the thin paper sacks held a simple kind of adventure for me. I developed an eye for measuring how full a silver-looking ladle of flour, mash, meal, sugar or corn had to be to push the scale indicator over to eight ounces or one pound. When I was absolutely accurate our appreciative customers used to admire: "Sister Henderson sure got some smart grandchildrens." If I was off in the Store's favor, the eagle-eyed women would say, "Put some more in that sack, child. Don't you try to make your profit offa me." 1

Then I would quietly but persistently punish myself. For every bad judgment, the fine was no silver-wrapped Kisses, the sweet chocolate drops that I loved more than anything in the world, except Bailey. And maybe canned pineapples. My obsession with pineapples nearly drove me mad. I dreamt of the days when I would be grown and able to buy a whole carton for myself alone. 2

Until I was thirteen and left Arkansas for good, the Store was my favorite place to be. Alone and empty in the mornings, it looked like an unopened present from a stranger. Opening the front 3

doors was pulling the ribbon off the unexpected gift. The light would come in softly (we faced north), easing itself over the shelves of mackerel, salmon, tobacco, thread. It fell flat on the big vat of lard and by noontime during the summer the grease had softened to a thick soup. Whenever I walked into the Store in the afternoon, I sensed that it was tired. I alone could hear the slow pulse of its job half done. But just before bedtime, after numerous people had walked in and out, had argued over their bills, or joked about their neighbors, or just dropped in to give Sister Henderson a "Hi y'all," the promise of magic mornings returned to the Store and spread itself over the family in washed life waves.

Momma opened boxes of crispy crackers and we sat around the meat block at the rear of the Store. I sliced onions, and Bailey opened two or even three cans of sardines and allowed their juice of oil and fishing boats to ooze down and around the sides. That was supper. In the evening, when we were alone like that, Uncle Willie didn't stutter or shake or give any indication that he had an "affliction." It seemed that the peace of a day's ending was an assurance that the covenant God made with children, Negroes and the crippled was still in effect. 4

Throwing scoops of corn to the chicken and mixing sour dry mash with leftover food and oily dish water for the hogs were among our evening chores. Bailey and I sloshed down twilight trails to the pig pens, and standing on the first fence rungs we poured down the unappealing concoctions to our grateful hogs. They mashed their tender pink snouts down into the slop, and rooted and grunted their satisfaction. We always grunted a reply only half in jest. We were also grateful that we had concluded the dirtiest of chores and had only gotten the evil-smelling swill on our shoes, stockings, feet and hands. 5

Late one day, as we were attending to the pigs, I heard a horse in the front yard (it really should have been called a driveway, except that there was nothing to drive into it), and ran to find out who had come riding up on a Thursday evening when even Mr. Steward, the quiet, bitter man who owned a riding horse, would be resting by his warm fire until the morning called him out to turn over his field. 6

The used-to-be sheriff sat rakishly astraddle his horse. His nonchalance was meant to convey his authority and power over even dumb animals. How much more capable he would be with Negroes. It went without saying. 7

His twang jogged in the brittle air. From the side of the Store, Bailey and I heard him say to Momma, "Annie, tell Willie he better lay low tonight. A crazy nigger messed with a white lady today. Some of the boys'll be coming over here later." Even after the slow drag of years, I remember the sense of fear which filled my mouth with hot, dry air, and made my body light. 8

The "boys"? Those cement faces and eyes of hate that burned the clothes off you if they happened to see you lounging on the main street downtown on Saturday. Boys? It seemed that youth had never happened to them. Boys? No, rather men who were covered with graves' dust and age without beauty or learning. The ugliness and rottenness of old abominations. 9

If on Judgment Day I were summoned by St. Peter to give testimony to the used-to-be sheriff's act of kindness, I would be unable to say anything in his behalf. His confidence that my uncle and every other Black man who heard of the Klan's coming ride would scurry under their houses to hide in chicken droppings was too humiliating to hear. Without waiting for Momma's thanks, he rode out of the yard, sure that things were as they should be and that he was a gentle squire, saving those deserving serfs from the laws of the land, which he condoned. 10

Immediately, while his horse's hoofs were still loudly thudding the ground, Momma blew out the coal-oil lamps. She had a quiet, hard talk with Uncle Willie and called Bailey and me into the store. 11

We were told to take the potatoes and onions out of their bins and knock out the dividing walls that kept them apart. Then with a tedious and fearful slowness Uncle Willie gave me his rubber-tipped cane and bent down to get into the now-enlarged empty bin. It took forever before he lay down flat, and then we covered him with potatoes and onions, layer upon layer, like a casserole. Grandmother knelt praying in the darkened Store. 12

It was fortunate that the "boys" didn't ride into our yard that evening and insist that Momma open the Store. They would have surely found Uncle Willie and just as surely lynched him. He moaned the whole night through as if he had, in fact, been guilty of some heinous crime. The heavy sounds pushed their way up out of the blanket of vegetables and I pictured his mouth pulling down on the right side and his saliva flowing into the eyes of new potatoes and waiting here like dew drops for the warmth of morning. 13

Considering Ideas

1. Who are "the boys"? How does Angelou feel about them?
2. The "boys" whom the sheriff refers to are actually men. What effect is created when these men are called boys?
3. Why is Angelou not grateful for the sheriff's warning?
4. What point does the narration make? That is, what is its significance?

Considering Technique

1. Angelou does not begin her narration until paragraph 6. What purpose do the first five paragraphs serve?
2. Paragraph 3 is largely descriptive. Cite an example of concrete sensory detail (see page 147). Cite an example of a simile (see page 148).

3. What purpose does the dialogue in paragraph 8 serve?
4. What purpose does paragraph 9 serve? Paragraph 10?
5. "The Boys" closes with an image of Uncle Willie in the vegetable bin. Is this an effective conclusion? Explain.

For Group Discussion or Journal Writing

Imagine that you are Momma, having that "quiet, hard talk with Uncle Willie" (paragraph 11). What do you think Momma might have said in order to convince Uncle Willie to hide? What might Uncle Willie have said in return?

Combining Patterns of Development

The Telephone

ANWAR ACCAWI

Originally from Magdaluna, a village in southern Lebanon, Anwar Accawi wrote "The Telephone" as part of his 1999 book The Tower of the Moon. *In this essay, Accawi combines narration with several other patterns of development to explain what happened when his small village acquired a telephone and became connected to the outside world. As you read, notice that the core narration does not begin immediately, and determine the purpose of the paragraphs before the narration.*

When I was growing up in Magdaluna, a small Lebanese village in the terraced, rocky mountains east of Sidon, time didn't mean much to anybody, except maybe to those who were dying, or those waiting to appear in court because they had tampered with the boundary markers on their land. In those days, there was no real need for a calendar or a watch to keep track of the hours, days, months, and years. We knew what to do and when to do it, just as the Iraqi geese knew when to fly north, driven by the hot wind that blew in from the desert, and the ewes knew when to give birth to wet lambs that stood on long, shaky legs in the chilly March wind and baaed hesitantly, because they were small and cold and did not know where they were or what to do now that they were here. The only timepiece we had need of then was the sun. It rose and set, and the seasons rolled by, and we sowed seed and harvested and ate and played and married our cousins and had babies who got whooping cough and chicken-pox—and those children who survived grew up and married *their* cousins and had babies who got whooping cough and chicken-pox. We lived and loved and toiled and died without ever needing to know what year it was, or even the time of day. 1

It wasn't that we had no system for keeping track of time and of the important events in our lives. But ours was a natural—or, rather, a divine—calendar, because it was framed by acts of God. Allah himself set down the milestones with earthquakes and droughts and floods and locusts and pestilences. Simple as our calendar was, it worked just fine for us. 2

Take, for example, the birth date of Teta Im Khalil, the oldest woman in Magdaluna and all the surrounding villages. When I first met her, we had just returned home from Syria at the end of the Big War and were living with Grandma Mariam. Im Khalil came by to welcome my father home and to take a long, myopic look at his foreign-born wife, my mother. Im Khalil was so old 3

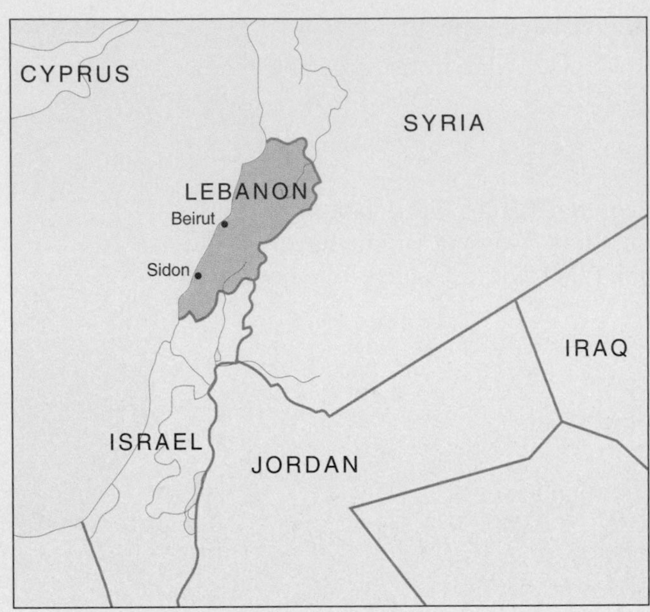

that the skin of her cheeks looked like my father's grimy tobacco pouch, and when I kissed her (because Grandma insisted that I show her old friend affection), it was like kissing a soft suede glove that had been soaked with sweat and then left in a dark closet for a season. Im Khalil's face got me to wondering how old one had to be to look and taste the way she did. So, as soon as she had hobbled off on her cane, I asked Grandma, "How old is Teta Im Khalil?"

Grandma had to think for a moment; then she said, "I've been told that Teta was born shortly after the big snow that caused the roof on the mayor's house to cave in." 4

"And when was that?" I asked. 5

"Oh, about the time we had the big earthquake that cracked the wall in the east room." 6

Well, that was enough for me. You couldn't be more accurate than that, now, could you? Satisfied with her answer, I went back to playing with a ball made from an old sock stuffed with other, much older socks. 7

And that's the way it was in our little village for as far back as anybody could remember: people were born so many years before or after an earthquake or a flood; they got married or died so many years before or after a long drought or a big snow or some other disaster. One of the most unusual of these dates was when Antoinette the seamstress and Saeed the barber (and tooth puller) got married. That was the year of the whirlwind during which fish and oranges fell from the sky. Incredible as it may sound, the story of the fish and oranges was true, because men—respectable men, like Abu George the blacksmith and Abu Asaad the mule skinner, men who would not lie even to save their own souls—told and retold that story until it was incorporated into Magdaluna's calendar, just like the year of the black moon and the year of the locusts before it. My father, too, confirmed the story for me. He told me that he had been a small boy himself when it had rained fish and oranges from heaven. He'd gotten up one morning after a stormy night and walked out into the yard to find fish as long as his forearm still flopping here and there among the wet navel oranges. 8

The year of the fish-bearing twister, however, was not the last remarkable year. Many others followed in which strange and wonderful things happened: milestones added by the hand of Allah to Magdaluna's calendar. There was, for instance, the year of the drought, when the heavens were shut for months and the spring from which the entire village got its drinking water slowed to a trickle. The spring was about a mile from the village, in a ravine that opened at one end into a small, flat clearing covered with fine gray dust and hard, marble-sized goat droppings, because every afternoon the goatherds brought their flocks there to water them. In the year of the drought, 9 that little clearing was always packed full of noisy kids with big brown eyes and sticky hands, and their mothers—sinewy, overworked young women with protruding collarbones and cracked, callused brown heels. The children ran around playing tag or hide-and-seek while the women talked, shooed flies, and awaited their turns to fill up their jars with drinking water to bring home to their napping men and wet babies. There were days when we had to wait from sunup until late afternoon just to fill a small clay jar with precious, cool water.

Sometimes, amid the long wait and the heat and the flies and the smell of goat dung, tempers 10
flared, and the younger women, anxious about their babies, argued over whose turn it was to fill up her jar. And sometimes the arguments escalated into full-blown, knockdown-dragout fights; the women would grab each other by the hair and curse and scream and spit and call each other names that made my ears tingle. We little brown boys who went with our mothers to fetch water loved these fights, because we got to see the women's legs and their colored panties as they grappled and rolled around in the dust. Once in a while, we got lucky and saw much more, because some of the women wore nothing at all under their long dresses. God, how I used to look forward to those fights. I remember the rush, the excitement, the sun dancing on the dust clouds as a dress ripped and a young white breast was revealed, then quickly hidden. In my calendar, that year of drought will always be one of the best years of my childhood, because it was then, in a dusty clearing by a trickling mountain spring, I got my first glimpse of the wonders, the mysteries, and the promises hidden beneath the folds of a woman's dress. Fish and oranges from heaven . . . you can get over that.

But, in another way, the year of the drought was also one of the worst of my life, because 11
that was the year that Abu Raja, the retired cook who used to entertain us kids by cracking walnuts on his forehead, decided it was time Magdaluna got its own telephone. Every civilized village needed a telephone, he said, and Magdaluna was not going to get anywhere until it had one. A telephone would link us with the outside world. At the time, I was too young to understand the debate, but a few men—like Shukri, the retired Turkish-army drill sergeant, and Abu Hanna the vineyard keeper—did all they could to talk Abu Raja out of having a telephone brought to the village. But they were outshouted and ignored and finally shunned by the other villagers for resisting progress and trying to keep a good thing from coming to Magdaluna.

One warm day in early fall, many of the villagers were out in their fields repairing walls or 12
gathering wood for the winter when the shout went out that the telephone-company truck had arrived at Abu Raja's *dikkan,* or country store. There were no roads in those days, only footpaths and dry streambeds, so it took the telephone-company truck almost a day to work its way up the rocky terrain from Sidon—about the same time it took to walk. When the truck came into view, Abu George, who had a huge voice and, before the telephone, was Magdaluna's only long-distance communication system, bellowed the news from his front porch. Everybody dropped what they were doing and ran to Abu Raja's house to see what was happening. Some of the more dignified villagers, however, like Abu Habeeb and Abu Nazim, who had been to big cities like Beirut and Damascus and had seen things like telephones and telegraphs, did not run the way the rest did; they walked with their canes hanging from the crooks of their arms, as if on a Sunday afternoon stroll.

It did not take long for the whole village to assemble at Abu Raja's *dikkan.* Some of the rich 13
villagers, like the widow Farha and the gendarme Abu Nadeem, walked right into the store and stood at the elbows of the two important-looking men from the telephone company, who proceeded

with utmost gravity, like priests at Communion, to wire up the telephone. The poorer villagers stood outside and listened carefully to the details relayed to them by the not-so-poor people who stood in the doorway and could see inside.

"The bald man is cutting the blue wire," someone said. 14

"He is sticking the wire into the hole in the bottom of the black box," someone else added. 15

"The telephone man with the mustache is connecting two pieces of wire. Now he is twisting the ends together," a third voice chimed in. 16

Because I was small and unaware that I should have stood outside with the other poor folk to give the rich people inside more room (they seemed to need more of it than poor people did), I wriggled my way through the dense forest of legs to get a firsthand look at the action. I felt like the barefoot Moses, sandals in hand, staring at the burning bush on Mount Sinai. Breathless, I watched as the men in blue, their shirt pockets adorned with fancy lettering in a foreign language, put together a black machine that supposedly would make it possible to talk with uncles, aunts, and cousins who lived more than two days' ride away. 17

It was shortly after sunset when the man with the mustache announced that the telephone was ready to use. He explained that all Abu Raja had to do was lift the receiver, turn the crank on the black box a few times, and wait for an operator to take his call. Abu Raja, who had once lived and worked in Sidon, was impatient with the telephone man for assuming that he was ignorant. He grabbed the receiver and turned the crank forcefully, as if trying to start a Model T Ford. Everybody was impressed that he knew what to do. He even called the operator by her first name: "Centralist." Within moments, Abu Raja was talking with his brother, a concierge in Beirut. He didn't even have to raise his voice or shout to be heard. 18

If I hadn't seen it with my own two eyes and heard it with my own two ears, I would not have believed it—and my friend Kameel didn't. He was away that day watching his father's goats, and when he came back to the village that evening, his cousin Habeeb and I told him about the telephone and how Abu Raja had used it to speak with his brother in Beirut. After he heard our report, Kameel made the sign of the cross, kissed his thumbnail, and warned us that lying was a bad sin and would surely land us in purgatory. Kameel believed in Jesus and Mary, and wanted to be a priest when he grew up. He always crossed himself when Habeeb, who was irreverent, and I, who was Presbyterian, were around, even when we were not bearing bad news. 19

And the telephone, as it turned out, was bad news. With its coming, the face of the village began to change. One of the first effects was the shifting of the village's center. Before the telephone's arrival, the men of the village used to gather regularly at the house of Im Kaleem, a short, middle-aged widow with jet-black hair and a raspy voice that could be heard all over the village, even when she was only whispering. She was a devout Catholic and also the village *shlikki*—whore. The men met at her house to argue about politics and drink coffee and play cards or backgammon. Im Kaleem was not a true prostitute, however, because she did not charge for her services—not even for the coffee and tea (and, occasionally, the strong liquor called arrack) that she served the men. She did not need the money; her son, who was overseas in Africa, sent her money regularly. (I knew this because my father used to read her son's letters to her and take down her replies, as Im Kaleem could not read and write.) Im Kaleem was no slut either—unlike some women in the village—because she loved all the men she entertained, and they loved her, every one of them. In a way, she was married to all the men in the village. Everybody knew it—the wives knew it; the itinerant Catholic priest knew it; the Presbyterian minister knew it—but nobody objected. Actually, I suspect the women (my mother included) did not mind their husbands' 20 visits to Im Kaleem. Oh, they wrung their hands and complained to one another about their men's unfaithfulness, but secretly they were relieved, because Im Kaleem took some of the pressure off them and kept the men out of their hair while they attended to their endless chores. Im Kaleem was also a kind of confessor and troubleshooter, talking sense to those men who were having family problems, especially the younger ones.

Before the telephone came to Magdaluna, Im Kaleem's house was bustling at just about any time of day, especially at night, when its windows were brightly lit with three large oil lamps, and the loud voices of the men talking, laughing, and arguing could be heard in the street below—a reassuring, homey sound. Her house was an island of comfort, an oasis for the weary village men, exhausted from having so little to do. 21

But it wasn't long before many of those men—the younger ones especially—started spending more of their days and evenings at Abu Raja's *dikkan.* There, they would eat and drink and talk and play checkers and backgammon, and then lean their chairs back against the wall—the signal that they were ready to toss back and forth, like a ball, the latest rumors going around the village. And they were always looking up from their games and drinks and talk to glance at the phone in the corner, as if expecting it to ring any minute and bring news that would change their lives and deliver them from their aimless existence. In the meantime, they smoked cheap, hand-rolled cigarettes, dug dirt out from under their fingernails with big pocketknives, and drank lukewarm sodas they called Kacula, Seffen-Ub, and Bebsi. Sometimes, especially when it was hot, the days dragged on so slowly that the men turned on Abu Saeed, a confirmed bachelor who practically lived in Abu Raja's *dikkan,* and teased him for going around barefoot and unshaven since the Virgin had appeared to him behind the olive press. 22

The telephone was also bad news for me personally. It took away my lucrative business—a source of much-needed income. Before the telephone came to Magdaluna, I used to hang around Im Kaleem's courtyard and play marbles with the other kids, waiting for some man to call down from a window and ask me to run to the store for cigarettes or arrack, or to deliver a message to his wife, such as what he wanted for supper. There was always something in it for me: a ten- or even a twenty-five-piaster piece. On a good day, I ran nine or ten of those errands, which assured a steady supply of marbles that I usually lost to Sami or his cousin Hani, the basket weaver's boy. But as the days went by, fewer and fewer men came to Im Kaleem's, and more and more congregated at Abu Raja's to wait by the telephone. In the evenings, no light fell from her window onto the street below, and the laughter and noise of the men trailed off and finally stopped. Only Shukri, the retired Turkish-army drill sergeant, remained faithful to Im Kaleem after all the other men had deserted her; he was still seen going into or leaving her house from time to time. Early that winter, Im Kaleem's hair suddenly turned gray, and she got sick and old. Her legs started giving her trouble, making it hard for her to walk. By spring she hardly left her house anymore. 23

At Abu Raja's *dikkan,* the calls did eventually come, as expected, and men and women started leaving the village the way a hailstorm begins: first one, then two, then bunches. The army took them. Jobs in the cities lured them. And ships and airplanes carried them to such faraway places as Australia and Brazil and New Zealand. My friend Kameel, his cousin Habeeb, and their cousins and my cousins all went away to become ditch diggers and mechanics and butcher-shop boys and deli owners who wore dirty aprons sixteen hours a day, all looking for a better life than the one they had left behind. Within a year, only the sick, the old, and the maimed were left in the village. Magdaluna became a skeleton of its former self, desolate and forsaken, like the tombs, a place to get away from. 24

Finally, the telephone took my family away, too. My father got a call from an old army 25
buddy who told him that an oil company in southern Lebanon was hiring interpreters and instructors. My father applied for a job and got it, and we moved to Sidon, where I went to a Presbyterian missionary school and graduated in 1962. Three years later, having won a scholarship, I left Lebanon for the United States. Like the others who left Magdaluna before me, I am still looking for that better life.

Considering Ideas

1. In your own words, state the thesis of "The Telephone."
2. How was the passage of time marked in Magdaluna before the arrival of the telephone? The villagers did not need to know the precise time of day, the exact day of the week, or even the current year as we are accustomed to marking these units of time. Why?
3. Specifically, how did the arrival of the telephone affect Magdaluna and the villagers? Why did it affect the village and its inhabitants as it did?
4. Explain the significance of the last sentence of the essay, and note what it implies about the author's opinion of the arrival of the telephone.
5. For what purpose did Accawi write "The Telephone"?

Considering Technique

1. In what paragraph does the primary narration begin? In what paragraph does it end?
2. Why are the first 10 paragraphs devoted to how the villagers marked time? How does that information help the author achieve his purpose for writing?
3. *Combining patterns:* Paragraphs 3–7 and 8–9 are developed with exemplification (using examples). How does the exemplification help the author achieve his purpose for writing?
4. *Combining patterns:* Accawi uses a great deal of description in "The Telephone." Cite three examples of description, and explain how it helps him achieve his purpose for writing.
5. *Combining patterns:* Cause-and-effect analysis is a pattern that writers use to show why an event occurred or what the results of an event were. Comparison-contrast is a pattern that writers use to show the similarities and differences between two items or events. Explain how "The Telephone" is partly a cause-and-effect analysis and partly a comparison-contrast.

For Group Discussion or Journal Writing

The telephone had a significant impact on the villagers of Magdaluna. What about other technological advancements? Select one other than the telephone, and consider its impact, both positive and negative.

PUNCTUATION NOTE

Parentheses

Sometimes when we speak, we lower our voices and whisper a tidbit of extra information. When you write, you can "whisper in your reader's ear," by using parentheses the way Maya Angelou does in paragraph 6 of "The Boys":

> Late one day, as we were attending to the pigs, I heard a horse in the front yard (it really should have been called a driveway, except that there was nothing to drive into it), and ran to find out who had come riding up on a Thursday evening when even Mr. Steward, the quiet, bitter man who owned a riding horse, would be resting by his warm fire until the morning called him out to turn over his field.

The material in parentheses is extra, nonessential information that Angelou presents as an aside. For more on parentheses, see page 640.

NARRATION IN AN IMAGE

Read the *Peanuts* cartoon on the next page and then answer the questions.

Considering the Image

1. Is Snoopy's opening in the cartoon likely to create interest in his narration? Why or why not?
2. How could Snoopy create a more interesting opening?
3. Does Snoopy use dialogue effectively? Explain.
4. If you were advising Snoopy, which would you suggest: idea generation activities or revision activities? Explain.

SUGGESTIONS FOR WRITING

Writing Narration

1. Relate an occurrence that caused you to change your opinion of someone or something, making sure you note your opinion both before and after the event.
2. Tell of an event that had a significant impact on you. Make clear what the impact was/is. You can also tell why the event affected you as it did.
3. Tell a story that describes a single, specific school experience. If you like, use a humorous approach.
4. Tell of a time when things did not go as you, or another, expected them to.
5. Write a narration about a specific job experience you have had.
6. Tell the story of a time you were happy or unhappy with your family life.

7. Narrate a moment or event that marked a turning point in the life of someone you know.
8. Tell of a time when you (or another) were treated unjustly.
9. Write an account of the time you were the angriest you have ever been.
10. Tell of an event that caused you to feel regret. If you like, you can write about a missed opportunity.
11. Relate an incident that caused you to realize something for the first time. Explain what the effect of that realization has been.
12. Tell a story of a time you witnessed (or displayed) courage.
13. Relate a memorable experience you have had in a sports competition.
14. Tell the story of some first-time experience.

Reading Then Writing Narration

1. In "In Line at the Post Office," Steven Doloff tells a story about a time he had to wait in line. Narrate an account of a time you had to wait. Be sure your narration makes a point.
2. In "The Boys," Maya Angelou narrates an account of an injustice. Tell of a time when you (or another) were treated unjustly, and go on to explain what can be learned from the event.

3. Discuss the effects on society of some piece of technology, such as the MP3 player, the cell phone, the digital camera, or the personal computer. Explain whether the effects have been mostly positive or mostly negative.

Narration beyond the Writing Classroom

Assume that you have been invited to speak to the college-bound graduating seniors at your high school alma mater. You have been asked to give them an idea of what to expect from college life. Write the speech, using one or more narrations to help your audience understand what college is like.

Responding to Theme

1. In "The Boys," Uncle Willie is forced to hide even though he is not guilty of a crime. Discuss another example of injustice that you are aware of, and try to explain the cause of that injustice.
2. Like Steven Doloff in "In Line at the Post Office," discuss what prompts people to identify with specific groups. Alternatively, discuss the effects of group identification.
3. In "The Telephone," Anwar Accawi notes the high price of technology. What price do you think we pay for progress? Is that price ever too high? Explain.
4. In the *Peanuts* cartoon on page 204, Snoopy is writing a narration that could be part of a romance novel. Romance novels are very popular. Explain why. As an alternative, select another popular kind of writing, such as horror stories, science fiction, or blogs, and explain why they are popular.
5. *Connecting the readings:* In "The Boys," and "In Line at the Post Office," the authors tell stories that speak to race and class distinctions. Discuss the role of race and/or class in one aspect of society, such as education, sports, television programming, or product marketing.

Writing Narration

The strategies here are not meant to replace your own effective procedures. They are here to try as you work to improve your writing process.

www.mhhe.com/tsw
For further help with writing narration, go to Catalyst 2.0 > Writing > Writing Tutors > Narration

PROCESS GUIDELINES

Think like a Writer: Generating Ideas, Considering Audience and Purpose, and Ordering Ideas

- If you need help thinking of a story to tell, complete one of these sentences:
  - I'll never forget the time I __________.
  - I was never so embarrassed (or proud) as when __________.
  - The time I __________ I learned __________.

- To establish a purpose and audience for your narration, answer these questions:
  - What point do I want my narration to make?
  - Who would be interested in my story?
  - Who could learn something from my story?
  - Who could be influenced by my story?
- To help you assess your reader's needs, answer these questions:
  - Does my reader already know the answer to any of the journalist's questions?
  - Has my reader had an experience similar to the one I am narrating?
- To generate ideas, answer these questions:
  - Who was involved?
  - Who was affected?
  - What happened?
  - How did it happen?
  - When did it happen?
  - Could it happen again?
  - Where did it happen?
  - Why is it important?
  - Why did it happen?
  - What was learned?
  - What was the effect?
  - Was it expected to happen?
- List features of people or scene to describe. Concentrate on details important to the narration or on its significance.
- List the events in the order they happened. Now rearrange the list to reflect a chronological order that includes one flashback. Which sequence works better?

Think like a Writer: Drafting

- Look for opportunities to include dialogue that advances the narration or lends insight into a person's character or motivation.
- Think about coherence, and include transitions to show a change of time or scene.

Think like a Critic; Work like an Editor: Revising

- Underline the sentence that states the significance of your narration or the point it makes. If you have no written statement of the significance or point, be sure it is strongly implied, or revise to add this information.
- If any answers to the journalist's questions are missing, decide whether they are needed based on your audience and purpose.
- Decide whether to add description to create interest and to help your reader visualize scene or people.
- Decide whether to add dialogue to create interest, give your reader insight into the nature of people who are part of your story, or move the narration at a quicker pace.
- To get reader response, see page 105. In addition, ask your reader to note any places where you should comment on or explain the significance of an event. Then ask your reader to write out the point of your narration so you can be sure it is stated or implied clearly.

Think like a Critic; Work like an Editor: Correcting Errors and Proofreading

- If you use dialogue, check your punctuation and capitalization against the models beginning on page 179.
- Be sure to proofread the final copy before handing it in. If you are submitting an electronic copy, proofread from a paper copy. If you are submitting a paper copy, check with your instructor about whether you can ink in minor corrections.

Remember

- Avoid rambling by eliminating extraneous details or discussions that do not advance the narration or help you achieve your purpose.

LOOKING AHEAD

In this chapter, you will learn how to use examples to achieve all the purposes for writing: to entertain, to express feelings, to relate experiences, to inform, and to persuade. Examples are so useful for achieving these goals that you will use them yourself and encounter them often. To appreciate the value of examples, consider this advertisement, and answer these questions:

- What kind of examples appear?
- How many examples are used?
- Why does the ad include this particular number of examples? Should there be more examples? Fewer?
- Are the examples grouped in any particular way?
- What do the examples have in common? How do the examples differ?
- What is the purpose of the examples? How well do the examples achieve their intended purpose?

Exemplification

In a column for the online magazine *Salon,* Eric Boehlert opened with this statement:

> The war on terrorism has produced some strange reversals.

If you read that sentence online and wondered what Boehlert could possibly mean, you did not have to wonder for long because his next sentence began with the words "For instance." Those words signaled that a helpful example would follow:

> For instance, one year ago Pakistan's Gen. Pervez Musharraf was an isolated, ostracized general who appointed himself president. Today, he's welcoming the British prime minister and American cabinet members, all seeking the ear of the influential Afghan neighbor.

Once you read the example, you understand what Boehlert means when he refers to "strange reversals" produced by the war on terrorism. And that is why writers use examples so often—nothing helps a reader understand a writer's point better than an example. Examples are part of most writing, no matter what the predominant pattern of development is. However, you can also develop a thesis by relying almost exclusively on examples, in which case the pattern of development is **exemplification.**

WHY IS EXEMPLIFICATION IMPORTANT?

Even our most routine communications rely heavily on examples to make their point. Suppose a friend asks you which professor to take for geology and you reply, "Take Chung's class; Chung's the most reasonable." Your friend might say, "What do you mean?" and you might explain by providing examples: "His tests are graded on the curve, he requires only one research paper, and he's always in his office to help students." Even the question "What do you want to do tonight?" can prompt the use of examples. If you reply, "Something relaxing," your answer will not be as clear as it would be if you added examples: "Something relaxing like a movie or a quiet dinner."

Exemplification adds clarity. It allows you to nail down a generalization by providing specific instances of ways that generalization is true. Consider, for example, the following four sentences:

> It is not easy today for a young married couple to get off to a good start. Credit is tight, making home ownership almost impossible, so the couple may spend many years in a cramped apartment. High-paying jobs are hard to find, so many couples cannot secure their income. Perhaps most significant, young marrieds find that financial worries cause tensions that strain the marriage bond.

The first sentence expresses a generalization, and the next three sentences provide examples that bear out the generalization. In the discussion of supporting detail in Chapter 3, you were cautioned to *show* rather than *tell*. Examples can help you do that by providing details to make generalizations concrete.

In addition to providing clarity and concreteness, examples add vitality and create reader interest by relating ideas to your readers' experience, understanding, or interests. For example, if you want to show that even nice people lie, and your audience is your co-workers, you can illustrate the point by saying that people call in sick when they merely want a day off. If your audience is college students, you can offer as an example the fact that some students say they missed class because of illness when they really overslept.

Essays developed primarily with examples can serve the full range of purposes for writing, as shown in this chart.

Purposes for Exemplification

Purpose	**Sample Exemplification**
To entertain	Amusing examples of blind dates that have gone badly
To share feelings and experiences	Examples of what causes you to feel stress on the job

To inform (of the lack of respect we have for the elderly)	Examples of incidents when the elderly have been treated with disrespect
To persuade (to convince the reader to vote against allowing casino gambling)	Examples of the negative effects of casino gambling in communities that have allowed it

Exemplification across the Disciplines and Beyond

Exemplification in the Classroom

Exemplification is critical in all your classes because your examinations and papers will often require you to cite examples to show you understand concepts. In a biology class, you might define and give examples of *natural selection.* In an art history class, you might use exemplification to show ways wood carving was important to colonial Americans. In an education class, you might explain and give examples of different learning styles. *As you read your textbooks and listen to lectures in your other classes, notice how often examples are used. Would the material be more difficult to understand or less interesting without the examples? How many of those examples will you be expected to know and include in papers and exams?*

Exemplification in Daily Life

Exemplification is likely to be a common component of writing you do in your personal life. E-mail to friends and family about your life will include examples of what you have been doing. A condolence letter might include examples of fond memories you have of the deceased. A letter to your residence life director about problems in your residence hall will include examples to illustrate the problems. *Make a list of the writing you do on a regular basis outside the classroom and workplace. How can examples help you achieve your purposes for that writing?*

Exemplification on the Job

Exemplification is an important component of workplace writing. For example, physical and occupational therapists write instructions for patients with examples of activities to engage in and to avoid. Safety officers and trade union officials write documents with examples of unsafe workplace conditions. Teachers write instructions that include examples of what is required to complete assignments. Stockbrokers send letters to clients with examples of different financial instruments available for investment. *How do you think you would use examples in a résumé? How would you use them in a recommendation letter for a friend or colleague? Select three of the following and indicate how you think they use examples: architects, police officers, nutritionists, child care workers, accountants, marketing directors.*

COMBINING EXEMPLIFICATION WITH OTHER PATTERNS

Because examples are so important for clarifying points and supporting generalizations, you will use them in most of your writing, no matter what its primary method of development may be. A narration of the time a tornado hit your town might include examples of the damage done by the storm. A process analysis about how to grow a beautiful flower garden might include examples of suitable plants for different soil, light, and climate conditions. A classification of personal digital assistants (PDAs) will include examples of the different kinds. An analysis of the causes of eating disorders can include examples of media messages that undermine a healthy body image. And a comparison-contrast of stock and bond funds will offer examples of the funds.

SELECTING DETAIL

In the next sections, you will learn about selecting the right kind of examples, using an appropriate number of examples, and developing examples in an adequate amount of detail.

Consider Examples from a Variety of Sources

Your examples can come from a variety of sources, including personal reading, your own experiences and observations, class readings and lectures, web surfing, television viewing, and research. Notice how each generalization below is followed by an example taken from a different source.

Generalization:	Too often, young children believe that what they see on television is an accurate representation of reality.
Example from personal reading:	I recall years ago reading of a young child who died after jumping from a window and trying to fly like the Superman character he had seen on TV.
Generalization:	Americans are unmoved by the plight of the homeless.
Example from observation:	I watched at least 50 people walk past an obviously sick, homeless man on Federal Street without noticing him.
Generalization:	Being a salesperson, especially at Christmastime, is difficult.
Example from experience:	Last Christmas I worked at the jewelry counter of a local department store. Although it is supposed to be a season of goodwill, Christmas made ordinarily pleasant people pushy and demanding. Once, a woman insisted that I bring out every watch in the stockroom just so she could verify that all the styles were on display.
Generalization:	Many of the early immigrants to this country found life harder here than it was in their homeland.

Example from class reading or lecture:	My history instructor, for example, explained that many of those who made the Atlantic crossing spent their lives in sweatshops, working for low wages.
Generalization:	Unfortunately, we are becoming a nation of cheaters.
Example from web surfing:	For example, insidehighered.com reports that as many as two-thirds of our high school students admitted to cheating in the last year.
Generalization:	People in high-pressure jobs can reduce their risk of heart attack.
Example from television viewing:	A recent television documentary explained that workers could strengthen their hearts by parking a mile from their office and walking to work with a heavy briefcase.
Generalization:	In the twenty-first century, Americans will make dramatic changes in the way they live.
Example from research:	The U.S. Census Bureau reports that each year, older Americans are 1 percent more likely to live alone than in the previous year, a statistic that points to an important lifestyle shift.

If you use an example from research, acknowledge the source according to the conventions given in Chapter 17.

Use Description and Narration as Examples

You can draw on description to provide examples. Consider an essay developing the thesis "Many of the early immigrants to this country found life harder here than it was in their homeland." As part of the examples of the hardships, you could note the difficulty of earning a living in sweatshops. Then you could describe the working conditions in those sweatshops. Your information might come from books and documentaries about sweatshops, from a local museum, or from a lecture in your history class.

Stories can also be illustrative, so some of your examples may be brief narrations, or **anecdotes.** For example, an exemplification essay with the thesis "Being a salesperson, especially at Christmastime, is difficult" will provide examples of the difficulties. One of those examples could be a narration of the time you spent over an hour helping a man who could not make up his mind about which necklace to purchase for his wife.

Use Hypothetical Examples

Hypothetical examples are not *actual* instances, but examples that are representative of common experience—so much so that their actual occurrence is plausible. Consider, for example, this generalization: "Magazine advertisements create an unrealistic image of the ideal woman." You could give examples from actual ads as support, but you could also create a hypothetical example that is sufficiently similar to actual ads, like this one:

> The woman in makeup and fashion advertisements is thin beyond what is desirable—and achievable—for the average woman. She wears designer clothes that most of us cannot afford and sports a hairdo that few can accomplish without a salon of experts showing up to help every morning. Then there is that makeup: eyeliner, eye shadow, foundation, powder, blush, lip liner, lipstick, mascara, brow liner. What woman has the time (or the skill) to put all that on? As if that isn't enough, the model is backlit for maximum effect.

While the above example is not a specific ad from any particular magazine, it is enough like what typically appears to be representative of actual occurrence.

Use the Right Number of Examples

How many examples to use is a key decision. If you use too few examples, you may fail to clarify your generalization and provide the necessary concreteness. If you use too many examples, you may be guilty of overkill.

You can provide just a few examples and develop each one in great detail, or you can provide quite a few examples and develop each one in far less detail. You can also provide a moderate number of examples, each developed to a degree somewhere between the two extremes. Whatever number of examples you have, it must be enough to explain and support your generalization adequately; and to whatever degree you develop an illustration, you must have enough detail that your reader appreciates the point you are making.

Consider Your Purpose and Audience

Audience is an important consideration because who your reader is will affect your selection of examples. For instance, assume you are writing about why your college is superior to other colleges, and you plan to present examples to illustrate some of your school's strengths. If you are writing for an academically oriented audience that does not care much for sports, you will not give the example that your football team is the conference champion. Similarly, a paper aimed at parents of prospective students will not give the example of wild parties on Saturday nights.

Taken together, your purpose and audience will profoundly influence the examples you include. For instance, assume you are writing about the benefits of running. To express why you enjoy running to your friends, who think you are odd because you run four miles a day regardless of the weather, you might provide examples of the benefits you get from this activity. However, if your purpose is to inform the average reader that running can control depression and anxiety, you might provide examples of people who have improved their outlook by running.

BEING A RESPONSIBLE WRITER

Sometimes writers get panicky and end up using examples irresponsibly. For instance, writers who wait until the last minute may be in a rush to meet the deadline, so they conjure up examples that mislead readers because they are not true. A writer who aims to convince readers that half-day kindergartens are better than all-day kindergartens cannot manufacture the example of a child who developed a sleep disorder after attending an all-day kindergarten. Remember, you cannot make up an example to support your thesis unless the example is sufficiently representative to be hypothetical.

A panicked writer who feels particularly desperate may import examples from the Internet, copy them from other sources, or record them from television. However, using published examples without acknowledging the source is a form of plagiarism. Remember to document examples you take from sources using the conventions explained in Chapter 17. (To see how source examples are acknowledged, read "Media Stereotyping of Arabs and Muslims as Terrorists" on page 223.)

Be a responsible writer when you write examples by asking yourself these questions:

- Are my actual and hypothetical examples sufficiently representative of reality?
- Are examples from outside sources properly acknowledged?

ORGANIZING EXEMPLIFICATION

The thesis can express your generalization, and the body paragraphs can present and develop the examples of that generalization.

Often a progressive order is used for the examples. If some of your examples are more compelling than others, you can save your strongest example for last in order to build to a big finish. Or you can begin with your second-best example to impress your reader right off with the validity of your generalization. You can also begin with your *best* example to impress your reader initially, while reserving your second-most-effective example for last to ensure a strong final body paragraph.

Other orders can also be effective. Suppose your thesis is that the fans at local high school basketball games are rowdy. You could arrange your examples chronologically by first giving examples of rowdiness before the game begins, then examples of rowdiness during the game, and finally examples of rowdiness after the game. You can also sequence your examples in a spatial order. If you are developing the generalization that the playground in the city park was not really designed with children in mind, you could begin at one end of the playground and work your way around, ordering your examples to correspond with this movement through space. If some of your examples come from your own

USING SOURCES FOR A PURPOSE

The quotation supports the writer's point that punishing or limiting offensive speech will threaten the free speech of everyone.

The paragraph below is a body paragraph for a letter to the editor of a campus newspaper. The letter argues that the campus administration should not prevent—as it plans to do—a neo-Nazi speech and demonstration on campus. The paragraph illustrates one way to use sources from this book in your writing. This paragraph includes a quotation from paragraph 24 of "Speech Codes: Alive and Well at Colleges" on page 230. (For more information on using quotations, see Chapter 17.)

THESIS IDEA: There are better ways to react to the planned campus neo-Nazi demonstration than to ban it.

WRITING PURPOSE AND AUDIENCE: To convince the campus administration not to ban the demonstration.

[1]If nothing else, campus efforts to stifle offensive speech prove that the road to hell is paved with good intentions. [2]Certainly, the desire to ensure that everyone in a diverse student population feels comfortable is well motivated, and the stated antipathy for hate speech is admirable, but our constitutional guarantee of free speech comes with an important caveat: To have *free* speech, we must tolerate *offensive* speech. [3]If neo-Nazis want to spew their venom in the campus commons, we must let them. [4]We don't have to agree

firsthand experience, some from your own observation, and some from the experience of others, you can group together the examples from the same source.

You can help readers keep track of your examples by introducing them in topic sentences. For instance, the writer of "Gardens for Growing Hope" on page 219 uses examples to support the thesis that urban gardens can reinvigorate neglected city neighborhoods. Here are three topic sentences that introduce three different examples:

> In New York City, for example, an organization called Green Guerillas has helped people to reclaim empty lots and abandoned spaces in the inner city by providing the tools and advice for transforming these dangerous spaces into flourishing small gardens.
>
> On the West Coast, urban gardens have helped to rebuild communities torn apart by violence or mistrust.
>
> One of the most successful examples of the transformative capability of an urban garden is the Carroll Street Garden in San Francisco.

with them, but we have to let them speak because banning their speech threatens the speech rights of everyone else. [5]If offensive speech is punished or otherwise stifled, students will fear saying anything controversial for fear of similar punishment. [6]As Harvey A. Silverglate and Greg Lukianoff explain in "Speech Codes: Alive and Well at Colleges," "Students, seeing what is banned . . . will play it safe and avoid engaging in speech that, even though constitutionally protected, may offend . . ." (233).

Avoiding Plagiarism

The paragraph illustrates some points about using quotations and avoiding plagiarism.

- **Use ellipses (. . .) to signal words omitted from the middle of a sentence.** As sentence 6 illustrates, use three spaced periods when words are omitted from the middle of a quotation.
- **Use ellipses and a period when words are omitted at the end of a sentence.** As sentence 6 shows, when words are omitted at the end of a sentence, add a period in the appropriate place.

Myths about Sources

MYTH: If words are omitted from a quotation, it is not necessary to provide a parenthetical citation or a works-cited entry.

FACT: Quotations with omitted words must be documented according to the conventions in Chapter 17, which means both a parenthetical citation and a works-cited entry must be included.

EXERCISE Writing Exemplification

1. Locate two published essays or articles that include examples. (You might check your textbooks, newsmagazines, and newspapers.) Photocopy the selections and answer these questions:
   a. Is exemplification or some other pattern the primary method of development?
   b. What is the source of the examples: personal experience, observation, research, or other?
   c. Are the examples adequately detailed? Do they support their generalization adequately? Explain.
   d. Are any of the examples hypothetical? How can you tell? If so, are they plausible?
2. For each of the following subjects, write one generalization that can be supported with examples.
   a. Education
   b. Television
   c. Sports

Visualizing an Exemplification Essay

The chart that follows can help you visualize one structure for an exemplification essay. Like all good models, this one can be altered as needed.

Introduction

- Creates interest
- States the thesis, which is the generalization you will explain or prove with examples

First Body Paragraph

- Gives one or more examples
- May include a topic sentence to introduce the example or examples
- Develops the example or examples with description, narration, or explanation
- Arranges details in progressive or some other logical order

Next Body Paragraphs

- May continue the example from the previous paragraph
- May give another example or examples
- May include a topic sentence to introduce the example or examples
- Develop the example or examples with description, narration, or explanation
- Arrange details in progressive or some other logical order
- Continue until all the examples are presented and developed

Conclusion

- Provides closure
- Leaves your reader with a strong final impression

3. Select one of the generalizations you wrote for number 2, and establish a possible audience and purpose for an essay that uses that generalization as a thesis.
4. To support the thesis/generalization, discover one example to fit each of the categories listed below. If you are unable to think of an example for a particular category, try to come up with two for another category. Also, one example may fill more than one category. For instance, one example may be both a narration and an event from personal experience.
   a. Example from personal experience
   b. Example from observation
   c. Example from personal reading

d. Example from a class reading or lecture
e. Example from television viewing
f. Narrative example
g. Descriptive example ■

LEARNING FROM OTHER WRITERS: Student Essays

The first student essay, "Gardens for Growing Hope," appears with marginal notes that point out features explained in this chapter. As you read, notice the number of examples the writer uses and the degree to which she develops each example.

The second student essay, "Let's Just Ban Everything," was written for the *Rocky Mountain Collegian,* Colorado State University's student newspaper. This essay uses examples for a persuasive purpose. Ask yourself how convincing these examples are.

"Media Stereotyping of Arabs and Muslims as Terrorists," the third student essay, includes research material as part of its supporting details. Be sure to consider how that research helps the writer achieve his purpose.

Gardens for Growing Hope

Cathy Levito

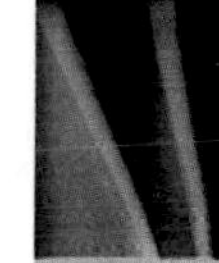

1 Many of our core inner-city neighborhoods have decayed into impoverished, high-crime areas. Most people agree that these areas can and should be transformed, but they also believe that doing so requires political initiative and a great deal of money. However, as I learned in my sociology class, there is one simple, inexpensive, effective action people can take to help reinvigorate neglected city neighborhoods: They can start an urban garden.

Paragraph 1
This is the introduction. The thesis, the last sentence, is the idea that will be supported with examples. Background information helps engage reader interest.

2 In New York City, for example, an organization called Green Guerillas has helped people to reclaim empty lots and abandoned spaces in the inner city by providing the tools and advice for transforming these dangerous spaces into flourishing small gardens. The Liz Christy Memorial Garden was started by a group of community activists in a vacant lot near the corner of Houston Street and the Bowery in Lower Manhattan, a part of the city with poor housing opportunities and few amenities. Local residents got together, cleared the lot, and planted flowers, trees, and vegetables. The City of New York agreed

Paragraph 2
The first sentence is the topic sentence. It states the first example that will support the thesis: the gardens started by Green Guerillas. Notice the transition, "for example," and that the details include information researched on the Internet.

to rent the lot to the Green Guerillas for a token sum, and the success of the garden inspired many other New Yorkers to plant gardens.

Paragraph 3
The first sentence is the topic sentence. It states the next example that will support the thesis: the A. Badillo Community Rose Garden. Notice the transition, "Another example."

Another example of urban renewal through gardening is the A. Badillo Community Rose Garden in the Bronx. When a building on a deteriorating block in the Bronx was demolished, local resident Irma Badillo used her own money to plant roses and other flowers, as well as trees, in the empty lot as a memorial to her father, who loved to garden. She recruited neighbors to help with the garden, and taught local children—many of whom had never been in a garden in their lives—how to care for plants. In the fifteen years since she established the garden, her Bronx neighborhood has attracted new mixed-income housing developments, and the crime rate has dropped. 3

Paragraph 4
The first sentence is the topic sentence. It states that the next examples will come from the West Coast. Notice that here and throughout the essay, the examples are real and not hypothetical.

On the West Coast, urban gardens have helped to rebuild communities torn apart by violence or mistrust. For instance, after the 1992 civil disturbances in Los Angeles, a group of students from Crenshaw High School in South-Central Los Angeles worked with a teacher and a community volunteer to transform a vacant lot behind their school into a vegetable garden. With volunteer support, the students began a for-profit company, "Food from the 'Hood," that began selling its products at a local farmer's market and eventually created its own line of salad dressings. Students learned to cooperate with local businesses, took pride in their community, and earned money for college scholarships. 4

Paragraph 5
The first sentence, the topic sentence, gives the next example: the Carroll Street Garden. The transition "One of the most successful examples" suggests a progressive order.

One of the most successful examples of the transformative capability of an urban garden is the Carroll Street Garden in San Francisco. Formerly an abandoned lot, the area is now a thriving herb and vegetable garden tended by former prisoners from the San Francisco County jail. Transforming abandoned urban spaces into gardens not only improves a neighborhood but also offers some of society's outcasts a new opportunity for joining in. A counselor at the jail had begun a garden there to teach prisoners gardening skills that they could use to find work when they were released; she expanded the program to the Carroll Street Garden to help released prisoners continue to practice their skills while earning a wage. Local restaurants and bakeries 5 purchase the garden's produce and have even hired graduates of the gardening program.

Urban gardens bring beauty and relaxation to troubled communities. They help reclaim neighborhoods, and they provide food, recreation, and learning opportunities to residents. As a creative and relatively low-cost investment, urban gardens can be an important first stage in the renewal of urban communities. 6

Paragraph 6
The conclusion provides a satisfying finish by restating the benefits of an urban garden.

Let's Just Ban Everything

Ken Hamner

As someone who's lost two grandparents to tobacco-related cancer, I was intrigued by the statistics presented by last Friday's *Collegian* article related to secondhand smoking and its associated health-risk statistics. 1

According to these statistics, secondhand smoke is a really bad thing, at least for people predisposed to cancer. These statistics make a lot of people sad, but there is an easy solution—ban smoking! That's right, folks—let's abolish secondhand smoke from its firsthand sources and overthrow the tyranny of those capitalistic tobacco dogs pushing them on innocents everywhere. It's justified—the personal freedoms of a few don't outweigh the long-term personal right to longevity of the many. 2

But wait! We should be consistent in our elimination of risks to our immortality. We tried alcohol prohibition once, but did we give it a fair chance? With modern science as our ally, we have found alcohol produces physiological and psychological addiction, cancer, heart disease, immune suppression and brain damage, all in addition to the evil things drunk people might do. This sounds bad, so we should get rid of alcohol. 3

Oh, did someone mention heart disease? Cholesterol is mean to some people and saturated fat isn't much better. In this case, how can we possibly 4 let our grocers sell us steaks and hamburgers without the proper health labels? And even with such warnings, what of our youth? How can we allow corporations like McDonald's to continue addicting our innocent youth to harmful hamburger products at an early age, using slick advertising techniques and cute corporate symbols like Grimace and Ronald McDonald?

This is an outrage! And what of the Blue Bonnet girl? She's a definite ploy 5
by the dairy industry to get young teenage males to eat more butter.

Guns provide obvious short-term health risks, so we should get rid of 6
them—along with sharp knives (won't need them if we ban red meat), broken bottles, automobiles, wet bathtubs, baseball bats (sorry World Series fans) and all potentially dangerous devices ad infinitum.

Playgrounds, offices and sidewalks should all be coated with soft, rubbery 7
materials because a significant percentage of clumsy people out there might trip and cut themselves, opening the door for many harmful pathogens to enter the bloodstream. Speaking of the environment, we had better halt all industry.

Pollution, though apparently not as dangerous as secondhand smoke, is 8
definitely a hazard. And what about water? It sounds far-fetched, but it is true that if you drink water every day for the rest of your life you will die. Life itself is hazardous. I questioned several people on this topic and every single one of them believed they would die sometime in their lives. You know what this means? Life is a leading cause of death! We should therefore ban life as quickly as possible. Or maybe we should be smart about this. What it all boils down to is personal, intelligent choices.

If you don't like being a patron or a waiter in a smoke-filled environment, 9
stop being a waiter in or a patron of that restaurant. There are dozens of alternative places to work and eat. The same goes for other health risks. But don't impose your "physiological morality" on everyone else. I wish my grandparents had taken a good look in the mirror in their 40s and seen the signs of tobacco-related decay that led to their deaths years later, but I'm also happy they had the right to choose for themselves how to live and how to die.

EXERCISE Considering "Let's Just Ban Everything"

1. What is the thesis of "Let's Just Ban Everything"?
2. Why does Hamner open by stating that he has "lost two grandparents to tobacco-related cancer"? What do you think of that opening?
3. What are the sources of the examples in the essay?
4. Are Hamner's examples effective? That is, do they do a good job of convincing an audience of college students?
5. Which paragraph uses hypothetical examples? Are these examples convincing? Why or why not? ■

Student Essay with Research

Media Stereotyping of Arabs and Muslims as Terrorists

Thomas Baird

Because the media shape what we believe, negative media portrayal of an ethnic group or social class can be detrimental. According to "Public Expresses Mixed Views of Islam, Mormonism," a report recently published by the Pew Forum on Religion & Public Life, 32% of the general public and 48% of people with anti-Muslim sentiments claim that the media have affected their opinions of Muslims more than anything else (4–5). Through the deliberate portrayal of the Islamic faith as one of violence, the media, especially Hollywood films and television, stereotype Muslims as radical terrorists, and because Americans tend to think that all Muslims are Arabs and vice versa, the cinematic stereotyping extends to all Arabs, not just those who are Muslim. 1

Numerous examples of Hollywood films throughout the industry's history have contributed to the distorted image of Muslims on the big screen. In his book *Reel Bad Arabs: How Hollywood Vilifies a People,* Jack G. Shaheen examines the negative portrayal of Muslims in hundreds of American films. Shaheen concludes: 2

> Seen through Hollywood's distorted lenses, Arabs look different and threatening. Projected along racial and religious lines, the stereotypes are deeply ingrained in American cinema. From 1896 until today, filmmakers have collectively indicated all Arabs as Public Enemy #1—brutal, heartless,

> uncivilized religious fanatics and money-mad cultural "others" bent on terrorizing civilized Westerners, especially Christians and Jews. (2)

By characterizing the Muslim as "other," Hollywood contributes to the general public sentiment that Muslims and Arabs represent the opposite of American ideals of freedom, civility, and tolerance. According to Shaheen, Hollywood has made it okay to condemn Muslims and Arabs based on an unrealistic and deeply prejudiced depiction of the Islamic faith.

Depicting Muslims as terrorists was routine in pre-9/11 movies. For example, in the 1996 movie *Executive Decision,* Muslims hijack a passenger jet, terrorize passengers, kill a flight attendant, and prepare to unload enough lethal nerve gas to kill the millions of residents of Washington, D.C., and the neighboring East Coast. Throughout the movie, Islam itself is equated with violence. At one point, a Muslim enters the dining room of a ritzy London hotel and massacres innocent couples. He is shown holding the holy Qur'an in one hand and a bomb in the other. In the 1994 movie *True Lies,* Muslims are portrayed as murderous terrorists plotting to incinerate Miami with an atomic bomb. In one scene, an Uzi tossed down a flight of stairs unintentionally cuts down a roomful of Arabs. Sadly, the scene was intended to be comical. The accidental murder of a roomful of innocent Arabs is supposed to stir laughter because, after all, all Arabs are Muslims, and all Muslims are terrorists. Although these movies are many years old, they continue to feed the popular stereotype because they show up repeatedly on both cable and broadcast networks. 3

More recent movies and television shows also feed the stereotype. In the action movie *Rules of Engagement* (2000), a marine officer gives the order to kill 83 Muslim men, women, and children who are threats because they are engaged in anti-American protests and shootings at the American embassy. Once again, Arabs are portrayed as terrorists. Then there is the immensely popular, post-9/11 television program *24.* In this program, Muslims engage in suicide bombings in U.S. cities, a Muslim terrorist detonates a nuclear bomb near Los Angeles, and a seemingly normal Muslim-American family is depicted as part of a lethal sleeper cell in the United States. In the 2002 4 made-for-television movie *The President's Man: A Line in the Sand,* Muslims from the Middle East attempt to explode a nuclear bomb in Texas—with the assistance of Arab-Americans.

5 To be fair, I must note that several recent documentaries have tried to alert the public to the difficult and dangerous Muslim-American experience. Documentaries such as *Persons of Interest* (2004), *Whose Children Are These?* (2004), *Midwest Muslim* (2006), and *Out of Status* (2006) depict real Muslims trying to lead normal lives in the face of blatant discrimination and prejudice. However, because documentaries like these are not Hollywood blockbusters and therefore reach a relatively small audience, the effect they have in counteracting the negative portrayal of Muslims is limited at best.

6 It is difficult for many Americans to consider Islamic stereotyping unjust, not just because some Muslims are terrorists but because movie and television repeatedly reinforce the mistaken notion that *all* Muslims and Arabs want to destroy us. However, just as true Catholics do not embrace priests who sexually abuse children, true Muslims reject the ranting of extremists. Islam is a religion of peace. The violence of some extremists does not justify the stereotyping of Muslims in movies and other media.

Works Cited

"Public Expresses Mixed Views of Islam, Mormonism." *The Pew Forum on Religion & Public Life.* Pew Research Center, 25 Sept. 2007. Web. 29 May 2008.

Shaheen, Jack G. *Reel Bad Arabs: How Hollywood Vilifies a People.* New York: Olive Branch-Interlink, 2001. Print.

EXERCISE Considering "Media Stereotyping of Arabs and Muslims as Terrorists"

1. What is the thesis of the essay?
2. What do you judge to be the author's purpose for writing? Do you think he achieves his purpose? Why or why not?
3. What are the sources of the writer's examples? Are the examples good ones?
4. How does the writer use research material to help him achieve his purpose for writing? ■

THINK LIKE A CRITIC; WORK LIKE AN EDITOR: The Student Writer at Work

When you reach your conclusion, you may feel the sense of relief that comes from having the finish line in view and fail to give your last paragraph the attention it deserves. However, a weak conclusion can leave your reader with a poor final impression and detract from your essay as a whole.

Cathy Levito let down when she drafted the conclusion of "Gardens for Growing Hope." Here is the first version of her conclusion:

First draft

> Thus, urban gardens, as I learned in my sociology class, are an effective, accessible solution to the difficult problems of many inner-city neighborhoods.

Cathy said that she thought her conclusion was satisfactory—good but not great—but a writing center staff member felt the conclusion was much weaker than the rest of her draft. Still, Cathy felt her approach was the right one: She wanted to end by reemphasizing the value of urban gardens. She decided to create the emphasis she wanted by stating explicitly what the benefits of the gardens are.

Reread "Gardens for Growing Hope," substituting the first-draft version of the conclusion. Is Cathy's final version an improvement or equally good?

LEARNING FROM OTHER WRITERS: Professional Essays

Fox's Flapdoodle MICHAEL SHERMER

Michael Shermer, the founding publisher of Skeptic *magazine, uses examples to examine the allegation in a Fox network television program that the moon landing never occurred. As you read the essay, which first appeared in* Scientific American *in 2001, think about why some Americans find it hard to believe that the lunar landing actually occurred.*

The price of liberty is, in addition to eternal vigilance, eternal patience with the vacuous blather occasionally expressed from behind the shield of free speech. It is a cost worth bearing, but it does become exasperating, as when the Fox Broadcasting Company aired its highly advertised special "Conspiracy Theory: Did We Land on the Moon?" NASA, viewers were told, faked the Apollo missions on a movie set. 1

Such flummery should not warrant a response, but in a free society, skeptics are the watchdogs against irrationalism—the consumer advocates of ideas. Debunking is not simply the divestment of bunk; its utility is in offering a better alternative, along with a lesson on how thinking goes wrong. The Fox show is a case study, starting with its disclaimer: "The following program deals with a controversial subject. The theories expressed are not the only possible explanation. Viewers are invited to make a judgment based on all available information." That information, of course, was not provided, so let's refute Fox's argument point by point in case the statistic at the top of the show—that 20 percent of Americans believe we never went to the moon—is accurate. 2

Claim: Shadows in the photographs taken on the moon reveal two sources of light. Given that the sun is the only source of light in the sky, the extra "fill" light must come from studio spotlights. *Answer:* Setting aside the inane assumption that NASA and its co-conspirators were too incogitant to have thought of this, there are actually *three* sources of light: the sun, the earth (reflecting the sun) and the moon itself, which acts as a powerful reflector, particularly when you are standing on it. 3

Claim: The American flag was observed "waving" in the airless environment of the moon. *Answer:* The flag waved only while the astronaut fiddled with it. 4

Claim: No blast crater is evident underneath the Lunar Excursion Module (LEM). *Answer:* The moon is covered by only a couple of inches of dust, beneath which is a solid surface that would not be affected by the blast of the engine. 5

Claim: When the top half of the LEM took off from the moon, there was no visible rocket exhaust. The LEM instead leaped off its base as though yanked up by cables. *Answer:* First, the footage clearly shows that there was quite a blast, as dust and other particles go flying. Second, without an oxygen-rich atmosphere, there is no fuel to generate a rocket-nozzle flame tail. 6

Claim: The LEM simulator used by astronauts for practice was obviously unstable—Neil Armstrong barely escaped with his life when his simulator crashed. The real LEM was much larger and heavier and thus impossible to land. *Answer:* Practice makes perfect, and these guys practiced. A bicycle is inherently unstable, too, until you learn to ride it. Also, the moon's gravity is only one sixth that of the earth's, so the LEM's weight was less destabilizing. 7

NASA, viewers were told, faked the Apollo missions on a movie set.

Claim: No stars show in the sky in the photographs and films from the moon. *Answer:* Stars don't routinely appear in photography shot on the earth, either, They are simply too faint. To shoot stars in the night sky, even on the moon, you need to use long exposures. 8

The no-moonic mongers go on and on in this vein, weaving narratives that include the "murder" of astronauts and pilots in accidents, including Gus Grissom in the Apollo 1 fire before he was about to go public with the hoax. Like most people with conspiracy theories, the landing naysayers have no positive supporting evidence, only allegations of cover-ups. I once asked G. Gordon Liddy[1] (who should know) about conspiracies. He quoted *Poor Richard's Almanack:* "Three people can keep a secret if two of them are dead." To think that thousands of NASA scientists would keep their mouths shut for years is risible rubbish. 9

[1]G. Gordon Liddy was the White House operative behind the break-in into the Democratic headquarters in the Watergate building in 1972. The subsequent cover-up led to the resignation of President Richard Nixon. Liddy was convicted of conspiracy for his role.

Considering Ideas

1. Explain the meaning of the title. Is it a good one? How does it hint at Shermer's attitude?
2. In paragraph 2, Shermer gives the disclaimer that the Fox network ran at the top of the program. Does that disclaimer adequately defend the broadcast? Why or why not?
3. What do you judge to be the author's purpose? Are the readers of *Scientific American,* where the essay first appeared, an appropriate audience for that purpose?

4. Why does Shermer think it is important to debunk the claim that Americans never landed on the moon?
5. In paragraph 2, Shermer calls skeptics "the consumer advocates of ideas." What does he mean?

Considering Technique

1. What is Shermer's thesis? That is, what generalization is he supporting with examples?
2. How do his examples support Shermer's thesis?
3. What is the source of the author's examples?
4. Shermer refers to the content of the Fox program as "flapdoodle," "flummery" (paragraph 2), and "risible rubbish" (paragraph 9). What is the effect of these word choices?
5. What approach does Shermer take in his conclusion? Does the conclusion bring the essay to a satisfying finish? Explain.

For Group Discussion or Journal Writing

In paragraph 2, Shermer says that "skeptics are the watchdogs against irrationalism." Exactly how do skeptics play the watchdog role? What other "irrationalism" do skeptics take on? Is there any irrationalism you think they should take on as soon as possible?

Shoddy Service Sows the Seeds of Discontent

Dawn Turner Trice

"Shoddy Service Sows the Seeds of Discontent" originally appeared in the Chicago Tribune *in February 2002. Notice that the examples are laced with humor, but ask yourself whether Trice has a serious message beneath the humor.*

Customer Service Gripe No. 1: I'm in the supermarket the other day, nearing the end of my checkout and listening to Gladys Knight and the Pips croon "Midnight Train to Georgia." 1

I'm humming, because I'm notorious for not knowing the words to any song, when I realize I've forgotten milk. (For a family of three, we consume so much milk we'd be better off owning a 2 percent cow.) 2

Anyway, because I'm forever cognizant of my fellow 15-items-or-less linemates, I ask the cashier, whom I'll call Broom Hilda, to add the milk to my tab. I tell her I can go back to fetch it. 3

She sucks her teeth and rolls her eyes before saying she cannot possibly add milk to my tab because she has to scan the jug. So she waves for a bag boy, a teenager who shuffles over in his stylish but sagging pants. She tells him to run back to the dairy to get milk. 4

Even I know he can't possibly run in those pants. "Uh," he says, swiping the back of his hand against nose drippings. He then reaches (with his snotty hand, mind you) under the counter. "Uh, she can have this one." He pulls out a gallon of milk. 5

Confession: I have food issues. I totally admit it. I worry about refrigeration. I religiously check expiration dates. I'm so unnerved by the prospect of salmonella and E. coli contamination that I cook meat until it has the elasticity of a baseball. 6

Naturally, the bag boy, Broom Hilda and the growing mob in the express line behind me don't know this so they'd simply prefer I grab the milk and run. 7

Seconds tick past as I feel the bottom of the jug, taking its temperature. Broom Hilda folds her arms across her bosom and balls her face up like a fist. 8

As I suspected, the milk is room temperature. "You want the milk or not?" she says. 9

"No, I do not want the milk." I ask her to scan it and I tell her I'll run back to get another gallon, which I'm sure had been sitting out earlier and now is cold again. 10

She rolls her eyes and tosses me my change. 11

Customer Service Gripe No. 2: I'm having lunch with a girlfriend at a nice restaurant. I assume it's a nice restaurant because we have linen napkins and more than one fork. 12

We get our water. Mine has a poppy seed bobbing around in it, or what I hope is a poppy seed. I point this out to a young man, who says "Oh" (which is far more refreshing than "Uh") and hurries to bring me another glass. 13

During my meal, a wonderful combination of chicken and bow tie pasta with spinach in a light and airy cream sauce, I ask for more water. 14

The server comes over with a pitcher. As she pours, a little piece of a red onion dribbles out into my glass. Silently, I watch it settle near an ice cube. 15

I point this out to the server, who says the onion bit must have already been in the glass. I assure her that it wasn't and I remind her that I didn't order anything with onions. 16

She freezes as though unplugged, then asks, "So, you want another glass?" 17

"Well, duh?" 18

She takes my glass back and when she returns—and I swear this is true—it has a poppy seed in it. 19

Yet Another Gripe: A friend told me she took her favorite dress, a tasteful yet slinky satin number, to a new dry cleaner, and when she brought it home and inspected it, she noticed a scorch mark near the tush area. She returned to the dry cleaners and told the nice lady behind the counter, who promptly replied: "Don't blame that on us. You must have brought it here like that." 20

I could go on but I won't. So here's my point. I understand fully that dealing with the public can be a grueling and thankless job. We (not me, of course) customers are sometimes a surly bunch of malcontents (especially those consuming beer) who treat customer service folk like crud. 21

While I do recognize that there are many in the service industry doing a bang-up job, there's a handful who aren't, and for some reason I've been running into you a lot lately. So please take note: It would be nice to be treated with a dose of decency and respect, since we are paying customers. 22

This, of course, means that if we're getting something for free, it's OK to treat us with the utmost disdain. 23

Considering Ideas

1. In your own words, state the thesis of "Shoddy Service Sows the Seeds of Discontent." Where in the essay is that thesis best expressed?
2. The essay was written for the *Chicago Tribune*. For what purpose do you think Trice wrote it? Do you think she was likely to achieve her purpose with her original audience? Why or why not?
3. Do you think Trice is fair to the service workers she mentions in the essay? Explain.
4. Is Trice serious in the last paragraph? Explain.

Considering Technique

1. What is the source of Trice's examples?
2. Does Trice use enough examples in enough detail to support her thesis? Explain.
3. *Combining patterns:* "Shoddy Service Sows the Seeds of Discontent" includes specific, descriptive detail. For example, in paragraph 4, Trice refers to the boy's "sagging pants," and in her opening, she refers to the specific song she was humming: "Midnight Train to Georgia." How do the description and specific detail help Trice achieve her writing purpose?
4. Trice includes humor. Cite an example of that humor. What purpose does the humor serve? Despite the humor, is the author making a serious point?

For Group Discussion or Journal Writing

How do you think the service workers mentioned in "Shoddy Service Sows the Seeds of Discontent" would respond to Trice? Would they have their own version of events? If so, what might it be?

Combining Patterns of Development

Speech Codes: Alive and Well at Colleges

HARVEY A. SILVERGLATE AND GREG LUKIANOFF

The authors combine exemplification with cause-and-effect analysis and definition to make a point about freedom of speech on college campuses, a point you may find surprising. This essay first appeared in 2003 in The Chronicle of Higher Education, *a publication for university faculty and administrators. As you read, consider whether the examples are particularly suited to the authors' intended audience.*

Five years ago, a higher-education editor for *The New York Times* informed one of us, Harvey Silverglate, that Neil L. Rudenstine—then president of Harvard University—had insisted that Harvard did not have, much less enforce, any "speech codes." Silverglate suggested the editor dig deeper, because virtually any undergraduate could contest the president's claim. 1

A mere three years earlier, the faculty of the Harvard Law School had adopted "Sexual Harassment Guidelines" targeted at "seriously offensive" speech. The guidelines were passed in response to a heated campus controversy involving a law student parody of an expletive-filled *Harvard Law Review* article that promoted a postmodernist, gender-related view of the nature of law. In response to an outcry by outraged campus feminists and their allies, a law professor lodged a formal complaint against the parodists with the college's administrative board. 2

When the board dismissed the charge on the technicality that the law school had no speech code that would specifically outlaw such a parody, the dean at the time appointed a faculty committee to draft the guidelines, which remain in force today. The intention was to prevent, or punish if necessary, future offensive gender-related speech that might create a "hostile environment" for female law students at Harvard. As far as Silverglate (who lives and works near the Harvard campus and follows events there closely) has observed, there has not been a truly biting parody on hot-button issues related to gender politics at the law school since. 3

Last fall, officials at Harvard Business School admonished and threatened with punishment an editor of the school's student-run newspaper for publishing a cartoon critical of the administration. He resigned in protest over the administration's assault on the paper's editorial independence. 4

At virtually the same time, after a controversy in which a law student was accused of racially insensitive speech, a cry went up for adopting "Discriminatory Harassment Guidelines" to parallel the code that outlawed gender-based insults. As the controversy progressed, some students accused two professors of insensitivity for trying to discuss the issues in class. Soon after the Black Law Students Association demanded that one of those professors be disciplined and banned from teaching required first-year classes, he announced that he would not teach his course for the rest of the semester. The other professor insisted on continuing to teach, but the dean's office announced that all of his classes had to be tape-recorded so that any students who felt offended being in his presence could instead listen to the recorded lecture. 5

All of that at a university that, as President Rudenstine supposedly assured *The New York Times,* did not have, much less enforce, a speech code. 6

Today, many in higher education still share Rudenstine's apparent belief that a speech code exists only if it is prominently stamped SPEECH CODE in the student handbook. To them, any speech code is an anachronism, a failed relic of the 1980s that has disappeared from all but the most repressive backwaters of academe. 7

But speech codes are alive and well, if one is realistic about what makes a campus regulation a speech code. The Foundation for Individual Rights in Education [FIRE] defines a speech code as *any campus regulation that punishes, forbids, heavily regulates, or restricts a substantial amount of protected speech.*[1] Thus defined, speech codes are the rule rather than the exception in higher education. 8

Why does virtually no college call its speech code by that name? For one thing, in the 1980s and 90s, every legal challenge of a clearly identified speech code at a public institution was successful. To maintain a weapon against speech that is "offensive" or "uncivil" (or merely too robust), the authors of the current stealthier generation of speech codes have adopted highly restrictive "speech zone" policies, e-mail policies that ban "offensive" speech, "diversity statements" with provisions that punish those uttering any "intolerant expression," and, of course, the ubiquitous "harassment policies" aimed at "hostile" viewpoints and words that operate by redefining speech as a form of conduct. 9

FIRE initiated, in April, a litigation project aimed at abolishing such codes at public colleges and universities, beginning with a lawsuit charging that various policies at Shippensburg University are unconstitutional. Shippensburg promises only to protect speech that does not "provoke, harass, demean, intimidate, or harm another." Shippensburg's "Racism and Cultural Diversity" statement (modified by the university after FIRE filed suit) defined harassment as "unsolicited, unwanted conduct which annoys, threatens, or alarms a person or group." Shippensburg also has "speech zones" that restrict protests to only two areas on the campus. 10

In a recent *Chronicle* article, Shippensburg's president, Anthony F. Ceddia, complained that FIRE had "cobbled together words and expressions of different policies and procedures." That is true; it found unconstitutional provisions in many different places—the student handbook and the university's Web site, to cite just two—and is challenging all of them. 11

FIRE has been developing an online database of policies that restrict speech on both private and public campuses. Given the longstanding

[1]Protected speech is the communication guaranteed free—and hence unregulated—by the First Amendment to the Constitution.

assumption that academic freedom at liberal-arts colleges protects offensive and unpopular speech, the number and variety of such policies are startling. FIRE's still-in-progress survey and analysis demonstrates that a clear majority of higher-education institutions have substantial speech restrictions and many others have lesser restrictions that still, arguably, infringe on academic freedom. 12

Some codes, of course, are worse than others. Some are patently unconstitutional; others, artfully written by offices of general counsels, seek to obfuscate their intention to prohibit or discourage certain speech. However, there is no excuse for a liberal-arts institution, public or private, to punish speech, no matter how impolite, impolitic, unpopular, or ornery. 13

No one denies that a college can and should ban true harassment—but a code that *calls* itself a "racial-harassment code" does not thereby magically inoculate itself against free-speech and academic-freedom obligations. The recent controversy over "racial harassment" at Harvard Law School has been replicated on campuses across the country, often with outcomes as perilous to academic freedom. For example, in 1999, a professor at the Columbia University School of Law administered a criminal-law exam posing a complex question concerning the issues of feticide, abortion, violence against women, and consent to violence. Some women in the class complained to two faculty members, who then told the law-school dean that the professor's exam was so insensitive to the women in the class that it may have constituted harassment. The dean brought the case to Columbia's general counsel before concluding—correctly of course—after a dialogue with FIRE that academic freedom absolutely protected the professor. 14

Such examples demonstrate the persistence of the notion that administrators may muzzle speech that some students find "offensive," in the name of protecting civil rights. Further, the continuing existence of these codes relies on people's unwillingness to criticize any restriction that sports the "progressive" veneer of preventing racial or sexual "harassment"—even when the codes themselves go far beyond the traditional boundaries of academic and constitutional freedom. Fortunately, some see these codes for what they are and recognize that there is nothing progressive about censorship. 15

It should be obvious that allowing colleges to promulgate broad and amorphous rules that can punish speech, regardless of the intention, will result in self-censoring and administrative abuses. Consider the case of Mercedes Lynn de Uriarte, a professor at the University of Texas at Austin. In 1999, after filing an employment grievance, she received notice that the campus's office of equal employment opportunity had chosen to investigate her for "ethnic harassment" of another professor in her department. Both de Uriarte and the accusing professor were Mexican-American. The facts suggest that the ethnic-harassment accusation was little more than an excuse for the university to retaliate against de Uriarte for filing the grievance. After nine months of pressing de Uriarte to answer personal questions about her beliefs and why she disliked the other professor, the EEO office concluded that there was no evidence of "ethnic harassment" but scolded de Uriarte for "harboring personal animosity" toward the other professor and for not being sufficiently cooperative with the investigating dean. 16

In 2001 at Tufts University, a female undergraduate filed sexual-harassment charges against a student publication, citing a sexual-harassment code and claiming a satirical cartoon and text made her a "sex object." A vocal member of the Student Labor Action Movement, she was offended when the paper mocked "oh-so-tight" slam tank tops (amid other jokes about Madonna and President Bush). Hearings were initiated. FIRE successfully persuaded the hearing panel to reject the attempted censorship. 17

Those are just two examples among dozens that FIRE has seen recently where speech codes are used against students or faculty members. They illustrate not only that these codes are enforced, but that they are enforced against speech that would be clearly protected in the larger society. 18

Moreover, virtually none of the cases that FIRE has dealt with have followed the paradigm that "hate-speech codes" were supposedly crafted to combat: the intentional hurling of an epithet at a member of a racial or sexual minority. Overwhelmingly, speech codes are used against much milder expression, or even against expression of a particular unpopular or officially disfavored viewpoint. 19

The situation of Steve Hinkle, a student at California Polytechnic State University, is another case in point. In the fall of 2002, he posted fliers for a speech by C. Mason Weaver, the author of *It's OK to Leave the Plantation.* In his book, Weaver, an African-American writer, argues that government assistance programs place many black people in a cycle of poverty and dependence similar to slavery. The flier included the place and time of the speech, the name of the book, and the author's picture. When Hinkle tried to post a flier in one public area, several students approached him and demanded that he not post the "offensive" flier. One student actually called the campus police, whose reports note that the students complained of a "suspicious white male passing out literature of an offensive racial nature." Hinkle was subjected to administrative hearings over the next half year and was found guilty of "disruption" for trying to post the flier. 20

Unless one considers posting a flier with factually accurate information a "hate crime," it is clear such speech codes are used to punish speech that administrators or students simply dislike. That should not come as a surprise to any student of history. When broad powers and unchecked authority are granted to officials—even for what are claimed to be the noblest of goals—those powers will be abused. Indeed, the Supreme Court has ruled unequivocally that "hate-speech laws," in contrast to "hate-crimes laws," are unconstitutional. Yet most of the speech prosecuted on college campuses does not even rise to the level of hate speech. 21

Some argue that speech codes communicate to students the kind of society to which we all *should* aspire. That is perhaps the most pernicious of all justifications, for it makes unexamined assumptions about the power of administrators to reach intrusively into the hearts and consciences of students. There is nothing ideal about a campus where protests and leaflets are quarantined to tiny, remote "speech zones," or where being inoffensive is a higher value than intellectual engagement. 22

Yet even if one agrees with such "aspirations," it is antithetical to a liberal-arts college to coerce others into sharing them. The threat of sanctions crosses the clear line between *encouraging* such aspirations and *coercing* fealty to them, whether genuine or affected. An administrator's employing the suasion of the bully pulpit differs crucially from using authority to bully disfavored opinions into submission. 23

Some people contend that the codes are infrequently enforced. The facts demonstrate otherwise, but even if a campus never enforced its speech code, the code would remain a palpable form of coercion. As long as the policy exists, the *threat* of enforcement remains real and will inevitably influence some people's speech. In First Amendment law, that is known as a "chilling effect":[2] Merely by disseminating the codes in student handbooks, administrators can prevent much of the speech they disfavor. Students, seeing what is banned—or even guessing at what might be banned as they struggle with the breadth or vagueness of the definitions—will play it safe and avoid engaging in speech that, even though constitutionally protected, may offend a student or a disciplinary board. 24

In the long run, speech codes—actively enforced or not—send the message that it is OK to ban controversial or arguably ugly expressions that some do not wish to hear. Students will not forget that lesson once they get their diplomas. A whole generation of American students is learning that its members should hide their deeply held unpopular beliefs, while other students realize that they have the power, even the right, to censor opinions they dislike. 25

Take the case at Ithaca College last spring, when the College Republicans brought to campus

[2]A "chilling effect" occurs when regulations or a particular atmosphere discourages free speech.

Bay Buchanan, the sister of Patrick Buchanan, for a speech entitled "The Failures of Feminism." Instead of protesting the speech or debating Buchanan's points, several students demanded that the campus police stop the event and declare it a "bias-related incident"—a punishable offense. The "Bias-Related Incidents Committee" ultimately declared the speech protected but then announced that it would explore developing policies that could prohibit similar future speeches. Outrageous though it seems, the students' reaction is understandable. Ithaca College teaches that it is okay to ban "biased" speech. The "Bias-Related Incidents Committee" shunned free speech as a sacred value and instead sought ways to punish disagreeable viewpoints in the future. 26

FIRE generally eschews litigation in favor of reasoning with campus administrators in detailed philosophical, academic, and moral arguments made in memorandums and letters. However, speech codes have proved remarkably impervious to reasoned arguments, for while FIRE often can snatch individual students from the jaws of speech prosecutions, administrators rarely abandon the codes themselves. (A happy exception was when in 1999 the Faculty Senate of the University of Wisconsin at Madison voted to repeal the long-standing code that restricted faculty speech.) FIRE thus initiated its litigation campaign. 27

Shippensburg is the beginning. In cooperation with FIRE's Legal Network, attorney Carol Sobel in May challenged a speech code at Citrus College, in California, where students were allocated three remote areas—less than 1 percent of the campus—for protest activities. Even if they were to protest within the ironically named "free speech area," students had to get permission in advance, alert campus security of the intended message, and provide any printed materials that they wished to distribute, in addition to a host of other restrictions. Further, this free-speech area was open only from "8 A.M. through 6 P.M. Monday through Friday." Citrus's student conduct code banned "lewd, indecent, obscene or offensive conduct [and] expression," and included a number of other highly restrictive provisions. Just two weeks after the lawsuit was filed, the administration yielded and rescinded all of the provisions listed above. It is unfortunate that it took a lawsuit to demonstrate that restrictions on words have no place on the modern liberal-arts campus. 28

Colleges must recognize that growth, progress, and innovation require the free and occasionally outrageous exchange of views. Without speech codes, students are more likely to interact honestly. Having one's beliefs challenged is not a regrettable side effect of openness and intellectual diversity, but an essential part of the educational process. And, in fact, liberty is more than simply a prerequisite for progress; it is, at the deepest level, a fundamental and indispensable way of being human. 29

Considering Ideas

1. What is the thesis of the essay? Where is that thesis best expressed?
2. For what purpose did Silverglate and Lukianoff write "Speech Codes: Alive and Well at Colleges"?
3. Do you think Neil L. Rudenstine was lying when he said that Harvard did not have any speech codes? Explain.
4. Many people would be surprised to learn that colleges have speech codes. Why?
5. What are speech zones? How do speech zones affect free speech on campuses?
6. Why do you think colleges adopt speech codes?

Considering Technique

1. *Combining patterns:* The examples in paragraphs 2–5, 10, 11, and 14 help the authors achieve their purpose for writing in the same way. What is it? How do the examples in paragraphs 16, 17, 20, and 26 help the authors achieve their purpose for writing?
2. Silverglate and Lukianoff use quite a few examples in their essay. Does their intended audience require this many examples? Why or why not?
3. *Combining patterns:* How does the cause-and-effect analysis in paragraphs 22–26 help the authors achieve their purpose for writing?
4. *Combining patterns:* Why do the authors include definition in paragraphs 8–10 and 24?
5. Is the conclusion a strong, effective one? Why or why not?

For Group Discussion or Journal Writing

Speech codes are a form of political correctness. Write a definition of political correctness, and note its positive and negative aspects.

Sarcasm

STYLE NOTE

Sarcasm is saying something that seems positive or neutral on the surface, but that is really intended to be critical. Dawn Turner Trice uses sarcasm in the last paragraph of "Shoddy Service Sows the Seeds of Discontent." After stating that as paying customers we should be treated with respect, Trice writes: "This, of course, means that if we're getting something for free, it's OK to treat us with the utmost disdain."

Trice does not really believe that people who get something for free should be treated with disdain. Instead, she is criticizing anyone who treats a customer—paying or not—with disdain.

EXEMPLIFICATION IN AN IMAGE

The print on page 236, titled "Golden Rule," was painted by beloved American painter Norman Rockwell (1894–1978).

Considering the Image

1. What do the people in the image exemplify?
2. What is the relationship between the people in the print and the Golden Rule written on the print? (The Golden Rule, an ethical principle in most religions, states, "Do unto others as you would have them do unto you.")

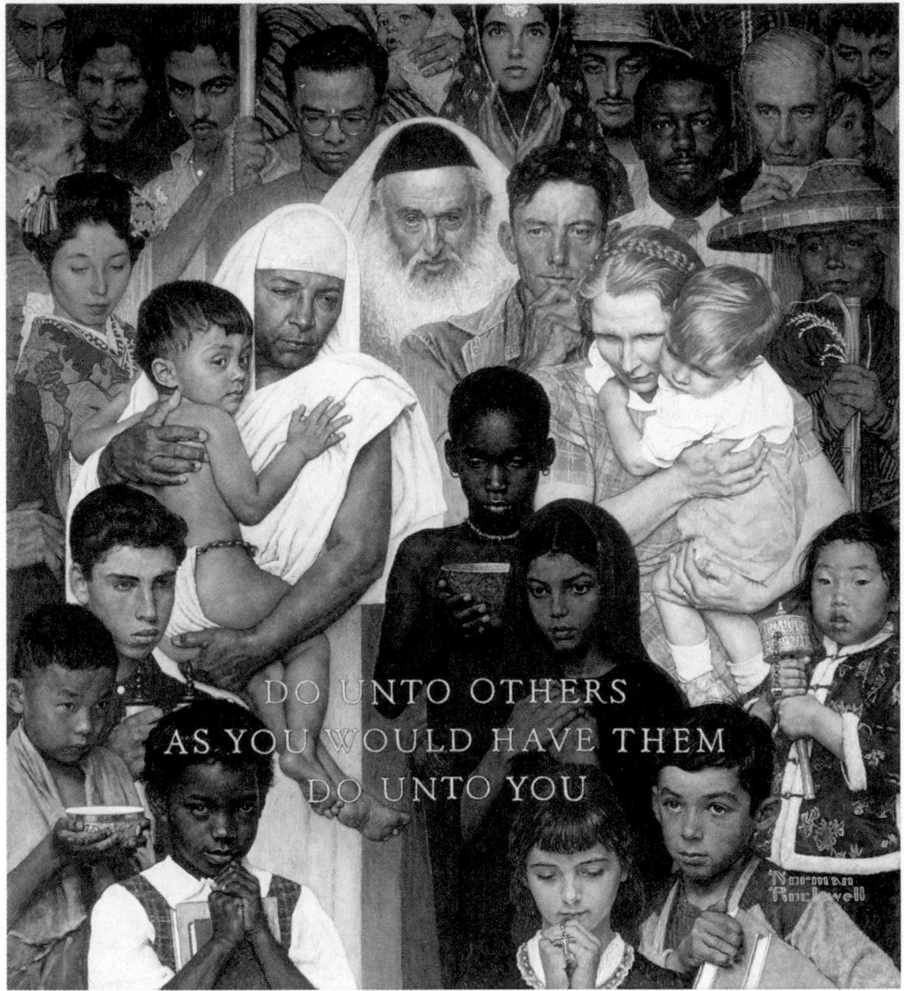

3. Rockwell organizes his examples—that is, he arranges the people—with the younger people in the foreground and the older people behind. Why do you think he uses that organization? Is there more to it than the need to put shorter people in the front?
4. Why are the people in the print not smiling?

SUGGESTIONS FOR WRITING

Writing Exemplification

1. Write an essay to illustrate that the Web improves (or hinders) human interaction.
2. Write an essay to illustrate that your campus or local newspaper is (or is not) doing a good job of covering important stories.

3. Write an essay to illustrate that appearances can be deceiving.
4. Write an essay illustrating the fact that something mostly positive, such as exercise or ambition, has some disadvantages.
5. Write an essay to illustrate one of the following:
   a. Things do not always go as planned.
   b. Sports are too violent.
   c. Businesses often take advantage of consumers.
   d. Advertising leads people to view luxuries as necessities.
6. Select a modern device, such as computer, television, PDA, answering machine, cell phone, or pager, and write an essay illustrating the problems the device can cause.
7. Illustrate how some condition in your life affected you dramatically. You might write about being an only child (oldest child, middle child, etc.), about being the child of divorced parents, about being a member of a minority group, about being tall or short for your age, about being athletic (or musically inclined or artistic), about being the class clown, and so on.

Reading Then Writing Exemplification

1. In "Shoddy Service Sows the Seeds of Discontent," Dawn Turner Trice gives examples of poor treatment of paying customers. Turn the tables by using exemplification to illustrate times when customers treated employees badly. Your examples can come from your own observation, from your own experience if you had or have a job that requires you to deal with the public, or from interviews with people who serve the public.
2. In "Fox's Flapdoodle," Michael Shermer debunks the notion held by perhaps 20 percent of Americans that we never landed on the moon. Select some other commonly held belief, and use examples to debunk it. You might consider a belief such as that college is easy, that the teen years are the best years of a person's life, that college athletes get a free ride in the classroom, or that recycling doesn't do much to help our environment.
3. In "Speech Codes: Alive and Well at Colleges," Harvey A. Silverglate and Greg Lukianoff argue that speech codes are a form of censorship and that they have a chilling effect on free speech at many colleges. Cite examples to illustrate why you do or do not feel that you can speak and write freely on your campus.

Exemplification beyond the Writing Classroom

Select a principle that you have learned in another class you are taking or have taken in the past, and write an essay that uses examples to illustrate that principle. For example, if you learned in a psychology class that people repeat behavior that is rewarded, give examples of times people have repeated rewarded behavior. You might tell about the class clown in your high school who would continue to disrupt classes because other students rewarded him with laughter. Similarly, if you learned in a business class that employees tie their productivity to the productivity of others in similar positions, you would provide examples to illustrate that principle.

Responding to Theme

1. In "Fox's Flapdoodle," Michael Shermer says that the Fox broadcast "Conspiracy Theory: Did We Land on the Moon?" was irrational. To what extent is television programming irrational, and how much harm does that programming cause?
2. Why do you think the employees in "Shoddy Service Sows the Seeds of Discontent" behaved the way they did? Is their behavior typical of the way people treat each other? Explain.
3. In "Speech Codes: Alive and Well at Colleges," Harvey A. Silverglate and Greg Lukianoff explain that speech codes rooted in misguided political correctness have a detrimental effect because they limit free speech. Think about whether you agree, and then write guidelines for your campus newspaper that cover one or more of the following: hate speech, profanity, politically correct speech, or any other speech you think needs to be addressed. Explain why your guidelines are appropriate for the publication.
4. The message of Norman Rockwell's painting is "Do unto others as you would have them do unto you." This saying, an ethical principle in many religions, is the "Golden Rule." Use examples to show that people either do or do not live according to the Golden Rule.
5. *Connecting the readings:* Using the information in "Fox's Flapdoodle" and "Speech Codes: Alive and Well at Colleges," along with your own experience and observation, discuss the price of free speech.

www.mhhe.com/tsw
For further help with writing exemplification, go to Catalyst 2.0 > Writing > Writing Tutors > Exemplification

Writing Exemplification

The following strategies are not meant to replace your own successful procedures. They are here to try as you develop your own effective writing process.

Think like a Writer: Generating Ideas, Considering Audience and Purpose, and Ordering Ideas

- For a generalization/topic you can support with examples, try these strategies:
  - Fill in the blanks in this sentence, altering words as you need to: ______ ______ is the most ______ I know. For example, one generalization might be, "Taking a three-year-old on a car trip is the trickiest thing I know." Another might be, "Finding a reliable Internet service provider is the biggest hassle I know."

  - Take a common saying and show that it is *not* true. For example, provide examples to show that honesty is *not* always the best policy or that patience is *not* a virtue.
- Determine your purpose by asking these questions:
  - Do I want to describe my reaction to or feelings about my topic?
  - Do I want to help my reader understand why I respond to my topic as I do?
  - Do I want to clarify the nature of my topic?
  - Do I want to convince my reader of something?
- Use these questions to help you assess your audience:
  - Will my reader respond best to examples from any particular sources?
  - Will my reader react well to hypothetical examples?
- To generate possible examples, answer these questions:
  - What have I done that illustrates my generalization?
  - What have I observed that illustrates my generalization?
  - What have I learned in school that illustrates my generalization?
  - What have I read, seen on television, or heard on the radio that illustrates my generalization?
  - What have others experienced that illustrates my generalization?
  - What can I narrate or describe to illustrate my generalization?
  - What can I research to illustrate my generalization?
- To develop an informal outline, list your examples and number them in the order they are to appear in your draft.

Think like a Writer: Drafting

- Using your informal outline as a guide, write your draft. If you have trouble, turn your informal outline into a more detailed outline and try again.
- Consider using topic sentences so that your reader will understand how the example or examples in the paragraph illustrate the thesis generalization.

Think like a Critic; Work like an Editor: Revising

- Be sure your examples are adequately detailed.
- Consider how your audience is likely to react to each example and how each will serve your writing purpose.
- Consider whether each example is representative and whether hypothetical examples are plausible.
- Be sure descriptive examples include concrete sensory detail and specific words, as explained in Chapter 6. Be sure narrative examples answer the appropriate journalist's questions and include appropriate dialogue, as explained in Chapter 7.
- To obtain reader response for revision, see page 105. Also, ask your reader to do the following:
  - Place a checkmark where more detail is needed.
  - Place a question mark where something is unclear.
  - Place an exclamation point next to any particularly strong examples.

Think like a Critic; Work like an Editor: Correcting Errors

- If you introduce examples with transitions such as *for example* or *for instance,* use commas to set off these transitional phrases.
- If you introduce examples with *including* or *such as,* use a comma before—not after—these words:

Yes: The bakery had many breakfast pastries, including scones, muffins, and brioche.

Yes: The bakery had many breakfast pastries, such as scones, muffins, and brioche.

No: The bakery had many breakfast pastries, including, scones, muffins, and brioche.

No: The bakery had many breakfast pastries, such as, scones, muffins, and brioche.

No: The bakery had many breakfast pastries including, scones, muffins, and brioche.

No: The bakery had many breakfast pastries such as, scones, muffins, and brioche.

Remember

Avoid using too few examples. The cumulative impact of your examples must provide convincing support of your thesis. Thus, to support the thesis that parking is a problem on your campus, you must do more than give two examples of times you had difficulty parking—even if those examples are highly detailed.

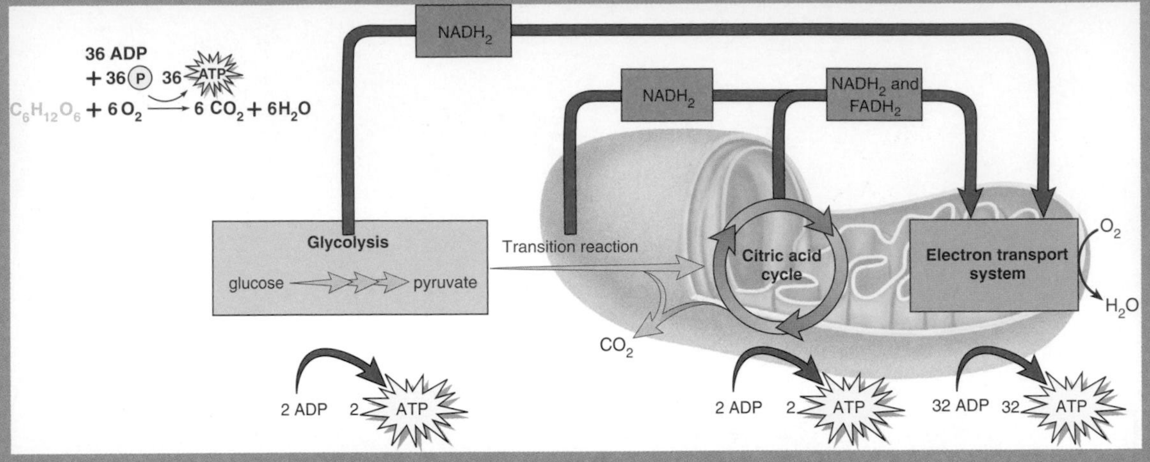

LOOKING AHEAD

People want to understand how things work, how things are made, and how things are done—that is, we want to understand the *processes* that are part of our lives. In fact, some of our most important scientific discoveries and some of our most useful inventions are the result of people analyzing processes to learn more about them. Our curiosity about processes even explains why one of the most popular destinations on the Web is howstuffworks.com. Because understanding and examining processes is important, in your classes, you will study processes such as cell division, electrical circuit completion, photosynthesis, inflation, and checks and balances—processes often depicted in diagrams like this one showing cellular respiration, from a biology textbook. In this chapter, you will learn about writing process analysis essays. Before doing so, consider the processes you are curious about, and list 10 that you would like to learn more about.

Process Analysis

When is a recipe more than a recipe? When it includes commentary along with the steps the cook should follow. Here, for example, is the first part of a chocolate chip cookie recipe that "will serve as sturdy companion through disappointment, great and small." The recipe with its commentary appeared in the *Chicago Tribune Magazine.*

> Melt 1 cup of butter. Other recipes expect you to drum your nails on the countertop while butter attains room temperature. Don't bother. Melting butter over low heat is blasphemous, but better. Remove from heat. Add 1½ cups brown sugar. Standard practice calls for a mix of white and brown. Standard practice yields unyielding cookies. Unadulterated brown sugar makes cookies more pliant and empathetic.
>
> Leah Eskin, "Round Comfort" (sidebar from "The Tao of Dough"), *Chicago Tribune Magazine,* Oct. 21, 2001, p. 23.

A recipe, like any writing that explains how something is made or done, is a **process analysis.** A process analysis can use straightforward "this is how you do it" writing, or it can include the writer's evaluation of the process, as the above recipe does.

WHY IS PROCESS ANALYSIS IMPORTANT?

There are two kinds of process analyses, and both are important. A **directional process analysis** gives the steps in a process that the reader can perform if he or she wants to. The directions that explain how to assemble the toy you bought your nephew are a directional process analysis. The instructions in your biology lab manual explaining how to prepare a slide are also a directional process analysis—as are the directions for programming your cell phone, the magazine article explaining how to land the perfect job, and instructions for building a personal web page.

An **informational process analysis** explains how something is made or done, but the reader is not likely to perform the process. An explanation of how brain surgery is performed is an informational process analysis because the reader is not likely to perform brain surgery. Similarly, explanations of how the body converts carbohydrates to energy, how plants manufacture chlorophyll, and how lightning occurs are all informational process analyses. Informational process analyses are important because they add to our knowledge, satisfy our curiosity, and help us appreciate complex or interesting processes.

Directional and informational process analyses can serve many purposes, as the following chart points out.

Purposes for Process Analysis

Purpose	**Sample Process Analysis**
To entertain	A humorous explanation of how to make a bad impression on a first date
To share feelings and experiences	An explanation of what the writer did to overcome an eating disorder
To inform (to help the reader learn how to do something)	An explanation of how to hang wallpaper so the reader does not have to pay someone to do it
To inform (by increasing the reader's knowledge)	An explanation of how computers work
To persuade (to convince the reader that a particular way to do something is superior to another way)	An explanation of how debit cards work (to show that using a debit card is better than using cash or credit cards)

OCCASIONS FOR WRITING

Process Analysis across the Disciplines and Beyond

Process Analysis in the Classroom

Every subject involves the study of how things occur, how they are made, or how they are done, so process analysis is a common component of writing across the disciplines. In science lab reports, you often explain the process to complete an experiment. In a paper for a political science class, you might explain how a bill moves through Congress. In a homework assignment for an electrical trades class, you might explain how to read a blueprint. In a homework assignment for a business class, you might explain how to develop a marketing report. *Think about your own courses. What processes are you likely to learn about? Look through the textbooks for those classes, and notice the processes that are explained in them. What are they? Are they directional or informational?*

Process Analysis in Daily Life

Process analysis will be part of the writing you do in your personal life. When you write directions to your house, you are writing process analysis, as you are when you share your homemade pizza recipe with a friend. If you e-mail instructions to a classmate for installing and updating antivirus software, you are also writing process analysis. *Tell about a situation in which you used process analysis. What were the circumstances? Which of the purposes for writing did your process analysis fulfill?*

Process Analysis on the Job

You are likely to use process analysis in the workplace. Employees often write job descriptions that explain how they perform aspects of their jobs. Human resources managers write procedures for taking vacations and sick leave. Safety officers write explanations of what to do in the event of various emergencies. *How might a teacher use process analysis? A quality control manager? A nurse or physician's assistant? A religious cleric? Think of two careers not already mentioned here, and note how writing process analysis might be involved.*

COMBINING PROCESS ANALYSIS WITH OTHER PATTERNS

Whenever you need to explain how something is made or done, you will use process analysis, regardless of the dominant pattern of development. For example, if you are writing a definition of *electoral college*, part of your essay will explain how the electoral college works to elect a president. If you are explaining the causes and effects of anorexia nervosa, you may also explain by what process the condition can lead to death. If you are contrasting two exercise programs, you might explain how each one works.

Even when process analysis is your dominant pattern, you are likely to use other methods of development. For example, to explain how to choose the best running shoes, you might give examples of the best ones to buy. To explain the process that causes leaves to change color in autumn, you might include a description of the various colors of the leaves.

SELECTING DETAIL

Most of the detail in a process analysis will be the steps in the process, but you do not merely write out the steps in list fashion. Instead, follow these guidelines.

Include All the Important Steps

Omitting a step is a common pitfall when you are writing about a process with which you are so familiar that you take steps for granted. If you omit steps in a directional process analysis, your reader may not be able to perform the process properly. Suppose you are writing a directional process analysis to explain how to begin a weight-lifting program. Suppose, too, that you have been lifting weights yourself for many years. You may forget all about the step of resting between exercises because for you that step is so habitual that you do it without thinking. Omit the step, and your reader could be injured. If you omit steps in an informational process analysis, your reader may fail to understand the process sufficiently. If, for instance, you are explaining how bees find food, you might indicate that scouts go out in search of food and then alert other bees to what they find. However, if you do not indicate how the scouts communicate the location of the food, your explanation of the process is incomplete.

Explain How a Step Is Performed

To ensure that your reader performs a process successfully, you may need to explain how to perform one or more steps. Think again about an explanation of how to begin a weight-lifting program. If you mention the need to rest between exercises, you should also mention how long the rest period should be. Otherwise, your reader may rest too long, not work the muscle enough, or risk injury.

In an informational process analysis, you may need to explain how a step is performed to be sure your reader understands the process. Suppose you are explaining how bees locate food, and you indicate that the insects use a dance to guide other bees to the food source. For your reader to understand the process, you must explain how that dance works. So you explain that if the food is closer than 10 yards, the bee will dance quickly in a circle. As the distance approaches 100 yards, the dance becomes sickle-shaped. Farther than 100 yards, the dance slows and becomes a figure eight.

Explain the Significance of a Step or Why It Is Performed

Explain why a step in a directional process analysis is performed if you think your reader will fail to appreciate its importance and skip it or perform it carelessly. For example, assume you are explaining how to find a job in a period of high unemployment, and you mention the need to send a thank-you note to the interviewer after the interview. If your reader might not appreciate the importance of this step, explain that sending the note impresses the interviewer with the applicant's courtesy and follow-through.

In an informational process analysis, you need not worry about failure to perform a step, but you may want to ensure that your reader appreciates the significance of a step. Think again about the explanation of how bees locate food. If you want your reader to appreciate the significance of the dance bees perform to guide other bees to food, you could say that this dance is actually a form of symbolic language.

Explain Trouble Spots and What *Not* to Do

Pointing out a possible problem can help the reader to avoid it. Think again about the explanation of how to find a job in a period of high unemployment. When you tell a job applicant to write a thank-you note after an interview, you can caution her or him to avoid a letter that looks unprofessional, because it is written on inappropriate stationery, perhaps something with a *Dilbert* cartoon or picture of kittens on it. If an aspect of an informational process analysis can be difficult or troublesome, pointing out that fact can help your reader appreciate the complexity of the process. For example, an explanation of how bees find food might note that on the first visit to the general area of a new source of food, bees may need to search for many minutes before finding the food. Then they must memorize sights and scents in order to find their way back on future trips.

If you fear your reader could take unnecessary or incorrect actions, your directional process analysis can point out something that should *not* be done. For example, you may want to caution your reader *not* to smile too much during a job interview because too much smiling can make an applicant seem frivolous or insincere.

Mention Necessary Items and Define Unfamiliar Terms

If your reader needs certain materials to perform the process, mention items that are needed early in your directional process analysis, so your reader can assemble them. Because it is convenient to have the items mentioned early on, most recipes begin with a list of the ingredients.

If you use technical terms or other unfamiliar vocabulary, provide definitions. For example, if you are explaining how to take blood pressure, you will need to define *systolic pressure* and *diastolic pressure.*

Include Examples and Description

To clarify all or part of a process, you can include examples and description. For instance, if you are explaining how a person should behave in a job interview, you might mention the advisability of asking questions about the nature of the job. To clarify this point, provide examples of appropriate questions, such as "Will I have an opportunity to learn new skills?" and "Do you encourage additional education?" If you are explaining how animals communicate in a paper for a linguistics class, you can illustrate the processes you describe with the songs of the European robin, the facial expressions of wolves, and the sounds and gestures of monkeys.

Use Visuals

A graph, picture, chart, or drawing can help your reader understand all or part of a process, particularly when the process is complex or your explanation is long. The visual cannot take the place of a written explanation, but it can provide a graphic summary. You may have noticed that textbooks often use visuals with process analyses to help students understand and remember explanations. This book includes essay organization charts (see page 251, for example) to help you visualize the structure of essays. Or consider this excerpt from a public speaking textbook. As part of the explanation of how to prepare visual aids for a speech, the author cautions to limit the number of fonts, colors, and graphics because too many can distract the audience. To prove and illustrate the point, the author includes this visual:

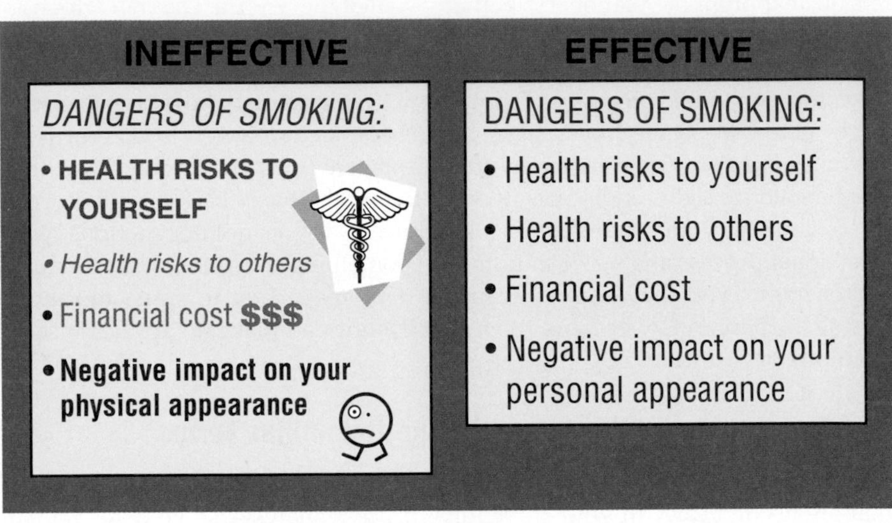

Consider Your Purpose and Audience

Your audience and purpose will determine whether you explain how to perform a step, indicate the significance of a step, note a trouble spot, and so on. Let's say you are explaining how people can protect their credit rating, and you note that people should limit the number of credit cards they use. If your audience is college students, you can point out this trouble spot: Credit card companies set up tables on college campuses and actively recruit students to sign up for their cards, so students must resist these efforts. For an audience that is not attending college, you would not point out this trouble spot.

Now let's say you are explaining how computer viruses are spread, and your purpose is to help the reader avoid contracting a virus. After explaining that e-mail attachments can spread viruses, you might warn the reader not to open e-mail attachments without scanning them for viruses. However, if your purpose is merely to inform the reader of the way viruses spread, you need not include this statement of what not to do; you need only state that viruses can be spread when infected e-mail attachments are opened.

BEING A RESPONSIBLE WRITER

The fact that it is *possible* to explain a process does not necessarily mean it is *wise* to explain that process. Our constitutional guarantee of free speech allows books and websites to explain how to do things that can hurt people, including make bombs, hack into computers, and commit hate crimes. However, you should never write a process analysis that can cause harm.

USING SOURCES FOR A PURPOSE

The paragraph below is a body paragraph for an essay about how students can interact effectively with their instructors. The essay explains that if students approach and interact with instructors in specific ways, they can forge enriching, helpful relationships with them. The paragraph, which warns students to make their requests in an appropriate manner, includes a paraphrase of paragraph 12 of "How to E-Mail a Professor" on page 258. (For more information on writing paraphrases, see Chapter 17.)

THESIS IDEA: To have the best possible college experience, students must know how to approach and interact with their instructors.

WRITING PURPOSE AND AUDIENCE: To inform first-year students, who may be intimidated by professors, about how to approach and interact with their instructors

[1]Although instructors are happy to help students in many ways, you should seek that help in an appropriate manner. [2]If you are working on a paper at 9:00 at night and suddenly wonder whether you are on the right track, do not e-mail the draft to your instructor and ask that he or she review it for you and send it back asap. [3]Doing so, as one experienced instructor admonishes, is rude (Leddy 259), and it assumes that professors have nothing better to do than sit around and wait for students to send them work. [4]There is, however, an appropriate way to get the help you seek. [5]As Leddy says, e-mailing an unsolicited paper is "bad form," but you can see your instructor during scheduled office hours or set up an appointment (259). [6]In short, be considerate about when and how you approach your instructors.

The paraphrase in sentence 3 helps support the idea that students should not e-mail unsolicited papers. The paraphrase in sentence 5 explains what students *should* do.

Avoiding Plagiarism

The paragraph illustrates some points about using source material and avoiding plagiarism.

- **Introduce your source material.** Sentences 3 and 5 illustrate that introductions are important because they help readers separate your own ideas from those of others. (The introductions help readers see that part of sentence 3 and all of sentence 5 include source material, but sentence 4 includes the writer's own idea.) Note that you need not always introduce with the author's name or the title of the source you are using. Sentence 3 gives the author's credentials (an experienced instructor) instead. Sometimes, giving the credentials adds extra authority or credibility to the source material.
- **Place key words and key phrases in quotation marks.** Paraphrase using your own wording and style, but as sentence 5 shows, you can include some of the source's exact words if you place them in quotation marks.

Myths about Sources

MYTH: The parenthetical citation must always come at the end of the sentence.

FACT: Sentence 3 shows that when the source material appears in the middle of a sentence, the parenthetical citation is also placed in the middle so that it is at the end of the paraphrase, quotation, or summary.

In addition, the Internet makes it easy to engage in some processes that are either forms of plagiarism or illegal. You should neither engage in nor write about how to engage in the downloading and pirating of music or videos for which you should pay. You should not download and submit as your own papers or source material written by others, nor should you write about how to do so. Always ask yourself these questions:

- Is there anything about my process analysis that could create problems for anyone?
- Is there anything about my process analysis that is illegal or a form of plagiarism?

ORGANIZING A PROCESS ANALYSIS

The introduction of your process analysis can include a thesis that mentions the process you will explain. It can also note the importance of understanding the process.

Thesis mentioning the process

`There is only one efficient way to clean a basement.`

Thesis mentioning the process and why it is important

`Car owners can save a great deal of money if they learn to change their own points and plugs.`

To create interest, your introduction can explain why understanding the process is important (if your thesis does not do this). You can also tell why you are qualified to explain the process, arouse the reader's curiosity about how the process is performed, or combine approaches.

Your conclusion can take any of the approaches given for the introduction. However, a separate conclusion may be unnecessary if the last step in the process provides sufficient closure.

Arrange your details in chronological order when your reader needs the steps presented in the order they are performed. Other times, chronological order is not necessary. For example, if you are explaining how to dress for success, the order of steps may not be significant.

If you are explaining what should *not* be done, do so near the step the caution is related to. For example, a cake recipe would explain not to overbake at the point baking time is mentioned. If your process analysis includes several statements of what not to do, you can group all the cautions together in their own paragraph.

If you define a term, do so the first time the term is used. If you explain a troublesome aspect of the process, do so just after presenting the step under consideration. If you explain why a step is performed, do so just before or after your explanation of the step. If necessary materials are listed, group this information together in an early paragraph, perhaps even in the introduction.

EXERCISE Writing Process Analysis

1. Explain how you might use process analysis as part of each of the following essays:
   a. A definition of a *good driver*
   b. The causes and effects of premature birth
   c. A classification of the ways advertisements influence consumers

Visualizing a Process Analysis Essay

The chart that follows can help you visualize one structure for a process analysis. Like all good models, this one can be altered as needed.

Introduction

- Creates interest, perhaps by noting the importance of the process, telling why you are qualified to explain the process, or arousing the reader's curiosity about the process
- States the thesis, which gives the process you will explain and which may note the importance of the process

First Body Paragraph

- Gives the first step in the process
- May explain how or why the step is performed
- May explain the significance of the step
- May explain what not to do or a trouble spot
- May explain items needed and unfamiliar terms
- May include examples and description
- May arrange details chronologically

Next Body Paragraphs

- Give the remaining steps in the process
- May explain how or why the step is performed
- May explain the significance of the step
- May explain what not to do or a trouble spot
- May explain items needed and unfamiliar terms
- May include examples and description
- May arrange details chronologically

Conclusion

- Creates closure
- Leaves the reader with a strong final impression

2. Think of two processes you perform well (shop for bargains, make friends, plan a party, buy used cars, etc.). List the steps in each process (in the order they are performed, if chronological order is important).
3. Assume you will write a process analysis for each of the processes you identified for number 2, and identify a purpose and audience for each.
4. For each process, answer the following questions, keeping your audience and purpose in mind. Be prepared to explain your answers.
   a. Is it necessary to explain *how* any steps are performed?
   b. Is it necessary to explain *why* any steps are performed?
   c. Will the reader understand better if I explain something that should *not* be done?
   d. Are there troublesome aspects that should be explained?
   e. Are any materials needed?
   f. Should any terms be defined?
   g. Is it possible to describe anything?
   h. Is it possible to use examples? ■

LEARNING FROM OTHER WRITERS: Student Essays

The first student essay, "A Visit to Candyland," is a directional process analysis that appears with marginal notes pointing out features explained in this chapter. The author makes her feelings apparent, so you can easily tell how much she enjoys completing the process. Look for the first clue to how the author feels about the process.

The second essay, "Going Green on Campus," is also a directional process analysis, but it does not give every step in the process because doing so is not possible. As you read, consider how many of the steps you already implement and how many you will implement in the future.

A Visit to Candyland

Debi McKinney

Paragraph 1
The introduction provides background information. The thesis is not stated, but the paragraph suggests a focus on making gingerbread houses.

1 You may have been to the supermarket around Christmastime and seen a gingerbread house kit. It probably involved graham-cracker slabs meant to be stuck together with thick white frosting and decorated with gumdrops. In my family, making gingerbread houses is a long-standing tradition, and one that involves far more than simply slapping some cookies and frosting together. Each year, in early December, we decide on a theme and go on to create an elaborate gingerbread structure that reflects the season and our interests. Our

cardinal rule in gingerbread house making often comes as a surprise to the friends who visit to marvel at our creations: absolutely everything in the gingerbread house must be edible, and not only edible, but tasty.

We begin by coming up with a concept. One year, it was a crèche scene with Mary, Joseph, the baby Jesus, and various animals, shepherds, and angels. Another year, it was a covered bridge under snow, with a horse-drawn carriage. Once we've decided on a theme, we might visit the library or go on the Internet to find visual ideas we can incorporate into our design. Then, after we've done some preliminary sketches, we make a pattern, measuring carefully with a ruler to make sure each piece will fit with the others. These pattern pieces are drawn onto thin paper and then precisely cut out with sharp scissors. We've found it helps to note on each pattern piece how many need to be made—a roof, for example, is usually made of two equal rectangles, and only one pattern piece is needed. 2

Paragraph 2
The paragraph gives the first two steps in the process. The details include examples of the first step and information on how the second step is performed.

The next step is to make the gingerbread. We use an old family recipe that produces a sturdy but extremely tasty gingerbread cookie, flavored with molasses, cinnamon, ground cloves, and lots of ginger. In order to make a really tough cookie, we incorporate many cups of flour into the batter. Once all the flour has been added, the dough is so dense it's almost impossible to stir, so we hand it off to my father, whose arms are the strongest. After the dough is finished, it has to sit in the refrigerator for a time period ranging from several hours to a week. This cooling period makes the dough easier to handle and the finished cookie even tougher. 3

Paragraph 3
The first sentence is the topic sentence. It gives the next step in the process. Some details explain why part of the step is performed.

Once the dough is ready to bake, it's time to make the pieces of the house. We do this by rolling out the dough onto sheets of tinfoil. We try to avoid handling the dough too much—if it gets warm before it goes into the oven, it loses some of its resilience. The dough is rolled until it's a little less than a quarter of an inch thick. Then we place the pattern pieces onto the rolled dough. Using a small knife, we cut around the pattern piece, discarding the excess dough. After we've cut out the windows on the wall pieces, we fill the holes with broken bits of hard candy. In the oven, these candy pieces melt and harden, forming what 4

Paragraph 4
The topic sentence (the first sentence) gives the next step in the process. Notice the transitions "once the dough is ready to bake," "then," and "once that's done."

looks like stained glass. Once that's done, we slide the tinfoil with the cookie pieces on it onto a cookie sheet and put them into the oven.

Paragraph 5
The topic sentence (the first sentence) gives the next step and includes a transition.

Seven to ten minutes later, the cookies are done, and we slide them onto 5
wire racks to cool. After they've cooled, we peel off the tinfoil backing and admire the colored light through the little stained-glass windows. Now we're ready for the hardest part of the whole process: putting the house together. Frosting is simply not tough enough for the elaborate structures we make, so instead we use melted sugar. We sprinkle regular granulated sugar into a wide, flat pan and heat it over a medium-high flame. In a few minutes it forms a glossy, dark-brown liquid. The ends of the gingerbread pieces that are to be stuck together have to be dipped very quickly into the melted sugar and then speedily and precisely joined to their intended mates. If this process is done too quickly, there may not be enough sugar to make the pieces stick, or we may stick them on at the wrong angle. If it's done too slowly, the sugar can harden, its sticking powers completely lost. When my brothers and I were little, we were not allowed to participate in the melted-sugar operation, but now we've developed the necessary manual dexterity and nerves of steel.

Paragraph 6
The topic sentence (the first sentence) gives the next step and includes a transition. Are you noticing the chronological order?

Now the house is assembled and ready for everyone's favorite stage: 6
decoration. We make frosting out of butter, confectioner's sugar, and food coloring, and add a base coat to the parts of the house that seem to need it, like the roof. We generally leave the sides bare, because the dark brown gingerbread is such a pretty color, but we add details with frosting piped out of a wax-paper tube. Then we add decorations. In the past we've used raisins, cinnamon sticks, star anise, nuts, and, of course, many different kinds of candy. Necco wafers, broken in half, make particularly good shingles.

Paragraph 7
The conclusion provides closure by explaining what is done with the gingerbread house and by highlighting a family tradition.

When we're finished, we've usually consumed a substantial quantity of 7
decorations, spoonfuls of frosting, and cookie scraps. Naturally we make gingerbread men to live in the house, but their lifespans tend to be extremely short—sometimes they don't even get frosted. We're too full to do anything but sit and admire our handiwork. A few days later, however, we host our

annual holiday party, where the final part of the tradition comes into play. The youngest child at the event (apart from babies, of course) is handed an orange suspended from a red satin ribbon. This is the gingerbread wrecking ball, and it's swung at the house until total destruction has been achieved. We're always sorry to see the house ruined, but then we have the pleasure, along with our guests, of eating our annual masterpiece.

Going Green on Campus

Nina Schwartz

College campuses across the country are going green. In fact, their efforts to be eco-friendly are so pervasive that a ranking system published by the Princeton Review now lists the top American colleges and universities according to their environmental policies, procedures, and courses. However, the attention to environmentally sound practices cannot be solely an institutional responsibility. College campuses are home to millions of students who live, work, consume, and produce day after day. By taking specific steps, we students can make a significant environmental difference on campus. 1

The first and most important step for students in becoming green is recognizing the impact of our actions on the world around us and behaving accordingly. Even if we live alone in a dorm room or apartment, we must realize that our living space is a shared living space. For example, the products we use to clean our rooms affect the quality of the air and water that we share with others. Using ecologically friendly cleaning supplies rather than harsh chemicals is an acknowledgement of our personal impact on a broader space and on an interconnected quality of life. Learning about the hazards of what we throw away is another way to recognize the environmental impact of our actions and behave responsibly. For example, we should understand the harmful effects of improper battery disposal and dispose of batteries so that harmful substances 2 do not seep into the environment. A good way to do so is by setting up convenient drop-off sites for used batteries on campus and then taking the filled containers to designated disposal sites. Going green is first and foremost about learning the effects of our choices on the surrounding environment and then acting to protect that environment.

As students, we can also make small changes in our personal habits 3
that collectively will create a significant difference. Many of these changes will not disrupt our current lifestyles. For instance, reducing our daily shower time by just a couple of minutes will conserve millions of gallons of water per year. We can unplug unused appliances in order to prevent small energy leaks and turn off lights when not in use. We should also stop using regular light bulbs. Instead, we should purchase environmentally friendly compact fluorescent light (CFL) bulbs for lamps we use every day. Although more expensive than regular light bulbs, CFLs last significantly longer and use significantly less energy. We should wear gently worn clothing more than once before washing it and wait to do laundry until we have a full load in order to reduce the amount of water and energy used. Choosing the cold water setting whenever possible will also help cut energy use. When drying clothes in a common space, we should choose a machine that was recently used in order to recycle heat. We should avoid overfilling the dryer so that clothes dry more quickly, and clean the lint filter before each load for better heating efficiency. We can also recycle and reuse as much as possible and carry around a reusable water bottle that can be washed and refilled. We can also be careful to buy, take, and use only what we need. For example, rather than grabbing a handful of paper napkins from a restaurant dispenser, we should take just one or two. Finally, we should restore or donate used items rather than throw them away. With small changes in our personal habits such as these, we can have a big collective impact on the environment.

We can also take steps in our academic lives to conserve and reuse. We 4
can minimize the amount of paper and energy used to print e-mails, web pages, and computer documents. Instead of printing, we can save files to a

portable USB flash drive. Whenever possible, we should print documents double-sided and recycle waste paper. Rather than driving to campus, we should use a bicycle or walk. For longer trips, carpooling or using public transportation will reduce pollution and roadway congestion. If driving is necessary, we should consider using hourly car rental services like Zipcar. But before getting in a car or on a bus, we should determine if we really need to leave at all. Often, it is far easier and more energy and time efficient to use the Internet to pay bills, watch tutorials, or chat with librarians and tutors.

As students, we can take steps to help others become green as well. 5
Many schools offer environmentally focused workshops, events, and courses that we can participate in to reach out and help others go green. We can also organize student groups to discuss and implement green strategies on campus and to bring more attention to the need for campus-wide green efforts, including efforts to harness solar and wind energy and to institute large-scale recycling and composting programs. To get started with campus outreach, we can use online resources such as the website for the Association for the Advancement of Sustainability in Higher Education (AASHE).

For efforts to protect the environment to be successful, all of us must 6
participate. That means students cannot let campus officials and institutional policies carry the full load of eco-friendly measures. We must act as individuals to be a part of the process.

EXERCISE Considering "Going Green on Campus"

1. Which sentence states the thesis of "Going Green on Campus"?
2. In what two places does the author explain why understanding the process is important?
3. In which paragraphs does the author tell how to perform a step?
4. How does the author use examples? How do the examples help explain the process?
5. How does the author use topic sentences? Do they make the process easier to follow? Explain.
6. Do you think the author explains the process in enough detail? Explain. ■

THINK LIKE A CRITIC; WORK LIKE AN EDITOR: The Student Writer at Work

Like most student writers, the author of "A Visit to Candyland" was aware of the importance of the thesis. However, multiple attempts at a stated thesis failed to produce a version the writer was satisfied with. Here is what her early versions looked like:

Early drafts of the thesis

> To make an awe-inspiring Christmas tradition, do what my family does and create a gingerbread house every year.
>
> Creating a gingerbread house for Christmas can be the start of a wonderful tradition.
>
> Christmas should bring families together, and nothing brings my family together more than creating our annual gingerbread masterpiece.

When she repeatedly failed to draft a thesis she felt worked well with the rest of her introduction, she decided to complete her draft without a stated thesis. Afterward, she felt her thesis was strongly enough implied, so she decided to forgo a stated thesis. What do you think of this decision?

LEARNING FROM OTHER WRITERS: Professional Essays

How to E-Mail a Professor MICHAEL LEDDY

Writer and college English professor Michael Leddy gives the teacher's point of view in this discussion of the protocol students should follow when they e-mail their instructors. As you read this 2005 post from Leddy's popular blog, Orange Crate Art, *consider the e-mail you have sent your own instructors and to what extent you have or have not followed Leddy's advice.*

I've read enough e-mails to know that many college students could benefit from some guidelines for writing an e-mail to a professor. Here they are: 1

Write from your college or university e-mail account. That immediately lets your professor see that your e-mail is legitimate. The cutesy or salacious personal e-mail address that might be okay when you send an e-mail to a friend is not appropriate when you're writing to a professor. 2

Include the course number in your subject line. "Question about 3009 assignment" is clear and sounds genuine, while "a question" looks like spam. "Question about English assignment" or "question about assignment," without identifying the class you're in, may leave your professor with the chore of figuring that out. For someone teaching large lecture classes, that might mean reading through hundreds of names on rosters. But even for a professor with smaller classes, it's a drag to get an e-mail that merely says "I'm in your English class and need the assignment." All of your professor's classes are English classes; she or he still needs to know which one is yours. 3

Consider, in light of this advice, the following examples:

> An e-mail from "qtpie2005" with the subject line "question."
>
> An e-mail from a university account with the subject line "question about English 2011 essay."

Which one looks legitimate? 4

Think about what you're saying. Most students are not accustomed to writing to their professors. Here are some ways to do it well: 5

Choose an appropriate greeting. "Hi/Hello Professor [Blank]" is always appropriate. Substitute "Dear" and you've ended up writing a letter; leave out "Hi" and your tone is too brusque. 6

Avoid rote apologies for missing class. Most professors are tired of hearing those standard apologies and acts of contrition. If you missed class because of some especially serious or sad circumstances, it might be better to mention that in person than in an e-mail. 7

Ask politely. Direct requests tend to sound more like orders in e-mail. For instance, "Please send me the next assignment." Even worse: "I need the next assignment." It's much better to ask a question: "Could you e-mail me with the page numbers for the next reading? Thanks!" is a lot better than "I need the assignment." 8

Proofread what you've written. You want your e-mail to show you in the best possible light. 9

Sign with your full name, course number, and meeting time.

> Maggie Simpson
> English 3703, MWF 10:00

Signing is an obvious courtesy, and it eliminates the need for stilted self-identification ("I am a student in your such-and-such class"). 10

One don't, and one last do: 11

Don't send unexpected attachments. It's bad form. Attaching an essay with a request that your professor look it over is very bad form. Arrange to meet your professor during office hours or by appointment instead. It's especially bad form to send an e-mail that says "I won't be in class today," with a paper or some other coursework attached. Think about it: Your professor is supposed to print out your essay because you're not coming to class? 12

When you get a reply, say thanks. Just hit Reply and say "Thanks," or a little bit more if that's appropriate. The old subject line (which will now have a "Re:" in front) will make the context clear. I don't think that you need to include a greeting with a short reply, at least not if you refer to your professor in your reply. And you don't need to identify yourself by course number and meeting time again. 13

Many e-mail messages end up never reaching their intended recipients, for reasons of human and technological error, so it's always appropriate to acknowledge that someone's message got through. It's also plain courtesy to say thanks. (Your professor will remember it too.) When you reply, you should delete almost everything of your professor's reply (quoting everything is rarely appropriate in e-mail). Leave just enough to make the original context clear. 14

So, what would a good e-mail to a professor look like?

> Hi Professor Leddy,
>
> I'm working on my essay on William Carlos Williams and I'm not sure what to make of the last stanza of "Spring and All." I'm stuck trying to figure out what "It" is. Do you have a suggestion? Thanks!
>
> Maggie Simpson
> Eng 3703, MWF 10:00 15

And a subsequent note of thanks:

> > "It" is most likely spring, or life itself. But have you
> > looked up "quicken"? That'll probably make
> > "It" much clearer.
>
> It sure did. Thanks for your help, Professor.
> Maggie Simpson 16

Considering Ideas

1. For what purpose did Leddy write his process analysis? Who is his intended audience?
2. Why is a "cutesy or salacious personal e-mail address" (paragraph 2) inappropriate for an e-mail to a professor? How does using such an address demonstrate a lack of audience awareness?
3. Do you think it is fair for instructors to form opinions about their students on the basis of their e-mail? Why or why not?
4. Explain the reference to Maggie Simpson in paragraphs 10 and 15. Why do you think Leddy includes this reference?

Considering Technique

1. In paragraph 1, Leddy suggests his credentials and his purpose for writing the process analysis. Given his audience, is this opening effective? Explain.
2. In which paragraphs does Leddy explain how to perform a step? Why does he do so?
3. In which paragraphs does the author say what *not* to do? Why does he do so?
4. In which paragraphs does the author explain why a step is performed? Why does he do so?
5. *Combining patterns:* Leddy uses a number of examples throughout his piece. How does this exemplification help him achieve his purpose for writing?

For Group Discussion or Journal Writing

What, if anything, did you learn about the process of e-mailing an instructor as a result of reading "How to E-Mail a Professor"? Did you find anything surprising about Leddy's procedures?

Wicked Wind BEN MCGRATH

Do you pay much attention to the sound effects in movies you enjoy? If not, you may begin to do so after reading "Wicked Wind." In this essay, which first appeared in The New Yorker *in 2003, Ben McGrath explains how Richard King, the sound designer for a popular, award-winning movie, created some of the sound effects. You may be surprised by the lengths King went to in order to capture just the right sound.*

If you want to re-create the auditory experience of being in a storm aboard a nineteenth-century British frigate, get yourself a pickup truck, some wood, a few acoustic blankets, and about a thousand feet of rope. Then drive out to the Mojave Desert and build a large wooden frame in the bed of the truck. String the rope back and forth around the frame, using a turnbuckle to make it good and taut, until all thousand feet have been spent. Face the truck head-on into a thirty-mile-an-hour wind, and lean hard on the gas pedal. Once you hit seventy, you're in business; the sound of the air meeting the lines of rope ought to approximate the shrieking of the wind in the frigate's rigging—

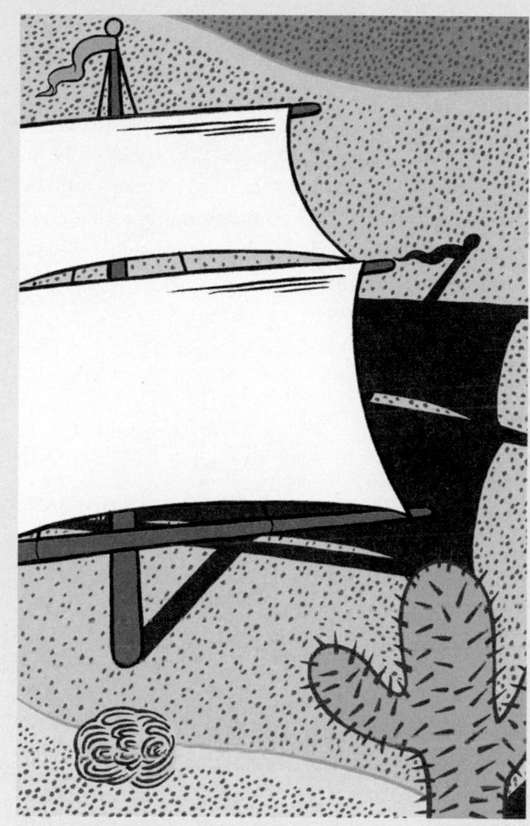

a foretaste of what the novelist Patrick O'Brian might call "a coming dissolution of all natural bonds, an apocalyptic upheaval, a right dirty night." For added effect, try holding a barbecue grill out the window and turning it at various angles as you cruise. Muffle any peripheral truck noise, as needed, with the blankets. 1

This, at least, is the approach that Richard King came up with recently as the sound designer for "Master and Commander: The Far Side of the World," the forthcoming adaptation of O'Brian's nautical series, set aboard the Royal Navy's H.M.S. Surprise during the Napoleonic Wars. King, who is forty-nine years old and a lifelong sailor, was charged not only with the task of supervising the editing of the film's soundtrack (distinct from any musical score or accompaniment) but also with recording all the individual sounds—musket fire, sloshing bilge, creaking wood—that need to be incorporated. In some cases, this requires creating the sounds from scratch. 2

Thus the trip to the desert. "Nobody wants to take their ships out in a gale," King said. "I actually tried to get myself on a ship somewhere in the world that would put itself in that situation." The Mojave, it turns out, is a convenient substitute, because it gets very windy, and the wind patterns are predictable, typically blowing from the southwest. King didn't limit his Mojave recording sessions to truck work, either. "We got some sails off a big square-rigger and took them out to the desert and built a giant framework—a mast, essentially—and rigged the sails so we could get them to flap at various intensities," he said. "So we got discrete sail flaps without any sound of water in the background." 3

King and his crew of eight editors made it a point of pride not to rely on "library" files, a standard collection of movies-ready sounds (car honks, airplanes taking off). Given that "Master and Commander" features extended battle scenes with plenty of cannon fire, forgoing the library necessitated still more ingenuity. "All the sounds I had heard in period movies of cannons going off were just big loud booms," King said. "But something O'Brian refers to a lot is the screaming of shot flying overhead." So he found a group of artillery collectors in northern Michigan who had cannons that were capable of firing vintage ammunition, and set to work re-creating the types of shot described in O'Brian's novels: round shot ("basically, their ship-to-ship—when they wanted to punch a hole in the hull"), chain shot ("two cannonballs connected by a two-foot piece of chain, which would spin around and take out the rigging and sails and mast"), grapeshot ("canisters with a number of smaller balls inside—anti-personnel weapons that would shoot across the deck to kill as many men as they could"). Then, in January, King and his crew set up a firing range at a National Guard base nearby that had all but closed for the winter. ("They had to snowplow the range for us to shoot.") They fired eighty rounds, recording both the initial explosions and, following another lead from O'Brian, the in-flight racket, which proved to be almost as loud as the booms themselves. "There was a concrete berm five hundred yards downrange which we could get behind and set up mikes and fire over," King said. "Nobody, as far as I know, had ever recorded any of this stuff. It sounded like nothing I've ever heard before." Imagine a cross between a piece of paper being ripped and a racecar speeding by. 4

Not all the work required of a sound designer is so elaborate. "The other day, I was trying to get a sound for a sail," King said. "It's kind of a mysterious scene in the film, where we look up and we see a sail, kind of loose, very softly moving in the light breeze. And I'm thinking, What would be cool there? I have a microphone in my room, and I turned on the recorder and did a *hawwwww*—a low breathing sound—and added some reverb to it. It worked." 5

Considering Ideas

1. The thesis of the essay is implied rather than stated. In your own words, write out the thesis.
2. For what purpose do you think McGrath wrote the essay? Who is his intended audience?
3. Why was it "a point of pride" for King that he did not use library files (paragraph 4)?
4. Make a list of at least four words or phrases that describe Richard King.
5. If you have seen *Master and Commander: The Far Side of the World,* do you have an increased appreciation for the movie as a result of reading the essay? If you have not seen the movie, does the essay make you want to see it? Explain.

Considering Technique

1. The essay opens with a process analysis rather than a lead-in and thesis. Why? Does that opening paragraph engage your interest in the essay? Why or why not?
2. Paragraph 4 mentions something that is *not* done. Why does McGrath include that information? How does it help him achieve his writing purpose?
3. Paragraph 4 also explains how a step is performed. How does that information help him achieve his writing purpose?
4. McGrath closes the way he opens—with a process analysis. Is the conclusion a good one? Why or why not?

For Group Discussion or Journal Writing

How important are sound effects to a movie? How aware are you of sound effects and other sound elements of a movie? If King had used library files, would it *really* have mattered much?

Annie Smith Swept Here

Eric L. Wee

Eric Wee combines narration and comparison-contrast with process analysis to explain how Washington D.C.'s best hotel housekeeper performs her job. "Annie Smith Swept Here" originally appeared in the Washington Post *in 2002.*

It never ceases to amaze me how hotel rooms mysteriously clean themselves.

—Quote on the Omni Shoreham Hotel sign that guests use to have their rooms cleaned

The cleaning begins around 6 A.M. She starts with the kitchen and makes her way to the bedroom. Then she scrubs the tub. Then the toilet. Then the sink. Then she crouches down and polishes the bathroom floor as she inches her way out the door. Then Washington's best hotel housekeeper heads to work. 1

Annie Smith's workday starts when she pulls open a worn wooden door on the side of the Omni Shoreham Hotel that guests never see. She strides past the signs that line the halls, reminding employees of how they should act. 2

Be natural and appropriately friendly. 3

Always maintain your smile even though your customer may not. 4

She waves to colleagues, then walks down a set of concrete stairs to her locker, where the hot, humid air smells of soap and bleach from the nearby laundry. There, her gray uniform with a white apron waits. 5

Soon she and 55 other women pack into a small windowless room two floors underground. It's been a while since the hotel, on Calvert Street NW, has needed this many of them. Canceled conventions and empty rooms recently have meant no work for most. Annie's been one of the lucky ones. 6

Most of the workers here are black. A few are Asian or Hispanic. Some are new from places like Ethiopia and El Salvador. Others, like Birdie and Precious and Dorothy, have started each morning like this with Annie for 24 years. Each will typically have 15 rooms to clean in this 836-room convention hotel. That means they need to finish a room every 30 minutes to punch out by their 4:30 P. M. deadline so the hotel won't have to pay overtime. Shortly after that, they have to be off the property. 7

In the center stands the new housekeeping director, a young, eager man named Quentin. He tells them he's worried about broken remote controls and light bulb problems. Five remotes didn't work yesterday. Six rooms had bad bulbs. He tells them that Model Search America is coming this weekend. A low groan emanates. They know that means teenagers with messy rooms and makeup-stained towels. Then before they grab their room assignments and fan out, the director wishes them "a wonderful Omni day." 8

For Annie, it's another shift of restoring her set of rooms on the sixth floor's east wing to the way she left them. And they are her rooms. She's looked after them for nearly two decades. Among these tubs, these beds, these nightstands, she finds a kind of inner peace. They have become an extension of her. 9

This morning Annie is sick with the flu, but she doesn't want to admit it. She loads her cart with two sizes of ivory-colored linens, hangs her blue vacuum cleaner on its edge and drags her supplies to her first stop. She's a lean, strong-looking woman who seems younger than her 48 years and bigger than her five-foot frame. She moves in quick, impatient steps, as if she's late to get somewhere. And once she's in her rooms she seems constantly preoccupied, mumbling to herself about a missing padded hanger or a bathmat. 10

She strips the sheets from Room 614's king-size bed with a few efficient strokes and stuffs them into a bright blue laundry bag. She airs the bed out while spraying every corner of the bathroom with a purple disinfectant. Then she sits on the tub's edge and starts scrubbing. 11

What Annie does in a room isn't fundamentally different from what other housekeepers do. It's how she does it that sets her apart. Another might lightly wipe down the shower wall. Annie scours it every day until a lather builds. Others dust. She polishes each piece of furniture from the chair legs to the armoire top. Her bosses say they can walk in and know it's an Annie Smith room. They can smell it. But the bed is the giveaway. Everything is perfect from the pillows to the bed skirts. The sheets are vise-tight. And the top is smooth like a pane of glass. 12

Annie entered a citywide bed-making contest several years ago. For six rounds, she and 92 others from more than two dozen hotels scurried around makeshift cots, tucking and folding. When it was over, she'd won the first-place ticket to Antigua. Her time: 1 minute 42 seconds with a perfect 10 quality score. The next year the American Hotel and Motel Association crowned her the nation's "Roomkeeper of the Year." Off she went to Hawaii. On trips like these she never allows a housekeeper to clean her hotel room. Instead she washes the tub with shampoo and a towel every morning. She makes her own bed, then tips the housekeeper $10 a day. 13

She likes to describe her job as an honest living. At $12.20 an hour, she's been able to raise a son and help send him to college. But she could be making more as a room supervisor. The hotel has offered her that job several times. She's always said no. She doesn't want to inspect other housekeepers' rooms. She wants to clean. 14

Annie's first rooms always take her longer, but she gradually picks up momentum. By 11:10 A.M. she's in Room 610's bathroom. She's moving from the mirror to the sink to the tub in hyper-speed. 15

"When I finish a room and I give it a last sweep, it's almost like it smiles at me. It looks brighter." 16

She raises herself up from wiping the bathroom floor and looks around the bedroom that she's cleaned more than 4,000 times. 17

"Maybe I'm not making the forty or fifty thousand dollars a year but I'm proud of what I'm doing because I'm showing off my masterpiece. Sometimes you feel like an artist or painter when you come into these rooms. It takes experience, it takes time, it takes everything that you have—I'm painting a picture." 18

She smiles at that thought, then moves to the bed and starts laying out the sheets. She wrestles with the bedspread, tugging on each side. She runs her hand over the top searching for any rogue wrinkles, then steps back and looks it over. 19

"It could be cloudy outside and if I made that bed good and I set everything up here the way it's supposed to be, it's almost like the sun is shining." 20

It's 3 P.M. and Annie is behind schedule, with four rooms still to finish. She looks worried but forces a smile. In Room 606 she finds a woman who's here for a transportation convention, staring at stacks of papers covering the floor. 21

"It's a mess in here but, believe it or not, it's somewhat organized," she tells Annie. She mulls over whether she wants her room cleaned, then decides against it. Annie refills the toilet paper, carries out a half-eaten deli sandwich and moves on. 22

Housekeepers love people who give them a break. And they love tippers. On a good day Annie will make $25. A woman from the World Bank once left $150. Today she'll only make an extra dollar. But she covets a simple compliment even more. 23

Housekeepers' dislikes are equally clear. They hate late checkouts. They hate DNDs (Do Not Disturbs) who want their rooms done late. They hate it when people call them maids.

And they cringe whenever they hear crowds of teenagers. 24

By the time she gets to Room 604, Annie's face looks drawn. She's slowing down. The rooms and the flu are overtaking her. 25

"I've got to do what I have to do," she says as she tugs her trolley past the door, pulling off the sheets from the bed and plunging her yellow-gloved right hand into another toilet. She knows if she rests, she'll never finish. 26

Before she steps out of the room, she makes sure each notepad is aligned with the right edge of the phone and the pen lies diagonally from left to right, with the Omni logo showing. The floral-scented conditioner and chamomile shampoo stand on the side of the toiletry basket nearest the shower. Each lampshade is straight, its seam in back and out of sight. And she's folded the first tissue into a triangle. 27

It's a few minutes before 4 P.M. when she enters her last room. Two unmade beds lie tangled. She snaps open a fresh new sheet, gradually bringing order to the chaos. Then as the hot water runs and she stands on her tiptoes to reach the far shower walls, the sweat from the strain and fever begins dripping down her face. By 4:20 P.M. the room smells like fresh snowflakes and lemon. She gives it a final scan. 28

"Excellent," she says softly and lets the door slide shut. She hauls the pillowcases full of crumpled sheets down the hall. The bulging garbage bag follows. She hurries toward the unmarked doors that lead to the service elevator and the clock she needs to punch. Her shoulders slump, and her head hangs as she trudges toward the exit. She passes more Omni motivation signs. 29

Smile and make eye contact. 30

Stay up! Be energetic! Take good care of ourselves! 31

Outside, her boyfriend's car waits to take her home. She sinks into the passenger seat and exhales deeply as she lets her head fall back. She wipes the last beads of sweat off her forehead and leans over to kiss him. 32

"We made it, baby," she says. "We made it." 33

Considering Ideas

1. How does Annie feel about the rooms she cleans? Why do you think she feels that way?
2. Wee says that Annie is Washington's best hotel housekeeper. What makes her better than other housekeepers?
3. In paragraph 13, Wee says that when Annie travels, she does not let anyone clean her room for her—and then she leaves a big tip. What does that information reveal about Annie?
4. Although Annie had the flu, she went to work. Why didn't she call in sick?
5. For what purpose do you think Wee wrote "Annie Smith Swept Here"?

Considering Technique

1. Why does Wee open with a quotation from a sign?
2. In which paragraph does the process analysis begin?
3. Wee uses descriptive language to explain Annie's process. For example, in paragraph 19, he refers to "rogue wrinkles," and he says that Annie "wrestles with the bedspread." How does the descriptive language help the author achieve his purpose?

4. *Combining patterns:* How does Wee use narration (storytelling) in "Annie Smith Swept Here"? How does he use comparison-contrast (showing similarities and differences)? How do these patterns help Wee achieve his purpose?
5. Explain the wordplay in the title.

For Group Discussion or Journal Writing

Annie Smith takes great pride in her work. Do you think most people display a similar pride in their work? Cite examples to support your view. Then explain why you think people do or do not take pride in their work.

STYLE NOTE

Point of View

Your **point of view** is determined by your pronouns. Use the first-person pronouns *I, me, my, mine, we, our,* and *ours* to write from the point of view of the writer. Use the second-person pronouns *you, your,* and *yours* to write from the point of view of the reader. Use the third-person pronouns *he, she, it, him, her, his, hers, its, they,* and *theirs* to write from the point of view of an outsider, someone who is not you and not your reader.

First person: To calm the dog, I reach down and offer my hand to smell.

Second person: To calm the dog, you reach down and offer your hand to smell.

Third person: To calm the dog, he reached down and offered his hand to smell.

Directional process analyses often use the second-person point of view because the writer is explaining to the reader a process the reader might perform, as this example from "How to E-Mail a Professor" illustrates:

> When you reply, you should delete almost everything of your professor's reply (quoting everything is rarely appropriate in e-mail).

Informational process analyses often use the third-person point of view because the writer is explaining a process performed by someone other than the reader or a process the reader is not likely to perform. Here is an example from "Annie Smith Swept Here":

> The cleaning begins around 6 A.M. She starts with the kitchen and makes her way to the bedroom. Then she scrubs the tub.

Finally, if you are explaining a process the way you perform it, either alone or with others, you will use the first-person point of view, as this excerpt from "A Visit to Candyland" illustrates:

> Once we've decided on a theme, we might visit the library or go on the Internet to find visual ideas we can incorporate into our design. Then, after we've done some preliminary sketches, we make a pattern.

PROCESS ANALYSIS IN AN IMAGE

The picture on page 268 comes from the HowStuffWorks website (www.howstuffworks.com). True to its name, the site explains how many things work, including the pop-up turkey timer shown in the picture.

Considering the Image

1. Does the picture included with the process analysis help you better understand how the pop-up turkey timer works? What, if anything, does the picture add?
2. The process analysis includes the technical term *binary*. Is the term adequately defined? Explain.
3. The process analysis concludes with a little-known fact. What does that fact add to the process analysis?

SUGGESTIONS FOR WRITING

Writing Process Analysis

1. Explain a process you perform well so that someone else can perform it—how to change the oil in a car, how to train for an athletic competition, how to build a campfire, how to buy a used car, and so forth. Your responses to the exercise on page 251 may help you here.
2. Explain any of the following processes to help first-year students at your school:

how to register	how to select a major	how to meet people
how to study for an exam	how to select an advisor	how to live with a roommate

3. Think of something you know how to make, and describe the process so that someone else can make it.
4. Explain a process that can save a life (CPR, first aid, the Heimlich maneuver, etc.).
5. Explain one of the following processes:

how to survive adolescence	how to buy the perfect gift
how to plan the perfect party	how to choose the right college
how to buy running shoes	how to buy a computer

6. Identify a problem that exists on your campus, and then explain a process for solving the problem.

Reading Then Writing Process Analysis

1. In "Annie Smith Swept Here," Eric Wee explains a process that many people take for granted or fail to value—the job performed by a hotel

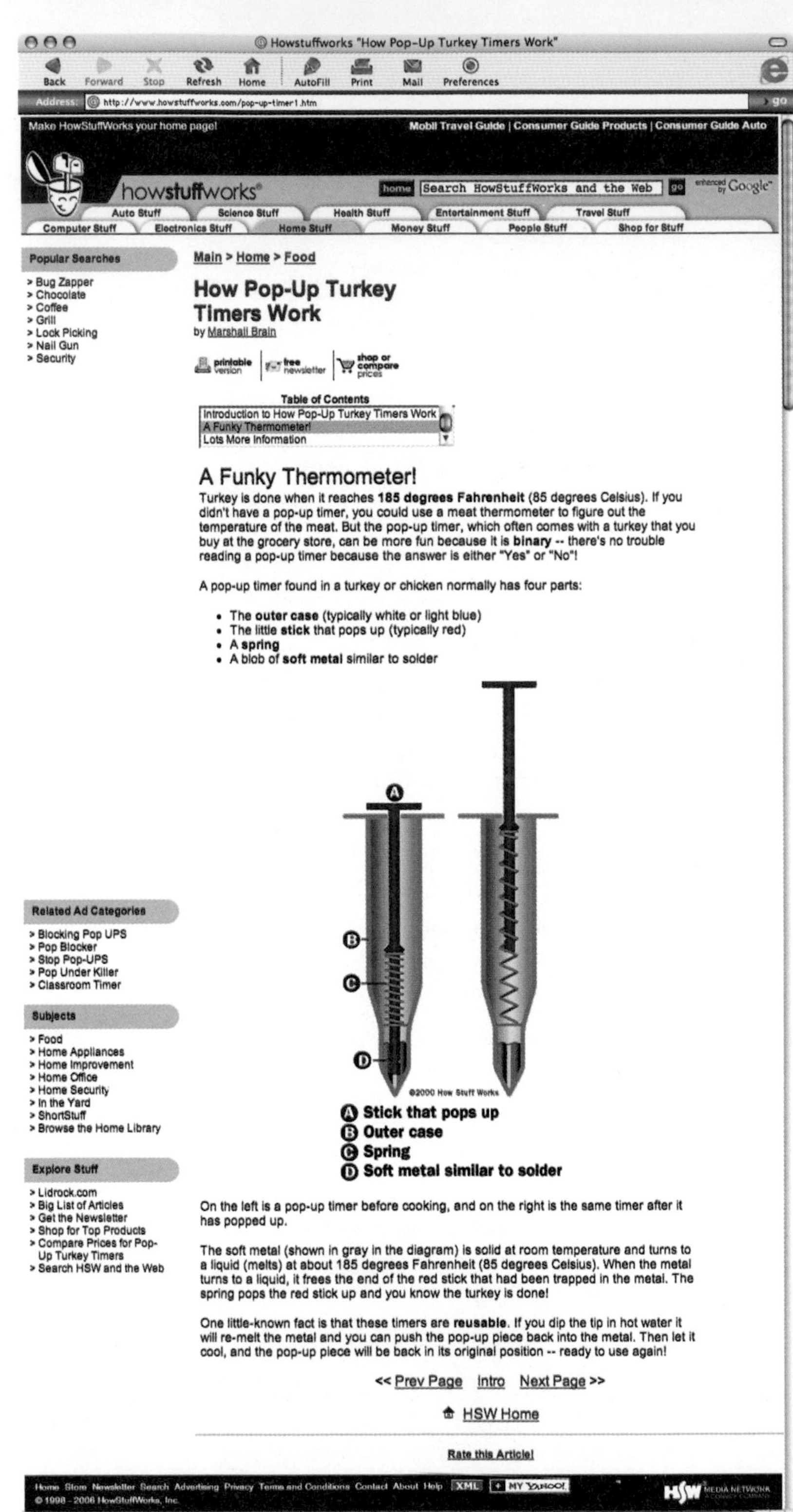

Howstuffworks "How Pop-Up Turkey Timers Work"

Back Forward Stop Refresh Home AutoFill Print Mail Preferences

Address: http://www.howstuffworks.com/pop-up-timer1.htm

Make HowStuffWorks your home page! Mobil Travel Guide | Consumer Guide Products | Consumer Guide Auto

howstuffworks® home Search HowStuffWorks and the Web go enhanced by Google

Auto Stuff Science Stuff Health Stuff Entertainment Stuff Travel Stuff

Computer Stuff Electronics Stuff Home Stuff Money Stuff People Stuff Shop for Stuff

Popular Searches

- Bug Zapper
- Chocolate
- Coffee
- Grill
- Lock Picking
- Nail Gun
- Security

Main > Home > Food

How Pop-Up Turkey Timers Work

by Marshall Brain

printable version | free newsletter | shop or compare prices

Table of Contents

- Introduction to How Pop-Up Turkey Timers Work
- A Funky Thermometer!
- Lots More Information

A Funky Thermometer!

Turkey is done when it reaches **185 degrees Fahrenheit** (85 degrees Celsius). If you didn't have a pop-up timer, you could use a meat thermometer to figure out the temperature of the meat. But the pop-up timer, which often comes with a turkey that you buy at the grocery store, can be more fun because it is **binary** -- there's no trouble reading a pop-up timer because the answer is either "Yes" or "No"!

A pop-up timer found in a turkey or chicken normally has four parts:

- The **outer case** (typically white or light blue)
- The little **stick** that pops up (typically red)
- A **spring**
- A blob of **soft metal** similar to solder

A Stick that pops up
B Outer case
C Spring
D Soft metal similar to solder

On the left is a pop-up timer before cooking, and on the right is the same timer after it has popped up.

The soft metal (shown in gray in the diagram) is solid at room temperature and turns to a liquid (melts) at about 185 degrees Fahrenheit (85 degrees Celsius). When the metal turns to a liquid, it frees the end of the red stick that had been trapped in the metal. The spring pops the red stick up and you know the turkey is done!

One little-known fact is that these timers are **reusable**. If you dip the tip in hot water it will re-melt the metal and you can push the pop-up piece back into the metal. Then let it cool, and the pop-up piece will be back in its original position -- ready to use again!

<< Prev Page Intro Next Page >>

HSW Home

Rate this Article!

Related Ad Categories

- Blocking Pop UPS
- Pop Blocker
- Stop Pop-UPS
- Pop Under Killer
- Classroom Timer

Subjects

- Food
- Home Appliances
- Home Improvement
- Home Office
- Home Security
- In the Yard
- ShortStuff
- Browse the Home Library

Explore Stuff

- Lidrock.com
- Big List of Articles
- Get the Newsletter
- Shop for Top Products
- Compare Prices for Pop-Up Turkey Timers
- Search HSW and the Web

Home Store Newsletter Search Advertising Privacy Terms and Conditions Contact About Help XML MY YAHOO!

© 1998 - 2006 HowStuffWorks, Inc.

HSW Media Network

Internet zone

housekeeper. Think of another process that people take for granted or do not value, and explain it in a way that helps your reader appreciate it more.

2. If you play an instrument, sing, dance, paint, or otherwise practice one of the arts, do what Ben McGrath does in "Wicked Wind," and explain a process associated with the art. For example, if you paint, you can describe the process of mixing paints to achieve certain effects.
3. Like the author of "A Visit to Candyland," explain a process you complete with your family, such as cooking Thanksgiving dinner, celebrating Grandma's birthday, participating in the annual park cleanup, or driving to the mountains. Convey your feelings about the process.

Process Analysis beyond the Writing Classroom

Process analysis can be a helpful problem-solving strategy. To appreciate this fact, identify a problem you are currently experiencing, such as procrastination, too much time online, an unhappy job situation, smoking, or loneliness. Then write out a detailed explanation of how you can solve that problem. Be specific. If you say that one step you will take to improve an unhappy job situation is to speak to your supervisor, indicate exactly what you will say and when and where you will say it. Also, be realistic. Do not say that you will look for another job if finding one is unlikely, given your school schedule.

Responding to Theme

1. In "How to E-Mail a Professor," Michael Leddy explains a process for communicating effectively in an e-mail. Tell about a time one of your e-mail communications with someone created a problem. Your essay should teach something about effective or ineffective communication.
2. "How to E-Mail a Professor" says something about the importance of audience awareness when students communicate with their professors. Discuss the importance of audience awareness in other forms of academic communication, such as classroom discussions, group activities, or student–teacher conferences.
3. The HowStuffWorks website (www.howstuffworks.com), from which the image on page 268 is taken, is extremely popular. In fact, in 2002, *Time* magazine named it one of the 50 best websites. The site is successful partly because we are so interested in learning about processes and because it explains these processes so clearly. In an essay, explain what process you would like to learn more about, why you would like to learn it, and how you can go about doing so, in addition to studying the website.
4. *Connecting the readings:* "How to E-Mail a Professor" says something about being a professor, "Wicked Wind" says something about being a sound designer, and "Annie Smith Swept Here" says something about being a hotel housekeeper. Drawing on those pieces and your own observation, explain how we ascribe status and value to jobs.

www.mhhe.com/tsw
For further help with writing process analysis, go to Catalyst 2.0 > Writing > Writing Tutors > Process Analysis

Writing Process Analysis

The following strategies are not meant to replace your own successful procedures. They are here to try as you work to improve your writing process.

Think like a Writer: Generating Ideas, Considering Audience and Purpose, and Ordering Ideas

- Consider past experiences and activities. If you were involved in athletics, perhaps you can describe how to coach Little League or how to prepare mentally for a big game. If you were a scout, maybe you can explain how to prepare for a hike or how to survive in the wilderness.
- To determine your purpose, answer these questions:
  - Do I want to inform my reader about a better way to do something or convince my reader to do something a different way?
  - Do I want to explain a process so my reader can perform it?
  - Do I want to explain a process so my reader appreciates it more?
- To identify and assess your audience, answer these questions:
  - Who does not know how to perform the process or fully understand or appreciate it?
  - Who needs to learn a better way to perform the process?
  - Does my reader appreciate the importance or beauty of the process?
  - Has my reader had any experience with the process? Will the steps be difficult for my reader to perform or understand?
  - Does my reader need any terms defined?
  - Would my reader find visuals helpful?
  - Will my reader react well to hypothetical situations?
- To generate ideas:
  - List every step in the process—in the order it is performed if chronological order is appropriate.
  - Review your list in light of your audience and purpose. Place an "H" next to a step if you should explain how it is performed. Place a "W" next to a step if you should explain why it is performed. Place a "T" next to a step if you should explain a troublesome aspect. Place a "D" next to a step if you should define a term.
  - Make a note about anything you should describe and any visuals you should provide. Should you explain anything that should not be done?
- Turn your list of steps and letters into a formal outline. Alternatively, complete an outline worksheet.

Think like a Writer: Drafting

- Draft a preliminary thesis that states the process you are explaining and why understanding that process is important.
- Using your outline as a guide, write your draft.

Think like a Critic; Work like an Editor: Revising

- Underline the statement that explains the significance of the process. If you have no such statement, be sure the significance is strongly implied.

- Checkmark paragraphs where you explain how to perform a step, why to perform a step, or what not to do. If you have no check marks or very few, evaluate whether you need more detail.
- If you have used any technical terms, be sure they are defined.
- Ask whether your process analysis seems boring. If so, try adding description or some lively examples. Explain the importance or beauty of the process.
- To obtain reader response for revision, see page 105. In addition, ask your reader whether there are any aspects of the process that are hard to follow.

Think like a Critic; Work like an Editor: Correcting Errors

- If you are writing a directional process analysis and want to address your reader, use the second-person pronouns *you, your,* and *yours*.
- If you do not want to address your reader directly, use the third-person pronouns *he, she, it, they, him, her, them, his, hers, its, their,* and *theirs*. Or, if you are explaining how you perform the process, use the first-person pronouns *I, me, my, mine, we, us, ours,* and *our*.
- Be careful not to mix first-, second-, and third-person pronouns inappropriately, or you will have an error called **person shift**. Here is an example of the error:

  Those who decide to take up the sport of rock climbing should do exercises to increase the strength and flexibility of *their* fingers. Many climbers learn exercises at a climbing gym, but *they* can also learn some from books on the subject. In addition, *you* can speak to a personal trainer.

Remember

Choose a process that is interesting or important to your reader. Avoid explaining how to wash a car or tie shoes unless you can find a way to make the process fresh, entertaining, or informative.

LOOKING AHEAD

We compare and contrast all the time. To decide which computer to buy, we compare and contrast the price and features of different models; to decide which candidate to vote for, we compare and contrast the qualifications and platform of each person. Sometimes, comparison-contrast pops up in surprising places, such as in this *Ziggy* cartoon. Before studying how to write a comparison-contrast essay, answer these questions about the cartoon:

- What items are compared and contrasted?
- What is the main point of similarity? Of difference?
- How does the comparison and contrast contribute to the cartoon's humor?

Comparison-Contrast

Globalization means that cultural influences no longer stop at the border; they often reach countries on the other side of their world of origination. Spider-Man is a case in point. In 2004, Marvel Comics launched "Spider-Man India," described in *Newsweek* as "the first ethnic adaptation of the popular comic book series." As with most adaptations, there are similarities and differences between the original and the reworking. The following excerpt from *Newsweek* points out some of them:

> Peter Parker of New York City becomes Pavitr Prabhakar of Mumbai, Mary Jane becomes Meera Jain and the villainous Norman Osbourne (a.k.a. the Green Goblin) turns into Nalin Oberoi. But the reinvention goes further than just translation: Spider-Man's been transformed from an allegorical figure representing the dangers of scientific experimentation, which grew out of anxieties from the nuclear age, into a hero trying to navigate a modern India still steeped in Hindu mysticism. His alter ego, Prabhakar, wears the white dhoti favored by Hindu-temple devotees. "I was trying to capture the essence of India," says Jeevan Kang, the 26-year-old former architect hired to write and draw the series.

The excerpt allows readers to draw conclusions about the blending of cultural influences.

When you place two items—like two versions of a superhero—next to each other to examine their similarities and/or differences, you are comparing and contrasting. In common usage, to *compare* is to look at both similarities and differences. However, strictly speaking, when you **compare,** you examine similarities; when you **contrast,** you examine differences; and when you **compare and contrast,** you examine both.

The items you compare and contrast should have enough in common to warrant side-by-side consideration. Usually, this means that the subjects belong to the same category. You can compare and contrast two jobs, two Halloween celebrations, or two ways to study, but not learning to use a computer and learning to roller-skate. Sometimes, however, writers use subjects from different categories in a special form of comparison-contrast called **analogy.** For example, an analogy might compare the human eye to a camera to explain how the eye works.

WHY IS COMPARISON-CONTRAST IMPORTANT?

To appreciate how fundamental comparison-contrast is to thinking about the world, consider how often you say or think things like, "This television show is not as good as the one I saw last week"; "Your schedule is very similar to mine"; "This soap dries my skin more than my cleansing cream"; and "Professor James is every bit as interesting as Professor Aqueros."

We make these comparisons and contrasts to understand one thing in terms of another. Sometimes we compare and contrast to understand something we do not know much about. For example, when we ask the table server what the octopus tastes like, and he says, "It tastes like chicken, only tougher," we can decide whether to order based on this comparison-contrast. Sometimes understanding one thing in terms of another gives us a new appreciation for something familiar or brings both into sharper focus. You may know about the baseball talent of Derek Jeter and Alex Rodriguez, but comparing their playing styles can give you a new appreciation for one or both players.

In addition to providing a strategy for thinking about the world, comparison-contrast is important to the decision-making process. To decide whether to buy one car over another, to rent an apartment near campus or a cheaper one across town, or to go to summer school or get a job, we often compare and contrast the advantages and disadvantages of each option before deciding.

The following chart will give you a better idea of the range of purposes comparison-contrast can serve.

Purposes for Comparison-Contrast

Purpose	Sample Comparison-Contrast
To entertain	A comparison-contrast of hosting a birthday party for three-year-olds and herding ducks in a humorous analogy

To share feelings and experiences	A comparison-contrast of how you felt before and after you learned you were adopted
To inform (of the nature of the less familiar sport of rugby)	A comparison-contrast of American football and rugby
To inform (to lend fresh appreciation for letter writing)	A comparison-contrast of communicating by e-mail and by letter
To persuade (to convince the reader to vote for a particular candidate)	A comparison-contrast of the platforms of two mayoral candidates to convince the reader that one is better than the other

COMBINING COMPARISON-CONTRAST WITH OTHER PATTERNS

Comparison-contrast is often combined with other patterns of development. If you are describing blues music, you can compare and contrast its rhythm with jazz rhythm to help your reader understand its qualities. If you are writing an extended definition of old age, you can compare and contrast the activities that the elderly enjoy with those that younger adults enjoy to help explain what old age is like. If you are explaining a better process for determining which patients are chosen to receive organ transplants, you can contrast your procedure with the existing one to show the superiority of your process.

Even when comparison-contrast is the dominant method of development, it may be combined with other patterns. A comparison-contrast of two football players can include a process analysis explaining the way each athlete plays defense. A contrast of two colleges that notes differences in the degree of political activism on campus can explain the effects of the activism and give examples of it.

Comparison-Contrast across the Disciplines and Beyond

Comparison-Contrast in the Classroom

Because comparison-contrast requires you to analyze subjects and draw conclusions, it is an important part of writing in college classes. In a paper for a political science class, you might contrast the rulings of two Supreme Court justices on states' rights issues. In a business class, you might write a research paper that compares and contrasts two management strategies. For an essay examination in an art appreciation class, you might explain Monet's use of light by comparing two of his paintings. *Think about three classes you are taking this term or expect to take soon. What instances of comparison-contrast might be part of the reading and writing for those classes? How will comparison-contrast help you to analyze and understand important ideas in your major?*

Comparison-Contrast in Daily Life

Comparison-contrast will be part of the writing you do in your personal life. For example, to decide whether to transfer to another school, you might write a comparison of both schools in your journal to determine whether transferring is a good idea. To convince a friend to become a vegetarian, you might contrast how you felt before and after becoming a vegetarian yourself. *If you have an important decision to make, how can you use comparison-contrast to help make a wise decision? Why will the comparison-contrast be helpful?*

Comparison-Contrast on the Job

Comparison-contrast is an important part of writing in the workplace. Department heads contrast two phone plans to determine which one the company should use. Human resources managers compare and contrast two applicants to determine who to hire. Union representatives compare and contrast contract offers during labor negotiations. *Name three jobs that are likely to involve comparison-contrast. How will people who have these jobs use comparison-contrast? Will comparison-contrast be a part of the career you hope to pursue after finishing school? How will comparison-contrast be useful in this job?*

SELECTING DETAIL

In many cases, you cannot mention every point of comparison or contrast without writing an unwieldy essay. A comparison of the presidencies of Ronald Reagan and Richard Nixon, for example, could take up a book. To limit your topic and make your comparison more manageable, choose a **basis of comparison,** which is a specific aspect of your subjects, and compare just those aspects. Your basis of comparison of Reagan and Nixon could be their foreign policies. If that topic still gives you too much to write about, you could limit the basis of comparison further, perhaps to a comparison of their Asian trade policies. In addition, remember the following points.

Include Enough Points of Comparison or Contrast

The number of points of comparison or contrast will vary from essay to essay, but usually, you should make at least three points. If you have only one or two points of comparison or contrast, you probably have too little to say about your subjects—unless those points are significant and require several paragraphs of explanation. Suppose you are contrasting the way men and women view friendship. You could note that women need to talk to their friends about their personal lives, while men prefer sharing activities rather than conversation. That point alone does not say very much about the differences between your subjects, so you would need to bring up other points of contrast.

Draw on Other Patterns to Explain Points of Comparison and Contrast

You often need to do more than mention similarities and differences—you need to *explain* the points of comparison and contrast. For this, you can draw on the patterns of development. Say you want to compare the ways you have celebrated Christmas before and after you left home for college. This may involve you in two narrations—one of a celebration before you left home, and one of a celebration after. If you want to contrast independent films and big-studio films, you may find yourself explaining with examples of different movies. If you contrast study techniques, you can use process analysis to explain how each technique works. If you compare and contrast two cars, you may describe the safety features of the vehicles.

Maintain Balance between the Points Discussed

Any point you discuss for one subject you should also mention for the other. Suppose you are comparing your family life before and after your parents divorced for the purpose of arguing that children can be better off if their parents end an unhappy marriage. If you describe the squabbling at mealtimes before the divorce and how it made you tense and afraid, then you should say something about what mealtime was like after the divorce.

To maintain balance, you need not give each point the same amount of development for each subject. You may describe the mealtime squabbling that occurred before the divorce extensively to give your reader a clear picture of its nature and effect on you. Then you can mention the peaceful meals you enjoyed after the divorce in just two or three sentences. Similarly, you may find that either the comparison or the contrast is more detailed, or that one of the subjects gets more development than the other. This variation is fine as long as each point treated is developed *adequately*.

Consider Your Audience and Purpose

Your purpose will influence details you include. Suppose you are contrasting dating practices today and those of 50 years ago. If your purpose is to reveal that women are more assertive now, you can note that they take the initiative today but that 50 years ago they seldom asked men out or paid expenses. If your purpose is to argue that dating was easier 50 years ago, you might mention that relationships were simpler before prescribed codes of conduct relaxed and blurred.

Like your purpose, your audience affects detail selection, so identifying and assessing your reader is important. How much your reader knows about your subjects, how your reader feels about your subjects, and how strong these feelings are—these all influence the details. For example, consider the essay that contrasts dating practices today with those of 50 years ago. Say your purpose is to convince your reader that dating was harder 50 years ago. If your reader is a feminist, you will note that 50 years ago men and women had more rigidly prescribed gender roles. As a result, women could not ask men out, they were expected to behave in specific ways, and they did not

USING SOURCES FOR A PURPOSE

The paragraph below is a body paragraph for an essay informing readers that video games are sometimes designed for harmful purposes. The paragraph illustrates one way to use sources from this book in your writing. This paragraph includes paraphrase and quotation from paragraphs 4, 7, and 10 of "The Army's Killer App" on page 293. (For more information on writing paraphrases and quotations, see Chapter 17.)

THESIS IDEA: Parents need to know that video games are sometimes designed to influence young people inappropriately.

WRITING PURPOSE AND AUDIENCE: To inform parents about video games that spread harmful propaganda, so they can help their children recognize and avoid succumbing to that propaganda

The paraphrase and quotation help the writer show how America's Army crosses a line and becomes dangerous.

[1]Video games can be more than entertainment; they can also be educational. [2]However, when the games cross a line from education to propaganda and seduction, they become dangerous. [3]Consider, for example, America's Army, a video game that simulates combat in a highly realistic fashion. [4]In "The Army's Killer App," Lev Grossman characterizes the game as "a giant ad" intentionally designed to recruit young people into the army (294). [5]Using a form of play to lure young people into a potentially lethal situation such as combat is dangerous because it blurs the boundaries between harmless fun and deadly reality. [6]After all, as Grossman explains, "Video games can't . . . convey the human cost of combat. [7]They pass along the adrenaline rush, the thrill of the fight, and leave out the rest" (295). [8]Nonetheless, America's

have a say in what they did on a date. However, if your reader is a teenager, you might mention that teenagers dated under the watchful eyes of parents, and they rarely went out in groups the way they do today.

BEING A RESPONSIBLE WRITER

Sometimes writers omit important points of comparison or contrast in order to achieve their writing purpose. For example, a financial services company might advertise its credit card as allowing a low household income and a fairly high credit limit in order to convince students to sign up for their product. However, a full comparison might show that the company's interest rate is extremely high. This information may be intentionally left out because consumers who care about managing their debt might not sign up for the credit card.

To be a responsible writer, do not attempt to achieve your purpose for writing by omitting important points of comparison or contrast. Instead, mention the negative points in a straightforward way, but emphasize the positive ones, like this:

Army seduces young people with the game and then, according to Grossman, invites them to click on a link taking them to the Army recruiting website (294)—a dangerous and immoral tactic, indeed.

Avoiding Plagiarism

The paragraph illustrates some points about using quotations and avoiding plagiarism.

- **Do not attribute your own ideas to sources.** Sentence 4 is a paraphrase (with a key phrase in quotations) attributed to Grossman, and sentences 6 and 7 are a quotation attributed to Grossman. Sentence 5, however, is the author's material that expresses a personal opinion, supported by the quotation in the next two sentences; therefore, it is not attributed to Grossman. Also notice that the information in sentence 8 before the dash is Grossman's and so is attributed to him; the information after the dash is the author's opinion and thus is not attributed.
- **Reintroduce as necessary.** As sentence 6 shows, when you return to a source you used earlier (in this case, in sentence 4), you should reintroduce the source so your reader understands that you have come back to it.

Myths about Sources

MYTH: You must document anything you use in your writing that you encounter in a source.

FACT: There is no need to document common knowledge. Common knowledge includes dates of historical record (when Lincoln was born and when Pearl Harbor was bombed), information that people agree on (the terrorist attacks of September 11, 2001, changed American air travel), and information that most people know (London is the capital of England). The information in sentence 1 is common knowledge because most people who know anything about video games agree about the point.

Although the interest rate is higher than that of Credit Card X, our card allows a lower household income and offers a higher credit limit. If you pay off your balance each month, the higher interest rate will not be a problem.

Also, do not omit qualifying points of comparison or contrast when you quote or paraphrase from sources, if doing so changes the meaning of the source material. When you change the meaning, you are not using the source material responsibly; you can even fall into the plagiarism trap.

Source: Hypnosis is often more effective for smoking cessation than willpower alone, but only when the patient genuinely wants to quit because hypnosis cannot force people to do things they really do not want to do.

Unacceptable paraphrase: Those who want to quit smoking will find that hypnosis is more successful than just using willpower.

Acceptable paraphrase: Those who want to quit smoking will find that hypnosis is more successful than just using willpower. However, the smoker must want to stop smoking for the hypnosis to be effective.

To be a responsible writer, ask yourself these questions:

- Have I left out any important points of comparison or contrast?
- If so, will their omission unfairly influence my reader?

ORGANIZING COMPARISON-CONTRAST

Your thesis for a comparison-contrast essay can state the subjects you are considering and whether you are comparing, contrasting, or doing both.

Thesis indicating that subjects will be compared

> People think that adolescence is more difficult for females than it is for males, but teenage males suffer many of the same anxieties that females do.

Thesis indicating that subjects will be contrasted

> Attending high school in Japan for two years gave me a firsthand look at the most important differences in our educational systems.

Thesis indicating that subjects will be compared and contrasted

> The differences between comedian Jon Stewart's *The Daily Show* and nightly network news broadcasts are significant, but the similarities are just as important.

Your thesis can also include the points of comparison or contrast that you will make.

Thesis indicating the points of contrast

> People think that adolescence is more difficult for females than it is for males, but teenage males suffer many of the same anxieties about their appearance, about dating, and about peer pressure that girls do.

Comparison-contrast is often organized using a subject-by-subject or point-by-point pattern. With a **subject-by-subject pattern,** you make all your points about your first subject, and then you make all your points about your second subject.

An outline for an essay with subject-by-subject organization could look like the following:

Thesis: People think that adolescence is more difficult for females than it is for males, but teenage males suffer many of the same anxieties that teenage females do.

I. Females
   A. Anxiety about appearance
   B. Anxiety about dating
   C. Anxiety about peer pressure

II. Males
   A. Anxiety about appearance
   B. Anxiety about dating
   C. Anxiety about peer pressure

Note the balance in the outline. The points discussed for females (anxiety about appearance, dating, and peer pressure) are also discussed for males. You need not develop each point equally, but you should treat the same points for each subject and do so in the same order.

The subject-by-subject organization works best for an essay that is not long, complex, or developed with a great many points. Otherwise, the reader working through your points on the second subject must keep too many points about the first subject in mind.

Longer, more complex essays can be organized following the **point-by-point pattern.** With this pattern, you make a point about your first subject and then treat the corresponding point about your second subject. Then you treat the next point about your first subject and follow it with the corresponding point about your second subject. You continue in this alternating fashion until all your points have been presented and developed.

An outline for an essay with point-by-point organization could look like the following:

Thesis: People think that adolescence is more difficult for females than it is for males, but teenage males suffer many of the same anxieties that teenage females do.

I. Anxiety about appearance
   A. Females
   B. Males

II. Anxiety about dating
   A. Females
   B. Males

III. Anxiety about peer pressure
   A. Females
   B. Males

You can tell from the outline that balance is important in point-by-point development. You must treat the same points for both subjects, although you need not give the same degree of development to each point for each subject.

For essays that show both similarities and differences, you can explain first the similarities and then the differences—or you can reverse this order. Generally, you should discuss last whichever is more significant, the similarities or differences, using the subject-by-subject or point-by-point pattern.

EXERCISE Writing Comparison-Contrast

1. For each pair of subjects, identify a possible audience and purpose for a comparison-contrast essay.
   a. Two places
   b. What college is like and what you thought it would be like
   c. Two times of life
   d. Two athletes
   e. Two job applications
   f. Two movies or television shows
2. Select one of the subject pairs in number 1, and write a suitable thesis for a comparison-contrast.
3. What other patterns of development might appear in comparison-contrast essays on the subject pairs in number 1? How would the patterns be used?

Visualizing a Subject-by-Subject Comparison-Contrast Essay

The chart that follows can help you visualize the subject-by-subject pattern of a comparison-contrast essay. Like all good models, this one can be altered as needed.

Introduction

- Creates interest
- States the thesis, which can indicate the subjects under consideration; whether you are comparing, contrasting, or doing both; and the points of comparison or contrast you will discuss

First Body Paragraph(s)

- Will make and explain all the points about the first subject
- Can include other patterns

Next Body Paragraph(s)

- Will make and explain all the points about the second subject, which correspond to the points made and explained for the first subject
- Will make and explain points in the same order used for the first subject
- Can include other patterns

Conclusion

- Provides closure
- Leaves the reader with a strong final impression

4. Assume you will write a comparison-contrast essay about your current writing process and the one you used at some point in the past (perhaps before this term began). Then do the following:
   a. Make one list of the similarities and one list of the differences.
   b. Based on your lists from item a, decide whether you would rather write an essay about similarities, differences, or both.
   c. Establish an audience and purpose, and write a preliminary thesis.
   d. Write two outlines, one with a subject-by-subject pattern and one with a point-by-point pattern. Decide which organization is better for your essay. ■

LEARNING FROM OTHER WRITERS: Student Essays

The first student essay, "The Human and the Superhuman: Two Very Different Heroes," appears with marginal notes to point out key features. It is a contrast developed with a point-by-point pattern. Meant to inform, the essay's

Visualizing a Point-by-Point Comparison-Contrast Essay

The next chart will help you visualize the point-by-point pattern of a comparison-contrast essay. Like all good models, this one can be altered as needed.

Introduction

- Creates interest
- States the thesis, which can indicate the subjects under consideration; whether you are comparing, contrasting, or doing both; and the points of comparison or contrast you will discuss

▼

First Body Paragraph(s)

- Will make the first point about the first subject and the corresponding point about the second subject
- Can include other patterns

▼

Next Body Paragraph(s)

- Will make and explain the next point about the first subject and the corresponding point about the second subject
- Can include other patterns
- Will continue until all the points are made about both subjects

▼

Conclusion

- Provides closure
- Leaves the reader with a strong final impression

contrasts are also a comment on our society. See if you agree with the author's assessments of why Superman and Batman appeal to the public.

The second essay, "Roll Back Prices or Just Roll On In?" is a contrast developed with a subject-by-subject pattern. The author's contrasts make a point about the retail landscape, a point you may or may not agree with.

The Human and the Superhuman: Two Very Different Heroes

Gus Spirtos

Paragraph 1
The introduction engages interest with historical background. The thesis (sentences 2 and 3) notes that the subjects are Superman and Batman and that the two will be contrasted: One is godlike, the other is human.

In the late 1930s a small company in the fledgling comic book business decided to create something new and different for the public: the superhero. Two of the first characters to be created were opposites of one another. One had the powers of a god while the other was only a man, yet Superman and Batman were the mythic creations that set the stage for all who followed. 1

Paragraph 2
This paragraph begins a point-by-point pattern. The first points are made about the first subject (Superman). The points are why Superman was created, what he was like ("immensely powerful"), and why he appealed to people (he represented idealism).

Superman was created in 1938 by two imaginative young men named Jerry Siegel and Joe Schuster. They wanted to create a character that was immensely powerful. What emerged was someone "faster than a speeding bullet, more powerful than a locomotive, and able to leap tall buildings in a single bound." The powers that Superman possessed created much reader interest. The story of the sole survivor of a doomed planet coming to earth to battle the forces of evil embodied the idealism people wanted during those post-Depression days. Although times have changed, the public still enjoys a bit of idealism once in a while, and Superman provides it. 2

Paragraph 3
This paragraph covers the same points made in paragraph 2, but for the second subject (Batman): why he was created (for vengeance), what he was like (human, not "immensely powerful"), and why he appealed to people (he was a warrior). Note the topic sentence (the first) with its transition.

Unlike Superman, Batman was not created for idealistic purposes, but rather for vengeance. While Superman was flying far above society, Batman was stalking the seedy underside of Gotham, preying on the criminal element. Bob Kane created Batman in 1939 with the human element in mind. The public enjoyed the idea of having a hero as human as they. Also, the concept of revenge associated with the murder of Batman's parents struck a chord with the public's conscience. This troubled hero has become more popular than Superman in recent years because the rise in crime that is prevalent in society today has been represented in the Batman books. With urban society becoming increasingly violent, Batman's methods of combating crime have 3 changed accordingly. Batman is not an idealistic role model, but rather a warrior fighting a never-ending battle.

The major differences between Superman and Batman revolve around the former's benevolence and the latter's malevolence. Superman acts with restraint and exudes a noble, benevolent attitude. Criminals do not fear Superman because of his personality, but rather they fear his power. Batman, on the other hand, strikes fear into the criminal element with his methods and obvious modus operandi: the dark, threatening bat. Criminals are afraid of Batman simply because they don't know what he will do if he apprehends them. This psychological factor is employed by Batman because of his vulnerability. Fear makes the criminal sloppy, and that sloppiness makes it much easier for Batman to apprehend him or her. Because of Superman's obvious invincibility, he does not bother with such tactics. Also, because of Batman's methods, he is not much of a team player. He would rather work alone than with a group of his fellow costumed heroes. Superman, however, enjoys working with, and sometimes leading, his fellow superheroes. He is a group player. 4

Paragraph 4
The topic sentence (the first) presents the last point of contrast: (one is benevolent and one is malevolent). The words "major differences" suggest progressive order. Notice that transitions help the writer move smoothly between subjects.

Superman and Batman have both survived for over 50 years. The reasons for their longevity are simple. Each was a pioneer character in the comic book medium. Superman showed readers that a man could fly. Batman showed them that being human isn't all that bad. The influence of each character on American culture will help both heroes survive at least another 50 years. 5

Paragraph 5
The conclusion creates closure by making a determination and looking to the future.

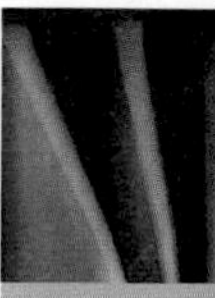

Roll Back Prices or Just Roll On In?

Joshua Tam

A recent Wal-Mart advertising campaign suggests that consumers should shop at corporate big-box discount stores rather than at locally owned, independent shops. The ads in the campaign claim that in a struggling economy, shopping at big-box discount stores like Wal-Mart will save consumers money and time and give them peace of mind. This assertion seems to be a direct 1 challenge to the image that local stores try to project: that they offer value, convenience, and a pleasant shopping experience. In the battle between the big-box discount stores and the locally owned, smaller stores, the big-box stores seem to be winning, but is that a good thing?

Big-box discount stores such as Wal-Mart, Costco, and Sam's Club pride themselves on offering the maximum value for consumers' money. For example, Wal-Mart's slogan, "Save money. Live better," makes the claim that the quality of consumers' lives will actually improve because they spend less on products they buy at Wal-Mart. Indeed, big-box stores do offer lower prices on many products, from cosmetics to appliances. Further, big-box stores are making an increasing effort to offer discounted products with recognizable and sought-after brand names to compete with higher-end stores that offer the same or similar goods. When value is simply a matter of cost-savings, big-box stores have the edge—particularly during times of recession and high unemployment. 2

Big-box stores also like to characterize themselves as convenient, as offering one-stop shopping destinations that save time, in addition to money. Shoppers can purchase everything from groceries to clothing. Because they are often located outside of city centers to accommodate their mammoth size, however, big-box stores may actually not be the closest and most convenient places to shop unless they truly do serve as one-stop shopping destinations. Then, big-box stores offer a level of product selection and availability—and, ultimately, convenience—that a single local store simply cannot compete with. But for consumers who need to shop at multiple stores, big-box discount stores may save neither time nor money. 3

Once in a big-box discount store, consumers often have a harried shopping experience. The huge size of the store makes finding items difficult, and the small number of employees makes getting help even more difficult. A customer with a question is likely to be frustrated. Purchasing items is also a hassle, as customers must stand in long checkout lines and wait to be treated impersonally. Of course, some companies try to personalize the shopping experience. A Wal-Mart greeter, for example, is the first, friendly face consumers see 4 when they enter the otherwise foreboding terrain of the mega-store, but once past the greeter, shoppers are on their own. Consumers must fend for themselves trying to maneuver through the crowded and seemingly endless aisles to find what they need without assistance from store employees.

In contrast to their big-box counterparts, locally owned and operated 5
stores tend not to assert a claim of cost-savings. Although local stores do, like big-box stores, promote the value of their products, they redefine value as something other than cheap prices. Rather than simply being a matter of lower prices, value is directly tied to the quality of goods and the company's standing behind that quality. For example, a recent television advertisement for a local jeweler in a rural Michigan town emphasizes the three generations that have carried on a tradition of quality and service. The ad implies that the quality of the items offered by the local store and the long-standing service offered by the employees will outweigh any cost-savings consumers might find at big-box stores. An opal ring purchased at the locally owned jewelry store may cost more than one at the big-box discount store, but the local jeweler will certify that the stone is superior and will guarantee to clean the ring and check the mounting for free whenever the owner wants. A big-box store typically will not do that. Value, for local stores, is less about a dollar figure and more about quality, reliability, and full service.

Because they are often clustered in accessible sections of town, local 6
stores can claim greater convenience over their big-box counterparts. Workers can easily walk or drive to local stores during their lunch breaks to purchase a last-minute birthday gift or to drop off film for developing. Indeed, many local advertisements make a point of emphasizing the stores' downtown or nearby strip plaza location. In terms of accessibility, then, local stores often come out ahead. But, when convenience refers to the sheer range of products offered by a single store, regardless of the distance shoppers must drive, local stores provide no contest. Indeed, many consumers prefer making a single trip out of town to do all the shopping to staying in town and shopping at multiple stores, no matter how close together they are.

Shoppers' overall shopping experience is likely to be more pleasant in smaller local stores. Finding items and checking out is generally less harrying, and the higher employee-to-customer ratio in local stores allows shoppers to get their questions answered and make their purchases more quickly and with personalized service. Still, many consumers are lured by the anonymity of mall culture, the greater assurance that they can browse a big-box store without an employee's continued insistence to help, without coming across anyone they know. In this sense, big-box stores offer a form of consumer escape, a mini vacation from the realities and relationships of small-town life. The ideal shopping experience seems to coincide, then, with the values, desires, and whims of the individual shopper. 7

Both big-box and local stores try to entice shoppers with their own definitions of value, convenience, and the ideal shopping experience. Is one better than the other? Consumers may not have a chance to decide because big-box discount stores are pushing out local merchants. Many, like me, find the loss of choice to be most unfortunate. 8

EXERCISE Considering "Roll Back Prices or Just Roll On In?"

1. What is Joshua's purpose for writing?
2. Does he compare, contrast, or do both? How does his choice help him achieve his writing purpose?
3. Joshua uses a subject-by-subject pattern. What do you think of this choice? Could he have used a point-by-point pattern equally well?
4. What sentence marks the transition from his first subject to his second?
5. What are Joshua's points of contrast? Does he maintain balance between his points? ■

THINK LIKE A CRITIC; WORK LIKE AN EDITOR: The Student Writer at Work

Organizing the details in a comparison-contrast essay often requires considerable thought and extensive revision. For Gus Spirtos, organizing—and reorganizing—was a primary part of his revision of "The Human and the Superhuman." An early draft of paragraph 2 looked like this:

Early draft

Superman and Batman were the products of different inspirations. In 1938, Jerry Siegel and Joe Schuster envisioned an immensely powerful character with super powers and abilities. This character became Superman, a hero motivated by idealism, who was "more powerful than a locomotive." Unlike Superman, Batman was created with the human element in mind. In 1939, Bob Kane envisioned a hero motivated by avenging the murder of his parents. The public responded to the concept of revenge. It still responds to this concept, as urban society becomes increasingly violent. Whereas Batman is a warrior fighting a never-ending battle against crime, Superman is an idealistic role model who fights crime for high idealistic purposes.

The paragraph is structured well enough: The first sentence is the topic sentence indicating that the point of contrast is the different inspirations. However, Gus felt that the details were "squashed" into the paragraph. He also felt that using the point-by-point pattern in the paragraph made it hard to develop points. He kept feeling the need to alternate back and forth too quickly. At his instructor's suggestion, Gus reorganized to create two paragraphs. Compare the above version with paragraphs 2 and 3 in the final essay. Does the final version work better? Should Gus have made other changes?

LEARNING FROM OTHER WRITERS: Professional Essays

A Fable for Tomorrow

Rachel Carson

Rachel Carson was one of the pioneers of modern environmentalism. Her book Silent Spring *(1962) made the general public aware of the effects of chemical weed and insect killers. "A Fable for Tomorrow," which is an excerpt from* Silent Spring, *uses contrast to warn of the dangers of chemical pesticides.*

There was once a town in the heart of America where all life seemed to live in harmony with its surroundings. The town lay in the midst of a checkerboard of prosperous farms, with fields of grain and hillsides of orchards where, in spring, white clouds of bloom drifted above the green fields. In autumn, oak and maple and birch set up a blaze of color that flamed and flickered across a backdrop of pines. Then foxes barked in the hills and deer silently crossed the fields, half hidden in the mists of the fall mornings. 1

Along the roads, laurel, viburnum and alder, great ferns and wildflowers delighted the traveler's eye through much of the year. Even in winter the roadsides were places of beauty, where countless birds came to feed on the berries and on the seed heads of the dried weeds rising above the snow. 2

The countryside was, in fact, famous for the abundance and variety of its bird life, and when the flood of migrants was pouring through in spring and fall people traveled from great distances to observe them. Others came to fish the streams, which flowed clear and cold out of the hills and contained shady pools where trout lay. So it had been from the days many years ago when the first settlers raised their houses, sank their wells, and built their barns.

Then a strange blight crept over the area and everything began to change. Some evil spell had settled on the community: mysterious maladies swept the flocks of chickens; the cattle and sheep sickened and died. Everywhere was a shadow of death. The farmers spoke of much illness among their families. In the town the doctors had become more and more puzzled by new kinds of sickness appearing among their patients. There had been several sudden and unexplained deaths, not only among adults but even among children, who would be stricken suddenly while at play and die within a few hours. 3

There was a strange stillness. The birds, for example—where had they gone? Many people spoke of them, puzzled and disturbed. The feeding stations in the backyards were deserted. The few birds seen anywhere were moribund; they trembled violently and could not fly. It was a spring without voices. On the mornings that had once throbbed with the dawn chorus of robins, catbirds, doves, jays, wrens, and scores of other bird voices there was now no sound; only silence lay over the fields and woods and marsh. 4

On the farms the hens brooded, but no chicks hatched. The farmers complained that they were unable to raise any pigs—the litters were small and the young survived only a few days. The apple trees were coming into bloom but no bees droned among the blossoms, so there was no pollination and there would be no fruit. 5

The roadsides, once so attractive, were now lined with browned and withered vegetation as though swept by fire. These, too, were silent, deserted by all living things. Even the streams were now lifeless. Anglers no longer visited them, for all the fish had died. 6

In the gutters under the eaves and between the shingles of the roofs, a white granular powder still showed a few patches; some weeks before it had fallen like snow upon the roofs and the lawns, the fields and streams. 7

No witchcraft, no enemy action had silenced the rebirth of new life in this stricken world. The people had done it themselves. 8

This town does not actually exist, but it might easily have a thousand counterparts in America or elsewhere in the world. I know of no community that has experienced all the misfortunes I describe. Yet every one of these disasters has actually happened somewhere, and many real communities have already suffered a substantial number of them. A grim specter has crept upon us almost unnoticed, and this imagined tragedy may easily become a stark reality we all shall know. 9

Considering Ideas

1. What point does Carson's contrast make? Where in the essay does she make her point known?
2. The town in the fable does not exist. Does that fact undermine the author's point? Why or why not?
3. "A Fable for Tomorrow" was published in 1962. Is the essay still relevant today? What does your answer say about the environmental movement?

4. In paragraph 4, Carson says it was "a spring without voices." Explain the significance of the phrase.
5. What is the "white granular powder" of paragraph 7?
6. Would you (or do you) pay money for food grown without chemicals? Why or why not?

Considering Technique

1. What subjects is Carson contrasting? Is the treatment of subjects balanced? Explain.
2. What pattern does Carson use to arrange her details?
3. Carson develops her discussion of the town after the blight in greater detail than she does her discussion of the town before the blight. Why does she do this?
4. *Combining patterns:* How does Carson use narration? Description?
5. How does Carson make the transition from the first subject to the second?
6. How does Carson conclude her essay? Is the conclusion effective? Explain.

For Group Discussion or Journal Writing

Do you think we are doing enough to protect the environment? Explain.

That Lean and Hungry Look[1] SUZANNE BRITT

In "That Lean and Hungry Look," which first appeared in Newsweek *in 1978, Suzanne Britt pronounces skinny people "crunchy and dull, like carrots" and infinitely inferior to fat people. This view is not common in American society, where fat people are often the targets of social discrimination.*

Caesar was right. Thin people need watching. I've been watching them for most of my adult life, and I don't like what I see. When these narrow fellows spring at me, I quiver to my toes. Thin people come in all personalities, most of them menacing. You've got your "together" thin person, your mechanical thin person, your condescending thin person, your tsk-tsk thin person, your efficiency-expert thin person. All of them are dangerous. 1

In the first place, thin people aren't fun. They don't know how to goof off, at least in the best, fat sense of the word. They've always got to be adoing. Give them a coffee break; and they'll jog around the block. Supply them with a quiet evening at home, and they'll fix the screen door and lick S & H green stamps. They say things like "there aren't enough hours in the day." Fat people never say that. Fat people think the day is too damn long already. 2

Thin people make me tired. They've got speedy little metabolisms that cause them to bustle briskly. They're forever rubbing their bony hands together and eying new problems to "tackle." I like to surround myself with sluggish, inert, easygoing fat people, the kind who believe that if you clean it up today, it'll just get dirty again tomorrow. 3

Some people say the business about the jolly fat person is a myth, that all of us chubbies are neurotic, sick, sad people. I disagree. Fat people may not be chortling all day long, but they're a

[1] The title refers to a line in Shakespeare's *Julius Caesar*. Caesar is suspicious of Cassius because, he says, Cassius has "a lean and hungry look" and "such men are dangerous." Caesar was right, as Cassius helps kill Caesar.

hell of a lot *nicer* than the wizened and shriveled. Thin people turn surly, mean and hard at a young age because they never learn the value of a hot-fudge sundae for easing tension. Thin people don't like gooey soft things because they themselves are neither gooey nor soft. They are crunchy and dull, like carrots. They go straight to the heart of the matter while fat people let things stay all blurry and hazy and vague, the way things actually are. Thin people want to face the truth. Fat people know there is no truth. One of my thin friends is always staring at complex, unsolvable problems and saying, "The key thing is . . ." Fat people never say that. They know there isn't any such thing as the key thing about anything. 4

Thin people believe in logic. Fat people see all sides. The sides fat people see are rounded blobs, usually gray, always nebulous and truly not worth worrying about. But the thin person persists. "If you consume more calories than you burn," says one of my thin friends, "you will gain weight. It's that simple." Fat people always grin when they hear statements like that. They know better. 5

Fat people realize that life is illogical and unfair. They know very well that God is not in his heaven and all is not right with the world. If God was up there, fat people could have two doughnuts and a big orange drink anytime they wanted it. 6

Thin people have a long list of logical things they are always spouting off to me. They hold up one finger at a time as they reel off these things, so I won't lose track. They speak slowly as if to a young child. The list is long and full of holes. It contains tidbits like "get a grip on yourself," "cigarettes kill," "cholesterol clogs," "fit as a fiddle," "ducks in a row," "organize" and "sound fiscal management." Phrases like that. 7

They think these 2,000-point plans lead to happiness. Fat people know happiness is elusive at best and even if they could get the kind thin people talk about, they wouldn't want it. Wisely, fat people see that such programs are too dull, too hard, too off the mark. They are never better than a whole cheesecake. 8

Fat people know all about the mystery of life. They are the ones acquainted with the night, with luck, with fate, with playing it by ear. One thin person I know once suggested that we arrange all the parts of a jigsaw puzzle into groups according to size, shape and color. He figured this would cut the time needed to complete the puzzle by at least 50 percent. I said I wouldn't do it. One, I like to muddle through. Two, what good would it do to finish early? Three, the jigsaw puzzle isn't the important thing. The important thing is the fun of four people (one thin person included) sitting around a card table, working a jigsaw puzzle. My thin friend had no use for my list. Instead of joining us, he went outside and mulched the boxwoods. The three remaining fat people finished the puzzle and made chocolate, double-fudged brownies to celebrate. 9

The main problem with thin people is they oppress. Their good intentions, bony torsos, tight ships, neat corners, cerebral machinations and pat solutions loom like dark clouds over the loose, comfortable, spread-out, soft world of the fat. Long after fat people have removed their coats and shoes and put their feet up on the coffee table, thin people are still sitting on the edge of the sofa, looking neat as a pin, discussing rutabagas. Fat people are heavily into fits of laughter, slapping their thighs and whooping it up, while thin people are still politely waiting for the punch line. 10

Thin people are downers. They like math and morality and reasoned evaluation of the limitations of human beings. They have their skinny little acts together. They expound, prognose, probe and prick. 11

Fat people are convivial. They will like you even if you're irregular and have acne. They will come up with a good reason why you never wrote the great American novel. They will cry in your beer with you. They will put your name in the pot. They will let you off the hook. Fat people will gab, giggle, guffaw, gallumph, gyrate and gossip. They are generous, giving and gallant. They are gluttonous and goodly and great. What you want when you're down is soft and jiggly, not muscled and stable. Fat people know this. Fat people have plenty of room. Fat people will take you in. 12

Considering Ideas

1. "That Lean and Hungry Look" is an amusing essay. Does Britt's contrast also make a serious point? Explain.
2. What evidence does Britt offer to support her contention that fat people are better than thin people? That is, what are her chief points of contrast between fat and thin people? Are her generalization and points of contrast fair? Explain.
3. What is Britt's opinion of logic? How can you tell?
4. Britt says, "Fat people will take you in" (paragraph 12). What does she mean?
5. In paragraph 4, Britt says that thin people are "crunchy and dull, like carrots." What is interesting about comparing thin people to carrots?

Considering Technique

1. What pattern of organization does Britt use for her essay? Is this pattern a better choice than the alternative? Explain.
2. Is Britt's treatment of both subjects balanced? Explain.
3. In paragraphs 4 and 9, Britt refers to a person she knows. What purpose does this detail serve?
4. Britt frequently repeats the phrases "thin people" and "fat people." Why?
5. The conclusion of the essay includes alliteration, which is the repetition of an initial consonant sound. What purpose does the alliteration serve?

For Group Discussion or Journal Writing

What attitudes do people have about fat people? About thin people? What stereotypes about fat and thin people are common?

Combining Patterns of Development

The Army's Killer App LEV GROSSMAN

Using comparison-contrast, cause-and-effect analysis, narration, and description, Lev Grossman considers the appropriateness of the U.S. Army's use of a video as a recruitment tool. As you read this essay, which first appeared in Time *magazine in 2005, answer the question the author poses in paragraph 8: "Is it fair to let young people think they can learn about the realities of armed combat from a video game?"*

A military convoy—two humvees, an ambulance and three five-ton trucks full of civilian evacuees—is bumping its way along a snow-swept high-plains dirt road. Suddenly a shout comes down the line: "Contact front!" It's an ambush, with gunmen on both sides of the road. Soldiers on top of the five-tons return fire with mounted machine guns. The clatter is deafening. The truck beds fill up with hot, bouncing, jingling brass shell casings. 1

A few of the civilians wave at the attackers, who continue to blast away. The convoy drives on, past the fray. The rear humvee, its driver obviously bored with the proceedings, wanders off the road to chase a cow. 2

This isn't a real ambush, and the convoy isn't in Iraq or Afghanistan. It's in Guernsey, Wyo., about 90 miles north of Cheyenne. The attack was staged by the U.S. Army for the benefit of about 35 computer programmers—the civilian evacuees—who work on a government-sponsored video game called America's Army. It's a handy training tool for soldiers, but the game's primary mission is to recruit: to persuade the millions of young people who play it on their home computers to go from virtual soldiers to real ones. The programmers are in Guernsey to make sure that the game is as realistic as it can be. But is it real enough? 3

America's Army, in which the military has invested $16 million, is the brainchild of Colonel Casey Wardynski, director of the Army's Office of Economic and Manpower Analysis. "In 1999 the Army had had two bad years of recruiting," Wardynski explains. The Army's square, earnest message of honor and patriotic duty wasn't connecting with the next generation of potential soldiers. "This was a solution to the problem." The military has a long history of playing around with war games for their educational benefits, but America's Army was a different animal altogether. The game is also a giant ad aimed at the public—at the 13-to-24-year-old demographic, to be specific, and it has hit its target squarely. Since it was released on July 4, 2002, America's Army has signed up 4.6 million registered players, and it adds 100,000 new ones every month. According to an Army study, 30% of Americans ages 16 to 24 say that some of what they know about the Army comes from the game. 4

Two things separate America's Army from most other video games. One, it's free: anybody who wants to can download it gratis at www.americasarmy.com or pick up a disc from an Army recruiter. The second is its extreme emphasis on authenticity. All weapons and vehicles in the game are meticulous virtual models of the real thing. "We don't want it to be like, 'He's not holding that right. That button isn't right,' " says Phillip Bossant, the game's art director. "We don't want the shell to eject from the wrong side." Players have to go through simulated Army training before they can enter combat, and the game emphasizes teamwork and the rules of engagement over freelance gunplay. If you shoot civilians or your fellow "soldiers," you'll be sent to a virtual Fort Leavenworth. 5

Realism is why the programmers, many notably plumper and longer-haired than regulation soldiers, have come to Guernsey. The Army releases updates and expansions for America's Army three or four times a year, and to keep the programmers on point it holds events like these—they're known internally as green-ups—every few months. Over the course of three days, they eat MREs (the consensus: chili macaroni good, black bean and rice burrito very very bad), ride in Black Hawks ("That feeling has to be there," Bossant says. "We need that zoom!") and wander around a frozen meadow in the dark wearing night-vision goggles. One of the game designers noticed that the goggles throw off less green light than he expected. That will be reflected in the next version of the game. They drink $1.75 Coors at the All-Ranks Club and climb in and out of the backs of trucks ("It took four people to hoist me in, and I still pulled a muscle," said one ruefully). Then there's that mock ambush. "I wanted them to be shocked," says Major Randy Zeegers, a tall, poster-perfect Green Beret who functions as a liaison between the Army and the designers. "They'll take that and put it in the game." 6

There's another key difference between America's Army and other games. Unlike with, say, Halo 2 or Doom 3, it's a relatively small step from virtual combat to the real thing. You can click a button in the game menu and go straight to an Army recruiting website. Theoretically, the Army can even track your performance in the game and use the information it harvests to evaluate your potential as a soldier. "That's part of the plan, but we haven't done it yet," says Wardynski. "Ultimately, if a kid comes to the Army and signs up, the recruiter could say, 'Have you ever played America's Army?' And with that you could see how they did in the game. Say they've done really well with the medical stuff—are you sure they don't want to be a medic? Of course, most of the kids want to be Green Berets." 7

Is it fair to let young people think they can learn about the realities of armed combat from a video game? Right now America's Army is available only on computers, but this summer it will be out for gaming consoles like Xbox and PlayStation 2, which reach a broader, more recreational audience. No question, the programmers are doing their best to make as accurate a representation as they can, within the limits of the medium. But in the fog of virtual war the lines between education, entertainment and propaganda can get pretty blurry. After I took part in a heated session on a combat simulator, dodging RPGs[1] and blasting away at street fighters in a nameless desert city, Major Zeegers asked me, "So, is killing Afghans fun?" It was hard to tell whether he was joking. 8

Colonel Wardynski is quick to point out that in games generally, when you die, you magically come back to life right away. Not in America's Army, he says. "In our game, there are penalties. In our game, if you're wounded or killed, you're out till the game starts over. The level of casualties your team incurs or inflicts on noncombatants—all those things come home as bad things to do. We don't want them to think it's Rambo."[2] 9

But video games can't—or can't yet—convey the human cost of combat. They pass along the adrenaline rush, the thrill of the fight, and leave out the rest. Games are supposed to be fun, but war isn't. "The violence, the combat—we recognize that's the part of the game people want to play," says Major Chris Chambers, deputy director of the America's Army development team. "We treat it openly and honestly. We have a death animation. We don't sugarcoat it. It's real—" He stops and corrects himself. "It's not real; it's simulated. But we're simulating reality." But it has to be fun too, right? "Bottom line, it's gotta be fun," Chambers agrees. "If it's not fun, you don't have a game." 10

[1]An RPG is a rocket-propelled grenade launcher.
[2]Rambo is a fictional Green Beret played by Sylvester Stallone in a series of movies. The character is known for risk-taking and bravery in the face of great odds.

Considering Ideas

1. What problem is the video game America's Army meant to solve?
2. Why do you think America's Army has been successful?
3. What is the significance of the question Major Zeegers poses at the end of paragraph 8? Do you think he was joking?
4. Paragraph 5 refers to the "extreme emphasis on authenticity" that characterizes America's Army. Why is this emphasis on authenticity important?
5. Does America's Army treat violence and combat "openly and honestly" (paragraph 10)?

Considering Technique

1. For what purpose and audience do you think Grossman wrote "The Army's Killer App"?
2. What elements of comparison-contrast occur in the essay?
3. *Combining patterns:* What purpose do the narration and description in paragraphs 1 and 2 serve?

4. *Combining patterns:* How does Grossman use cause-and-effect analysis to help achieve his writing purpose?
5. Where is the best indication of Grossman's opinion about America's Army?
6. Explain the wordplay in the essay's title

For Group Discussion or Journal Writing

Do you think it is fair and accurate to call America's Army a game? Do you think it is "fair to let young people think they can learn about the realities of armed combat from a video game" (paragraph 8)? Be sure to give reasons for your beliefs.

COMPARISON-CONTRAST IN AN IMAGE

Comparison-contrast is a common component of advertisements because advertisers often compare products to the competition. However, the State Farm Insurance advertisement on page 297 uses comparison a different way.

Considering the Image

1. What subjects does the advertisement consider? Are these subjects compared, contrasted, or both compared and contrasted?
2. In what way does the advertisement say the subjects are similar?
3. What assumptions does the advertisement make about the reader?
4. A comparison is at the heart of the slogan used by State Farm Insurance: "Like a good neighbor, State Farm is there." Do you think the slogan is an effective one? Explain.

DEVELOPMENT NOTE

Dialogue

You learned in Chapter 7 that dialogue is useful when you write narration. However, it is also useful with other patterns of development, particularly to illustrate a point. For example, Suzanne Britt uses dialogue in "That Lean and Hungry Look" to illustrate that thin people believe in logic:

> Thin people believe in logic. Fat people see all sides. The sides fat people see are rounded blobs, usually gray, always nebulous and truly not worth worrying about. But the thin person persists. "If you consume more calories than you burn," says one of my thin friends, "you will gain weight. It's that simple."

Lev Grossman uses dialogue in "The Army's Killer App" to illustrate the authenticity of the video game America's Army:

> All weapons and vehicles in the game are meticulous virtual models of the real thing. "We don't want it to be like, 'He's not holding that right. That button isn't right,'" says Phillip Bossant, the game's art director. "We don't want the shell to eject from the wrong side."

WE SEE YOUR NEED FOR
LIFE INSURANCE GROWING EVERY DAY.
WE LIVE WHERE YOU LIVE.™

As your family grows, so does your need for protection. From Whole Life Insurance to Term Insurance, nobody helps you provide that protection like State Farm. We're there to help you with your other financial needs too, like *State Farm Mutual Funds.*™

LIKE A GOOD NEIGHBOR

STATE FARM IS THERE.™

Call your State Farm agent or visit us at *statefarm.com.*®

Life insurance issued by: State Farm Life Insurance Company (not licensed in NY or WI), State Farm Life and Accident Assurance Company (licensed in NY and WI), Home Offices: Bloomington, Illinois. • For more complete information about State Farm Mutual Funds, including charges and expenses, ask a Registered State Farm Agent for a free prospectus. Read it carefully before you invest or send money. State Farm Mutual Funds are offered by State Farm VP Management Corp. 1-800-447-4930. State Farm VP Management Corp. is a separate entity from those State Farm entities which provide auto, life, fire and health insurance products. L2002-02 04/02

SUGGESTIONS FOR WRITING

Writing Comparison-Contrast

1. Write an essay that compares and/or contrasts two books, television shows, or movies that have similar themes.
2. Contrast the styles of two athletes who play the same sport.
3. Select two movies, television shows, or songs, and use comparison and/or contrast to show how they reflect the values of two different groups of people or the social climates of two different eras. For example, contrast *Leave It to Beaver* and *The Simpsons* to show that the former reflects the 1950s and the latter the present.
4. Compare and/or contrast life as it is today with life as it would be without some modern fact of life, such as cars, telephones, antibiotics, professional football, airplanes, or computers. Be careful not to dwell on the obvious.
5. Compare and/or contrast the way you view something or someone now with the way you did when you were a child.
6. Compare and/or contrast two magazine ads or two television commercials for the same kind of product (wine, cigarettes, cars, jeans, cold remedies, etc.).
7. If you have lived in two cities or states or countries, write a comparison-contrast of some aspect of life in those two places (school, dating, treatment of the elderly, etc.).
8. Write a comparison-contrast of one of the following:
    a. The way you thought something would be and the way it really was
    b. Two political figures
    c. Two people you admire
9. Write a humorous essay comparing and/or contrasting some feature of soap operas with the same feature in real life (the way problems are solved, the way friends interact, the way crimes are solved, etc.).

Reading Then Writing Comparison-Contrast

1. A fable is a story, written in a simple style, with a moral or lesson. Write a fable in the style of Rachel Carson's "A Fable for Tomorrow" that compares and/or contrasts life today with life as it would be if population growth continued unchecked, if drug usage continued to escalate, or if some other problem continued unresolved. Be sure your moral or lesson is apparent.
2. Select two popular politicians, musicians, actors, or comedians with very different styles. Like Gus Spirtos in "The Human and the Superhuman," contrast the two and explain why each appeals to the public.
3. If you play video games, select one, such as Grand Theft Auto or The Sims, and like Lev Grossman in "The Army's Killer App," use comparison-contrast to demonstrate how realistic the game is.

4. Select two opposite types, such as the health nut and the junk food addict, the procrastinator and the planner, the impetuous and the thoughtful, or the studious and the slacker. Like Suzanne Britt, write a humorous contrast that shows the superiority of the one generally looked down upon.

Comparison-Contrast beyond the Writing Classroom

If you have a job, interview your boss and ask him or her to discuss the similarities and differences between your company or business and a competitor's. Then write up the comparison-contrast for a training manual that explains to new employees how the company stacks up against a competitor. If you do not have a job, interview the owner or manager of a company in your community, and complete the same assignment.

Responding to a Theme

1. In "A Fable for Tomorrow," Rachel Carson points out that we are destroying our environment. "Fable" first appeared in Carson's *Silent Spring* in 1962. Do you think our treatment of the environment has improved since the essay was published? Cite specific examples to support your view.
2. Suzanne Britt may have been prompted to write "That Lean and Hungry Look" in part because our society favors thin people over fat people. In an essay, explain and illustrate some of the ways society conveys its anti-fat messages.
3. Using the information in "The Army's Killer App," explain how America's Army blurs the lines that separate education, entertainment, and propaganda. Then discuss the impact this blurring of lines has on society.
4. The advertisement on page 297 uses comparison to sell life insurance. Consider insurance company advertisements that you find in print, on television, or on the radio. Then write an essay that explains what strategies are used and why.
5. *Connecting the readings:* Although we know not to judge a book by its cover, many times we form impressions of people and situations based on their appearance. Write an essay that explores how we react to appearances. You can consider your own experience and observations, along with the ideas in "That Lean and Hungry Look" and "The Army's Killer App."

Writing Comparison-Contrast

The following strategies are not meant to replace your own successful procedures. They are here to try as you work to improve your writing process.

www.mhhe.com/tsw

For further help writing comparison-contrast, go to Catalyst 2.0 > Writing > Writing Tutors > Comparison/Contrast

PROCESS GUIDELINES

Think like a Writer: Generating Ideas, Considering Audience and Purpose, and Ordering Ideas

- For a topic, consider the similarities between two subjects generally thought of as different, or consider the contrasts between two subjects generally viewed as similar. For example, an essay noting the differences between getting a degree and getting an education can clarify the real essence of education, despite the fact that "getting a degree" is commonly equated with "getting an education."

- Determine your purpose by asking yourself these questions:
  - Do I want to clarify the nature of one unfamiliar subject by placing it next to a more familiar subject?
  - Do I want to lend a fresh insight into one subject by placing it next to another?
  - Do I want to bring one or both of my subjects into sharper focus?
  - Do I want to show that one of my subjects is superior to the other?
- To identify and assess your audience, answer the questions on page 42.
- To generate ideas, list every similarity and difference you can think of for your subjects without evaluating your ideas.
- Do you need a specific basis of comparison? If so, write that out.
- Remember that a formal outline can make organizing comparison-contrast easier. Be sure to check your outline for balance.

Think like a Writer: Drafting

- Draft a working thesis that mentions your subjects and whether you will compare, contrast, or do both. Now draft a second working thesis that also mentions your points of comparison or contrast. Which thesis do you prefer?
- Using your outline as a guide, write your draft.
- As you draft, think about using topic sentences so that your reader will understand which points and subjects you are dealing with every step of the way.

Think like a Critic; Work like an Editor: Revising

- Be sure you are discussing the same points for each subject of your essay.
- Read your draft aloud. If you hear awkward shifts from subject to subject or from point to point, add transitions like *similarly, in the same way, on the other hand,* or *in contrast.* Or repeat key words.
- To obtain reader response for revision, see page 105. In addition, ask your reader to place a check mark where more detail is needed.

Think like a Critic; Work like an Editor: Correcting Errors

Use the **comparative form** of adjectives and adverbs to compare and contrast two items and the **superlative form** to compare and contrast more than two items.

Base Form	Comparative Form	Superlative Form
old	older	oldest
eager	more eager	most eager
swiftly	more swiftly	most swiftly
good	better	best

No: Both the machinists union and the flight attendants union are negotiating new contracts, but the machinists have the *best* chance of receiving a pay raise.

Yes: Both the machinists union and the flight attendants union are negotiating new contracts, but the machinists have the *better* chance of receiving a pay raise. [Only two unions are compared, so use the comparative form.]

No: Of all the East Coast hospitals with trauma centers, our city medical center admitted *more* burn victims.

Yes: Of all the East Coast hospitals with trauma centers, our city medical center admitted *the most* burn victims. [More than two hospitals with trauma centers are compared, so use the superlative form.]

For more on comparative and superlative forms, see page 621.

Remember

Avoid stating the obvious. For example, if you are comparing two cars, you need not mention that both cars have engines, although mentioning the size of the engines is appropriate.

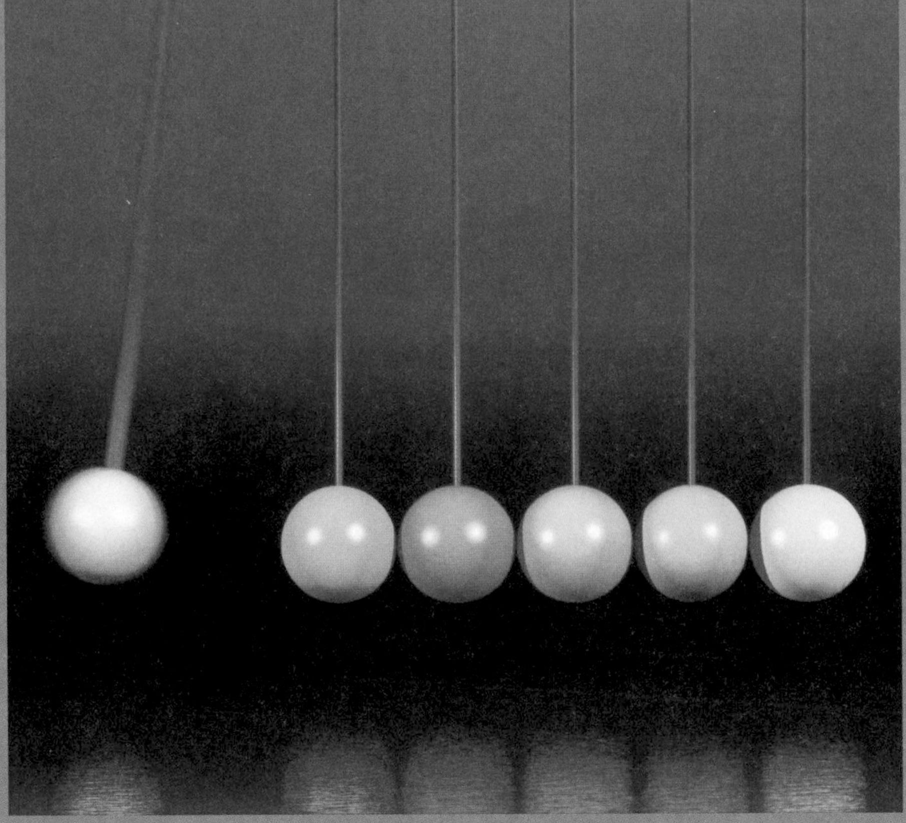

LOOKING AHEAD

Because we are uncomfortable with uncertainty, we want to know why events occur and what the results of events will be. Why have there been so many hurricanes lately? What will happen to the housing market if interest rates rise? Why do prescription drugs cost so much? Why doesn't your car get better mileage? How are the new scholarship guidelines affecting athletic recruiting? When we answer questions like these to determine the reasons for or the results of events, we engage in cause-and-effect analysis. Before learning how to write cause-and-effect analyses, consider the pictured apparatus, known as Newton's Cradle. When a ball on the end is swung as a pendulum into the next ball, the ball on the opposite end is hit away at the same speed as the first ball—but the middle balls barely move. The same phenomenon occurs if two balls are knocked into the others: Two balls on the other end are hit away at the same speed, but the middle balls barely move.

Newton's Cradle is commonly used for demonstration in physics classes. Why would physicists be interested in the cause-and-effect relationship demonstrated by Newton's Cradle?

Newton's Cradle is a popular desktop toy for business executives. What cause-and-effect relationship explains that popularity?

Cause-and-Effect Analysis

Many cities and states have banned smoking in public places, including bars. The cause of the ban is usually concern for public health. The effect of the ban, however, may be more complex than legislators expected, as the article from *The Atlantic* on the next page points out.

When we ask why an event or action occurs or occurred, such as why smoking bans in bars may increase the number of fatal car accidents, we consider **causes.** When we ask what results or resulted from an event, such as what happens when smoking is banned in bars, we consider **effects.** The study of causes, effects, or both causes and effects is **cause-and-effect analysis.**

WHY IS CAUSE-AND-EFFECT ANALYSIS IMPORTANT?

We enjoy a good mystery novel or movie, but we don't like mysteries in real life. If we do not understand why something happens or what might result from an event, we don't say, "What a good mystery!" Instead, we feel unsettled, even anxious. Thus, an understanding of causes and effects helps us make sense of the world and live more comfortably in it. For example, cause-and-effect analysis can help us understand the past if we identify the causes of the stock market crash of 1929 and go on to determine how that event affected our country and its people. Cause-and-effect analysis can help us envision the future, as when we predict the effects of the current air pollution levels on the quality of life 20 years from now.

PUBLIC HEALTH

Smoke 'Em If You Got 'Em

Can smoking cigarettes actually *save* lives? When some state and local governments banned smoking in bars, the number of fatal car accidents involving drunk drivers rose by about 13 percent, two economists recently showed. In the most extreme result, they found that fatal accidents in Jefferson County, Colorado, increased by more than 40 percent after neighboring Boulder County instituted a ban. Although a portion of the smoking population simply stays at home to drink after bans are enacted, the researchers argue that many other smokers seek out bars in locales where simultaneously imbibing and inhaling remains legal. Given the greater distance to a bar in a neighboring county or state, the authors surmise that smokers in towns with bans log more drunk-miles, leading to more alcohol-related accidents. Growing evidence from neurological research also suggests that smoking lessens a drinker's level of intoxication, and that nicotine deprivation can sharpen the urge to drink. As a result, the authors say, smokers who comply with the ban and elect to booze close to home may be drinking more, or getting more drunk from the same number of drinks. While a national smoking ban could offset some of the increase in fatalities, perhaps alcohol, like coffee, is simply best (and safest) when enjoyed with cigarettes.

—*"Drunk Driving After the Passage of Smoking Bans in Bars," Scott Adams and Chad Cotti,* Journal of Public Economics

Cause-and-effect analysis can also help us plan, make decisions, and implement important changes. For example, by considering the effect of investing a certain amount of money every month, a person can estimate the amount of money available upon retirement and decide whether to save additional money. By examining the reasons for a poor grade on a test, a student can adjust study habits for the next exam. Cause-and-effect analysis even helps keep us safe. For example, an understanding of the effects of high cholesterol levels can lead us to avoid certain foods.

The chart that follows illustrates the range of purposes that cause-and-effect analysis can serve.

Purposes for Cause-and-Effect Analysis

Purpose	Sample Cause-and-Effect Analysis
To entertain	A humorous account of the effects of technology on the average person

To share feelings and experiences	An explanation of the effects of being the child of a military parent and moving to a new town every few years
To inform	An explanation of what causes the consumer price index to rise and fall
To persuade (to convince the reader that your city government is not responsible for the blight downtown)	An explanation of the causes of the blight downtown

Cause-and-Effect Analysis across the Disciplines and Beyond

Cause-and-Effect Analysis in the Classroom

Cause-and-effect analysis is one of the most frequently used patterns in college writing. For instance, in a paper for an economics class, you might explain what causes the federal government to raise and lower the prime interest rate. In a midterm history exam, you might explain the causes and effects of the Industrial Revolution. In a research paper for a botany class, you might explain the effects of logging on plant diversity. *How do you think students might use cause-and-effect analysis in an examination for an education class? In an essay for a history class? In a research paper for a psychology class? Why do you think cause-and-effect analysis is so useful in so many courses?*

Cause-and-Effect Analysis in Daily Life

Cause-and-effect analysis is very common in personal writing. For example, in a letter to the editor of your local newspaper, you might write about what will happen if voters do not pass a bond issue. In a letter to a customer service representative, you might note the reasons for your dissatisfaction with a product. In a family newsletter, you might give the effects of your decision to move to a new city or change jobs. *When you have a difficult decision to make, how can writing cause-and-effect analysis help you make that decision?*

Cause-and-Effect Analysis on the Job

Many professions involve writing cause-and-effect analysis. A sales representative might give the reasons for a sales decline. A human resources officer might write a report predicting the effects of changing insurance plans. A nurse will chart the effects of a particular treatment on a patient. *How might a marketing manager use cause-and-effect analysis? What about an advertising executive? A school principal?*

COMBINING CAUSE-AND-EFFECT ANALYSIS WITH OTHER PATTERNS

Other patterns of development often help support cause-and-effect analysis. Suppose you are explaining the effects of moving to a new town when you were in seventh grade, and one of those effects was that you felt like an outsider. You could support this point with the example of the time no one wanted to sit with you at lunch. If you are discussing the effects of dumping industrial waste into rivers, you can describe the appearance of a river that has had industrial waste dumped into it.

Narration can also appear in a cause-and-effect analysis. Say you are explaining why there has been a call for better-trained airport security personnel in the wake of the September 11, 2001, terrorist attacks. To support this point, you can tell the story of the time a major airport was shut down because security staff had left a metal detector unplugged.

Process analysis can also be used. Assume you are explaining the long-term effects of using pesticides, and you mention that pesticides work their way into the food chain. To support this point, you can describe the process, showing your readers how the pesticide goes from soil to plant to animal to human.

You will also encounter cause-and-effect analysis in essays developed primarily with other patterns. If you are narrating an account of your visit to your childhood home, you might include a discussion of how you were affected by the visit. If you are explaining the process of batiking, you might note what causes the cracking effect of the finished art. If you are comparing and contrasting two cities, you might explain what causes the crime rate to be lower in one of them. Cause-and-effect analysis can be a part of any essay, no matter what the dominant pattern of development.

SELECTING DETAIL

The following strategies will help you choose your details for cause-and-effect analysis.

Report Multiple Causes and Effects

A cause can have many effects; an effect can have many causes. If you overlook these multiple causes and effects, you will be oversimplifying. Consider, for example, the construction of a shopping plaza on a quiet street. The effects may be many, including increased traffic congestion, more automobile accidents, higher taxes paid to the local government, more part-time jobs for teenagers, and the need for increased police protection. Omit discussing any of these effects, and your analysis is incomplete. Now consider the announced tuition increase at your college. The causes for the increase are likely to be several, including a reduction in state subsidies, reduced enrollment, the need to pay higher salaries to attract the best professors, and the rising cost of health care benefits. Omit discussing any of these causes, and your reader will fail to understand the full motivation for the increase.

Identify Underlying Causes and Effects

Some causes and effects are obvious; others are beneath the surface, so they are *underlying* causes or effects. Be sure you identify and discuss these underlying causes and effects. For example, if you are examining the causes of the high divorce rate, you might note the increase in two-career marriages. This would be an obvious cause. A closer examination of this cause, however, would reveal underlying causes: Two-career marriages mean less clearly defined roles, less clearly defined divisions of labor, added job-related stress, and increased competition between partners. If you are discussing effects, then you should consider underlying effects. Suppose you are examining the effects of being the youngest child in a family. One obvious effect is that the youngest is considered "the baby." Look beyond that obvious effect to the underlying effects: The youngest can come to view him- or herself as the baby and hence as less capable, less mature, and less strong; the youngest, viewed as a baby, may not be taken seriously by other family members.

Prove That Something Is a Cause or an Effect

You must do more than merely state that something is a cause or an effect; you must provide evidence to prove it. Remember that to have adequate detail and convince your reader, you must show and not just tell. Suppose you are analyzing the effects of low teacher pay, and you note that low pay causes talented people to spurn teaching as a career. To back up this statement, you could survey bright students you know and ask them whether they would consider teaching as a career. Ask those who say they would not choose teaching why. If a significant percentage cites low pay, you can mention that cause.

Identify Immediate and Remote Causes

Immediate causes occur near the time of an event, while *remote* causes occur in a more distant time. For example, consider a cause-and-effect analysis of the shortage of nurses in your area. An immediate cause is that managed care has reduced the income of nurses in local hospitals and thereby has reduced the number of nurses in your area. A more remote cause is the post–World War II baby boom that has given us record numbers of aging Americans in need of medical care. It is tempting to assume that immediate causes are more significant than remote ones, but that is not always true. In the case of the shortage of nurses, the remote cause is the more important one.

Reproduce Causal Chains

A **causal chain** occurs when a cause leads to an effect and that effect becomes a cause, which leads to another effect that becomes a cause leading to another effect, and so on. To understand causal chains, consider the effects of raising the cost of a stamp.

First, the government raises the price of a postage stamp. What is the effect? Once the cost of the stamp goes up, it costs more to mail a letter. That is the first effect. This effect becomes a cause: It causes business expenses to rise for companies. What is the effect of this cause? The cost of doing business increases. This effect becomes a cause: It causes companies to raise the prices on their goods and services. What is the effect? Consumers cannot afford the increase, so they buy less. This effect becomes a cause: It causes the economy to slow down. Causal chains like this one are often part of a cause-and-effect analysis.

Sample Causal Chain

Cause		**Effect**
Government increases price of stamp	→	Cost of mailing letter increases
Cost of mailing letter increases	→	Business expenses increase
Business expenses increase	→	Cost of doing business increases
Cost of doing business increases	→	Companies raise prices of goods and services
Companies raise prices of goods and services	→	Consumers buy less
Consumers buy less	→	Economy slows

Explain Why Something Is or Is Not a Cause or an Effect

Sometimes you should explain why something is a cause or an effect. For example, suppose you state that one effect of divorce on young children is to make them feel responsible for the breakup of their parents' marriage. You should go on to explain why: Young children think that if they had behaved better, their parents would not have fought so much and would have stayed married.

Sometimes you must explain that something is *not* a cause or an effect. Say you are explaining the causes of math anxiety among women. If your reader believes that women are genetically incapable of excelling in math, then you should note that this explanation is untrue and explain *why* it is not true: No studies have shown that anyone is good or bad at mathematics because of gender.

Consider Your Audience and Purpose

Your audience and purpose will determine the details you include. For example, if you are explaining what causes the consumer price index to rise and fall to inform your classmates in intermediate economics, you need not define *consumer price index* because intermediate economics students have learned the definition already. However, a definition would be helpful to the average reader of your city newspaper because, while readers have heard of the consumer price index, they may be unsure of what it is. If you are analyzing the effects of advertising aimed at children in order to share your experience with your own child, you might narrate an account of how your child reacted to advertisements for sweetened cereal. However, if your purpose is to convince your reader that advertising should not be aimed at children, one parent's experience with one child is insufficient, so you might research to find data on how children in general react to advertisements for sweetened cereal.

BEING A RESPONSIBLE WRITER

Sometimes writers exaggerate causes or effects to achieve their writing purpose. You see this often in advertising, where the effect of, say, a new detergent is said to be "dazzling" whites or the effect of a moisturizer is said to be "a radiant, youthful appearance." We try these products and are disappointed when we do not need sunglasses to view our white clothes or when we are not asked to show an ID to see an R-rated movie. Clearly, such exaggeration is misleading.

Writers also mislead if they omit causes or effects to achieve their writing purpose. Say you are analyzing the effects of computers on higher education because you want to convince your university to put computers in every residence hall room. You may be tempted to omit mentioning that students can become distracted by surfing the Internet for extended periods of time because this effect does not help you achieve your purpose. However, the omission contributes to an incomplete analysis. Rather than omit it, you should mention it and counter it in some way, perhaps like this: "With easy access to computers, students may be tempted to surf the Internet for extended periods. However, that is not necessarily wasted time because Net surfing offers important relaxation for students."

To be a responsible writer, ask yourself these questions:

- Have I exaggerated any causes or effects?
- Have I identified and explained multiple causes or effects?
- Have I omitted any causes or effects?

In many of the "Being a Responsible Writer" sections in Part 2, you learned ways to avoid plagiarism. In this section, it seems logical to discuss one of the chief causes of plagiarism: Many students knowingly commit acts of plagiarism because they mistakenly believe that plagiarism is a victimless offense, that it is harmless to others. However, plagiarism can create a causal chain with effects that *can* harm other students. Honest students may not be able to compete successfully with students who cheat, and they may have lower grades as a result, causing them to lose out on scholarships, recommendations, and jobs.

ORGANIZING CAUSE-AND-EFFECT ANALYSIS

Your thesis for a cause-and-effect analysis can indicate the subject you will analyze. It can also note whether you will discuss causes, effects, or both causes and effects.

Thesis indicating that the essay will analyze causes

```
To solve the problem of teenage drug abuse, we must
first understand what leads teenagers to take drugs.
```

USING SOURCES FOR A PURPOSE

The paragraph below is the introduction to an essay for a business administration class, an essay about how to incorporate stress reduction strategies into a business model. The paragraph, which illustrates one way to use sources from this book in your writing, includes paraphrase from paragraphs 3, 5, 12, and 13 of "Our Schedules, Ourselves" on page 323. (For more information on writing paraphrases and quotations, see Chapter 17.)

THESIS IDEA: Let's look at how Walljasper's ideas can be incorporated into a successful business model.

WRITING PURPOSE AND AUDIENCE: To inform classmates in a business administration class about how to include stress reduction techniques in a business model

The paraphrase in sentences 3–7 helps the writer create interest by explaining Walljasper's ideas and leading in to the thesis idea that stress reduction can be included in a business model.

[1]Pick up any popular magazine, and you will likely find an article about stress—about how stressed we are, about the health risks associated with stress, about why we are so stressed, or about how to cope with stress. [2]Jay Walljasper understands the problem and its solution. [3]In "Our Schedules, Ourselves," he explains that we are victims of our schedules and our technology. [4]We fill our days with too many activities that are rigidly scheduled. [5]Further, Walljasper says that the computers and cell phones that were supposed to give us free time have, instead, made it possible for bosses to reach us when we are on vacation or dining after work. [6]To reduce stress, Walljasper believes we must think about time differently and look for opportunities to abandon our schedules. [7]He even recommends the benefits of committing to unscheduled time (325). [8]Assuming Walljasper is right, let's look at how his ideas can be incorporated in a successful business model.

Avoiding Plagiarism

The paragraph illustrates the following points about using paraphrase and avoiding plagiarism.

- **Restate the author's ideas accurately.** Compare the paraphrase in sentences 3–7 to paragraphs 3, 5, 12, and 13 of the source to see that the writer of the paraphrase does not add any meaning that is not in Walljasper's essay and does not change Walljasper's meaning in any way.
- **Use your own words and style.** Compare the paraphrase in sentences 3–7 to paragraphs 3, 5, 12, and 13 to see that the writer does not copy Walljasper's wording or style.
- **Reintroduce as necessary.** As sentences 5–7 show, when your paraphrase spans several sentences, reintroduce the source strategically so that the reader will know you are still using outside material.

Myths about Sources

MYTH: Only quotations have to be documented; paraphrases can be used without citation.

FACT: You need to document *all* material from sources according to the conventions discussed in Chapter 17. The exception is common knowledge, as explained on page 279.

Thesis indicating that the essay will analyze effects

```
Not everyone realizes the effects unemployment has
on a person's self-image.
```

Thesis indicating that the essay will analyze both causes and effects

```
The reasons Congress is cutting aid to the homeless
are understandable, but the effects of this action
will be devastating.
```

You can arrange the detail for your cause-and-effect analysis a number of ways. Often a progressive order is best, whereby you give the most significant or obvious causes or effects first and work progressively to the least significant or obvious causes or effects. You can also move from the least significant or obvious to the most significant or obvious.

A chronological arrangement is possible if the causes or effects occur in a particular time order. If you are reproducing causal chains, a chronological order is a likely choice since one cause will lead to effects and other causes that occur in a particular time sequence.

Sometimes you will group causes and effects in particular categories. Suppose you are explaining what causes high school students to drop out of school. You could group together all the causes related to home life, then group together all the causes related to peer pressure, and then group together all the causes related to academic environment.

The introduction of a cause-and-effect analysis can be handled in any of the ways described in Chapter 3. Another approach is to explain why understanding the cause-and-effect relationship is important. For example, if you want to provide reasons for adolescent drug use, your introduction could note that understanding the reasons for the problem is a first step toward solving the problem.

If your essay will treat the causes of a problem, your introduction can provide a summary of the chief effects. Say you will explain why fewer people are entering the teaching profession. Your introduction can note some of the chief effects of this phenomenon: fewer qualified teachers, a decline in the quality of education, and larger class sizes. Similarly, if your essay will explain the effects of something, your introduction can note the chief causes. For example, if your essay will discuss the effects of increased tuition fees at your school, your introduction can briefly explain the causes of the increase: lower enrollment generating less income, higher operating costs, or perhaps an expensive building program.

The conclusion of a cause-and-effect analysis can be handled in any of the ways explained in Chapter 3. Often a cause-and-effect analysis ends with a conclusion drawn from the cause-and-effect relationship. For example, if your essay has shown what the causes of teenage drug abuse are, it could end with the conclusion you have reached about the best way to combat the problem. A summary can also be an effective way to end. If the cause-and-effect relationship is complex, with several causal chains, your reader may appreciate a final reminder of the complete picture.

EXERCISE Writing Cause-and-Effect Analysis

1. Check your textbooks in other courses, as well as newsmagazines and newspapers, for a piece of writing that includes cause-and-effect analysis. Read the selection and answer these questions:
   a. Does the cause-and-effect analysis form the primary pattern of development, or is it part of a piece developed primarily with another pattern?
   b. Are causes, effects, or both causes and effects discussed?
   c. What purpose does the cause-and-effect analysis serve?
2. Pick an important decision you made sometime in your life, such as quitting the football team, choosing a college, joining the army, or moving

Visualizing a Cause-and-Effect Analysis

The chart that follows can help you visualize one structure for a cause-and-effect analysis. Like all good models, this one can be altered as needed.

Introduction

- May engage interest by noting important effects if you are analyzing causes or by noting important causes if you are analyzing effects
- Includes a thesis that mentions the subject and whether causes, effects, or both will be discussed

First Body Paragraph

- Will state the first cause or effect
- May reproduce causal chains
- May explain why something is or is not a cause or an effect
- May identify underlying causes and effects or remote causes
- Will arrange details in a progressive or other logical order

Next Body Paragraphs

- Give remaining causes and/or effects
- May reproduce causal chains
- May explain why something is or is not a cause or an effect
- May identify underlying causes and effects or remote causes
- Will arrange details in a progressive or other logical order

Conclusion

- May draw a conclusion from the cause-and-effect relationship
- May summarize if the cause-and-effect relationship is complex

away from home. Make one list of everything that caused you to make your decision. Then make a second list of all the effects of your decision.

3. Study your list, try to identify one causal chain, and list every cause and effect in that chain.
4. Study your list again. If you were to write an essay from the list, would you treat causes, effects, or both? Why? What audience and purpose would you use for the essay?
5. Would you note anything that is not a cause or an effect? If so, what? ■

LEARNING FROM OTHER WRITERS: Student Essays

The two cause-and-effect analyses that follow were written by students. The first, "Mom, There's a Coyote in the Backyard!" is annotated to help you study its key features. This essay considers effects. As you read, notice how the writer uses topic sentences to present each effect.

The second cause-and-effect analysis, "Athletes on Drugs: It's Not So Hard to Understand," explains the reasons some professional athletes use drugs. Notice how well the author of this essay explains the causes.

Mom, There's a Coyote in the Backyard!

Cammie Bullock

1 Not so long ago, the howl of the coyote was associated only with the deserts and plains of the American Wild West. However, the coyote was considered vermin in its native Western habitat and was nearly eradicated by hunting through the early twentieth century. The clever animal simply hit the road and found hunting grounds in the suburbs of large midwestern and East Coast cities, including the suburbs of St. Louis, where I live. Coyotes find plenty of prey in these new areas, particularly where cleared land borders on forest or park. Unfortunately, their ability to scavenge and hunt anywhere has made them an increasing nuisance.

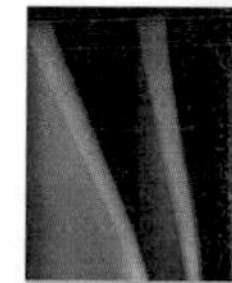

Paragraph 1
The introduction gives important background information. The thesis, the last sentence, indicates that the essay will discuss the nuisance effects of the coyote's move to the suburbs.

Notice that the introduction explains a cause—the reason the coyote has migrated eastward to the suburbs.

2 Increasingly, coyotes in their new habitats are coming in close contact with pets, often attacking them. Several years ago, a coyote killed former talk-show host Kathy Lee Gifford's bichon frise (a small, fluffy white dog)

Paragraph 2
The topic sentence, the first sentence, states the first effect: attacks on pets. Notice the use of example in the supporting detail.

in the backyard of her Greenwich, Connecticut, estate. Here in the St. Louis area, there have been numerous reports of coyotes attacking and killing small dogs left unattended in backyards. Although there do not seem to be any cases of coyotes attacking humans, people in the suburb of Ladue have reported seeing packs of five or six coyotes that seem to be less afraid of people, even coming close to backyards when people are outside.

Paragraph 3
The topic sentence, the first sentence, states the second effect: the spread of distemper and rabies, which could lead to attacks on people. Notice the transition that signals effect, "consequently."

There is also increasing concern here that rabies and canine distemper might spread to coyotes, which would make them more likely to attack people. Consequently, my veterinarian urges all dog owners (I have a terrier) to have their dogs vaccinated against rabies and canine distemper, and to be aware that coyotes seen in the daytime might be infected. She told me that in Texas, where rabies has wiped out most of the native coyotes, authorities have been spreading vaccine-laced bait where the remaining coyotes can get it; this isn't a good idea for a suburban area, though, where domestic animals and even children could come in contact with the bait. 3

Paragraph 4
The topic sentence, the first sentence, states the next effect: scavenging. Notice that the effect is also a cause: It causes the writer to secure her garbage cans with bungee cords.

Scavenging is another problem associated with coyotes. They are attracted to the smell of garbage and scavenge at a town dump site. My garbage cans have been raided a few times each year by raccoons, but coyotes are not as skilled at knocking over or opening trash cans. Even so, our local waste collection company distributes a flyer every year suggesting ways to keep garbage cans secure from scavenging coyotes. (I use bungee cords to keep the lids secure on my trash cans.) 4

Paragraph 5
The conclusion provides a satisfying ending by explaining how the coyote problem can be addressed.

Now that coyotes appear to have settled comfortably into their new ecological niche, a debate is growing about the most effective way to monitor and control the population. By carefully monitoring and vaccinating our own domestic animals, keeping garbage cans covered and secure, and working toward cruelty-free methods of wild animal population control (such as trap and release), we can learn to enjoy the occasional howl of the "song dog" even at a backyard barbecue. 5

Athletes on Drugs: It's Not So Hard to Understand

John Selzer

On June 17, 1986, Len Bias, a basketball star from the University of Maryland, was the second pick in the National Basketball Association amateur draft. Bias had everything going for him; he was a 22-year-old kid about to become a millionaire and superstar. He was on top of the world (or so it seemed). Forty hours later Len Bias was dead—from an overdose of drugs. The Len Bias story is tragic, but it is just one of many cases. Just eight days following the Bias tragedy, Cleveland Browns all-pro safety Don Rogers, then 23, died of a drug overdose. Steve Howe, once a dazzling pitcher, found himself out of baseball because of his drug problems. And the list goes on. Why? Why are professional athletes, people who have money, success, fame, and power, destroying their lives with drugs? 1

To most people the life of professional athletes is filled with glamour. All they see are the sports cars, the million-dollar contracts, and the adoring fans. People do not realize the mental anguish that is involved with being a professional athlete. The loneliness, the fear of failure, and the insecurities of their jobs are just a few of the pressures that athletes have to deal with every day. In some sports, such as baseball, basketball, and hockey, the teams play five to seven games a week, so the athletes must travel to two or three different cities. This constant travel has an adverse effect on athletes' ability to cope with daily pressures. They begin to miss family and friends, often becoming lonely and depressed. As an alternative to this depression, they turn to drugs. 2

In most cases, professional athletes of today have been the best in their sports since childhood. They have won honors and awards for their talents all through their lives. They have seldom been failures, and fear of becoming one is their worst nightmare. The athletes are surrounded by family, friends, and coaches who tell them they are the best. These people attempt to make the athletes feel flawless, incapable of making a mistake. Therefore, when players do have a bad day, they not only let themselves down but those people too. Again, in order to deal with the pressure, drugs become an option. 3

For most of today's professional athletes, sports is all they know. Many 4
do not have a college education, and, more than likely, without sports they would not have a career. Athletes must remain above the competition to keep their jobs. In some cases, when the God-given ability is not enough, the player uses drugs for improvement. Athletes have found that some drugs, such as amphetamines, can increase their physical abilities. These drugs help the athlete to perform better, therefore giving her or him a greater chance of success. For example, steroids have almost become a norm in some sports. Bodybuilders and football players have discovered that these drugs speed up the development of strength and muscles. In professional football, large numbers of offensive and defensive linemen claim to have used steroids at least once in their careers. Those professional athletes who refuse to use amphetamines and steroids are no doubt at a disadvantage.

In today's sports athletes are bigger, stronger, and faster; therefore, more 5
injuries are occurring. Injuries are part of the game, and all players have suffered at least one in their careers. The most discomforting fact about injuries for professional athletes of today is not the pain but the drugs that are used to ease their discomfort. In many cases, coaches and trainers strongly encourage the use of such drugs. In the high-priced world of sports, time is money. Athletes cannot afford to sit out and allow their injuries to heal properly. They often turn to drugs to help speed up the healing process. Often these drugs are illegal; sometimes they are more dangerous than the injury itself, but for the athlete the use of the drug appears to be the only choice. Without the drugs, the players face the loss of thousands of dollars as well as their livelihoods.

The professional athlete has to deal with a great deal of pressure. As the 6
mental struggles begin to mount and the aches and pains begin to multiply, the athlete becomes more susceptible to drug use. Drug use should never be accepted, but in the case of the professional athlete, condemning the problem will not solve it. The fans, owners, and especially the players themselves must reexamine the pressures and stop the drug problem before it destroys more people's lives.

EXERCISE Considering "Athletes on Drugs: It's Not So Hard to Understand"

1. In paragraph 1, John expresses his thesis as a question. How well does this strategy work? Explain.
2. Does the author do a good job of explaining why the factors he mentions are causes? Explain your view.
3. Does John omit any important causes? Explain.
4. Does John convince you that drug use by athletes is understandable? Why or why not?
5. What strategies does John use for his introduction and conclusion? ■

THINK LIKE A CRITIC; WORK LIKE AN EDITOR: The Student Writer at Work

When Cammie Bullock read over the first draft of "Mom, There's a Coyote in the Backyard!" she was concerned about her transition from discussing the threat of coyotes to pets, to discussing the threat to humans.

First draft

> Coyotes in their new habitats are coming in contact with pets and attacking them. Several years ago, a coyote killed former talk-show host Kathy Lee Gifford's small dog in the backyard of her Greenwich, Connecticut, estate. Here in St. Louis, coyotes have attacked and killed small dogs left unattended in back yards. It hasn't happened yet, but there is concern that rabies and canine distemper might spread to coyotes, which would make them more likely to attack people. Consequently, my veterinarian recommends that dog owners have their dogs vaccinated and watch out for coyotes in the daytime that might be infected. She said that in Texas, where rabies has wiped out most of the native coyotes, authorities are spreading bait with vaccine in it where the coyotes can get it, but this idea will not work for a suburban area because of domestic animals and children.

Cammie realized that the paragraph was trying to make two separate points, one about the threat to pets and one about the threat to people. Neither point was developed well. She addressed the problem by putting each point in its own paragraph and adding detail in the first paragraph to pave the way for the second paragraph.

Second draft

Coyotes in their new habitats are coming in contact with pets and attacking them. Several years ago, a coyote killed former talk-show host Kathy Lee Gifford's small dog in the backyard of her Greenwich, Connecticut, estate. Here in St. Louis, coyotes have attacked and killed small dogs left unattended in backyards. Although there do not seem to be any cases of coyotes attacking humans, people in Ladue have reported seeing packs of coyotes that seem to be less afraid of people.

There is also concern that rabies and canine distemper might spread to coyotes, which would make them more likely to attack people. Consequently, my veterinarian recommends that dog owners have their dogs vaccinated and watch out for coyotes in the daytime that might be infected. She said that in Texas, where rabies has wiped out most of the native coyotes, authorities are spreading bait with vaccine in it where the coyotes can get it, but this idea will not work for a suburban area because of domestic animals and children.

Cammie made other changes in the next draft, but she felt the transition from the threat to pets to the threat to people was now better. What do you think? Is the transition better? Is it good enough?

LEARNING FROM OTHER WRITERS: Professional Essays

Eight Reasons Plagiarism Sucks JACK SHAFER

In this analysis of effects, Jack Shafer, who is editor-at-large for the online publication Slate, *explains the harm done by journalists who plagiarize. The article, which first appeared in* Slate *in 2008, mentions reporter Alexei Barrionuevo, who admitted to taking two lines from a* Miami Herald *piece and including them in his* New York Times *article. He was also accused of lifting material from Bloomberg News.*

Readers have stormed my inbox, accusing me of "picking nits" in the latest of my two columns about the plagiarism of *New York Times* reporter Alexei Barrionuevo (Feb. 27 and March 5). One reader found my charge "hyperactive." Another insisted that Barrionuevo's lifting from Bloomberg News was akin to "repeating the bus schedule," hence no foul. Another ridiculed me, saying I exist inside an "echo chamber" of journalists, academics, and bloggers who "care about this crap." 1

As I read that last note, I realized that I needed to explain in detail why plagiarism matters and why journalists, academics, and bloggers are right to care about it. In order of importance, here are my eight reasons plagiarism sucks: 2

It swindles readers. One of my correspondents mistakenly thought that what disturbed me most about plagiarism was that it robs other writers of their labors. That's the least of my problems. Plagiarism burns me up because it violates the implied warranty that comes with every piece of journalism. Unless qualified with citations or disclaimers such as "compiled from wire reports," news articles are supposed to be original work. 3

When a reporter appropriates the words of another without credit, he gives the reader the mistaken impression that he has independently verified the primary facts in his story. So, if the first reporter got stuff wrong—dates, names, places, events—the lazy and corrupt second reporter will end up cheating the reader out of the true story. 4

(Plagiarism aside, some editors discourage their reporters from milking Nexis[1] for research not because they worry about their guys pinching but because they worry about their guys inadvertently retransmitting other guys' mistakes and clichés, setting them ever deeper in stone.) 5

Journalism is about truth, not lies. I cringe at writing those precious words, but like Samantha Power[2], I've released them and can't yank them back. A reporter who abducts the work of another reporter without giving credit tells a sleazy lie with every keyboard stroke. "I wrote that," he lies. The plagiarist's fraud dissolves the trust between his publication and its reader; it injures the reader (of course), the plagiarist's publication, the plagiarist's colleagues, and the plagiarist's profession. (Good lord, am I starting to sound like a weepy Committee of Concerned Journalists parishioner?) 6

It corrupts the craft. This is really a corollary of "Harms Readers" and "Truth, Not Lies." Every plagiarism bust reinforces the view of readers and viewers who already believe the profession is filled with lying, psychopathic scum. Bank robbers injure only the banks they rob. Plagiarists injure the entire journalism profession, even the most scrupulous and honest of practitioners. 7

It promotes the dishonest. One path to journalistic success is productivity. Another is writing deeply sourced stories. The industrious plagiarist combines both techniques, routinely out-producing his colleagues with stolen, excellent copy. When the time comes to appoint a new London bureau chief or a new deputy editor for metro, who is going to get the slot: the good reporter or the supercharged, not-yet-apprehended plagiarist? Nobody will deny that rewarding cheaters for cheating sucks. But again, the greatest injury isn't done to other journalists but to readers. When the less-talented fellow gets the better job, the paper (or magazine or Web site or broadcast) suffers, and that suffering is inflicted upon readers. 8

It denigrates the hard work of others. How often do convicted plagiarists or their apologists attempt to blot away the plagiarists' crimes by saying, "Oh, the borrowing was trivial." Or, "That was just a boilerplate story." They'll insist that there are only so many ways to write "Joe Doe, the famous rope climber, died in his bed last night from a gunshot wound," and that such news story similarities are inevitable. 9

The problem with the boilerplate excuse is that news stories written by nonplagiarists almost never overlap the way the stories written by plagiarists do. I thought I made this point in my last Barrionuevo story by publishing a sidebar that stacked the opening paragraphs from his "mad cow" story against those from the Bloomberg story he lifted from and the accounts published by the globeandmail.com

[1]Nexis is a content provider for professionals in law, business, education, and government.

[2]Samantha Power was a member of Barack Obama's 2008 campaign team until she called rival Hillary Clinton "a monster."

and the *Omaha World-Herald.* Except for Barrionuevo, each journalist quoted in the sidebar brought to the alleged boilerplate their unique news judgment. 10

If you think it's easy to write compelling boilerplate, just try. 11

It's not what we paid for. No *New York Times* subscriber should have to pay in excess of $600 a year for rewritten Bloomberg News copy. 12

It's not theft—it's something worse. Lots of people hate plagiarism because they consider it theft. I'm not really a member of that party, even if I've used the words *theft, stealing, crime,* and the like in my plagiarism columns. There is no crime called "plagiarism." If somebody publishes an entire paragraph of mine without credit, you can't really say that he's *stolen* it from ***Slate***. My words can still be found at the same old URL, and the local sheriff can't charge the perpetrator with felony theft even if he thinks the perp nicked my piece. (However, a word-thief can be served with a civil complaint alleging copyright infringement, or if the pilfering is grand enough a U.S. attorney may decide to charge him with the felony of willful copyright infringement.) 13

The reason plagiarism is worse than theft is because the only real remedies for it are shame and ostracism, both of which have proved very poor deterrents. Most plagiarists find a way back into the business, as Trudy Lieberman reported in the *Columbia Journalism Review.* 14

It's vampiric. Before anybody points the plagiarism gun at me, please allow me to credit my ***Slate*** colleague David Plotz with that witty formulation. "The plagiarist is, in a minor way, the cop who frames innocents, the doctor who kills his patients. The plagiarist violates the essential rule of his trade. He steals the lifeblood of a colleague," Plotz observed. 15

To put it in the modern vernacular, plagiarism sucks. 16

Considering Ideas

1. "Eight Reasons Plagiarism Sucks" is one of a series of *Slate* pieces that Shafer wrote about Alexei Barrionuevo's plagiarism (see headnote). For what purpose do you think he wrote this particular article?
2. Why does Shafer think that plagiarism is worse than theft (paragraph 13)?
3. How does plagiarism swindle readers?
4. Shafer says that he gives his eight reasons "in order of importance." Do you agree with his ranking of reasons? Explain.

Considering Technique

1. Paragraphs 1 and 2 form the introduction of Shafer's article. What approach does he take to that introduction?
2. Which sentence is Shafer's thesis, and which words indicate that he will discuss effects?
3. Shafer presents the effects in boldface topic sentences that open paragraphs. Why do you think he does so?
4. What causal chain appears in paragraph 8?
5. Why does Shafer use the informal term *suck* for a subject as serious as plagiarism?

For Group Discussion or Journal Writing

Do you think plagiarism should be a crime punishable in the same way as other theft? Why or why not?

It's Not Just How We Play That Matters **Suzanne Sievert**

Suzanne Sievert is concerned about a new trend: contests and games with no winners. In this cause-and-effect analysis, which first appeared in 2001 in Newsweek*'s "My Turn" column, Sievert asserts that children do not suffer from competition; in fact, they benefit from it.*

Last Halloween my 5-year-old son entered a pumpkin-decorating contest at his school. He was so proud of his entry—a wild combination of carvings, paint and feathers he had constructed all by himself with his own kindergartner's sense of art. He lugged it proudly to the school cafeteria and we placed it among the other entries, a very creative bunch of witch pumpkins, snowman pumpkins, scary pumpkins, even a bubble-gum blowing, freckle-faced pumpkin wearing a baseball cap. "Wow," I thought to myself, "the judges are going to have a tough time choosing a winner." 1

I guess the judges must have thought the same thing because they didn't choose one. When we returned to the school cafeteria for the annual fall dinner that evening, we saw that all the pumpkins had been awarded the same black and gold ribbon. My son, eagerly searching to see if he'd won, kept asking me, "Which pumpkin won? Where's the winner?" 2

What could I say? "Well, it looks like everyone won. Look: you got a ribbon, honey!" 3

Kids are smart. That didn't satisfy him. "Yeah, but who *won*?" he asked. I could sense his disappointment and my own disappointment as well. What's the point of having a contest if you're not going to pick a winner? 4

I understand what the school was trying to do. The judges meant to send the message that all the children had done a great job and deserved to be recognized. I worry that a different message was sent, one that said losing is a hardship that no one should have to go through. 5

I've noticed this trend a lot lately: adults' refusing to let children fail at something. It's as if we grown-ups believe that kids are too fragile to handle defeat. Last year I purchased a game for my son and his 4-year-old brother that I'd found in a catalog. It was touted as teaching kids to work together to reach an end goal, with lots of fun problem-solving along the way. "Great!" I thought, and ordered it right away. The game arrived and I played it with my boys. The trouble was that everyone won this game. We all arrived at the end together. This sounds great in theory, but where's the incentive to keep playing? We played that game twice, and it has sat gathering dust ever since. 6

Without a potential winner, a game or contest loses its excitement. If there's nothing to compete for, the drive to do our best is replaced by a "What's the point?" attitude. Competition is symbiotic with motivation. It's part of human nature to be competitive; after all, survival of the fittest is the basis of evolution. A competitive spirit is key to our success as adults, so why shouldn't we foster it in our children? 7

I'm not suggesting we pit our children against each other in fierce competitions in all aspects of life. We should be wary of overzealous coaches who lose the spirit of good sportsmanship in the heat of the game. But in the right situations, a healthy rivalry can teach our kids a lot about life. While games and contests illustrate the importance of drive and determination, they also teach our children how to lose. And with that comes other invaluable lessons—about learning from mistakes, searching for ways to improve and finding the will to try again. 8

As a parent I know the easier route is to keep kids from losing at something rather than to face

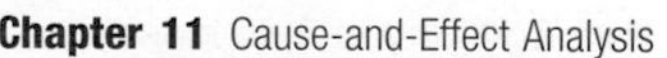

their frustration when it happens. I'm guilty of purposely letting my boys win at Candyland, and when we occasionally have a race to see who can get dressed first, I sometimes declare, "You're both the winners!" rather than listen to them taunt one another, "Ha ha, you lose. I'm the winner!" But when I do hear those taunts, I try to use them to my advantage. I once said to the loser in a game we were playing, "Well, he may be the winner, but *you* are a good sport." This was a new term for my boys at the time, but when I explained what it meant, my "good sport" was very proud of himself. And the next time we played a game, my other son deliberately lost just so he could be a good sport, too. 9

Kids can endure failure. My son understood that he might not win the pumpkin contest. He would have been fine if he hadn't gotten a ribbon; he would have tried again next year. The let-down for him was that no winner was chosen at all. I'm certain there were a lot of hopeful entrants who felt unsatisfied when no one walked away with first prize. Too bad my kindergartner wasn't the judge. The following morning he asked me again, "Mommy, who really won the pumpkin contest?" 10

"They didn't pick one winner," I explained again. 11

"Well, *I* think the snowman won," he said with a nod. And then he was satisfied. 12

Considering Ideas

1. What cause-and-effect relationship is Sievert analyzing? For what purpose does she analyze this relationship?
2. Why did the school decide not to declare a winner in the pumpkin decorating contest? Why does the author think the school was wrong not to declare a winner?
3. Why does Sievert believe that competition is important? Do you agree with her? Explain.
4. Does Sievert discuss all the effects of competition, or are there some that she omits? Are the effects of competition that she *does* discuss sufficiently convincing? Explain.

Considering Technique

1. Both the introduction and the conclusion narrate an account of the pumpkin-decorating contest. How does this narration help the author achieve her writing purpose?
2. In paragraph 6, Sievert includes an example of a game played without competition. How does the example help the author achieve her writing purpose?
3. Sievert admits to letting her children win at Candyland. Why does she mention that fact? Does it contradict her philosophy on children's competition? Explain.
4. Does Sievert develop the effects she discusses in adequate detail? Explain.

For Group Discussion or Journal Writing

In paragraph 8, Sievert says that contests and games "teach our children how to lose." Is it important for children to learn how to lose? Why or why not?

Our Schedules, Ourselves

JAY WALLJASPER

Do you feel pressured because you have too much to do? If so, you are not alone, because many of us are doing more than we should. In this essay, which first appeared in the Utne Reader *in 2003, Jay Walljasper explains both the reasons for and the effects of the very full schedules that govern the lives of so many. As you read, notice how the author combines exemplification, process analysis, and contrast along with cause-and-effect analysis.*

DAMN! You're 20 minutes—no, more like half an hour—late for your breakfast meeting, which you were hoping to scoot out of early to make an 8:30 seminar across town. And, somewhere in there, there's that conference call. Now, at the last minute, you have to be at a 9:40 meeting. No way you can miss it. Let's see, the afternoon is totally booked, but you can probably push back your 10:15 appointment and work through lunch. That would do it. Whew! The day has barely begun and already you are counting the hours until evening, when you can finally go home and happily, gloriously, triumphantly, do nothing. You'll skip yoga class, blow off the neighborhood meeting, ignore the piles of laundry and just relax. Yes! . . . No! Tonight's the night of the concert. You promised Nathan and Mara weeks ago that you would go. *DAMN!* 1

Welcome to daily grind circa 2003—a grueling 24-7 competition against the clock that leaves even the winners wondering what happened to their lives. Determined and sternly focused, we march through each day obeying the orders of our calendars. The idle moment, the reflective pause, serendipity of any sort have no place in our plans. Stopping to talk to someone or slowing down to appreciate a sunny afternoon will only make you late for your next round of activities. From the minute we rise in the morning, most of us have our day charted out. The only surprise is if we actually get everything done that we had planned before collapsing into bed at night. 2

On the job, in school, at home, increasing numbers of North Americans are virtual slaves to their schedules. Some of what fills our days are onerous obligations, some are wonderful opportunities, and most fall in between, but taken together they add up to too much. Too much to do, too many places to be, too many things happening too fast, all mapped out for us in precise quarter-hour allotments on our Palm Pilots or day planners. We are not leading our lives, but merely following a dizzying timetable of duties, commitments, demands, and options. How did this happen? Where's the luxurious leisure that decades of technological progress was supposed to bestow upon us? 3

The acceleration of the globalized economy, and the accompanying decline of people having any kind of a say over wages and working conditions, is a chief culprit. Folks at the bottom of the socio-economic ladder feel the pain most sharply. Holding down two or three jobs, struggling to pay the bills, working weekends, no vacation time, little social safety net, they often feel out of control about everything happening to them. But even successful professionals, people who seem fully in charge of their destinies, feel the pinch. Doctors, for example, working impossibly crowded schedules under the command of HMOs, feel overwhelmed. Many of them are now seeking union representation, traditionally the recourse of low-pay workers. 4

The onslaught of new technology, which promised to set us free, has instead ratcheted up the rhythms of everyday life. Cell phones, e-mail, and laptop computers instill expectations of instantaneous action. While such direct communication can loosen our schedules in certain instances (it's easier to shift around an engagement on short notice), overall they fuel the trend that every minute must be accounted for. It's almost impossible to put duties behind you now, when the boss or committee chair can call you at a rap show or sushi restaurant, and documents can be e-mailed to you on vacation in Banff or Thailand. If you are never out of the loop, then are you ever not working? 5

Our own human desire for more choices and new experiences also plays a role. Just like hungry diners gathering around a bountiful smorgasbord, it's hard not to pile too many activities on our plates. An expanding choice of cultural offerings over recent decades and the liberating sense that each of us can fully play a number of different social roles (worker, citizen, lover, parent, artist, etc.) has opened up enriching and exciting opportunities. Spanish lessons? Yes. Join a volleyball team? Why not. Cello and gymnastics classes for the kids? Absolutely. Tickets to a blues festival, food and wine expo, and political fundraiser? Sure. And we can't forget to make time for school events, therapy sessions, protest rallies, religious services, and dinner with friends. 6

Yes, these can all add to our lives. But with only 24 hours allotted to us each day, something is lost too. You don't just run into a friend anymore and decide to get coffee. You can't happily savor an experience because your mind races toward the next one on the calendar. In a busy life, nothing happens if you don't plan it, often weeks in advance. Our "free" hours become just as programmed as the work day. What begins as an idea for fun frequently turns into an obligation obstacle course. Visit that new barbecue restaurant. *Done!* Go to tango lessons. *Done!* Fly to Montreal for a long weekend. *Done!* 7

We've booked ourselves so full of prescheduled activities there's no time left for those magic, spontaneous moments that make us feel most alive. We seldom stop to think of all the experiences we are eliminating from our lives when we load up our appointment book. Reserving tickets for a basketball game months away could mean you miss out on the first balmy evening of spring. Five p.m. skating lessons for your children fit so conveniently into your schedule that you never realize it's the time all the other kids in the neighborhood gather on the sidewalk to play. 8

A few years back, radical Brazilian educator Paulo Freire was attending a conference of Midwestern political activists and heard over and over about how overwhelmed people felt about the duties they face each day. Finally, he stood up and, in slow, heavily accented English, declared, "We are bigger than our schedules." The audience roared with applause. 9

Yes, we are bigger than our schedules. So how do we make sure our lives are not overpowered by an endless roster of responsibilities? Especially in an age where demanding jobs, two-worker households or single-parent families make the joyous details of everyday life—cooking supper from scratch or organizing a block party—seem like an impossible dream? There is no set of easy answers, despite what the marketers of new convenience products would have us believe. But that doesn't mean we can't make real steps to take back our lives. 10

Part of the answer is political. So long as Americans work longer hours than any other people on Earth we are going to feel hemmed in by our schedules. Expanded vacation time for everyone, including part-time and minimum wage workers, is one obvious and overdue solution. Shortening the work week, something the labor movement and progressive politicians successfully accomplished in the early decades of the 20th century, is another logical objective. There's nothing preordained about 40 hours on the job; Italy, France, and other European nations have already cut back working hours. An opportunity for employees outside academia to take a sabbatical every decade or so is another idea whose time has come. And how about more vacation and paid holidays? Let's start with Martin Luther King's birthday, Susan B. Anthony's birthday, and your own! Any effort to give people more clout in their workplaces—from strengthened unions to employee ownership—could help us gain much-needed flexibility in our jobs, and our lives. 11

On another front, how you think about time can make a big difference in how you feel about life. . . . Note how some of your most memorable moments occurred when something in your schedule fell through. The canceled lunch that allows you to spend an hour strolling around town. Friday night plans scrapped for a bowl of popcorn in front of the fireplace. Don't be shy about shucking your schedule whenever you can get away with it. And with some experimentation, you may find that you can get away with it a lot more than you imagined. 12

Setting aside some time on your calendar for life to just unfold in its own surprising way can also nurture your soul. Carve out some nonscheduled hours (or days) once in a while and treat them as a firm commitment. And resist the temptation to turn every impulse or opportunity into another appointment. It's neither impolite nor inefficient to simply say, "let me get back to you on that tomorrow" or "let's check in that morning to see if it's still a good time." You cannot know how crammed that day may turn out to be, or how uninspired you might feel about another engagement, or how much you'll want to be rollerblading or playing chess or doing something else at that precise time. 13

In our industrialized, fast-paced society, we too often view time as just another mechanical instrument to be programmed. But time possesses its own evershifting shape and rhythms, and defies our best efforts to corral it within the tidy lines of our Palm Pilots or datebooks. Stephen Rechtschaffen, author of *Time Shifting,* suggests you think back on a scary auto collision (or near miss), or spectacular night of lovemaking. Time seemed almost to stand still. You can remember everything in vivid detail. Compare that to an overcrammed week that you recall now only as a rapid-fire blur. Keeping in mind that our days expand and contract according to their own patterns is perhaps the best way to help keep time on your side. 14

Considering Ideas

1. The thesis of "Our Schedules, Ourselves" is implied. Write out the thesis.
2. For what purpose did Walljasper write the essay?
3. According to the essay, why are we overscheduled? That is, what causes us to try to do so much?
4. What are the effects of our overcrowded schedules?
5. How does the author propose solving the problem of overscheduling? Do you think his solution is practical?
6. Explain the meaning of the title.

Considering Technique

1. The opening paragraph begins and ends with the word *damn.* Explain the effect of that strategy.
2. What metaphor do you see in paragraph 2? (Metaphors are explained on page 148.) What simile do you see in paragraph 6? (Similes are explained on page 148.)
3. In what way is the essay a cause-and-effect analysis?
4. *Combining patterns:* How does the author use exemplification in paragraphs 1, 6, and 7? Why are the examples so brief? How does he use exemplification in paragraphs 12 and 13?

5. Why does the author tell the anecdote about Paulo Freire in paragraph 9?
6. *Combining patterns:* How does the author use process analysis? How does he use contrast?

For Group Discussion or Journal Writing

How much of what Walljasper says applies to the lives of students? Cite examples to support your view.

DICTION NOTE

Specific Diction

In Chapter 5, you learned the importance of specific diction for conveying ideas as precisely as possible. In addition, specific diction gives a sentence energy and contributes to a lively style. Using specific verbs will help you achieve specific diction, as these underlined examples from "Eight Reasons Plagiarism Sucks" illustrate:

> Readers have stormed my inbox . . . (paragraph 1)
>
> I cringe at writing those precious words, but like Samantha Power, I've released them and can't yank them back. (paragraph 6)

Suzanne Sievert also uses specific verbs in "It's Not Just How We Play That Matters":

> [The game] was touted as teaching kids to work together to reach an end goal . . . (paragraph 6)
>
> I'm not suggesting we pit our children against each other . . . (paragraph 8)
>
> Kids can endure failure. (paragraph 10)

And Jay Walljasper uses specific verbs in "Our Schedules, Ourselves":

> Determined and sternly focused, we march through each day . . . (paragraph 2)
>
> Friday night plans scrapped for a bowl of popcorn in front of the fireplace. (paragraph 12)
>
> But time possesses its own evershifting shape and rhythms, and defies our best efforts to corral it . . . (paragraph 14)

CAUSE-AND-EFFECT ANALYSIS IN AN IMAGE

Pay attention to advertisements, and you will notice how often cause-and-effect analysis appears as a component. The antismoking advertisement on the next page is another example.

Considering the Image

1. The advertisement considers both causes and effects. What cause is considered? What effects?
2. What audience does the advertisement hope to reach? How can you tell?
3. What is the purpose of this advertisement?
4. How does the photograph help the advertisement achieve its purpose?
5. What causal chain is reproduced in the advertisement?

SUGGESTIONS FOR WRITING

Writing Cause-and-Effect Analysis

1. Explain either the causes or the effects of racial or religious prejudice.
2. Analyze the effects of some technological innovation, such as the DVD player, the cell phone, the Global Positioning System (GPS), video games, or the personal digital assistant (PDA).
3. Explain the causes of increased violence among spectators at sporting events.
4. Select a popular trend and analyze its causes and/or effects.
5. Explain why some college students cheat.
6. Analyze the causes and/or effects of one of your bad habits.
7. Explain the effects college has had on your life.
8. Where we grow up has an enormous effect on who and what we become. How did the place where you grew up affect you?
9. Explain how the way we dress affects how people perceive us.
10. Explain how television influences our view of the world.
11. Explain the long-term effects of a childhood experience.
12. If you or a family member has been unemployed, explain the effects of this unemployment.
13. Identify a problem on your campus (inadequate housing, crowded classes, outdated requirements, high tuition, etc.), and analyze its causes and/or effects.

Reading Then Writing Cause-and-Effect Analysis

1. In "Eight Reasons Plagiarism Sucks," Jack Shafer explains some of the effects of plagiarism by journalists. Write an essay that explains the effects of plagiarism among students.
2. In an essay, explain why college students plagiarize.
3. In "It's Not Just How We Play That Matters," Suzanne Sievert claims that competition is "key to our success as adults." Do you agree? Write an essay that analyzes the effects of competition.
4. In "Our Schedules, Ourselves," Jay Walljasper says that we need to change the way we view time. Explain how you view time, and give the reasons you have that view.
5. In "Athletes on Drugs: It's Not So Hard to Understand," the student author discusses the causes of drug abuse among professional athletes. Explain the causes of some other problem behavior, such as cheating on exams, smoking, overeating, shoplifting, or road rage.

Cause-and-Effect Analysis beyond the Writing Classroom

Write an analysis of the causes and effects of procrastination among college students, and explain how to avoid the problem. Your essay should be suitable for inclusion in a handbook to help first-year students adjust to college. If you need help with ideas, interview other students to learn about their experiences with procrastination.

Responding to Theme

1. In "Eight Reasons Plagiarism Sucks," Jack Shafer argues that plagiarism is a serious offense with serious consequences. Do you agree? State and support your assertion.
2. The student author of "Athletes on Drugs: It's Not So Hard to Understand" explains why athletes turn to drugs. What do you think can be done to solve the problem? Describe a specific plan to address the issues in the student's essay and any other issues you find pertinent.
3. Suzanne Sievert derives the title of her essay from this common expression: "It's not whether you win or lose; it's how you play the game that matters." Which is more accurate, Sievert's title or the expression it is drawn from?
4. The billboard advertisement on page 327 implies that children are harmed when their parents use tobacco products. Should schools educate students about the risks of using tobacco and encourage them to urge their parents to quit? If so, devise a program suitable for students in grade 6. If not, explain why not.
5. *Connecting the readings:* Although we understand the risks, we often do things that are not good for ourselves. We smoke, drink, drive too fast, eat poorly, and otherwise compromise our health and well-being. In an essay, explain why. You can draw on the ideas in "Athletes on Drugs: It's Not So Hard to Understand," "Our Schedules, Ourselves," and "Let's Just Ban Everything" (page 221), and on your own experience and observation.

Writing Cause-and-Effect Analysis

Try the following guidelines, or rely on your own tried-and-true procedures if you prefer.

www.mhhe.com/tsw
For further help writing cause-and-effect analysis, go to Catalyst 2.0 > Writing > Writing Tutors > Causal Analysis

PROCESS GUIDELINES

Think like a Writer: Generating Ideas, Considering Audience and Purpose, and Ordering Ideas

- If you need help finding a topic, try one of the following:
  - Think of something you do well or do badly, such as run track, do math, or make friends. Then consider why you do this activity well or badly and how your ability or lack of it has affected you.
  - Identify something about your personality, environment, or circumstances, and assess how this factor has affected you. You could analyze the effects of poverty, shyness, a large family, moving, and so forth.
- To establish and assess your audience, answer the questions on page 42.

- To determine your purpose, answer the questions on page 40.
- To generate ideas, try the following:
  - List every cause and/or effect you can think of without censoring yourself.
  - To discover underlying causes and effects, ask *why?* and *then what?* after every cause and effect in your list. For example, if you listed difficulty making friends as an effect of shyness, ask *then what?* and you may get the answer "I was lonely." This answer could be an underlying effect of your shyness. If you listed "strong legs" as a reason for your success at running track, ask *why?* and you may get the answer "I lifted weights to increase leg strength." This would give you an underlying cause. Asking *then what?* will also help you discover causal chains.
  - Number your causes and effects in the order you will write them up in your draft. Remember that a progressive order is often effective.
  - Ask yourself why understanding the cause-and-effect relationship is important. The answer can be stated in your introduction, thesis, or conclusion.

Think like a Writer: Drafting

- As you draft, refer to your list of numbered causes and effects.
- Use topic sentences to introduce each cause or effect so that your reader can follow along easily.

Think like a Critic; Work like an Editor: Revising

- To determine whether you should add detail, answer these questions about each cause and effect:
  - How do I prove that this is a cause or effect? Is the proof adequate?
  - Is there an underlying cause or effect? If so, should it be included?
  - Is there a remote cause? If so, should it be included?
  - Is this part of a causal chain? If so, should the chain be reproduced?
  - Is there anything my reader mistakenly thinks is a cause or effect?
- To secure reader response, see page 105. In addition, have your reader ask *why?* and *then what?* after all your causes and effects. If doing so leads your reader to any underlying causes or effects you should discuss, ask your reader to note them on the draft.

Think like a Critic; Work like an Editor: Correcting Errors

Recognize that "the reason is because" is redundant since "the reason" *means* "because." If you have used this expression, change it to either "the reason is that" or simply "because."

No: Financial aid checks were late this term. The reason is because the computer center experienced systems problems.

Yes: Financial aid checks were late this term. The reason is that the computer center experienced systems problems.

Yes: Financial aid checks were late this term because the computer center experienced systems problems.

Remember

Do not assume that an earlier event caused a later one. Enrollment may have declined at your college after a tuition increase was instituted, but you cannot automatically assume that one caused the other. Other factors may have been involved. Perhaps the job outlook became brighter, so more high school graduates went to work rather than to college.

LOOKING AHEAD

In this chapter, you will learn about writing definitions, but not the kind of definitions you read in a dictionary. You will learn how to write longer definitions that go beyond dictionary definitions to include your personal sense of terms and their significance. Before beginning the chapter, try your hand at definition. Consider this picture of Venus Williams and Thailand's Tamarine Tanasugarn at the quarterfinals of the 2008 Wimbledon tournament. Then, in a paragraph, write a definition of good sportsmanship. Or, if you prefer, write a definition of athletic competition.

Definition

With online dictionaries, pocket dictionaries, collegiate dictionaries, and specialized dictionaries for specific subjects, checking the meaning of a word has never been easier. However, a dictionary does not always explain the special associations a word has for *you* or the significance of its meaning in society. For that you need an **extended definition,** which goes beyond the concise formal definition in a dictionary to explain the nature of that word, including its associations, significances, nuances, or complexities.

Consider, for example, the term *jazz.* You probably know what jazz is when you hear it, and you could look it up in the dictionary and learn that it is "music originating in New Orleans around the beginning of the 20th century." However, to understand the characteristics of jazz, you need an extended definition, something like this excerpt from *The World of Music* by David Willoughby:

- To be jazz, the music must swing. This is the feel of jazz—the jazz rhythm.
- To be jazz, the music must be improvised. Improvisation is at the heart of jazz, but much jazz music is not improvised. . . .
- To be jazz, the rhythm must be syncopated. Although jazz has a considerable emphasis placed on syncopated rhythms, not all of it will have these off-beat rhythms. . . .
- To be jazz, the music has to be played on certain "jazz" instruments. Some instruments, such as the saxophones (saxes), trumpets, trombones, drums, bass, and piano, are characteristically jazz instruments when they are played a certain way in a certain context. . . .

WHY IS DEFINITION IMPORTANT?

To discover what a word means, you go to the dictionary, but sometimes the dictionary is not enough. A dictionary gives the meaning of a word like *fun*, but what is fun to you may not be fun to someone else, and so the full meaning of that word will vary among individuals. Some words symbolize abstractions, with subtleties that cannot all be compressed into a few lines of space in a dictionary. What, for example, does *justice* mean? Certainly, it is a concept with complexities far beyond its neat dictionary definition. In addition, some words have meanings so complex that a dictionary definition can touch on only the high points, leaving much unexplained. *Democracy* is such a word. Not only is its meaning complex, but it varies greatly depending on which country's democracy is referred to. In cases like these, extended definition is helpful.

Extended definition can serve a variety of informational purposes. Obviously, a definition can inform your reader about something not commonly understood. For example, you might define *creative accounting* for a reader who does not know what it is and who wants to learn more about illegal corporate accounting practices. An extended definition can clarify a complex, multifaceted concept such as *wisdom* or *freedom,* specifying the way you are using the word. An extended definition can also provide a fresh appreciation for something familiar. For example, an extended definition of *free speech* can give readers a new way of looking at a freedom they may take for granted. An extended definition can even comment on something beyond the subject defined. For instance, a definition of *senior citizen* can lead to an understanding of what it means to grow old in this country. In fact, a definition can serve the full range of writing purposes, as illustrated in the following chart.

Purposes for Definition

Purpose	**Sample Definition**
To entertain	A definition of *commuter* that points to the humor of balancing a work and home life
To share feelings and experiences	A definition of *friendship* that includes your childhood experiences with your best friend
To inform	A definition of *manifest destiny*
To inform (and give a fresh appreciation for the familiar)	A definition of *coach* to help the reader understand everything a coach does for an athlete
To persuade	A definition of *poverty* to convince the reader to do something about it

Definition across the Disciplines and Beyond

Definition in the Classroom

Most courses introduce new terminology and important concepts, so definition will be a frequent component of your college writing. In a philosophy class, for instance, you might need to define *epistemology.* Often you will combine definition with another pattern. For example, in a political science class, you might be asked to define and give examples of *gerrymandering.* In a finance class, you might need to define and explain the effects of *bear* and *bull markets. Look through a chapter in two textbooks for your other classes. How many terms and concepts are in boldface type and defined? Is there a glossary at the back of the book that includes definitions of important terms? How likely is it that exam questions will require you to write definitions of these terms?*

Definition in Daily Life

Definition can be an important part of your personal writing. As editor of a newsletter for your religious congregation, you might define *charity* to encourage congregants to be more charitable. If you e-mail a friend a recipe that calls for a Madeleine pan, you might need to define *Madeleine pan.* In a letter to your representative in Congress, you might define *domestic violence* to encourage that person to support legislation to help victims of domestic violence. *How might you use definition in your personal journal? How might you use definition in a letter to the editor about Internet pornography? What purpose would the definition serve?*

Definition on the Job

Definition is often a part of workplace writing. A nutrition counselor might define *eating disorder* in a newsletter for clients. A sales manager might define *sales resistance* in a training manual for new salespeople. A safety officer might define *disaster preparedness* in an e-mail to all employees. *How might you use definition in the job you hope to have after graduation? For whom might you write a definition? Which of the purposes for writing will that definition fulfill?*

COMBINING DEFINITION WITH OTHER PATTERNS

Definition can combine with other patterns of development to help you achieve your purpose for writing. For example, to inform your reader, you might first define *pornography* and then use cause-and-effect analysis to explain its effects. To convince your reader that even upper-middle-class people can become homeless, you can define *homelessness* and then go on to use process analysis to explain how one can become homeless. An essay on heroism can first define *heroism* and then classify the types of heroism. An essay on stress can combine three patterns by first defining *stress,* then explaining its causes, and finally noting what can be done to cope with it.

An essay developed primarily with extended definition will likely draw on other patterns of development to support its points. This aspect of combining patterns is explained in the discussion of selecting detail that follows.

SELECTING DETAIL

An extended definition explains the characteristics of the term being defined. If you are defining *anorexia nervosa,* for example, you should explain that the victim of this eating disorder tries to eat as little as possible, behavior that can eventually lead to death. You might also explain that poor body image may be involved, along with the victim's compulsive need to control some aspect of his or her life. To develop these points, you can use some or all of the following strategies.

Write a Stipulative Definition

You can include a **stipulative definition** to restrict the parameters of your explanation. If a word has more than one meaning or if its meaning includes many aspects, a stipulative definition can narrow your scope by establishing the boundaries of your definition. For example, the term *pornography* means different things to different people. To set the scope of your discussion of its meaning, you can include a stipulative definition like this: "Pornography is any material in any medium that sexually arouses some people but creates a threat to the well-being of others." This stipulative definition works well in a cause-and-effect essay that demonstrates the harm pornography causes.

Draw on Other Patterns of Development

An extended definition can include any of the patterns of development or combination of patterns. If you are defining *Christmas spirit,* for example, you could develop the definition using one or more of the following patterns:

Description:	Use sensory details to describe how Christmas spirit makes people feel, or describe the decorations, music, and foods that help create the mood that contributes to the spirit.
Narration:	Tell a story about a person who demonstrated Christmas spirit.
Exemplification:	Provide examples to illustrate the nature of Christmas spirit.
Process analysis:	Explain what retailers do to create Christmas spirit in shopping malls.
Comparison-contrast:	Compare and contrast Christmas spirit with the feelings people get on other holidays in order to clarify the nature of the spirit.

Cause-and-effect analysis: Explain how people are affected by Christmas spirit.

Classification-division: Classify the various kinds of Christmas spirit or the various ways it is manifested; divide the spirit into its components.

Argumentation: Argue that the spirit of Christmas is being lost to commercialism.

Compare or Contrast the Term with Related Words

Sometimes you can clarify a term by showing how it is similar to or different from another term. For example, in "Parenthood: Don't Count on Sleeping Until They Move Out," on page 343, Maria Lopez compares her subject to another term: "First and foremost, a parent is a guesser." If you were defining *maturity,* you could contrast the term with a related one, like this: "Maturity is not merely adulthood, for many people over 21 lack real maturity."

Explain What Your Term Is *Not*

Sometimes you will want to explain what your subject is *not.* For example, if you are defining *freedom,* you may want to say that freedom is *not* doing anything you want, it is *not* a privilege, and it is *not* necessarily guaranteed to everyone. From here you could go on to explain what you believe freedom *is.* This technique can be useful for making important distinctions or dispelling common misunderstandings.

Consider Your Audience and Purpose

Your purpose will influence the details you include. Suppose you are defining *fear* to give your reader a fresh outlook on this feeling by showing that fear is really a positive emotion. You might note that fear is adaptive because it ensures our survival. You might also note instances when we would endanger ourselves needlessly were it not for fear. However, a different purpose would call for different details. If you want your definition to show that fear keeps us from realizing our potential, you might include details that show how lack of achievement is related to fear of failure and fear of risk taking.

Audience also affects detail. Assume that you are writing an essay defining *teenager,* and your purpose is to make your reader aware of how difficult the teen years are. If your reader is 25 and so more likely to remember adolescence, you can explain less than if your audience is much further removed from those years and needs to be reminded of a few things. Similarly, if your audience is a neighbor who has been expressing concern over "what the youth in this country have come to," you may want to explain why teenagers behave as they do in order to address and dispel your reader's negative feelings. However, if your audience is a teenager, there will be no ill will to overcome, so you might instead include details that will reassure the teen that he or she is not alone in the struggle.

BEING A RESPONSIBLE WRITER

Definition is important. For example, how the government defines *disability* affects who is covered under the Americans with Disabilities Act. How your college defines *financial need* determines who gets scholarship money.

When terms and concepts are not defined responsibly, the consequences can be serious. For example, when an employer unfairly defines *qualified* as being "male," women are excluded from the top ranks of an organization. How we define people is particularly significant. Consider hate groups, for example. On their websites and in their print material, they define various religious and ethnic groups in irresponsible ways in order to fuel prejudice. African-Americans are defined as inferior, Arabs as evil terrorists, and Jews as greedy manipulators. Other groups also fall victim to irresponsible definitions: Feminists are called man-haters, and the poor are called lazy, for instance.

If you use a definition from a dictionary, avoid plagiarism by acknowledging this source material, using quotation marks, and including a works-cited entry at the end of your paper.

USING SOURCES FOR A PURPOSE

The paragraph below is the introduction for an essay that aims to convince readers that athletes should not be considered heroes. This paragraph, which includes a paraphrase and quotation from paragraph 4 of "Hero Inflation" on page 347, illustrates one way to use sources from this book in your writing. (For more information on writing paraphrases and quotations, see Chapter 17.)

THESIS IDEA: Turning athletes into heroes is harmful.

WRITING PURPOSE AND AUDIENCE: To convince the average reader that we should not think of athletes as heroes

The paraphrase in sentence 1 and the quotation in sentence 4 help the writer set up a comparison between elevating victims and athletes to hero status.

[1]Without a doubt, Americans suffer from "hero inflation," which is the elevation of victims to hero status, as Nicholas Thompson explains the tendency (347). [2]However, promoting victims (such as those who died in the terrorist attacks of 9/11) to the status of heroes is not the only form of hero inflation Americans engage in. [3]The phenomenon is evident in the sports world, where those with superior athletic ability are rewarded not just with inflated paychecks but also with overblown public adulation. [4]Just as Thompson says that turning victims into heroes "diminish[es] the idea of role models who perform truly extraordinary acts" (347), turning athletes into heroes is also harmful.

Avoiding Plagiarism

The paragraph illustrates the following points about avoiding plagiarism.

1. Acknowledge the source and use quotation marks:

    The *Random House College Dictionary* defines cybernetics as "the study of human control functions and of mechanical and electric systems designed to replace them."

2. Provide a works-cited entry:

    "Cybernetics." *Random House College Dictionary*. 10th ed. 2001. Print.

For more on these procedures, see Chapter 17.

To be a responsible writer, ask yourself these questions:

- What are the possible consequences of my definition? (If your definition can cause harm to a group of people, you are not being responsible.)
- Does my definition consider both positive and negative aspects of the term? (If you are considering only positive or only negative aspects, you may not be a responsible writer.)
- Where necessary, have I acknowledged the source, used quotation marks, and included a works-cited entry?

- **Attribute quotations correctly.** The attribution most often appears before the paraphrase or quotation, but as sentence 1 shows, it can also appear after the source material.
- **Understand how to quote part of a sentence.** As sentence 4 illustrates, when you quote part of a sentence, you must not alter the original meaning. (See paragraph 4 on page 347 to check the full sentence in the source.)

Myths about Sources

MYTH: Source material is authoritative, so it stands on its own and does not have to be linked to details around it.

FACT: You achieve coherence with transitions, repetition of key words and ideas, and synonyms so your source material connects to your other ideas. To illustrate, the introduction is reprinted below with some of the coherence devices underlined. (See pages 100–104 on coherence.)

Without a doubt, Americans suffer from "hero inflation," which is the elevation of victims to hero status, as Nicholas Thompson explains the tendency (347). However, promoting victims (such as those who died in the terrorist attacks of 9/11) to the status of heroes is not the only form of hero inflation Americans engage in. The phenomenon is evident in the sports world, where those with superior athletic ability are rewarded not just with inflated paychecks but also with overblown public adulation. Just as Thompson says that turning victims into heroes "diminish[es] the idea of role models who perform truly extraordinary acts" (347), turning athletes into heroes is also harmful.

ORGANIZING DEFINITION

Your thesis can indicate what you are defining and what point can be drawn from the definition like this:

> Christmas spirit is not what it used to be.
> Christmas spirit is a natural high.

Your thesis can also note your subject and the characteristics you will explain, like these:

> A good teacher gives every student a chance to succeed, allows every student free expression, and challenges every student to explore new ideas.

This thesis indicates that a good teacher will be defined with an explanation of three characteristics: giving students a chance to succeed, allowing students free expression, and challenging students to explore new ideas.

Each of your body paragraphs can present a characteristic of what you are describing, which can be noted in the topic sentence. For example, if you are defining *jealousy,* you could use topic sentences like these:

> Jealousy is an all-consuming emotion.
> Jealousy causes people to behave in hurtful ways.
> Jealousy destroys friendships.

Your supporting detail for each paragraph can explain and clarify the characteristic noted in the topic sentence.

If your body paragraphs are developed with particular patterns of development, follow the organization principles that govern these techniques. Otherwise, a progressive arrangement is frequently effective, perhaps beginning and ending with your strongest points.

Your introduction can engage your reader's interest with a variety of techniques. You can explain what many people believe your subject means if you plan to show that it means something else, either because the meaning has changed or because people have misconceptions. For example, if you are defining *dating,* you can explain that many people think that dating still involves the male asking the female out, picking her up, deciding what to do, making the arrangements, and paying for the evening. Your essay, then, can discuss meeting online, group dating, women asking men out and paying for the date, and so on. Often an anecdote about your subject can prepare readers for a definition. If you are defining *couch potato,* for instance, you can tell a story about the time your brother spent an entire weekend watching ESPN.

Generally, you should avoid dictionary definitions in your introduction. Your reader will know, at least approximately, how your subject is defined in *Webster's,* so a formal definition is likely to be boring.

Your conclusion can be an effective place to elaborate on the significance of your definition by explaining the points to be drawn from it. For instance, after defining *dating,* you can explain that today's dating practices allow people to get to know each other before they spend time alone

Visualizing a Definition Essay

The chart that follows can help you visualize one structure for an extended definition. Like all good models, this one can be altered as needed.

Introduction

- Creates interest, perhaps by explaining what people believe your subject means (if you will show it means something else) or by telling an anecdote about your subject
- States the thesis, which gives the term and the characteristics you will explain or the point to be drawn from the definition

▼

First Body Paragraph

- Gives the first characteristic
- May include other patterns of development
- May include a stipulative definition
- May compare or contrast the term with another term
- May explain what the term is *not*
- May arrange details progressively or in another logical order

▼

Next Body Paragraphs

- Give the remaining characteristics
- May include other patterns of development
- May include a stipulative definition
- May compare or contrast the term with another term
- May explain what the term is *not*
- May arrange details progressively or in another logical order

▼

Conclusion

- May elaborate on the significance of the definition
- Creates closure

because they first chat online and go out in groups. You can then draw a conclusion about whether this fact makes dating better than it was in the past.

EXERCISE Writing Definition

1. Select a concept (freedom, justice, good taste, sportsmanship, etc.), object (a smartphone, a surfboard, a backpack, etc.), person (a good teacher, a friend, etc.), or movement (environmentalism, feminism, etc.) to define.

2. What is the most distinguishing characteristic of the subject you selected for number 1? The second-most distinguishing characteristic? What patterns of development could you use to explain each of those characteristics in an essay?
3. Come up with three additional points you could make to help define your subject by answering any of the following questions that are pertinent:
   a. What story can I tell to help define my subject?
   b. What features of my subject can I describe?
   c. What examples would help define my subject?
   d. To what can I compare my subject? With what can I contrast it?
   e. What is my subject *not*?
4. Write out a thesis that includes your subject and a point that could be drawn from your definition.
5. Read the following paragraph, and evaluate how effective it would be as an introduction for an extended definition. Be prepared to cite reasons for your view.

   Although I feel that it is not extremely difficult for two people to establish a relationship, maintaining that relationship may not be quite as easy. Undoubtedly, we all have our faults and flaws, our marks of imperfection, and as two people come to know more about each other, these flaws become more and more evident. It is the degree of emphasis placed on these flaws that determines whether or not a relationship blossoms into a true friendship. If a person is truly your friend, then even after coming to know a lot about you, he or she will still care very much for you. A true friend is fun to be with, trustworthy, and reliable. ■

LEARNING FROM OTHER WRITERS: Student Essays

The next two essays, written by students, are examples of extended definition. The first, "Parenthood: Don't Count on Sleeping Until They Move Out," appears with marginal notes that point out key features. Written to inform and express some of the author's feelings, the definition is developed with examples, many of them hypothetical. (For more on hypothetical examples, see page 213.) Ask yourself whether these examples work well to develop the definition.

The second essay, "What Is Writer's Block?" defines a condition you probably have experienced. The definition includes vivid descriptive language—how well does it describe the writer's block you are familiar with? Also, the author uses sentence fragments deliberately—what do you think of them?

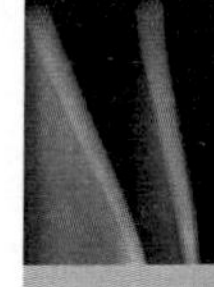

Parenthood: Don't Count on Sleeping Until They Move Out

Maria Lopez

Before I had children, I thought I had a crystal clear understanding of the word "parents." Parents were those people who fed me, clothed me, put a roof over my head, and took me to the doctor when I was ill. They were not, however, people who should be inquiring into my personal life, worrying about the choices I made as I grew into my teens and demanded more freedom. Most of all, they were insensitive people whose feelings could not be hurt by anything I said or did. Yes, I thought I knew all about parents—right up until the time my first child was born. That's when I discovered that my assumptions about parents were dead wrong. A parent, I've learned, is a person both blessed and cursed with the world's most difficult job. 1

Paragraph 1
The introduction—the author engages reader interest by explaining what she used to think the term *parents* meant. The thesis (the last sentence) notes that the term has come to mean something different to her. The thesis includes what will be defined and the point to be drawn (the parent has the "world's most difficult job").

First and foremost, a parent is a guesser. At best, the guess is an educated one; at worst, it's a blind shot in the dark. An educated guess, for example, would be Mom's choice of the right toy for an eight-year-old boy's birthday gift, based on what every other eight-year-old boy in the neighborhood owns. Simple, right? The educated guess, however, can get scarier: Should a child be taken to the emergency room at midnight with an earache and a fever, or can treatment safely be delayed until morning? The sleepless parent, rocking the sleepless child through the night, makes and unmakes the decision. Yes, little Jen has had earaches before, and she's usually better by morning. But what if this time is different? What if she's worse? What if she loses her hearing? But it's rainy and miserable outside. What if taking her out makes her worse? What if she has to wait hours in the emergency room? What if . . . well, you get the picture. As if the educated guess isn't bad enough, though, a parent often must also be a guesser in the dark, blindly hoping that some of the guesses are the right ones. Was it right or wrong to ground the thirteen-year-old for lying? How about for screaming in her mother's face? And what's the appropriate curfew for a seventeen-year-old, anyway? How much freedom is too much? 2

Paragraph 2
The topic sentence (the first) notes the first characteristic of the term being defined (the parent is a guesser). The rest of the paragraph is the supporting detail to develop the topic sentence. Note the use of questions to convey the sense of uncertainty and the hypothetical situations to illustrate the need for guessing.

How much is too little? Is the parent encouraging rebellion and possibly dangerous behavior by being too strict or too permissive? The awful truth, of course, is seldom voiced: Parents are people who NEVER, EVER learn whether all those blind guesses were right or wrong, foolish or wise, helpful or damaging.

Paragraph 3
The topic sentence (the first) gives the next characteristic (vulnerability). The supporting detail is examples. The last sentence gives another characteristic (silent sufferers) that is an effect.

All of this guessing helps parents become sensitive souls, exquisitely vulnerable to their offspring. The flinching probably starts with the first child's departure for kindergarten (or maybe even preschool) without a backward glance at Mom and Dad, standing tearfully at the door. Then there's that terrible moment of truth when a child first realizes that parents aren't really gods, that they don't have all the answers, even on fourth-grade homework. What can hurt worse than the astonished look on a child's face that says, "You let me down, Mom" or "I always thought you knew everything, Dad"? I'll tell you what hurts worse: the teenaged boy who finds his mother's mere presence a total embarrassment, the teenaged girl who tells her father that he doesn't understand ANYTHING, or the five-year-old who screams, "I hate you! I hate you!" Eventually, to avoid those painful scenes, many parents become silent sufferers, developing high blood pressure as well as a high tolerance for mental anguish. 3

Paragraph 4
The last paragraph gives another characteristic in the first sentence ("anxious bargainers with God"), and the second-to-last sentence gives another characteristic ("grateful believers"). The last sentence provides the closure.

Finally, as they lay exhausted in the dark at midnight, or pace the floor at 3:00 A.M., many parents become anxious bargainers with God. If You just let her come home safely, God, I'll never swear at her again. If You'll just help him stop drinking, God, I promise I'll spend more time with him. Then, when the door cracks open and footsteps creak up the stairs, every parent—whatever the religious background—becomes a grateful believer. Thankfully, we whisper, "Someday, if there's a God, you'll have a kid JUST LIKE YOU." 4

What Is Writer's Block?

Melissa Greco

I have writer's block. For the last two days I have sat at this table, staring at a blank piece of paper. My mother calls to ask what I'm doing, and I say I'm writing. She asks me what, and I say nothing, for I have writer's block. "Well, write something," she replies. Something? Obviously, she does not understand writer's block. 1

Writer's block is pacing. Up and down in front of the table with pen in hand. Wearing a ragged trail in an otherwise OK carpet. Pacing. Palms sweating. Knowing you have a deadline that is creeping up on you like a fairy tale troll, following behind, and steadily getting closer and closer with each tick of the clock. 2

Writer's block is trying. Sitting down ready and willing to work. Picking up a freshly sharpened pencil and advancing on a clean, crisp piece of paper only to have a sense of emptiness come over me. The pencil falters above the paper, and the words stubbornly refuse to leave their hiding places in the recesses of my mind. Now the sweaty hand forces the pencil down onto the paper. Write something. Doodles. Lots and lots of doodles. Squiggly little lines. Bold black circles. Delicate little spiderwebs. Angry dots! Names . . . Julie . . . Mike . . . John . . . Jimmy. Why won't the words come? What are they afraid of? Try, make those sweaty palms produce. Deadlines. 3

Writer's block is doubting myself, being convinced I can't write. It is waiting, waiting for the block to recede. It is starting, stopping, starting over, stopping again. 4

Writer's block is anticipation. I know they will come, if I can just be patient a few more minutes. I can feel them; the words are there. As soon as they're ready, they will come spilling out, tumbling all over each other, mixing letters and vowels in their rush to be heard. Then the pencil will have to restrain them and take them one by one and put them in their proper order. 5

Until that time, I can only see a dam. I can feel the force of the words straining behind it. I can see them bouncing off the tall, unyielding walls. Occasionally, one or two escape through the overflow. Open those floodgates, and let them flow. 6

EXERCISE Considering "What Is Writer's Block?"

1. Which sentence is the thesis of "What Is Writer's Block?"? What does that thesis accomplish?
2. The definition of writer's block includes the chief characteristics of the term. What organizational device does the author use to introduce each characteristic?
3. What does the essay accomplish that a dictionary definition of writer's block cannot achieve?
4. Paragraph 3 describes and simulates freewriting. How does this strategy help define writer's block?
5. What metaphor does the author use to help define writer's block? (Metaphors are explained on page 148.) ■

THINK LIKE A CRITIC; WORK LIKE AN EDITOR: The Student Writer at Work

"Parenthood: Don't Count on Sleeping Until They Move Out" has this thesis:

> A parent, I've learned, is a person both blessed and cursed with the world's most difficult job.

You may have noticed when you read the essay that the author does not say anything about the blessings of parenthood. That was not the case in an earlier draft of the essay, which included this paragraph as the conclusion:

Early draft of conclusion

> No matter how difficult parenting becomes, small moments surface to make the pain bearable. Your kindergartner rushes in from school and announces, "I missed you, Mommy," and you start to glow from your heart out to your skin. Your teenager tosses the car keys on the table and says, "I filled up the tank for you, Dad," and you start to think that maybe there's hope for the boy yet. We hear that more and more couples are choosing to be childless, but enough of us

are becoming parents that the moments of joy must be carrying the day.

The author decided she liked the current conclusion better and opted not to revise the above paragraph for inclusion in the final version. Did she do the right thing? Should she have revised the thesis?

LEARNING FROM OTHER WRITERS: Professional Essays

Hero Inflation

NICHOLAS THOMPSON

In this opinion piece that first appeared in the Boston Globe *in 2002,* Globe *correspondent Nicholas Thompson challenges our definition of hero, claiming that elevating the victims of the September 11, 2001, attacks to hero status is a misapplication of the term. As you read, ask yourself how his view was likely to be received a year after the attacks.*

Since Sept. 11, America has become a nation of heroes. Stevie Wonder, Willie Nelson, and Bruce Springsteen played a "tribute to heroes" that raised $150 million for victims of the attacks. Firefighters and rescue workers have earned acclaim for heroism, but so has nearly everyone who directly suffered on that horrible morning. 1

"The fatalities of that day are all heroes and deserve to be honored as such," said Thomas Davis, a Republican congressman from Virginia, while successfully working to obtain a full burial plot in Arlington National Cemetery for the former National Guardsman who piloted the plane that crashed into the Pentagon. 2

The victims of the terrorist attacks deserve tremendous sympathy. They died tragically and often horrifically. But not all died in a way that people have previously described as heroic. And even the heroism attributed to the rescue workers stems as much from the country's needs in responding to the disaster as from what actually happened in the collapsing buildings. 3

It is long overdue that Americans appreciate their public servants. It is also necessary to honor those who died simply for being in America. But changing the definition of hero to accommodate tragic victims may actually weaken us by diminishing the idea of role models who perform truly extraordinary acts. 4

To the ancient Greeks, "heroes," such as Hercules or Odysseus, performed great deeds, frequently challenged the gods, and were immortalized after death. Heroes lived in times and realms halfway between gods and men and often were deemed to have brought prosperity to the people who praised them. 5

That definition gradually evolved in this country as Americans adapted it to the people most respected here. Heroes won that standing by courageously transforming the world—Martin Luther King Jr. or Mother Teresa for example. Or heroes could earn that title simply for incredible acts of bravery several steps above the call of duty—Oskar Schindler[1], a young girl who plunges into a dangerous icy river and saves a stranger's life, or maybe someone from battle such as Henry Johnson who fought off 20 Germans with a knife and a couple of hand grenades in World War I. 6

Roughly speaking, American heroes first needed bravery. But bravery is not sufficient because evil people can be brave, too. So, the second trait in American historical lore is nobility. Heroes must work toward goals that we approve of. Heroes must show ingenuity. Lastly, they should be successful. Rosa

[1]Using blackmail, bribery, and forgery, Oskar Schindler (1908–1974) saved the lives of 1300 Polish Jews working in his factory during World War II.

Parks[2] wouldn't have been nearly as much of a hero if she hadn't sparked a boycott that then sparked a movement. Charles Lindbergh[3] wouldn't have been nearly as heroized if the Spirit of St. Louis had crashed into the Atlantic, or if scores of other people had made the flight before. 7

Recently though, a fourth trait—victimhood—seems to have become as important as anything else in determining heroic status. Today heroes don't have to do anything; they just need to be noble victims. 8

For example, if J. Joseph Moakley was known at all nationally, it was as a hard-working Massachusetts congressman who almost always followed the Democratic Party line. But when he was stricken with leukemia, he became a national hero, earning praise from the president and seemingly everyone else in Washington. He was cited from the balcony, traditionally the spot reserved for heroes, by President Bush during the State of the Union message. (This paper even wrote about a letter received at his house addressed simply to "Joe Moakley, Hero.") His death earned almost as much newspaper coverage as the death this year of the 98-year-old Mike Mansfield, a giant of the U.S. Senate who served as majority leader longer than anyone in history and initiated the Senate Watergate Committee. 9

But that shouldn't surprise us. Books about overcoming adversity clog the bestseller lists, and perseverance during illness—any illness—is grist for the heroic mill. If John F. Kennedy wanted to run for president today, he might constantly mention his struggle against Addison's disease as opposed to emphasizing his exploits on his PT boat in the Pacific. 10

Of course, victimhood hasn't completely eclipsed action in our national selection of heroes. The biggest heroes have many of the virtues of traditional heroes but also are victims—for example, the 350 firefighters who died in the World Trade Center and who now stand atop our national pantheon. These men have been honored everywhere from the current cover of *Sports Illustrated* to a recent best-selling comic book that makes them into superheroes. They even inspired thousands of Halloween costumes. 11

But although the firemen who died in the Trade Center bravely fought the flames and led the evacuation, they did so as workers doing the best they could in their jobs—people trained by the city to rush into buildings and save others. Firefighters chose a very worthy line of work, but to die while doing it isn't completely different from, say, the computer programmers who stayed in the Trade Center and perished while desperately trying to preserve the data backing people's financial portfolios. Just after Christmas, a New Bedford policeman carried a woman out of a burning building. "I'm not a hero," he said upon emerging outside. "I'm just a worker." 12

There were no doubt some unconditional individual heroes on Sept. 11, including some of the people on United Flight 93 who fought the hijackers and individual firefighters and police who went well beyond the requirements of the job, but most of the other people who died in the attacks were simply victims, much like the tens of thousands of innocent people killed in home fires, or on highways, every year. 13

They deserve our grief and their families and communities merit great sympathy. But it's time for a little more perspective when Congress almost unanimously passes a bill called the "True American Heroes Act" awarding Congressional Gold Medals—the highest honor that body can give—to every government official who died in the attacks, including Port Authority employees who were killed in their World Trade Center offices. 14

[2] In 1955, in Montgomery, Alabama, Rosa Parks (1913–2005) refused to give up her seat on a bus to a white passenger, an event that many mark as the beginning of the civil rights movement.

[3] In 1927, Charles Lindbergh (1902–1974) made the first nonstop solo flight from New York to Paris in his plane the *Spirit of St. Louis*.

Of course, some of the hero-making is born of necessity. In the aftermath of the attacks, we needed to turn the narrative away from the horror of the images on television and our clear vulnerability. As soon as the buildings came down, we needed to build the victims up. It also helped to reclassify everyone on the opposing side as incorrigibly demonic and everyone on our side as paragons of virtue. After the 11th, the first part was easy and the second part took a little bit of work. 15

That wasn't of course a wholly bad thing. The inflation of the heroism of Sept. 11 surely helped the nation recover and pull together. Moreover, America probably didn't have enough heroes. An August *U.S. News and World Report* poll revealed that more than half of all Americans didn't consider a single public figure heroic. Right before the attacks, Anheuser-Busch[4] planned an ad campaign titled "Real American Heroes" that, among other things, saluted the inventor of the foot-long hot dog. 16

But just because the sometimes false focus on heroism helped the nation salve its wounds doesn't make such attitudes wholly good either. Heroes often end up as role models, a task not well suited for victims. Moreover, by lowering the bar for heroism, we cheapen the word and, in some ways, the exploits of people who have earned the right to be called that in the past. 17

Finally, when people earn classification as heroes, those acting in their names often try to take it a step too far. Last month, for example, the federal government announced plans to disburse about as much money this year to families of attack victims as the entire international aid community has slated to give to Afghanistan over the next decade—and that money will come in addition to incredible amounts of charitable aid also already raised. Nevertheless, a spokesman for a victims' lobby group immediately dissented, demanding more. "We are exploring our legal options and lining up attorneys," he said. Almost no criticism could be found in response. 18

Emerson once wrote that "every hero becomes a bore at last." Well, at least their lawyers and lobbyists do. 19

[4]Anheuser-Busch is the brewing company that manufactures Budweiser beer.

Considering Ideas

1. Which sentence is the thesis of "Hero Inflation"?
2. According to Thompson, why did we become "a nation of heroes" after the September 11 attacks?
3. What are the characteristics of the American hero?
4. For what purpose did Thompson write "Hero Inflation"? How do you think Thompson's original *Boston Globe* audience reacted to the essay?
5. Why does Thompson object to elevating victims to hero status?

Considering Techniques

1. In paragraphs 5 and 6, Thompson traces the historical definition of *hero*. How does this information help him achieve his purpose for writing?
2. *Combining patterns:* What is the purpose of the examples in paragraphs 6 and 7? In paragraphs 9 and 10?
3. Why does Thompson develop what a hero is *not* in such detail? How does that detail help him achieve his writing purpose?

4. *Combining patterns:* In what paragraphs does Thompson contrast *hero* with another term?
5. How does paragraph 18 help Thompson make his point about heroes?

For Group Discussion or Journal Writing

Who are your heroes? What makes these people heroes in your eyes?

My Way!

Margo Kaufman

In this excerpt from her 1993 book 1-800-Am-I-Nuts, *Margo Kaufman defines* control freak. *She draws heavily on the control freaks in her life to illustrate their typical behavior. At first, she is critical of control freaks, but by the end of the essay, she has softened her view.*

Is it my imagination, or is this the age of the control freak? I'm standing in front of the triceps machine at my gym. I've just set the weights, and I'm about to begin my exercise when a lightly muscled bully in turquoise spandex interrupts her chest presses to bark at me. "I'm using that," she growls as she leaps up from her slant board, darts over to the triceps machine, and resets the weights. 1

I'm tempted to point out that, while she may have been planning to use the machine, she was, in fact, on the opposite side of the room. And that her muscles won't atrophy if she waits for me to finish. Instead, I go work on my biceps. Life's too short to fight over a Nautilus machine. Of course, *I'm* not a control freak. 2

Control freaks will fight over anything: a parking space, the room temperature, the last pair of marked-down Maude Frizon pumps, even whether you should barbecue with the top on or off the Weber kettle. Nothing is too insignificant. Everything has to be just so. 3

Just so *they* like it. "These people compulsively have to have their own way," says Los Angeles psychologist Gary Emery. "Their egos are based on being right," Emery says, "on proving they're the boss." (And it isn't enough for the control freak to win. Others have to lose.) 4

"Control freaks are overconcerned with the means, rather than the end," Emery says. "So it's more important that the string beans are the right kind than it is to just enjoy the meal." 5

"What do you mean just enjoy the meal?" scoffs my friend Marc. "There's a right way to do things and then there's everything else." It goes without saying that he, and only he, has access to that Big Right Way in the Sky. And that Marc lives alone. 6

"I really hate to be in any situation where my control over what I'm doing is compromised," he admits. "Like if somebody says, 'I'll handle the cooking and you can shuck the corn or slice the zucchini,' I tell them to do it without me." 7

A control freak's kitchen can be his or her castle. "Let me show you the right way to make rice," said my husband the first time I made the mistake of fixing dinner. By the time Duke had sharpened the knives, rechopped the vegetables into two-inch squares, and chided me for using the wrong size pan, I had decided to surrender all control of the stove. (For the record, this wasn't a big sacrifice. I don't like to cook.) 8

"It's easier in a marriage when you both don't care about the same things," says Milton Wolpin, a psychology professor at the University of Southern California. "Otherwise, everything would be a battle." 9

And every automobile would be a battleground. There's nothing worse than having two control freaks in the same car. "I prefer to drive," my friend Claire says. "But no sooner do I pull out 10 of the driveway than Fred starts telling me what to do. He thinks that I'm an idiot behind the wheel and that I make a lot of stupid mistakes."

She doesn't think he drives any better. "I think he goes really, really fast, and I'm sure that someday he's going to kill us both," she says. "And I complain about it constantly. But it's still a little easier for me to take a back seat. I'd rather get to pick him apart than get picked on." 11

My friend Katie would withstand the abuse. "I like to control everything," she says. "From where we're going to eat to what we're going to eat to what movie we're going to see, what time we're going to see it, where we're going to see it, where we're going to park. Everything!" 12

But you can't control everything. So much of life is beyond our control. And to me, that's what makes it interesting. But not to Katie. "I don't like having my fate in someone else's hands," she says firmly. "If I take charge, I know that whatever it is will get done and it will get done well." 13

I shuffle my feet guiltily. Not too long ago I invited Katie and a bunch of friends out to dinner to celebrate my birthday. It was a control freak's nightmare. Not only did I pick the restaurant and arrange to pick up the check, but Duke also called in advance and ordered an elaborate Chinese banquet. I thought Katie was going to lose her mind. 14

"What did you order? I have to know," she cried, seizing a menu. "I'm a vegetarian. There are things I won't eat." Duke assured her that he had accounted for everybody's taste. Still, Katie didn't stop hyperventilating until the food arrived. "I was very pleasantly surprised," she confesses. "And I would trust Duke again." 15

"I'm sure there are areas where you're the control freak," says Professor Wolpin, "areas where you're more concerned about things than your husband." *Me?* The champion of laissez-faire? "You get very upset if you find something visible to the naked eye on the kitchen counter," Duke reminds me. "And you think you know much better than me what the right shirt for me to wear is." 16

But I'm just particular. I'm not a control freak. 17

"A control freak is just someone who cares about something more than you do," Wolpin says. 18

So what's wrong with being a control freak? 19

Considering Ideas

1. What characteristics of the control freak does Kaufman discuss?
2. Why does it go "without saying . . . that Marc lives alone" (paragraph 6)? What is Kaufman implying when she mentions that he lives alone?
3. The author's friend Katie likes to take control because that way she knows that "'whatever it is will get done and it will get done well'" (paragraph 13). What view of people does Katie have?
4. Why does Kaufman ask, "So what's wrong with being a control freak?" (paragraph 19)?
5. Paragraph 18 includes a stipulative definition of *control freak.* Do you think it is accurate? Why or why not?

Considering Technique

1. What approach does Kaufman use to engage interest in her introduction? Does it do a good job of engaging reader interest? Explain.
2. For what purpose do you think Kaufman defines *control freak*?

3. Kaufman quotes Los Angeles psychologist Gary Emery. How does the quotation help her achieve her writing purpose?
4. How does Kaufman use exemplification to help develop her definition?

For Group Discussion or Journal Writing

In paragraph 13, Kaufman says, "So much of life is beyond our control. And to me, that's what makes it interesting." Agree or disagree, citing examples to support your view.

Combining Patterns of Development

I Remember Masa[1]

José Antonio Burciaga

In this 1988 essay from his collection Weedee Peepo, *José Burciaga combines several patterns with definition in an appreciation for that staple of Mexican cuisine, the tortilla. As you read the selection, think about what would prompt the author to write about an item of food that has been part of the Mexican diet for thousands of years.*

1 My earliest memory of *tortillas* is my *Mamá* telling me not to play with them. I had bitten eyeholes in one and was wearing it as a mask at the dinner table.

2 As a child, I also used *tortillas* as hand warmers on cold days, and my family claims that I owe my career as an artist to my early experiments with *tortillas*. According to them, my clowning around helped me develop a strong artistic foundation. I'm not so sure, though. Sometimes I wore a *tortilla* on my head, like a *yarmulke,*[2] and yet I never had any great urge to convert from Catholicism to Judaism. But who knows? They may be right.

3 For Mexicans over the centuries, the *tortilla* has served as the spoon and the fork, the plate and the napkin. *Tortillas* originated before the Mayan civilizations, perhaps predating Europe's wheat bread. According to Mayan mythology, the great god Quetzalcoatl, realizing that the red ants knew the secret of using maize as food, transformed himself into a black ant, infiltrated the colony of red ants, and absconded with a grain of corn. (Is it any wonder that to

[1]Masa is a dough, often made with dried corn.
[2]A yarmulke is a skullcap worn by religious Jewish men and boys.

this day, black ants and red ants do not get along?) Quetzalcoatl then put maize on the lips of the first man and woman, Oxomoco and Cipactonal, so that they would become strong. Maize festivals are still celebrated by many Indian cultures of the Americas.

When I was growing up in El Paso, *tortillas* were part of my daily life. I used to visit a *tortilla* factory in an ancient adobe building near the open *mercado*[3] in Ciudad Juárez. As I approached, I could hear the rhythmic slapping of the *masa* as the skilled vendors outside the factory formed it into balls and patted them into perfectly round corn cakes between the palms of their hands. The wonderful aroma and the speed with which the women counted so many dozens of *tortillas* out of warm wicker baskets still linger in my mind. Watching them at work convinced me that the most handsome and *deliciosas tortillas* are handmade. Although machines are faster, they can never adequately replace generation-to-generation experience. There's no place in the factory assembly line for the tender slaps that give each *tortilla* character. The best thing that can be said about mass-producing *tortillas* is that it makes it possible for many people to enjoy them. 4

In the *mercado* where my mother shopped, we frequently bought *taquitos de nopalitos,* small tacos filled with diced cactus, onions, tomatoes, and *jalapeños*. Our friend Don Toribio showed us how to make delicious, crunchy *taquitos* with dried, salted pumpkin seeds. When you had no money for the filling, a poor man's *taco* could be made by placing a warm *tortilla* on the left palm, applying a sprinkle of salt, then rolling the *tortilla* up quickly with the fingertips of the right hand. My own kids put peanut butter and jelly on *tortillas,* which I think is truly bicultural. And speaking of fast foods for kids, nothing beats a *quesadilla,* a *tortilla* grilled-cheese sandwich. 5

Depending on what you intend to use them for, *tortillas* may be made in various ways. Even a run-of-the-mill *tortilla* is more than a flat corn cake. A skillfully cooked homemade *tortilla* has a bottom and a top; the top skin forms a pocket in which you put the filling that folds your *tortilla* into a taco. Paper-thin *tortillas* are used specifically for *flautas,* a type of taco that is filled, rolled, and then fried until crisp. The name *flauta* means *flute,* which probably refers to the Mayan bamboo flute; however, the only sound that comes from an edible *flauta* is a delicious crunch that is music to the palate. In México *flautas* are sometimes made as long as two feet and then cut into manageable segments. The opposite of *flautas* is *gorditas,* meaning *little fat ones*. These are very thick small *tortillas*. 6

The versatility of *tortillas* and corn does not end here. Besides being tasty and nourishing, they have spiritual and artistic qualities as well. The Tarahumara Indians of Chihuahua, for example, concocted a corn-based beer called *tesgüino,* which their descendants still make today. And everyone has read about the woman in New Mexico who was cooking her husband a *tortilla* one morning when the image of Jesus Christ miraculously appeared on it. Before they knew what was happening, the man's breakfast had become a local shrine. 7

Then there is *tortilla* art. Various Chicano artists throughout the Southwest have, when short of materials or just in a whimsical mood, used a dry *tortilla* as a small, round canvas. And a few years back, at the height of the Chicano movement, a priest in Arizona got into trouble with the Church after he was discovered celebrating mass using a *tortilla* as the host. All of which only goes to show that while the *tortilla* may be a lowly corn cake, when the necessity arises, it can reach unexpected distinction. 8

[3]A mercado is a market.

Considering Ideas

1. Burciaga defines *tortilla*. What characteristics of his subject does he mention?

2. Why are tortillas so important to Burciaga?
3. Why does the author consider peanut butter and jelly on a tortilla to be a bicultural phenomenon?
4. In paragraph 7, the author says that tortillas have "spiritual and artistic qualities." Is he serious? That is, can food really be spiritual and artistic?

Considering Technique

1. The thesis of the essay is not in the introduction. What is the thesis and where is it found? What point does it say can be drawn from the definition?
2. For what purpose do you think Burciaga writes about tortillas?
3. For what audience do you think Burciaga is writing? How familiar is that audience with tortillas?
4. *Combining patterns:* The author uses description in paragraphs 4–6. How does that description help him achieve his writing purpose? He uses narration in paragraph 3 and exemplification in paragraphs 7 and 8. How do each of those patterns help him achieve his writing purpose?

For Group Discussion or Journal Writing

Part of "I Remember Masa" notes the importance of tortillas in the author's family life as a child. In general, how important is food in family life? Cite examples to support your opinion.

STYLE NOTE

Questions

Writers can use two kinds of questions: those that are asked and answered in print, and those that are asked in print but not answered. José Antonío Burciaga writes the first kind of question in paragraph 2 of "I Remember Masa." He asks whether his family is correct that his career as an artist is a result of his early play with tortillas:

> But who knows?

The answer follows the question and suggests that his family may be correct:

> They may be right.

The second kind of question is a **rhetorical question.** A rhetorical question is asked for effect; the writer does not answer it because the answer is obvious. Margo Kaufman asks a rhetorical question to conclude "My Way!":

> So what's wrong with being a control freak?

Because she asks this question after she discovers that she may be a control freak, the writer clearly intends—and the reader realizes—that the answer is "Nothing."

DEFINITION IN AN IMAGE

This Princeton University Press advertisement appeared in *Scientific American* in 2001. Note its use of definition.

Considering the Image

1. What subject does the advertisement define? What stipulative definition is included in the ad?
2. What is the purpose of the definition in the advertisement?
3. What pattern of development helps develop the definition?
4. The advertisement appeared in *Scientific American.* What features of the advertisement and its definition take that audience into consideration?

SUGGESTIONS FOR WRITING

Writing Definition

1. Write a definition of a stereotype depicted on television or in a magazine advertisement, such as lawyers, doctors, teachers, fathers, or teenagers.
2. Define one of the following:

situation comedy	frustration	spam
being in the zone	tackiness	apathy
maturity	adolescence	success
patriotism	cyberspace	greed
geek	celebrity	inner strength
Christmas spirit	stereotyping	cynicism
sportsmanship	jealousy	leader

3. Define *superhero* (Wonder Woman, Superman, Batman, Spider-Man, etc.).
4. Define the nature of a successful (popular, not necessarily good) television show.
5. Define an ethnic term (*chutzpah, machismo, gringo,* etc.).

Reading Then Writing Definition

1. Like Nicholas Thompson in "Hero Inflation," write a definition of *hero.*
2. Using "What Is Writer's Block?" for a guide, write an essay with the title "What Is Inspiration?"
3. Using "Parenthood: Don't Count on Sleeping Until They Move Out" as a guide, write a definition of *son* or *daughter.* As an alternative, write a definition of *only child, firstborn, middle child,* or *baby of the family,* whichever designation applies to you.
4. In "I Remember Masa," José Antonio Burciaga defines *tortilla.* Write your own definition of a food that is an important part of your ethnicity or an important part of a holiday celebration or that was an important part of your childhood. Like Burciaga, use some description with the definition.

Definition beyond the Writing Classroom

Assume you are the manager of a department store and that you anticipate hiring extra salespeople to work the busy holiday period from November to mid-January. To help train these new hires, you plan to develop a manual that explains company policies and procedures. For the introduction to the manual, write a 500- to 700-word definition of "a good sales associate." Alternatively, imagine that you and your classmates have been asked to work as peer counselors at a local high school. With a group of classmates, write a 500- to 700-word definition of "a healthy friendship" based on what you each experienced as adolescents. Remember that your audience is teenagers and your purpose is to provide helpful and compassionate guidance.

Responding to a Theme

1. If you disagree with Nicholas Thompson's thesis in "Hero Inflation," write an essay arguing that the definition of hero should include victims, particularly the victims of the September 11 terrorist attacks.
2. In "My Way!" Margo Kaufman notes the need that some people have to control every aspect of a situation. In an essay, explain to what extent students do—and do not—have control over situations in their lives.
3. In "I Remember Masa," José Antonio Burciaga notes the importance of tortillas in Mexican culture. Discuss the role of a particular food or drink—such as the hamburger, turkey, or Coca-Cola—in American culture.
4. Explain whether you think the Princeton University Press advertisement is an effective one. Describe the characteristics of the audience the advertisement targets, and explain how well it addresses that audience and achieves its purpose.
5. *Connecting the readings:* In "My Way!" Margo Kaufman discusses the controlling nature of the control freak; in "Speech Codes: Alive and Well at Colleges" (page 230), Harvey Silverglate and Greg Lukianoff discuss the controlling nature of speech codes. And in "Our Schedules, Ourselves," (page 323), Jay Walljasper notes that we can be controlled by our schedules. Drawing on the ideas in these essays and your own experiences and observations, discuss how much control Americans have over their lives.

Writing Definition

The following guidelines are not meant to replace your own effective procedures. They're here for you to try as you work to improve your writing process.

www.mhhe.com/tsw

For further help writing definition, go to Catalyst 2.0 > Writing > Writing Tutors > Definition

Think like a Writer: Generating Ideas, Considering Audience and Purpose, and Ordering Ideas

- If you need help finding a topic, try one of the following:
  - Leaf through a dictionary and consider the entries. List words you might like to explore through extended definition, and then choose one term from this list.

PROCESS GUIDELINES

- Consider your own experience. What moods or emotions have you known lately? Depression, anger, anticipation, love—these can be defined using narration and examples from your life.
- Think of people you have observed or interacted with recently. Coaches, teachers, salespeople, doctors—these roles can be defined using your observations and experiences for details.

- To target a specific audience, answer these questions:
  - Who has a different opinion about the term than I do?
  - Who does not fully understand the term?
  - Who takes my subject for granted?
- To determine your purpose, answer these questions:
  - Do I want to clarify the nature of a complex subject?
  - Do I want my reader to appreciate something taken for granted?
  - Do I want to inform my reader about something not well understood?
  - Do I want to make a statement about something related to the term?
  - Do I want to express my feelings or relate my experience?
  - Do I want to convince my reader of something?
- To generate ideas, answer all the pertinent questions:
  - What are the three most important characteristics of my subject?
  - What three words best describe my subject?
  - How does my subject work?
  - What are some examples of my subject?
  - What is my subject like and different from?
- Complete an outline worksheet. (See page 66.)

Think like a Writer: Drafting

- As you draft, refer to your outline worksheet. Think about your audience and purpose, departing from your outline as necessary to meet the needs of your audience and fulfill your purpose.
- Use topic sentences to introduce each characteristic of the term, so your reader can follow along easily.

Think like a Critic; Work like an Editor: Revising

- Place a check mark each time you mention a distinguishing characteristic. Do you have at least two check marks? Study the detail you give to explain each characteristic to be sure it is adequate.
- Find the sentence or sentences that explain the significance of your definition. If you have not stated the significance, should you?
- To secure reader response, see page 105.

Think like a Critic; Work like an Editor: Correcting Errors

Eliminate circular definitions. A **circular definition** restates the term without adding helpful information.

Circular: Freedom of speech is being able to speak freely.

Better: Freedom of speech is the one constitutional guarantee without which no democracy can survive because it guarantees healthy dissent and public debate on important issues.

Remember

- Use your own writing style, not one found in dictionaries. If you write that "Christmas spirit is that seasonal mood of ebullience and feeling of goodwill and generosity characteristic of and emanating from the yearly celebration of the birth of Jesus," you will not sound natural.
- Avoid using "according to *Webster's*" unless citing the dictionary definition serves an important purpose—perhaps as a contrast to the definition you give.

LOOKING AHEAD

Classification essays group items according to their characteristics, and division essays give the components of a single item. You will learn how to write both kinds of essays in this chapter. Before doing so, however, think about the examinations you take as a college student. True-false exams, like the one Peppermint Patty is taking in this *Peanuts* cartoon, are just one kind of examination. Assume you are going to classify the kinds of exams college students take, and name all the types you can think of. Next, pick one of those kinds of exams, and assume you will divide it into its components. List three of those components.

Classification and Division

Scientists are always placing items in groups because doing so makes it easier to study and understand them. For example, *The Handy Science Answer Book*™ groups the kinds of volcanoes this way:

> *Cinder cones* are built of lava fragments. They have slopes of 30 degrees to 40 degrees and seldom exceed 1,640 feet (500 meters) in height. Sunset Crater in Arizona and Paricutín in Mexico are examples of cinder cones.
>
> *Composite cones* are made of alternating layers of lava and ash. They are characterized by slopes of up to 30 degrees at the summit, tapering off to five degrees at the base. Mount Fuji in Japan and Mount St. Helens in Washington are composite volcanoes.
>
> *Shield volcanoes* are built primarily of lava flows. Their slopes are seldom more than 10 degrees at the summit and two degrees at the base. The Hawaiian Islands are clusters of shield volcanoes. Mauna Loa is the world's largest active volcano, rising 13,653 feet (4,161 meters) above sea level.
>
> *Lava domes* are made of viscous, pasty lava squeezed like toothpaste from a tube. Examples of lava domes are Lassen Peak and Mono Dome in California.

Just as placing items in groups aids understanding, so does identifying the components of an item. For example, upon learning that a fancy wedding cake can cost as much as $5,000, you may wonder why it costs so much. Part of the answer lies in knowing what goes into the cake. Here is that information, taken from a *USA Today* article:

What Goes into a $5,000 Wedding Cake?

Eggs: 192
Sugar: 38 pounds
Butter: 22.2 pounds
Flour: 12.63 pounds
White chocolate: 7.7 pounds
Fresh strawberries: 17 pints
Simple syrup: 2 liters
Fondant: About 50 pounds
Fondant "tiles": Nearly 20,000
Fondant "flowers": 150

Labor: Three people working 135 hours; extra worker brought in on Saturday to help at the last minute

When you group items or information according to their characteristics—the way volcanoes are grouped in the preceding example—you are **classifying.** When you take a single entity and break it down into its parts—the way the wedding cake is broken down—you are **dividing.** Classification and division can be performed separately, but they can also be performed together. For example, scientists must identify the components of a volcano (slopes, lava, ash, etc.) before they can group them into various categories. Or consider the way the telephone book's yellow pages are organized. First, businesses are *classified* by type, so there are listings for restaurants, insurance companies, automobile sales, hair salons, and so on. Then each classification is *divided* into components, so restaurant listings include Jimmy's Pizza Parlor, Fifth Avenue Steak House, Bagels and More, and so on.

WHY ARE CLASSIFICATION AND DIVISION IMPORTANT?

Life is filled with information about people, places, things, devices, facts, and figures. Without some way to group and order all these elements, each new item we encounter would baffle us. Classification and division help provide a mechanism for grouping and organizing information.

Imagine a library without a division and classification system. If you wanted to read a mystery by a particular author, you would have to scan the shelves until you got lucky and came across the book. Fortunately, libraries have classification and division systems, so you can go quickly to the area where mysteries are shelved and then to the mysteries by a particular author. Shopping too would be daunting. Imagine taking your list to a grocery store that shelved items randomly, instead of grouping baking goods together, produce together, dairy products together, and so forth. Or imagine trying to find a DVD in a store that did not classify and divide movies by type (science fiction, action, drama, comedy, etc.) and then by title.

Classification can serve a number of informational purposes. People often classify because ordering information *makes for easier study.* In biology, grouping animals into classifications such as mammals, birds, reptiles, and amphibians allows scientists to study animal life more efficiently.

In addition, classification is a way to *clarify similarities and differences.* For example, if you classified diet programs, you would discover how these programs are similar and different. Such information could help you decide which program is best for you. In addition, such a classification could point out which features are shared by successful programs. Knowing this information can help you predict the chances of success for any program you encounter.

Further, classification can *provide a fresh way of viewing something.* For example, television programs are usually classified as dramas, sitcoms, reality shows, game shows, soap operas, variety shows, and so forth. However, an essay that classifies programs according to how they portray women can lead to a greater awareness of how television influences our perception of women.

Division can also serve informational purposes. A laboratory analyzes blood and reports its findings by dividing a sample into its components. Division can be a way *to explain something not well understood.* For example, to explain how a desktop computer works, you could divide it into its components and explain each one.

The chart that follows illustrates the range of purposes that classification and division can serve.

Purposes for Classification and Division

Purpose	**Sample Classification and Division**
To entertain	A classification of your eccentric relatives according to their amusing traits, or a division of a disastrous family reunion into its parts for comic effect
To share feelings and experiences	A division of a grieving process you went through into its components
	A classification of your childhood birthday parties
To inform (clarify similarities and differences)	A classification of the models of bicycles (racing, touring, dirt bikes, etc.) according to their chief characteristics (price, frame design, tire size, etc.)
To inform	A division of a good health club into its components so the reader can choose a health club wisely
To persuade	A classification of telephone solicitors according to the reasons they take the job (those who are unprepared for other work, those who are housebound, and those who are disabled) to convince the reader to treat solicitors with more respect; or a division of the job of telephone solicitation into its components to show how difficult it is and thereby convince the reader to be more respectful

Classification and Division across the Disciplines and Beyond

Classification and Division in the Classroom

Classification and division will be important components of your college writing. In an exam for a speech class, you might be asked to classify persuasive rhetorical strategies, or you might identify the components of an effective speech. For a biology midterm, you might be asked to divide a cell into its parts. In a paper for an advertising class, you might explain the components of a successful advertising campaign, or you might classify the most successful kinds of campaigns. *How might you use classification and/or division in an education paper about remedial reading programs? In your major or in classes you are taking this term?*

Classification and Division in Daily Life

Classification and division can be a part of your personal writing. To make a decision about the best health maintenance organization to join, you can divide the possibilities into their components to determine which offers the best benefits. In an advertisement for a garage sale, you can classify the items you are selling according to type, such as kitchenware, children's clothing, and books. As fund-raising chair of an organization, you can classify kinds of fund-raisers to help your committee decide which kind you should have. *If you had to make an extended shopping trip to many stores for many items, such as drugstore items, grocery items, and clothing, how might you write a list using classification and division?*

Classification and Division on the Job

Classification and division is part of workplace writing. Investment counselors classify the kinds of mutual funds to help their clients decide which to invest in. Human resources managers divide insurance plans into their components to help employees understand their coverage. A movie reviewer for a newspaper evaluates a movie with division by considering its parts, such as the director, the actors, the script, and the cinematography. *How might you use classification and division in the job you hope to have after graduation? For whom will you write the classification and division? Which of the purposes for writing will that classification and division fulfill?*

COMBINING CLASSIFICATION AND DIVISION WITH OTHER PATTERNS

When you classify, you set up categories. For example, to classify baby-sitters according to the quality of care they give, you could use these categories: the slovenly teen sitter, the cleanliness nut, the inattentive sitter, the nervous sitter, and the elderly sitter. To explain the characteristics of the elements in the categories, you could rely heavily on various patterns of development. For example, in a humorous classification of baby-sitters, you could describe the appearance of the slovenly teen sitter, narrate an account of the time the cleanliness nut scrubbed the children *and* the bathroom, and illustrate the inattentive sitter with the example of the sitter who talked on the phone while the child wandered through the neighborhood. You could also explain nervous sitters with a process analysis of the elaborate procedure they go through to guard against the child's choking when being fed, compare the elderly sitter to a doting grandparent, and define the perfect sitter.

Similarly, division can rely on other patterns. For example, an essay that divides the cell into its components could describe the parts and use process analysis to explain what they do.

Classification and division can also appear in essays developed primarily with other dominant patterns. An essay explaining the effects of social stratification might first explain the socioeconomic categories people fit into; an essay noting the causes of cheating among college students could begin with a classification of kinds of cheating; and an essay that explains how employers can effectively communicate with employees might divide an effective e-mail into its parts.

SELECTING DETAIL

Writing can include just classification or just division, but the two patterns of development are often used together. For example, in an essay about kinds of television shows, you might first classify the kinds (sitcoms, dramas, reality shows, game shows, talk shows, etc.). Then you might use division to explain the parts of each kind of show. The following strategies can help you write essays that include both classification and division or that include classification alone. Some of the strategies also apply to division used by itself.

Have a Principle of Classification or Division

A classification must group elements according to some principle that provides the logic for the classification. Consider, for example, a classification of teachers. One group could be those who lecture, one could be those who use a question-and-answer format, and one could be those who guide student discussion. The principle of classification in this case is instructional methods.

When you classify, place elements in groups according to your principle of classification. Your supporting details can indicate what the groups are, what elements are in each group, and what the characteristics of the elements are. Assume, for example, that you are classifying aerobics classes according to the amount of impact they have on the joints. You could support this classification by noting your categories (perhaps high impact, moderate impact, and low impact) and indicating which classes (perhaps dance aerobics, step aerobics, and walk aerobics) fit into each category. Finally, you could describe the relevant aspects of the classes in each category (perhaps kind of movements, speed of movements, and number of repetitions). In other words, you support your classification by arranging items in groups and explaining what the elements in the group are like.

With division, you may or may not need a principle of division. If you are dividing shampoo into its components to analyze what is in the product, you need no principle because you will mention every component. However, if you are discussing what makes up a successful game-show host, you will need a principle—perhaps the qualities of the on-air personality that make the host, and by extension the show, watchable. Do not think that you must develop each grouping in equal detail, for some groupings may need more explanation than others. As long as all groupings are explained *adequately*, they need not be explained *equally*.

Be Sure All Categories or Components Conform to Your Principle of Classification or Division

Suppose you are classifying American voters according to how they make up their minds, and you establish these categories: people who make decisions based on the issues, people who make decisions based on the personalities of the politicians, people who make decisions based on what friends and family think, and people who do not make decisions because they do not vote. The last category does not conform to the principle of classification and, therefore, should not be included.

Use Mutually Exclusive Categories

If an item can fall into more than one grouping, your categories are not mutually exclusive, a problem that creates an unreliable classification. Suppose you are classifying news shows, and you establish these categories: cable, network, hard news, and soft news. Because these categories are not mutually exclusive, some shows can be placed in more than one group. *NBC Nightly News*, for instance, is both hard news and network.

Explain Each Category or Component

For adequate detail, you must explain each category or component, perhaps with details about the characteristics of each one. Look, for example, at paragraph 2 of "Grocery Shoppers" on page 371. The category identified is a particular kind of grocery shopper that the author calls "The Mother." Notice that the paragraph takes pains to explain what members of this category are like.

Consider Your Audience and Purpose

Most things can be classified or divided according to more than one principle. To decide which principle to use, consider your audience and purpose. Kinds of education curricula, for example, can be classified according to several principles, including cost-effectiveness and the number of students who stay in the profession for more than five years. If your audience is college deans, you could use cost-effectiveness as your principle of classification. Your purpose could be to inform deans of how to structure education curricula to save money. However, if you want to convince members of local boards of education that they should consider the kind of program teacher applicants graduated from, then a better principle of classification will be students who stay in the profession for more than five years.

Your audience and purpose will also affect your supporting detail. Say you are classifying home computers to inform a reader who knows little about computers. You may have to define terms like *byte* and *hard drive.* Similarly, how extensively you use examples may depend on your purpose and audience. For instance, if you are classifying video games to inform parents who have never played them, you may need to give many examples of each type; however, if your readers are teenagers who play the games often, fewer examples will be called for.

BEING A RESPONSIBLE WRITER

Responsible writers do not omit categories or items in categories to achieve their purpose. Consider the store owner who classifies kinds of laptop computers in a sales brochure. If the store owner omits a particular kind of computer from the classification because the profit margin is low on that type, customers get an incomplete classification—and one that steers them away from one purchasing option.

Responsible writers also do not unfairly or inappropriately classify people or things negatively. When classifying religions, for example, a responsible writer would not classify Western religions as enlightened and Eastern religions as unenlightened.

To be a responsible writer, ask yourself these questions:

- Have I included every category and division relevant to my principle of classification or division?
- Have I included every item that belongs in each category?
- Are any of my classifications unfairly negative?

ORGANIZING CLASSIFICATION AND DIVISION

The introduction of classification and division can be handled a number of ways. For example, you can explain the value of the classification or division. If you are classifying movies recently released on DVD and your audience consists of parents, you can explain that the classification is important because it helps parents choose suitable movies for their youngsters. If you are dividing sugared breakfast cereal into its components for parents, you can explain that the division is important because parents should understand what they are feeding their children. Your introduction can also explain why you are qualified to classify or divide your subject. Thus, if you are classifying cookbooks or dividing a good cookbook into its parts, you can explain that you have been a cookbook collector and gourmet cook for many years. This approach gives your classification and division credibility because you establish yourself as knowledgeable. Another approach is to explain how you discovered the classification or division. If you are classifying baseball coaches or explaining what makes a good coach, you can note that you arrived at your conclusions after years of observing your children's coaches.

USING SOURCES FOR A PURPOSE

Below is a body paragraph for an online posting for a social psychology class arguing that lying is not necessary for maintaining peaceful social interaction. The paragraph follows paragraphs explaining that even little white lies are unnecessary for keeping interaction running smoothly. It argues that a particular kind of lie more serious than the little white lie is also unnecessary for smooth social interaction. It includes quotation and paraphrase from paragraphs 34 and 44 of "The Truth about Lying" on page 379. (For more information on writing quotations and paraphrases, see Chapter 17.)

THESIS IDEA: Contrary to what many say, peaceful social interaction is not dependent on the telling of certain kinds of lies.

WRITING PURPOSE AND AUDIENCE: To convince students in a social psychology class that lying is not necessary for smooth social interaction

The paraphrase in sentence 2 presents a kind of lie some people think is acceptable, for the reason given in the quotation in sentence 6.

[1]Although most people are not disturbed by little white lies, they should be. [2]They should also be disturbed by a more serious lie, what Judith Viorst calls the "trust-keeping [lie]," which occurs when one person tells a lie to a second person in order to protect a confidence shared by a third person (381). [3]Without the trust-keeping lie, some would argue that we would betray confidences, and doing so would cause those who shared the confidences to be angry with us. [4]You might be thinking that trust-keeping lies could be avoided if we refused to hear confidences, and that is true. [5]However, then we would

Your thesis can indicate your subject and state that you are classifying or dividing, like this:

```
Many commercial weight-loss programs are available,
but the best ones have the same components.
```

This thesis states that the best commercial weight-loss programs will be divided into their parts. Your thesis can also include your principle of classification or division:

```
Some students classify teachers according to how
difficult they are, but a better way to classify
them is according to their teaching techniques.
```

This thesis states that teachers will be classified and that the principle of classification is teaching techniques. Another approach is to state your groupings in your thesis:

```
White lies can be harmless, embarrassing, or
hurtful.
```

In your body paragraphs, topic sentences can introduce each grouping or component as it is presented. For example, the following topic sentences could appear in a classification of white lies:

lose an invaluable (and therapeutic) feature of human interaction: the ability to share personal, sensitive information with a friend. [6]Viorst believes that "once we've promised to keep a trust, we must tell lies to keep it" although "we can't tell Watergate lies [i.e., lies with serious, harmful consequences]" (382). [7]I disagree with Viorst, however. [8]We don't have to lie to keep the confidence. [9]We can avoid betraying the third person's confidence by simply telling the second person, "That's not something I'm comfortable talking about."

Avoiding Plagiarism

The paragraph illustrates some points about using source material and avoiding plagiarism.

- **Use brackets when you alter the syntax of a quotation to work it into your sentence smoothly.** For example, in sentence 2, *lie* appears in brackets because in the source, Viorst uses the word *lies.* (See paragraph 34 on page 381.) The writer of the essay uses the singular form to work the quoted material into the sentence.
- **Use brackets to add explanatory information to a quotation.** As sentence 6 illustrates, use brackets to add material to a quotation for clarity.

Myths about Sources

MYTH: Students should not disagree with ideas in source material.

FACT: Critical readers evaluate material thoughtfully and form their own opinions. You can disagree with what you read, as long as you support your assertion.

```
Most white lies are harmless.

At times, white lies prove embarrassing to the teller.

Unfortunately, a small percentage of white lies are hurtful.
```

After the topic sentence that presents the grouping, you can provide the supporting details that give the characteristics of the elements in the group or components.

At times, you can arrange your groups or components in a progressive order. For example, in the classification of white lies, the groupings can be arranged according to how serious the consequences of the lies are. You can discuss the harmless lies first, then the embarrassing ones, and then the hurtful ones. In an essay that explains the components of the best commercial weight-loss programs, you can discuss the components in their order of effectiveness.

Sometimes you can arrange groups in chronological order. For example, if you are classifying ways to discipline children, you might do so according to the age of the child.

Many times, you can present your groupings or components in a random order because no organizational pattern is apparent or called for. However, if you discuss the same characteristics for each grouping, use the same order each time. For example, if you classify salespeople and discuss personality, technique, and willingness to help for each group, present these aspects in the same order each time. Doing so provides consistency and helps your reader to make comparisons among your groupings.

To provide closure in your conclusion, you can indicate the value of your classification or division if you did not do so in your introduction. Otherwise, you can use one of the strategies explained beginning on page 88.

Visualizing Classification and Division

The chart that follows can help you visualize the organization of classification and division. Like all good models, this one can be altered as needed.

Introduction

- May engage interest by explaining
  - The value of the classification or division
  - Why you are qualified to classify or divide the subject
  - How you discovered the classification or division
- Includes a thesis that can state
  - The subject and whether you are classifying or dividing
  - The principle for classifying or dividing
  - Why you are qualified to classify or divide the subject
  - How you discovered the classification or division

First Body Paragraph

- Gives the first grouping or component in a topic sentence
- Specifies the grouping or component according to the principle of classification or division
- Explains the grouping or component, using the appropriate patterns of development
- Arranges details in a progressive or other logical order

Next Body Paragraphs

- Give the remaining groupings or components, according to the principle of classification or division
- Explain the groupings or components, using the appropriate patterns of development
- Arrange details in a progressive or other logical order

Conclusion

- May elaborate on the significance of the classification or division
- Provides closure

EXERCISE Writing Classification and Division

1. For one 24-hour period, list every classification and division that you encounter.
2. List as many principles of classification as you can for an essay that classifies restaurants. Now list possible principles of division for an essay that divides restaurants into their components.
3. Identify a principle of classification or division for each of these subjects: friends, teachers, students.
4. Write a thesis for each subject and principle of classification or division from number 3. Each thesis should include words that indicate you will classify or divide, or words that present the principle of classification or division.
5. Note the categories or components that could appear in an essay using one of the thesis statements from number 4.
6. Pick one of the categories identified in number 5, and list the elements in that category.
7. What patterns of development could you use to help explain the elements noted in number 6? ■

LEARNING FROM OTHER WRITERS: Student Essays

The two essays that follow were written by students. The first, "Grocery Shoppers," classifies the people who shop in grocery stores, primarily to entertain the reader. Annotations in the margin point out its key features. As you read, notice how much supporting detail the author provides to develop each category.

The second essay, "Horror Movies," is an informative classification that comments on both its subject and the people who watch horror movies. This essay has less detail than "Grocery Shoppers." Do you think it needs more?

Grocery Shoppers

Anita Selfe

While entering Giant Eagle to do my usual Saturday grocery shopping, I found myself behind a trim young woman with three children in tow, their ages approximately one, three, and five. Although I have been shopping for groceries for well over 30 years, it was only then that I realized that grocery shoppers fall into several basic categories. 1

Paragraph 1
The introduction engages interest with background information and gives the author's qualifications (she has shopped for over 30 years). The thesis (last sentence) gives the subject (grocery shoppers) and words indicating that classification will occur ("fall into several basic categories").

The woman I entered behind fit perfectly into the category I call "The Mother." Technically, a mother can be any woman shopping with a child. However, shopping with only one kid presents no substantial challenge, so 2

Paragraph 2
The topic sentence (the first) notes the first category (The Mother). The supporting detail (the characteristics of the category) is a narrative example. Note the specific detail and word choice.

"The Mother" must be accompanied by at least two children. "The Mother" I entered behind illustrated that women in this category have two organizational problems. The first is where to find space in the cart to pile the groceries. In the case of "The Mother" I entered behind, child #1, the eldest, was instructed to sit on the bottom shelf of the grocery cart, while #2 child sat in the carriage, and #3 child, the youngest, in the child seat. This arrangement temporarily controlled the number-two problem: how to restrain the six extra hands she had brought along. It was not long, however, before #2 child became buried in Pampers, tissues, and cereal boxes. Child #2 was then transferred to the bottom shelf, freeing #1 to walk and help Mommy. "See, Mommy, I can count the eggs," piped a little voice. "Cleanup in aisle seven," sounded the P.A. system. Such announcements are a sure indicator that "The Mother" is in the store. The bottom shelf of a shopping cart is not without hazard for the child riding thereupon. That day, "The Mother," mumbling to herself something about not forgetting the laundry detergent, abruptly turned left at the end of an aisle, while child #2, anticipating another pass through the cereal section, inclined right. Cries of pain and surprise rang out (another sure indicator that "The Mother" is in the store), as child #2's head unceremoniously clunked to the floor. "The Mother" administered loving kisses and murmured assurances that "Yes, we will go find the Crispy Mermaid Cereal right now." During this disturbance, the youngest child remained calm and occupied by carefully peeling the little red price stickers from the grocery items within her reach.

Paragraph 3
Discussion of the first category continues. The topic sentence (the first) notes the focus on solving the problem of hungry kids. The supporting detail is narration.

Seeing all the food in the store typically makes the children hungry, so "The Mother" I was observing solved the problem as many of her kind do. A stop at the delicatessen for packages of bologna and cheese, and another at the produce department for apples and grapes, and lunch was served. A box of vanilla wafers, its top unceremoniously ripped open, became dessert. With six little hands busy feeding three little mouths, "The Mother" now hurried to finish the rest of her shopping. 3

Another category of shopper is the "Mother's Helper." "Mothers' Helpers" 4
are preteens sent to the store by their mothers for some urgently needed item. An unusual phenomenon happens when "Mothers' Helpers" enter a grocery store—they suddenly become avid readers! Cereal boxes are removed from the shelves and are read front and back. After scrutinizing the candy-bar labels (as well as smelling and palpitating the contents), the "Mothers' Helpers" usually find time to read the comic books and muscle magazines. Of course, the final stop before making their purchase is the video department, where they avidly review any new titles and some of their old favorites as well. You probably have seen "Mothers' Helpers" on their way home—pedaling slowly with hands, not on the handlebars, but carefully clutching the urgently needed item for Mom.

Paragraph 4
The topic sentence (the first) notes the second category (Mother's Helper). Notice the transition ("another category"). The supporting detail explains the chief characteristics of the items in the category. Notice the specific word choice.

Another frequently seen shopper is "Ms. Organization." "Ms. Orga- 5
nization" is identifiable by the coupon box (usually the size of a small fishing tackle box) in the child seat of the grocery cart, her 32-function solar calculator, her pencil chiseled to a lethal point, and her detailed grocery list with items arranged in the order of aisles in the store. The list, I am sure, was compiled while consulting the recipe cards for next week's menus. Methodically, "Ms. Organization" moves up and down each aisle, scanning prices, matching items to coupons, recording each purchase on her calculator, then canceling the item from her list with a neat, impeccably straight line. Never get behind "Ms. Organization" at the checkout because she never lets the clerk ring anything up until everything is out of the cart. Then she monitors the ringing up of each item and finds a reason to demand a price check. Even worse, she is known to demand a recheck of an entire register tape, so out comes every item from the bags, and out comes the "Use Next Lane" sign. On the way out of the store, "Ms. Organization" can be seen clutching her purse while giving instructions in economics to the boy helping her take her groceries to the car.

Paragraph 5
The topic sentence (the first) notes the third category (Ms. Organization). Notice that the sentence begins with a transition. The supporting detail to give characteristics is description. Notice that the classification's principle of organization is the behavior of shoppers. The writer's purpose is to entertain.

Paragraph 6
The topic sentence (the first) presents the next category (Hapless Husband). The supporting detail notes the chief characteristics (by contrasting Hapless Husband with Ms. Organization) and includes description.

At the other end of the spectrum from "Ms. Organization" is the "Hapless Husband," a male who has been coerced into grocery shopping. Far from organized, he walks erratically up and down the aisles, head and eyes inclined upward to read each aisle's contents. His disorganized list, often scrawled on the back of an envelope, is so illegible that he must often guess whether he is to buy Frosted Flakes or french fries. Unlike "Ms. Organization," he has no clue how the store is set up, so he is frequently seen doubling back, repeatedly pushing the cart up and down the same aisle, and stopping other shoppers to ask where the toilet paper or some other item is. When he does manage to find what he needs, "Hapless Husband" grabs it with no regard for price and, with great relief, tosses it into the cart. Once he makes it to the checkout, he pays no attention to the prices being punched into the register, pays whatever the clerk tells him to, and leaves the store dazed and confused. While you do not want to get behind "Ms. Organization," you do want to be behind "Hapless Husband" because he never challenges anything at the checkout. 6

Paragraph 7
The conclusion provides closure by giving the significance of the classification—the types are part of us all.

In truth, there is a little bit of each kind of shopper in all of us. At times, each of us can be as frazzled as "The Mother," as easily distracted as the "Mother's Helper," as efficient as "Ms. Organization," or as confused as the "Hapless Husband," which makes all shoppers fall into the largest category of all—"The Human Being." 7

Horror Movies

Ray Harkleroad

Horror movies started out harmless enough, but they have developed over the years into stomach-turning trash. 1

The first popular horror movies were the mass destruction movies. These include *The Blob, Invasion of the Body Snatchers,* and the classic *War of the* 2

Worlds. In these movies the human race is threatened with destruction by odd creatures, usually from another planet. The early mass destruction movies are the least gory of the horror flicks. There is no graphic violence, murder, or mutilation. The camera cuts away at the moment someone is done in, and eerie music hints at the mayhem that occurs. The early mass destruction movies give an audience plenty of frightening moments without turning anyone's stomach. They are harmless fun for those who like a good scare.

The supernatural thrillers came next. These movies tend to be very scary and even more nauseating. They deal with the satanic and the occult, and vampires and evil spirits are often wreaking havoc on unsuspecting, average human beings. In *The Exorcist,* a young girl was possessed by the devil who caused her to vomit green goop, spin her head in a full circle, and otherwise disgust the audience. *The Omen* and *Rosemary's Baby* fit into this class of movies that cause knee-clanking fear while souring the stomach. 3

The worst group of horror movies is undoubtedly the psychopath chop 'em up group. These movies, unlike many of the supernatural thrillers, have weak plots. They rely solely on gore to keep the audience interested. Take, for example, the movie series *Friday the Thirteenth.* In these, indestructible Jason uses an ice pick and an axe to attack his victims. The violence is graphic; blood flies everywhere. *The Texas Chainsaw Massacre, Halloween,* and *Nightmare on Elm Street*—all of these depict mutilation, murder, and mayhem vividly and in detail. Strangely, these movies should be the most disturbing, but audiences love them, returning for sequel after sequel. What does this say about us? Why do the simple, scary mass destruction movies no longer provide sufficient thrills? Perhaps the answers to these questions are even scarier than the movies. 4

EXERCISE Considering "Horror Movies"

1. What is the author's principle of classification?
2. What categories does the author present? Are the categories mutually exclusive? Do they all conform to the principle of classification?
3. Is each of the categories developed in adequate detail? Explain.

4. What is the thesis of "Horror Movies"? Is the thesis effective? Why or why not?
5. Where does the author imply the significance of the classification? What is that significance? Does the author do an effective job of indicating the significance? Explain. ■

THINK LIKE A CRITIC; WORK LIKE AN EDITOR: The Student Writer at Work

As it stands in the final version, paragraph 6 was not originally in "Grocery Shoppers." Instead, Anita Selfe had written the following paragraph 6:

Early draft

> At the other end of the continuum from "Ms. Organization" is "Ms. Hit-and-Run," a generally twenty-something shopper who is interested only in getting in and out of the store as fast as possible. "Ms. Hit-and-Run" is busy, busy, busy and has no time for thoughtful planning, so she runs into the store on her way home from work, races up and down the aisles and grabs whatever she thinks she might need. Operating without a list, she typically goes for the convenience food. She fills her cart with frozen dinners, precooked meals from the deli, 20 cartons of yogurt, and 12-pack cans of Coke. If she doesn't see something she thinks she needs, she figures she will get along without it, since she has no time to double back and look again. Get out of the way of "Ms. Hit-and-Run" because she will drive her cart right up your heels in her haste. Generally in and out of the store in under ten minutes, Ms. Hit-and-Run is the shopper you want to be behind in the checkout because she is in too much of a hurry to challenge anything.

Anita thought she was just about finished with her essay when a classmate read it over. The reader had a comment that surprised Anita: She said that the essay seemed sexist because all the categories were female shoppers. At first, Anita rejected the comment because most grocery shoppers *are* women. Then she decided to ask her instructor, who recommended that Anita consider her purpose for writing. Anita wanted to entertain her readers and became concerned that some would be offended that women were singled out. She therefore omitted the paragraph and added the one that is there now. Do you think she did the right thing?

The Dog Ate My Disk, and Other Tales of Woe

Carolyn Foster Segal

"The Dog Ate My Disk, and Other Tales of Woe" first appeared in The Chronicle of Higher Education, *a publication for college teachers and administrators, in 2000. The original audience likely found the essay entertaining. As a college student, do you also find it entertaining?*

Taped to the door of my office is a cartoon that features a cat explaining to his feline teacher, "The dog ate my homework." It is intended as a gently humorous reminder to my students that I will not accept excuses for late work, and it, like the lengthy warning on my syllabus, has had absolutely no effect. With a show of energy and creativity that would be admirable if applied to the (missing) assignments in question, my students persist, week after week, semester after semester, year after year, in offering excuses about why their work is not ready. Those reasons fall into several broad categories: the family, the best friend, the evils of dorm life, the evils of technology, and the totally bizarre. 1

The Family. The death of the grandfather/grandmother is, of course, the grandmother of all excuses. What heartless teacher would dare to question a student's grief or veracity? What heartless student would lie, wishing death on a revered family member, just to avoid a deadline? Creative students may win extra extensions (and days off) with a little careful planning and fuller plot development, as in the sequence of "My grandfather/grandmother is sick"; "Now my grandfather/grandmother is in the hospital"; and finally, "We could all see it coming—my grandfather/grandmother is dead." 2

Another favorite excuse is "the family emergency," which (always) goes like this: "There was an emergency at home, and I had to help my family." It's a lovely sentiment, one that conjures up images of Louisa May Alcott's little women[1] rushing off with baskets of food and copies of *Pilgrim's Progress,*[2] but I do not understand why anyone would turn to my most irresponsible students in times of trouble. 3

The Best Friend. This heartwarming concern for others extends beyond the family to friends, as in, "My best friend was up all night and I had to (a) stay up with her in the dorm, (b) drive her to the hospital, or (c) drive to her college because (1) her boyfriend broke up with her, (2) she was throwing up blood [no one catches a cold anymore; everyone throws up blood], or (3) her grandfather/grandmother died." 4

At one private university where I worked as an adjunct, I heard an interesting spin that incorporated the motifs of both best friend and dead relative: "My best friend's mother killed herself." One has to admire the cleverness here: A mysterious woman in the prime of her life has allegedly committed suicide, and no professor can prove otherwise! And I admit I was moved, until finally I had to point out to my students that it was amazing how the simple act of my assigning a topic for a paper seemed to drive large numbers of otherwise happy and healthy middle-aged women to their deaths. I was careful to make that point during an off week, during which no deaths were reported. 5

The Evils of Dorm Life. These stories are usually fairly predictable; almost always feature the evil roommate or hallmate, with my student in the role of the innocent victim; and can be summed up as follows: My roommate, who is a horrible person, likes to party, and I, who am a good person, cannot concentrate on my work

[1]Louisa May Alcott wrote the novel *Little Women* (1868) about the adventures of the four March sisters.

[2]*Pilgrim's Progress* is a religious allegory written by the Puritan John Bunyan and published in two parts in 1678 and 1684.

when he or she is partying. Variations include stories about the two people next door who were running around and crying loudly last night because (a) one of them had boyfriend/girlfriend problems; (b) one of them was throwing up blood; or (c) someone, somewhere, died. A friend of mine in graduate school had a student who claimed that his roommate attacked him with a hammer. That, in fact, was a true story; it came out in court when the bad roommate was tried for killing his grandfather. 6

The Evils of Technology. The computer age has revolutionized the student story, inspiring almost as many new excuses as it has Internet businesses. Here are just a few electronically enhanced explanations:

- The computer wouldn't let me save my work.
- The printer wouldn't print.
- The printer wouldn't print this disk.
- The printer wouldn't give me time to proofread.
- The printer made a black line run through all my words, and I know you can't read this, but do you still want it, or wait, here, take my disk. File name? I don't know what you mean.
- I swear I attached it.
- It's my roommate's computer, and she usually helps me, but she had to go to the hospital because she was throwing up blood.
- I did write to the newsgroup, but all my messages came back to me.
- I just found out that all my other newsgroup messages came up under a different name. I just want you to know that its really me who wrote all those messages, you can tel which ones our mine because I didn't use the spelcheck! But it was yours truely:) Anyway, just in case you missed those messages or don't belief its my writting, I'll repeat what I sad: I thought the last movie we watched in clas was borring. 7

The Totally Bizarre. I call the first story "The Pennsylvania Chain Saw Episode." A commuter student called to explain why she had missed my morning class. She had gotten up early so that she would be wide awake for class. Having a bit of extra time, she walked outside to see her neighbor, who was cutting some wood. She called out to him, and he waved back to her with the saw. Wouldn't you know it, the safety catch wasn't on or was broken, and the blade flew right out of the saw and across his lawn and over her fence and across her yard and severed a tendon in her right hand. So she was calling me from the hospital, where she was waiting for surgery. Luckily, she reassured me, she had remembered to bring her paper and a stamped envelope (in a plastic bag, to avoid bloodstains) along with her in the ambulance, and a nurse was mailing everything to me even as we spoke. 8

That wasn't her first absence. In fact, this student had missed most of the class meetings, and I had already recommended that she withdraw from the course. Now I suggested again that it might be best if she dropped the class. I didn't harp on the absences (what if even some of this story were true?). I did mention that she would need time to recuperate and that making up so much missed work might be difficult. "Oh, no," she said, "I can't drop this course. I had been planning to go on to medical school and become a surgeon, but since I won't be able to operate because of my accident, I'll have to major in English, and this course is more important than ever to me." She did come to the next class, wearing—as evidence of her recent trauma—a bedraggled Ace bandage on her left hand. 9

You may be thinking that nothing could top that excuse, but in fact I have one more story, provided by the same student, who sent me a letter to explain why her final assignment would be late. While recuperating from her surgery, she had begun corresponding on the Internet with a man who lived in Germany. After a one-week, whirlwind Web romance they had agreed to meet in Rome, to rendezvous (her phrase) at the papal Easter Mass. Regrettably, the time of her flight made it impossible for her to attend class, but she trusted that I—just this once—would accept late work if the pope wrote a note. 10

Considering Ideas

1. How do you think most students would react to the cartoon on Segal's door, the one described in paragraph 1? Would they see it as the "gently humorous reminder" Segal intends it to be? Explain.
2. The original audience for the essay was college professors and administrators. What do you think the intended purpose of the essay is for that particular audience?
3. Does Segal achieve her original purpose with you and other students as her audience? Are the original audience and student readers likely to react differently to the essay? Explain.
4. Do you think all of the excuses given in the essay were *really* given to the author? Explain.

Considering Technique

1. Write out Segal's thesis. Underline the words that indicate the subject, double underline the words that indicate classification will occur, and bracket the words that indicate the groupings.
2. What is Segal's principle of classification? Do all the categories conform to that principle? Explain.
3. Segal's original audience probably found many of her examples humorous. How does Segal achieve her humor?
4. *Sarcasm* is stating one thing but meaning another, often to insult or scorn. Cite an example of sarcasm in the essay.
5. *Combining patterns:* How does Segal use exemplification in the essay? How does that exemplification help her achieve her writing purpose?

For Group Discussion or Journal Writing

Do you think instructors should accept late work? Write a policy that you think is fair to both students and teachers.

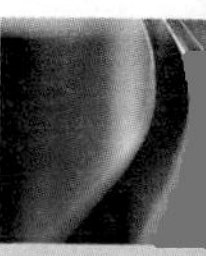

The Truth about Lying JUDITH VIORST

Judith Viorst is a poet and essayist. "The Truth about Lying" originally appeared in Redbook *in 1981. In the essay, which classifies lies, Viorst examines her position on lying and asks the reader to do the same.*

I've been wanting to write on a subject that intrigues and challenges me: the subject of lying. I've found it very difficult to do. Everyone I've talked to has a quite intense and personal but often rather intolerant point of view about what we can—and can never, *never*—tell lies about. I've finally reached the conclusion that I can't present any ultimate conclusions, for too many people would promptly disagree. Instead, I'd like to present a series of moral puzzles, all concerned with lying. I'll tell you what I think about them. Do you agree? 1

Social Lies. Most of the people I've talked with say that they find social lying acceptable and necessary. They think it's the civilized way for folks to behave. Without these little white lies, they say, our relationships would be short and brutish and nasty. It's arrogant, they say, to insist on being so incorruptible and so brave that you cause other people unnecessary embarrassment or pain by compulsively assailing them with your honesty. I basically agree. What about you? 2

Will you say to people, when it simply isn't true, "I like your new hairdo," "You're looking much better," "It's so nice to see you," "I had a wonderful time"? 3

Will you praise hideous presents and homely kids? 4

Will you decline invitations with "We're busy that night—so sorry we can't come," when the truth is you'd rather stay home than dine with the So-and-sos? 5

And even though, as I do, you may prefer the polite evasion of "You really cooked up a storm" instead of "The soup"—which tastes like warmed-over coffee—"is wonderful," will you, if you must, proclaim it wonderful? 6

There's one man I know who absolutely refuses to tell social lies. "I can't play that game," he says; "I'm simply not made that way." And his answer to the argument that saying nice things to someone doesn't cost anything is, "Yes, it does—it destroys your credibility." Now, he won't, unsolicited, offer his views on the painting you just bought, but you don't ask his frank opinion unless you want *frank,* and his silence at those moments when the rest of us liars are muttering, "Isn't it lovely?" is, for the most part, eloquent enough. My friend does not indulge in what he calls "flattery, false praise, and mellifluous comments." When others tell fibs he will not go along. He says that social lying is lying, that little white lies are still lies. And he feels that telling lies is morally wrong. What about you? 7

Peace-Keeping Lies. Many people tell peace-keeping lies; lies designed to avoid irritation or argument; lies designed to shelter the liar from possible blame or pain; lies (or so it is rationalized) designed to keep trouble at bay without hurting anyone. 8

I tell these lies at times, and yet I always feel they're wrong. I understand why we tell them, but still they feel wrong. And whenever I lie so that someone won't disapprove of me or think less of me or holler at me, I feel I'm a bit of a coward, I feel I'm dodging responsibility, I feel . . . guilty. What about you? 9

Do you, when you're late for a date because you overslept, say that you're late because you got caught in a traffic jam? 10

Do you, when you forget to call a friend, say that you called several times but the line was busy? 11

Do you, when you didn't remember that it was your father's birthday, say that his present must be delayed in the mail? 12

And when you're planning a weekend in New York City and you're not in the mood to visit your mother, who lives there, do you conceal—with a lie, if you must—the fact that you'll be in New York? Or do you have the courage—or is it the cruelty?—to say, "I'll be in New York, but sorry—I don't plan on seeing you"? 13

(Dave and his wife Elaine have two quite different points of view on this very subject. He calls her a coward. She says she's being wise. He says she must assert her right to visit New York sometimes and not see her mother. To which she always patiently replies: "Why should we have useless fights? My mother's too old to change. We get along much better when I lie to her.") 14

Finally, do you keep the peace by telling your husband lies on the subject of money? Do you reduce what you really paid for your shoes? And in general do you find yourself ready, willing, and able to lie to him when you make absurd mistakes or lose or break things? 15

"I used to have a romantic idea that part of intimacy was confessing every dumb thing that you did to your husband. But after a couple of years of that," says Laura, "have I changed my mind!" 16

And having changed her mind, she finds herself telling peace-keeping lies. And yes, I tell them too. What about you? 17

Protective Lies. Protective lies are lies folks tell—often quite serious lies—because they're convinced that the truth would be too damaging. They lie because they feel there are certain human values that supersede the wrong of having lied. They lie, not for personal gain, but because they believe it's for the good of the person they're lying to. They lie to those they love, to those who trust them most of all, on the grounds that breaking this trust is justified. 18

They may lie to their children on money or marital matters. 19

They may lie to the dying about the state of their health. 20

They may lie about adultery, and not—or so they insist—to save their own hide, but to save the heart and the pride of the men they are married to. 21

They may lie to their closest friend because the truth about her talents or son or psyche would be—or so they insist—utterly devastating. 22

I sometimes tell such lies, but I'm aware that it's quite presumptuous to claim I know what's best for others to know. That's called playing God. That's called manipulation and control. And we never can be sure, once we start to juggle lies, just where they'll land, exactly where they'll roll. 23

And furthermore, we may find ourselves lying in order to back up the lies that are backing up the lie we initially told. 24

And furthermore—let's be honest—if conditions were reversed, we certainly wouldn't want anyone lying to us. 25

Yet, having said all that, I still believe that there are times when protective lies must nonetheless be told. What about you? 26

If your Dad had a very bad heart and you had to tell him some bad family news, which would you choose: to tell him the truth or lie? 27

If your former husband failed to send his monthly child-support check and in other ways behaved like a total rat, would you allow your children—who believed he was simply wonderful—to continue to believe that he was wonderful? 28

If your dearly beloved brother selected a wife whom you deeply disliked, would you reveal your feelings or would you fake it? 29

And if you were asked, after making love, "And how was that for you?" would you reply, if it wasn't too good, "Not too good"? 30

Now, some would call a sex lie unimportant, little more than social lying, a simple act of courtesy that makes all human intercourse run smoothly. And some would say all sex lies are bad news and unacceptably protective. Because, says Ruth, "a man with an ego that fragile doesn't need your lies—he needs a psychiatrist." Still others feel that sex lies are indeed protective lies, more serious than simple social lying, and yet at times they tell them on the grounds that when it comes to matters sexual, everybody's ego is somewhat fragile. 31

"If most of the time things go well in sex," says Sue, "I think you're allowed to dissemble when they don't. I can't believe it's good to say, 'Last night was four stars, darling, but tonight's performance rates only a half.' " 32

I'm inclined to agree with Sue. What about you? 33

Trust-Keeping Lies. Another group of lies are trust-keeping lies, lies that involve triangulation, with *A* (that's you) telling lies to *B* on behalf of *C* (whose trust you'd promised to keep). Most people concede that once you've agreed not to betray a friend's confidence, you can't betray it, even if you must lie. But I've talked with people who don't want you telling them anything that they might be called on to lie about. 34

"I don't tell lies for myself," says Fran, "and I don't want to have to tell them for other people." Which means, she agrees, that if her best friend is having an affair, she absolutely doesn't want to know about it. 35

"Are you saying," her best friend asks, "that if I went off with a lover and I asked you to tell my husband I'd been with you, that you wouldn't lie for me, that you'd betray me?" 36

Fran is very pained but very adamant. "I wouldn't want to betray you, so . . . don't ask me." 37

Fran's best friend is shocked. What about you? 38

Do you believe you can have close friends if you're not prepared to receive their deepest secrets? 39

Do you believe you must always lie for your friends? 40

Do you believe, if your friend tells a secret that turns out to be quite immoral or illegal, that once you've promised to keep it, you must keep it? 41

And what if your friend were your boss—if you were perhaps one of the President's men—would you betray or lie for him over, say, Watergate? 42

As you can see, these issues get terribly sticky. 43

It's my belief that once we've promised to keep a trust, we must tell lies to keep it. I also believe that we can't tell Watergate lies. And if these two statements strike you as quite contradictory, you're right—they're quite contradictory. But for now they're the best I can do. What about you? 44

Some say that truth will out and thus you might as well tell the truth. Some say you can't regain the trust that lies lose. Some say that even though the truth may never be revealed, our lies pervert and damage our relationships. Some say . . . well, here's what some of them have to say. 45

"I'm a coward," says Grace, "about telling close people important, difficult truths. I find that I'm unable to carry it off. And so if something is bothering me, it keeps building up inside till I end up just not seeing them any more." 46

"I lie to my husband on sexual things, but I'm furious," says Joyce, "that he's too insensitive to know I'm lying." 47

"I suffer most from the misconception that children can't take the truth," says Emily. "But I'm starting to see that what's harder and more damaging for them is being told lies, is *not* being told the truth." 48

"I'm afraid," says Joan, "that we often wind up feeling a bit of contempt for the people we lie to." 49

And then there are those who have no talent for lying. 50

"Over the years, I tried to lie," a friend of mine explained, "but I always got found out and I always got punished. I guess I gave myself away because I feel guilty about any kind of lying. It looks as if I'm stuck with telling the truth." 51

For those of us, however, who are good at telling lies, for those of us who lie and don't get caught, the question of whether or not to lie can be a hard and serious moral problem. I liked the remark of a friend of mine who said, "I'm willing to lie. But just as a last resort—the truth's always better." 52

"Because," he explained, "though others may completely accept the lie I'm telling, I don't." 53

I tend to feel that way too. 54

What about you? 55

Considering Ideas

1. Of the four types of lies, which does Viorst find the most serious? Why? Do you agree?
2. Viorst presents lying in terms of "a series of moral puzzles" (paragraph 1). Explain how deciding whether to lie is like a "moral puzzle."
3. Even though it makes Viorst feel guilty, she will tell lies. Why?
4. If your best friend were having an affair, would you lie for him or her? Why or why not?

Considering Technique

1. Evaluate Viorst's approach to her introduction. There is no thesis that indicates that classification will occur. Is that a problem? Explain.
2. What is the principle of classification? In what order does Viorst arrange her categories?

3. *Combining patterns:* How does Viorst use each of the following to develop her classification: definition, exemplification, narration, cause-and-effect analysis?
4. Viorst repeatedly asks, "What about you?" Explain the purpose of this refrain.

For Group Discussion or Journal Writing

People disagree about when it is okay to lie and when it is not. They even disagree about whether it is *ever* okay to lie. What factors do you think determine the position an individual takes on lying?

Growing Up Asian in America

KESAYA E. NODA

Kesaya E. Noda is a college teacher and peace activist. In "Growing Up Asian in America," which first appeared in Making Waves: An Anthology by and about Asian American Women *(1989), Noda divides her identity into three components. As you read, notice the elements of cause-and-effect analysis and contrast in the essay.*

Sometimes when I was growing up, my identity seemed to hurtle toward me and paste itself right to my face. I felt that way, encountering the stereotypes of my race perpetuated by non-Japanese people (primarily white) who may or may not have had contact with other Japanese in America. "You don't like cheese, do you?" someone would ask. "I know your people don't like cheese." Sometimes questions came making allusions to history. That was another aspect of the identity. Events that had happened quite apart from the me who stood silent in that moment connected my face with an incomprehensible past. "Your parents were in California? Were they in those camps during the war?"[1] And sometimes there were phrases or nicknames: "Lotus Blossom." I was sometimes addressed or referred to as racially Japanese, sometimes as Japanese-American, and sometimes as an Asian woman. Confusions and distortions abounded. 1

How is one to know and define oneself? From the inside—within a context that is self-defined from a grounding in community and a connection with culture and history that are comfortably accepted? Or from the outside—in terms of messages received from the media and people who are often ignorant? Even as an adult I can still see two sides of my face and past. I can see from the inside out, in freedom. And I can see from the outside in, driven by the old voices of childhood and lost in anger and fear. 2

I Am Racially Japanese. A voice from my childhood says: "You are other. You are less than. You are unalterably alien." This voice has its own history. We have indeed been seen as other and alien since the early years of our arrival in the United States. The very first immigrants were welcomed and sought as laborers to replace the dwindling numbers of Chinese, whose influx had been cut off by the Chinese Exclusion Act of 1882. The Japanese fell natural heir to the same anti-Asian prejudice that had arisen against the Chinese. As soon as they began striking for better wages, they were no longer welcomed. 3

[1]On February 19, 1942, soon after the beginning of World War II, President Franklin Roosevelt signed an executive order calling for the internment of 120,000 Americans of Japanese heritage in one of 10 "relocation centers" in California, Idaho, Utah, Arizona, Wyoming, Colorado, and Arkansas. More than two-thirds of the Japanese who were interned were citizens of the United States.

Japanese-American internees line up for a meal at an internment camp in Puyallup, Washington.

I can see myself today as a person historically defined by law and custom as being forever alien. Being neither "free white," nor "African," our people in California were deemed "aliens, ineligible for citizenship," no matter how long they intended to stay here. Aliens ineligible for citizenship were prohibited from owning, buying, or leasing land. They did not and could not belong here. The voice in me remembers that I am always a *Japanese*-American in the eyes of many. A third-generation German-American is an American. A third-generation Japanese-American is a Japanese-American. Being Japanese means being a danger to the country during the war and knowing how to use chopsticks. I wear this history on my face. 4

I move to the other side. I see a different light and claim a different context. My race is a line that stretches across ocean and time to link me to the shrine where my grandmother was raised. Two high, white banners lift in the wind at the top of the stone steps leading to the shrine. It is time for the summer festival. Black characters are written against the sky as boldly as the clouds, as lightly as kites, as sharply as the big black crows I used to see above the fields in New Hampshire. At festival time there is liquor and food, ritual, discipline, and abandonment. There is music and drunkenness and invocation. There is hope. Another season has come. Another season has gone. 5

I am racially Japanese. I have a certain claim to this crazy place where the prayers intoned by a neighboring Shinto priest (standing in for my grandmother's nephew who is sick) are drowned out by the rehearsals for the pop singing contest in which most of the villagers will compete later that night. The village elders, the priest, and I stand respectfully upon the immaculate, shining wooden floor of the outer shrine, bowing our heads before the hidden powers. During the patchy intervals when I can hear him, I notice the priest has a stutter. His voice flutters up to my ears only occasionally because two men and a woman are singing gustily into a microphone in the compound, testing the sound system. A prerecorded tape of guitars, 6 samisens,[2] and drums accompanies them. Rock music and Shinto prayers. That night, to loud applause and cheers, a young man is given the award for the most *netsuretsu*—passionate, burning—rendition of a song. We roar our approval of the reward. Never mind that his voice had wandered and slid, now slightly above, now slightly below the given line of the melody. Netsuretsu. Netsuretsu.

In the morning, my grandmother's sister kneels at the foot of the stone stairs to offer her morning prayers. She is too crippled to climb the stairs, so each morning she kneels here upon the path. She shuts her eyes for a few seconds, her motions as matter of fact as when she washes rice. I linger longer than she does, so reluctant to leave, savoring the connection I feel with my grandmother in America, the past, and the power that lives and shines in the morning sun. 7

Our family has served this shrine for generations. The family's need to protect this claim to identity and place outweighs any individual claim to any individual hope. I am Japanese. 8

I Am a Japanese-American. "Weak." I hear the voice from my childhood years. "Passive," I hear. Our parents and grandparents were the ones who were put into those camps. They went without resistance; they offered cooperation as proof of loyalty to America. "Victim," I hear. And, "Silent." 9

Our parents are painted as hard workers who were socially uncomfortable and had difficulty expressing even the smallest opinion. Clean, quiet, motivated, and determined to match the American way; that is us, and that is the story of our time here. 10

"Why did you go into those camps?" I raged at my parents, frightened by my own inner silence and timidity. "Why didn't you do anything to resist? Why didn't you name it the injustice it was?" Couldn't our parents even think? Couldn't they? Why were we so passive? 11

I shift my vision and my stance. I am in California. My uncle is in the midst of the sweet potato harvest. He is pressed, trying to get the harvesting crews onto the field as quickly as possible, worried about the flow of equipment and people. His big pickup is pulled off to the side, motor running, door ajar. I see two tractors in the yard in front of an old shed: the flatbed harvesting platform on which the workers will stand has already been brought over from the other field. It's early morning. The workers stand loosely grouped and at ease, but my uncle looks as harried and tense as a police officer trying to unsnarl a New York City traffic jam. Driving toward the shed, I pull my car off the road to make way for an approaching tractor. The front wheels of the car sink luxuriously into the soft, white sand by the roadside and the car slides to a dreamy halt, tail still on the road. I try to move forward. I try to move back. The front bites contentedly into the sand, the back lifts itself at a jaunty angle. My uncle sees me and storms down the road, running. He is shouting before he is even near me. 12

"What's the matter with you?" he screams. "What the hell are you doing?" In his frenzy, he grabs his hat off his head and slashes it through the air across his knee. He is beside himself. "Don't you know how to drive in sand? What's the matter with you? You've blocked the whole roadway. How am I supposed to get my tractors out of here? Can't you use your head? You've cut off the whole roadway, and we've got to get out of here." 13

I stand on the road before him helplessly thinking, "No, I don't know how to drive in sand. I've never driven in sand." 14

"I'm sorry, uncle," I say, burying a smile beneath a look of sincere apology. I notice my deep amusement and my affection for him with great curiosity. I am usually devastated by anger. Not this time. 15

During the several years that follow I learn about the people and the place, and much more about what has happened in this California village where my parents grew up. The issei, our grandparents, made this settlement in the desert. Their first crops were eaten by rabbits and ravaged 16

[2]A samisen is a guitarlike instrument.

by insects. The land was so barren that men walking from house to house sometimes got lost. Women came here too. They bore children in 114-degree heat, then carried the babies with them into the fields to nurse when they reached the end of each row of grapes or other truck-farm crops.

I had had no idea what it meant to buy this kind of land and make it grow green. Or how, when the war came, there was no space at all for the subtlety of being who we were—Japanese-Americans. Either/or was the way. I hadn't understood that people were literally afraid for their lives then, that their money had been frozen in banks; that there was a five-mile travel limit; that when the early evening curfew came and they were inside their houses, some of them watched helplessly as people they knew went into their barns to steal their belongings. The police were patrolling the road, interested only in violators of curfew. There was no help for them in the face of thievery. I had not been able to imagine before what it must have felt like to be an American—to know absolutely that one is an American—and yet to have almost everyone else deny it. Not only deny it, but challenge that identity with machine guns and troops of white American soldiers. In those circumstances it was difficult to say, "I'm a Japanese-American." "American" had to do. 17

But now I can say that I am a Japanese-American. It means I have a place here in this country, too. I have a place here on the East Coast, where our neighbor is so much a part of our family that my mother never passes her house at night without glancing at the lights to see if she is home and safe; where my parents have hauled hundreds of pounds of rocks from fields and arduously planted Christmas trees and blueberries, lilacs, asparagus, and crab apples, where my father still dreams of angling a stream to a new bed so that he can dig a pond in the field and fill it with water and fish. "The neighbors already came for their Christmas tree?" he asks in December. "Did they like it? Did they like it?" 18

I have a place on the West Coast where my relatives still farm, where I heard the stories of feuds and backbiting, and where I saw that people survived and flourished because fundamentally they trusted and relied upon one another. A death in the family is not just a death in a family; it is a death in the community. I saw people help each other with money, materials, labor, attention, and time. I saw men gather once a year, without fail, to clean the grounds of a ninety-year-old woman who had helped the community before, during, and after the war. I saw her remembering them with birthday cards sent to each of their children. 19

I come from a people with a long memory and a distinctive grace. We live our thanks. And we are Americans. Japanese-Americans. 20

I Am a Japanese-American Woman. Woman. The last piece of my identity. It has been easier by far for me to know myself in Japan and to see my place in America than it has been to accept my line of connection with my own mother. She was my dark self, a figure in whom I thought I saw all that I feared most in myself. Growing into womanhood and looking for some model of strength, I turned away from her. Of course, I could not find what I sought. I was looking for a black feminist or a white feminist. My mother is neither white nor black. 21

My mother is a woman who speaks with her life as much as with her tongue. I think of her with her own mother. Grandmother had Parkinson's disease and it had frozen her gait and set her fingers, tongue, and feet jerking and trembling in a terrible dance. My aunts and uncles wanted her to be able to live in her own home. They fed her, bathed her, dressed her, awoke at midnight to take her for one last trip to the bathroom. My aunts (her daughters-in-law) did most of the care, but my mother went from New Hampshire to California each summer to spend a month living with Grandmother because she wanted to and because she wanted to give my aunts at least a small rest. During those hot summer days, mother lay on the couch watching the television or reading, cooking foods that Grandmother liked, and speaking little. Grandmother thrived under her care. 22

The time finally came when it was too dangerous for Grandmother to live alone. My relatives kept finding her on the floor beside her bed when they went to wake her in the mornings. My mother flew to California to help clean the house and make arrangements for Grandmother to enter a local nursing home. On her last day at home, while Grandmother was sitting in her big, overstuffed armchair, hair combed and wearing a green summer dress, my mother went to her and knelt at her feet. "Here, Mamma," she said. "I've polished your shoes." She lifted Grandmother's legs and helped her into the shiny black shoes. My Grandmother looked down and smiled slightly. She left her house walking, supported by her children, carrying her pocket book, and wearing her polished black shoes. "Look, Mamma," my mom had said, kneeling. "I've polished your shoes." 23

Just the other day, my mother came to Boston to visit. She had recently lost a lot of weight and was pleased with her new shape and her feeling of good health. "Look at me, Kes," she exclaimed, turning toward me, front and back, as naked as the day she was born. I saw her small breasts and the wide, brown scar, belly button to pubic hair, that marked her because my brother and I were both born by Caesarean section. Her hips were small. I was not a large baby, but there was so little room for me in her that when she was carrying me she could not even begin to bend over toward the floor. She hated it, she said. 24

"Don't I look good? Don't you think I look good?" 25

I looked at my mother smiling and as happy as she, thinking of all the times I have seen her naked. I have seen both my parents naked throughout my life, as they have seen me. From childhood through adulthood we've had our naked moments, sharing baths, idle conversations picked up as we moved between showers and closets, hurried moments at the beginning of days, quiet moments at the end of days. 26

I know this to be Japanese, this ease with the physical, and it makes me think of an old Japanese folk song. A young nursemaid, a fifteen-year-old girl, is singing a lullaby to a baby who is strapped to her back. The nursemaid has been sent as a servant to a place far from her own home. "We're the beggars," she says, "and they are the nice people. Nice people wear fine sashes. Nice clothes." 27

> If I should drop dead,
> bury me by the roadside!
> I'll give a flower
> to everyone who passes.
> What kind of flower?
> The cam-cam-camellia (*tsun-tsun-tsuhaki*)
> watered by Heaven:
> alms water.

The nursemaid is the intersection of heaven and earth, the intersection of the human, the natural world, the body, and the soul. In this song, with clear eyes, she looks steadily at life, which is sometimes so very terrible and sad. I think of her while looking at my mother, who is standing on the red and purple carpet before me, laughing, without any clothes. 28

I am my mother's daughter. And I am myself. 29

I am a Japanese-American woman. 30

Epilogue. I recently heard a man from West Africa share some memories of his childhood. He was raised Muslim but when he was a young man, he found himself deeply drawn to Christianity. He struggled against his inner impulse for years, trying to avoid the church yet feeling pushed to return to it again and again. "I would have done *anything* to avoid the change," he said. At last, he 31 became Christian. Afterwards he was afraid to go home, fearing that he would not be accepted. The fear was groundless, he discovered, when at last he returned—he had separated himself, but his family and friends (all Muslim) had not separated themselves from him.

The man, who is now a professor of religion, said that in the Africa he knew as a child and a young man, pluralism was embraced rather than feared. There was "a kind of tolerance that did not deny your particularity," he said. He alluded to zestful, spontaneous debates that would sometimes loudly erupt between Muslims and Christians in the village's public spaces. His memories of an atheist who harangued the villagers when he came to visit them once a week moved me deeply. Perhaps the man was an agricultural advisor or inspector. He harassed the women. He would say: "Don't go to the fields! Don't even bother to go to the fields. Let God take care of you. He'll send you the food. If you believe in God, why do you need to work? You don't need to work! Let God put the seeds in the ground. Stay home." 32

The professor said, "The women laughed, you know? They just laughed. Their attitude was, "'Here is a child of God. When will he come home?'" 33

The storyteller, the professor of religion, smiled a most fantastic tender smile as he told this story. "In my country, there is a deep affirmation of the oneness of God," he said. "The atheist and the women were having quite different experiences in their encounter, though the atheist did not know this. He saw himself as quite separate from the women. But the women did not see themselves as being separate from him. 'Here is a child of God,' they said. 'When will he come home?'" 34

Considering Ideas

1. According to the author, who is responsible for perpetuating the stereotype of the Japanese?
2. What are the three components of Noda's identity?
3. What do you think Noda means when she says that her "identity seemed to hurtle toward [her] and paste itself right to [her] face" (paragraph 1)?
4. What do paragraphs 3–8 suggest about how many Japanese feel about their ancestors?
5. Noda says that "when the war came, there was no space at all for the subtlety of being who we were—Japanese-Americans" (paragraph 17). What does she mean?

Considering Technique

1. Noda introduces each component of her identity in a topic sentence that is really a heading. What is the effect of this strategy?
2. In what order does Noda arrange the components?
3. *Combining patterns:* What patterns of development does Noda use to develop each of the components of her identity?
4. What purpose do paragraphs 8, 20, 29, and 30 serve? How do these paragraphs help the reader?
5. An *epilogue* is a concluding statement added on to an essay as an appendix. How does Noda's epilogue relate to the rest of her essay?

For Group Discussion or Journal Writing

Noda wonders whether she should define herself from the inside or from the outside. How do people's identities differ when considered from the inside and from the outside? What accounts for the difference?

Combining Patterns of Development

The Ways of Meeting Oppression

MARTIN LUTHER KING, JR.

Martin Luther King, Jr., who won the Nobel Peace Prize in 1964, was the most prominent civil rights leader of the 1950s and 1960s. In the following essay, taken from his book Stride toward Freedom, *King classifies responses to oppression and evaluates the effectiveness of those responses, relying, in part, on definition, exemplification, and cause-and-effect analysis.*

Oppressed people deal with their oppression in three characteristic ways. One way is acquiescence: The oppressed resign themselves to their doom. They tacitly adjust themselves to oppression, and thereby become conditioned to it. In every movement toward freedom some of the oppressed prefer to remain oppressed. Almost 2,800 years ago Moses set out to lead the children of Israel from the slavery of Egypt to the freedom of the promised land. He soon discovered that slaves do not always welcome their deliverers. They become accustomed to being slaves. They would rather bear those ills they have, as Shakespeare pointed out, than flee to others that they know not of. They prefer the "fleshpots of Egypt" to the ordeals of emancipation. 1

There is such a thing as the freedom of exhaustion. Some people are so worn down by the yoke of oppression that they give up. A few years ago in the slum areas of Atlanta, a Negro guitarist used to sing almost daily: "Been down so long that down don't bother me." This is the type of negative freedom and resignation that often engulfs the life of the oppressed. 2

But this is not the way out. To accept passively an unjust system is to cooperate with that system; thereby the oppressed become as evil as the oppressor. Noncooperation with evil is as much a moral obligation as is cooperation with good. The oppressed must never allow the conscience of the oppressor to slumber. Religion reminds every man that he is his brother's keeper. To accept injustice or segregation passively is to say to the oppressor that his actions are morally right. It is a way of allowing his conscience to fall asleep. At this moment the oppressed fails to be his brother's keeper. So acquiescence—while often the easier way—is not the moral way. It is the way of the coward. The Negro cannot win the respect of his oppressor by acquiescing; he merely increases the oppressor's arrogance and contempt. Acquiescence is interpreted as proof of the Negro's inferiority. The Negro cannot win the respect of the white people of the South or the peoples of the world if he is willing to sell the future of his children for his personal and immediate comfort and safety. 3

A second way that oppressed people sometimes deal with oppression is to resort to physical violence and corroding hatred. Violence often brings about momentary results. Nations have frequently won their independence in battle. But in spite of temporary victories, violence never brings permanent peace. It solves no social problem; it merely creates new and more complicated ones. 4

Violence as a way of achieving racial justice is both impractical and immoral. It is impractical because it is a descending spiral ending in destruction for all. The old law of an eye for an eye leaves everybody blind. It is immoral because it seeks to humiliate the opponent rather than win his understanding; it seeks to annihilate rather than to convert. Violence is immoral because it thrives on 5 hatred rather than love. It destroys community and makes brotherhood impossible. It leaves society in monologue rather than dialogue. Violence ends by defeating itself. It creates bitterness in the survivors and brutality in the destroyers. A voice echoes through time saying to every potential Peter, "Put up your sword."[1] History is cluttered with the wreckage of nations that failed to follow this command.

If the American Negro and other victims of oppression succumb to the temptation of using violence in the struggle for freedom, future generations will be the recipients of a desolate night of bitterness, and our chief legacy to them will be an endless reign of meaningless chaos. Violence is not the way. 6

The third way open to oppressed people in their quest for freedom is the way of nonviolent resistance. Like the synthesis in Hegelian philosophy, the principle of nonviolent resistance seeks to reconcile the truths of two opposites—the acquiescence and violence—while avoiding the extremes and immoralities of both. The nonviolent resister agrees with the person who acquiesces that one should not be physically aggressive toward his opponent; but he balances the equation by agreeing with the person of violence that evil must be resisted. He avoids the nonresistance of the former and the violent resistance of the latter. With nonviolent resistance, no individual or group need submit to any wrong, nor need anyone resort to violence in order to right a wrong. 7

It seems to me that this is the method that must guide the actions of the Negro in the present crisis in race relations. Through nonviolent resistance the Negro will be able to rise to the noble height of opposing the unjust system while loving the perpetrators of the system. The Negro must work passionately and unrelentingly for full stature as a citizen, but he must not use inferior methods to gain it. He must never come to terms with falsehood, malice, hate, or destruction. 8

Nonviolent resistance makes it possible for the Negro to remain in the South and struggle for his rights. The Negro's problem will not be solved by running away. He cannot listen to the glib suggestion of those who would urge him to migrate en masse to other sections of the country. By grasping his great opportunity in the South he can make a lasting contribution to the moral strength of the nation and set a sublime example of courage for generations yet unborn. 9

By nonviolent resistance, the Negro can also enlist all men of good will in his struggle for equality. The problem is not a purely racial one, with Negroes set against whites. In the end, it is not a struggle between people at all, but a tension between justice and injustice. Nonviolent resistance is not aimed against oppressors but against oppression. Under its banner consciences, not racial groups, are enlisted. 10

[1]The apostle Peter had drawn his sword to defend Christ from arrest. The voice was Christ's, who surrendered himself for trial and crucifixion (John 18:11).

Considering Ideas

1. Explain the advantages and disadvantages of each way of meeting oppression.
2. King says that some oppressed people accept their oppression because they "would rather bear those ills they have . . . than flee to others that they know not of" (paragraph 1). Why is this the case?
3. What does King mean when he says, "Under [nonviolent resistance's] banner consciences, not racial groups, are enlisted" (paragraph 10)?
4. King says, "To accept passively an unjust system is to cooperate with that system; thereby the oppressed become as evil as the oppressor" (paragraph 3). What does King mean? Do you agree with him? Why or why not?

Considering Technique

1. Which sentence is the thesis of the essay?
2. What is King's principle of classification? In what order does King present his groupings?
3. What is the purpose of King's classification? How do you know?
4. *Combining patterns:* What purpose does the cause-and-effect analysis in paragraphs 5 and 6 serve? What purpose does the cause-and-effect analysis in paragraphs 8–10 serve?
5. *Combining patterns:* What definition occurs in paragraph 7? What purpose does that definition serve? Which paragraphs include examples? What purpose do the examples serve?

For Group Discussion or Journal Writing

Martin Luther King, Jr., believed that nonviolent resistance was superior to violence because "violence never brings permanent peace" (paragraph 4). Are there ever times when violence is the best solution? Explain, using examples if possible.

STYLE NOTE

The Dash

You know that a comma signals a pause. Sometimes, however, you want a pause that is longer than the one a comma provides. In those cases, a dash is useful. The longer pause signaled by a dash provides emphasis or dramatic effect, as these examples from the readings illustrate:

> From "The Truth about Lying": "If your former husband failed to send his monthly child-support check and in other ways behaved like a total rat, would you allow your children—who believed he was simply wonderful—to continue to believe that he was wonderful?" (paragraph 28).

> From "Growing Up Asian in America": "I had not been able to imagine before what it must have felt like to be an American—to know absolutely that one is an American—and yet to have almost everyone else deny it" (paragraph 17).

> From "The Ways of Meeting Oppression": "So acquiescence—while often the easier way—is not the moral way" (paragraph 3).

For more on using the dash, see page 639.

CLASSIFICATION IN AN IMAGE

The feature on page 392 is from the culture-lifestyle section of *Wired* magazine.

The Geekster Handbook

A field guide to the identification of unique species in the nerd underground.

1. The Fanboy

DISPOSITION Speaks mostly in lines from *The Simpsons*, *Star Wars*, *Highlander*, and *Ghostbusters*. Enjoys arguing about whether Batman or Boba Fett would win in a fight. (Batman.) **BELIEFS** The Force exists, but midi-chlorians are bullshit. Han shot first. **TURN-ONS** Princess Leia in slave gear. Starbuck (male and female incarnations). *Amazing Fantasy* No. 15. Velour uniforms.

2. The Music Geek

DISPOSITION Would be really happy to introduce you to music better than that over-exposed crap you like. Always up for a show, but it'll totally suck. **BELIEFS** MP3s are not as good as CDs, which are not as good as vinyl LPs, which are not as cool as wax cylinders. What your speaker cables are made of matters. **TURN-ONS** A complete set of Sub Pop Singles Club 45s. VH1's *Behind the Music* (hair metal only). 0.0 scores on Pitchfork. Vacuum tubes.

3. The Gamer

DISPOSITION High DEX and INT scores, low CHA (thus, the lack of friends). Given to indecipherable insults ("I pwn3d u, n00b!"). **BELIEFS** The game *Real World* has a great physics engine, hi-res graphics, and convincing surround sound, but the learning curve is too steep. Girls should dress like Yuna in *Final Fantasy*. **TURN-ONS** Spawn points. Haptic feedback. Pac-Man ringtones. Morgan Webb. Split-screen co-op.

4. The Gadget Guy

DISPOSITION Sociable while waiting in line on launch day; ferocious in comments on Gizmodo. Seemingly unflappable in the face of early adopter's remorse (aka Apple Newton Syndrome). **BELIEFS** I can fix that. There's no god but MacGyver. The price will drop in a month, but I need it now. **TURN-ONS** Unboxing videos. Backup batteries. Blue LEDs. Laser pointers. People who RTFM. Things that make loud clicking sounds.

5. The Hacker

DISPOSITION Chronically crabby—then again, having such a superior intellect is a heavy burden. Paranoid tendencies. **BELIEFS** One shall stand, one shall fall. Sun allergy is a real condition. Cybersex: *not* utterly disgusting. Cory Doctorow is too soft on DRM. *2600* magazine has gotten too commercial. **TURN-ONS** Trinity. l33t fluency. Narc-spotting at DefCon.

6. The Otaku

DISPOSITION Alarmingly happy. Prefers to read right to left. **BELIEFS** Manga is a medium, not a genre. Furries aren't loathsome. I can learn Japanese from *Gundam*. Lynn Minmay is the most annoying character in the history of anything. The next major anime release will be a box office hit in the West—this time for sure. It's not all tentacle porn, OK? **TURN-ONS** Tentacle porn. Dirty Larping. Dating sims. All things *kawaii*.

—Troy Brownfield

Considering the Image

1. What does the feature classify? What is the principle of classification?
2. In what way is the image part of the classification? In what way are the words part of the classification? How do the words and image work together to create the classification?
3. What audience does the feature target? What purpose does it hope to achieve?
4. How do the picture and words work together to help the feature achieve its purpose?

SUGGESTIONS FOR WRITING

Writing Classification and Division

Use classification and/or division to develop an essay on one of these subjects:

- college students
- professors
- bosses
- roommates
- talk-show hosts
- your friends
- fads or trends of the past 10 years
- advertisements for a particular kind of product
- sitcoms
- part-time jobs
- needy friends
- automobile drivers
- salespeople
- table servers
- pet owners
- fast-food restaurants
- study techniques
- radio stations
- coaches
- movie comedies
- reality shows
- women's or men's magazines

Reading Then Writing Classification and Division

1. Like Carolyn Foster Segal in "The Dog Ate My Disk, and Other Tales of Woe," write a humorous classification of excuses for something, such as for breaking a date or being late to work.
2. In "The Truth about Lying," Judith Viorst classifies kinds of lies. Using her categories or your own, classify the kinds of lies told in school.
3. In "The Ways of Meeting Oppression," Martin Luther King, Jr., classifies the ways to deal with oppression and notes which of the ways is best. In similar fashion, write an essay that classifies the ways to deal with one of the following: sexual harassment, gender discrimination, stress, depression, or peer pressure. Be sure to note which way is the most effective.
4. In "Grocery Shoppers," Anita Selfe classifies kinds of grocery shoppers. Classify another kind of shopper, such as the car buyer or bargain hunter. As an alternative, divide the grocery shopper, car buyer, bargain hunter, or other kind of shopper into his or her components.
5. In "Horror Movies," Ray Harkleroad classifies kinds of horror movies. Write a classification of another movie genre, such as the science fiction

movie, the romantic comedy, the action movie, or the buddy movie. As an alternative, divide a particular movie genre into its components.

6. Like Kesaya Noda in "Growing Up Asian in America," divide your personality into its components. Alternatively, divide someone else's personality into its components.

Classification and Division beyond the Writing Classroom

Assume you have accepted a job as a resident advisor in a first-year residence hall, beginning next fall term. You know that the new students have much to learn about college life, and you want to help them. Write a handout to put in every room that classifies and explains study techniques, so the new students understand the dos and don'ts.

Responding to Theme

1. In "The Dog Ate My Disk, and Other Tales of Woe," Carolyn Foster Segal uses humor to explore the reasons students turn in assignments late. For an audience of college instructors, explain why students fail to meet deadlines. Your purpose is to help instructors better understand students and the pressures they experience.
2. Do you agree with those who, Judith Viorst says, find social lying "the civilized way for folks to behave" (paragraph 2)? Or do you take the position that it is morally wrong (paragraph 7)? Explain and defend your view.
3. Cite one or more examples of oppression that you have experienced or observed, and explain how that oppression could be addressed using the nonviolent resistance that Martin Luther King, Jr., advocates in "The Ways of Meeting Oppression."
4. *Connecting the readings:* In "The Truth about Lying," Judith Viorst classifies lies and indicates which ones she finds acceptable and which ones she finds morally wrong. In "The Dog Ate My Disk, and Other Tales of Woe," Carolyn Foster Segal classifies excuses (many of which are lies) for submitting late assignments. Combine the subjects of these two authors and classify the lies students tell, indicating which of them are acceptable and which are not. You need not limit yourself to lies students tell teachers or to lies about late assignments.

PROCESS GUIDELINES

www.mhhe.com/tsw

For further help writing classification and division, go to Catalyst 2.0 > Writing > Writing Tutors > Classification

Writing Classification and Division

The following guidelines are not meant to replace your successful procedures. They are here to try as you work to develop your own effective, efficient writing process.

Think like a Writer: Generating Ideas, Considering Audience and Purpose, and Ordering Ideas

- Try classifying kinds of soap opera characters, sportscasters, or dieters; or use division to identify the components of a successful website or telemarketer or a popular campus nightspot.

- Write each group on a separate index card. On the back of each card, list all the members of the group and the characteristics of the group members. Studying the cards will help you determine whether you want to classify or divide and what your principle of classification or division is.
- Determine your purpose by asking the questions on page 40.
- To identify and assess your audience, answer the questions on page 42.
- Create an outline. Because outlines are themselves forms of classification and division, they can be particularly helpful in planning.

Think like a Writer: Drafting

- Write a preliminary thesis that states your subject and whether you are classifying or dividing. If you like, you can also state your principle for classifying or dividing.
- Using your outline as a guide, write your draft.
- As you draft, think about using topic sentences to introduce your categories or components.

Think like a Critic; Work like an Editor: Revising

- Reread your draft to be sure everything conforms to your principle of classification (or division, if you used one).
- Check that your thesis states one of the following:
  - The subject and whether you are classifying or dividing
  - The subject and principle of classification or division
  - Your subjects and groupings
- Be sure you have included all relevant categories and divisions. Have you introduced each of these in a topic sentence?
- Identify your statement of the value or significance of the classification or division. If you do not have this statement, consider adding it.
- To obtain reader response for revision, see page 105.

Think like a Critic; Work like an Editor: Correcting Errors

If your thesis states your categories or divisions, use parallelism to express them in the same grammatical form. Refer to page 124 for an explanation of parallelism.

Remember

Be sure you have at least three groupings in your classification. If you have only two, you are probably writing a comparison-contrast essay.

LOOKING AHEAD

Many times, two or more patterns come together to create meaning. Consider, for example, the American flag. Three patterns—five-point stars, stripes, and a rectangle—come together to create a single powerful symbol that means "The United States of America." So far in this book, chapters have focused primarily on single patterns of development. In this chapter, however, you will learn about combining patterns to create meaning in a single essay. Before turning your attention to the chapter, look around you for instances when two or more patterns are combined in a single entity. You might consider elements such as nature, architecture, art, and clothing. List five instances when patterns are combined.

Combining Patterns of Development

In a travel piece he wrote for *Newsweek,* Paul Tolme discusses the pleasures of visiting the American desert during the fall and winter. Here are three paragraphs from that six-paragraph selection:

> The American desert may be forbidding in summer, when temperatures soar past 100 degrees. But in the fall and winter, when the mercury drops into the 70s and 80s, travelers can explore its unique landscape in comfort. Visitors can pose with 12-foot cactuses, view exotic wildlife, explore the region's famous rock formations and camp out under the stars.
>
> One of the hottest places on earth, Death Valley, becomes positively balmy in the fall. Visitors can set off on long excursions in the park, the lowest point in the Western Hemisphere. Stunning geological formations, mountain vistas and the ruts of pioneer wagon trains await those who venture off the main roads. A favorite hike is the four-mile loop up Mosaic Canyon, a narrow slot featuring smooth marble walls that tower overhead (entrance fee: $10 per vehicle; **nps.gov/deva** for more info). For $87, visitors can get a hotel room in Stovepipe Wells, which has a restaurant, general store and saloon.
>
> Joshua Tree National Park in southern California is another favorite with hikers. The higher Mojave region offers cooler temperatures for strolling amid the park's namesake trees—spiny, multilimbed plants that resemble something out of Dr. Seuss. Camping at night far from city lights, visitors can enjoy the night sky as they have never seen it (entrance fee: $10 per vehicle; **nps.gov/jotr**).

Although the excerpt is brief, it includes three patterns of development to help the author inform travelers that the desert is a desirable winter destination. Tolem *contrasts* the forbidding desert in summer with the comfortable desert in the fall and winter; he *describes* the desert; and he gives *examples* of activities visitors can engage in.

WHY IS COMBINING PATTERNS IMPORTANT?

To achieve your purpose for writing, you have the option of combining patterns of development. In fact, you are likely to combine patterns frequently, which is why each pattern chapter in Part 2 of the text also includes discussion and readings that show how to combine patterns to achieve the full range of writing purposes. As the examples in the following chart show, you can combine patterns to entertain, share feelings and experiences, inform, and persuade.

Purposes for Combining Patterns

Purpose	**Sample Pattern**
To entertain	An amusing narration about your first job with a description of your boss, and an explanation of the process you mistakenly followed
To share feelings and experiences	A blog entry that tells about your son's or daughter's wedding and that contrasts how you felt with how you thought you would feel and that explains the effect of his or her wedding on you
To inform	An explanation of the process whereby the 401(k) pension increases savings and a contrast of the plan with other pension plans
To persuade	A definition of the school voucher system with examples of its benefits to persuade readers to support vouchers

Combining Patterns across the Disciplines and Beyond

Combining Patterns in the Classroom

Every course that involves writing will afford the opportunity to combine patterns. For a psychology exam, you might need to define *operant conditioning* and use process analysis to explain how it works. In an art appreciation homework assignment, you might need to divide color into its properties and explain the effects of each of those properties on a painting. In a paper for a communications class, you might classify the problems associated with intercultural communication, give examples of those problems, and explain their causes and effects. *Skim a chapter in one of your textbooks, and identify the various patterns of development in that chapter. How does each of those patterns help you understand and learn important content?*

Combining Patterns in Daily Life

In your personal writing, you are likely to combine patterns. For example, in a letter about your travels, you might describe your hotel and narrate an account of a museum tour you took. A condolence note might give examples of the deceased's good deeds and how he or she affected others. A recipe you send to a friend will explain the process for making the dish, and it might describe what the finished product should look like. *How might you combine patterns in a letter to the editor of your campus newspaper, in which you try to convince students and faculty to donate money to a famine relief agency? What about in an e-mail to a friend to tell that person how you are?*

Combining Patterns on the Job

When you write on the job, you will often combine patterns. If you write the company newsletter, your profile of the employee of the month might narrate a story about a time the employee did something helpful to the company, and it might give examples of the employee's accomplishments. In a quarterly report, a district sales manager might contrast earnings for two quarters and explain a process for improving sales. *What writing will you do routinely on the job you hope to have after graduation? What patterns might you combine to complete that writing? How will those patterns help you achieve your purposes for writing?*

SELECTING AND ORGANIZING DETAIL

The principles you learned for selecting detail for each pattern still apply when you combine those patterns. However, when you combine patterns, you generally rely more heavily on one pattern than the others. You will likely have a *primary pattern* and one or more *secondary patterns.* For example, to convince your readers to support a recycling program, you might draw on description to create images of the litter that results when the community does not recycle, and you might use cause-and-effect analysis to explain the economic and ecological benefits of recycling. If cause-and-effect analysis is more likely to persuade your audience than description, cause-and-effect analysis will be your primary pattern, so the principles for selecting detail for cause-and-effect analysis will govern your writing more than the ones for selecting descriptive detail.

Similarly, when you combine patterns, you may also use more than one organizing principle for your details. To convince readers to support a recycling program, you might describe the litter problem using a spatial order and then give the economic and ecological effects of recycling using a progressive order. Because essays that combine patterns can be more complex than ones that rely on a single pattern, outlining is particularly helpful.

If you have trouble generating ideas for your essay, try answering these questions:

- What can I describe?
- What can I narrate?
- What illustrations can I give?
- What process can I explain?
- What can I compare or contrast?
- What causes or effects can I explain?
- What can I define?
- What can I classify or divide?

EXERCISE Combining Patterns

1. For a letter to your state legislators asking them to fund prenatal classes for low-income parents, how might you use each of these patterns? Which one is likely to be the primary pattern?
   a. Exemplification
   b. Contrast
   c. Cause-and-effect analysis
2. For a research paper for your criminal justice class about the nature and extent of looting following natural disasters, how might you use each of these patterns? Which one is likely to be the primary pattern?
   a. Classification-division
   b. Exemplification
   c. Definition
3. For a report to your supervisor about using virtual reality for training customer service representatives, how might you use each of these patterns? Which one is likely to be the primary pattern?
   a. Process analysis
   b. Cause-and-effect analysis
   c. Narration
4. For a paper giving guidelines for dealing with classroom bullies for your education class, how might you use each of these patterns? Which one is likely to be the primary pattern?
   a. Definition
   b. Exemplification
   c. Division

USING SOURCES FOR A PURPOSE

Below is an introduction for an essay that could be written for an education class, an essay that explains why current educational practices in many public schools do not encourage teachers to treat their students as individuals. The paragraph includes a quotation from paragraph 4 of "Boy Brains, Girl Brains" on page 413. (For more information on quotations, see Chapter 17.)

THESIS IDEA: The current system of public education does not encourage teachers to see their students as individuals.

WRITING PURPOSE AND AUDIENCE: To inform classmates of some common classroom practices that keep teachers from seeing their students as individuals

[1]The once-common strategy of segregating students by gender is becoming popular again. [2]Proponents of same-sex schools claim that they help students learn by eliminating distractions and by gearing instruction to the specific needs of each gender. [3]But is same-sex education really a good idea? [4]Not according to education professor David Sadker, who maintains that segregating students is not necessary: "'If you want to make schools a better place,' says Sadker, 'you have to strive to see kids as individuals'" (qtd. in Tyre 414). [5]Unfortunately, the current system of public education does not encourage teachers to see their students as individuals.

The quotation in sentence 4 creates interest and paves the way for the thesis.

Avoiding Plagiarism

The paragraph illustrates several points about using source material and avoiding plagiarism, including the following:

- **If you quote material that is cited in a second source, note the secondhand nature of the borrowing with "qtd. in" ("quoted in") in the parenthetical citation.** As sentence 4 illustrates, "qtd. in" lets the reader know you did not borrow the material from its original source.
- **Use double and single quotation marks correctly.** Double quotation marks indicate where the quotation from the secondary source begins and ends; single quotation marks indicate where double quotation marks appeared in the source from which you took the quotation.

Myths about Sources

MYTH: Because the source material was written in the past, it should be introduced with a past-tense verb.

FACT: Using present-tense verbs to introduce quotations, paraphrases, and summaries is conventional. Even though the source material was written in the past, the words "live on" into the present.

5. For a report for the school board on the benefits of school uniforms, how might you use each of these patterns? Which one is likely to be the primary pattern?
   a. Description
   b. Contrast
   c. Cause-and-effect analysis ■

LEARNING FROM OTHER WRITERS: Student Essay

In the following essay, Jason Fishman combines several patterns to explain that if we do not analyze statistics critically, we risk being manipulated by them. Annotations in the margin point out the patterns of development.

Paragraph 1
The introduction gives a hypothetical example that illustrates the thesis, which is the last sentence. The thesis indicates that a process will be explained.

Paragraph 2
This paragraph includes examples and cause-and-effect analysis. It also notes the importance of understanding the process.

Beware of Misleading Statistics

Jason Fishman

Pretend you have just read this statistic: 60% of all fatalities involving sport-utility vehicles are caused by rollovers. At first, this alarming statistic might cause you to feel outrage toward SUV manufacturers who produce such dangerous vehicles. However, before becoming incensed, know that this statistic raises several unanswered questions: How was this number determined? Which SUVs were taken into consideration? During which time period were the SUVs examined? What other factors (such as tire quality, brake performance, or seatbelt use) were taken into account in determining this percentage? It is tempting to believe a claim simply because a number is attached to it, especially when that number is shocking or extreme. But, as the SUV example demonstrates, statistics need to be weighed and evaluated like any other form of evidence. To determine the value of a particular statistic, critical readers and consumers must examine the reasoning (or lack of reasoning) behind that statistic, and the statistic may not withstand the process. 1

From magazine and newspaper articles to scientific, technical, and governmental reports, statistics are often used to persuade an audience. For example, a magazine article might claim that 35% of plastic bottles used to feed babies contain potentially harmful chemicals. Such a statistic would steer 2 mothers toward another method of feeding their babies. Or a Congressional candidate might assert that your state's 8% unemployment rate proves that the federal government needs to step in to help create more jobs and to prevent further job loss. As common as statistics are in American culture, they are often misused to lead an audience to purchase a particular product, to vote a particular way, or to take a particular action. It is crucial to recognize the most prevalent types of misused statistics, which threaten to ensnare the trusting consumer.

3 Misleading or inaccurate statistics can be the result of loaded survey questions. For example, consider the following question that might be asked of nonsmokers: "Taking into account the overwhelming research confirming the harmful effects of second-hand smoke, do you experience annoyance or discomfort when in the vicinity of a smoker?" The lead-in to this question, which emphasizes the detrimental effects of second-hand smoke, steers the respondent toward a particular response. It would be extremely difficult or impossible to say that no annoyance or discomfort is experienced when the respondent is asked to consider how smokers put their health in jeopardy. The first step in identifying a loaded question involves breaking the question down into its component words. In the sample nonsmoker survey question, the words "overwhelming," "harmful," "annoyance," and "discomfort" are key. Now that these key words have been identified, they can be evaluated for bias. Clearly, this question was formulated to elicit a negative response toward smokers. A more neutrally worded survey question might be, "How do you feel when in the vicinity of a smoker?" This question, unlike the first, does not reveal a particular bias. Loaded questions can be used to make a statistical claim that could in turn be used to sway public opinion or enact certain laws, such as a public smoking ban.

Paragraph 3
This paragraph includes cause-and-effect analysis, examples, process analysis, and contrast. Note how the examples are used to clarify.

4 Another type of misleading statistic can result from biased samples. For example, an analysis of the causes of homelessness in the United States would be biased if it looked only at individuals within a particular demographic. Imagine an analysis that reported that 63% of the homeless cases in

Paragraph 4
This paragraph includes process analysis with clarifying examples. Note the use of topic sentences in the body paragraphs.

America are caused by cuts to federally funded social welfare programs. If this analysis took into account only the experiences of people living within a particular part of the country (say, the Northeast) or having a particular socio-economic background (say, incomes below $30,000 for a family of 4), it would be biased. Another study that includes sample homeless populations from around the country with varied socio-economic backgrounds might find that only 32% of homeless cases are caused by program cuts. To determine if a sample used in generating a particular statistic is biased, consider the groups of people or things that were (and were not) included in the sample. Then, consider whether or not those omissions might significantly affect the statistic and, if so, whether the statistic has any remaining merit or value.

Paragraph 5
This paragraph includes examples, cause-and-effect analysis, and process analysis. Notice how "a third type of" provides transition and indicates that classification is also occurring.

5 A third type of misleading statistic involves false causality. Consider the following sample assertion: "85% of teenage girls who develop an eating disorder regularly read teen magazines. Therefore, teen magazines cause eating disorders in teenage girls." This example makes a false connection between reading magazines and developing psychological disorders. Such a claim would also have to sufficiently explain why some girls who read teen magazines do not develop eating disorders. A claim that links the pressures placed upon teenage girls to look and act a certain way with eating disorders would only hold up if it examined the specific and complex ways in which outside influences, such as the media, affect the psychological development of teenage girls. To determine if a statistic uses false causality, examine the statistic's claim about a particular cause and effect. Then, consider whether other, unmentioned factors might produce the same effect. It is often impossible to prove direct causality, but any valid claim must take a range of possible factors into account.

Paragraph 6
This paragraph includes examples and process analysis. The classification continues.

6 A fourth type of misused statistic stems from selective reporting and overgeneralization. For example, a report that examines the impact of standardized tests on middle-school students' grade-point averages might state, "In the small, rural town of Plainville, 8 out of 10 middle-school students whose grade-point averages were 3.0 or above further improved their grade-point

averages after preparing for an academic year to take a standardized test." These results could be selectively reported and overgeneralized as: "Standardized tests help to improve the grade-point averages of 80% of middle-school students." Such an overgeneralization would fail to take into account where the survey took place (a small, affluent American town), the fact that the student subjects were already high achievers, and that the preparation for the test, not the test itself, might have contributed to the higher grade-point averages. Whenever possible, try to find the original source of information (rather than a summary of that source) that forms the basis for a particular statistic. Additionally, examine the language used to report a statistic for bias or overgeneralization. Broad statements, such as "standardized tests" (Which tests? Conducted where?) and "80% of middle-school students" (All middle-school students?), reveal the holes in this sample statistic.

Regardless of their specific agendas, examples of misused statistics abound in American culture. Only by examining statistics closely do we have a chance of lessening the grip of the alluring, all-powerful—yet misleading—number. 7

Paragraph 7
The conclusion provides closure by noting the importance of understanding the process.

LEARNING FROM OTHER WRITERS: Professional Essays

Hold the Mayonnaise JULIA ALVAREZ

In "Hold the Mayonnaise," which appeared in the New York Times Magazine *in 1992, Julia Alvarez combines cause-and-effect analysis, comparison-contrast, and narration to explain how she felt when she became the Latina stepmother in an American household. As you read, notice that Alvarez blends the patterns so seamlessly that you may not immediately notice where each one begins and ends.*

"If I die first and Papi ever gets remarried," Mami used to tease when we were kids, "don't you accept a new woman in my house. Make her life impossible, you hear?" My sisters and I nodded obediently and a filial shudder would go through us. We were Catholics, so of course, the only kind of remarriage we could imagine had to involve our mother's death. 1

We were also Dominicans,[1] recently arrived in Jamaica, Queens, in the early 60's, before waves of other Latin Americans began arriving. So, when we imagined who exactly my father might possibly ever think of remarrying, only American

[1]Dominicans are people from Santo Domingo.

women came to mind. It would be bad enough having a *madrastra,*[2] but a "stepmother . . ." 2

All I could think of was that she would make me eat mayonnaise, a food I identified with the United States and which I detested. Mami understood, of course, that I wasn't used to that kind of food. Even a madrastra, accustomed to our rice and beans and tostones and pollo frito, would understand. But an American stepmother would think it was normal to put mayonnaise on food, and if she were at all strict and a little mean, which all stepmothers, of course, were, she would make me eat potato salad and such. I had plenty of my own reasons to make a potential stepmother's life impossible. When I nodded obediently with my sisters, I was imagining not just something foreign in our house, but in our refrigerator. 3

So it's strange now, almost 35 years later, to find myself a Latina stepmother of my husband's two tall, strapping blond, mayonnaise-eating daughters. To be honest, neither of them is a real aficionado of the condiment, but it's a fair thing to add to a bowl of tuna fish or diced potatoes. Their American food, I think of it, and when they head to their mother's or off to school, I push the jar back in the refrigerator behind their chocolate pudding and several open cans of Diet Coke. 4

What I can't push as successfully out of sight are my own immigrant childhood fears of having a *gringa*[3] stepmother with foreign tastes in our house. Except now, I am the foreign stepmother in a gringa household. I've wondered what my husband's two daughters think of this stranger in their family. It must be doubly strange for them that I am from another culture. 5

Of course, there are mitigating circumstances—my husband's two daughters were teenagers when we married, older, more mature, able to understand differences. They had also traveled when they were children with their father, an eye doctor, who worked on short-term international projects with various eye foundations. But still, it's one thing to visit a foreign country, another altogether to find it brought home—a real bear plopped down in a Goldilocks house. 6

Sometimes, a whole extended family of bears. My warm, loud Latino family came up for the wedding: my *tia*[4] from Santo Domingo; three dramatic, enthusiastic sisters and their families; my papi, with a thick accent I could tell the girls found it hard to understand; and my mami, who had her eye trained on my soon-to-be stepdaughters for any sign that they were about to make my life impossible. "How are they behaving themselves?" she asked me, as if they were 7 and 3, not 19 and 16. "They're wonderful girls," I replied, already feeling protective of them. 7

I looked around for the girls in the meadow in front of the house we were building, where we were holding the outdoor wedding ceremony and party. The oldest hung out with a group of her own friends. The younger one whizzed in briefly for the ceremony, then left again before the congratulations started up. There was not much mixing with me and mine. What was there for them to celebrate on a day so full of confusion and effort? 8

On my side, being the newcomer in someone else's territory is a role I'm used to. I can tap into that struggling English speaker, that skinny, dark-haired, olive-skinned girl in a sixth grade of mostly blond and blue-eyed giants. Those tall, freckled boys would push me around in the playground. "Go back to where you came from!" *"No comprendo!"*[5] I'd reply, though of course there was no misunderstanding the fierce looks on their faces. 9

Even now, my first response to a scowl is that old pulling away. (My husband calls it "checking out.") I remember times early on in the marriage when the girls would be with us, and I'd get out of school and drive around doing errands, killing time, until my husband, their father, would be leaving work. I am not proud of my fears, but I understand—as the lingo goes—where they come from. 10

[2]*Madrastra* is Spanish for "stepmother."
[3]*Gringa* is a disparaging term for a foreign woman, especially an American woman.
[4]*Tia* is Spanish for "aunt."
[5]*No comprendo* is Spanish for "I do not understand."

And I understand, more than I'd like to sometimes, my stepdaughters' pain. But with me, they need never fear that I'll usurp a mother's place. No one has ever come up and held their faces and then addressed me, "They look just like you." If anything, strangers to the remarriage are probably playing Mr. Potato Head in their minds, trying to figure out how my foreign features and my husband's fair Nebraskan features got put together into these two tall, blond girls. "My husband's daughters," I kept introducing them. 11

Once, when one of them visited my class and I introduced her as such, two students asked me why. "I'd be so hurt if my stepmom introduced me that way," the young man said. That night I told my stepdaughter what my students had said. She scowled at me and agreed. "It's so weird how you call me Papa's daughter. Like you don't want to be related to me or something." 12

"I didn't want to presume," I explained. "So it's O.K. if I call you my stepdaughter?" 13

"That's what I am," she said. Relieved, I took it for a teensy inch of acceptance. The takings are small in this stepworld, I've discovered. Sort of like being a minority. It feels as if all the goodies have gone somewhere else. 14

Day to day, I guess I follow my papi's advice. When we first came, he would talk to his children about how to make it in our new country. "Just do your work and put in your heart, and they will accept you!" In this age of remaining true to your roots, of keeping your Spanish, of fighting from inside your culture, that assimilationist approach is highly suspect. My Latino students—who don't want to be called Hispanics anymore—would ditch me as faculty adviser if I came up with that play-nice message. 15

But in a stepfamily where everyone is starting a new life together, it isn't bad advice. Like a potluck supper, an American concept my mami never took to. ("Why invite people to your house and then ask them to bring the food?") You put what you've got together with what everyone else brought and see what comes out of the pot. The luck part is if everyone brings something you like. No potato salad, no deviled eggs, no little party sandwiches with you know what in them. 16

Considering Ideas

1. Mayonnaise, which figures prominently in the essay, is a *symbol* (a representation of something else). What does mayonnaise symbolize for Alvarez?
2. Why did Alvarez introduce her stepchildren as her husband's daughters?
3. In your own words, explain the advice that the author's father gave her, the same advice that Alvarez thinks is good to follow in a stepfamily. Why do you think her Latino students would rebel at this advice?
4. Alvarez says that her wedding day was a day "full of confusion and effort" (paragraph 8). What does she mean?
5. For what purpose do you think Alvarez wrote "Hold the Mayonnaise"? What kinds of publications would be interested in reprinting the essay? Why?

Considering Technique

1. Does the introduction engage your interest? Why or why not? What strategy does Alvarez use to engage interest?
2. *Combining patterns:* What comparison-contrast does Alvarez include in the essay?

3. *Combining patterns:* What cause-and-effect analysis does Alvarez include?
4. *Combining patterns:* How does Alvarez use anecdotes (brief narrations) in paragraphs 1–3, 7, 8, and 12–14?
5. What metaphor appears in paragraph 6? Why is the metaphor a good one? What metaphor appears in paragraph 11? What simile appears in paragraph 16? (Metaphors and similes are explained on page 148.)

For Group Discussion or Journal Writing

Alvarez associates mayonnaise with white culture and tastes. Discuss a food that has a strong association for you. Explain the association and why it exists for you. For example, you might explain that lumpy mashed potatoes make you think of your grandmother, who cooked them every Sunday for family dinners. Then you could tell about the dinners.

Juvenile Injustice ANGIE CANNON

If you know little about juvenile correctional facilities, you may be flabbergasted by the information in "Juvenile Injustice," an article that originally appeared in U.S. News & World Report *in 2006. Using cause-and-effect analysis, exemplification, contrast, description, and narration, the author provides a shocking indictment of our juvenile justice system. As you read, think about what the current state of affairs says about our society.*

CHINO, Calif. At the Herman G. Stark Youth Correctional Facility here, the K & L disciplinary lockdown is known as "the Rock." Here dim corridors are lined with the steel doors of a dozen concrete cells. The air is dank, and the drip-drip of water echoes quietly, thanks to the perpetually leaking showers. On the mental health unit, shouts and curses bounce off the walls. In a cell, a young man with his head down paces silently, back and forth, back and forth. 1

Angry outbursts punctuate the din. One day, two youths—one black, the other Latino—passed each other and a racial slur was muttered. Both teens started swinging. A counselor screamed at them to stop, then blasted the pair with Mace. The smaller Latino boy knocked the black youth to the ground and kicked him. A guard ran up and slammed the Latino with his baton. Then, the black kid jumped up and pummeled the Latino. The guard flailed at the black youth with his baton and yelled: "Get off him! Get off him!" A second guard threw the black inmate to the ground. Finally, both kids were cuffed and sent off for a stretch in 23-hour lockdown. 2

It was just another day at Stark, the biggest, toughest prison in the California Youth Authority system. One expert has called the CYA system "a very dangerous place" with "an intense climate of fear." Last year, there were nearly 300 attacks at Stark—more than double the previous year's total. And that was just kids beating up other kids. There were also 52 assaults on staffers at Stark—also double the previous year's tally. "There's riots and fights all the time," says German Carranza, 23, a round-faced native of East Los Angeles who was sent to the Youth Authority at age 17 for a gang-related murder. "I don't feel safe here. But you get so used to it you don't feel fear. You're just alert all the time." 3

California is hardly unique. Juvenile justice facilities across the nation are in a dangerously advanced state of disarray, with violence an almost everyday occurrence and rehabilitation the exception rather than the rule. Abuse of juvenile

inmates by staff is routine. At the Charles H. Hickey Jr. School in Baltimore, staffers used force on juveniles 550 times between July 2002 and December 2003. At the Nevada Youth Training Center, staffers repeatedly punched boys in the chest, kicked their legs, and shoved them against walls. In Florida, a 211-page report issued in March faulted employees at the Miami-Dade Regional Juvenile Detention Center for failing to act as a 17-year-old begged for help but slowly died of a ruptured appendix over two days in June 2003. In Mississippi, suicidal girls at the Columbia Training School were stripped naked and placed in the "dark room," a locked, windowless isolation cell with no light and only a drain in the floor for a toilet; other kids were hogtied and pole-shackled and put on public display for hours. Girls were forced to eat their own vomit. Some staffers at Arizona's Adobe Mountain School sexually abused teens. Several states have had a disturbing spate of suicides among incarcerated kids. "Almost every place is experiencing major problems," says criminologist Barry Krisberg, author of a recent scathing report on the California Youth Authority. "There are cycles of abuse, reform, and abuse, and we are in a cycle of abuse." 4

It wasn't supposed to be this way. The nation's first juvenile court convened in Chicago, on July 3, 1899. To social reformers who pushed for the court, the premise was that kids were different from adults; the juvenile court aimed to rehabilitate, not punish, and the facilities where juveniles served their time were supposed to help that process along. Juveniles were then to be set free when they were deemed rehabilitated or reached 21, whichever came first. Records, generally, were kept confidential. 5

"Full-Court Press." But that, as they say, was then. As violent crime among juveniles rose during the late 1980s and early 1990s, a frightened public lost patience with the old system, and many states moved away from rehabilitation. Today, almost every state has laws making it easier to try kids as adults. Today, juvenile facilities nationwide hold some 104,000 offenders—both kids going through the court system and those adjudicated "delinquent," meaning they have committed crimes ranging from vandalism to homicide. Most states have more juveniles held for property crimes, drug offenses, and public disorder than anything else, but about a quarter of the kids are in for violent crimes. Most are minorities. 6

The philosophy behind locking kids up may have changed, but that's hardly a reason to excuse the violence and abuse experienced at so many of these facilities. Juvenile lockups typically are the provinces of states, which either run them or pay millions to private contractors to do the job. But the U.S. Department of Justice has recently begun attacking abuses in juvenile facilities in an aggressive way. The feds have active investigations or are monitoring settled cases in juvenile justice systems in 13 states or separate territories, including California, Georgia, Michigan, Virginia, and New Jersey. Preliminary inquiries are underway in Connecticut, Florida, New York, North Carolina, and Oklahoma. And more cases are on the horizon. "We have a full-court press on this," says R. Alexander Acosta, assistant attorney general for civil rights. Under a 1980 law, his attorneys have the power to investigate and sue to correct a pattern or practice of unlawful conditions at juvenile facilities. The 1994 federal crime act also allows the department to sue when administrators of juvenile justice systems violate kids' rights. The flurry of suits began during the Clinton administration, but John Ashcroft's[1] Justice Department has more than kept up the pace, doubling the number of new investigations. "No one deserves to be treated this way," says Brad Schlozman, deputy assistant attorney general for civil rights. "These aren't 17-year-old drug dealers. They are 14-year-olds who have run away or who've been truant." 7

At first glance, the depth of the current troubles seems almost counterintuitive. The arrest rate for juvenile violent crime in 2002 was down nearly 50 percent over the past decade. And with nearly every state making it easier to send older, more serious teen offenders off to adult prisons, juvenile facilities might have been expected to become less prone to violence and abuse, not more. 8

Obviously, that's not the case. Why? Lacking political clout, juvenile justice facilities are chronically short of money, which means fewer staff, more overcrowding—in short, more trouble. Then there's the problem of turnover. State juvenile corrections directors can be expected, on average, to stay in their jobs only about three years. The California Youth Authority, for instance, has had five directors since 1995. Similar problems affect the direct-care staff, whose annual salaries range from $20,000 to $32,000. About a quarter of Arizona's staff, for instance, has turned over annually in recent years. 9

Putting still more pressure on the facilities are the courts. Despite the fall in violent crime among minors, the juvenile-court caseload increased 43 percent between 1985 and 2000. 10

As if that weren't bad enough, the widespread closing of children's psychiatric hospitals has made things worse. In 1992, for instance, Massachusetts closed the Gaebler Children's Center in Waltham, which treated disturbed children mostly under age 14. As a result, says Ned Loughran, executive director of the Council of Juvenile Correctional Administrators, juvenile lockups "are getting a tremendous number of kids with mental health problems." 11

Mismatch. The numbers are staggering. A congressional report released in July found that two thirds of juvenile detention facilities hold kids who are waiting for community mental health treatment. In 33 states, youths with mental illness are held in detention centers without any charges against them. From January 1 to June 30, 2003, nearly 15,000 incarcerated youths were waiting for community mental health services, the report said. In addition, two thirds of juvenile detention facilities that hold youths waiting for mental health services report that some of these youths have attempted suicide or attacked others. "Judges are throwing up their hands," Loughran said, "and these kids have been flooding the juvenile corrections system." Studies suggest that about 60 percent to 70 percent of kids in detention or juvenile facilities suffer from a psychiatric disorder. "We don't think the prevalence was that high 10 or 15 years ago," says Thomas Grisso, a University of Massachusetts clinical psychologist studying the mental health of juvenile offenders. 12

[1]John Ashcroft was attorney general of the United States from 2001 to 2005.

Advocates applaud the Justice Department's muscle because it pressures states to pony up more money for juvenile-justice budgets. "The Justice Department is discovering what happens when you don't fund these places properly—they go to hell in a handbasket," says James Austin, director of George Washington University's Institute on Crime, Justice, and Corrections. Austin has helped monitor settlements between the Justice Department and troubled juvenile facilities in Georgia and Louisiana. In both states, he notes, prosecutors and judges were sending kids to those facilities who didn't need to go there. "In Georgia," he says, you would see 9-year-olds being sent for being disruptive in school." In both states, the first fixes, Austin explained, were to cut the number of kids in the system by half, add educational and mental health staff, and beef up internal avenues to investigate abuse allegations. In Louisiana, the state was spending about $50 million a year on juvenile justice before the legal settlement. After the settlement, in 2000, the state increased that to about $85 million annually. "The situation," Austin says, "has gotten a lot better in both Georgia and Louisiana." 13

But they are, it seems, the exception. Over the past few years, Maryland has provided a more depressingly familiar scenario: repeated scandals at violent, mismanaged detention facilities—followed by politicians' glib promises to clean things up. The state's "reform" legislation—passed in April—is considered weak by many, in part because it would take years to implement. That same month, the Justice Department found serious civil rights violations at two Maryland facilities after a 20-month investigation. At a recent gathering in Baltimore, mothers with sons in various Maryland juvenile lockups recited a litany of horrors. Erika recalls that the first time she visited her son at the Cheltenham Youth Facility, cited repeatedly by state monitors for "excessive violence," Jason cried and told her he could hear staffers punching and kicking another kid late at night. Jason, now 18, spent nearly a month at Cheltenham for marijuana possession and distribution. "There was one kid who was 12 or 13, and he was hyper and acting up, and one night, the staff went in and started choking him," Jason recalled. "I heard him screaming in his cell." 14

The stories are equally disturbing at the Hickey School in Baltimore, which has housed about 250 delinquent boys. Nestled on several rolling acres in rural Baltimore County, it's both a detention center for kids awaiting trial and a "training school" for boys already found delinquent by the courts. Since 1991, the state has paid tens of millions to two private companies—first Rebound, a Colorado company, then Youth Services International, a subsidiary of Correctional Services Corp.—to run the place. But the problems persisted. Behind Hickey's razor-wire fences, there are nearly three assaults a day, according to a recent state report. Of the more than 70 child abuse/neglect investigations there since July 1, 2002, a quarter of the allegations have been substantiated; in an additional 30 percent, there was not enough evidence to rule out the case but not enough to prove neglect or abuse. The state took over operations at Hickey on April 1. At the same time, Maryland lawmakers approved a package of reforms that include smaller facilities with only 48 beds, year-round education, and programs to ease kids back into their communities, though it has a years-long timetable and funding is uncertain. The state also plans to hire a new private contractor to run the facility. On a visit by a reporter to Hickey, the place seemed clean and calm, if grim. Several teens said they had not witnessed any violence there. Ken Montague, who heads the Department of Juvenile Services, says his department has tried to train staff not to be violent. But he concedes that the challenges at a place like Hickey are immense, with 50 percent to 70 percent of the kids there suffering mental-health or substance-abuse problems. "We have to work on this," Montague says, "and make sure these kids get the help they need." 15

What many kids get instead of help, however, is experience—of the wrong kind. Ralph Thomas, who runs the governor's office that monitors Maryland's juvenile facilities, says the system is churning out even more troubled kids: "Many of these kids come out worse for their experience in these facilities. They're more likely to prey on society." 16

And not just in Maryland. Back in California, at the Southern Youth Correctional Reception Center and Clinic in Norwalk, Mark Alvarado, 19, is a depressing illustration of the state of juvenile justice. Alvarado says he set his grandmother's house on fire at age 5. At 9, he says he joined a gang; his older brother had "Natural Born Killer" tattooed on his collarbone. He was in and out of juvenile hall for years for what he calls "little stuff—burglaries and robberies and arson." He was thrown in the CYA at 16 for auto theft. There, he says, he learned new skills—how to hot-wire a car and how to break into houses. "I came out a better criminal," he says. "That's how it is for most people." Alvarado was paroled in June. 17

Considering Ideas

1. For what purpose do you think the author wrote "Juvenile Injustice"?
2. Today's juvenile justice system has strayed from its initial intent. What was that intent, and how has it strayed?
3. Why have we moved away from the original intent of the juvenile justice system? Is the reason understandable? Why or why not?
4. Why are conditions in juvenile correctional facilities so bad?
5. What do you think the current state of juvenile justice facilities—and the reasons for that state—say about our society?

Considering Technique

1. The thesis of the essay is delayed for several paragraphs. What is the thesis, and where is it located?
2. *Combining patterns:* What patterns does the author combine before stating the thesis in order to engage readers' interest? Is the strategy effective? That is, would the lead-in likely engage the interest of the readers of *U.S. News & World Report*?
3. *Combining patterns:* How does the author use exemplification to support the thesis and achieve her writing purpose? How does she use contrast?
4. *Combining patterns:* Which pattern does the author rely on the most heavily? How does she use that pattern to achieve her purpose for writing?
5. What strategy does the author use for the conclusion? Is that strategy a good one? Explain.

For Group Discussion or Journal Writing

Juveniles accused of violent crimes are often tried as adults. That means they are tried in adult courts, given adult sentences, and sent to adult prisons. What do you think of this practice? Why?

Boy Brains, Girl Brains **Peg Tyre**

Do boys and girls learn differently? Peg Tyre combines comparison-contrast, cause-and-effect analysis, process analysis, and exemplification to report research indicating that they do. In this article that originally appeared in Newsweek *in 2005, Tyre reports on an important implication of this research for education. As you read, notice how Tyre uses multiple patterns in the same paragraph.*

Three years ago, Jeff Gray, the principal at Foust Elementary School in Owensboro, Ky., realized that his school needed help—and fast. Test scores at Foust were the worst in the county and the students, particularly the boys, were falling far behind. So Gray took a controversial course for educators on brain development, then revamped the first- and second-grade curriculum. The biggest change: he divided the classes by gender. Because males have less serotonin in their brains, which Gray was taught may cause them to fidget more, desks were removed from the boys' classrooms and they got short exercise periods throughout the day. Because females have more oxytocin, a hormone linked to bonding, girls were given a carpeted area where they sit and discuss their feelings. Because boys have higher levels of testosterone and are theoretically more competitive, they were given timed, multiple-choice tests. The girls were given multiple-choice tests, too, but got more time to complete them. Gray says the gender-based curriculum gave the school "the edge we needed." Tests scores are up. Discipline problems are down. This year the fifth and sixth grades at Foust are adopting the new curriculum, too. 1

Do Mars and Venus[1] ride the school bus? Gray is part of a new crop of educators with a radical idea—that boys and girls are so biologically different they need to be separated into single-sex classes and taught in different ways. In the last five years, brain researchers using sophisticated MRI and PET technology have gathered new information about the ways male and female brains develop and process information. Studies show that girls, for instance, have more active frontal lobes, stronger connections between brain hemispheres and "language centers" that mature earlier than their male counterparts. Critics of gender-based schooling charge that curricula designed to exploit such differences reinforce the most narrow cultural stereotypes. But proponents say that unless neurological, hormonal and cognitive differences between boys and girls are incorporated in the classroom, boys are at a disadvantage. 2

Most schools are girl-friendly, says Michael Gurian, coauthor with Kathy Stevens of a new book, *The Minds of Boys: Saving Our Sons from Falling Behind in School and Life*, "because teachers, who are mostly women, teach the way they learn." Seventy percent of children diagnosed with learning disabilities are male, and the sheer number of boys who struggle in school is staggering. Eighty percent of high-school dropouts are boys and less than 45 percent of students enrolled in college are young men. To close the educational gender gap, Gurian says, teachers need to change their techniques. They should light classrooms more brightly for boys and speak to them loudly, since research shows males don't see or hear as well as females. Because boys are more-visual learners, teachers should illustrate a story before writing it and use an overhead projector to practice reading and writing. Gurian's ideas seem to be catching on. More than 185 public schools now offer some form of single-sex education, and Gurian has trained more than 15,000 teachers through his institute in Colorado Springs. 3

To some experts, Gurian's approach is not only wrong but dangerous. Some say his curriculum is part of a long history of pseudoscience

[1]A reference to the book *Men Are from Mars, Women Are from Venus: A Practical Guide for Improving Communication and Getting What You Want in Your Relationships* by John Gray. The book discusses fundamental differences between men and women.

aimed at denying equal opportunities in education. For much of the 19th century, educators, backed by prominent scientists, cautioned that women were neurologically unable to withstand the rigors of higher education. Others say basing new teaching methods on raw brain research is misguided. While it's true that brain scans show differences between boys and girls, says David Sadker, education professor at American University, no one is exactly sure what those differences mean. Differences between boys and girls, says Sadker, are dwarfed by brain differences within each gender. "If you want to make schools a better place," says Sadker, "you have to strive to see kids as individuals." 4

Natasha Craft, a fourth-grade teacher at Southern Elementary School in Somerset, Ky., knows the gender-based curriculum she began using last year isn't a cure-all. "Not all the boys and girls are going to be the same," she says, "but I feel like it gives me another set of tools to work with." And when she stands in front of a room of hard-to-reach kids, Craft says, another set of tools could come in handy. 5

Considering Ideas

1. What are the chief arguments for single-sex classrooms?
2. What are the chief arguments against single-sex classrooms?
3. Why are most schools girl-friendly? In your earlier schooling, were your classrooms girl-friendly?
4. David Sadker opposes single-sex education, saying that there are more differences within genders than between them (paragraph 4). What do you think these differences are?

Considering Technique

1. The thesis of "Boy Brains, Girl Brains" is implied rather than stated. In your own words, write out the thesis. For what purpose do you think the essay was written?
2. *Combining patterns:* The essay opens with exemplification. Does that exemplification create an effective beginning? Why or why not?
3. *Combining patterns:* How does Tyre use cause-and-effect analysis in paragraphs 1 and 3? How does she use comparison-contrast in paragraphs 1 and 2?
4. *Combining patterns:* How does Tyre use process analysis in paragraph 3?
5. Does Tyre treat both sides of the issue with equal emphasis and detail? Explain.

For Group Discussion or Journal Writing

David Sadker says that we can improve schools if we "see kids as individuals" (paragraph 4). Discuss several ways that teachers and administrators can see children as individuals. How well do we currently treat children as individuals?

PUNCTUATION NOTE

Hyphens

Use a hyphen between two or more words when the words together form a noun or when they form an adjective that comes before a noun. These uses of the hyphen are illustrated in "Boy Brains, Girl Brains":

> So Gray took a controversial course for educators on brain development, then revamped the first- and second-grade curriculum. (paragraph 1)
>
> ... they were given timed, multiple-choice tests (paragraph 1)
>
> Eighty percent of high-school dropouts are boys ... (paragraph 3)
>
> Natasha Craft ... knows the gender-based curriculum ... isn't a cure-all. (paragraph 5)
>
> And when she stands in front of a room of hard-to-reach kids, Craft says, another set of tools could come in handy. (paragraph 5)

COMBINING PATTERNS IN AN IMAGE

Study the advertisement on page 416 to identify the elements of both exemplification and definition that it includes.

Considering the Image

1. What persuasive purpose does the advertisement have?
2. What informational purpose does the advertisement have?
3. What element of definition appears in the advertisement, and how does that definition help the ad achieve its purpose?
4. What element of exemplification appears in the advertisement, and how does that exemplification help the ad achieve its purpose?

SUGGESTIONS FOR WRITING

Writing with Multiple Patterns

1. *Combining process analysis and exemplification:* Explain a process you perform well, and give examples of ways the process is useful or efficient.
2. *Combining narration and cause-and-effect analysis:* Narrate an account of a time you experienced a success or a failure, and explain the causes and/or the effects of the outcome.
3. *Combining definition and classification:* Define *stereotype,* and classify the ways stereotypes affect our thinking about other people.
4. *Combining comparison-contrast and description:* Compare and contrast some aspect of yourself or your life now and that same aspect several years ago, being sure to describe that aspect in the present and in the past. For

example, you can describe where you live now and where you lived before college, or how you look now and how you looked when you were in high school.

5. *Combining cause-and-effect analysis and exemplification:* Select something that is currently popular in society, such as podcasts, reality television, rap music, or football. Give reasons for its popularity and examples of how it affects society.

Reading Then Writing with Multiple Patterns

1. All of us have felt like outsiders at times, whether it has been as the new student in school, a stranger in a roomful of people who know each other, or a new employee on the job. Like Julia Alvarez does in "Hold the Mayonnaise," use multiple patterns to tell about a time you tried to fit into a group of people when you felt like an outsider.
2. Like Angie Cannon does in "Juvenile Injustice," combine patterns to tell about a situation that you think is wrong and needs to be changed. The situation can exist on campus, in your community, or in your workplace.
3. Like Peg Tyre does in "Boy Brains, Girl Brains," combine patterns to explain a way to improve education.

Combining Patterns beyond the Writing Classroom

Assume you are applying for an important job, and as part of the application process, you must write an essay explaining what you hope to accomplish in the next 10 years. Drawing on whatever patterns you need to, explain what your goals are, why they are important, and how you plan to accomplish them.

Responding to a Theme

1. In "Hold the Mayonnaise," Julia Alvarez discusses the role of a stepparent. Explain how the presence of stepparents and stepchildren has altered the nature of the American family.
2. In "Juvenile Injustice," the author paints a bleak picture of the juvenile justice system. Part of the problem is the increased pressure on the system created by youths who commit violent crimes. Some people say that bullying in schools is one of the reasons young people commit these violent crimes. What do you think can be done to address the problem of bullying in our schools?
3. In "Boy Brains, Girl Brains," arguments for single-sex education are presented. Argue for or against single-sex education in high school.
4. The advertisement for the American Indian College Fund attempts to dispel the common stereotype of native Americans. Create an advertisement of your own that dispels a common stereotype of some other group of people.
5. *Connecting the readings:* Much is made of the problems with American education. "Boy Brains, Girl Brains" points to one problem, and "School Is Bad for Children" on page 8 points to another. Despite the many criticisms of our system of education, much is right with the way we educate our youths. Write an essay in which you discuss what is *right* with American education.

PROCESS GUIDELINES

www.mhhe.com/tsw

For further help combining patterns, go to Catalyst 2.0 > Writing > Writing Tutors > Blended Essay

Combining Patterns

The following guidelines are not meant to replace your own effective procedures. They are here for you to try as you work to improve your writing process.

Think like a Writer: Generating Ideas, Considering Audience and Purpose, and Ordering Ideas

- Recognize that an assigned topic may suggest certain patterns. For example, the assigned topic "gender bias in the media" suggests that you will define *gender bias* and give examples of its occurrence.
- Use the patterns if you need help narrowing your topic or generating ideas by answering the questions given earlier in this chapter, on page 400.
- If necessary, answer the "Questions for Establishing Purpose" on page 40 and the "Questions for Identifying and Assessing Audience" on page 42.
- To order your ideas, assess whether the patterns you combine suggest particular arrangements. For example, if you combine process analysis and cause-and-effect analysis, you will likely combine chronological and progressive orders.
- Write a formal outline, which can be particularly helpful when you are using more than one order for your ideas.

Think like a Writer: Drafting

- If you have trouble beginning, start with your thesis and then write the first point to develop that thesis.
- Keep the characteristics of the patterns you are using in mind as you draft.

Think like a Critic; Work Like an Editor: Revising

- Consult the graphic visualizations of each pattern in Chapters 6–13 for a quick review of the characteristics of each pattern you use.
- When you move from one pattern to another, achieve coherence with transitions and repetition.

Think like a Critic; Work like an Editor: Correcting Errors

- Use the "Guide to Frequently Occurring Errors" for reference, and check with a writing center tutor if you are unsure about a grammar, usage, or punctuation point.
- Check one extra time for the kinds of mistakes you are in the habit of making.

Using the Patterns of Development

PART 3

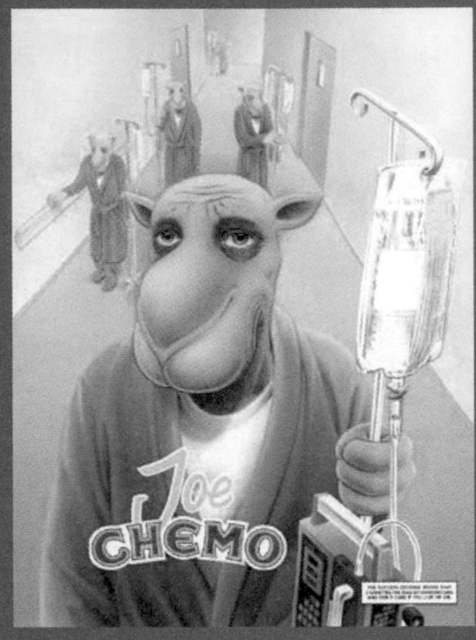

LOOKING AHEAD

In this chapter, you will learn strategies for argumentation. That is, you will learn persuasive techniques for convincing readers to think or act in a particular way. An interesting aspect of argumentation is that no matter what the issue, people will take opposing views. The images here, for example, represent opposing views. The first image is a popular Joe Camel advertisement meant to persuade people to buy Camel cigarettes. The second advertisement is a parody of Joe Camel, "Joe Chemo," meant to persuade people *not* to smoke Camels—or any cigarettes. Before turning your attention to the chapter, consider the two advertisements, and answer the following questions:

- How does the Joe Camel ad work to persuade people to smoke Camels?
- How does the Joe Chemo ad work to persuade people *not* to smoke?
- What specific audience is the Joe Camel ad addressing? Is the Joe Chemo ad trying to reach the same audience?
- How well does each advertisement achieve its purpose? Explain.

Argumentation

As social beings, we are moved to express our opinions and try to convince others of their truth, the way the author of the following letter to the editor of the *Dallas Morning News* does.

> **Foolish to subsidize**
>
> Your July 9 editorial, "Summer rain—Misery and benefit come from Texas storms," missed the point. There are two issues here: The first one is that people should not be allowed to build in known flood plains, period. If no building were allowed, no damage would occur. Second, the federal government should not be in the flood insurance business. These people cannot afford private flood insurance, so because of the (as usual) misguided efforts of the federal government, they can purchase cheap flood insurance from the government (me). My tax dollars are subsidizing their foolishness.
>
> The local government should not issue building permits to anyone in a known flood plain, unless that person can and does obtain private flood insurance.

The letter writer has strong opinions about whether people should be allowed to build on a flood plain and whether the federal government should issue flood insurance—those are her *issues.* Her belief is that people should not build on flood plains, but if they do they should have private flood insurance—those are her *claims.* Whether the writer convinced her readers to agree with her claims about the issues depends, in part, on how well she argued her case. In other words, in **argumentation,** the writer offers evidence to support a claim about an issue. The more convincing the evidence, the more convincing the argument and the more likely readers will agree.

WHY IS ARGUMENTATION IMPORTANT?

Argumentation, which works to convince readers to think or act a particular way, is everywhere. Magazine advertisements work to convince you that the surest path to popularity is using the right deodorant; letters from banks try to persuade you that owning their credit cards will allow you to buy as much as you want without penalty; campaign literature works to convince you to vote for candidates; travel brochures aim to persuade you to visit Belize for the vacation of a lifetime; movie posters try to entice you to buy a ticket to the latest James Bond film; college websites urge you to attend their schools; newspaper editorials try to persuade you of the dangers of tax reform; public service billboards work to persuade you to buckle your seat belt; and book reviews try to convince you of the quality—or lack of quality—of the latest best-seller.

Because so many people are trying to convince you to adopt certain views or take certain actions, understanding how argumentation works will make you more aware of how people are trying to move you and, thus, better able to evaluate their arguments. In addition, you will have many occasions to write argumentation yourself (as the next sections explain), so understanding the principles of argumentation is important for that reason.

Argumentation is not fighting, and it need not involve conflict. While its purpose is to persuade, it can serve a variety of persuasive purposes, some of which are given in the following chart.

Purposes for Argumentation

Purpose	**Sample Argumentation**
To reinforce an existing view and create sentiment to maintain the status quo	A report to a department supervisor explaining the benefits of the four-day workweek option that the department instituted a year ago
To call readers to action	A newspaper editorial urging people to sign a petition in support of a piece of legislation
To change people's minds	A campaign brochure urging voters in a predominantly Republican district to vote for a Democratic candidate

To lessen an objection	An e-mail to your parents, who do not want you to transfer to another college, convincing them that a transfer will not be as expensive as they think
To earn support for a position	A letter to the editor of a newspaper arguing that mandatory drug testing is an invasion of privacy

Argumentation across the Disciplines and Beyond

Argumentation in the Classroom

Many courses, particularly after the introductory level, require you to write argumentation. For example, for a paper in an ethics class, you might argue for an equitable procedure for allocating transplant organs. For an American history paper, you might argue for or against the payment of reparations to Native Americans. On a class website for a business management class, you might argue for or against the use of flextime. *What important issues are commonly argued in your major? How likely are you to write essays that argue claims about these issues? How might you use argumentation in the classes you are taking this term?*

Argumentation in Daily Life

In your personal writing, you are likely to use argumentation often. For example, you might write a letter to the editor of your local paper to persuade readers to adopt your position on an issue, or you might write an e-mail to convince a friend to take a day off and go to the beach with you. If you have problems with a product you bought, you might write a letter to a customer service representative arguing for a refund. *How might you use argumentation as chair of a membership committee for your city's children's museum? As a member of the ticket sales committee for a theater group? As a volunteer worker on a political campaign?*

Argumentation on the Job

The writing you do at work is likely to include argumentation. Union leaders, for example, write letters to persuade their members to vote for or against contracts. Attorneys write opening and closing arguments to convince juries; social workers write reports to convince judges to rule in clients' behalf; real estate brokers write listings to persuade people to consider buying property. *How might you use argumentation in the job you hope to have after graduation? For whom will you write the argumentation? How important will this writing be to your success on the job?*

FINDING AN ISSUE AND ESTABLISHING YOUR CLAIM

An argument essay gives evidence to support a claim about an issue. An **issue** is a concern or problem about which people disagree, and a **claim** is the writer's opinion about the issue. If you argue that the tax on cigarettes should be increased, your issue is the cigarette tax, and your claim is that the tax should be increased. If you argue that animals should not be used to test the safety of cosmetics, your issue is testing cosmetics with animals, and your claim is that such testing should not occur. As you work to find an issue and establish your claim, be sure they are debatable and sufficiently narrow.

First, your issue and claim must be debatable. That is, they must be controversial rather than a statement of fact or personal preference. You cannot argue, for example, that cigarettes are harmful because medical science has already proven this—the matter is not debatable. Nor can you argue that women look better without makeup—the matter is one of personal preference.

In addition to being debatable, your issue and claim must be sufficiently narrow. How narrow they should be depends on your purpose and audience. You will not be able to argue convincingly for censorship in a five-page paper for your media class. There are simply too many kinds of censorship. However, you *can* narrow your issue and claim to argue for censorship of the Internet. For an even shorter paper, you can narrow further to argue for censorship of the Internet in high schools with wired classrooms. In a letter to the editor of your campus newspaper, you do not have space to argue convincingly against the college's new five-year plan, but you can argue against the recommended annual tuition hikes. If you are a guest columnist with more space, you can argue that the five-year plan places more importance on new buildings than on quality instruction.

Consider Your Audience and Purpose

Your audience will affect how you establish your issue and claim. First, you should determine which of three kinds of readers you are writing for: supportive, wavering, or hostile.

Supportive readers. These readers are already sympathetic to your claim. If you want your college to begin a campuswide recycling program, supportive readers would include members of the campus environmental club. Because this audience is already on your side, your purpose will focus more on moving your readers to act rather than to think a certain way. Thus, rather than argue that your school should begin a recycling program, you might want to argue that your readers should begin a letter-writing campaign to urge the administration to launch the program.

Wavering readers. These readers are not committed to your claim but can be brought to your side. They may need more information, may not yet have made up their minds, or may not care much about the issue. With wavering readers, you should identify the reasons for resistance and address them.

Wavering readers for an argument essay urging campuswide recycling might include students who think that recycling is too much trouble. You can address this concern by explaining that conveniently located recycling bins make recycling easier than they think and that any moderate inconvenience is a small price to pay for a cleaner environment.

Hostile readers. These readers are strongly opposed to your claim or are difficult to persuade for another reason, perhaps apathy or anger. Because hostile readers are the most difficult to persuade, you must have a realistic writing purpose for this audience. You may not be able to change these readers' minds, so you may have to settle for lessening their objections. For example, your college's chief financial officer may be strongly opposed to recycling because the school has no money to run the program and layoffs are on the horizon. In that case, your purpose may be to convince your reader to consider recycling when the school's financial picture improves, or to present evidence that a recycling program can be financially beneficial to some aspect of the school.

Your audience will also affect the purpose of your argument essay. While you want to convince your readers to see things just as you do, this may be an unreasonable expectation. If you favor gun control and are writing to the membership of the National Rifle Association, a realistic purpose would be to convince them of the need for stricter enforcement of existing laws. An unrealistic purpose would be to convince them that handguns should be banned.

Sometimes a particular audience is so opposed to your claim that the best you can hope for is that readers will consider your points and agree that they have some merit. For example, if you are writing to the president of the local teachers' union about the hardships of teachers' strikes, you cannot expect your reader to come out against such strikes. However, if you present a good enough case, your reader may come to understand something he or she never realized before and become more sympathetic to your claim. Perhaps this new understanding will influence the reader's thinking and actions in the future.

The following can help you settle on a purpose compatible with your audience.

Audience and Purpose Compatibility

Audience	**Possible Purpose**
Is well informed and strongly opposed to your claim	To lessen the opposition by convincing the audience that some of your points are valid and worth consideration
Is poorly informed and opposed to your claim	To inform the audience and change their view

(continued)

Would find it difficult to perform the desired action	To convince the audience that it is worth the sacrifice or convince them to do some part of what is desired
Should not find it difficult to perform the desired action	To convince the audience to perform the action
Has no interest one way or the other in the issue	To arouse interest and persuade the audience to agree

EXERCISE Considering Audience, Identifying Issues, and Making Claims

1. For each of the following claims, note whether the indicated audience is likely to be supportive, wavering, or hostile. Explain your view.
   - **a.** In order to graduate from college, students should be required to perform 40 hours of community service. *(audience = college students)*
   - **b.** In order to graduate from college, students should be required to perform 40 hours of community service. *(audience = college administrators)*
   - **c.** Building a water tower on Cadillac Drive will help water reach the north quarter of the township, allowing new businesses to locate there and revitalize the area. *(audience = homeowners on Cadillac Drive)*
   - **d.** Building a water tower on Cadillac Drive will help water reach the north quarter of the township, allowing new businesses to locate there and revitalize the area. *(audience = township administrators)*
   - **e.** Establishing a curfew for people under 18 will help keep our youth out of trouble. *(audience = parents)*
   - **f.** Establishing a curfew for people under 18 will help keep our youth out of trouble. *(audience = teenagers)*
2. For three of the following subjects, identify two issues suitable for consideration in an argument essay. Then make a claim about each issue.

   Example: Television

   Issue: Sexual content on prime-time television programs

   Claim: Prime-time television programs have too much explicit sexual content.

   Issue: Advertising on children's programs

   Claim: Programs aimed at children under age five should be free of advertising.

   - **a.** Sports
   - **b.** College life
   - **c.** Rock music
   - **d.** Graduation requirements
   - **e.** Politics ■

KINDS OF SUPPORT

Because an argument essay is written on a debatable issue, there is no absolute right or wrong side. In fact, all sides of the issue are likely to have some merit. To convince readers, you must support your claim to demonstrate that it is *more correct* than opposing ones. Three kinds of support can help you do this: logical appeals, emotional appeals, and ethical appeals.

Logical Appeals

To convince your readers by appealing to their sense of logic, offer compelling reasons and evidence for your claim. **Reasons** explain why you believe your claim about the issue. Suppose you are arguing that juveniles who commit violent crimes should not stand trial in adult courts. Your reasons—why you believe that juveniles should not be tried in adult courts—could include these:

- Adult courts do not offer juveniles the age-appropriate protections that juvenile courts do.
- Juveniles sentenced in adult courts go to adult prisons, where they are often abused.
- Adult sentences are too long for juveniles.
- Juveniles sentenced in adult courts are not rehabilitated.

No matter how compelling they are, reasons alone are not enough to convince thoughtful readers: You must back up each of these reasons with evidence. **Evidence** is specific facts, statistics, examples, quotations, personal experience, observations, and explanations that demonstrate the truth of the reasons. For example, to back up the reason that juveniles who are sentenced in adult courts go to adult prisons, where they are often abused, you can cite statistics about the rate of abuse of juvenile offenders by adult inmates. You could then use cause-and-effect analysis to explain that as a result of the abuse, the juveniles are likely to become more psychologically impaired than they were when they entered prison.

Sources of Reasons and Evidence

Reasons and evidence to support your claim can come from a variety of sources, including your own experience and observation, reading and television viewing, class lectures, the experience of others, research, and the testimony of authorities. Here are some examples.

Issue: Testing students for drugs

Claim: High school students should be tested regularly.

Personal experience and observation. A friend of yours overdosed in high school. His death suggests a reason for your claim: Regular drug testing might have led to a rehabilitation that could have saved his life. As evidence to back up this reason, you can use narration to tell about your classmate, who was a regular drug user from his sophomore year until his death on the morning of high school graduation. You can then use cause-and-effect analysis to show that drug testing could have prevented the tragedy.

Reading and television viewing. A news report that over half of teenagers surveyed admitted to regular drug use suggests a reason for your claim: With drug use that common, drug testing is needed to identify users and get them help. As evidence to back up this reason, you can cite the news report as proof of how widespread adolescent drug use is and then use process analysis to explain how the testing would lead to helpful intervention.

Class lectures. Learning in a sociology class that drug testing has been a deterrent among Olympic athletes suggests deterrence as a reason for your claim. As evidence to back up this reason, you can cite the information as an example. You can also use comparison to explain that if drug testing keeps Olympic athletes from using drugs, it can do so for high school students as well.

The experience of others. A classmate who transferred from a private school in another state tells you that he was afraid to use drugs there because of drug testing, but he feels free to use them in your school, where no drug testing exists. This information also suggests deterrence as a reason for your claim. As evidence to back up this reason, you can cite your classmate's experience.

Research. An Internet search or library reading turns up statistics that show teenage drug use as a leading cause of violent crime. This information suggests a reason for your claim: If drug testing reduces drug use among teenagers, it will also reduce the amount of violence that plagues our high schools. As evidence to back up this reason, you can use cause-and-effect analysis to show how reducing the amount of drug use will reduce the amount of violence. (Be sure to document research material according to the conventions explained in Chapter 17.)

Testimony of authorities. Interviewing high school principals and drug counselors who favor drug testing can give you additional reasons and evidence for support.

Inductive and Deductive Reasoning

An appeal to logic should show the progression of thought that led you to the conclusion expressed in your claim. Two frequently used patterns of reasoning are induction and deduction.

Induction. With **induction,** the progression is from specific evidence to the general conclusion given in the claim.

Specific evidence: The number of adolescent suicide attempts is increasing.

Specific evidence: In the last year, the local high school reported four attempted suicides.

Specific evidence: Guidance counselors in middle school and high school are counseling more students for depression than ever before.

Specific evidence: Today's high school students are under a great deal of stress.

Conclusion: Our high school should institute a suicide prevention program.

Inductive reasoning allows you to argue your claim by showing how specific evidence (facts, statistics, cases, examples, etc.) lead to the point you want to convince your reader of. Thus, if you wanted to convince your reader that the local high school should institute a suicide prevention program, you could do so by stating and explaining each piece of evidence that leads to your conclusion that the program is a good idea.

In inductive reasoning, your conclusion is sound only if it is based on sufficient evidence and only if that evidence is accurate. Thus, you cannot reasonably conclude that today's teens are suicidal solely on the basis of the fact that there were four attempted suicides in one high school. Nor can you draw that conclusion if you are wrong about the amount of depression counselors are seeing in teenagers.

Induction can be used in an entire essay or in part of one. Here is a paragraph developed with induction. Notice that the evidence appears first, and the conclusion drawn from that evidence appears last.

> *evidence* [Maxine Phillips reports that approximately 9.5 million preschoolers have mothers with jobs outside the house.] *evidence* [Many of these mothers are the sole support of their children, so they cannot stay home, although they may want to.] *evidence* [An alarming number, says Phillips, also cannot afford quality day care, so their children are in substandard situations or worse—unsupervised.] *evidence* [Given the compelling evidence that the child's early years are key to good development, we must ensure that those years are spent in sound, enriching environments like the ones quality day care can provide.] *evidence* [Yet, if that day care is not affordable, large numbers of children will suffer.] [That is something we have it in our power to prevent:] *conclusion* [The federal

government should subsidize day care programs for single parents.]

Deduction. A second progression of thought leading to a conclusion is deduction. **Deduction** is a form of reasoning that moves from a generalization (known as a major premise) to a specific case (known as a minor premise) and on to a conclusion. Deduction works like this:

Generalization (major premise):	Our city has a serious unemployment problem.
Specific case (minor premise):	A proposed federal prison would create 500 new jobs.
Conclusion:	If the new federal prison is built in our city, we could put 500 people to work.

Deductive reasoning can help you organize the argument for your claim about an issue. Suppose you want to convince your reader that your city should compete for the new federal prison. You can support your claim by reproducing your deductive reasoning: The city needs jobs, and the prison will provide them.

To argue well, however, you must avoid the illogical conclusions that result from inaccurate or sweeping generalizations. Notice the problems with the following deductive reasoning:

Generalization (major premise):	All students cheat at one time or another.
Specific case (minor premise):	Lee is a student.
Conclusion:	Lee cheats.

This conclusion is illogical because the first generalization is inaccurate—all students do not cheat.

Generalization (major premise):	Foreign cars are better made than American cars.
Generalization (minor premise):	My car was made in Germany.
Conclusion:	My car is better made than American cars.

This conclusion is illogical because the first generalization is sweeping—many foreign cars are not better made than American cars. Remember, your conclusion is valid only when your premises are valid.

Deduction can be used in an entire essay or in part of one. Here, for example, is a paragraph developed with deduction. Notice that the major premise appears first, followed by the minor premises and the supporting evidence. The conclusion the deduction leads to appears last.

major premise

[No one argues with the fact that preschool children require a nurturing environment.] *minor premise* [No one disagrees either that the best nurturing environment is a stable home combined, if necessary, with a quality day care center.] *minor premise* [Lately, however, evidence suggests that many preschoolers are not getting the nurturing they need because their mothers work to make ends meet and there is too little money for adequate day care.] *evidence for minor premise* [Maxine Phillips reports that over half the mothers of preschoolers are in the workforce. She also explains that many of these mothers, who are the sole support of their children, cannot afford to stop working, nor can they afford adequate day care, so children end up in substandard environments or unsupervised.] *conclusion* [In light of this, the need for federally subsidized day care becomes apparent.]

Avoiding Logical Fallacies

Because any appeal to logic must have sound thinking at its core, errors in reasoning, called **logical fallacies,** weaken an argument. If the logical fallacies are serious or frequent enough, your readers will reject your claim, and you will not achieve your purpose for writing. When you read about induction and deduction, you learned three types of faulty logic: basing a conclusion on insufficient evidence, using sweeping generalizations, and using inaccurate generalizations. In addition, when you revise, check for the following logical fallacies.

1. Do not attack an idea on the basis of the people associated with that idea. This faulty logic is **guilt by association.**

   Example: Only liberals oppose balancing the federal budget, and we all know the mess they've gotten this country into.

   Explanation: The people who do or do not champion an idea or action have nothing to do with the validity of that idea or action.

2. Avoid name calling or attacks on personalities rather than ideas. This is ***ad hominem*** (to the man).

   Example: The president of this college is so out of touch with students that he thinks they will sit still for another tuition increase.

   Explanation: It is legitimate to criticize what people do or think, but it is unfair to attack the personalities of the people themselves.

3. Do not defend or attack an idea or action on the grounds that people have always believed that idea or performed that action.

   Example: Children have always learned to read in first grade, so why should we begin teaching them any earlier now?

   Explanation: Everything believed and done in the past and present is not always for the best. Perhaps new research in education indicates that children are capable of reading before the first grade.

4. Avoid illogical comparisons, also called **false analogy.**

   Example: The voters in this city have not passed a school levy for seven years. They will never vote for a teacher to become our next senator.

   Explanation: How voters feel about school levies has nothing to do with how they feel about a political candidate who happens to be a teacher. The comparison is not logical.

5. Do not assume that what is true for one person will be true for everybody. This is a **sweeping generalization.**

   Example: When I was a child, my parents spanked me regularly, and I turned out just fine. Clearly, there is no harm in spanking as a punishment.

   Explanation: It does not hold that just because one person suffered no ill effects from spanking, no one will suffer ill effects from spanking.

   To avoid sweeping generalizations, you need not avoid using evidence from your personal experience. You should, however, be careful of what you conclude from this evidence. Do not make more of it than it is.

6. Do not offer an unproven statement as the truth, or you will be guilty of **begging the question.**

   Example: Unnecessary programs like shop and home economics should be eliminated to balance the new school budget.

   Explanation: The importance of shop and home economics is debatable, so you cannot assume they are unnecessary and argue from there. You must first prove they are unnecessary.

7. Avoid drawing a conclusion that does not follow from the evidence. This is called a **non sequitur.**

   Example: Feminism is still a potent social force in the United States. No wonder our divorce rate is so high.

   Explanation: Many factors contribute to the divorce rate; no logical reason establishes feminism as the sole cause or even one cause.

8. Do not present only two options when more than two exist. This is the **either/or fallacy.**

   Example: Either you support the strike or you are opposed to organized labor.

   Explanation: The sentence ignores other possibilities, such as opposing the strike but believing the union's demands should be met, or opposing the strike but calling for further negotiations.

9. Avoid **bandwagon appeals** that argue that everyone believes something, so the reader should, too.

   Example: All the professors I spoke to in the political science department favor the trade agreement with Japan, so it must be a good idea.

   Explanation: The issue should be argued on the merits of the trade agreement, not on the basis of who favors it.

10. Do not assume that an event that precedes another event is the cause of that event. This is called a **post-hoc fallacy.**

    Example: After students read *The Catcher in the Rye,* the number of teen pregnancies in our school increased. The book causes promiscuity.

    Explanation: Although the pregnancies followed the reading of the book, other factors may have caused the increase in the pregnancy rate.

11. Do not digress from the matter at hand by introducing a distraction, called a **red herring.**

    Example: We should not spend more money on AIDS research because so many AIDS victims chose to put themselves at risk.

    Explanation: The behavior of some people who contract AIDS is not the issue but a distraction (red herring) meant to direct the reader's attention away from the issue—whether more money should be spent on AIDS research.

EXERCISE Recognizing Logical Fallacies

Directions: Each of the following includes one or more logical fallacies. Identify what they are.

1. The proposed assisted-living facility is an unnecessary expenditure of public funds. The elderly in this city have always been cared for by family members or in nursing homes.
2. Those who favor school prayer are the same reactionaries who bomb abortion clinics.

3. The last generation has seen a marked increase in the number of working mothers, which explains the similar increase in the rate of violent crime.
4. Because football players care less about their schoolwork than their sport, the university should eliminate athletic scholarships.
5. How can any union member not vote for Chris Politician? After all, every major labor group in the country has endorsed him. ■

Emotional Appeals

Sound logic and compelling reasons and evidence will help you argue your claim by appealing to your readers' rational side. However, logical appeals are not all that influence a person—emotion also plays a role. After all, when we make up our minds about something, how we *feel* about the issue, along with what we *think* about it, can influence our decision. For this reason, charities that seek your money often include heart-wrenching pictures of hungry children along with their request. The pictures are calculated to move your emotions.

Emotional appeals focus on readers' values and needs. For example, the belief that anyone who is willing to work hard can get ahead is a fundamental American value. To appeal to this value, an essay arguing for the election of Chris Politician can mention that Politician grew up in poverty, worked during high school to help pay the rent, and made it through college by working three jobs to pay tuition. This appeal to readers' values makes Politician seem to embody a core American virtue—the willingness to work hard to advance oneself.

Emotional appeals also focus on needs. For example, human beings need to feel attractive. Thus, the writer of a toothpaste advertisement may claim that using the product results in fewer cavities *and* a brighter smile. Our intellect makes us understand the importance of fewer cavities, so that is an appeal to logic. However, our emotional need to be attractive makes us want a brighter smile.

The toothpaste advertisement illustrates that together, logical and emotional appeals can be more convincing than either appeal would be alone. However, a critical reader will recognize when emotional appeals are the sole or primary thrust of an argument and become wary. While an appeal to emotions can be both effective and appropriate, it cannot replace appeals to logic.

To appreciate the persuasive quality of emotional appeals, consider an essay that argues the claim that young children should not be playing organized baseball. In addition to giving reasons and evidence, the essay can include this emotional appeal to the reader's desire to protect children from emotional distress:

> To me, there is nothing more heartbreaking than watching a 6- or 7-year-old baseball player crying because he just struck out, he missed the ball, or he got yelled at by his manager. I guess I'm old-fashioned—I prefer games that make children laugh and leave them smiling.

Ethical Appeals

No matter how strong your support is, you cannot convince a reader who does not trust you. To earn your reader's trust, you must establish your authority and present yourself as reliable. Doing so enables you to come across as ethical. For a strong ethical appeal, present compelling reasons and evidence, write a well-reasoned argument that avoids logical fallacies, and avoid overusing emotional appeals. In addition, if you have knowledge or experiences that particularly qualify you to write about your subject, mention them. For example, if you are arguing that nursing homes should be required to install surveillance cameras in patients' rooms to help prevent abuse, you can explain that you have volunteered in a nursing home for five years and have firsthand knowledge of the need for the surveillance.

Two other important strategies for appealing to readers' ethics are raising and countering objections, and creating goodwill.

Raising and Countering Objections

No matter what claim you make about an issue, some reasonable people will disagree with you. Ignoring their opposing views will weaken your position because you will not come across as someone who has weighed all sides before drawing conclusions. However, if you acknowledge and come to terms with the most significant arguments on the other side, you help incline your reader to accept your claim because it appears more carefully thought out. Further, even if you ignore the opposition's points, your reader will have them in mind. To be convincing, then, you must deal with the chief objections head-on to dispel some of your reader's disagreement. The process of acknowledging and coming to terms with opposing views is called **raising and countering objections.**

Raising and countering objections is a two-part operation. First, state the opposition's point; this is *raising the objection.* Then, make the point less compelling by introducing a point of your own; this is *countering the objection.*

Let's return to the paper written to convince a reader to vote for Chris Politician to see how raising and countering objections works. Your first step is to identify your reader's most compelling objections. Let's say they are these:

- Politician lacks experience in city government.
- Politician's proposed safety forces budget is inflationary.
- Politician's health problems will undermine his effectiveness.

After identifying the chief objections, you must lessen their force in one of two ways: by offering an equally compelling point of your own to balance out the opposition or by showing that the opposition's point is untrue. Here are some examples:

Offering an equally compelling point

> Some people claim that Politician's lack of experience in municipal government will make him a poor city manager. (*objection raised*) Although he has not

had actual experience in city government, 10 years as president of City Bank have provided Politician with all the managerial skills any mayor could need. Furthermore, our current mayor, who came to the job with five years of experience on the City Council, has mismanaged everything from Street Department funds to the city's public relations efforts. Thus, experience in city government does not guarantee success. *(objection countered)*

Although some contend that the increased safety forces budget that Politician supports is inflationary, *(objection raised)* the fact remains that without adequate police and fire protection, we will not attract new industry to our area. *(objection countered)*

Showing that the opposition's point is untrue

Some of Politician's detractors say that he is not well enough to do the job. *(objection raised)* However, Politician's physical examination last month shows he is in perfect health, and any discussion to the contrary is based on rumor and falsehood. *(objection countered)*

As the examples show, an objection is sometimes countered in a single sentence and sometimes in several sentences. If an objection is particularly compelling, you may need to devote one or more paragraphs to countering it. Usually, you need not raise and counter every objection to your claim. You can identify your reader's most important objections and deal with those.

EXERCISE Raising and Countering Objections

Directions: Select one of the following claims, and assume your audience is members of the local school board. Write out two likely objections to the claim. Then explain a strategy for countering each objection.

- High school seniors should be required to pass a proficiency test in order to graduate.
- High school seniors should not be required to pass a proficiency test in order to graduate. ■

Creating Goodwill

If your audience includes hostile or wavering readers, your ethical appeal should create some goodwill between you and them. No matter how misguided you think their views are, a confrontational stance will only alienate these readers further, making it harder for you to achieve your persuasive purpose. However, establishing some common ground can make it easier for them to consider your claim objectively. Suppose you are arguing for mandatory drug testing of high school students. You can establish common ground with hostile or wavering readers by noting that you both want to ensure the safety and well-being of young people. Once your readers recognize that you share a goal, you are positioned closer together and have less opposition to overcome.

A second way to create goodwill is to demonstrate that you understand your reader's viewpoint and take it seriously. Doing so validates your reader's view and makes that person less defensive and less inclined to dig in and hold fast to a position at all costs. For example, when arguing for mandatory drug testing of teenagers, you could say something like this to show that you understand and respect your reader's view: "Mandatory drug testing does raise important privacy issues and presents a challenge to the Bill of Rights, facts that make the issue a particularly thorny one."

Using the Patterns of Development

The patterns of development will help you present the logical, emotional, and ethical appeals that support your claim. The following chart demonstrates the usefulness of the patterns by showing some of the ways a writer can use them in an essay arguing the claim that voters should elect Chris Politician.

Using the Patterns of Development to Argue a Claim

Claim: Voters Should Elect Chris Politician

Support	Pattern
Politician will eliminate the downtown blight.	**Describe** the blight so readers appreciate the importance of eliminating it.
Politician has integrity.	**Narrate** an account of a time Politician showed integrity.
Politician is a creative problem solver.	Give **examples** of problems Politician has solved creatively.
Politician has a plan for reducing the city's deficit.	Use **process analysis** to explain how the plan works.
Politician is better qualified than his opponent.	**Compare and contrast** the qualifications of Politician and the opponent.
Politician has powerful connections in state government.	Use **cause-and-effect analysis** to explain the benefits of having connections in state government.
Politician is a political sophisticate.	**Define** *political sophisticate*, so readers understand the importance of being one.
Politician would be an exemplary mayor.	Use **classification-division** to explain the components of being mayor and show that Politician has those components.

USING SOURCES FOR A PURPOSE

Below is a body paragraph for an essay arguing for a complete ban on torture. To help support the thesis, the paragraph, which includes a long quotation from paragraph 11 of "Torture Warrants?" on page 458, raises and counters the objection that occasional torture is acceptable if torture warrants are issued. (For more information on writing quotations, see Chapter 17.)

The writer uses the long quotation to counter the objection that torture warrants will reduce the frequency of torture. The sentence after the long quote makes explicit the point to be drawn from the quotation. Note the use of "brutal" to help make clear the writer's view of torture.

THESIS IDEA: The United States should adopt as policy a complete ban on the use of torture.

WRITING PURPOSE AND AUDIENCE: To convince general readers that the United States should ban torture

[1]Some people think the way around the torture debate is to call for court approval for torture by requiring officials to secure a "torture warrant" before brutalizing someone in custody. [2]Those who favor torture warrants don't really favor their routine use. [3]They are more likely to find torture necessary under extreme circumstances and, therefore, advocate for the use of warrants only infrequently. [4]These people believe that torture warrants will reduce the frequency with which torture is used, but they should heed Harvey A. Silverglate's argument:

> [5][I]nstitutionalizing torture will give it society's imprimatur, lending it a degree of respectability. [6]It will then be virtually impossible to curb not only the increasing frequency with which warrants

An argument essay often will draw on multiple patterns of development. For example, to convince people to vote for Chris Politician, you might give examples of problems Politician has solved creatively, contrast his qualifications with those of his opponent, and explain the effects of his connections in state government.

BEING A RESPONSIBLE WRITER

Responsible writers use emotional appeals fairly and with restraint. They do not play on a reader's vulnerabilities to manipulate emotions in order to achieve their purpose. Thus, as a responsible writer, you can call upon the reader's patriotism to earn support for defense spending, but you should not whip up emotions by saying that anyone who does not support the spending is un-American and supports terrorists. To do so is unfair, untrue, and inflammatory. It also preys on the reader's fear of undermining the country's safety.

will be sought—and granted—but also the inevitable rise in *unauthorized* use of torture. [7]Unauthorized torture will increase not only to extract life-saving information, but also to obtain confessions (many of which will then prove false). [8]It will also be used to punish real or imagined infractions, or for no reason other than human sadism. (459–60)

[9]As Silverglate's argument shows, torture warrants are no substitute for banning torture outright.

Avoiding Plagiarism

The paragraph illustrates several points about using source material and avoiding plagiarism.

- **Know how to handle a long quotation.** A long quotation is one that runs more than four typed lines in your paper. As sentences 5–8 illustrate, double-space a long quotation and indent it instead of using quotation marks. Do not indent the first word more than the rest, even if it begins a paragraph in the source. Place the parenthetical citation after the final period. As sentence 4 shows, follow the introduction with a colon.
- **Reproduce italics in a quotation.** When words appear in italics in the source, duplicate those italics in your quotation, as sentence 6 illustrates.

Myths about Sources

MYTH: If you copy material from the Internet and paste it into your paper, you do not have to document the material.

FACT: Material copied and pasted from the Internet is treated the same way as material taken from print sources. Document it according to the conventions explained in Chapter 17.

To be a responsible writer, ask yourself these questions when you appeal to your reader's emotions:

- What aspect of my reader's emotions, values, or needs am I appealing to?
- Is it fair to appeal to this aspect, or am I taking advantage of a vulnerability?
- Is my emotional appeal only a small part of my supporting detail?

ORGANIZING AN ARGUMENT ESSAY

The thesis for an argument essay expresses your issue and claim. The issue must be debatable, and your claim must express your stand on the issue. Here are two examples:

Thesis: Because rottweilers and pit bulls have a history of attacking people without provocation, private citizens should be prohibited from owning these dog breeds.

Issue: Owning rottweilers and pit bulls

Claim: Private citizens should not be allowed to own these breeds.

Thesis: In order to graduate with a bachelor's degree, all college students should be tested for proficiency in a foreign language.

Issue: Graduation requirements

Claim: Bachelor's degree candidates should be tested for foreign language proficiency.

Your introduction can be written with any of the strategies explained beginning on page 75. In particular, you can engage your reader's interest by showing why your issue is important. For example, if you are arguing that college students should be required to become proficient in a foreign language, you could explain that globalization demands that we find ways to understand each other better, and speaking each others' language helps achieve that goal.

If you possess particular qualifications for writing about the issue, you can mention them in your introduction as part of your ethical appeal. For example, if you want to convince your reader that private citizens should not be allowed to own rottweilers and pit bulls, you can explain in your introduction that you were a volunteer at an animal shelter for five years and learned a great deal about the breeds.

To organize your body paragraphs, you must consider how best to combine several elements:

- Your pattern of reasoning—whether you are using induction or deduction
- Your reasons and evidence
- Your patterns of development
- The objections you raise and counter, and other ethical appeals you make
- Your emotional appeals

If all or part of your argument involves inductive or deductive reasoning (or a combination of these), follow the progression characteristic of that pattern of reasoning. If you are following an inductive pattern, you will present your specific evidence and follow it with a conclusion drawn from that evidence. If you are following a deductive pattern, you will write a major premise, follow it with a minor premise, and then write the conclusion.

For your reasons and evidence, a progressive order from the least to the most compelling point is effective because the force of your argument builds gradually. To help your reader follow your argument, you can state each reason in a topic sentence. If you develop evidence with a particular pattern of development, use the order best suited to the pattern. Thus, narration and process analysis will follow a chronological order, and comparison-contrast will follow a subject-by-subject or point-by-point order.

As part of your organizational strategy, you will need to determine the most effective place to raise and counter objections. Most often, you can raise and counter at the points where the objections logically emerge. Suppose you are arguing that children should not be allowed to play with toy guns, and you explain that violent play leads to violent behavior. At that point, you can raise and counter the objection that playing with toy guns can serve to vent violent tendencies harmlessly and thus reduce violent behavior.

If your claim is an unpopular one, with many objections to it, you might want to raise the objections in your introduction or first body paragraphs. Then the rest of your essay can counter the objections. This strategy might be effective, for example, if you are arguing the unpopular claim that military service should be required of all 18-year-olds. You could explain all the reasons people are opposed to such military service and then go on to show why your claim is more compelling.

Ethical and emotional appeals can be placed where they will have the most strategic value for your argument. If a particular emotional appeal creates a strong ending, place it in your last body paragraph or in your conclusion. If explaining why you are qualified to write on the issue is important for persuading a wavering reader, include that information in the introduction or first body paragraph.

You can conclude with any of the strategies explained in Chapter 3. Often it is effective to restate your claim about the issue to emphasize it. If you include many arguments, you can summarize them in the conclusion. Finally, you can craft an effective conclusion by calling your reader to action, recommending a solution to a problem, or explaining what would happen if your claim were not adopted.

EXERCISE Analyzing an Argument

Directions: Alone or with two classmates (as your instructor directs), select an editorial that makes an argument from your local or campus newspaper. Analyze the chief strengths and weaknesses of the editorial. Consider the following:

- How clearly the issue and claim are stated
- The logical appeals
- The sources of reasons and evidence
- The emotional appeals
- The ethical appeals
- Whether the editorial achieves its purpose ■

LEARNING FROM OTHER WRITERS: Student Essays

The next three argument essays were written by students. The reasons and evidence in all of them come from the writers' experience or observation and their thoughtful consideration of the issues. In addition, the third essay includes research that helps support the writer's claim.

In "It's Just Too Easy," Michael Weiss argues that we should make it more difficult for teenagers to get driver's licenses. The essay is annotated as a study aid. First, the author argues that a particular problem exists. Then, he argues for the adoption of his solution. Be sure to notice the appeal to ethics in the essay.

www.mhhe.com/tsw

For more examples of student argument essays, go to Catalyst 2.0 > Writing > Writing Samples > Sample Argument Papers

Visualizing an Argument Essay

The chart that follows can help you visualize one structure for an argument essay. Like all good models, this one can be altered as needed.

Introduction

- Creates interest, perhaps by explaining why the issue is important, by providing necessary background information, or by giving your qualifications
- May state objections that will be countered in your essay
- States the thesis, which includes the issue and claim

First Body Paragraph

- May give a reason to support your claim and evidence to back up your reason
- May raise and counter an objection, create goodwill, or appeal to emotions
- May include ethical appeals
- May include other patterns of development
- May arrange details in a progressive order, an inductive order, a deductive order, or any order appropriate to the pattern used

Next Body Paragraphs

- Continue until all the reasons, evidence, and other supporting details are given
- May raise and counter objections, create goodwill, or appeal to emotions
- May include ethical appeals
- May include other patterns of development
- May arrange details in a progressive order, an inductive order, a deductive order, or any order appropriate to the pattern used

Conclusion

- May restate your claim
- May summarize the arguments
- May call your reader to action, recommend a solution to a problem, or explain what will happen if your claim is or is not adopted

In "What's for Lunch? Fast Food in the Public Schools," Cheryl Sateri argues her claim that fast-food restaurants have a place in high schools. Her supporting details are mostly reasons backed up by evidence.

In "Should Obscene Art Be Funded by the Government?" Mary E. Fischer argues inductively that the federal government should not restrict funds to the National Endowment for the Arts. When you read this selection, pay careful attention to how the research material helps the writer achieve her persuasive purpose. You will learn more about research, and researched writing, in the following chapters.

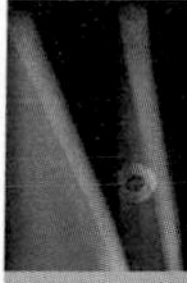

It's Just Too Easy

Michael Weiss

1 As their adolescent children approach driving age, parents lie awake at night staring at the ceiling. Why? Terror keeps them awake and wide-eyed. Sure, the convenience of having an extra driver around to run to the drugstore, pick up little Sally at her dance lesson, and swing by the dry cleaners sounds heavenly, yet the appeal of the extra driver is offset by the sobering reality that driving poses a threat to the safety of teenagers and those around them. It was explained to me by one of my driver's education instructors that teenagers cause a disproportionate number of accidents. Although they represent only 7 percent of the drivers on the road, they are responsible for 16 percent of all accidents and 14 percent of all fatal crashes. I would not have admitted this when I got my own license and began to drive a few years ago, but in the interest of everybody's safety, we need tough guidelines for licensing teenage drivers.

Paragraph 1
The introduction creates interest with images of parents, and it demonstrates the importance of the issue with statistics on teen accidents from the testimony of an authority. The thesis is the last sentence. It includes the issue (licensing teenage drivers) and the claim (the guidelines for granting licenses should be tough).

2 Immediately, teenagers and others are probably thinking that this is a classic case of discrimination, that young people are not inherently worse drivers than people in any other age group and should not be singled out. Of course, teenagers have all the natural ability to be as safe as anyone else on the road (and maybe even safer than the octogenarians out there driving), but they do lack experience behind the wheel, and that is what causes their accidents. The standards I am proposing will do nothing more than give teens the experience they need to be among the safest motorists out there.

Paragraph 2
This paragraph raises an objection in the first sentence (the topic sentence) and counters it in the rest of the paragraph with an equally compelling point. This paragraph explains part of the problem: Teens lack driving experience.

3 When I got my driver's license, it was a joke. The day of my sixteenth birthday, I took a written test so easy that an impaired chimpanzee would have passed. I did not even study, and I got a 90 percent. That entitled me to get a learner's permit for a modest fee. Now I could drive anywhere, anytime, as long as I was with a licensed driver. My parents were strict, so I could only drive with them or my driver's ed instructor, but many of my friends were out driving with older brothers and sisters (not older by much) and with other friends. It was the blind leading the blind because the licensed drivers were only barely

Paragraph 3
The first sentence is the topic sentence. This paragraph includes personal experience to demonstrate part of the problem: Getting a license is currently too easy. Evidence is developed with narration. Note the inductive reasoning.

more experienced than the ones with the learner's permits. To get my real license, I took six hours of driver's education. I had three teachers who rotated taking me out on the road. One of them was a loser who was just one rung above a derelict. We went out three times, two hours at a time, and bingo I was allowed to take my driver's test. I passed—barely. Next thing I knew, I was licensed and on the road anytime I could wheedle the car out of my parents. Although I did not know it then, I was no more ready to drive than to be an astronaut.

Paragraph 4
This paragraph uses the author's experience and that of others to continue to prove that there is a problem: Teens have accidents and do not drive safely. Evidence is developed with exemplification.

Soon my friends and I were having accidents, nothing serious, but they could have been. I rear-ended a van on an exit ramp. My best friend got a speeding ticket. His girlfriend changed lanes, cut off a pickup, and narrowly escaped injury. Others I know had freeway collisions, parking lot fender-benders, and various moving violations. We were all accidents waiting to happen because we had no experience and no appreciation for the damage we could inflict. What I am proposing would give teenagers more driving experience before they strike out on their own, and it would help them better appreciate what it means to drive. 4

Paragraph 5
The last two sentences raise and counter an objection. The counter is an equally compelling point. Paragraphs 1–4 argue that there is a problem; paragraphs 5–8 argue for a solution. Note that the solution is specific and detailed. Evidence also includes the reasons the solution would work.

First, the test for securing a learner's permit should be rigorous. In addition to covering all rules of the road and all traffic signs, it should present various driving scenarios and ask what the proper response should be. Passing this test should not be easy. People should have to study, and they should have to score in the 90s. Then, we could be sure that people who get their learner's permit at least have a certain basic knowledge. Some people might think this test would be unfair to people who are not very bright and have trouble taking tests. Is it any more fair to put unknowledgeable people behind the wheels of cars, where their lack of information could cause injury and death? 5

Paragraphs 6–8
Note the use of cause-and-effect analysis to show what would happen if the writer's solution were adopted.

Once a teenager has a learner's permit, he or she should have to have a great deal of experience behind the wheel before being permitted to take the test for a permanent license. At least 20 hours would not be unreasonable, with at least five hours at night and five hours on a busy highway or interstate. This requirement would help ensure that teens are experienced in a variety of 6 driving situations and know what to do and how to respond in tricky driving situations. Even better would be to increase the requirement to 22 hours and require two hours of driving in inclement weather—rain, snow, fog, and so forth. This way young drivers could learn about handling skids, driving on wet pavement, increasing stopping time, and all the other precautions necessary in less-than-ideal conditions.

Until they have their permanent licenses, teenagers should not be able to drive with anyone other than a parent, guardian, driver's education instructor, or person over 21. This requirement would serve two purposes. First, it would help ensure that teens were getting their driving hours in with responsible, experienced drivers. Second, it would encourage more parental involvement in the driver's education process. 7

Finally, passing the actual driving test should be difficult. Teenagers should have to demonstrate ability on the highway, in heavily trafficked areas, and at night. They should also demonstrate the ability to maneuver a car in tight areas, operate safely in reverse, and park. If they can do that, then we will be putting more experienced, capable drivers on the road. 8

Young people are at risk today from so many sources, including drugs, alcohol, stress, street violence, and broken homes. Anything we can do to protect them should be a top priority. Of course, on the road, teens are not the only ones at risk. With tougher requirements for getting a driver's license, we can protect young drivers and everybody else in a vehicle. 9

Paragraph 9
The conclusion includes an emotional appeal and a restatement of the thesis.

What's for Lunch? Fast Food in the Public Schools

Cheryl Sateri

Americans are getting fatter. Statistics and studies are not needed to prove this observation. The news media are full of stories about people suing McDonald's for making them fat, and the local mall is crowded with people who probably shouldn't "supersize" their next meal. Out of concern for the health of young 1 people, some parents at the high school I attended tried to force healthy eating habits on students by removing snack-food and soda vending machines from the student lunchroom. These same parents are also opposing the local school board's efforts to contract with a fast-food franchise to take over part of the food service at the high school lunchroom. However, I believe that a fast-food restaurant can provide a convenient, profitable service that will improve the diets of high school students.

Lunchtime at my former high school (and probably at most public high schools around the country) was never a leisurely, relaxing meal. Each grade had lunch for a thirty-minute period. Students stood in line for fifteen or twenty minutes waiting for some warmed-over "pizza" or "burrito," which they then had to gulp down as fast as possible. A fast-food franchise, which likely has the experience and the equipment to serve many people quickly and efficiently, would eliminate the unreasonable wait. 2

A fast-food franchise would also offer greater variety and healthier choices. 3 In my school cafeteria, fresh vegetables and fruits were rarely offered, but fatty, sauce-drenched mystery casseroles were. The only drinks were tiny cartons of warm milk and sugary juice drinks. However, the McDonald's franchise in my college student union offers ice-cold milk in large cartons, yogurt, fresh fruit, crispy salads, and grilled chicken sandwiches. Although I don't know what franchise would eventually move into my former high school, the school board could make healthy choices and variety a condition of the contract.

Along with vending machines, a fast-food franchise in the student lunch- 4 room would keep student dollars on campus, since a portion of the profits would be returned to the school. At my high school, everyone looked forward to senior year because of off-campus lunch privileges (most seniors in good standing had a free period immediately after lunch). If students were not currently serving a detention, they were allowed to leave the building to purchase lunch. Of course, everyone walked two blocks up to the KFC or the Subway and spent their money there. If seniors could purchase such food on campus, a percentage of the money now spent off campus would go to the school's student activity funds. During my senior year, funds from the vending machines helped to pay for the Club Latino's trip to Mexico. Additional funds from a franchise could help pay for more after-school sports programs or for renovating the gym, which would benefit the health of students.

The current school lunch program is not providing convenient, healthy 5
choices for students, nor is it helping students have a pleasant, leisurely lunch. Of course, if the food in the cafeteria were improved, vending machines and a franchise restaurant would be unnecessary. However, this would cost money, and since there is never enough money to reduce class size, I do not see the school board putting in a salad bar any time soon. As an alternative, a fast-food restaurant is an option that benefits everyone.

EXERCISE Considering "What's for Lunch? Fast Food in the Public Schools"

1. What is the thesis of "What's for Lunch? Fast Food in the Public Schools"? What does the thesis state as the issue? As the writer's claim?
2. Which paragraph presents a problem and then argues for a particular solution? How does that strategy help the writer argue her claim?
3. What objection does the writer raise? How does she counter the objection? Does she effectively soften the objection? Explain. Should any other objections be raised and countered?
4. Does the author give enough reasons with enough evidence? Explain.
5. Does the essay include inductive reasoning, deductive reasoning, or both?
6. What element of ethical appeal exists in the essay? ■

Student Essay with Research

Should Obscene Art Be Funded by the Government?

Mary E. Fischer

Knowledge of music, literature, painting, and sculpture is fundamental to 1
understanding culture, for the art we produce reflects our society. Recognizing art's importance, Congress established the National Endowment for the Arts (NEA)

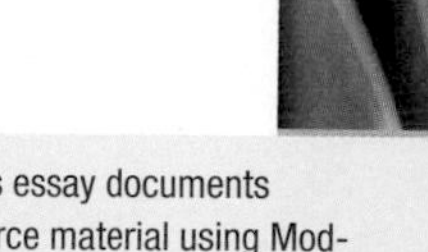

This essay documents source material using Modern Language Association (MLA) style, explained on pages 506–26.

in 1965 to fund artistic organizations. Over the years, this funding has been crucial to many ballets, concerts, and gallery showings. In fact, the funding has been the key to the survival of many museums and other arts organizations.

In the last few years, a number of lifestyles outside the mainstream have become more visible, even more accepted. These include homosexuality, promiscuity, and what is euphemistically called "alternative lifestyles." As we would expect, artists have begun to portray these lifestyles in their work. However, some have deemed these artworks obscene, and they have asked whether taxpayers have an obligation to fund these "obscene" artworks. But what is "obscene"? This topic is repeatedly addressed in Congress, and as William Olcott explains in "Senate Cuts NEA Funds," in 1989 the U.S. Senate took action: 2

> [The Senate] approved restrictions proposed by [North Carolina Senator] Jesse Helms that would prohibit federal funds from being used to "promote, disseminate, or produce obscene or indecent materials, including but not limited to depictions of sadomasochism, homoeroticism, the exploitation of children or individuals engaged in sex acts; or material which denigrates the objects or beliefs of the adherents of a particular religion or nonreligion; or material that denigrates, debases, or reviles a person, group, or class of citizens on the basis of race, creed, sex, handicap, age, or national origin." (8)

On March 31, 1998, the Clinton Justice Department argued before the Supreme Court concerning a standard for awarding grants by the NEA. According to Martin Garbus in "The Indecent Standard," the Supreme Court concluded that "the art must meet general standards of decency and respect for the diverse beliefs and values of the American public" (7). Yet this standard is vague. What are these standards of decency and who is to set them? Many artists and organizations are outraged by these restrictions. They question the qualifications of the government to judge artistic merit. In fact, many of these artists and organizations have protested the restrictions by not applying for or 3 accepting NEA grants. They maintain that the very idea that restrictions are set is a violation of our fundamental rights as United States citizens.

Many people believe that government funding of obscene art should be restricted. According to Irving Kristol in "Offensive Art Should Not Be Funded by the Government," the NEA was founded in a different time, and the fact that the role of art in American life has changed should be considered (30-33). The popular argument states that artists of today are abusing their freedom of expression. In contrast to a time when patrons dictated the creation of art, the artist dictates today's art. This artistic dictatorship may be an important advancement in the history of art, but this art is no longer intended for the public. So why should the public be expected to fund something that its members may not agree with? Many say that it is time for this obscene art to be stopped, at least if it is produced at society's expense. Although the elimination of the NEA may violate our fundamental rights, the argument continues, who considers the rights of the people who are forced to fund it? 4

Kristol makes some valid points; however, the argument in support of funding obscene art is more compelling. By restricting funding of obscene art, the government is practicing censorship and thus violating our rights, by dictating what the artist can say. In actuality it is saying that artists are free to express themselves, but it will not support this freedom financially. In this respect the government is dictating to society exactly what art is acceptable. Is Congress qualified to judge this artwork? Too often people interpret artwork as obscene without taking into account the moral and political reflections that it offers. For example, Andres Serrano's photograph entitled "Piss Christ" was merely seen as a crucifix submerged in the artist's urine. At first glance, this may be true, but upon deeper reflection, one realizes that it is making a statement about the commercialization of Christianity. Perhaps if people were more educated about the artwork and its interpretation, they would not jump to false conclusions. 5

In the article "Congress Should Fund the NEA without Restrictions," Major R. Owens states that with help from the media, the problem surrounding the 6 funding of the NEA has been blown out of proportion (62-64). The NEA is responsible for the success of many cultural events throughout this country. Without this program, people in small towns as well as large cities would not have the opportunity to participate in events that improve the quality of their lives. The NEA aids in funding children's television programs and art education programs, as well as children's art festivals, thus making it possible to learn about self-expression, creativity, and self-esteem through the arts.

Furthermore, of all art produced in America, only a small percentage is 7
considered obscene or questionable. According to John E. Frohnmayer, the former chairman of the NEA, only 30 of the 95,000 grants that have been awarded have been considered controversial (58). If people take offense to this art, they have the freedom to avoid it. The vast majority of artwork is not considered obscene and is freely available to all who oppose controversial art. Why should the minority be penalized? Even if a person's beliefs do not coincide with the belief of the majority, does he or she not have the right of self-expression? By penalizing the minority, we are contradicting the fundamental ideas that our country was founded upon.

As one scholar reminds us, our founding fathers encouraged governmental 8
support of the arts and humanities. George Washington called for the establishment of a national university, and Thomas Jefferson, among others well versed in art, helped to legislate funds for centers of scholarship and learning (Frohnmayer 57-58). Our country is built on the foundation of freedom. The art that is produced will reflect our diverse society. We must not fear new or different ways of expression if we are to grow as a society.

The artist's purpose is to explore and express ideas, however unpopular 9
they may be. Art is intended to appeal to the senses and emotions as well. As humans, we experience emotions other than happiness and contentment. Hate, fear, insecurity, lust, jealousy, and revulsion deserve a proper depiction, recognition, and celebration as well. The very fact that a particular work of art disgusts an onlooker indicates that the purpose of the artwork is fulfilled. In a land where we deem liberty sacred, we should support the

artist's right to create and express and welcome any and all explanations of the art. All in all, art brings communities together. The NEA is a fundamental institution that educates and brings opportunities to people who would otherwise have few chances to appreciate art, music, and the performing arts. Restricting funding to the NEA would have devastating effects on our growth as a society.

Works Cited

Frohnmayer, John E. "The Content of Art Should Not Influence Government Funding." *Free Speech.* Ed. Bruno Leone. San Diego: Greenhaven, 1994. 57-61. Print.

Garbus, Martin. "The Indecent Standard." *The Nation. Academic Search Premier,* 13 April 1998. Web. 17 Nov. 2008.

Kristol, Irving. "Offensive Art Should Not Be Funded by the Government." *Free Speech.* Ed. Bruno Leone. San Diego: Greenhaven, 1994. 30-33. Print.

Olcott, William. "Senate Cuts NEA Funds." *Fund Raising Management* 20.7 (1989): 8. *ProQuest Central*. Web. 14 Nov. 2008.

Owens, Major R. "Congress Should Fund the NEA without Restrictions." *Free Speech.* Ed. Bruno Leone. San Diego: Greenhaven, 1994. 62-64. Print.

The list of works cited should appear on a separate page.

EXERCISE Considering "Should Obscene Art Be Funded by the Government?"

1. What is the thesis of the essay? What is the issue, and what is the claim?
2. How does the research material help the author achieve her persuasive purpose? What does it contribute to her logical appeals? To her ethical appeals?
3. How does the author appeal to her readers' emotions? Does that emotional appeal help her achieve her persuasive purpose? Why or why not?
4. Do you think a wavering reader would be persuaded by the essay? What about a hostile reader? Explain.
5. What is the purpose of the first three paragraphs? Are these paragraphs important? Explain. ■

THINK LIKE A CRITIC; WORK LIKE AN EDITOR: The Student Writer at Work

When he wrote the early drafts of "It's Just Too Easy," Michael Weiss put most of his energy into paragraphs 5–8, the ones that argue for his solution to the problem of how easy it is for teenagers to get a driver's license. A classmate who read the early draft felt that Michael didn't prove that there really *was* a problem. The classmate said that Michael needed more evidence. Here, for example, is an early draft of paragraph 3:

Early draft of paragraph 3

> When I got my driver's license, it was a joke. The day of my sixteenth birthday, I took a ridiculously easy test and got a learner's permit. Now I could drive as long as I was with a licensed driver. My parents were strict, so I could only drive with them or my driver's ed instructor, but many of my friends were out driving with older brothers and sisters and with other friends. To get my real license, I took only six hours of driver's education and then a driver's test, which I passed. Next thing I knew, I was licensed and on the road anytime I could get the car.

Michael worked to address the issue his classmate raised. He added evidence that he thought proved the existence of the problem. What do you think of his final version of paragraph 3? Is it convincing enough now? What about the other paragraphs that argue that the problem exists? Are they convincing?

LEARNING FROM OTHER WRITERS: Professional Essays

Why I Dread Black History Month WAYNE M. JOSEPH

In this essay, which first appeared in 1994 in Newsweek, *middle school principal Wayne M. Joseph argues that Black History Month misses the point that black history cannot be separated from American history.*

Every year when the month of February approaches, I'm overcome with a feeling of dread. February is hailed as Black History Month, a national observance that is celebrated neither at the school in which I am the principal nor in my own home. This may come as a surprise to the even casual observer, since I am black. In my humble estimation Black History Month is a thriving monument to tokenism which, ironically, has been wholeheartedly embraced and endorsed by the black community. 1

For at least 28 days we are bombarded by the media with reminders of great black Americans. Teachers across America dust off last year's lesson plans and speak of African kings and queens. Dr. Martin Luther King's "I Have a Dream" speech is played repeatedly and there are festivities where people wear traditional African garb and may even speak a few words of Swahili. 2

So, you might ask, what is wrong with this? 3

Black contribution to American history is so rich and varied that attempting to confine the discussion and investigation to four weeks a year tends to trivialize the momentous impact that blacks have had on American society. 4

There is also a tendency to somehow feel that "black" history is separate from "*American*" history. "Black" history *is* American history—they are not mutually exclusive. The struggles of black people in America strike at the core of our country's past and its development. One cannot, for instance, hope to thoroughly study the factors leading to the Civil War or Reconstruction without investigating the issue of slavery and the emancipation of those slaves. American music and dance has little significance without the recognition of black influences. Spirituals, jazz, and the blues are a vital and important part of American culture. To speak of the experience of black people in America (as some are inclined to do during the month of February) as independent of the American social, political, and economic forces at work in our country is a misreading of history at best and a flagrant attempt to rewrite it at worst. 5

Of course very few people will be courageous enough during February to say that it's irrelevant whether or not Cleopatra and Jesus were black, since their experiences have not the slightest kinship with those of black Americans. 6

It is not very difficult to understand why the distant (usually African) past is used as a way to give blacks a sense of cultural identity. In the final analysis, however, it's a hollow attempt to fill a vacuum that was created by the institution of slavery. It is widely acknowledged that one of the more insidious aspects of American slavery was that Africans of different cultures and languages were stripped of their cultural base and were forced to learn the enslaver's tongue to survive. Unlike the German, Italian, and Jewish immigrants who came to this country with their own languages, religions, and customs, Africans of different backgrounds were compelled to eschew their own roots in order to survive on American soil. 7

Slavery and Segregation

Instead of African kings and queens who never set foot in America, it is the black people who survived the infamous "middle passage" and endured slavery who should be heralded as "kings" and "queens" for their courage and perseverance. After slavery, there were scores of blacks who endured beatings, lynchings, and daily degradations indigenous to the system of discrimination in both the North and the South; yet these paragons of endurance are seldom lauded. It's as if the words "slavery" and "segregation" are to be mentioned only fleetingly during February. We should look to our own grandfathers and grandmothers to find examples of real heroism. Unfortunately, the significance of these black men and women as well as the traditional black icons—Dr. King, Malcolm X, Jackie Robinson, et al.—are lost in a month in which people are studied in isolation instead of within the historical context that produced them. 8

Black parents must try to instill in children a sense of their own history. This should include a sense of family—the accomplishments of parents, grandparents, and ancestors have more relevance than some historical figure whose only connection to the child is skin color. We in the schools are often expected to fill the gaps that parents have neglected in their child's development; but for every child a knowledge of identity and self-worth must come from home to be meaningful and long-lasting. For the black child, a month-long emphasis on black culture will never fill that void. 9

There will be those, I'm sure, who will say that I should feel pleased that black people are recognized one month out of the year, knowing the difficulty black Americans have historically encountered validating their accomplishments. But being black does not entitle one to more or less recognition based solely on heritage. In a multicultural society, there is a need to celebrate our cultural differences as well as our commonalities as human beings. No one group has a monopoly on this need. 10

One month out of every year, Americans are "given permission" to commemorate the achievements of black people. This rather condescending view fails to acknowledge that a people and a country's past should be nurtured and revered; instead, at this time, the past of black Americans is handled in an expedient and cavalier fashion denigrating the very people it seeks to honor. 11

February is here again, and I'll be approached by a black student or parent inquiring as to what the school is doing to celebrate Black History Month. My answer, as always, will be that my teachers and I celebrate the contributions of *all* Americans *every* month of the school year. 12

Considering Ideas

1. What reasons does Joseph give for his opposition to Black History Month?
2. Do you find the evidence that backs up Joseph's reasons to be convincing? Why or why not?
3. Do you think Joseph's position on Black History Month is popular among African-Americans? Why or why not?
4. Joseph dwells on the negative aspects of Black History Month. What positive aspects are associated with it? Do the positive aspects outweigh the negative? Explain.

Considering Technique

1. In paragraph 1, Joseph identifies himself as a black school principal. Why does he do so? Is this identification an ethical appeal? How does it influence your reading of the argument?
2. What emotional appeal appears in paragraphs 1 and 2? In paragraph 11? What does the emotional appeal contribute to the persuasive quality of the essay?
3. What objection does Joseph raise, and how does he counter it? Is the counter effective? Are there any other objections that he should have raised and countered?
4. How does Joseph use examples in paragraph 5? What do the examples contribute to the persuasive quality of the essay?
5. How does Joseph create goodwill in paragraph 7?

For Group Discussion or Journal Writing

Joseph says that an alternative to Black History Month is for children to learn about their own family histories. What can be gained when people study their own family histories? Is this endeavor a suitable alternative to Black History Month?

The Case for Torture Warrants **ALAN M. DERSHOWITZ**

Alan Dershowitz is an attorney and member of the faculty of Harvard Law School. Although opposed to torture in principle, Dershowitz argues that sometimes torture is called for. In those instances, we should require court approval for torture in the form of torture warrants. This essay was first posted on the author's Harvard website in 2002. As you read it, pay close attention to the reasons he gives for his claim.

Now that it has been disclosed that our government had information of "undetermined reliability," from an agent whose code name is Dragonfire, that New York City may have been targeted for a 10 kiloton nuclear weapon, the arguments for empowering law enforcement officials to do everything necessary to prevent a catastrophic terrorist attack are becoming more compelling.[1] In the immediate aftermath of the September 11th attacks, FBI officials leaked a story about their inability to obtain information from suspected terrorists by conventional means, such as buying the information by offers of cash or leniency, or compelling the information by grants of immunity and threats of imprisonment for contempt of court. Those who leaked the story suggested that there may come a time when law enforcement officials might have to resort to unconventional means, including non-lethal torture. Thus began one of the most unusual debates in American legal and political history: should law enforcement be authorized to torture suspects who are thought to have information about a ticking bomb? 1

This ticking bomb scenario has long been a staple of legal and political philosophers who love to debate hypothetical cases that test the limit of absolute principles, such as the universal prohibition against the use of torture which has long been codified by international treaties. The ticking bomb case has also been debated, though not as a hypothetical case, in Israel, whose security services long claimed the authority to employ "moderate physical pressure" in order to secure real time intelligence from captured terrorists believed to know about impending terrorist acts. The moderate physical pressure employed by Israel was tougher than it sounds, but not nearly as tough as the brutal methods used by the French in interrogating suspected terrorists during the Algerian uprisings. The Israeli security service would take a suspected terrorist, tie him to a chair in an uncomfortable position for long periods of time with loud music blaring in the background, and then place a smelly sack over his head and shake him violently. Many tongues were loosened by this process and several terrorist acts prevented, without any suspects being seriously injured. 2

Torture, it turns out, can sometimes produce truthful information. The Israeli experience suggested that information obtained as a result of torture should never be believed, unless it can be independently confirmed, but such information can sometimes be self-proving, as when the subject leads law enforcement to the actual location of the bomb. 3

Nonetheless, the Israeli Supreme Court outlawed all use of even moderate, non-lethal physical pressure. It responded to the ticking bomb scenario by saying that if a security agent thought it was necessary to use physical pressure in order to prevent many deaths, he could take his chances, be prosecuted, and try to raise a defense of "necessity." In my book *Shouting Fire,* I wrote critically of this decision on the ground that it places security officials in an impossible dilemma. It would be better if any such official could seek an *advanced* ruling from a judge, as to whether physical pressure is warranted under the specific circumstances, in order to avoid being subject to an after the fact risk of imprisonment. Thus was born the proposal for a torture warrant. 4

Actually it was a rebirth, because half a millennium ago torture warrants were part of the law of Great Britain. They could be sought only

[1]Ultimately, investigators determined that Dragonfire's information was false.

in cases involving grave threats to the Crown or the Empire and were granted in about one case a year. Judges even in those times were extremely reluctant to authorize the thumb screw. 5

Why then should we even think about returning to an old practice that was abolished in England many years ago? The reason is because if we ever did have a ticking bomb case—especially a ticking nuclear bomb case—law enforcement officials would in fact resort to physical force, even torture, as a last resort. In speaking to numerous audiences since September 11th—audiences reflecting the entire breadth of the political and ideological spectrum—I have asked for a show of hands as to how many would favor the use of non-lethal torture in an actual ticking bomb case. The vast majority of audience members responded in the affirmative. So have law enforcement officials to whom I have spoken. If it is true that torture would in fact be used in such a case, then the important question becomes: is it better to have such torture done under the table, off the books and below the radar screen—or in full view, with accountability and as part of our legal system? This is a very difficult question with powerful arguments on both sides. On the one hand, we have had experience with off the book policies such as President Nixon's "plumbers"[2] and Oliver North's "foreign policy initiatives."[3] In a democracy, accountability and visibility must be given high priorities. On the other hand, to legitimate torture and make it part of our legal system, even in extreme cases, risks reversion to a bad old time when torture was routine. 6

One key question is whether the availability of a torture warrant would, in fact, increase or decrease the actual amount of torture employed by law enforcement officials. I believe, though I cannot prove, that a formal requirement of a judicial warrant as a prerequisite to non-lethal torture would decrease the amount of physical violence directed against suspects. Judges would require compelling evidence before they would authorize so extraordinary a departure from our constitutional norms, and law enforcement officials would be reluctant to seek a warrant unless they had compelling evidence that the suspect had information needed to prevent an imminent terrorist attack. Moreover the rights of the suspect would be better protected with a warrant requirement. He would be granted immunity, told that he was now compelled to testify, threatened with imprisonment if he refused to do so and given the option of providing the requested information. Only if he refused to do what he was legally compelled to do—provide necessary information which could not incriminate him because of the immunity—would he be threatened with torture. Knowing that such a threat was authorized by the law, he might well provide the information. If he still refused to, he would be subjected to judicially monitored physical measures designed to cause excruciating pain without leaving any lasting damage. A sterilized needle underneath the nail might be one such approved method. This may sound brutal, but it does not compare in brutality with the prospect of thousands of preventable deaths at the hands of fellow terrorists. 7

Let me cite two examples to demonstrate why I think there would be less torture with a warrant requirement than without one. Recall the case of the alleged national security wiretap being placed on the phones of Martin Luther King by the Kennedy administration in the early 1960s. This was in the days when the Attorney General could authorize a national security wiretap without a warrant. Today no judge would issue a warrant in a case as flimsy as that one. When Zacarias Moussaoui was detained after trying to learn how to fly an airplane, without wanting to

[2]President Nixon's "plumbers" were a group of operatives charged with "stopping leaks." The plumbers were responsible for the 1972 break-in at the Democratic Party's national headquarters in the Watergate Hotel.

[3]Oliver North was a deputy director of the National Security Council in 1981, during the Reagan administration. He was implicated in the Irangate scandal, involving the supply of arms to Iran in exchange for U.S. hostages.

know much about landing it, the government did not even seek a national security wiretap because its lawyers believed that a judge would not have granted one. If Moussaoui's computer could have been searched without a warrant, it almost certainly would have been. 8

It is a great tragedy that we have to be discussing the horrors of torture. Some even believe that any discussion of this issue is beyond the pale of acceptable discourse in 21st century America. But it is far better to discuss in advance the kinds of tragic choices we may encounter if we ever confront an actual ticking bomb terrorist case, than to wait until the case arises and let somebody make the decision in the heat of the moment. 9

An analogy to the shooting down of a passenger-filled hijacked airliner heading toward a crowded office building will be instructive. Prior to September 11th it might have been a debatable issue whether the plane should be shot down. Today that is no longer debatable. But would anyone suggest that the decision should be made by a low ranking police officer? Of course not. We all agree that this should be a decision made at the highest level possible—by the President or the Secretary of Defense, if there is time to have such a dreadful decision made by accountable public figures. The use of torture in the ticking bomb case, like the shooting down of the hijacked airplane, involves a horrible choice of evils. In my view this choice should be made with visibility and accountability, either by a judicial officer or by the President of the United States. It should not be made by nameless and unaccountable law enforcement officials, risking imprisonment if they guess wrong. 10

Considering Ideas

1. The thesis of "The Case for Torture Warrants" is implied. What is that thesis? What is the issue? What is the claim?
2. If you were writing the legislation authorizing torture warrants in ticking-bomb scenarios, how would you define *ticking bomb scenario*?
3. What reasons does Dershowitz give to support his claim?
4. What evidence does Dershowitz give to back up his reasons? Is the evidence convincing? Explain.

Considering Technique

1. What is Dershowitz's major premise? His minor premise? His conclusion?
2. What purpose do paragraphs 1–4 serve?
3. What element of emotional appeal do you notice in paragraph 1? How does that emotional appeal help Dershowitz achieve his writing purpose? What ethical appeal do you notice in paragraph 6, and how does it help him achieve his writing purpose?
4. What objection does Dershowitz raise in paragraph 9, and how does he counter that objection? Is the counter effective? Explain.
5. *Combining patterns:* How is exemplification used in paragraph 8 to help Dershowitz achieve his writing purpose? How is comparison-contrast used in paragraph 2 to help him achieve his writing purpose?

For Group Discussion or Journal Writing

One argument states that with torture warrants, we are giving up a measure of our civil rights in order to have more security. Are you willing to give up some of your civil rights to feel safer? Explain.

Torture Warrants? HARVEY A. SILVERGLATE

Like Alan Dershowitz does in the previous essay (which is not the Dershowitz Los Angeles Times *piece that Silverglate refers to in paragraph 2), attorney Harvey A. Silverglate takes on the issue of torture warrants, but he argues a different claim. This essay first appeared in 2001 on Phoenix.com. As you read it, consider whether you agree with Silverglate, Dershowitz—or neither author.*

Among the unsettling effects of the September 11 terrorist attacks on New York and Washington and the anthrax mailings that followed is their triggering, seemingly overnight, of a national debate over whether the United States should practice torture—as a matter of national policy—to combat terrorism. The pro-torture camp wants to authorize law-enforcement agents to inflict intense physical pain in order to extract information from suspected terrorists (the word "suspected" is often conveniently omitted by the law's proponents) where that information might pinpoint the location of a "ticking bomb" or otherwise avert some imminent act of mass carnage. 1

So imagine the surprise of many long-time legal observers when Harvard Law professor Alan Dershowitz published an op-ed piece in the *Los Angeles Times* on November 8, arguing that "if we are to have torture, it should be authorized by the law" and that the authorities should be required to apply to judges for "torture warrants" in each case. A careful reading of his op-ed indicates that Dershowitz did not actually go so far as to say he favors torture. And in subsequent lectures and interviews he placed on record his personal opposition to torture. But the piece drew a firestorm of criticism from both liberals and libertarians, who argued that Dershowitz had indirectly sanctioned the use of torture and should now be regarded as a turncoat in the battle to preserve civil liberties. 2

Nonetheless, Dershowitz's op-ed makes a fairly powerful, though flawed, argument that torture would be ruled constitutional. Under the right circumstances, he claims, torture, while "very troubling," would pass a test the Supreme Court has sometimes used to determine the constitutionality of the government's use of an extreme law-enforcement technique: whether it "shocks the conscience." 3

"Consider a situation in which a kidnapped child had been buried in a box with two hours of oxygen," suggests the law professor, ever the master of the difficult hypothetical. "The kidnapper refused to disclose its location," he continues. "Should we not consider torture in that situation?" 4

Dershowitz, clearly uncomfortable with his own rhetorical question, does not quite give a direct answer. In order to avoid an ugly answer to an impossibly difficult moral and legal question, he takes another route. Since there is "no doubt that if an actual ticking bomb situation were to arise, our law enforcement authorities would torture," he says, "the real debate is whether such torture should take place outside of our legal system or within it." The answer to this question is clear and easy for Dershowitz: "If we are to have torture, it should be authorized by law" because "democracy requires accountability and transparency." 5

Besides, Dershowitz argues, the Constitution poses no obstacle to legal, court-authorized, supervised torture. That's because the Fifth Amendment's protection against self-incrimination does not protect against requiring someone to testify and disclose information; it merely protects against the use of such information against the person interrogated. Thus, in the face of a court-issued "immunity" order, any citizen may be forced to testify in a judicial forum, or suffer imprisonment for the refusal to do so. Nor does Dershowitz believe that any "right of bodily integrity" that might be read into the Bill of Rights prohibits, say, the injection of "truth serum," since the Supreme Court has already authorized the forcible drawing of blood from a suspect for alcohol testing. "Certainly there can be no constitutional distinction" he argues, "between an injection that removes a liquid and one that injects a liquid." (This particular argument is spurious, and Dershowitz should know better: he is a long-time opponent of the death penalty, where the current preferred method of execution is the injection of deadly poisons into the veins of the convict.) 6

Dershowitz fails to mention altogether another amendment—the Eighth, which states quite plainly that no "cruel or unusual punishments [shall be] inflicted." The modern-era Supreme Court has ruled that this standard, which is inherently subjective, must be interpreted according to society's evolving standards of decency. It is likely that the pre–September 11 Court would have ruled that techniques all would agree constitute "torture" would qualify as "cruel" and (for our society, at least) "unusual." But in the atmosphere created by the ghastly attacks of September 11, the Court might now rule that it is neither cruel nor unusual to torture a convict, a prisoner, or even a mere suspect, if the information that might be wrung from that person could save thousands of innocent lives. (After all, the Supreme Court did uphold the constitutionality of President Franklin D. Roosevelt's transfer of Japanese-Americans from the West Coast into "relocation camps" after Pearl Harbor, and of his using a military tribunal to try—and execute—German saboteurs who landed on our shores intending to destroy strategic targets.) War does change mindsets, even of the courts—and understandably so. 7

But leaving aside his interpretation (or neglect) of inherently vague constitutional provisions, Dershowitz's conclusion is clear: if torture is to be administered, it should require "torture warrants" issued by judges before whom the government must lay out reasons why torture—and only torture—could extract life-saving information. "Thus we would not be winking an eye of quiet approval at torture while publicly condemning it," he says. 8

Some advocates of torture justify their position on the simple ground that monsters like those who helped level the World Trade Center deserve to be tortured, ostensibly to get information that might prevent future catastrophic destruction of human life. (Of course, if the pain inflicted also goes a small way toward exacting some retribution for the WTC carnage, though the suspected terrorist had nothing to do with September 11 but is planning an entirely new attack, some would view it as a just bonus.) But Dershowitz is not in that camp. He understands that in the real world, when law-enforcement authorities have reason to believe that a suspect has information that can save lives, individual cops and agents will resort to torture no matter what. After all, we have long struggled to control the gratuitous use of torture by police on suspects from whom they seek to extract confessions, and by sadistic prison guards against inmates for no apparent practical purpose whatsoever. Can there be any real doubt that a law-enforcement officer, or, for that matter, most of us, would probably be willing to resort to the torture of a person who knew where to find our kidnapped child or where to locate an atomic bomb ticking away in some major American city? 9

So what, then, is wrong with a system that requires torture warrants—especially if an opponent of torture like Dershowitz can argue for their constitutionality? The answer is threefold. 10

First, institutionalizing torture will give it society's imprimatur, lending it a degree of respectability. It will then be virtually impossible to curb not only the increasing frequency with which warrants will be sought—and granted—but also the inevitable rise in *unauthorized* use of torture. Unauthorized torture will increase not only to extract life-saving information, but also to obtain confessions (many of which will then prove false). It will also be used to punish real or imagined infractions, or for no reason other than human sadism. This is a genie we should not let out of the bottle. 11

Second, we should think twice before entirely divorcing law from morality. There can be little doubt that until now, Americans have widely viewed torture as beyond the pale. The US rightly criticizes foreign governments that engage in the practice, and each year our Department of State issues a report that classifies foreign nations on the basis of their human-rights records, including the use of torture. Our country has signed numerous international treaties and compacts that decry the use of torture. We tamper with that hard-won social agreement at our grave moral peril. 12

Third, our nation sets an example for the rest of the world: we believe not only in the rule of law, but in the rule of *decent* laws, and in a government composed of decent men and women who are accountable to a long tradition. There may be more efficient ways of governing, but our system is intentionally inefficient in certain ways in order to protect liberty. Our three co-equal branches of government immediately come to mind. Also, government can almost always proceed more efficiently if it is not dogged by an independent press protected by the First Amendment. But we have found from long experience that, as Jefferson famously said, if one were forced to choose between government without the press or the press without government, the latter might well be preferable. Trials by jury are long, inefficient, expensive, and sometimes lead to the acquittal of defendants whom the state is convinced are guilty and wants very much to incarcerate or even execute. Some of those acquitted are indeed guilty. Yet trial by jury remains the best (albeit imperfect) system ever devised for ascertaining truth while curbing government excess and abuse of power. Torture may sometimes offer an efficient means of obtaining information, but efficiency should not always trump other values. 13

Yet we still face Dershowitz's "ticking bomb" hypothetical. How do we deal with that? Is it really moral, after all, to insist on having "clean hands" and to refrain from torture, when thousands or even hundreds of thousands of people could die as a result of our pious and self-righteous morality? 14

The answer to this quandary lies in a famous criminal-law decision rendered in Victorian England by the British appeals court known as the Queen's Bench. It is a case studied by virtually every American law student at virtually every law school. In *Regina* [the Queen] *v. Dudley and Stephens,* the court dealt with one of the most difficult criminal cases in English legal history. 15

In July 1884, four crewmen of a wrecked English yacht were set adrift in a lifeboat more than 1000 miles from the nearest land mass. They had no water and no food except for two one-pound tins of turnips. Three of the men—Dudley, Stephens, and Brooks—were "able-bodied English seamen," while the fourth lifeboat passenger was an 18-year-old boy who was less robust than the others and soon showed signs of weakening. As they drifted, severe hunger and thirst set in. It became clear, as the trial court found, that unless the three stronger seamen killed the boy—who by then had deteriorated substantially and was on the verge of dying anyway—and then ate his body and drank his blood, all four of them would die. "There was no appreciable chance of saving life except by killing one for the others to eat," and the boy seemed the most logical candidate since he was "likely" to die anyway, as the trial court put it. Dudley and Stephens followed this course, with Brooks dissenting. Once the boy was killed, all three partook of his flesh and blood. Four days later, the three survivors, barely alive, were rescued by a passing ship. 16

The Queen's Bench was faced with the question of whether, under English law, the three were guilty of murder, or whether the homicide was justified by a "defense of necessity." The judges concluded that they were guilty of murder and should be sentenced to death. "[T]he absolute divorce of law from morality would be of fatal consequence," they wrote, "and such divorce would follow if the temptation to murder in this case were to be held by law an absolute defense of it." Were this bright line against murder abandoned, warned the court, it might "be made the legal cloak for unbridled passion and atrocious crime." The genie, in other words, would have escaped from the bottle, with unimaginable consequences. 17

But since this case is a very hard one and the outcome—the death penalty—would strike most civilized people as excessive under the circumstances, the judges suggested a way out of the dilemma. The judges claimed that it is left "to the Sovereign"—in this instance, the Queen—"to exercise that prerogative of mercy which the Constitution has intrusted to the hands fittest to dispense it." In other words, executive clemency offers a way to trim the harsh edges of the law in the truly exceptional case. 18

The lesson of this case for the use of torture warrants is clear. When a law-enforcement officer truly believes that a suspect possesses life-saving information, and commits the perfectly human act of torturing the suspect to obtain that information, the officer *should* be tried for the crime of violating the suspect's constitutional rights, or for some related crime such as assault and battery or mayhem (willful bodily mutilation). If the jury, acting as the conscience of the community, decides that the officer does not deserve to be convicted and punished under the circumstances, it will acquit. Indeed, under our system of unanimous jury verdicts in federal and most state criminal trials, a single juror who refuses to vote for conviction can "hang" the jury and prevent a verdict and hence a conviction. In our legal history, there have even been instances where juries, exercising what is known as "jury nullification," have refused to convict or have acquitted obviously guilty defendants. Such verdicts are hardly unknown, as in cases of mercy killings or the medical use of marijuana. 19

Further, even when a conviction has been handed down in a hard case, the government's chief executive (the president of the United States or, on the state level, usually the governor) may exercise his or her constitutional authority to commute (or terminate) the sentence and free the defendant, or even pardon the defendant and thereby wipe clean his or her criminal record. In the *Dudley and Stephens* case, in fact, Queen Victoria commuted the sentence to six months' imprisonment. This is how a civilized nation upholds civic decency and the rule of law while allowing for those exceptional situations when normal human beings break the law for some greater good or under conditions of overwhelming necessity. 20

We do not need, and should not dare to enact, a system of torture warrants in the United States. Our legal system is perfectly capable of dealing with the exceptional hard case without enshrining the notion that it is okay to torture a fellow human being. 21

Considering Ideas

1. Which sentence is Silverglate's thesis? What does that thesis state as the author's issue and claim?
2. What reasons does Silverglate give for his claim?
3. What is the source of the evidence to support the reasons? Do you find the evidence convincing? Explain.
4. Do you think Silverglate's essay would convince a wavering audience? A hostile audience? Explain.
5. In paragraph 4, Silverglate refers to Dershowitz's example of a kidnapped child. What element of emotional appeal does this example include? Would the example be effective if the kidnapped victim were an elderly person?

Considering Technique

1. In paragraphs 2–6, Silverglate is not arguing his claim. What is he doing in those paragraphs, and how do they help him earn goodwill and achieve his persuasive purpose?
2. In which paragraphs does Silverglate raise and counter objections? What are those objections, and how does he counter them?
3. Part of Silverglate's argument is made by deduction. What is his major premise? His minor premise? His conclusion?
4. What ethical appeal do you notice in the essay?
5. Who do you think is more convincing—Dershowitz or Silverglate? (The question does not ask who you agree with; it asks who makes the more convincing argument.) Explain your view.

For Group Discussion or Journal Writing

Do you agree with the judges' ruling in the *Regina v. Dudley and Stephens* case? Why or why not?

STYLE NOTE

Emphasis

Setting an idea off in a one-sentence paragraph can emphasize the idea. In paragraph 4 of "Why I Dread Black History Month," Wayne Joseph uses that strategy to emphasize a reason he disapproves of Black History Month:

> Black contribution to American history is so rich and varied that attempting to confine the discussion and investigation to four weeks a year tends to trivialize the momentous impact that blacks have had on American society.

ARGUMENTATION IN IMAGES: A CASEBOOK

A casebook of visual arguments begins on page 463. The images, all related to global climate change, illustrate some of the forms visual arguments can take: photojournalism pictures, political cartoons, and advertisements. As you study the images, note the different appeals they employ, and consider how the images function similarly to and differently from written arguments.

Considering the Images

1. Write out a claim the photograph of the polar bear could support.
2. We often think of photographs as being "objective" representations of reality. Does the photograph of the polar bear make an emotional appeal? How?
3. Describe the claims in the two political cartoons. How do they use humor to bolster their claims?

4. Which of the three appeals—logical, emotional, and ethical—does the "Drowning of the Penguins" cartoon make? How is this cartoon similar to the photograph of the polar bear?

Photograph and accompanying text in a photo essay on climate change in *Time* magazine in 2006.

Political cartoon by Ken Catalino.

Political cartoon by Gary Varvel.

By permission of Gary Varvel and Creators Syndicate, Inc.

5. Describe the audience you think the Prius advertisement is targeting.
6. The face mask in the Prius ad is made from a vegetable leaf. How does that image help the advertisement fulfill its persuasive purpose?
7. The poster on page 466 for *An Inconvenient Truth,* Al Gore's movie about global warming, is a visual depiction of the argument advanced in the film, that global warming poses a grave threat to the planet. How does the poster make its visual argument?

Print advertisement for the Toyota Prius, a car that runs on a combination of gasoline and electricity.

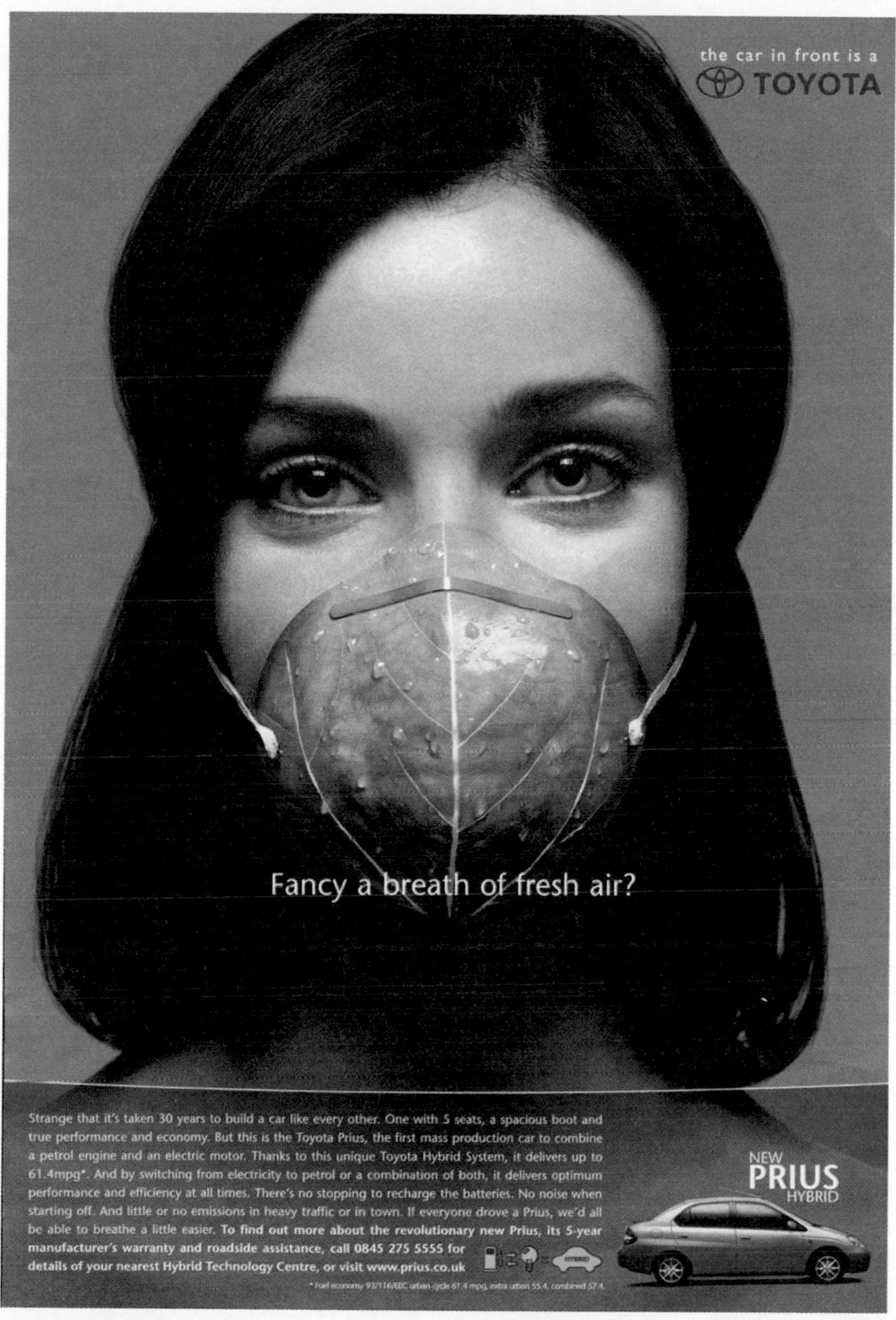

Poster for *An Inconvenient Truth.*

Screenshot from Catalyst 2.0 visual rhetoric tutorial.

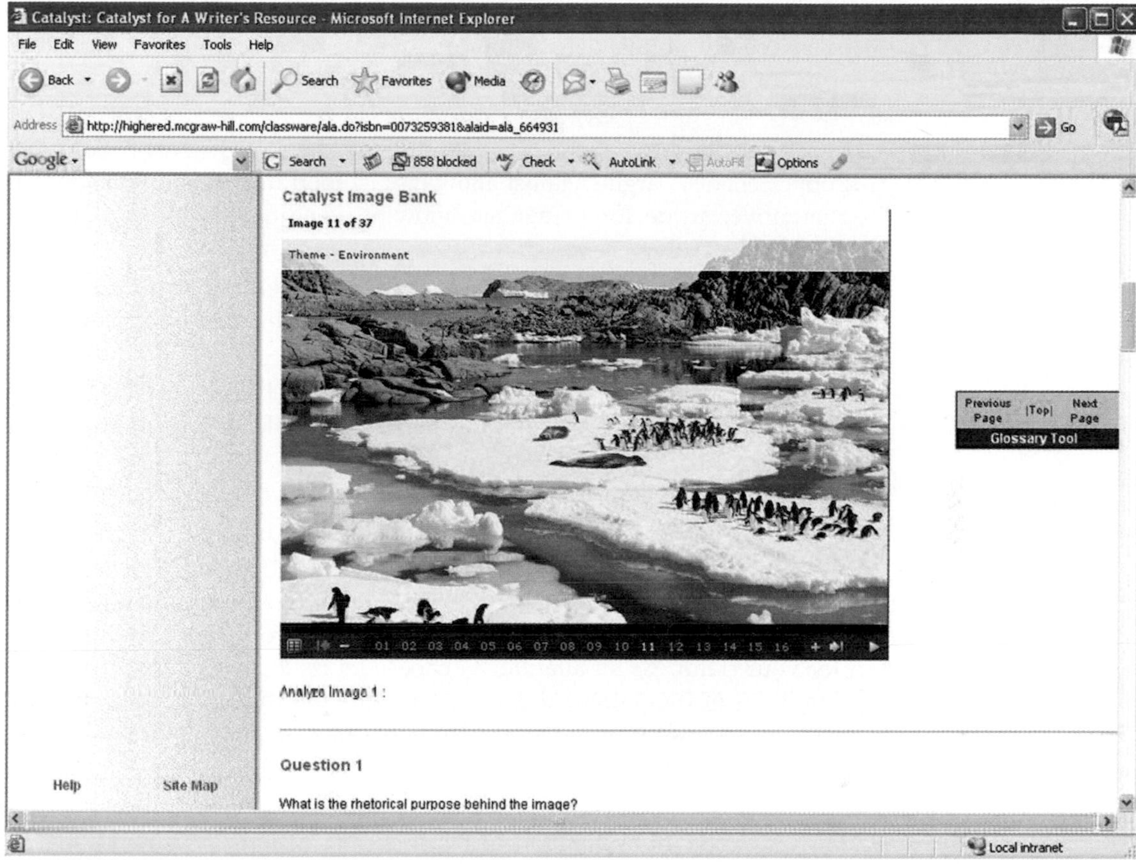

To see more images like the one above and to learn more about visual rhetoric, visit the Catalyst 2.0 Visual Rhetoric Tutorial by way of *The Student Writer*'s Online Learning Center—www.mhhe.com/tsw. Here you will find comprehensive coverage of visual analysis, as well as many more examples of visual argument in the Catalyst Image Bank. Check out Catalyst > Writing > Visual Rhetoric Tutorial.

SUGGESTIONS FOR WRITING

Writing Argumentation

Make and argue a claim about one of these issues:

school prayer
athletic scholarships
the movie rating system
a longer school year
graduation requirements
a campus issue
homeland security
censorship of the Internet
proficiency testing as a graduation requirement
revealing the identity of a biological mother to an adopted child
immigration laws

Reading Then Writing Argumentation

1. Like Michael Weiss in "It's Just Too Easy," argue against the continuation of an activity young people commonly engage in with parental or government approval, such as working while attending school, drinking at age 21, or voting at age 18.
2. Making the opposite claim argued in "What's for Lunch? Fast Food in the Public Schools," argue against allowing fast food in public schools. As an alternative, argue for or against allowing vending machines in public schools.
3. Making the opposite claim argued in "Why I Dread Black History Month," argue that Black History Month is a positive celebration of black culture and accomplishment.
4. Making the opposite claim argued in "Should Obscene Art Be Funded by the Government?" argue that restrictions should be placed on the art funded by the National Endowment for the Arts.

Argumentation beyond the Writing Classroom

Pick an issue currently being debated on your campus, and write an argument that could be published as a letter to the editor of your campus newspaper or as a guest editorial. Be sure to articulate the issue, your claim, and the support for your claim. As an alternative, choose an issue being debated in your community or in the nation, and write an argument that could be published as a letter to the editor of the local newspaper or as a guest editorial.

Responding to a Theme

1. In paragraph 7 of "Why I Dread Black History Month," Wayne M. Joseph notes that African-Americans were stripped of their cultural base. Explain why that was the case, and go on to explore what happens when people lose their cultural base.
2. Before the terrorist attacks of September 11, 2001, we had little reason to debate the use of torture, as Alan Dershowitz and Harvey A. Silverglate do in their essays. Discuss something else that has changed dramatically since the attacks, and explain how American society or values have been affected by that change.
3. Automobiles are a major source of air pollution. The advertisement on page 465 draws on that fact by emphasizing that the Toyota Prius is good for the environment. Assume that Congress is considering a bill that would reduce highway speed limits to 50 miles per hour, provide monetary incentives to employers with carpooling programs, increase the gasoline tax by 10 percent, and increase income tax rates to build high-speed trains in all major metropolitan areas. How do you think the lifestyles of Americans would change?
4. *Connecting the readings:* In paragraph 13 of "Torture Warrants?" Harvey Silverglate says, "Our nation sets an example for the rest of the world: we believe not only in the rule of law, but in the rule of *decent* laws. . . ."

Discuss the difficulty of maintaining a commitment to the belief Silverglate mentions when we are faced with difficult threats and problems. To respond, you can draw on your own experience and observation, "The Case for Torture Warrants," "Torture Warrants?" "Growing Up Asian in America" (which discusses the internment of Japanese-Americans during World War II) on page 386, and "Juvenile Injustice" on page 408.

Writing Argumentation

These guidelines are suggestions to try as you develop your own effective writing process. They are not meant to replace your own successful procedures.

www.mhhe.com/tsw
For further help writing argument essays, go to Catalyst 2.0 > Writing > Writing Tutors > Arguments

PROCESS GUIDELINES

Think like a Writer: Generating Ideas, Considering Audience and Purpose, and Ordering Ideas

- For an issue and claim, try the following:
  - Choose an issue you are interested in and know something about.
  - Review your campus and local newspapers for controversial issues and aims that are important to you or that you have an opinion about.
  - Fill in the blank: It is wrong that ________. If, for example, you complete the sentence by saying that "students cannot strike," you can argue that students should be permitted to strike.
- To identify your audience, answer these questions:
  - Who thinks the issue is important but hasn't made up his or her mind?
  - Who might disagree with my claim?
  - Who could be convinced to agree with me?
  - Who could be convinced to take an action I favor?
- To assess your audience, answer these questions:
  - Is my audience supportive, wavering, or hostile?
  - Why is my audience supportive, wavering, or hostile?
- To determine your purpose, answer these questions:
  - Can I lessen opposition?
  - Can I convince my readers to agree with me?
  - Can I change my readers' minds about some aspect of my issue?
  - Can I convince my readers to take a particular action?
- List reasons that support your claim.
- To generate ideas for logical appeals, answer these questions:
  - Why is the issue important?
  - What would happen if my claim were (or were *not*) adopted?
  - What story can I tell to support my claim? What examples can I provide?
  - What comparisons or contrasts can I make to support my claim?
  - Do any cause-and-effect relationships support my claim?
- To generate ideas for ethical appeals, answer these questions:
  - What qualifies me to write about the issue?
  - What objections are my readers likely to have? How can I counter those objections?
  - What common ground do I share with my readers?

- To generate ideas for emotional appeals, answer these questions:
  - What needs and values are important to my readers?
  - How can I appeal to those needs and values?
- Develop a list of ideas for your draft, and write an outline. Consider the following:
  - Whether some or all of your support follows an inductive or deductive pattern
  - Whether some or all of your support should follow a progressive order
  - What the best places are to raise and counter objections

Think like a Writer: Drafting

- Draft a working thesis that mentions your debatable issue and claim.
- Using your outline as a guide, write your draft. If you have trouble writing your introduction, explain why the issue is important and/or why you are qualified to write about the issue.
- If you have trouble writing your conclusion, try explaining what would happen if your claim were—or were not—adopted. If appropriate, call for your readers to take a particular action.
- Think about using topic sentences to state the reasons for your claim.

Think like a Critic; Work like an Editor: Revising

- Be sure your reasons, evidence, emotional appeals, and ethical appeals are geared to the characteristics of your readers.
- Examine the evidence that supports each of your reasons. If you have only a sentence or two, consider how the patterns of development can help you include more evidence.
- Ask whether you have raised and countered important objections. If not, consider doing so.
- If your audience is wavering or hostile, think about what you have done to create goodwill.
- If some of your evidence comes from research, follow the conventions explained in Chapter 17.
- To obtain reader response for revision, see page 105. In addition, ask your reader to explain whether your argument is convincing and why.

Think like a Critic; Work like an Editor: Correcting Errors

You may have occasions to refer to people in general. Be careful to use pronouns correctly by modeling these examples. For more on pronouns, see Chapter 24.

> If a *person* objects to the content of a television program, *he or she* [not *they*] should write the sponsor.
>
> *People* often object to the content of a television program. When *they* [not *you*] do, *they* [not *you*] should write the sponsor.

If *someone* objects to the content of a television program, *he or she* [not *they*] should write the sponsor.

Everybody who objects to the content of a television program should write the sponsor [not *their* sponsor].

Anyone who objects to the content of a television program should write the sponsor [not *their* sponsor].

Remember

- Avoid clauses such as "most people agree," "as anyone can see," and "anyone who understands the issue believes." You will alienate readers who disagree, do not see, or fail to believe, making it harder to achieve your purpose.
- Do not argue both sides of an issue. You should raise and counter compelling objections, but do not present all the arguments on one side of the issue and then all the arguments on the other side.

LOOKING AHEAD

Calvin, the little boy in the *Calvin and Hobbes* cartoon, does not appreciate the value of research. Nevertheless, research is such an important component of education—particularly higher education—that you will learn about it both in this chapter and in the next one. Although you are learning about research here in your college writing class, make no mistake—research matters in every subject you study. Before you begin the first of the research chapters, consider the importance of research by responding to the following:

- Why should college students learn how to research?
- In your major or a subject you might major in, what issues or topics are actively being researched? Why is that research important?
- What are three subjects you will take before graduation that will likely require you to incorporate research findings into your writing projects?

Conducting Research

Peg Tyre wrote "Smart Moms, Hard Choices" for *Newsweek* in 2006 to consider the decision women make about whether to pursue careers or to stay at home full-time to raise their children. Tyre did research in order to present all sides of the issue. Although much of the discussion about the subject had been sparked by the book *Mommy Wars,* Tyre went beyond that single source and addressed the topic from a variety of perspectives.

Here is an excerpt that includes some of the information she gathered in her research:

> While the raw emotionalism of the debate is compelling, economists and sociologists who study women in the work force complain that books like *Mommy Wars* can obscure an important reality: *most* women with children work outside the home. Women who are most likely to stay home with their children are younger than 24 and have obtained high-school diplomas, according to the U.S. Census. Older, more educated moms are more likely to keep working. When women quit to raise kids, they rarely retire for good. According to a report issued in December by the Census, 75 percent of women with school-age children are employed or looking for work. By the time their children are 12 or older, that number rises to 80 percent. "The nature of the economy," says Kathleen Gerson, a New York University sociologist, "means that only a very tiny percentage of women—very wealthy ones," can afford to leave the work force entirely.
>
> Which is not to say that the landscape for working moms isn't changing. While the number of working moms rose dramatically in the 1970s and

1980s, those numbers peaked at 73 percent in 2000. Since then, the number of working mothers has dropped about 1.6 percent.

Tyre's article is strengthened by a quotation, census data, statistics, and the perspective of economists and sociologists who did not contribute to *Mommy Wars.* All this information provides credibility and depth.

Researched writing is among the most important writing you will do, both in school and in the workplace. This chapter and the next one will help you master the research process so you can sift through the wealth of resources to find information on your topic and use that information responsibly. You will learn how to use the tools of research, including your campus library and the Internet, to discover authoritative information on any topic. You will also learn how to integrate that information into your writing and document it in the proper form.

WHEN TO RESEARCH

You probably already do a considerable amount of research, or fact-finding, without realizing it. When you question your friends to learn which courses they recommend taking, you are researching—as you are when you check the classified advertisements for the best prices on used cars, call local electronics stores to find the best place to purchase an MP3 player, and use the Internet to learn how to fix your leaking faucet. In addition, researching and including source material is a common component of writing done in most college courses. Sometimes you will include a source or two in an essay to support your own ideas, and sometimes you will use sources extensively in a research paper.

Using Sources in an Essay to Support Your Own Ideas

Information gathered through research can help support the main points of an essay written for almost any purpose.

- **Important statistics.** For a paper arguing in favor of gun control legislation, written for a criminal justice class, you can research to discover the number of handgun deaths per year in the United States.
- **Specialized procedures or technical information.** For an essay explaining a procedure for matching organs and donors, written for an ethics class, you can research the procedures currently used to decide which patients receive the limited number of available organs.
- **Background information.** For a paper about the dangers of some herbal remedies, written for a health class, you can research why the Food and Drug Administration does not regulate these substances.
- **The view of an authority.** For a paper explaining the benefits of vegetarianism, written for a nutrition class, you can research what the National Institutes of Health says about a vegetarian diet.

- **Relevant explanation.** For a paper about teacher preparation, written for an education class, you can research the effectiveness of alternative certification programs.
- **Supporting detail.** For a paper about the drawbacks of legalized gambling, written for an urban sociology class, you can research the negative effects of gambling on towns that have already legalized it.

For two examples of essays that use sources to support the author's ideas, see pages 223 and 447.

Using Sources in a Research Paper

The academic research paper presents a thorough exploration of a topic. Unlike an essay, in which you use sources to support your own ideas, the research paper requires you to investigate and present a range of sources on your topic.

- For a labor studies course, you can write a research paper about the effectiveness of mutual gains bargaining.
- For an environmental science course, you can write a research paper about the effects of beach erosion on sea turtles.
- For a nursing course, you can write a research paper about the effects of the nursing shortage on nurses' work environment.
- For a child care class, you can write a research paper about the effects of day care on toddlers' socialization processes.
- For a psychology class, you can write a research paper about the causes of depression in college students and its effect on them.

For an example of a research paper, see page 535.

THE RESEARCH PROCESS

The procedures explained in this chapter can help you plan a timeline for creating your paper and help you locate, analyze, and organize sources. Some of the procedures are suitable for finding sources to support your own ideas in an essay; others will help you write a research paper.

Create a Timeline for Your Research Paper

A research paper is a complex assignment that cannot be completed quickly. You should create a timeline to manage your time and stay organized while working through the planning, research, drafting, and citation phases of your paper. Using the chart on page 476, set deadlines for yourself for each step in the research process based on the amount of time you have to complete the paper, and you will stay on track and avoid last-minute panic.

Completion Date	Step in Process
	Choose a broad topic (see page 476).
	Narrow your topic and draft a preliminary thesis (and, if necessary, have the topic or thesis approved by your instructor) (see page 477).
	Locate sources in the library, on the Internet, and through field research (see pages 479, 487, and 492).
	Compile a working bibliography (see page 494).
	Evaluate your sources (see page 495).
	Take notes (see page 496).
	Create an outline (see page 503).
	Write a first draft (see page 504).
	Check your in-text documentation and create a works-cited or references page (depending on whether you are using MLA or APA style) (see page 506).
	Revise and edit your draft (see page 532).
	Format and submit your final paper (see page 535).

Choose a Broad Research Paper Topic

Choose a topic that interests you, so you do not become bored. Perhaps you are curious about the civil rights movement in the 1960s, or maybe you wish you knew more about the space program. A research paper presents the perfect opportunity to indulge your curiosity.

If an interesting topic does not strike you right off, try some of these strategies:

1. Browse through newspapers and magazines for ideas. Online, browse the newspapers, journals, and magazines listed at www.aldaily.com.
2. Review your class notes for topics and issues your professor has discussed.
3. Consider what you have read lately. Have you read about the dropping of the atomic bomb on Hiroshima at the end of World War II in history class? Have you come across a newspaper article on Internet fraud? Either of these topics can be an excellent starting point.
4. Leaf through a general-knowledge encyclopedia like *World Book Encyclopedia.* Online, you can browse *Encarta* at encarta.msn.com.
5. Surf the Internet, especially reference sites. For a good starting point, visit www.refdesk.com. In addition, you can type a broad subject, such

as "Charter Schools," into a search engine such as www.yahoo.com or www.google.com and see what surfaces.

Some topics are not suitable for a research paper and should be avoided. If you are uncertain about the suitability of your topic, consult with your instructor. Here are some cautions:

1. Avoid topics that do not require research because they have been thoroughly documented, with few recent discoveries or controversies. These are subjects like "the circulatory system" and "the life of Abraham Lincoln."
2. Avoid topics that lack scientific foundation, such as UFOs, the Bermuda Triangle, reincarnation, and ESP.
3. If you do not have Internet access, avoid topics that are very current or regional because finding print sources for these can be difficult.
4. Be aware that some instructors prefer students to avoid religious topics. If such a topic interests you, be sure to talk it over with your teacher.
5. Avoid topics that have little academic significance. Instead of researching the many moods of Britney Spears, research how Spears has shaped popular culture.

Narrow Your Topic

Broad topics like "media violence" cover so much territory that you cannot treat them adequately in a standard research paper. Narrower topics like "the effects of cartoon violence on preschoolers" allow for a more in-depth discussion at a manageable length. When you move from broad topic to narrow topic, remember these guidelines.

Understand Your Purpose

Has your instructor asked you to write a problem–solution paper, an argument essay, or an explanatory report? Notice how differently the broad topic "televised violence" can be narrowed based on the purpose of the assignment:

Problem–solution paper: How parents can limit their preschoolers' exposure to televised violence

Argument essay: Why the government should limit the violence on television

Explanatory report: The nature and amount of violence on prime-time network television

Understand the Terms of the Assignment

Are there requirements for length, kinds of sources, or number of sources? When is the paper due? Answers to questions like these will help you make decisions about how to narrow your topic. Consider the broad topic "pollution." If you are expected to submit a six-page paper in three weeks, you do not want to research the topic of "industrial pollution"—that involves too many kinds of pollution in too many industries. Even the narrower topic of "automobile emissions" would probably be too broad. Writing about "the effectiveness of California's laws limiting automobile emissions," however, may work very well.

Use Strategies for Narrowing a Topic

In Chapter 2, you learned strategies for narrowing a broad topic. Use one or more of these strategies to help you narrow your research paper topic. For example, you might use mapping to help you narrow the broad topic "televised violence":

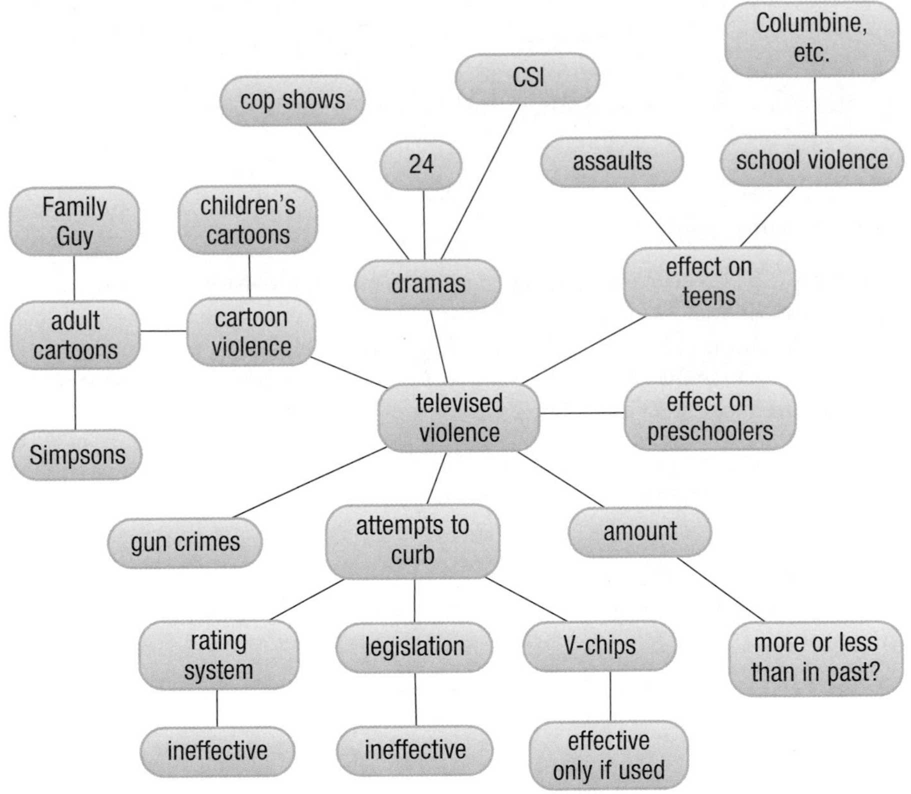

Possible narrow topic: the reasons attempts to regulate the amount of violence children view on television have been ineffective

Skim Source Materials

You can get ideas for narrowing a broad topic by skimming source materials in the following ways:

1. Review the tables of contents of books on your broad topic. You can find books using your library's online catalog.
2. Using the previewing strategies explained in Chapter 1, skim encyclopedia articles on your broad topic, either in the library or online.
3. Look up your broad topic in *The New York Times Index.* The titles of articles on your topic can suggest ways to narrow.
4. Type in your broad topic into your favorite search engine and into www.findarticles.com. The titles that come up will suggest ways to narrow your topic.
5. Note that your campus library will probably have *ProQuest, InfoTrac, EBSCOhost,* or some other online database listing magazine articles. Topics and subtopics given there can suggest ways to narrow your topic.

Draft a Preliminary Thesis

Based on your narrow topic, draft a preliminary thesis to guide your research. Your preliminary thesis focuses your research by helping you decide what material will be useful to you (and, therefore, what material you should take notes on) and what material you can pass by. Here are three examples of suitable preliminary thesis statements:

```
Charter schools offer a positive alternative to
traditional public schools.

Preschoolers exposed to televised violence are
more aggressive with their siblings and peers.

Paying women to be stay-at-home mothers would
reduce the number of people on welfare.
```

Always remember that your preliminary thesis is subject to change in light of information your research brings forth. Thus, if during your research you discover that certain kinds of charter schools work better than others, you can amend your thesis:

```
Charter schools that specialize in helping at-risk
students offer a strong alternative to traditional
public schools.
```

Use the Library to Locate Sources

www.mhhe.com/tsw

For further information on researching in the library, go to Catalyst 2.0 > Research > Using the Library

The information in the next sections will help you locate sources to supplement your own ideas in an essay or for a research paper. However, before getting under way, you should familiarize yourself with your campus library and its resources. Check to see whether your library offers a self-guided tour or a library-use workshop. Taking the tour or participating in the workshop will save you significant time by showing you how to locate the sources you need as efficiently as possible. You should also become familiar with your library's website.

Consider the Kind of Information You Need

Perhaps you are looking for a statistic or quotation to supplement your own ideas by backing up one of your points. Or maybe you are seeking historical background about an issue to use in the introduction of an essay you are writing on that issue. If you are writing a research paper, you may be looking for all the causes of the high divorce rate in the United States. Keeping your research needs in mind will help you decide what to look at and what to pass by.

Use the Computer Catalog to Locate Books

You can find books on your topic by using your library's computer catalog, which contains information on every book the library has. In most libraries, this computer catalog has replaced the card catalog. This makes searching faster and often more convenient, since most libraries allow access to their computer catalog both at terminals in the library and via the library's web page.

The computer catalog can be searched by author, by title, by ISBN (International Standard Book Number), by keyword, or by a subject term listed in the *Library of Congress Subject Headings (LCSH)*. The *LCSH* is usually located near the computer catalog terminals. (The Library of Congress system of headings is used in most academic libraries, though the Dewey decimal system is still used in some public libraries.)

When you are first looking for sources for a research paper or to supplement your ideas in an essay, you will probably search the catalog via the subject entries. A search of this kind is similar to the keyword search you may already be familiar with from search engines such as Google or Yahoo! To search by subject, follow the directions on the computer catalog screen, or ask a librarian. If you are unsure what word to use to start your search, consult the *LCSH* for topic headings used in your library. Once you have searched for your chosen term, you will get one or more screens listing the titles of books that your library has on the topic you typed in. See the figure on page 481 for an example of how this screen can look (but note that no two computer catalogs look exactly the same!).

Many academic library catalogs let you perform advanced searches, in which you can specify the type of material returned in the search, such as books, maps, dissertations, or scores, or the copyright dates between which you want to search.

When performing a subject search, you may have to experiment with the words you choose. Suppose your research topic is how corporations have profited from genetically modifying the food we eat. If you use the too-broad "food," you could end up with over 12,000 entries. However, if you use the too-narrow "corporations and genetically modified food," you might end up with only one entry. Using the phrase "genetically modified foods" produces a more acceptable number of entries.

The computer catalog entry for a specific book contains many useful pieces of information including the call number of the book (which gives the location of the book in the library); its availability; bibliographic information

Results of a Computer Catalog Search. The search term "genetically modified foods" produces this list of resources related to the topic.

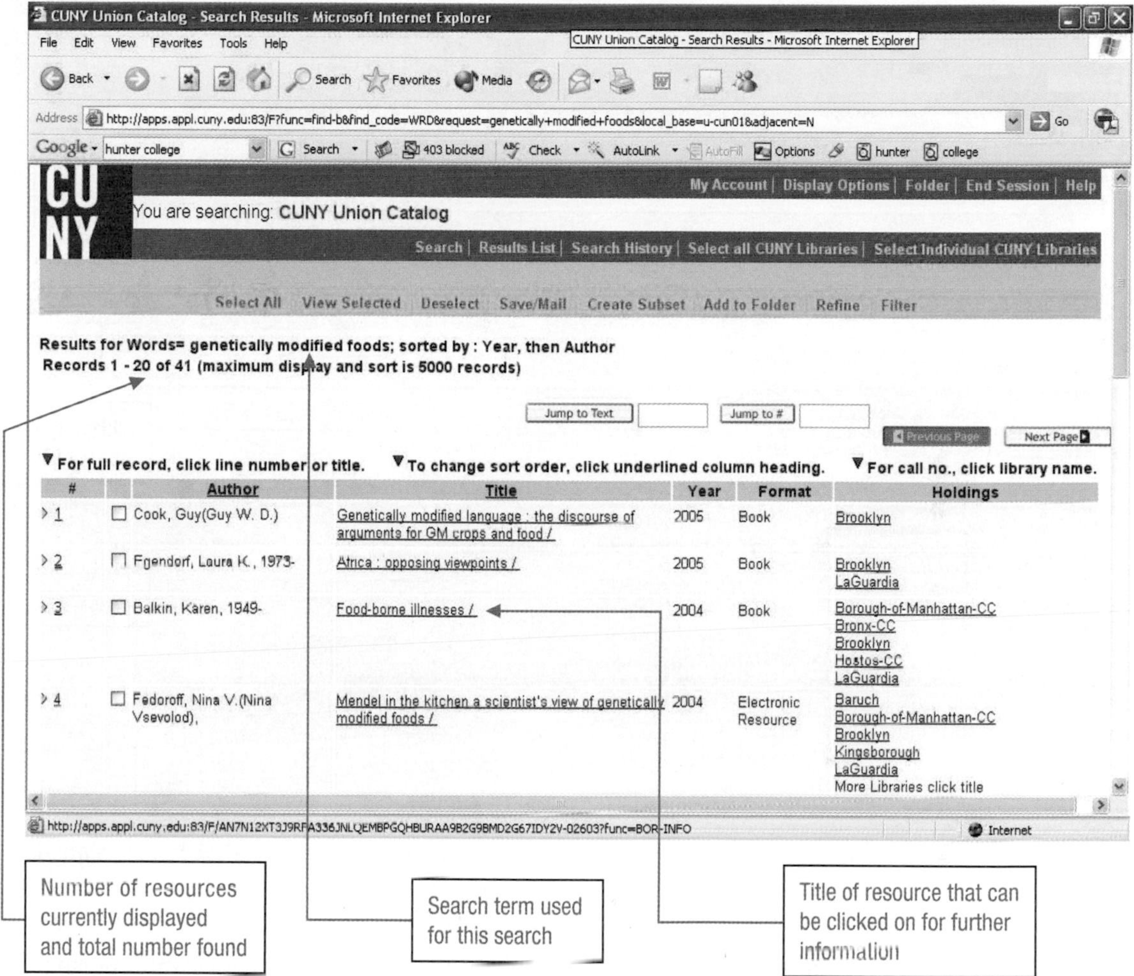

such as the title, author, publisher, and date of publication; and related *LCSH* terms. Usually, you can access this additional information by clicking on the title of the book on the results page.

Take a look at the information for a book found during our search on "genetically modified foods" in the figure on page 482.

If the catalog is not computerized, you will use the traditional card catalog. Like the computer version, the card catalog files every book in the library three ways: by author, by title, and by one or more subjects. Some catalogs file all the cards together, and some catalogs have two parts. First, the catalog file of books is alphabetized according to author and title. Second, the card catalog has a subject file that arranges books alphabetically according to the subjects they treat.

Entry for a Book Listed in a Computer Catalog. This screen provides detailed information on a particular book in the library, including its subjects, bibliographic information, and call number.

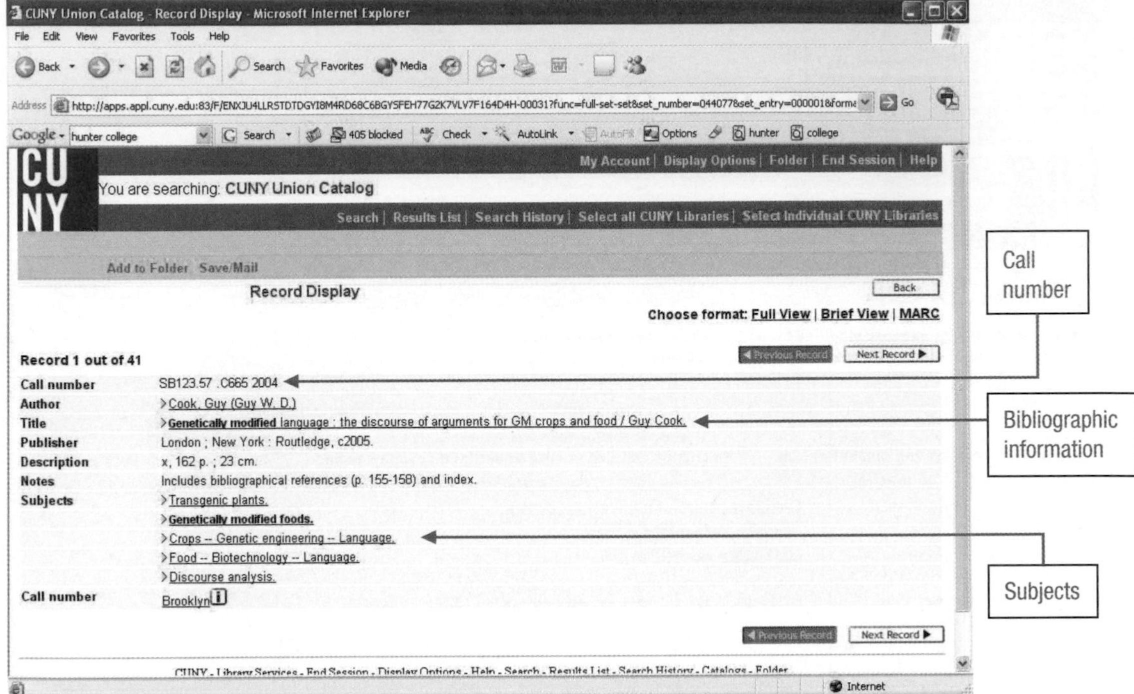

Reprinted with permission from CUNY.

Use Reference Works

When you are looking for specific information—perhaps a particular statistic—turn to reference works. These works may be on CD-ROM or in a specific area of the library's reference room. Useful works include the following:

- *Information Please Almanac* and *Facts on File* give statistics and information on current events.
- The *Congressional Record* has information about what has transpired in Congress.
- The *Statistical Abstract of the United States,* published by the Bureau of the Census, gives information on the population and on American institutions.
- *Current Biography* and *Webster's New Biographical Dictionary* contain articles on people you may need information about.

Some of the most useful reference works are encyclopedias.

Be sure to look at both the general-knowledge encyclopedias, such as *Encyclopedia Britannica,* and the relevant specialty encyclopedias, like *Encyclopedia of Economics.* You can find the names of specialty encyclopedias under the appropriate subject headings of the computer catalog. Here is a partial list:

Encyclopedia of American Ethnic Groups
Encyclopedia of American Political History

Encyclopedia of Economics
Encyclopedia of Education
Encyclopedia of Feminism
Encyclopedia of Film and Television
Encyclopedia of Judaica
Encyclopedia of Psychology
Encyclopedia of World Art
International Encyclopedia of Social Sciences
World Encyclopedia of Film

Encyclopedias are designated in the computer catalog with "Ref." before the call number. They are shelved in the reference room.

Many library catalogs also include links to online encyclopedias. Some of these online encyclopedias are available for general use (such as the *Britannica* concise, available from Yahoo! Education), while others require a password to access. Passwords can generally be obtained from a reference librarian.

Use Indexes and Databases to Locate Periodical Material

Periodicals are magazines, newspapers, and journals published at regular intervals. They are important to the researcher because they contain the most current material available on a subject—unlike books, they are updated frequently.

Types of Periodicals. **General periodicals** are magazines and newspapers meant for the average reader. They include daily newspapers like the *Washington Post* and *Wall Street Journal* and magazines like *Time, Newsweek,* and *Sports Illustrated.* Think of general periodicals as the publications you can buy at a newsstand. These periodicals rarely provide in-depth treatment, as they are meant for the average reader.

Often such periodicals have extensive websites that include archives. For example, the *New York Times* site is updated throughout the day with world and regional news, and the site also allows you to search archives of articles dating back as far as 1851. The site provides full text for articles less than a week old and abstracts (or summaries) of articles older than one week. Full text of articles older than one week can be purchased for a small fee.

Journals are periodicals published by scholarly, professional organizations like the American Psychological Association and the Modern Language Association. They include titles such as *American Economic Review* and *Modern Fiction Studies.* They are not available at your local newsstand. The treatment of subjects in journals is more detailed because it is for readers knowledgeable in the given field. However, this fact should not discourage you from using journal articles, because they can be understood by college students. In fact, their more detailed discussions usually make them more satisfying than magazine articles.

Periodical Indexes. One way to find both general periodical and scholarly journal articles is through the use of indexes. Indexes catalog magazine and journal articles, most often by topic, so they are often the easiest way to find material related to your subject. Indexes are generally available in print form, on

CD-ROM, and through online, searchable databases. While this last format will probably be the one you use most frequently in your research, keep in mind that some articles written prior to 1985 might not be available through an electronic database. You should refer to a print index such as the *Readers' Guide to Periodical Literature* to find those articles.

Online databases like *EBSCOhost* and *ProQuest* that will lead you to periodicals differ in their specifics, but most allow you to search by title, author, or keyword. The figure below shows the results of a keyword search of an online database using the search term "genetically modified foods."

When searching an online database like *EBSCOhost*, keep in mind that the variety and number of keywords you use will affect the quantity and relevance of your results. After you have completed a search, click on the title

Results of an Online Periodical Database Search. This page shows the periodicals found in a search for "genetically modified foods."

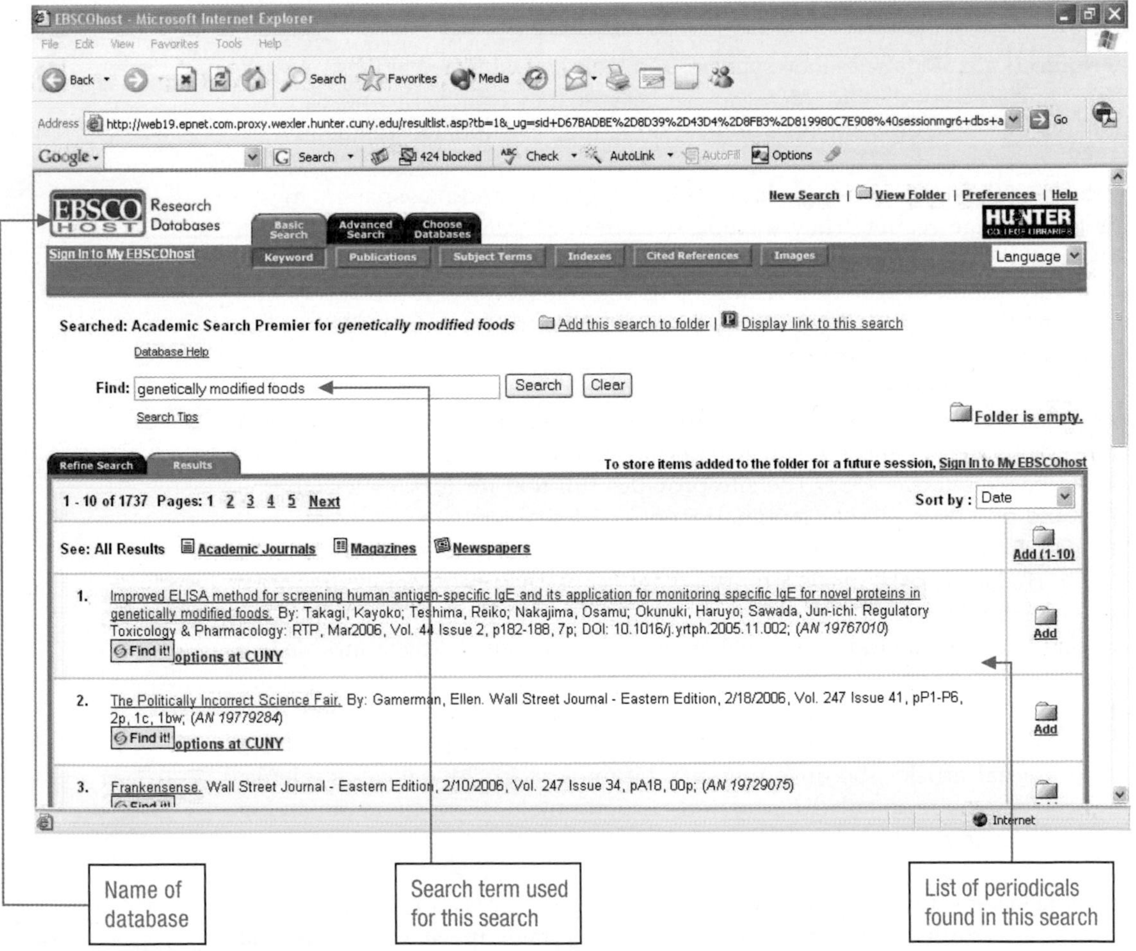

of an article to view complete citation information. The figure below shows what this might look like.

Often you can link directly to the full text of the article from its citation page. However, if the page does not offer a link, you should be able to find a print version of the complete piece in your library or obtain a copy through interlibrary loan.

Different libraries will use various online databases. Here is a list of some of the most popular ones:

- *EBSCOhost* accesses articles from more than 3,000 popular and scholarly periodicals in every academic subject. An important advantage of this useful resource is that it gives access to whole articles rather than abstracts.

Detailed Citation of an Article in an Online Periodical Database. This page gives further information on a listed article, including its publication information.

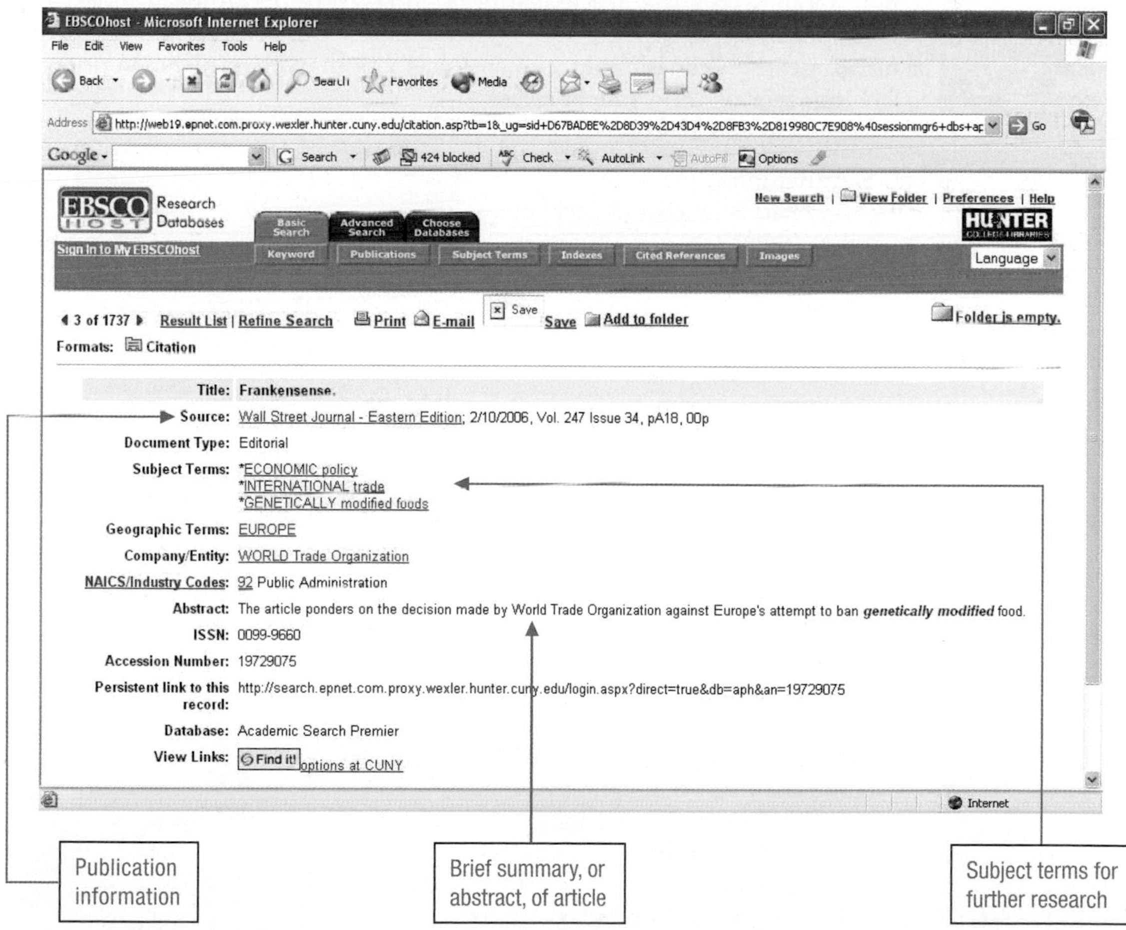

Reprinted with permission from EBSCO Host.

- *ProQuest* indexes more than 4,000 periodicals in its online form. An abstract is included for each article. Abstracts are useful because they allow you to judge how helpful the article is likely to be.
- *InfoTrac* indexes articles from over 1,100 magazines, journals, and newspapers by subject, title, and author. It is particularly helpful for very current topics.
- *LexisNexis* provides full-text articles from over 5,600 news, business, legal, and medical publications. It is particularly useful for searching newspapers.

Other helpful newspaper indexes include *The New York Times Index* and *ProQuest Newspaper Abstracts,* which indexes the *New York Times, Wall Street Journal, Christian Science Monitor, Washington Post,* and *Los Angeles Times.*

To discover useful journal articles, check the online or print indexes appropriate to your subject. In addition, check the abstracts and bibliographies. As touched on previously, an **abstract** lists articles by subject matter and provides a brief summary of each article's content in addition to information about where the article can be found. A **bibliography** includes both books and journal articles. The following is a list of some of the most common indexes, bibliographies, and abstracts that may be available in print, on CD-ROM, or on an online database.

ABC-CLIO (American history)
Agricultural Index
Applied Science and Technology Index
Art Index
Bibliography of Modern History
Bibliography on Women
Biological Abstracts
Business Periodicals Index
Chemical Abstracts
Drama Bibliography
Energy Index
Engineering Index
ERIC (education)
Film Index
General Science Index
GDCS (Government Documents Catalog Service)
Historical Abstracts
Humanities Index
Index to Economic Journals
Index to Religious Periodical Literature
International Bibliography of Geography
International Nursing Index
MLA Bibliography
Music Index
Nursing Literature Index
PAIS International (public and social policy, social sciences)
Philosopher's Index

PsycInfo
PubMed (biomedicine)
Social Science Index
Sociological Abstracts
Women: A Bibliography

Use the Internet to Locate Sources

www.mhhe.com/tsw
For further information on using the Internet to do research, go to Catalyst 2.0 > Research > Using the Internet

The Internet can be a useful research tool because it contains a variety of text, visual, and multimedia files that can be quickly searched. However, the Internet has many disadvantages. The changing nature of the Web means that a site you read yesterday might be gone tomorrow. Furthermore, quality control can be an issue, as *anyone* can post *anything* to a website. For instance, fiction can be presented as fact, images can be modified and tampered with, and 14-year-olds can masquerade as doctoral students in psychology. So how do you traverse this minefield of information? Let's start by examining the entry points for your research: basic and metasearch engines.

Searching the Internet

Basic search engines sift through the vast amounts of information and return the most relevant sites according to your keywords. **Metasearch engines** sort through several basic search engines at once. No single search engine covers the millions of pages available on the Internet, so use a few as you research. Also, search engines come and go with some frequency, so check with your reference librarian to learn whether there is a new search engine you should try.

Basic Search Engines

Altavista	www.altavista.com
Google	www.google.com
Lycos	www.lycos.com
MSN	www.msn.com
Yahoo!	www.yahoo.com

Metasearch Engines

Dogpile	www.dogpile.com
Ixquick	www.ixquick.com
Mamma	www.mamma.com
Metacrawler	www.metacrawler.com

The following figure shows the home page of the popular search engine Google.

Home Page of Google. Google is one of the most popular search engines on the Internet.

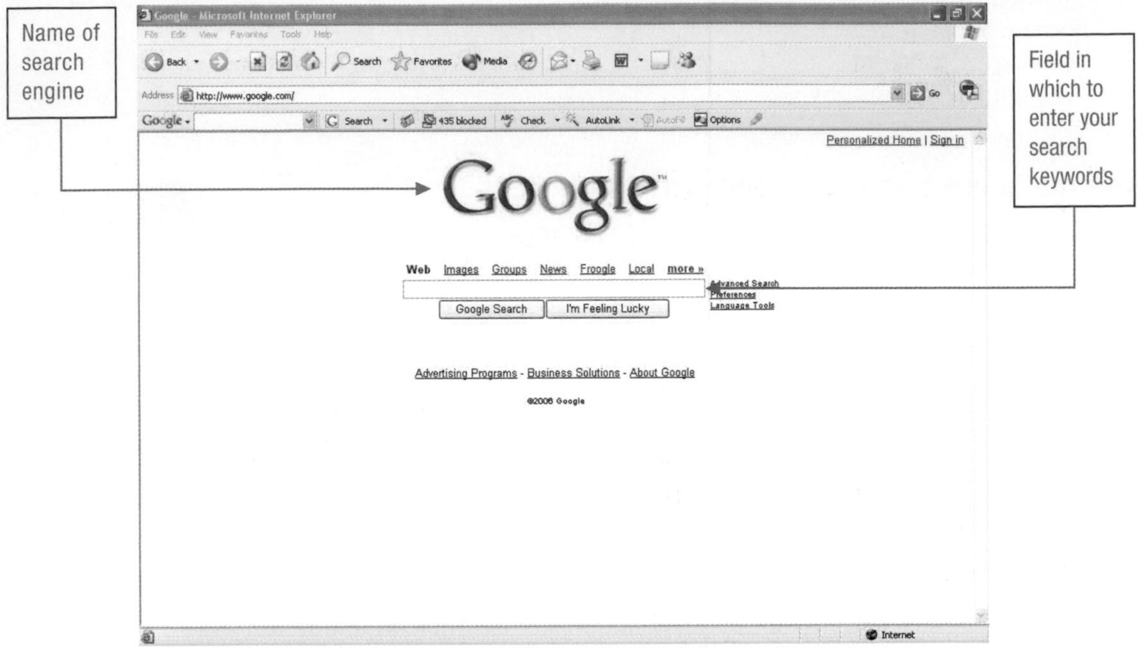

Search engines are powerful research tools when they are used correctly. The key to getting the best results from your Internet search is the keyword or keywords you use to focus your search. As with the search terms you use for a library catalog search, you want a keyword or keywords that are neither too broad nor too narrow. Be sure you spell your keywords correctly and use relevant terminology to ensure that your search retrieves the most relevant results.

You should also familiarize yourself with the following commands. Use them with your keywords to specify precisely what you are searching for and to weed out irrelevant results.

- **Quotation marks.** Keywords enclosed in quotation marks denote an exact word or phrase. So, if you want the search engine to look for only the complete phrase *genetically modified foods,* with those exact words in that exact order, you would enclose it in quotes: "genetically modified foods."
- **AND, OR, and NOT.** Using these words, in all-capital letters, between your keywords tells your search engine how to look for them. AND stipulates that both terms should be present in a source (e.g., genetically AND food). OR stipulates that at least one of the terms should be present (food OR produce). NOT excludes any source that includes that term (food NOT human).
- **+ and – signs.** The + and – signs function just like the AND and NOT commands. Include a + sign between two keywords, without spaces, to stipulate that both should be present in a source (genetically+food).

Include a – sign before a term, again without a space, to exclude sources that include it (food–human).

Experiment with these commands to understand how they function. Once you have mastered them, they will save you a great deal of time and improve your overall Internet research skills.

Once you have entered your keywords and conducted your search, the search engine will return a list of results. The figure below shows what this list can look like using Google. Clicking the links the search engine produces will take you to that web page.

Google Results Page. This shows the web pages Google found after a search for "genetically modified" AND "foods."

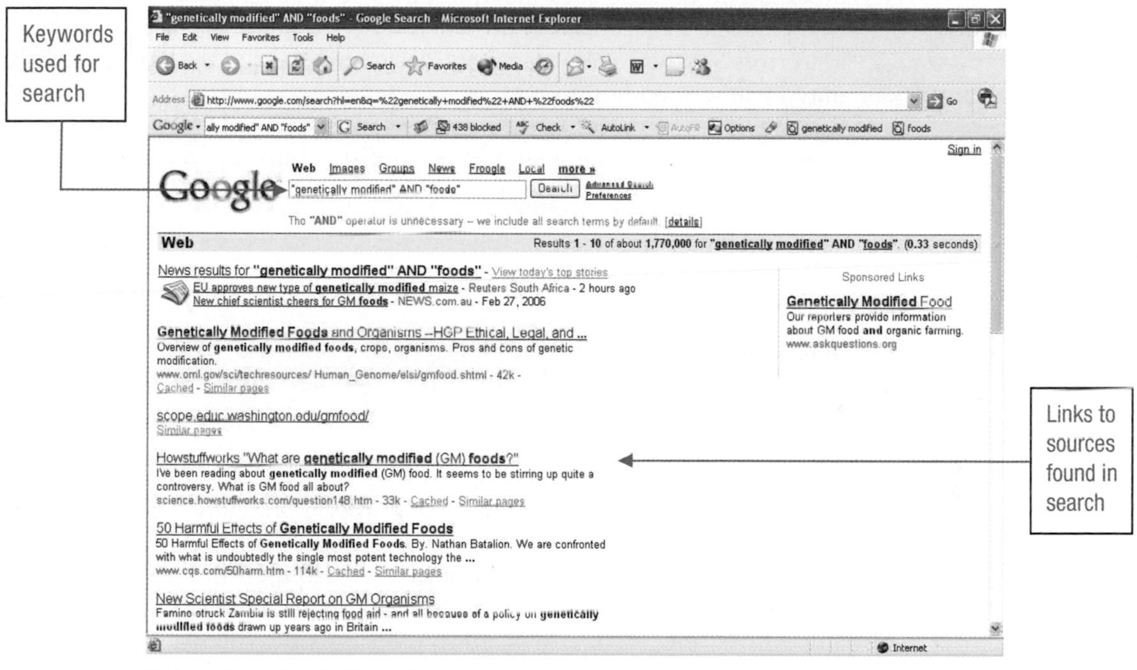

Evaluating Internet Sources

Internet sources present a special challenge because the quality of the material varies so greatly. No editor checks facts or assesses the logic of web pages. When evaluating Internet sources, ask the following questions:

- Who is sponsoring the website? Generally, you should work with informational sites (ones whose purpose is to present information). Sites sponsored by universities, the government, or research foundations are likely to be more reliable than for-profit sites. In addition, pages associated with major news and media organizations like CNN or the *Wall Street Journal* are reliable. URLs (universal resource locators) that end in *gov* are sponsored by the government, and ones ending in *edu* are sponsored by an educational institution. Remember, though, that anything posted by a student, like a paper or diatribe, will also end in.edu.

- Can the sponsor of the page be verified? Look for a phone number or postal address. Check the sponsor's credentials on the Web or in a print source. Does the sponsor have a particular bias? For example, a page sponsored by Planned Parenthood may have pro-choice leanings. If the page has particular leanings, are opposing points of view considered?
- When was the site last updated? The date may appear on the page. A very old page may no longer be reliable. If you use Internet Explorer, you can see the dates some sites were created and revised by clicking "File" and then "Properties."
- Does the site include links to credible sites? A site full of dead links or links to questionable sites may not be current or reliable.
- Does the site look professional? Do you notice grammar, usage, or spelling errors? Is the page attractively designed? A page that looks shoddy may include shoddy information.
- Can information on the site be verified in a print source? Controversial or surprising information should be confirmed for accuracy.

The figure on page 491 compares two websites—one reliable and credible, the other questionable.

Other Internet Resources

Searching for documents and sites relevant to your topic is not the only way to use the Internet as a research tool. The Web also allows people from all over the world to communicate through e-mail, listservs, newsgroups, and blogs.

E-mail. E-mail is very useful for conducting interviews with experts on your topic. Because an e-mail interview does not require scheduled, face-to-face time, an electronic interview format allows you to question people who do not live near you or who might not be able to spare the time for an in-person or phone interview. Also, e-mail interviews provide you with an accurate record of an expert's response to your questions.

Many people are wary about unsolicited questionnaires. Send a brief e-mail first, asking permission to send additional questions. In this initial e-mail, describe your project and your interest in the work of the interviewee. Be polite and professional in your follow-up e-mails, and send a thank-you e-mail after an interview has been completed.

Listservs and newsgroups. Electronic discussion groups such as listservs and newsgroups can be an excellent resource for conducting interviews and surveys. Topics for such groups range anywhere from child rearing to snowboarding, and most anyone can join any list or group. Once you subscribe to a list, you can post questions to the group via e-mail. Most group members have a great deal of knowledge about the group topic, so general questions that can be answered by other methods of research should not be posted. For example,

A Comparison of Two Websites. Here are two web pages, the first one reliable and credible, the second questionable in the accuracy of its content. When evaluating websites, look for information about the site's sponsor, the date it was last updated, and the general quality of its design and presentation.

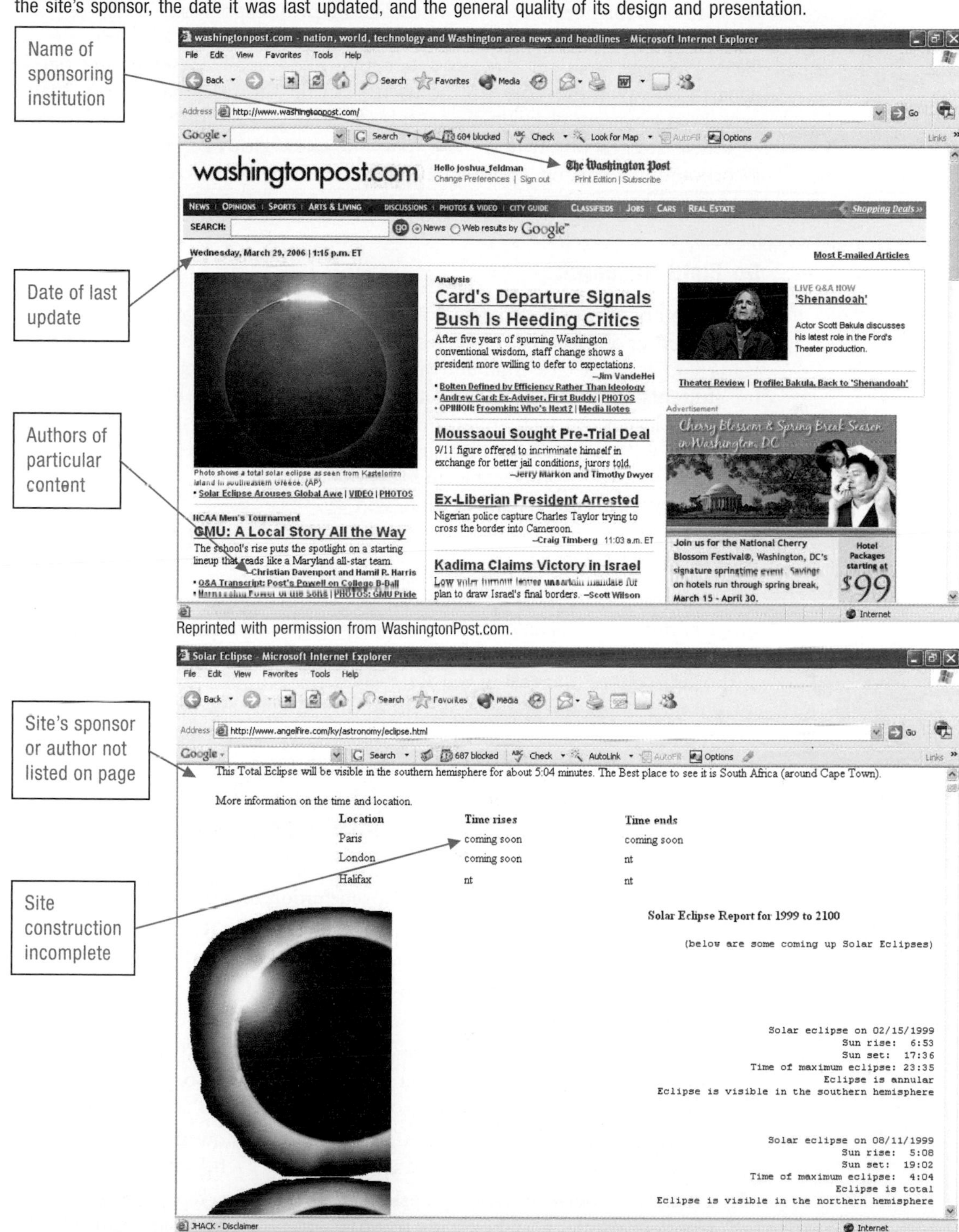

Reprinted with permission from WashingtonPost.com.

the question "How do you learn to snowboard?" might be ignored by members of a snowboarding listserv, but the more specific question "What types of bindings are best for freestyling?" should elicit helpful responses.

Blogs. Weblogs, or blogs, are not interactive like e-mail, listservs, and newsgroups; however, they can still be useful during the research process. Many experts in a variety of fields maintain blogs, and you might find helpful book or article suggestions within these diarylike sites. However, be careful about incorporating firsthand information from these sites within your paper. Blog entries can be based more on opinion than fact and can contain strong biases.

Do Field Research

So far, you have read about research that leads you to what other people have discovered about a topic. **Field research,** on the other hand, is inquiry that leads you to your *own* firsthand findings. The most practical field research for students to conduct is interviews and surveys. Topics based on campus and local issues are well suited to interviews and surveys, but those based on topics with a larger scope—such as international politics—may not be. After all, students, professors, and local leaders will be more available to interact with you than world leaders will be.

Conducting an Interview

Many people on or near campus can be worth interviewing. For instance, medical professionals have important perspectives on topics such as the AIDS epidemic and physician-assisted suicide; local businesspeople can speak authoritatively on increasing the state sales tax; school board members have information about the advantages and disadvantages of teachers' unions; and your classmates can discuss their experiences with test anxiety.

These guidelines can help you conduct an interview:

1. Decide whether open or closed questions will be more useful. **Open questions** allow for unlimited response; **closed questions** limit the respondents' answers.

   Open question: How will the proposed tuition increase affect you?

   Closed question: The proposed tuition increase will likely (a) cause me to drop out of school, (b) cause me to reduce my course load, (c) have no effect on me.

2. Make an appointment.
3. Write out your questions in advance so you are prepared and do not waste your interviewee's time. Although not required to do so, you can send the interviewee the questions ahead of time, so that he or she can prepare.
4. Although you will have written out questions, allow the interviewee to go in unexpected directions if doing so yields useful information.
5. Take careful notes. If necessary, ask the interviewee to repeat so you get the words just right. Or take a tape recorder and ask permission to use it.

6. Get permission to quote the interviewee, and document according to the form given on page 525.
7. Alternatively, conduct an "interview" via e-mail, allowing your subject to write responses to your questions. This is a useful strategy when your interview subject is very busy or if your topic is technical or complex.

Conducting a Survey

A **survey** is a questionnaire—a set of questions designed to gather information from a group of people. There are different kinds of surveys. In the social sciences, for example, surveys are conducted according to strict, rigorous procedures. Here, however, we are using a more informal methodology.

Surveys are useful when you want to get the general opinion or reaction of a particular group. For example, you may want to know how high school teachers feel about charter schools or to learn how much television college students watch. If you are conducting both surveys and interviews, be sure your choices of subjects do not overlap. In addition to asking for answers, you may want your respondents to indicate their age, gender, or other information if you want to compare responses. For example, if you are surveying students to learn whether they experience test anxiety, you might want to learn their class rank to see if seniors are more likely to be anxious than first-year students.

When you survey people, remember these guidelines:

1. Include a cover letter explaining who you are and the purpose of the survey.
2. Write clear questions. You might want to test them out on people to be sure they are clear.
3. Decide whether open or closed questions will be more useful. Open questions such as "Explain your experience with test anxiety" can give you answers that are difficult to interpret and tally. You will find it more productive to write closed multiple-choice or scale questions like these:

   How often do you experience test anxiety?

   a. Never
   b. Every time you take a test
   c. About half the time you take a test
   d. Less than half the time you take a test
   e. More than half the time you take a test

   If you experience test anxiety at least half the time you take a test, rate the typical level of your anxiety.

mild		*severe*		*debilitating*
1	*2*	*3*	*4*	*5*

4. If you use closed questions, be sure your choices do not overlap. For example, "less than half the time" and "rarely" overlap and undermine the usefulness of answers.

5. Keep value judgments out of your questions. If you write, "Have you ever engaged in the immoral practice of plagiarism?" your respondent will be forced to admit to being immoral if answering yes. Instead, write, "Have you ever quoted a passage without using quotation marks?"
6. Be sure your respondents are a representative sample of the group you are considering. Thus, if your campus is ethnically diverse, try to represent all ethnicities when you survey students about test anxiety. Also, use enough respondents. Asking 10 students about test anxiety will not tell you much about the student body, but asking 50 may give you reliable information about how many members of this group experience the problem.
7. Use e-mail if possible for the convenience of respondents.

Compile a Working Bibliography

A **working bibliography** is a list of potentially useful sources—sources you should look at closely later, when you take notes. To compile a working bibliography, follow these steps:

1. Look up your subject in the computer or card catalog, and create a bibliography card for any book that looks promising. Although some people place their working bibliography on notebook paper or in a computer file, index cards are a better choice. The wise researcher writes up the cards to follow the appropriate works-cited forms, which are given beginning on page 516. The following are examples of bibliography cards. The first card is for a book in print form; the second is for an online article.

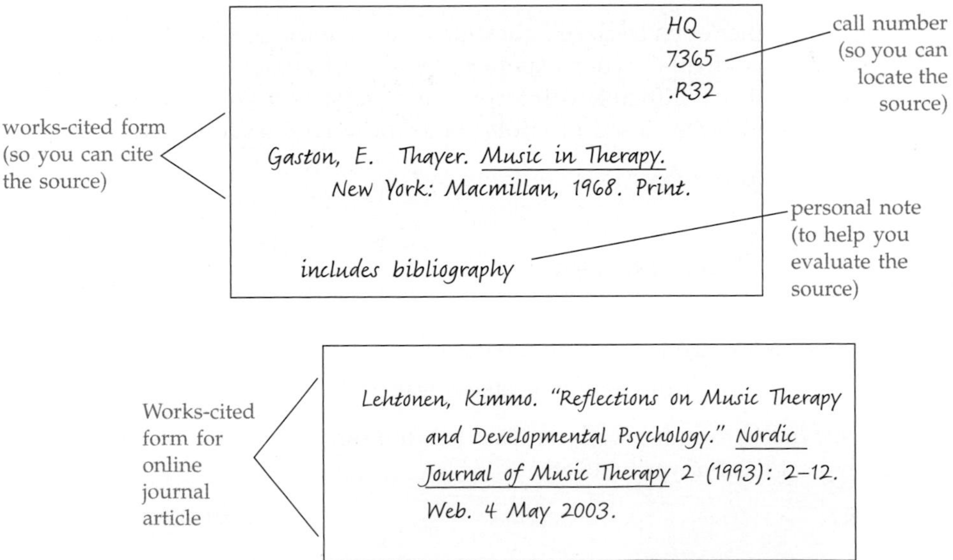

2. Look up your topic in the appropriate indexes, bibliographies, databases, and abstracts, and make bibliography cards for promising sources, following the forms beginning on page 516.

3. Check the Internet if you have access to it, and make bibliography cards for promising sources, following the forms beginning on page 520.

Admittedly, you will decide what to include in your working bibliography based on flimsy evidence: whether the title of the source sounds promising. For this reason, you should err on the side of caution, creating a card for any source that holds even a slight chance of usefulness. You can discard the source later if it proves disappointing.

EVALUATING AND USING YOUR SOURCES

www.mhhe.com/tsw
For further help evaluating sources, go to Catalyst 2.0 > Research > CARS Source Evaluation Tutor

Before taking notes, evaluate your sources to determine which of them are good enough to take notes on. Answering the following questions can help:

- Is the material recent enough? For some topics (e.g., General Sherman's Civil War strategy), older material may be fine, but other topics (e.g., the ethics of cloning) require the most up-to-date materials available.
- Does the author have suitable credentials? On the back cover, in the preface, or on the last page of a book, you can learn such things as an author's educational background and degrees earned, the relevant work or research history, the publications authored, and the awards received. Similar material is often available in headnotes or footnotes of articles and online.
- Is the author expressing a fact, an opinion, or both? Remember, a fact is verifiable information, and an opinion is the author's interpretation of the fact. Thus, it is a fact that the stock market is at a three-year low but an opinion that it will decline more before the end of the year.
- Does the material manipulate emotions? Is it written with a particular bias? If so, you must recognize a source's bias and take it into account. For example, an article on abortion that appears on the Planned Parenthood website will likely give one picture of a controversial subject, while one on a right-to-life website will likely give another.
- Is the material sufficiently scholarly, complete, and accessible? Skim to see if it includes references to relevant research. Look at the table of contents, index, and headings to check coverage. Read a few paragraphs to be sure the writing is not too technical or difficult for you to understand. At the same time, be sure the material is not too general and superficial.
- Does the source include material you need for your research?

Read Your Sources Strategically

Read *strategically* to find what is relevant to your research as quickly as possible. The first step is to determine the usefulness of a source. These strategies can help:

1. Read the title and major headings. If there is a table of contents, look it over. If there is an index, look up important words and phrases. If any of these suggest information relevant to your research, the source may be useful.

2. If there is a preface or introduction, or chapter or unit summaries, read them quickly. If they touch on your topic, the source may be useful.
3. Read the first sentence of every paragraph in an article and of every paragraph of a relevant chapter in a book, looking for an indication that the rest of the material is relevant to your topic.
4. Read the last paragraph of an article or relevant chapters of a book, looking for key ideas.
5. Note boldface, italicized, and underlined terms. Are any of these keywords for your topic?
6. Note graphics and read captions looking for indications that the material is relevant to your topic.

www.mhhe.com/tsw

For further help with notetaking and related research skills, go to Catalyst 2.0 > Research > Research Techniques

Take Notes

Some people take notes on index cards, and some people use their computers.

If you use index cards:

1. Avoid the temptation to fill each card. Instead, write one piece of information per card, as in the following figure, so you can shuffle your note cards into a suitable order later when you organize your paper.
2. On each card, indicate the source and page number the note is taken from, or any necessary URL, so you can document the material in your paper.
3. Be sure you have an entry in your working bibliography for each source.

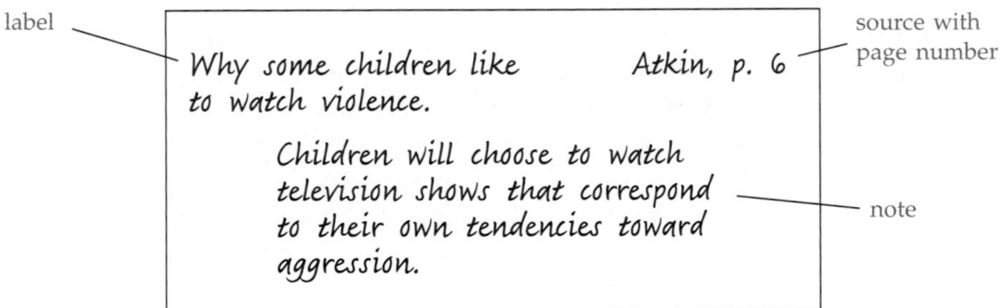

4. Label each card to categorize its content. Labels such as "Historical background," "Teen pregnancy rate," and "Possible solution" will help you organize your cards.
5. If you quote, be sure to use quotation marks.

If you use the computer:

1. Put all your notes in one file, create separate files for different headings or subtopics, or place each note in a separate file. Consider which method best lends itself to cutting and pasting your notes into a draft.
2. Keep backup copies of all your notes on a CD in case of hard drive failure. Losing all your notes is a catastrophic setback.

3. Avoid filling up screens with uninterrupted notes. Instead, write one item of information and then hit "control/enter" to create a page break, or start a new file for the next note. You want to be able to rearrange notes easily for your draft.
4. Indicate the source and page number the note is taken from or any necessary URL, so you can document the material in your paper.
5. Label each note to categorize its content.

If most of your sources are online, you may be tempted to cut and paste directly from the website into your notes—and from your notes into your paper. This practice is dangerous because it often leads to plagiarism, as explained on page 506. You should paraphrase, summarize, and quote as you take notes.

If you photocopy or download and print out sources:

1. Be sure the source and page numbers are on the photocopy. If you have not made a bibliography card for the source, write all the bibliographic information on the photocopy.
2. Underline or highlight the useful information, but avoid marking too much, or you will have trouble extracting what you need when you draft your paper.
3. In the margins, label your underlining or highlighting to indicate its content, your responses to the source, or how you might use the source in your paper.

There are four kinds of notetaking you should know if you take notes on note cards or on a computer: paraphrase notes, quotation notes, summary notes, and personal notes.

Paraphrase Notes

When you **paraphrase,** you restate an author's original ideas in your own words and style. Most of your notes should be paraphrases so that your paper has your own distinctive style. When you paraphrase, remember the following points:

- You must alter the style and wording of the original material.
- You may not add any ideas.
- You may not alter the meaning of the original material in any way.

A good procedure for paraphrasing is to read the original material several times until you understand its meaning. Then pretend to explain to a friend what you just read, and write the paraphrase in the way you would form the explanation. Check to be sure you have altered the style and wording without altering or adding to the meaning. To paraphrase a long passage, break it down into parts and write the paraphrase part by part.

To appreciate the difference between an acceptable and unacceptable paraphrase, study the following examples:

> From *Sociology* by Richard T. Schaefer, page 423: An economic system does not exist in a vacuum. Someone or some group makes important decisions about how to use resources and how to allocate goods, whether it be a

tribal chief or a parliament or a dictator. A cultural universal common to all economic systems, then, is the exercise of power and authority.

Unacceptable paraphrase: An economic system does not exist alone. A person or collection of people will make major decisions about how to use and distribute resources and allocate goods. Thus, power and authority are a cultural universal in all economies. This fact holds true regardless of whether the power or authority is benign or cruel (Schaefer 423).

Explanation: The paraphrase is unacceptable for two reasons: The style is too close to that of the original, and the last sentence of the paraphrase includes an idea that does not appear in the original.

Acceptable paraphrase: In every economy, one or more persons determine the use and distribution of resources and goods. Thus, economic systems do not function independent of people, and they do not function without the use of power (Schaefer 423).

Explanation: This paraphrase has a style different from that of the original, but the meaning of the original has not been changed, nor has any meaning been added.

When you paraphrase, you may find it necessary or desirable to retain a key word or phrase from the original. If the word or phrase is part of the author's distinctive style, place it in quotation marks, as this example illustrates:

> In every economy, one or more persons determine the use and distribution of resources and goods. Thus, economic systems do not function independent of people or "the exercise of power and authority" (Schaefer 423).

Quotation Notes

So that your paper retains your distinctive style, most of your notes should be paraphrases. However, if a source expresses a point in a particularly effective way, or if you encounter material that is very difficult to paraphrase, you can use quotation. When you quote, remember these Modern Language Association (MLA) guidelines:

1. With very few exceptions (noted below), do not alter the spelling, capitalization, punctuation, or wording of anything you quote.
2. Work short quotations (those fewer than five lines in your paper) into your sentence or paragraph.
3. Set long quotations (those five or more lines in your paper) off in a particular way:
   a. Start a new line and indent the quotation 10 spaces on the left.
   b. Indent the first word if the quotation marks the beginning of a paragraph in the source.
   c. Do not use quotation marks unless they appeared in the source, in which case use double quotation marks.

d. Follow the introduction to a long quotation with a colon.

e. Double-space the quotation.

f. Place the period before the parenthetical citation.

See page 537 for an example of a long quotation.

4. To omit some portion from the middle or end of a quotation, use an ellipsis mark (three spaced periods). Be sure when you omit words that you do not alter the original meaning. Here's an example:

Source: *Sociology* by Richard T. Schaefer, page 423: An economic system does not exist in a vacuum. Someone or some group makes important decisions about how to use resources and how to allocate goods, whether it be a tribal chief or a parliament or a dictator. A cultural universal common to all economic systems, then, is the exercise of power and authority. The struggle for power and authority inevitably involves *politics,* which political scientist Harold Lasswell (1936) tersely defined as "who gets what, when, and how."

Quotation with ellipsis mark "A cultural universal common to all economic systems . . . is the exercise of power and authority" (Schaefer 423).

If the omission comes at the end of a sentence, use the ellipsis mark and then a period.

Quotation with ellipsis mark: "Someone or some group makes important decisions about how to use resources and how to allocate goods . . ." (Schaefer 423).

5. When you must add a word or phrase to a quotation to clarify something or work the quotation into your sentence, place the addition inside brackets.

Quotation with addition: "A cultural universal common to all economic systems, then, is the exercise of power and authority [to determine how goods and resources will be used]" (Schaefer 423).

6. When part of the material you are quoting appears in italics, reproduce those italics. If you are writing by hand, underline words in italics.

Quotation with underlining: "The struggle for power and authority inevitably involves *politics* . . ." (Schaefer 423).

7. When all or part of what you are quoting is itself a quotation, use single quotation marks wherever double quotation marks appear in the source. Continue to use double quotation marks to mark the place where the quoted material begins and ends.

Quotation with single quotation marks: "The struggle for power and authority inevitably involves *politics,* which political scientist Harold Lasswell (1936) tersely defined as 'who gets what, when, and how'" (Schaefer 423).

8. When you work the quotation into your paper with an introduction containing the word *that,* do not capitalize the first word of the quotation (unless it is a proper noun), and do not use a comma after the introduction. If the introduction in your text does not have the word *that,* then use a comma and capitalize the first word of the quotation.

Example with *that:*	Schaefer says that "an economic system does not exist in a vacuum" (423).
Example without *that:*	Schaefer says, "An economic system does not exist in a vacuum" (423).

Combining Paraphrase and Quotation

Many passages lend themselves to a combination of paraphrase and quotation, as the following example shows.

Paraphrase and quotation:	In every economy, one or more persons determine the use and distribution of resources and goods. Thus, economic systems do not function independent of people, and they do not function without the use of power. "The struggle for [this] power . . . involves *politics,* which political scientist Harold Lasswell (1936) tersely defined as 'who gets what, when, and how'" (Schaefer 423).

Summary Notes

A **summary** is a condensed version of all or part of a source. The summary may condense a paragraph into a sentence or two, or multiple paragraphs into a single paragraph, or an entire essay into a paragraph or two. Like a paraphrase, a summary restates an author's ideas in your own words and style without altering or adding meaning.

Here are two summaries of paragraph 7 of "The Case for Torture Warrants" on page 455.

Unacceptable summary:	In "The Case for Torture Warrants," Alan M. Dershowitz claims that a requirement for a warrant to use non-lethal torture would decrease the amount of torture directed against suspects because compelling evidence would have to be shown before judges would authorize torture. Further, law enforcement officials would not ask for a warrant unless they had compelling evidence that the torture would prevent a terrorist attack. The warrants would also protect a suspect's rights and lead to judicially monitored, less brutal torture (456).

This summary is not as condensed as it could be, but more problematically, it does not sufficiently alter Dershowitz's wording. It is too similar to the original to be presented without quotation marks. In fact, it can be seen as plagiarism (see page 506). Now consider this example:

Acceptable summary: In "The Case for Torture Warrants," Alan M. Dershowitz claims that instituting torture warrants would decrease the incidence of torture, protect the rights of suspects, and result in less brutal torture techniques (456).

The author of this summary has sufficiently altered the wording of the original essay. It succinctly captures Dershowitz's ideas, but does so in the author's voice.

For more on how to write a summary, see page 12.

Personal Notes

As you take notes, ideas of your own will occur to you. You may think of a way to handle your introduction, or you may have an idea in response to what you have read, or you may see a connection between ideas in different sources, or you may think of a piece of information you should look up. When comments, insights, and other brainstorms strike you, write them on note cards too, so you do not forget them. Just be sure to label these ideas as your own, so you do not confuse them with borrowed information.

RECONSIDERING YOUR PRELIMINARY THESIS

After notetaking, you will know much more about your topic than you did when you wrote your preliminary thesis. As a result, you may want to rewrite your thesis to refine it or to take it in a new direction. First, review your note cards to refresh your memory about the information you collected. Then shape your thesis to reflect what you discovered in the library, on the Internet, or in field research. Even this version of your thesis is not final, however. You may continue to rework it during drafting and revising.

"Go ask your search engine."

LOOKING AHEAD

When you conduct research, whether you do so with electronic tools (such as a search engine) or with paper tools (such as a bound bibliography or index), you have a responsibility to treat your source material with respect. In the previous chapter, you learned to be respectful of source material by paraphrasing, quoting, and summarizing it appropriately. In this chapter, you will learn other important conventions for respectfully handling source material by acknowledging source material with appropriate documentation. Before doing so, respond to the following:

- How would you feel if you wrote a short story and shared it with a friend, who copied it over without your name on it and gave it to his girlfriend as a gift?
- How would you feel if your boss took your report and gave it to the company president, passing it off as her own work?
- Why do you think that responsible researchers believe that it is both fair and important to inform their readers of the source of their facts, statistics, and other researched information?

CHAPTER 17

Writing with Sources and Using Proper Documentation

In the previous chapter, you learned the steps of the research process and how to gather sources using the wealth of tools in the library, on the Internet, and beyond. In this chapter, you will learn to integrate your research findings into your writing. You will also learn how to document your sources correctly.

OUTLINING

Because writing a research paper is complex, you should write a detailed outline, even if you do not customarily do so. In outlining, consider the following:

1. Before outlining, read over your notes. Consider your source material and personal notes thoughtfully. In particular, think about how your notes support your preliminary thesis. Do your notes suggest that you should revise your thesis?
2. Look for a pattern as you review your notes and arrange your note cards or computer notes to reflect that order.
3. If ideas occur to you as you order your notes, work them into your order.
4. Using your ordered ideas as a guide, write a detailed outline to guide your first draft.
5. As you outline, consider whether you need additional information to support or explain a point. If so, do additional research.

WRITING YOUR FIRST DRAFT

Use organizational tools to guide your audience. Place your thesis in one of the introductory paragraphs, so your reader is aware of your focus from the start; use topic sentences to make the main idea of every paragraph clear for readers; and use transitions to guide the reader from point to point. Where you will write a paraphrase, quotation, or summary, you can paste your computer note into the draft or tape the note card on the draft.

As you draft, avoid stringing sources together one after another. Instead, comment on your paraphrases, quotations, and summaries by analyzing them, showing their significance, indicating their relationships to something else, and so forth. Here is an example paragraph. Notice that the student author comments on the source material by showing its application.

Paraphrase: Professor Charles Atkin explains another reason children should not be completely restricted from viewing violence. He suggests that children will choose to watch television shows that correspond to their own tendencies toward aggression (6).

Student comment on paraphrase: Thus, by observing the types of programs their children prefer, parents can gain a better understanding of their personalities. A child who continually elects to watch violence may have aggressive tendencies. Parents need to know whether their children are too aggressive so they can intervene, and one way they can discover this is to observe their children's viewing preferences.

Finally, when you draft, you must document source material by introducing paraphrases, quotations, and summaries; writing parenthetical text citations; and including a works-cited page. These issues are taken up in the next sections.

PLAGIARISM

www.mhhe.com/tsw
For further help avoiding plagiarism, go to Catalyst 2.0 > Research > Avoiding Plagiarism

When people think of **plagiarism,** a form of academic dishonesty, they often think of students illicitly downloading papers from the Internet or copying large passages from books and passing them off as their own work. In other words, they think of plagiarism as something intentionally dishonest. And, to be sure, such behavior is unethical and in some cases illegal.

There are other forms of plagiarism, though, that are equally unethical but that receive much less attention. Plagiarism occurs any time a student does not give proper credit for a fact, idea, or passage in his or her writing.

For this reason, you must be both honest and thorough in your academic writing; you must always alert your reader when an idea is not your own. Of course, to do so, you must be able to recognize when such an acknowledgment is necessary.

What to Document

In the sections that follow, you will find extensive coverage of how to give credit properly for outside sources in your writing. Providing this credit is called **documentation.**

Every time you use the words, ideas, or opinions of others, you must document that material. You must document facts that are not common knowledge, including statistics, references to studies, descriptions of experiments, an author's original ideas, an author's opinion, and an author's conclusion—regardless of whether this material appears in your paper as quotation, paraphrase, or summary.

You need not document facts that are common knowledge. Thus, you don't need to document that Abraham Lincoln was assassinated by John Wilkes Booth, that gravity holds the planets in orbit, or that plants bend toward the sun. Nor do you need to document dates that are not debatable, such as the date Lincoln was shot, or common sayings, such as "Fools rush in where wise men fear to tread."

If you are in doubt about whether to document a point, err on the side of caution. It is better to document too much than to document too little and plagiarize as a result. Of course, your instructor can advise you when you are unsure.

How to Avoid Plagiarism When You Paraphrase

One of the most common forms of plagiarism occurs when a student paraphrases a passage from a source but does not sufficiently alter the author's words and style. Even when you properly acknowledge that the material is borrowed, you will still be guilty of plagiarism if the paraphrase is too close to the original. Consider the following example:

> From *The American Tradition in Literature,* 11e, by George and Barbara Perkins, page 553: A former orator, Red Jacket (or Sagoyewatha) was skilled in humorous and sarcastic speeches in defense of the traditions of the Five Nations of the Iroquois, of which his Seneca tribe was a part.

Student paraphrase considered plagiarism

```
A former orator, Sagoyewatha, also
known as Red Jacket, was skilled
in witty and sarcastic speeches on
behalf of the Five Nations of the
Iroquois, of which his Seneca
tribe was a member (Perkins and
Perkins 553).
```

If you want to include the exact words of another writer, use quotation marks. Do not change every third word of a source and think that the writing is now your own. For more on paraphrasing, see pages 497–98.

How to Avoid Online Plagiarism

Be particularly careful to avoid plagiarism with online sources by paraphrasing, summarizing, quoting, and documenting appropriately when you download material. It is easy to copy sections from an online source and paste them into your paper, forgetting to use quotation marks and to document. You may think that you will add these later but forget to do so.

Also note that digital sources, because they are new and always changing, can be particularly tricky to document in the proper format. See pages 520–24 for details on correct digital documentation. If you have any questions, ask your instructor for guidance.

BEING A RESPONSIBLE WRITER

Plagiarism is a form of academic dishonesty that often carries serious penalties. To avoid plagiarism, do the following:

1. Always use quotation marks around someone else's words.
2. Be sure to quote accurately. Use the ellipsis mark when you omit words and brackets when you add them.
3. Never add or alter meaning when you paraphrase.
4. Use your own wording and style when you paraphrase.
5. Include the author and/or title of the source with each paraphrase, quotation, or summary.
6. Give a parenthetical citation and works-cited or references entry for every paraphrase, quotation, and summary.

www.mhhe.com/tsw

For further help with documentation, go to Catalyst 2.0 > Research > Research Techniques

DOCUMENTING SOURCE MATERIAL

Documentation refers to the system for acknowledging that you are using the words or ideas of another person. It is also the system of conventions for noting the source of your paraphrase, quotation, or summary so that your readers can locate this material if they want to. (These conventions will be discussed in the next sections.) In order to document responsibly using the Modern Language Association (MLA) guidelines, you must be diligent about doing the following for every paraphrase, summary, and quotation in your paper:

1. Introduce the source material with the name of the author or source.
2. Provide a parenthetical text citation for the source material.

3. Enclose all quotations in quotation marks.
4. Provide a "Works Cited" entry.

How to Document Using MLA Style

The next sections explain the MLA's conventions for documenting source material. They are appropriate for papers written in the humanities (including writing courses). These conventions include introducing paraphrases, quotations, and summaries; providing parenthetical text citations; and writing a "Works Cited" page. Keep in mind that all the rules are designed to make it clear to your reader what source material you are using and where that material can be found, and the rules will seem more logical and easier to remember.

Introduce Source Material

To distinguish your own ideas from those you have discovered in the library or on the Internet, introduce each paraphrase, quotation, and summary with a phrase that indicates its source. Consider, for example, the following passage from a student paper. The introductions are underlined as a study aid.

> Businesses in the United States and the world over lose great sums of money because of the alcoholic employee. <u>Estimates of the Department of Health, Education, and Welfare and a study done by Roman and Trice show that</u> the number of alcoholics ranges from as high as ten out of every one hundred workers to a low of three to four out of one hundred (Williams and Moffat 7). Alcoholism, <u>as Joseph Follman states</u>, is "a problem so far reaching and so costly [it] must have an effect upon the business community of the nation." <u>Follman goes on to say</u>, "The result is impaired production, labor turnover, and increased costs of operation" (78). In terms of impaired productivity, the cost in the United States alone is said to be $12.5 billion a year, <u>as the National Council on Alcoholism estimates</u> (Follman 81-82). Obviously, someone must pay these costs, and no doubt it is the consumer who pays higher prices for goods and services. Yet reduced productivity because of alcoholic employees and the resulting higher prices could be held in check by the sound implementation of company programs to rehabilitate the alcoholic employee.

The paragraph includes both source material and the writer's own ideas. Each paraphrase and quotation is introduced to identify it as someone else's words or ideas. A close look reveals these points about introducing source material:

- The introduction is in the present tense. This **present-tense convention** is followed because printed words live on, even if they were written long ago.
- Introductions usually appear before the source material, but they can also be placed in the middle or at the end.
- The verbs used in your introductions should be varied to avoid monotony. For example, instead of repeatedly writing "Smith says," use "Smith explains" (notes, reveals, demonstrates, believes, contends, etc.).
- An introduction can refer to the author of the source material ("Smith finds"), or to the credentials of the author ("one researcher believes" or "a prominent sociologist contends"), or to the title of the source ("according to *Advertising Age*").

Write Parenthetical Text Citations

In addition to introducing source material, you must cite your source of information within parentheses at a pause in the sentence as close to the cited material as possible. This is true whether your material is a paraphrase, a summary, or a quotation.

1. When your paraphrase, quotation, or summary has been introduced with the author's name, include the page number or numbers the material appears on in the source in parentheses; put the period after the citation:

   Ruth Caldersen agrees that corporal punishment is not a legitimate form of discipline in schools (104).

2. When the introduction does not include the author's name, note this name along with the appropriate page number or numbers in parentheses:

   One researcher remarks, "Corporal punishment teaches children to solve problems with violence" (Hayes 20).

3. If you quote something that is cited in a second source, note the second-hand nature of the borrowing with *qtd. in* (which means "quoted in"):

   One high school principal remarks, "I've never known corporal punishment to improve the behavior of unruly students" (qtd. in Hayes 16).

4. When more than one source by the same author is cited in your paper, include the author's name in the introduction, and use a short form of the title in the parenthetical citation:

   Rodriguez feels that a teacher who resorts to corporal punishment is acting out of frustration (*Discipline* 86).

The above title is a short form of *Discipline in the Public Schools.* It distinguishes the source from another of Rodriguez's works cited, *Education in an Enlightened Age.*

5. For online or other sources that do not have page numbers, place the author in parentheses. If the author is not given, place the title in parentheses:

   ```
   According to the American Academy of Pediatrics,
   all corporal punishment should be banned in
   schools ("Corporal Punishment in Schools").
   ```

Note: For a long quote that is set off by indentation, the citation appears *after* the period. (See page 498 on long quotes.)

Write the "Works Cited" Page

In addition to introducing source material and providing parenthetical text citations, proper documentation requires you to provide a "Works Cited" page (or pages) at the end of your paper. This is an alphabetical listing of all the sources from which you paraphrased, summarized, and quoted—it is *not* a listing of all the sources you consulted during your research. For an example of a "Works Cited" page, see page 541. Notice that you list the entries alphabetically by the author's last name. If the source has no known author, alphabetize the work according to the first important word in the title (excluding *a, an,* or *the*). Double-space each entry and double-space between each entry.

The following sections present forms you should model for papers written according to the style recommended by the Modern Language Association, which is explained in the *MLA Handbook for Writers of Research Papers* (7th ed., 2009). Most humanities papers are written according to MLA guidelines. Instructors in the social sciences may want you to use the style recommended by the American Psychological Association (APA) (see page 526), while science instructors may favor the Council of Science Editors (CSE) format. When in doubt, check with your instructor. If you want additional information on MLA style, go online to Purdue University's Online Writing Lab at owl.english.purdue.edu/owl/resource/557/01/.

Proper MLA works-cited entries require you to combine different pieces of information from a source into a single citation. The following figures will show you what some of the most important citation forms look like and where you can find their various parts within a source.

To further assist you in understanding which parts of a source match up with which parts of a citation, the citations in these figures are color-coded:

- Author information is highlighted in tan.
- Title information is highlighted in yellow.
- Publication data is highlighted in blue.

Note that you should *not* reproduce this coloring in your own citations. It is here only for your reference.

The figures are followed by a list of models of proper MLA forms. Consult these pages as you prepare your "Works Cited" page.

MLA Works-Cited Entry: Book with One Author. You can find the information for a book citation on the book's title page and copyright page.

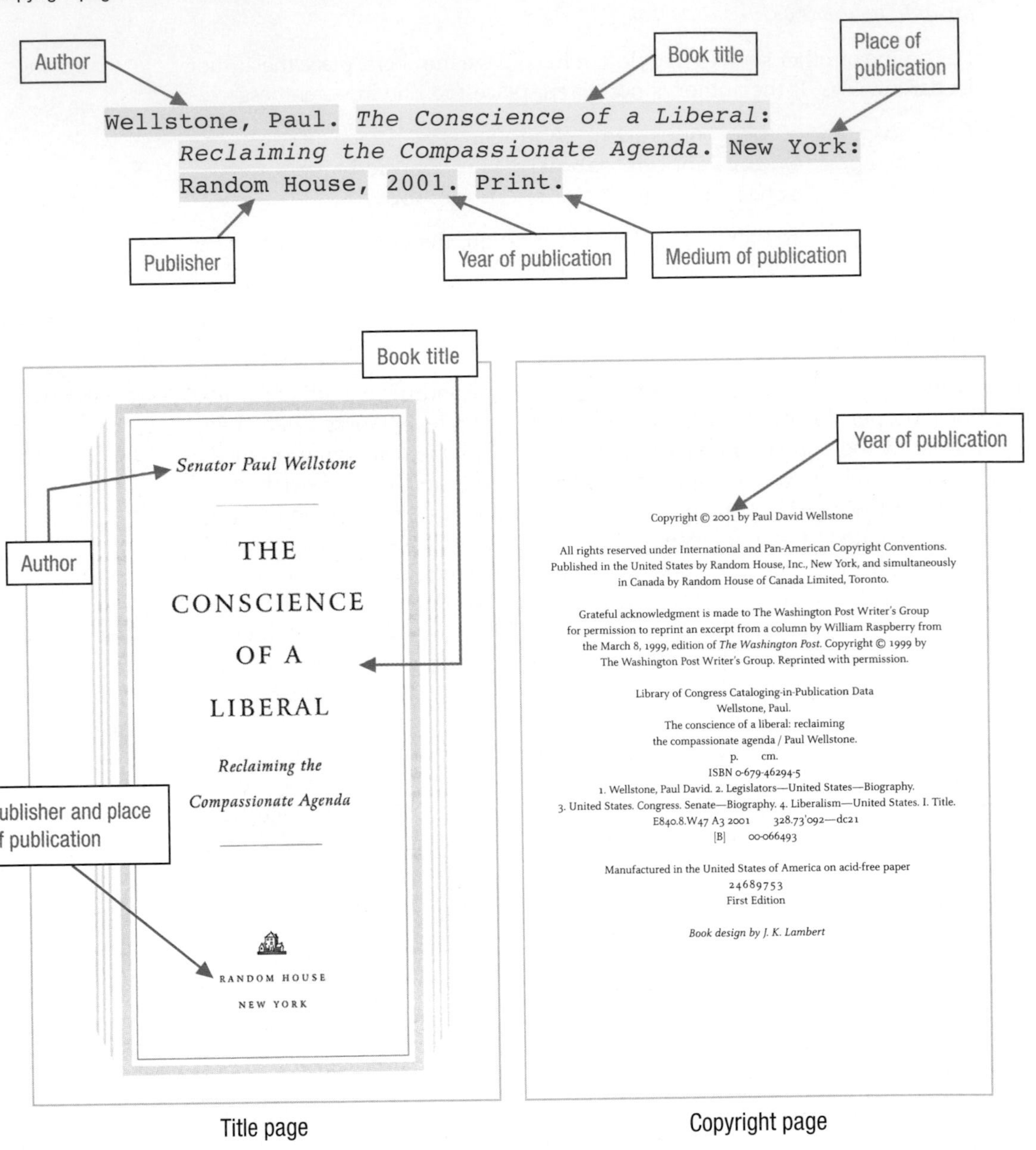

MLA Works-Cited Entry: Journal Article. Many journals, like the one shown below, provide the information needed for a citation on the first page of an article as well as on the cover or contents page. Note that this is a scholarly journal, so only the year of publication follows the volume and issue numbers. For citation of an article from a monthly or weekly magazine, see pages 519–20.

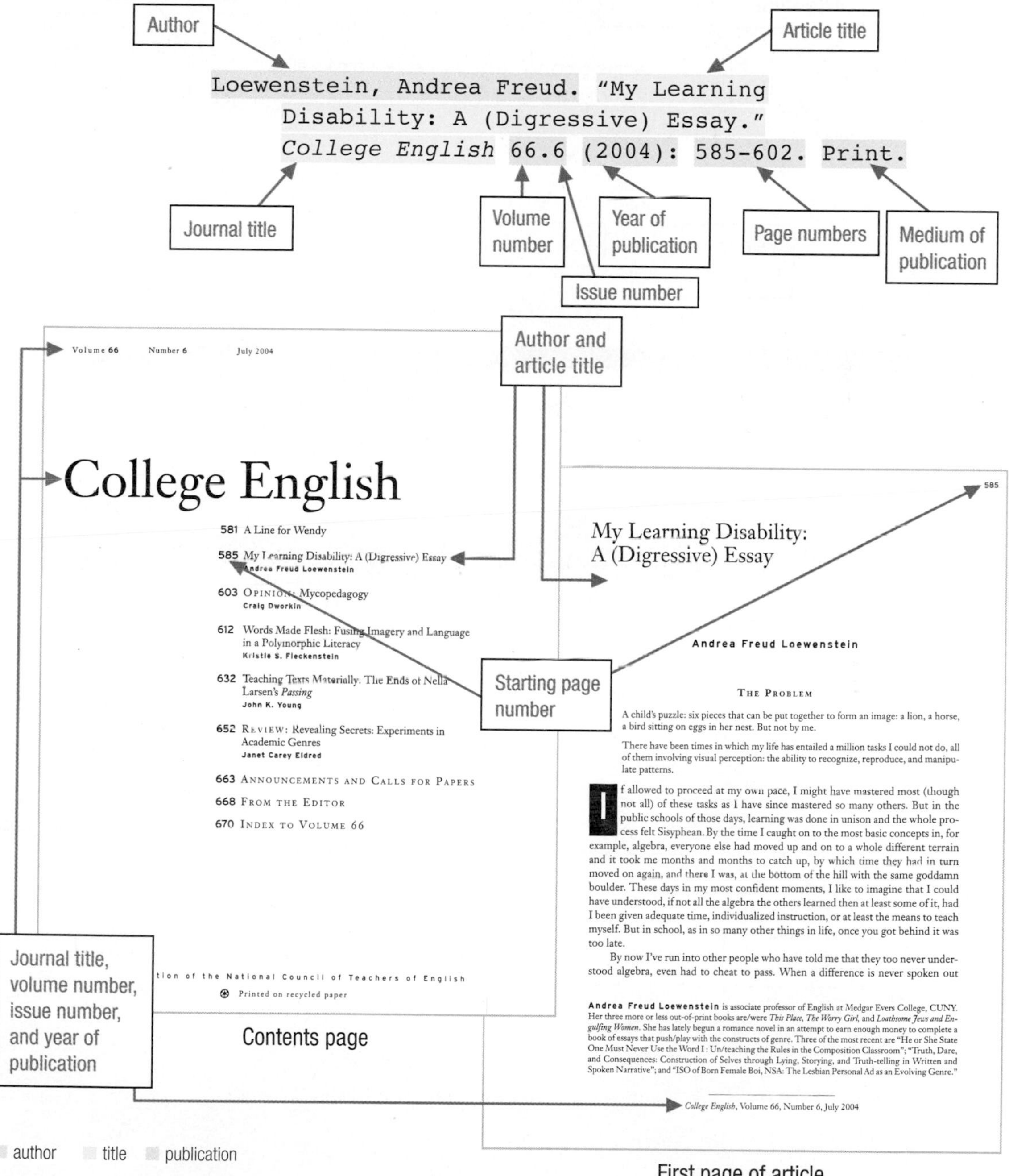

Volume 66 Number 6 July 2004

College English

...tion of the National Council of Teachers of English

Printed on recycled paper

Contents page

585

My Learning Disability: A (Digressive) Essay

Andrea Freud Loewenstein

The Problem

A child's puzzle: six pieces that can be put together to form an image: a lion, a horse, a bird sitting on eggs in her nest. But not by me.

There have been times in which my life has entailed a million tasks I could not do, all of them involving visual perception: the ability to recognize, reproduce, and manipulate patterns.

If allowed to proceed at my own pace, I might have mastered most (though not all) of these tasks as I have since mastered so many others. But in the public schools of those days, learning was done in unison and the whole process felt Sisyphean. By the time I caught on to the most basic concepts in, for example, algebra, everyone else had moved up and on to a whole different terrain and it took me months and months to catch up, by which time they had in turn moved on again, and there I was, at the bottom of the hill with the same goddamn boulder. These days in my most confident moments, I like to imagine that I could have understood, if not all the algebra the others learned then at least some of it, had I been given adequate time, individualized instruction, or at least the means to teach myself. But in school, as in so many other things in life, once you got behind it was too late.

By now I've run into other people who have told me that they too never understood algebra, even had to cheat to pass. When a difference is never spoken out

Andrea Freud Loewenstein is associate professor of English at Medgar Evers College, CUNY. Her three more or less out-of-print books are/were *This Place*, *The Worry Girl*, and *Loathsome Jews and Engulfing Women*. She has lately begun a romance novel in an attempt to earn enough money to complete a book of essays that push/play with the constructs of genre. Three of the most recent are "He or She State One Must Never Use the Word I: Un/teaching the Rules in the Composition Classroom"; "Truth, Dare, and Consequences: Construction of Selves through Lying, Storying, and Truth-telling in Written and Spoken Narrative"; and "ISO of Born Female Boi, NSA: The Lesbian Personal Ad as an Evolving Genre."

College English, Volume 66, Number 6, July 2004

First page of article

MLA Works-Cited Entry: Journal Article from an Online Database. Citing an article accessed via an online subscription database service like ProQuest or EBSCO requires information about the print version of the article and the database used.

Author and title of print version of the article

Name of database

Harker, Brian. "Louis Armstrong and the Clarinet." *American Music* 21.2 (2003): 137-58. *Academic Search Premier.* Web. 17 Nov. 2008.

Medium of publication

Date of access

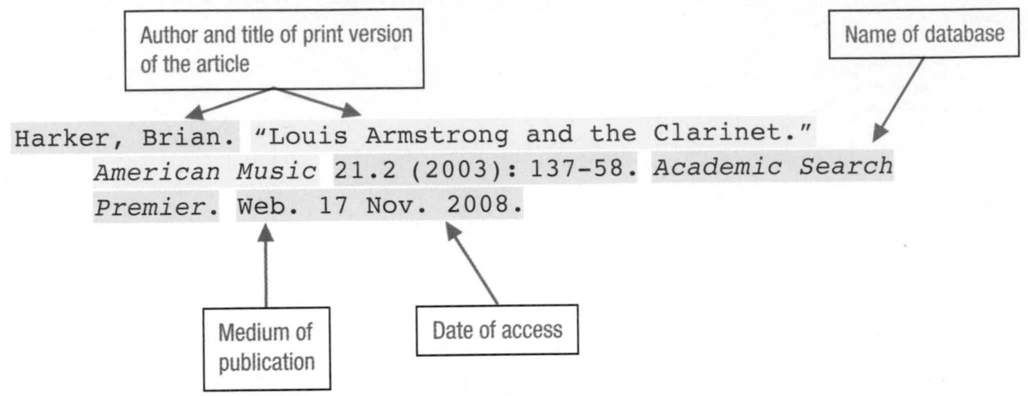

EBSCOhost - Microsoft Internet Explorer
Name of database service
EBSCO HOST Research Databases
New Search | View Folder | Preferences | Help
HUNTER
Basic Search
Advanced Search
Choose Databases
Sign In to My EBSCOhost
Keyword
Publications
Subject Terms
Indexes
Cited References
Images
Language
13 of 34 Result List | Refine Search
Print E-mail Save Add to folder
Article title
Folder is empty.
Formats: Citation
Title: Louis Armstrong and the Clarinet.
Author
Authors: Harker, Brian1
Source: American Music; Summer2003, Vol. 21 Issue 2, p137-158, 22p, 12 diagrams
Document Type: Article
Subject Terms: *CLARINET
*MELODY
*MUSIC -- Performance
*MUSICIANS
*STYLE, Musical
*ARPEGGIOS
Journal title, year of publication, volume number, issue number, and page range information
People: ARMSTRONG, Louis
Abstract: Focuses on musician Louis Armstrong's fascination with the clarinet. Traditional role as bearer of the melody; Style of music; Musical performances; Sawtooth pattern of descending and ascending arpeggios.
Author Affiliations: 1Brigham Young University
ISSN: 0734-4392
Abstract
Accession Number: 12103654
Persistent link to this record: http://search.epnet.com.proxy.wexler.hunter.cuny.edu/login.aspx?direct=true&db=aph&an=12103654
Internet

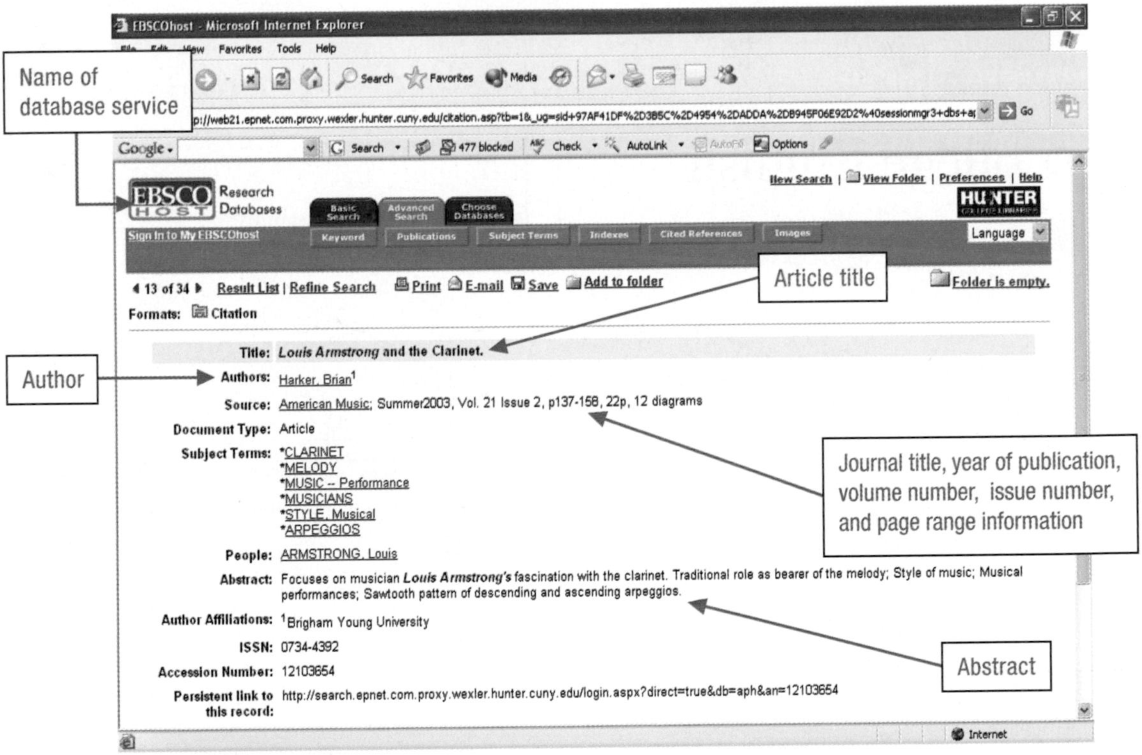

Reprinted with permission from EBSCO Host.

author title publication

MLA Works-Cited Entry: Scholarly Website. To cite a scholarly website as a whole—as opposed to a single page within it—include the editor (if any), the title of the site, the version number (if relevant), the sponsoring institution (or use n.p. if none is available), the date of publication or the most recent update (or n.d. if none is given), the medium of publication (Web), and the date you accessed the site. You may need to click through the site a bit to find all this information.

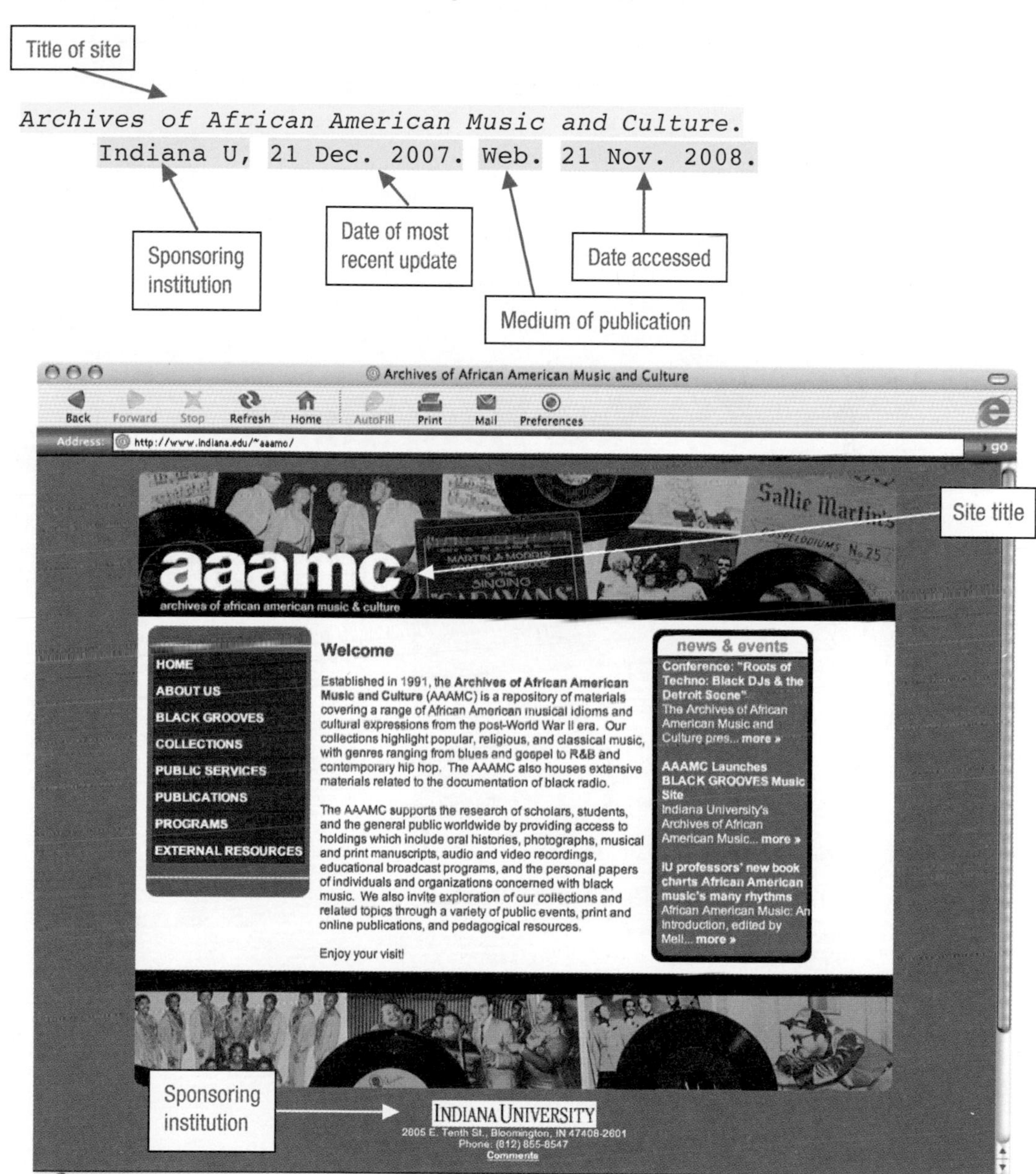

Reprinted with permission from Indiana University, Archives of African American Music and Culture.

author title publication

Elements of an MLA Works-Cited Entry: Newspaper Article. To find the citation information for a newspaper article, look on both the page or pages the article appears on and the front page of the newspaper (where you will find, for example, the edition of the newspaper).

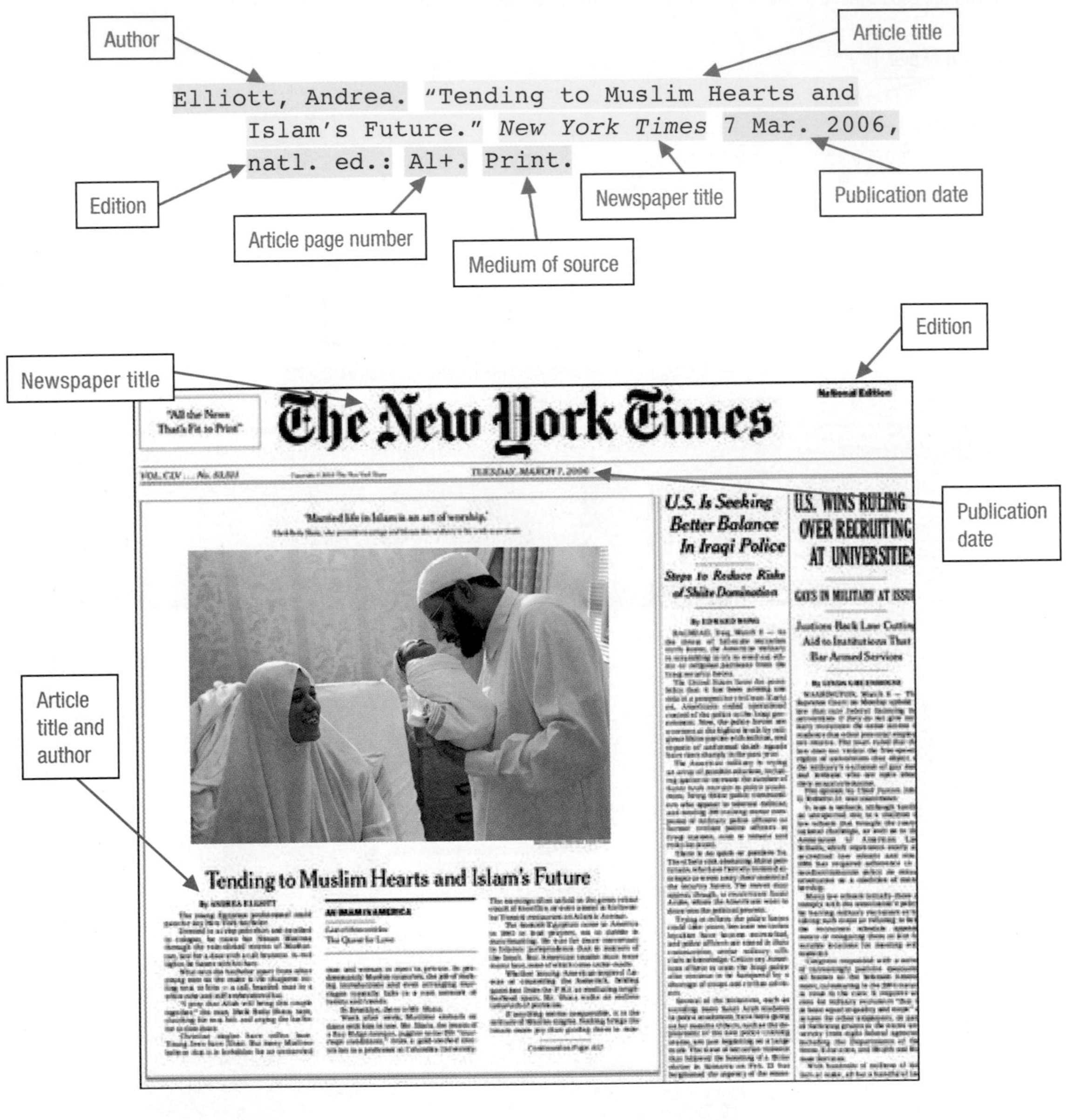

author title publication

MLA Works-Cited Models

Below you will find information on formatting various types of works for inclusion in an MLA "Works Cited" page. You will see that each entry includes, in addition to a sample, a color-coded model. This model is designed to show you how each part of a source fits into the citation. It should also help you understand the underlying structure of all MLA citations.

- Author information is highlighted in tan.
- Title information is highlighted in yellow.
- Publication data is highlighted in blue.

Note that you should *not* reproduce this color highlighting in your own citations. It is included here for your reference only.

MLA Works-Cited Entries: Directory to Models and Samples

Forms for Books

Forms for Periodicals

Forms for Electronic Sources

Forms for Other Sources

MLA Forms for Books

Book by One Author

Titles of books should be italicized. The city of publication but not the state should appear just before the publisher.

Author's Last Name, First Name. *Title.* Publication City: Publisher, Year of Publication. Medium of Publication.

Johnson, Paul. *Birth of the Modern: World Society 1815–1830*. New York: Harper, 1991. Print.

Book by Two or Three Authors

List the authors in the order in which they appear on the title page. Last name appears first for the first author only.

Book with two authors

First Author's Last Name, First Name, and Second Author's First and Last Names. *Title*. Publication City: Publisher, Year of Publication. Medium of Publication.

Book with three authors

First Author's Last Name, First Name, Second Author's First and Last Names, and Third Author's First and Last Names. *Title*. Publication City: Publisher, Year of Publication. Medium of Publication.

Fisher, Seymour, and Rhoda L. Fisher. *What We Really Know about Child Rearing*. New York: Basic, 1976. Print.

Book by More Than Three Authors

If a book has more than three authors, list the first author only, followed by *et al.,* which means "and others."

First Author's Last Name, First Name, et al. *Title*. Publication City: Publisher, Year of Publication. Medium of Publication.

Shafer, Raymond P., et al. *Marijuana: A Signal of Misunderstanding*. New York: NAL, 1972. Print.

Book by an Unknown Author

Title. Publication City: Publisher, Year of Publication. Medium of Publication.

Macmillan Science Library: Genetics. New York: Macmillan, 2002. Print.

author title publication

Book by an Author with an Editor

List the author, the title, and then *Ed.* followed by the name of the editor.

Author's Last Name, First Name. *Title.* Ed. Editor's First and Last Names. Publication City: Publisher, Year of Publication. Medium of Publication.

Arnold, Matthew. *Culture and Anarchy*. Ed. J. Dover Wilson. Cambridge: Cambridge UP, 1961. Print.

Book by an Editor

Treat the editor as an author, listing his or her name first, but follow the name with *ed.* If the book has more than one editor, use the plural *eds.*

Editor's Last Name, First Name, ed. *Title.* Publication City: Publisher, Year of Publication. Medium of Publication.

Marshall, Sam A., ed. *1990 Photographer's Market*. Cincinnati: Writer's Digest, 1989. Print.

Edition Other Than the First

Author's Last Name, First Name. *Title.* Name or Number of ed. Publication City: Publisher, Year of Publication. Medium of Publication.

Langacker, Ronald W. *Language and Its Structure: Some Fundamental Linguistic Concepts*. 2nd ed. New York: Harcourt, 1973. Print.

Multivolume Work

Indicate in your citation of a multivolume work whether you used only one volume or all the volumes. If you used only one volume, list the number of the volume you used, preceded by *Vol.,* after the title. If you used two or more of the volumes, give the total number of volumes, followed by *vols.*

One volume in a multivolume work

Author's Last Name, First Name. *Title.* Vol. Number Used. Publication City: Publisher, Year of Publication. Medium of Publication.

Reich, Warren. *Encyclopedia of Bioethics*. Vol. 2. New York: Macmillan, 1995. Print.

All volumes in a multivolume work

Author's Last Name, First Name. *Title.* Number of vols. Publication City: Publisher, Year of Publication. Medium of Publication.

author title publication

Lissauer, Robert. *Lissauer's Encyclopedia of Popular Music in America*. 3 vols. New York: Facts on File, 1996. Print.

Selection in an Anthology

Follow the author and title of the selection with the title of the anthology. Include *Ed.* and the name of the editor.

Author's Last Name, First Name. "Title of Work." *Title of Anthology*. Ed. Editor's First and Last Names. Publication City: Publisher, Year of Publication. Page(s). Medium of Publication.

Smith, Hale. "Here I Stand." *Readings in Black American Music*. Ed. Eileen Southern. New York: Norton, 1971. 286–89. Print.

Encyclopedia Article

"Title of Entry." *Title of Encyclopedia*. Name or Number of ed. Year of Publication. Medium of Publication.

"Tilbury Town." *The HarperCollins Reader's Encyclopedia of American Literature*. 2nd ed. 2002. Print.

Book with a Translator

List the author of the work, followed by the title. Place the translator's name after the title, with the abbreviation *Trans.*

Author's Last Name, First Name. *Title*. Trans. Translator's First and Last Names. Publication City: Publisher, Year of Publication. Medium of Publication.

Medvedev, Zhores A. *Nuclear Disaster in the Urals*. Trans. George Sanders. New York: Norton, 1979. Print.

More Than One Work by the Same Author

List the author's name in the first entry only. For subsequent works, replace the name with three hyphens and a period. Order the citations alphabetically by title.

First entry

Author's Last Name, First Name. *Title*. Publication City: Publisher, Year of Publication. Medium of Publication.

author title publication

Second entry

---. *Title.* Publication City: Publisher, Year of Publication. Medium of Publication.

Tannen, Deborah. *That's Not What I Meant!* New York: Ballantine, 1986. Print.

---. *You Just Don't Understand: Women and Men in Conversation.* New York: Ballantine, 1990. Print.

MLA Forms for Periodicals

Author Unknown

"Title of Article." *Name of Publication* Day Month Year: Page(s). Medium of Publication.

"Night of Horror." *Sports Illustrated* 13 Oct. 1980: 29. Print.

Article from a Scholarly Journal

Whether a journal is paginated by volume or issue, include the volume number and issue number, separated by a period. Put the year of the publication in parentheses, followed by the page numbers of the entire article and the medium of its publication. If you accessed the article online, you will need to include additional information. (See pages 520–24 for details on documentation of electronic sources.)

Author's Last Name, First Name. "Title of Article." *Title of Journal* Volume. Issue (Year): Page(s). Medium of Publication.

Crumley, E. Frank. "The Adolescent Suicide Attempt: A Cardinal Symptom of a Serious Psychiatric Disorder." *American Journal of Psychotherapy* 36.2 (1982): 158–65. Print.

Article in a Magazine Published Monthly

For an article in a monthly magazine, include the month and year of publication but no volume or issue number.

Author's Last Name, First Name. "Title of Article." *Title of Magazine* Month Year: Page(s). Medium of Publication.

Walker, Malcolm. "Discography: Bill Evans." *Jazz Monthly* June 1965: 20–22. Print.

author title publication

Article in a Magazine Published Weekly

For an article in a weekly magazine, include the day, month, and year of publication but no volume or issue number.

Author's Last Name, First Name. "Title of Article." *Title of Magazine* Day Month Year: Page(s). Medium of Publication.

> Kanfer, Stefan. "Doing Violence to Sport." *Time* 31 May 1976: 64–65. Print.

Article in a Newspaper

Include the day, month, and year of publication, as well as the edition if available (*natl. ed.* or *late ed.* for example) after the date. Give a section designation along with the page number when possible. When citing an article that appears on nonconsecutive pages, put a plus (+) sign after the first page number.

Author's Last Name, First Name. "Title of Article." *Name of Newspaper* Day Month Year, specific ed.: Page(s). Medium of Publication.

> Nossiter, Adam. "As Life Returns to New Orleans, So Does Crime." *New York Times* 30 Mar. 2006, natl. ed.: A1+. Print.

Editorial

To cite a newspaper editorial, add the word *Editorial* after the title of the article.

"Title." Editorial. *Name of Newspaper* Day Month Year, specific ed.: Page(s). Medium of Publication.

> "Patience on Panama." Editorial. *Philadelphia Inquirer* 12 May 1989, late ed.: A22. Print.

MLA Forms for Electronic Sources

The following examples are based on the most recent guidelines published by the Modern Language Association. Citation methods for electronic sources continue to be refined and modified. For the most up-to-date information on MLA forms for electronic sources, visit www.mla.org.

Due to the changeable nature of sources on websites versus printed publications, you must provide some additional information when citing online materials. You must include information about the website or the database where you found your sources and note at the end of your citation that the information was published on the Web and give the date you accessed the materials.

Note: Because researchers are most likely to locate sources by searching for titles or authors through a web search engine (like Google or Yahoo!) or through a library's subscription database service (like EBSCO or ProQuest), you do not

author title publication

need to include the URL in a citation unless it would be impossible to locate the source otherwise. If you do include it, it should be enclosed in angle brackets (< >), placed immediately after the date of access, and followed by a period.

> *Archives of African American Music and Culture.* Indiana U, 21 Dec. 2007. Web. 21 Nov. 2008. <http://www.indiana.edu/~aamc/>.

Scholarly Website

Begin with the name of the editor (if relevant), the title of the site, and the version number (if relevant), followed by the electronic publication data: the sponsoring institution (or *N.p.* if not available), the date of publication or most recent update (or *n.d.* if not available), and the medium of publication. End with your date of access.

Editor's Last Name, First Name, ed. *Title of Site.* Sponsoring Institution. Day Month Year Posted or Last Updated. Medium of Publication. Day Month Year of Access.

> Bahri, Deepika, ed. *Postcolonial Studies.* Emory University, 13 Nov. 2002. Web. 1 Dec. 2008.

Part of a Scholarly Website

When citing one page or part of a scholarly website, use the basic model above, but add to the beginning the author (if known) and the title of the page or part in quotes. If the author is unknown, begin with the title (in quotes). Move the editor after the title of the site.

Author's Last Name, First Name. "Title of Page or Part." *Title of Site.* Ed. Editor's First and Last Names. Sponsoring Institution, Day Month Year Posted or Last Updated. Medium of Publication. Day Month Year of Access.

> Ahmed, Aziza. "Victorian Women Travelers in the 19th Century." *Postcolonial Studies.* Ed. Deepika Bahri. Emory University, Fall 1998. Web. 1 Dec. 2008.

Professional or Personal Website

Name the person who created the site (if available), the title of the page or part, the overall site title (italicized), the name of the associated institution (or *N.p.* if none is given), the date posted or updated (or *n.d.* if none is available), the medium of publication, and your date of access. If no title is given, use a description like *Home page* or *Online posting* (but do not underline, italicize, or place in quotes).

author title publication

"Title of Page or Part." *Title of Site.* Sponsoring Institution, Day Month Year Posted. Medium of Publication. Day Month Year of Access.

"Bisphenol A in Your Body: How It Got There and How to Minimize Your Exposure." *Enviroblog.* Environmental Working Group, 26 Sept. 2007. Web. 1 Dec. 2008.

E-Mail

List the author first, then the subject line in quotation marks, followed by *message to* and the recipient, the date of the message, and then the medium of delivery.

Writer's Last Name, First Name. "Subject Line." Message to Recipient's First and Last Names. Day Month Year of Message. Medium of Delivery.

Ashley, David. "Bias in Local News." Message to Karen Hirschberg. 8 Sept. 2001. E-mail.

Article in an Online Newspaper

Provide the following information: the author's name (if available), the title of the article (in quotation marks), the name of the newspaper (underlined), the publisher or sponsor of the site, the publication date, the medium of publication, and the date of access.

Author's Last Name, First Name. "Title of Article." *Name of Newspaper.* Publisher, Day Month Year of Publication. Medium of Publication. Day Month Year of Access.

Tyson, Ann Scott. "Off Welfare, Yes. But No Job." *The Christian Science Monitor.* The First Church of Christ, Scientist, 9 April 1998. Web. 24 April 1998.

Article in an Online Magazine

Provide the following information: the author's name (if available), the title of the piece (in quotation marks), the name of the magazine (italicized), the publisher or sponsor (or *N.p.* if not available), the publication date, the medium of publication, and the date of access.

Author's Last Name, First Name. "Title of Article." *Title of Magazine.* Publisher, Day Month Year of Publication. Medium of Publication. Day Month Year of Access.

author title publication

Fromartz, Samuel. "Groovin' with Scofield, Medeski, Martin, and Wood." *All about Jazz*. All About Jazz, 3 April 1998. Web. 10 April 2004.

Article in an Online Journal

Provide information just as for a print journal: the author's name, the title of the work cited (in quotation marks), the name of the journal (italicized), and the publisher or sponsor (or *N.p.* if not available). Next provide the volume and issue numbers, separated by a period, and the journal's year of publication (in parentheses). Indicate the number of paragraphs in the article if the information is available. Follow this with the medium of publication and your access date.

Author's Last Name, First Name. "Title of Article." *Title of Journal* Volume. Issue Number (Year): Page(s). Medium of Publication. Day Month Year of Access.

Woodruff, Eliot Ghofur. "Metrical Phase Shifts in Stravinsky's *The Rite of Spring*." *Music Theory Online* 12.1 (2006): n. pag. Web. 3 Apr. 2006.

Material from a CD-ROM or DVD-ROM

Follow the basic instructions for citing books or parts of books, but add the medium of publication. If the name of the vendor or a date of release or update is available and different from the publisher and publication date, add this to the end of the citation.

"Title of Article or Section." *Title of CD-ROM or DVD-ROM.* Publication City: Publisher, Year of Publication. Medium of Publication. Name of vendor, Year of Publication or Update.

"Photosynthesis." *Microsoft Encarta Multimedia Encyclopedia*. Redmond: Microsoft, 1994. CD-ROM.

Work from an Online Database or Subscription Service

A citation for a work obtained from an online database or subscription service includes the print information about the work, followed by the name of the database (italicized), the medium of publication, and the date of access.

Journal article from online database

Author's Last Name, First Name. "Title of Article." *Title of Periodical* Volume. Issue (Year): Page(s). *Name of Database.* Medium of Publication. Day Month Year of Access.

author title publication

Harker, Brian. "Louis Armstrong and the Clarinet." *American Music* 21.2 (2003): 137–58. *Academic Search Premier*. Web. 17 Nov. 2008.

Newspaper article from online database

Author's Last Name, First Name. "Title of Article." *Name of Newspaper* Day Month Year, ed.: Page(s). *Name of Database.* Medium of Publication. Day Month Year of Access.

Jervis, Rick. "General Sees Rift in Iraq Enemy." *USA Today* 26 Jan. 2006: A1. *Academic Search Premier*. Web. 8 June 2006.

If you used a personal subscription service like America Online or MSN, provide the same information as for a library subscription service: Identify the service, the medium of publication, and the date of access.

"Title of Document." *Title of Longer Work.* Date of Publication. Service Used. Medium of Publication. Day Month Year of Access.

"Photosynthesis." *World Book Online Reference Center*. 2005. America Online. Web. 5 Nov. 2005.

Weblog ("Blog") Posting

Cite an entry or comment from a Weblog as you would an article or page of a website. If the entry has no title, use the label "Weblog entry" or "Weblog comment" (without quotes).

Author's Last Name, First Name. "Title of Posting." *Name of Blog.* Publisher or Sponsor (or N.p.). Day Month Year of Posting. Medium of Publication. Day Month Year of Access.

Gladwell, Malcolm. "NBA Heuristics." *Gladwell.com*. 10 Mar. 2006. Web. 21 May 2006.

Online Posting to a Listserv or Newsgroup

Author's Last Name, First Name. "Title or Subject Line of Post" (use Online posting if post has no title). Title of Site. Publisher or Sponsor, Day Month Year of Post. Medium of Publication. Day Month Year of Access.

Taylor, Richard. "Meat Eaters Are More Likely to Have B12 Deficiencies." Vegetarians. Google Groups, 22 Aug. 2002. Web. 1 Dec. 2008.

author title publication

MLA Forms for Other Sources

Radio or Television Show

Include the specific episode title, the title of the program, the series title (if necessary—note that in the example below there is none). Then give any important information about the program, such as the writer (*By*), the director (*Dir.*), or the host (*Host*). Then give the name of the network that is responsible for the show and the medium ("Radio" or "Television").

"Title of Episode." *Title of Program.* Series Title. Name of Network. Broadcast Station, City. Day Month Year of Broadcast. Medium.

"The Meth Epidemic." *Frontline*. PBS. WNET, New York. 4 Apr. 2006. Television.

If you accessed the broadcast online, provide the information on the program as above, but then include the network, the title of the website, the medium (*Web*), and the date you accessed the program.

"Title of Episode." *Title of Program.* Host. Host's First and Last Names. Name of Network. *Name of Website.* Medium of Publication. Date of Access.

"Lincoln's Strategy to Turn Rivals into Allies." *Fresh Air*. Host Terry Gross. National Public Radio. *NPR.org*. Web. 2 Dec. 2008.

Film or Video

Include the title (italicized), the director (*Dir.*) and lead actors (*Perf.*) or narrator (*Narr.*), the distributor, the year of the film's release, and the medium (*Film, DVD, Videocassette*).

Title of Film. Dir. Director's First and Last Names. Perf. Lead Actor's First and Last Names. Distributor, Year of Film's Release. Medium of Publication.

The Matrix. Dir. Andy Wachowski and Larry Wachowski. Perf. Keanu Reeves, Laurence Fishburne, and Carrie-Anne Moss. Warner Bros., 1999. DVD.

Personal Interview

List the name of the person you interviewed, followed by *Personal interview* and the date on which the interview took place.

Subject's Last Name, First Name. Personal interview. Day Month Year of Interview.

Humphrey, Neil. Personal interview. 1 May 2006.

author title publication

Published Interview

First, list the name of the person interviewed, followed by the title of the interview (if there is a title) and *Interview with* and the name of the interviewer (if known and relevant). Then list the name and publication information for the source where you found the interview.

Subject's Last Name, First Name. "Title of Interview" or Interview. Interview with Interviewer's First Name and Last Name. Citation Information for Source of Interview. Medium of Publication.

Comerford, Cris. "Home Cooking." Interview with Richard Wolffe. *Newsweek* 3 Apr. 2006: 10. Print.

Lecture or Speech

Speaker's Last Name, First Name. "Title of Lecture." Sponsoring Institution. Venue. City. Day Month Year of Presentation. Type of Event.

Franco, Jose. "Effects of Globalization on Germany." Columbia University. Hamilton Hall, New York. 13 Nov. 1999. Lecture.

Podcast

Digital audio content, downloaded or listened to online, should be cited as you would a page or part of a website, specifying the medium of delivery (whether *Web* or *MP3 file*) before your date of access.

Writer or Speaker's Last Name, First Name. "Title of File." *Title of Website.* Publisher or Sponsor, Day Month Year of Publication. Medium of Publication. Date of Access.

Polatajko, Helen. "The Science of Practice: Can Data Trump Lived Experience?" *NYU Steinhardt Podcasts*. NYU, n.d. Web. 2 Dec. 2008.

How to Document Using APA Style

The methods for documenting source material explained so far have been those of the Modern Language Association (MLA). For papers written in the social sciences, your instructor may want you to follow the American Psychological Association (APA) format, which is explained in the APA's *Publication Manual of the American Psychological Association* (5th ed., 2001) and the *APA Style Guide to Electronic References* (2007). The APA format for handling parenthetical citations and the final list of sources is different from the MLA format.

author title publication

Parenthetical Citations

In the APA format, the conventions for parenthetical citations are different from those used in the MLA format. Also, parenthetical citations for paraphrases are handled differently from those for quotations.

In the APA format, parenthetical citations include the publication date, but page numbers are *required* for quotations only. You may use page numbers or other locators (like *para.* for paragraphs or *chap.* for chapters) if they will help your readers locate passages in longer works. Also, *p.* or *pp.* is used before the page number(s). There is another difference as well: A comma appears between the name of the author and the year, and between the year and the page number. For example, when you introduce source material with the author's name, place the year of publication in parentheses after the name. For a quotation, add the page number with a *p.* in parentheses at the end.

Paraphrase

For mutual gains bargaining to work, Haines (1991) believes that everyone involved must have extensive training in how to resolve conflict without confrontation.

In the same paragraph, references to the author do not need to repeat the publication year if you make it clear that the same source is referred to.

Mutual gains bargaining has not become popular because, as Haines points out, the required training is costly and time-consuming.

Quotation

Haines (1991) says that for mutual gains bargaining to work, "all parties must undergo rigorous training in nonconfrontational dispute resolution" (p. 40).

If you do not introduce the source material with the author's name, you must follow the material with the author's last name, a comma, and the publication year for a paraphrase. Add the page number for a quotation. Place this information in parentheses.

Paraphrase

For mutual gains bargaining to work, everyone involved must have extensive training in how to resolve conflict without confrontation (Haines, 1991).

Quotation

For mutual gains bargaining to work, "all parties must undergo rigorous training in nonconfrontational dispute resolution" (Haines, 1991, p. 40).

Note: Electronic documents should be cited just like any other reference. However, publication dates and page numbers are sometimes not available. When there is no date, use *n.d.* When there are paragraph numbers but no stable page numbers, use *para.* or the paragraph symbol (¶) followed by the number. When there are no page or paragraph numbers but the document contains headings, use the heading title (with no quotes or italics), and indicate which paragraph under the heading (Intro. section, para. 2).

List of References

Rather than a "Works Cited" page, APA format calls for a list of sources with the heading "References." The "References" page includes the same information as the "Works Cited" page, but it is presented in a different format, as the examples in the next sections illustrate. If you want additional information on APA style, go online to Purdue University's Online Writing Lab at http://owl.english.purdue.edu/owl/resource/560/01/.

APA Reference Entries: Directory to Models and Samples

APA Forms for Books

Book with One Author

Author's Last Name, Initial(s). (Year of Publication). *Title.* Publication City: Publisher.

Dretske, F. (1988). *Explaining behavior: Reasons in a world of causes.* Cambridge: MIT Press.

author title publication

Book with Two or More Authors

First Author's Last Name, Initial(s), & Second Author's Last Name, Initial(s). (Year of Publication). *Title.* Publication City: Publisher.

Bosworth, J., & Toller, T. N. (1898). *An Anglo-Saxon dictionary.* New York: Oxford University Press.

Edition Other Than the First

Author's Last Name, Initial(s). (Year of Publication). *Title* (name or number ed.). Publication City: Publisher.

Creech, P. J. (1975). *Radiology and technology of the absurd* (3rd ed.). Boston: Houghton-Mifflin.

Edited Book or Anthology

Editor's Last Name, Initial(s). (Ed.). (Year of Publication). *Title.* Publication City: Publisher.

Higgins, J. (Ed.). (1988). *Psychology.* New York: Norton.

Item in an Anthology or Chapter in an Edited Book

Item or Chapter Author's Last Name, Initial(s). (Year of Publication of Item or Chapter). Title of item or chapter. In Editor's Initial(s) and Last Name (Ed.), *Title of edited book* (pp. pages). Publication City: Publisher.

Rubenstein, J. P. (1967). The effect of television violence on small children. In B. F. Kane (Ed.), *Television and juvenile psychological development* (pp. 112–134). New York: American Psychological Society.

APA Forms for Periodicals

Article from a Scholarly Journal (Continuous Pagination through Volumes)

Author's Last Name, Initial(s). (Year of Publication). Title of article. *Title of Journal, volume,* page(s).

Crumley, E. F. (1982). The adolescent suicide attempt: A cardinal symptom of a serious psychiatric disorder. *American Journal of Psychotherapy, 26,* 158–165.

author title publication

Article from a Scholarly Journal (Separate Pagination in Each Issue)

Author's Last Name, Initial(s). (Year of Publication). Title of article. *Title of Journal, volume*(issue), page(s).

Tong, T. K. (1988). Temporary absolutisms versus hereditary autocracy. *Chinese Studies in History, 21*(3), 3–22.

Article in a Magazine Published Weekly

If the magazine has a volume number, include it after the title. If it does not, follow the title with the page numbers (as in the example below).

Author's Last Name, Initial(s). (Year, Month Day of Publication). Title of article. *Title of Magazine, volume,* page(s).

McIntyre, R. S. (1988, April 2). The populist tax act of 1989. *The Nation, 445,* 462–464.

Article in a Magazine Published Monthly

If the magazine has a volume number, include it after the title. If it does not, follow the title with the page numbers (as in the example below).

Author's Last Name, Initial(s). (Year, Month of Publication). Title of article. *Title of Magazine, volume,* page(s).

Chandler-Crisp, S. (1988, May). "Aerobic writing": A writing practice model. *Writing Lab Newsletter,* 9–11.

Article in a Newspaper

Author's Last Name, Initial(s). (Year, Month Day of Publication). Title of article. *Title of Newspaper,* p(p). page(s).

Farrell, W. E. (1976, December 9). Ex-Soviet scientist, now in Israel, tells of nuclear disaster. *New York Times,* p. A8.

APA Forms for Electronic Sources

The following examples are based on the most recent guidelines published by the American Psychological Association. Citation methods for electronic sources continue to be refined and modified. For the most up-to-date information on APA forms for electronic sources, visit www.apa.org.

author title publication

Article from on Online Periodical or Database with a DOI

Most scholarly journals now assign articles a Digital Object Identifier (DOI), an alphanumerical label that provides a persistent link to the article's location online. Use this DOI instead of the URL when possible.

Author(s)'s Last Name, Initial(s) (up to six). (Year of Publication). Title of article. *Title of Journal, volume* (issue if paginated by issue), page(s). doi: DOI Number

Strouse, G., and Troseth, G. (2008). "Don't try this at home": Toddlers' imitation of new skills from people on video. *Journal of Experimental Child Psychology, 101,* 262–280. doi:10.1016/jecp.2008.05.010

Article from an Online Periodical or Database with No DOI

When a DOI is not available, provide the URL of the article if it is open-access or the site where the article can be retrieved (either the journal home page or the database) and the document number assigned by the site (if any).

Author(s)'s Last Name, Initial(s) (up to six). (Year of Publication). Title of article. *Title of Journal, volume* (issue if paginated by issue), page(s). Retrieved from URL or Title of Database (document number, if any).

Thomas, J., Gerber, T., Brockman, T., Patten, C., Schroeder, D., and Offord, K. (2008). Willingness among college students to help a smoker quit. *Journal of American College Health, 57,* 273–279. Retrieved from ProQuest (1592649871).

Document on a Website

Include as much information as possible: the author's name, the date of publication (or *n.d.* if not available), the title of the document, and a URL that will take your reader directly to the source. (Do not use a period after the URL.) Provide a retrieval date if there is no date for the document or if it is likely to change.

Author's Last Name, Initial(s). (Year, Month Day of Publication or n.d.). *Title of Document.* Retrieved Month, Day, Year of Access (if subject to change), from URL

Watson, D. (2005, May 15). *Photosynthesis: How life keeps going*. Retrieved April 2, 2006, from http://www.ftexploring.com/photosyn/photosynth.html

author title publication

Newspaper or Magazine Article

For online versions of print newspapers or magazines with searchable databases, you need only provide the URL of the main website.

Author's Last Name, Initial(s). (Year, Month Day of Publication). Title of article. *Title of Periodical.* Retrieved from URL

Nordland, R. (2006, April 3). Sadir strikes. *Newsweek*. Retrieved from http://www.newsweeek.com

For articles from online magazines or newspapers with no print versions, use *[Online exclusive]* between the article title and the magazine title.

Author's Last Name, Initial(s). (Year, Month Day of Publication). Title of article. [Online exclusive]. *Title of magazine.* Retrieved Month, Day, Year of Access, from URL

Merron, J. (2006, March 31). What's a nervous breakdown? [Online exclusive]. *Slate*. Retrieved May 12, 2006, from http://www.slate.com/id/2139052/?nav=tap3

Weblog ("Blog") or Online Posting

If online postings are archived online, provide as much standard information as possible and replace *Retrieved from* with *Message posted to.*

Author's Last Name, Initial(s). (Year, Month Day of Posting). Title or Subject of post. Message posted to URL

Gladwell, M. (2006, March 6). NBA Heuristics. Message posted to http://www.gladwell.typepad.com/gladwellcom/2006/03/nba_heuristics.html

E-Mail, Personal Interviews, and Personal Communications

Do not include in reference lists personal communications that are not archived. They are cited within the text only—for example, "L. Capri (personal communication, October 4, 2001)."

www.mhhe.com/tsw

For a wealth of electronic editing resources, go to Catalyst 2.0 > Editing

REVISING AND EDITING YOUR RESEARCH PAPER

Once you have completed a draft of your research paper, you will want to revise it carefully, rewriting sections for clarity and effectiveness, checking over your documentation to ensure that it is thorough and properly formatted, and

author title publication

finally eliminating errors of grammar and punctuation. You should expect that this process will take time. Even the best writers must go through many drafts and be vigilant in correcting careless mistakes.

To help you revise and edit your researched writing, ask yourself the following questions:

1. Have I fully explained or proven my thesis? Is it backed up by sufficient evidence?
2. Have I revised for effective expression including sentence variety?
3. Is my level of diction appropriate? Have I avoided colloquialisms and clichés? Is my language gender-neutral and inoffensive?
4. Does my paper include a sufficient number and variety of sources?
5. Have I correctly documented anything in my paper that comes from another source? Are my paraphrases sufficiently changed from their original source? Have I been especially careful in documenting any online material sources I used?
6. Are the citations in my essay properly formatted for the documentation style I am using? Have I included a properly formatted "Works Cited" or "References" page at the end of my paper?
7. Have I eliminated any typos, spelling errors, and grammatical mistakes?

EXERCISE Writing Research

1. Assume that you are writing a paper on how magazine advertisements influence people to buy, and you are seeking explanations of specific persuasive techniques used. With this in mind, do the following:
   a. Check the computer catalog, and write two bibliography cards for two promising books.
   b. Refer to the list on pages 486–87, and name the abstracts, bibliographies, and indexes you should check.
   c. Check the titles you named for item b, and write bibliography cards for two promising articles.
2. Examine the following excerpt from *The Readers' Guide to Periodical Literature,* and respond to the questions that follow.

   Economic conditions
   Displaced homemaker. A. McCarthy. Commonweal 103:38+ Ja 16 '76
   Employment
   Job strategies '76. N. A. Comer. Mademoiselle 82:112–15 F '76
   Women on the job. McCalls 103:68+ F '76
   See also
   Women—Occupations

   a. What is the title of the article about economic conditions? Who is the author?

b. In what periodical does the article appear? In what issue? On what page does the article begin?

c. Write a bibliography card for the article.

3. Assume you are interested in the general subject "The president of the United States." Look up the subject in a general-interest encyclopedia, and list five aspects of the general topic that you could explore further if you were working to narrow to a topic.

4. Write correct works-cited citations in MLA style for the following:

   a. A book titled *Into the Flames,* by Irene Gut Opdyke, published by San Bernardino, California, publisher Borgo Press in 1992

   b. A book edited by Ronald Catanare titled *Alcoholism: The Total Treatment Approach,* published by Springfield, Illinois, publisher Charles C. Thomas in 1977

   c. An article from the *Washington Post,* titled "NFL Tests Replays for Officials," that appeared March 9, 1977, on page 7

   d. An article you looked at on December 13, 2008, titled "Who Is to Blame?" by Barrett Sheridan, that appeared online at newsweek.com December 10, 2008

   e. An article titled "The Free Verse Spectrum," by Eleanor Berry, that appeared in the journal *College English,* volume 59, issue 8, in December 1997 on pages 873–897

5. Paraphrase paragraphs 3 and 4 of "The Environmental Issue from Hell" on page 21. If you like, you may include some quotations. Be sure to introduce the paraphrase and alter style but not meaning.

6. Quote directly the first sentence of "The Environmental Issue from Hell." Introduce the quotation with the author's name and *that.* Then rewrite the quotation without *that* in the introduction.

7. Quote the first sentence of paragraph 3 of "The Environmental Issue from Hell," omitting the words "the great moral crisis of our time." Remember to use ellipses and introduce the quotation.

8. Quote the first sentence of paragraph 7 of "The Environmental Issue from Hell," adding *global warming* after *It's.* Remember to use brackets and to introduce the quotation.

9. With a classmate, select a passage from one essay in this book. Each of you should summarize the passage. Then compare your summaries to see how they are similar and how they are different. Discuss the differences. ■

www.mhhe.com/tsw

For more examples of student research papers, go to Catalyst 2.0 > Research > Sample Research Papers

LEARNING FROM OTHER WRITERS: A Student Research Paper

Cooper 1

Julie Cooper

Professor Hansen

English 101

4 September 2008

> Note the double-spacing, heading, centered title, and page number.

> The paper follows MLA style to document its research.

Genetically Modified Food: Watching What We Eat

1 When most people eat out at restaurants or in their homes, they do not stop to consider that scientists have modified the genes in many of the ingredients in their meals. The ripe tomatoes in their salads may contain fish genes, the chemical makeup of their salmon or beef entrées may have been manipulated to cause these animals to grow four times as fast as their species would develop in the wild, and the pie they enjoy for dessert might consist of apples embedded with chicken genes. Genetically altered food is not new—for years, farmers have fused strains of plants of the same species to create hybrids that were less prone to disease or more appealing in taste or appearance. What is different about many of today's genetically modified foods is that they have been reengineered by scientists using genes from different species to create altogether new entities. Henri E. Cauvin cautions that such alterations could have far-reaching consequences, although scientific testing has not demonstrated that all such foods are unsafe for human consumption (A6). Current international regulation of genetically modified (GM) foods has been weakened by the economic and political influence of the biotech industry and an overall lack of understanding about the process of genetic engineering. New federal regulations need to be put in place to protect Americans from the uncertain environmental and health effects of genetically modified food.

> The introduction gives background information.

> The paraphrase helps establish the reason for the author's argument. The paraphrase is introduced with the author's name and followed by a parenthetical citation.

> Thesis.

2 Genetically modified crops are now widespread in the United States. According to the Campaign to Label Genetically Engineered Foods, in 1999, one fourth of crops were genetically modified, including 35% of corn and 55%

> The source material helps establish the extent of the issue and why it is important.

Cooper 2

The parenthetical citation includes a shortened title. There is no page number because the source is a website.

of soybeans, and these figures continue to increase ("Meteoric"). Worldwide, genetically modified crops are also on the rise (Fig. 1). GM crops in the United States currently undergo field tests overseen by a division of the U.S. Department of Agriculture that determine their impact on the ecosystem and nontarget species, or species that are not directly involved in the genetic engineering. Records interpreted by Richard Caplan of the Public Interest Research Group (PIRG) show that in 1990, the USDA recognized eighty-one field site tests, and by the year 2000, 4,549 field tests were permitted, a 56-fold increase in a decade (4). Some critics argue that the development of GM foods is progressing at such a rapid rate that rigorous testing by the government cannot keep pace with the technology.

Note the explicit introduction showing that the information did not originate with Caplan.

Topic sentence.

Environmental groups like Greenpeace and Friends of the Earth claim 3
that the USDA has designed their regulations to promote the biotech industry at the expense of the safety of the American public. Ralph Nader, the consumer advocate and founder of PIRG, has also voiced this complaint:

Fig. 1 Line graph indicating the global surge in genetically altered crops. Pew Initiative on Food and Biotechnology, University of Richmond, August, 2004.

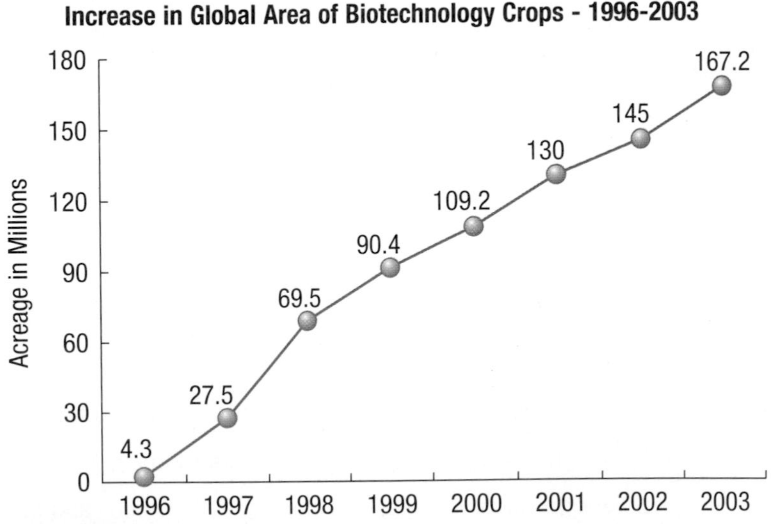

> The U.S. Department of Agriculture has been handing out tax dollars to commercial corporations, including co-funding the notorious terminator-seed project, in order to protect the intellectual property of biotechnology firms from some farmers. You can expect nothing but boosterism from that corner.
>
> The creation of pervasive unknowns affecting billions of people and the planet should invite, at least, a greater assumption of the burden of proof by corporate investigators that their products are safe. Not for this industry. It even opposes disclosing its presence to consumers in the nation's food markets and restaurants. Against repeated opinion polls demanding the labeling of genetically engineered foods, these companies have used their political power over the legislative and executive branches of the government to block the consumer's right to know and to choose. (xi–xii)

Quotation of more than four lines is set off, introduced with a colon, and indented. The period comes before the parenthetical citation.

Nader's reference to the "terminator-seed project" alludes to one of the more insidious forms of genetically modified or engineered foods: an organism bred so that it is programmed to kill its own seeds, effectively eliminating a plant's ability to regenerate. The testing for this "seed suicide" technology, according to one source, was funded by the USDA and Delta and Pine Land Co. (McHughen 192). Some argue that because plants grown from terminator technology do not generate seeds for farmers to save for reuse in their next planting, it undoes the very processes in nature that have enabled agriculture to flourish since time immemorial. If plants no longer regenerate themselves, human beings will be dependent on the large biotech firms that profit, in turn, by selling them more seeds.

Notice the synthesis of sources: The McHughen paraphrase explains the Nader quotation.

The author's name is included in the parenthetical citation because it is not part of the introduction.

Other GM foods may threaten the health of the people who consume them. 4
This issue, which has generated great controversy in the European Union, has only recently received the same level of attention in the United States. As the PBS video *Harvest of Fear* explains, when it was revealed that the company Aventis had created a kind of GM corn called Starlink that Taco Bell used in its taco shells, many Americans were indignant. Most of them had no idea that

Topic sentence.

they were regularly consuming numerous bioengineered products. Starlink corn was different from other genetically modified foods approved for the nation's dinner tables, however. In July of 2000, Larry Bohlen, a member of the environmental group Friends of the Earth, had read on the Environmental Protection Agency's website that Starlink was a kind of GM corn "not approved for human consumption . . . only animal consumption." The film goes on to explain that Bohlen decided to send twenty-three different corn-based products that he bought at his local supermarket to a laboratory to determine whether or not they had been made with Starlink corn. The lab found that Starlink corn, deemed unfit for human consumption by the EPA because it contained the Cry9C, a protein that elevates risks of allergic reaction, had entered a widely available supermarket product. These findings disturbed many consumers and made headlines in the United States. Taco Bell later vowed that they would end their use of Starlink corn in their products (*Harvest*).

Reintroduction makes it clear that the paraphrase is ongoing.

5 Such concerns about the existence of allergens in genetically altered organisms (GMOs) have practical repercussions in countries far from the United States. Cauvin reports that since its discovery in Taco Bell's taco shells, Starlink corn has been found in Japan, Korea, the United Kingdom, and Denmark (*Harvest*). In Zambia, where 13 million people are presently suffering from a severe famine, an international aid effort to donate GM corn has resulted in a political standoff. Cauvin reports that Zambian officials have "banned the distribution of food produced with genetically modified organisms" (A6). Martin Teitel and Kimberly A. Wilson note that the debate has centered on the human and environmental impact of GM corn. To date, there have been no documented cases of deaths due to allergic reactions caused by genetically modified foods (47). But it has been impossible to assess whether fatalities due to food allergies have increased as a result of genetically modified ingredients because most foods are not labeled with detailed genetic information. Charles Arntzen of Cornell University asserts that users of GM foods have never "had so

Topic sentence.

Source material is introduced with the author's name and the present tense.

Note the synthesis of multiple sources.

much as a headache," from genetically engineered foods, and that because these products are "science-driven" they are extremely safe (*Harvest*). But the assurance of scientists and biotech firms that their products are safe is not enough to calm growing fears. Mundia Sikatana, the Zambian Minister of Agriculture, asks: "What else would you call an allergy caused by a substance? That substance is poisonous" (qtd. in Cauvin A6). As a result, thousands of tons of GM corn shipped to Zambia by the United States and administered by the United Nations World Food Program are sitting in freezers on the orders of the Zambian president.

Key words in paraphrase are placed in quotation marks.

The parenthetical citation for material from one source is quoted in a second source.

In addition to the risk of allergic reactions in consumers, *Harvest of Fear* cautions that the GM corn offered by the United States presents a threat of cross-pollination with Zambia's non-modified varieties of corn. Such a crossover would endanger the country's exports to the European Union, which requires the labeling of all GM products. The video explains that such contamination issues concern many members of the environmental community. They worry that if disease-resistant GM foods become dominant, they may wipe out non-modified versions of the same food, thus eliminating the variety of foods available to the human race. In some cases, such as that of B.t. corn, a GM corn that contains a toxic gene that deters corn borers and caterpillars, the diversity of the ecosystem is threatened. The gene in B.t. corn kills not only crop pests, but a so-called "non-target species," the larvae stage of monarch butterflies that feed on the milkweed plants that grow near cornfields (*Harvest*). As Stephen Nottingham notes in his book *Eat Your Genes,* "Because plants produce the toxin continuously," resistance to B.t. will develop much faster using genetically modified plants than using B.t. sprays (56). The fact that the genetic makeup of our plants can be toxic to certain species is alarming to the general public, and for good reason. 6

The reintroduction makes it clear that the paraphrase is ongoing.

The last sentence of the paragraph combines common knowledge and the author's evaluation.

One of the only ways to avoid consuming genetically modified produce is to eat organically grown plants and vegetables. Unlike genetically modified agriculture, which uses cutting-edge gene manipulation in its plants, organic farming promotes a "back to the land" philosophy, in which plants are grown 7 naturally, using compost and other organic substances as fertilizer and little or no chemical pesticides. But even if consumers could eat organic produce exclusively, such a radical approach to protecting themselves from GMO consumption is not assured. The seeds or pollen of GMOs easily contaminate organic plants. The Campaign to Label Genetically Engineered Foods reports that in 1999, the Wisconsin-based company Terra Prima was forced to destroy 87,000 bags of organic chips at a cost of almost $150,000, after a European importer determined that they were contaminated with GM corn ("Organic"). Genetically modified foods pose legitimate threats to the organic agricultural industry. In their book *The Rubbish on Our Plates,* Fabien Perucca and Gerard Pouradier argue that the only way consumers can advance the organic movement is to encourage and reward organic farmers by patronizing their farm-stands and purchasing their products (208). If consumers send a clear economic message to the agriculture giants who devote a great deal of their financial resources to developing new GM products and the governments that allow those products on the global market, perhaps the flood of GM products can be slowed.

Even though the source is given in the introduction, the title appears in the parenthetical citation because the source is a website without page numbers, and something is needed to mark the end of the paraphrase.

Note the synthesis of source material with the author's own ideas.

Americans are definitely interested in knowing more about whether or not the foods they eat have been genetically modified. A poll conducted by ABC News in June of 2001 revealed that 93% of 1,024 people surveyed believe "the federal government should require labels on food saying whether it's been genetically modified or bioengineered" ("Behind the Label"). The long-term environmental and health effects resulting from the growth and consumption of genetically modified foods remain unknown. This uncertainty, coupled with the eagerness on the part of the American people to know when the food they are eating has been genetically modified, suggests that a new course of action needs to be charted. The federal government is expected to protect its citizens from bioterror and biohazards. Therefore, the federal government must not give the biotech industry free reign in its creation of GMOs. New restrictions and clearer genetic labeling will give the American public the security of knowing that what they eat is good for them. 8

The conclusion restates the thesis to reassert the author's claim.

The source material helps establish the point that Americans support the writer's claim.

Works Cited

"Behind the Label: Many Skeptical of Bio-Engineered Food." *ABC News.* ABC News, 20 June 2001. Web. 20 Aug. 2006.

Caplan, Richard. *Raising Risk: Field Testing of Genetically Engineered Crops in the U.S.* Washington: U.S. Public Interest Research Group, June 2001. Print.

Cauvin, Henri E. "Between Famine and Politics, Zambians Starve." *New York Times* 30 Aug. 2002, natl. ed.: A6. Print.

"Genetically Modified Crops in the United States." *Pew Initiative on Food and Biotechnology.* U. of Richmond, Aug. 2004. Web. 8 June 2006.

Harvest of Fear. Dir. Jon Palfreman. Prod. WGBH Educational Foundation. PBS Video, 2001. Videocassette.

McHughen, Alan. *Pandora's Picnic Basket: The Potential and Hazards of Genetically Modified Foods.* New York: Oxford UP, 2000. Print.

"Meteoric Growth: GE Foods Now Are Almost Everywhere You Look—GE Foods Tutorial." *The Campaign.* Campaign to Label Genetically Engineered Foods, n.d. Web. 8 Aug. 2006.

Nader, Ralph. Foreword. *Genetically Engineered Food: Changing the Nature of Nature.* By Martin Teitel and Kimberly A. Wilson. Rochester: Park Street, 1999. ix–xiii. Print.

Nottingham, Stephen. *Eat Your Genes: How Genetically Modified Food Is Entering Our Diet.* New York: Zed, 1998. Print.

"Organic Foods at Risk—GE Foods Tutorial." *The Campaign.* The Campaign to Label Genetically Engineered Foods, n.d. Web. 2 Dec. 2008.

Perucca, Fabien, and Gerard Pouradier. *The Rubbish on Our Plates.* London: Prion, 1996. Print.

Teitel, Martin, and Kimberly A. Wilson. *Genetically Engineered Food: Changing the Nature of Nature.* Rochester: Park Street, 1999. Print.

The title is centered. Double-space before the first entry.

Works-cited entries are double-spaced. The first line is flush left, and subsequent lines are indented five spaces.

Alphabetize entries according to the author's last name. If no name appears, use the first important word in the title.

Reprinted by permission of L. J. Kopf.

LOOKING AHEAD

Tests are a fact of every college student's life, and how well you perform on those tests is largely a function of how well you have learned the material being tested. However, your performance is also a function of how good your test-taking strategies are. There are many kinds of tests, and some of them are depicted in the cartoon. The kind of test that requires the best test-taking strategies is the essay examination. This chapter will help you become better at writing essay exam answers for all of your classes, and it will help you with a special kind of assessment often used in writing classes: the writing portfolio. Before turning your attention to this chapter, consider how well you currently write essay exam answers by responding to the following questions:

- Do you find essay exams more difficult or less difficult than other kinds of exams?
- When you take an essay exam, do you follow a specific procedure?
- What do you do well when you take essay exams? What could you do better?

Assessment: Assembling a Writing Portfolio and Writing Essay Exam Answers

As you know, at regular intervals, your instructors will assess your progress. This assessment takes many forms, and two of them are discussed in this chapter: assembling a writing portfolio and writing essay exam answers.

THE WRITING PORTFOLIO

A **portfolio** is a paper or electronic folder that includes samples of your work. Artists, photographers, and designers assemble portfolios to show prospective clients the nature and quality of their work. Writing instructors often ask students to assemble writing portfolios to display their best or most representative writing—and, in some cases, all of their writing. Instructors then read those portfolios to assess the progress students have made over the term. Students often participate in the assessment by writing an essay or letter reflecting on the writing in the portfolio.

The requirements for portfolios vary from instructor to instructor and from course to course. If you are assembling a portfolio, make sure you understand the requirements for your particular program. For example:

- You may be asked to include all of your writing, including your idea generation material and early drafts.
- You may be asked to include final essays only.
- You may be asked to show a sampling of your work in several specific patterns of development or genres (e.g., narration, cause-and-effect analysis, argumentation, response to a reading, and research).

- You may be asked to show work over time, perhaps one essay from early in the term, one from the middle, and one from the end.
- You may be asked to include a specific number of your best essays.
- You may be asked to include a self-evaluation of your writing and yourself as a writer.
- You may be asked to include your course journal.

The Purposes of a Writing Portfolio

A writing portfolio allows you to showcase a range of your writing so your instructor can assess your ability based on a variety of pieces for a number of purposes. Because a portfolio is more representative of your writing than one essay would be, it may give a truer picture of you as a writer.

A portfolio also gives you an opportunity for self-reflection and self-assessment, and for that reason, it is a learning experience. If you are asked to choose what work to include, you should read all of your writing and evaluate it to determine which pieces are the best. You may have forgotten what your writing was like at the beginning of the term, so the evaluation process may lead you to surprising—and happy—conclusions about what you have learned.

If you must include a self-reflection essay in your portfolio, you may consider such issues as what your individual writing process entails, how you feel about your essays, which assignments you prefer and why, what you have learned, and what you still need to learn. Such reflection can make you more conscious of yourself as a student and a student writer. It will help you when you write in your other courses by reminding you of important points such as ways to generate ideas, the importance of assessing audience, and the need to revise. It can also give you a sense of accomplishment as you recognize the progress you have made from essay to essay.

How to Assemble Your Portfolio

If your instructor requires a portfolio of your work, you will be told so early in the term, and you will be told to save all of your work. Assembling your portfolio, then, is a matter of reviewing your saved work, evaluating it, and compiling the portfolio according to your instructor's criteria. Be sure to allow plenty of time. Reading over your work, assessing it, and making decisions about what to include requires time to reflect. Also, if you are permitted to revise essays further before including them in your portfolio, you need ample time for rewriting.

Be sure to work steadily on your portfolio all term. The biggest mistake many students make is to let much of their revising go until the final week of the term. If you procrastinate, you will not enjoy the chief advantage of the portfolio system, which is the opportunity for ongoing feedback and revision.

Also, be sure you understand the requirements for the portfolio. What essays are you expected to submit? Should you include drafts, idea generation material, or a self-assessment essay? Should you include portions of your journal or excerpts from peer review? If a self-reflection essay is required, be sure you understand the requirements for its length and content.

The following strategies can help you assemble your portfolio:

1. Organize your papers or computer files by placing each essay with its related material, including idea generation material, peer reviews, early drafts, and teacher comments.
2. Read over each essay to form a general impression. Read as thoughtfully as possible, taking notes on a separate sheet. Your notes should offer your response to your writing, including your sense of its strengths and weaknesses, what further revisions you would like to make, whether it fulfills its purpose, and how it addresses its audience.
3. If you are permitted to revise further, choose the essays you will revise, using your notes as a guide.
4. Select the essays to include in your portfolio, using the portfolio requirements and your notes to guide your selection.
5. If a self-reflection essay is required, use your notes to help you write it.

What to Include in a Self-Reflection Essay

Your instructor may indicate specifically what to include in your self-reflection essay, or you may have the freedom to include whatever assessment and reflection information you wish. If you have the freedom to include what you like, consider these possibilities:

1. Explain what you have included in your portfolio, and why. If you have included your best work, tell why you think it is the best. You can also tell whether it was easy or difficult to decide what to include, and why.
2. Explain what you have learned about writing, and refer to the materials in your portfolio to illustrate that learning.
3. Explain what you still need to learn, and refer to portfolio materials as illustration.
4. Discuss aspects of your writing process. You can explain how it has evolved over the term and use materials in your portfolio to illustrate that evolution.
5. Explain how you see yourself as a writer. You can also compare and contrast your current view with the one you had at the beginning of the term.
6. Explain and evaluate your participation in class discussions, your contributions to reader response during revision or workshop sessions, and your use of the campus writing center.

ESSAY EXAM ANSWERS

Essay examination questions may require you to do more than know and repeat information; they may require you to consider that information thoughtfully, perhaps by analyzing it, demonstrating its significance, relating it to other information, or interpreting it. In addition, they may require you to do all that in an essay—and in a limited amount of time. In short, writing essay exam answers can be a sophisticated writing task, but one you can master with a combination of what you have already learned this term and what you will learn in this chapter.

PROCESS GUIDELINES

Writing Essay Exam Answers

The procedures explained next can help you write strong essay exam answers, but as with all writing procedures, you may alter them as circumstances and your own needs dictate.

Think like a Writer: Generating Ideas, Considering Audience and Purpose, and Ordering Ideas

- Read the directions carefully to be sure you understand what the essay question is asking you to do. Some questions ask you to respond using one of the patterns of development. These items read like this:
  - *Describe* conditions in early-twentieth-century sweatshops.
  - *Narrate* the events leading to the indictment of Enron officials, and *explain the effects* of those indictments on the economy.
  - *Define* checks and balances, and illustrate their importance.
  - *Compare and contrast* direct and representational democracies.
  - *Classify* methods of dispute resolution, and *describe the process* whereby each one works.
- You may also be asked to do one or more of the following:
  - *Agree* or *disagree*—Argue your claim about the issue.
  - *Assess, criticize,* or *evaluate*—Give your opinion about the merits of the subject.
  - *Discuss*—Examine in detail by stating all relevant points about the topic.
  - *Explain*—Clarify the meaning or significance of the topic, and perhaps give your interpretation.
  - *Prove*—Argue a claim about an issue to demonstrate that something is or is not true.
  - *Summarize*—State the main points about the topic.
- Recognize that your audience is your instructor, who expects a well-written, complete answer.
- Recognize that your purpose is to let your instructor know you have mastered the material by informing or persuading, as the question dictates.
- On scratch paper, the test booklet, or the exam sheet, quickly list the points you will include in your answer.
- Number the ideas on your list to form a scratch outline. Now you know the ideas you will include in your answer and the order you will write those ideas in.

Think like a Writer: Drafting

- Begin with a thesis statement that reflects the question. For example, if the question reads, "Explain the causes of the Civil War," you can begin with this thesis: "A number of events led to the Civil War." If the question reads, "Explain the controversy surrounding attention deficit disorder," you can begin with this thesis: "Attention deficit disorder is a controversial diagnosis because psychologists disagree about both its cause and its treatment."
- Organize simply. You do not need a lead-in or formal conclusion.
- Do not pad your answer with unnecessary information. A busy instructor has no time for padding and may penalize you for it.

Think like a Critic; Work like an Editor: Revising and Correcting Errors

- Rewrite quickly. You do not have the time to create a polished piece, and your instructor will not expect one. Focus on completeness, accuracy, and clarity.
- Check for grammar, spelling, and usage errors, but do not go too slowly. Your instructor understands that you are working fast and will tolerate a few mistakes.
- Because you do not have time to copy over, neatly cross out and add as you need to. Make sure your changes are legible.

Strategies for Reducing Anxiety

Everyone feels anxious during an essay exam. A little anxiety is helpful because it keeps you mentally sharp, but too much can cause you to freeze up. To avoid crossing the line into debilitating anxiety, try these strategies:

1. **Eat and sleep well.** Avoid all-night study sessions before the exam, and get a good night's rest instead. Eat bland, nutritious food an hour before the test. Avoid loading up on sugar and carbohydrates, so your energy does not fade mid-exam. You cannot perform well if you do not feel well.
2. **Think positively.** Psychologists have proven that all else being equal, positive thinkers outperform negative thinkers.
3. **Arrive early and get set up.** Avoid the added stress of a sprint to your exam site. Find a desk you like, get your supplies ready, settle in, and relax by focusing on your breathing.
4. **Read before you write.** Read over the entire exam to learn what is expected of you. While you are working on one question, a portion of your brain will be considering other questions, so you will be better able to answer them when you get to them.
5. **Budget your time.** If you need to answer four questions in an hour, allow 15 minutes for each question. If two questions are worth 40 points each and two are worth 10 points each, spend more time on the 40-point questions.

6. **If you run out of time, list the ideas you would have written up if you had more time.** You may get partial credit for demonstrating your knowledge.
7. **Keep track of the time.** If your room does not have a clock, wear a watch so you can mark when you should move on to the next question.

A Sample Essay Exam Answer

The following question is similar to one that might appear on an exam for a class on the psychology of learning.

> **Question:** Explain and illustrate how infants, from approximately 6 to 12 months, use their observation of adults' behavior to guide their exploration of their environment.

Study the following answer, using the marginal notes as a guide.

Paragraph 1
The answer opens with a thesis that reflects the question. The answer is organized chronologically, beginning with the child at 6 months. As the question requests, an example is included.

Paragraph 2
Chronological order continues with movement to "around 7 months." After the point is made, the answer gives an example, as the question requests.

Paragraph 3
Chronological order continues with movement to a one-year-old. A point is made in the first sentence, and an example, per the question's instructions, is given.

Paragraph 4
The last paragraph ties things together by reflecting the question asked and summarizing the points made.

Notice that the answer includes no unnecessary information.

From 6 to 12 months, infants use social cues from others to guide their 1
exploration of the environment. By 6 months, infants will copy the way adults act upon objects. For example, in one experiment, infants frequently rolled a ball after seeing their mothers roll it, and they frequently pounded a ball after seeing their mothers pound one.

Around 7 months, infants will follow adults' eyes and direct their own eyes 2
toward what the adult is looking at. The baby may then gaze at the object for a while or turn back to the adult, probably to check the adult's line of vision. This behavior helps infants learn what objects are important to adults. For example, adults in a hunting-and-gathering culture may look specifically at certain plants and animals, and the infant's tendency to follow the adults' view helps the babies learn about those items sooner than they otherwise would.

By the time they are a year old, infants look at adults' facial expressions 3
for clues about the safety or danger of their own actions. For example, in one experiment with 12-month-olds, the children did not play with a toy if the mother displayed a facial expression of disgust, but they readily played with it if her expression was one of joy or interest.

Although infants learn about their environment in many ways, their obser- 4
vation of adults' actions, direction of gaze, and facial expressions teaches them a great deal about the world they live in.

EXERCISE Writing Essay Exam Answers

1. Read or reread "The Case for Torture Warrants" on page 455. Then, to practice writing essay exam answers, give yourself 15 minutes to answer the following question: Summarize the reasons Alan M. Dershowitz advocates the use of torture warrants, and explain why you think the government has not accepted Dershowitz's suggestion that it use torture warrants.
2. Describe the process you followed to write the answer for number 1. How well did the process work? What changes, if any, do you think you should make in this process?
3. Select a reading in this book, and write an essay question for it that can be answered in 15 minutes. Then pair up with a classmate and answer each other's questions.
4. Describe the process you followed to write the answer for number 3. How well did the process work? What changes, if any, do you think you should make in this process? ■

LOOKING AHEAD

You already know that college students read a great deal, but you may think that only English majors read literature. Yes, college students read quite a bit, but much of that reading is literature—even in classes other than English. And, of course, college students are expected to write about the literature they read. This chapter will help you read and write about literature, but before turning your attention to that material, answer the following questions:

- Other than textbooks, what reading have you been asked to complete in your college classes? Has any of that reading been novels, short stories, biographies, or poems?
- What have you written in response to your non-textbook reading?
- Other than textbooks, what reading do you expect to complete in your classes in the next year? Will you have to write in response to that reading?

Writing about Literature

English majors are not the only students who write about literature. In fact, students in a variety of classes are asked to read and write about fiction and nonfiction. For example, history majors may be asked to read and write in response to Michael Shaara's novel about the Battle of Gettysburg, *The Killer Angels,* and business majors may be asked to read and respond to Upton Sinclair's literary exposé of the meat-packing industry, *The Jungle.*

HOW TO READ LITERATURE

As a creative venture, literature includes many elements, some that are not always found in essays. When you read literature, therefore, look for the following:

- **Similes and metaphors.** A **simile** compares two unlike things, using the words *like* or *as.* A **metaphor** compares two unlike things, without using the words *like* or *as.*

  Simile: After his growth spurt, 12-year-old Benjamin felt as awkward as a colt trying to stand for the first time.

  Metaphor: When Leah saw the blanket of snow from her bedroom window, she knew school would be cancelled for the day. [Snow is compared to a blanket.]

- **Irony. Irony** is a contrast between what is expected and what actually happens—as when a driver education instructor who forgets to renew his or her driver's license is forced to take a renewal test and fails it. Irony can also occur when there is a contrast between what the reader knows and what a character does or says—as when a character confides the details of a murder investigation to a friend the reader knows to be the murderer.

- **Symbols.** A **symbol** suggests an idea beyond its literal meaning. For example, white is literally a color, but it is also a symbol of purity in many cultures. Look for clues that something is a symbol, as when a birth is a symbol of hope. In the poem "Coca-Cola and Coco Frío," on page 554, Coca-Cola symbolizes the presence of U.S. culture.
- **Setting.** The **setting** for a literary work is where and when events take place. Setting can suggest something important about meaning, so notice whether the time is the present, past, or future and whether it is morning, afternoon, or evening. Also note where events unfold. You will notice in "Coca-Cola and Coco Frío," for example, that the fact of the action occurring in Puerto Rico is important to the meaning of the poem.
- **Plot** and **theme.** In a short story, play, or novel, the **plot**—the fictional narration—offers much to consider. Study it to determine whether there is conflict, resolution, moral dilemma, good battling evil, and so on. **Theme,** which is often revealed through plot, is the main idea considered in the literary work. Does the plot revolve around someone battling hardship? Then the theme might be the indomitable human spirit. Does an evil person lose everything? Then the theme might be the triumph of good over evil.
- **Characters.** The **characters** are the people depicted in the literary work. Try to determine what these people are like. Are they flawed, guilt-ridden, courageous, or fearful? Is there a narrator? If so, ask yourself how trustworthy this character is. Sometimes authors intentionally create unreliable narrators. Remember, too, that characters are usually multidimensional—like real people—so they may not be consistent, and they may have many characteristics. Determining what characters are like is not always easy. You often must consider their actions and words and then draw conclusions.

Literature demands much of a reader. These techniques can help you discover the richness of literary works:

1. **Read the work several times.** Literary works can be complex, requiring multiple readings. Your responses and understanding will emerge gradually with each reading, so be patient.
2. **Talk to your classmates and teacher.** Part of the fun of literature is discussing its complexity and your interpretations and responses. Ask questions and consider alternate views.
3. **Accept multiple interpretations.** There is no one "correct" meaning residing in the text for readers to ferret out. You and your classmates may disagree about the meaning of a symbol, the motivation of a character, or the author's point. That is fine as long as each of you can back up your interpretations with solid evidence from the text.
4. **Mark the text.** You learned about marking a text in Chapter 1. As you read a literary work, mark the text with your reactions and interpretations

and with your ideas about similes and metaphors, symbols, setting, plot, theme, and characters.

HOW TO WRITE ABOUT LITERATURE

When you write about literature, you can rely on the techniques you have developed for generating ideas, drafting, and revising. In addition, remember the following:

1. **Know what aspect of the work you are to consider.** Are you being asked to write about plot, theme, irony, symbolism, character, setting, your reaction, or something else? If the assignment is open-ended, keep your topic manageable by limiting it to one aspect of the work—perhaps the motivation of one character, the writer's use of one symbol, or the significance of a particular setting.
2. **Be aware of verbs commonly used in assignments about literature.** Three words often used in literary assignments are *interpret, analyze,* and *evaluate.*
   - **a.** *Interpret* means to "assign meaning to." You might be asked to interpret the significance of a character's actions, for example. When you interpret, remember that multiple meanings are possible. Your task is to support your interpretation with evidence from the text.
   - **b.** *Analyze* means to "examine in detail, often by dividing something into its parts." You might be asked to analyze a character's motivation, which will require you to study each element of the forces that compel the character to act a particular way.
   - **c.** *Evaluate* means to "examine the significance, often by considering relationships among parts or cause and effect." You might be asked to evaluate the effect of a character's childhood on his or her actions as an adult, or to evaluate what setting contributes to the work's dominant theme.
3. **Review your marked text for ideas.** For help narrowing a topic, developing a thesis, or discovering supporting detail, you can rely on the idea generation techniques you have been using. In addition, review the notes you made when you marked the text to find ideas you can develop.
4. **Trust your responses.** You do not have to be an experienced reader of literature, an English major, or a literary critic to have valid responses to literature. You need only to be able to support those responses with evidence from the work.
5. **Cite the text for evidence.** To explain and prove your points, quote from the work. To see how this is done, study the sample student essay on page 555. Also, be sure to follow the conventions for quoting and paraphrasing explained in Chapters 16 and 17. In addition, when you quote up to three lines of poetry, separate the lines of the poem with a slash (/), and indicate which lines are quoted in parentheses, like this:

   > Martin Espada opens his poem with a scene at a family gathering, where "the fat boy wandered / from table to table / with his mouth open" (lines 3–5).

Use the word "lines" with the line numbers the first time you quote from the poem; for subsequent quotations, use only the numbers. If you are quoting more than three lines, the quotation should begin a new line, and the lines you are quoting should each be indented 10 spaces or one inch.

6. **Research to learn about the author and work.** Learning about the author's life and social, political, and historical context can shed light on a work's theme and purpose. Learning what other readers say about a work can give you ideas to support your points or ideas to refute. Remember, though, to use research material responsibly by following the conventions explained in Chapters 16 and 17.

LEARNING FROM OTHER WRITERS: Student Essay

The essay in this section was written by a student in response to the poem that appears below. Read the poem and then the essay, which has marginal notes to point out key features.

Coca-Cola and Coco Frío

Martin Espada

On his first visit to Puerto Rico,
island of family folklore,
the fat boy wandered
from table to table
with his mouth open.
At every table, some great-aunt
would steer him with cool spotted hands
to a glass of Coca-Cola.
One even sang to him, in all the English
she could remember, a Coca-Cola jingle
from the forties. He drank obediently, though
he was bored with this potion, familiar
from soda fountains in Brooklyn.

Then, at a roadside stand off the beach, the fat boy
opened his mouth to coco frío, a coconut
chilled, then scalped by a machete
so that a straw could inhale the clear milk.
The boy tilted the green shell overhead
and drooled coconut milk down his chin;
suddenly, Puerto Rico was not Coca-Cola
or Brooklyn, and neither was he.

For years afterward, the boy marveled at an island
where the people drank Coca-Cola
and sang jingles from World War II

in a language they did not speak,
while so many coconuts in the trees
sagged heavy with milk, swollen
and unsuckled.

Symbol and Theme in "Coca-Cola and Coco Frío"

Michael Hambuchen

1 On the surface, "Coca-Cola and Coco Frío" is a narrative; it tells the story of a boy visiting Puerto Rico, his family's place of origin. Martin Espada, like the boy of the poem, is an American of Puerto Rican origin. As Judy Clarence explains in "A Mayan Astronomer in Hell's Kitchen," he is the son of a political activist and lawyer, and he has dedicated his life to the Hispanic community. Among his strongest feelings is his frustration about Puerto Rico's political status. In an article for *The Progressive,* Espada writes of how Puerto Rico has been controlled by other countries for the last 500 years. He mentions the voice of Puerto Ricans falling silent on American ears and calls Puerto Rico an "anachronism" because, in being a territory of the United States, it is much like a colony. Espada considers Puerto Rico's status undemocratic because while Puerto Ricans cannot vote for the President of the United States, the President can draft them into war. He also speaks of the annexation of Puerto Rico by the United States as being the end of the Puerto Rican culture and language.

Paragraph 1
The introduction gives background information on the author's life and politics. It comes from research and is correctly documented.

2 It is the importance of maintaining Puerto Rican culture that provides the theme of "Coca-Cola and Coco Frío." The poem tells the people of Puerto Rico that they should not adopt the American culture just because they are in American control. If they do so, they are abandoning a rich culture of their own.

Paragraph 2
This paragraph states the thesis of the essay.

3 In the poem, the boy wanders "from table to table / with his mouth open" (lines 4–5). The open mouth suggests wonderment; it suggests that the boy wants to learn about his heritage. However, rather than expose him to Puerto Rican food and drink, his relatives always lead him towards Coca-Cola, an

Paragraph 3
This paragraph is a summary of the narration in the poem. The second sentence gives the significance of one aspect of the poem: the boy's open mouth.

American product. He drinks the available beverage, but he does not learn anything that can quench his thirst for knowledge about his culture. One of his relatives even sings to him, in English, an American Coca-Cola song from a commercial. The boy really is sick of drinking Coke; he has it at home, and he has it often. However, later at a roadside stand, the boy gets to try coco frío, a Puerto Rican drink, and he instantly connects with his heritage.

Paragraph 4
The first sentence is the topic sentence. It states the paragraph's focus as the importance of symbolism in giving the poem's theme. The supporting details discuss symbolism. Notice the quotation used as explanation, and notice the parenthetical line citation.

The symbolism of the poem is important in presenting the theme of preserving Puerto Rico's heritage. The fat boy himself symbolizes Puerto Rico. The boy has a rich Puerto Rican heritage; he is of Puerto Rican blood, but living in the United States has forced a different culture on him. Saying the island is "of family folklore" (2), Espada reveals that the boy and Puerto Rico are living an American culture, and the Puerto Rican culture is nothing more than folklore. The boy has lived in the United States all his life, just as Puerto Rico has been possessed by the United States for much of its life. Both, it seems, have lost their Puerto Rican identity. 4

Paragraph 5
The first sentence is the topic sentence. It gives the paragraph's focus as Coca-Cola and Brooklyn as symbols. The supporting details explain the meaning of the symbols.

While Coca-Cola is a symbol of American culture, Brooklyn is a symbol of America itself. By saying that the fat boy is "bored with this potion, familiar / from soda fountains in Brooklyn" (12–13), Espada is saying that Puerto Rico, symbolized by the boy, is bored with the American influence. However, much like the boy who "drank obediently" (11), Puerto Rico is still obedient to the United States. 5

Paragraph 6
The first sentence is the topic sentence. It presents the paragraph's focus as what coco frío symbolizes. The supporting details are quotations from the poem and the author's own ideas.

Coco frío symbolizes the heritage of Puerto Rico. The fat boy realizes that "Puerto Rico was not Coca-Cola / or Brooklyn, and neither was he" (20–21) after he drinks the coco frío. The last stanza further shows that the coco frío represents Puerto Rican culture: The "many coconuts in the trees / sagged heavy with milk, swollen / and unsuckled" (26–28) are an abundant and rich heritage wasted. The author uses these symbols to tell the people of Puerto Rico that they are not Americans, they do not have an American culture, and they should not lose their culture to American influence. Until Puerto Ricans heed the author's advice, Espada will, like the boy in the poem, "[marvel] at an island" (22) where people supplant their heritage with someone else's. 6

For Martin Espada, as revealed in "Coca-Cola and Coco Frío," the best culture for Puerto Rican people is their own. Through symbol and theme, the poem urges Puerto Ricans to remember their heritage, despite attractive outside influences. 7

Paragraph 7
The conclusion restates the thesis.

Works Cited

Clarence, Judy. Rev. of "A Mayan Astronomer in Hell's Kitchen," by Martin Espada. *Library Journal* 1 Mar. 2000. *ProQuest*. Web. 20 Feb. 2001.

Espada, Martin. "¡Viva Vieques!" *The Progressive*. The Progressive Magazine, July 2000. Web. 20 Feb. 2001.

A SHORT STORY AND POEM FOR RESPONSE

For practice writing in response to literature, the short story and poem that appear next are each followed by a writing assignment.

The Open Window

Saki (H. H. Munro)

Saki (1870–1916), pronounced "Saw-key," is the pen name for journalist and short story writer Hector Hugh Munro. His stories are known for their strange twists and surprise endings. "The Open Window" is no exception.

"My aunt will be down presently, Mr. Nuttel," said a very self-possessed young lady of fifteen; "in the meantime you must try and put up with me." 1

Framton Nuttel endeavoured to say the correct something which should duly flatter the niece of the moment without unduly discounting the aunt that was to come. Privately he doubted more than ever whether these formal visits on a succession of total strangers would do much towards helping the nerve cure which he was supposed to be undergoing. 2

"I know how it will be," his sister had said when he was preparing to migrate to this rural retreat; "you will bury yourself down there and not speak to a living soul, and your nerves will be worse than ever from moping. I shall just give you letters of introduction to all the people I know there. Some of them, as far as I can remember, were quite nice." 3

Framton wondered whether Mrs. Sappleton, the lady to whom he was presenting one of the letters of introduction, came into the nice division. 4

"Do you know many of the people round here?" asked the niece, when she judged that they had had sufficient silent communion. 5

"Hardly a soul," said Framton. "My sister was staying here, at the rectory, you know, some four years ago, and she gave me letters of introduction to some of the people here." 6

7 He made the last statement in a tone of distinct regret.

8 "Then you know practically nothing about my aunt?" pursued the self-possessed young lady.

9 "Only her name and address," admitted the caller. He was wondering whether Mrs. Sappleton was in the married or widowed state. An undefinable something about the room seemed to suggest masculine habitation.

10 "Her great tragedy happened just three years ago," said the child; "that would be since your sister's time."

11 "Her tragedy?" asked Framton; somehow in this restful country spot tragedies seemed out of place.

12 "You may wonder why we keep that window wide open on an October afternoon," said the niece, indicating a large French window that opened on to a lawn.

13 "It is quite warm for the time of the year," said Framton; "but has that window got anything to do with the tragedy?"

14 "Out through that window, three years ago to a day, her husband and her two young brothers went off for their day's shooting. They never came back. In crossing the moor to their favourite snipe-shooting ground they were all three engulfed in a treacherous piece of bog. It had been that dreadful wet summer, you know, and places that were safe in other years gave way suddenly without warning. Their bodies were never recovered. That was the dreadful part of it." Here the child's voice lost its self-possessed note and became falteringly human. "Poor aunt always thinks that they will come back some day, they and the little brown spaniel that was lost with them, and walk in at that window just as they used to do. That is why the window is kept open every evening till it is quite dusk. Poor dear aunt, she has often told me how they went out, her husband with his white waterproof coat over his arm, and Ronnie, her youngest brother, singing, 'Bertie, why do you bound?' as he always did to tease her, because she said it got on her nerves. Do you know, sometimes on still, quiet evenings like this, I almost get a creepy feeling that they will all walk in through that window—"

15 She broke off with a little shudder. It was a relief to Framton when the aunt bustled into the room with a whirl of apologies for being late in making her appearance.

16 "I hope Vera has been amusing you?" she said.

17 "She has been very interesting," said Framton.

18 "I hope you don't mind the open window," said Mrs. Sappleton briskly; "my husband and brothers will be home directly from shooting; and they always come in this way. They've been out for snipe in the marshes today, so they'll make a fine mess over my poor carpets. So like you menfolk, isn't it?"

19 She rattled on cheerfully about the shooting and the scarcity of birds, and the prospects for duck in the winter. To Framton it was all purely horrible. He made a desperate but only partially successful effort to turn the talk on to a less ghastly topic; he was conscious that his hostess was giving him only a fragment of her attention, and her eyes were constantly straying past him to the open window and the lawn beyond. It was certainly an unfortunate coincidence that he should have paid his visit on this tragic anniversary.

20 "The doctors agree in ordering me complete rest, an absence of mental excitement, and avoidance of anything in the nature of violent physical exercise," announced Framton, who laboured under the tolerably widespread delusion that total strangers and chance acquaintances are hungry for the least detail of one's ailments and infirmities, their cause and cure. "On the matter of diet they are not so much in agreement," he continued.

21 "No?" said Mrs. Sappleton, in a voice which only replaced a yawn at the last moment. Then she suddenly brightened into alert attention—but not to what Framton was saying.

"Here they are at last!" she cried. "Just in time for tea, and don't they look as if they were 22
muddy up to the eyes!"

Framton shivered slightly and turned towards the niece with a look intended to convey sym- 23
pathetic comprehension. The child was staring out through the open window with dazed horror in her eyes. In a chill shock of nameless fear Framton swung around in his seat and looked in the same direction.

In the deepening twilight three figures were walking across the lawn towards the window; they 24
all carried guns under their arms, and one of them was additionally burdened with a white coat hung over his shoulders. A tired brown spaniel kept close at their heels. Noiselessly they neared the house, and then a hoarse young voice chanted out of the dusk: "I said, Bertie, why do you bound?"

Framton grabbed wildly at his stick and hat; the hall-door, the gravel-drive, and the front 25
gate were dimly noted stages in his headlong retreat. A cyclist coming along the road had to run into the hedge to avoid imminent collision.

"Here we are, my dear," said the bearer of the white mackintosh, coming in through the 26
window; "fairly muddy, but most of it's dry. Who was that who bolted out as we came up?"

"A most extraordinary man, a Mr. Nuttel," said Mrs. Sappleton; "could only talk about his 27
illnesses, and dashed off without a word of goody-bye or apology when you arrived. One would think he had seen a ghost."

"I expect it was the spaniel," said the niece calmly; "he told me he had a horror of dogs. He 28
was once hunted into a cemetery somewhere on the banks of the Ganges by a pack of pariah dogs, and had to spend the night in a newly dug grave with the creatures snarling and grinning and foaming just above him. Enough to make any one lose their nerve."

Romance at short notice was her specialty. 29

Writing in Response to "The Open Window"

Short story writers often use dialogue to advance narrative and to reveal character. Analyze the dialogue in "The Open Window," and explain what it reveals about Framton Nuttel, Vera, and Mrs. Sappleton.

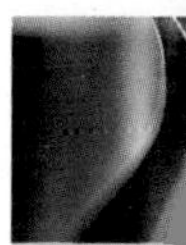

A Gathering of Deafs

John Heaviside

John Heaviside wrote "A Gathering of Deafs" as a student at Hunter College of the City University of New York. The poem, which conveys the rich expressiveness of American Sign Language, was published in Hunter College's student literary review in 1989.

By the turnstiles
in the station
where the L train greets
the downtown six
a congregation of deafs
passes forth
jive wild

and purely physical
in a world dislocated
from the subway howling
hard sole shoe stampede
punk rock blasted radio
screaming, pounding, honking
they gather in community
engaging
in a dexterous conversation

An Old Woman
of her dead husband tells
caressing the air
wrinkled fingers
tell the story
delicate, mellifluous motion
she places
gentle configurations
before the faces
of the group

A young Puerto Rican
describes a fight with his mother
emphasizing each word
abrupt, staccato movements
jerking his elbows
and twisting his wrists
teeth clenched
lips pressed
the story concluded
a fist into his palm

By the newsstand
two lovers
stroke the air
syllables
graceful and slow
their joining
the flow
of fingertips

Writing in Response to "A Gathering of Deafs"

Explain what "A Gathering of Deafs" says about the sign language of the deaf and how that language contrasts with the world of sound. Which world is presented in a more positive light, the world of sound or the world of the deaf?

A Brief Guide to Sentence Errors

PART 4

Word Choice

www.mhhe. com/tsw

For information and exercises on word choice, go to Catalyst > 2.0 > Editing > Word Choice

In Chapter 5, you learned much about word choice (diction), including choosing the appropriate level of diction, using specific words, choosing simple words, using gender-neutral language, avoiding wordiness, and eliminating clichés. In this chapter, you will learn about how to eliminate certain troublesome words and phrases, to eliminate double negatives, and to use frequently confused words correctly.

TROUBLESOME PHRASINGS (tp)

The words, phrases, and clauses discussed next are incorrect or inappropriate in many writing situations.

Phrasings That Announce Your Intent or Opinion

1. In your English compositions, eliminate phrasings like *as this paragraph will explain, my paper will prove, as I will show,* and *the following paragraphs will tell.* These announcements of intent are acceptable conventions in business, scientific, and technical writing, but in essays for the humanities, they are poor style.
2. Eliminate the phrase *in conclusion* when you have reached your last paragraph, and it is obvious that you are concluding.
3. Avoid phrases and clauses such as *I believe, in my opinion, it seems to me,* and *I think* when the ideas expressed are clearly your beliefs, opinions, and

thoughts. Use these expressions to distinguish your ideas from another person's.

Avoid: *In my opinion,* the mayor's refusal to endorse the safety forces' pay raise is shortsighted.

Use: The mayor's refusal to endorse the safety forces' pay raise is shortsighted.

Use: The city council president believes that the mayor is right to criticize the pay raise for the safety forces, but *I believe* the mayor's refusal to endorse the safety forces' pay raise is shortsighted.

Unnecessary or Faulty Modifiers

1. Do not use *very* to intensify things that cannot be intensified. The temperature can be *hot* or it can be *very hot,* but words like *dead, gorgeous, incredible, outstanding, unique,* and *perfect* cannot be made stronger by adding *very.*
2. Avoid unnecessary qualifications using words such as *really, different,* and *particular.* They add no meaning to your sentences and make them wordy.

   Avoid: In this *particular* case, I agree.

   Use: In this case, I agree.

   Avoid: She served three *different* kinds of sandwiches.

   Use: She served three kinds of sandwiches.
3. Avoid modifying nouns and adjectives with the suffix *-type.* Find the accurate word for what you mean.

   Avoid: She likes a *desert-type* climate.

   Use: She likes a *dry* climate.

Faulty Synonyms

1. Avoid *being as* or *being that* as synonyms for *since* or *because.*

   Avoid: *Being that* final exams begin next week, I must take a leave of absence from my job to study.

   Use: *Because* final exams begin next week, I must take a leave of absence from my job to study.

   Use: *Since* final exams begin next week, I must take a leave of absence from my job to study.
2. Avoid using *expect* as a synonym for *suppose.*

   Avoid: I *expect* dinner will be ready in an hour.

   Use: I *suppose* dinner will be ready in an hour.

3. Avoid using *real* to mean *very.*

Avoid: The weather was *real* hot in Arizona.

Use: The weather was *very* hot in Arizona.

4. Do not use *of* to mean *have.*

Avoid: He could *of* (should *of,* would *of*) gone if he had had the time.

Use: He could *have* (should *have,* would *have*) gone if he had had the time.

5. Do not use *plus* as a synonym for *and* to join main clauses.

Avoid: My car needs new tie rods *plus* the tires need to be rotated.

Use: My car needs new tie rods; *in addition,* the tires need to be rotated.

Etc.

1. *Etc., and more, and so forth,* and *and such* suggest that you could say more but do not want to. At times, these expressions are appropriate, but usually you *should* say whatever you *could* say.

Avoid: For his camping trip, Kevin bought a tent, a sleeping bag, a lantern, *etc.*

Use: For his camping trip, Kevin bought a tent, a sleeping bag, a lantern, *a stove, and a first-aid kit.*

2. Do not use *etc.* with *such as. Such as* notes that you are listing items representative of a group, so there is no need to use *etc.* to indicate that other things are included.

Avoid: For his camping trip, Kevin bought several items, *such as* a tent, a sleeping bag, a lantern, *etc.*

Use: For his camping trip, Kevin bought several items, *such as* a tent, a sleeping bag, and a lantern.

3. Do not use *and etc. Etc.* means "and so forth"; therefore, *and etc.* means "and and so forth."

Faulty Grammar and Usage

1. Avoid referring to people with the relative pronoun *which* or *that.* Instead, use *who* or *whom.*

Avoid: Donna is the woman *which* won the essay contest.

Avoid: Donna is the woman *that* won the essay contest.

Use: Donna is the woman *who* won the essay contest.

2. Do not use *irregardless.* Use *regardless* or *irrespective of.*

3. Eliminate *the reason is because.* Use *the reason is that* or *because* instead.

   Avoid: *The reason* fewer people are becoming teachers *is because* teachers' salaries are not competitive.

   Use: *The reason* fewer people are becoming teachers *is that* teachers' salaries are not competitive.

   Use: Fewer people are becoming teachers *because* teachers' salaries are not competitive.

4. Avoid using *so* as an intensifier unless it is followed by a clause beginning with *that.*

   Avoid: After studying for midterm exams, I was *so* tired.

   Use: After studying for midterm exams, I was *very* tired.

   Use: After studying for midterm exams, I was *so* tired *that I slept for 12 hours.*

5. Eliminate *vice versa.* If you want to indicate that the opposite is also true, write out exactly what that opposite is.

   Avoid: My mother is always criticizing me, and *vice versa.*

   Use: My mother is always criticizing me, *and I am always criticizing her.*

6. In general, replace *a lot* and *a lot of* with *many, much,* or *a great deal of.*

   Avoid: Juan earned *a lot of* respect when he told Peter he would not cheat for him.

   Use: Juan earned *a great deal of* respect when he told Peter he would not cheat for him.

   If you do find it appropriate to use *a lot* (in quoting dialogue, for example), remember that it is two words.

7. Use *try to* rather than *try and.*

   Avoid: *Try and* understand my position.

   Use: *Try to* understand my position.

ESL NOTE

Idioms

An **idiom** is an expression whose meaning cannot be determined from the meaning of the words that form it. For example, *on the ropes* is an idiom that means "to be close to failure." You cannot figure out that meaning from the meaning of the words *on, the,* and *ropes.* Learning a language's idioms takes time. If English is not your first language, be patient with yourself. Listen for idioms on television and radio and in the speech of your teachers and classmates. Look for them in newspapers and magazines. You can often learn their meaning by looking up the most important word in a dictionary; idioms with the word are often listed. For example, for *on the ropes,* you would look up "ropes."

EXERCISE Troublesome Phrasing

Directions: Correct the paragraphs to eliminate troublesome words and phrases:

1. [1]Irregardless of how busy you are, you can become more organized and efficient if you get in the habit of making a to-do list. [2]To keep the list from doing more harm than good, however, decide what you need to do plus establish a reasonable amount of time to allocate to each task. [3]A lot of people become frustrated because they make up lists with goals very impossible to achieve in a reasonable amount of time, such as cleaning the entire house, grocery shopping, studying, etc. in one day. [4]Being that a list that is too ambitious can add to your stress, your goals must be attainable. [5]In my opinion, you should identify reasonable goals, set priorities, allow flexibility, and cross items out as they are completed. [6]Most important, you should try and avoid annoyance if all your goals are not met, for another list can be made tomorrow. [7]The most productive people which I know are list-type people, but they content themselves with what they *do* accomplish and do not worry about what they do *not* accomplish.

2. [1]I was watching television recently and saw something very bizarre in a television commercial. [2]Miss Piggy was praising Denny's restaurant and its new Grand Slam Breakfast, which consists of a lot of food, including bacon and sausage. [3]I was immediately struck by the fact that a pig was selling pork-type food. [4]However, as the next examples show, strange product endorsers are not uncommon. [5]Consider the Pillsbury Dough Boy, which is both trademark and product endorser. [6]The boy is made out of dough, right? [7]He could of found another line of work, right? [8]Does he really have to promote the baking of his species? [9]In my opinion, the same can be said of the Chiquita Banana. [10]The reason I find it odd is because a banana is encouraging me to eat its kind. [11]I must be in the minority, however. [12]Being that Denny's, Pillsbury, and Chiquita Bananas are selling just fine, consumers must not be put off by these strange promotions. ■

DOUBLE NEGATIVES (dn)

The following words are **negatives** because they communicate the sense of *no.*

no	none	nothing	hardly
not	nowhere	no one	scarcely
never	nobody		

Be sure to use only *one* negative to express a single negative idea.

No (two negatives): *No one* can do *nothing* to help.

Yes (one negative): *No one* can do anything to help.

No (two negatives): I *cannot* go *nowhere* with you.

Yes (one negative): I *cannot* go *anywhere* with you.

Yes (one negative): I can *go nowhere* with you.

Contractions often include a form of *not,* which is a negative.

No (two negatives): She *can't hardly* wait for Leonard to arrive.

Yes (one negative): She *can't* wait for Leonard to arrive.

Yes (one negative): She can *hardly* wait for Leonard to arrive.

No (two negatives): Henry *wouldn't* be *nothing* without you.

Yes (one negative): Henry would be *nothing* without you.

Yes (one negative): Henry *wouldn't* be anything without you.

A sentence can include more than one negative idea. However, only *one* negative word should express each of these negative ideas, like this:

I will not go if you do not change your attitude.

EXERCISE Double Negatives

Directions: Rewrite to eliminate the double negatives. Two sentences are correct.

1. The school board will not never agree to abolish the dress code.
2. In the back row, we can't hardly hear what the actors are saying.
3. I don't know nothing about cars, but I will try to help you change your oil.
4. We baked so many cookies that the dozen we ate won't hardly be missed.
5. That stupid dog won't never learn to fetch my slippers.
6. The play would not be nearly as enjoyable without the innovative sets.
7. The department store can't hardly handle all the customers who have come for the six-hour clearance sale.
8. Once I took the pain medication, I did not feel nothing in my swollen toe.
9. I would not have made it to college if my grandparents had not helped me pay my tuition.
10. I don't know nothing about planting a garden, so I'm going to find a website to help me learn the best plants for this climate. ■

FREQUENTLY CONFUSED WORDS (fcw)

accept, except

Accept is a verb that means "to receive" or "to agree to":

Mary was pleased to *accept* the scholarship.

I *accept* the conditions of employment you explained.

Except is a preposition that means "excluding":

Except for the color, Joe liked the car.

advice, advise

Advice is a noun that means "a recommendation":

Harriet always values Jan's *advice.*

Advise is a verb that means "to recommend":

I *advise* you to quit while you are ahead.

affect, effect

Affect is a verb meaning "to influence":

The trade deficit *affects* the strength of our economy.

Effect is a noun meaning "result":

The *effects* of the drug are not fully known.

Effect is also a verb meaning "to bring about":

The new company president will *effect* changes in corporate policy.

all right, alright

Alright is nonstandard.

allusion, illusion

Allusion is a noun meaning "indirect reference":

I resent your *allusion* to my past.

Illusion is a noun meaning "something false or misleading":

Having money can create the *illusion* of happiness.

already, all ready

Already means "by this time":

I would stay for dinner, but I have *already* eaten.

All ready means "prepared":

Now that I have packed, I am *all ready* to leave.

among, between

Between is usually used to show the relationship of two things:

The animosity *between* Lee and Ann has existed for years.

Between can be used for more than two things when it means "within":

The floor *between* the stove, refrigerator, and table is hopelessly stained from years of wear.

Among is used to show the relationship of more than two things:

The friendship *among* Kelly, Joe, and Stavros began in third grade.

amount, number

Amount is used for a unit without parts that can be counted individually:

The *amount* of suffering in the war-torn nation cannot be measured.

Number is used for items that can be counted:

The *number* of entries in the contest will determine the odds of winning.

beside, besides

Beside means "next to":

Dad put his book down *beside* his glasses.

Besides means "in addition to" or "except for":

Besides a crib, the expectant parents bought a dresser.
I have nothing to tell you *besides* watch your step.

breath, breathe

Breath is a noun:

The skaters held their *breath* as the judges announced the scores.

Breathe is a verb:

At high altitudes it is more difficult to *breathe.*

coarse, course

Coarse means "rough":

Because wool is *coarse,* I do not like to wear it.

Course means "path," "route," or "procedure":

To speed your progress, summer school is your best *course.*

complement, compliment

Complement means "something that completes":

Red shoes will *complement* the outfit nicely.

Compliment means "praise" or "flattery":

Your *compliment* comes at the right time because I was depressed.

conscience, conscious

Conscience is an awareness of right and wrong:

> When in doubt, follow your *conscience.*

Conscious means "aware":

> Eleni is always *conscious* of the feelings of others.

dessert, desert

Dessert is the sweet at the end of a meal:

> Ice cream is everyone's favorite *dessert.*

Desert (deh-ZERT) is a verb meaning "abandon":

> Kim is a good friend because he never *deserts* me in my time of need.

Desert (DEZ-ert) is a noun meaning "dry, sandy land":

> When driving across the *desert,* a person should have a survival kit in the car.

different than, different from

Experienced readers are likely to prefer *different from.*

disinterested, uninterested

Disinterested means "impartial":

> In labor disputes, a federal mediator acts as a *disinterested* third party.

Uninterested means "lacking interest" or "bored":

> Giselle is *uninterested* in my problem because she has troubles of her own.

farther, further

Farther refers to distance:

> It is not much *farther* to the restaurant I told you about.

Further means "in addition" or "additional":

> The senator believed *further* that the tax favored the rich.
> Any *further* discussion is a waste of time.

fewer, less

Fewer is used for things that can be counted individually:

> There were *fewer* A's on the test than I expected.

Less is used for one unit without individual members that can be counted:

> The *less* you know about what happened, the happier you will be.

human, humane

Human refers to men and women and to the qualities they possess.

> If we did not make mistakes, we would not be *human.*

Humane means "compassionate":

> Our society is not known for *humane* treatment of the elderly.

imply, infer

Imply means "to suggest something without stating it":

> Your attitude *implies* that you do not care.

Infer means "to draw a conclusion from evidence":

> I can *infer* from your sarcasm that you do not agree with me.

it's, its

It's is the contraction of *it is* or *it has:*

> *It's* unfair to accuse Lee of lying without proof.
> *It's* been three years since George moved.

Its is a possessive pronoun:

> The dog buried *its* bone at the base of the oak tree.

lay, lie

Lay means "to put" or "to place." Both its past tense and past-participle forms are *laid:*

> I usually *lay* my keys on the table by the door as soon as I come into the apartment, but I must have *laid* them somewhere else last night.

Lie means "to recline" or "to be in a horizontal position." Its past-tense form is *lay* and its past-participle form is *lain:*

> I thought I would *lie* down on the couch for an hour to rest, but I *lay* there for three hours thinking about changing my major.

loose, lose

Loose means "unfastened" or "not tight":

> Joey's *loose* tooth made it hard for him to eat corn on the cob.

Lose means "misplace":

> Every time I buy an expensive pen, I *lose* it.

passed, past

Passed means "went by":

Summer *passed* far too quickly.

Past refers to previous time:

The *past* week was hectic because I had to work overtime at the store and study for final exams.

precede, proceed

Precede means "to come before":

A preface *precedes* the main part of a book.

Proceed means "continue":

I am sorry I interrupted you; *proceed* with your plan.

principal, principle

Principal, as a noun, refers to a school administrator; as an adjective, *principal* means "first in importance":

The *principal* suspended the students for fighting.
The *principal* issue here is whether we can afford the trip.

Principle is a truth or a moral conviction:

My *principles* will not allow me to lie for you.

set, sit

Set is a verb that takes a direct object:

For daylight saving time, *set* your clock ahead one hour.

Sit is a verb that does not take a direct object:

Sit near the door, and I will find you when I arrive.

stationary, stationery

Stationary means "unmoving" or "unchanging":

This fan is *stationary;* it does not rotate.

Stationery is writing paper:

More men are using pink *stationery* for personal correspondence.

than, then

Than is used for comparisons:

The car I bought is more fuel efficient *than* yours.

Then is a time reference; it also means "next":

I went to college in the 1970s; students were politically active *then.*
Spade the ground thoroughly; *then* you can plant the seeds.

there, their, they're

There indicates place; it is also a sentence opener:

> I thought my car was parked *there.*
> *There* are 12 people going on the ski trip.

Their is a possessive pronoun:

> Children rarely appreciate what *their* parents do for them.

They're is the contraction form of *they are:*

> Lyla and Jim said *they're* coming, but I will believe it when I see them.

threw, through, thorough

Threw is the past tense of *throw:*

> The pitcher *threw* the ball to third base.

Through means "finished" or "into and out of":

> We should be *through* by noon.
> When I drove *through* the Lincoln Tunnel, I forgot to put my headlights on.

Thorough means "complete":

> In the spring, many people give their houses a *thorough* cleaning.

to, too, two

To means "toward," and it is also used with a verb to form the infinitive:

> After five years, Kathleen saved enough money *to* go *to* Italy.

Too means "also" or "excessively":

> The child whined because he did not get to go skating *too.*
> When the curtain went up, I was *too* frightened to say my lines.

Two is the number:

> Lenny gets along well with his *two* roommates.

whose, who's

Whose is the possessive form of *who:*

> *Whose* books are on the kitchen table?

Who's is the contraction form of *who is* and *who has:*

> *Who's* going with you?
> *Who's* been in the cookie jar?

your, you're

Your is the possessive form of *you:*

Your car is parked in a tow-away zone.

You're is the contraction form of *you are:*

Let me know when *you're* coming with us.

EXERCISE Frequently Confused Words

1. Select five sets of frequently confused words that you are not completely comfortable using. Use each word in a sentence that you compose.
2. Correct the errors with frequently confused words.

[1]The San Francisco earthquake of April 18, 1906, struck at 5:12 A.M. [2]Its affects were devastating. [3]In the coarse of 65 seconds of tremblings and shocks, water and gas mains cracked. [4]The break in the gas lines caused a fire that lasted three days and destroyed two-thirds of the city. [5]The amount of lives lost was great: 3,000 of the 400,000 residents died. [6]Beside that, the entire business district was leveled, and 3 out of 5 homes were destroyed. [7]Its difficult to imagine, but almost 300,000 people were left homeless and 490 city blocks were destroyed. [8]The quake, which registered 8.3 on the Richter scale, through the city into a panic, but their were signs of normalcy as well. [9]The city's three major newspapers, whose offices burned, pulled together across the Bay in Oakland and printed a combined edition the next day. [10]As strong and devastating as that earthquake was, it's not as strong as the 9.0 earthquake that struck Lisbon, Portugal in 1755, demolishing the city and killing slightly less than 61,000 people. [11]It was felt further away than any other quake—all the way to Sweden. ■

Sentence Fragments (frag)

www.mhhe.com/tsw
For information and exercises on sentence fragments, go to Catalyst 2.0 > Editing > Sentence Fragments

A **sentence fragment** is a word group that cannot stand as a sentence—even if you give it a capital letter and end punctuation. A fragment results under several circumstances.

- A fragment results when the subject is omitted.

  Fragment: Fans were anxious for the concert to begin. *But waited patiently.*

  Sentence: Fans were anxious for the concert to begin. But *they* waited patiently.

- A fragment results when all or part of the verb is omitted.

  Fragment: The townspeople were angry that the hotel allowed bands to entertain guests outdoors. *Their amplifiers turned up so high that the noise carried to residential districts.*

  Sentence: The townspeople were angry that the hotel allowed bands to entertain guests outdoors. Their amplifiers *were* turned up so high that the noise carried to residential districts.

- A fragment results when the subject and the complete verb are omitted.

  Fragment: The parents spent over $500 on toys for their children. *Most of it on the two girls.*

  Sentence: The parents spent over $500 on toys for their children. *They spent* most of it on the two girls.

- A fragment occurs when a dependent clause is capitalized and punctuated as a sentence.

Fragment: *Since she was graceful as well as daring.* She was an excellent dancer.

Sentence: Since she was graceful as well as daring, she was an excellent dancer.

For a discussion of dependent clauses, see page 120.

FINDING SENTENCE FRAGMENTS

If you have a tendency to write sentence fragments, go over your paper a separate time, looking just for fragments. Read each word group aloud, and ask yourself whether it sounds like a complete sentence. If you are not sure, check to see if the word group has a subject and a complete verb and does not begin with a subordinating conjunction (see below). Do not move on to the next word group until you are sure the one you are leaving behind is a sentence. For this method to be effective, you must read slowly, listening to each word group independent of what comes before and after it. Otherwise, you may fail to hear a fragment because you complete its meaning with the sentence that comes before or after it.

Subordinating conjunctions often begin sentence fragments, so study any word group that begins with one of them. The following are common subordinating conjunctions:

after	as if	because	for example	such as	when
although	as long as	before	if	unless	whenever
as	as soon as	especially	since	until	whether
	as though	even though	so that		while

If you compose at the computer, use the search function to locate these words in your draft. Each time you locate a word group beginning with one of them, make sure you have a sentence rather than a fragment. Another computer tip is to isolate every word group you are calling a sentence by hitting the tab key twice before each capital letter that marks a sentence opening. Then read each word group separately to check for completeness. With word groups visually isolated this way, you are less likely to overlook a fragment by mentally connecting it to a sentence before or after it. After checking everything, reformat your draft.

If your computer's grammar checker highlights a sentence for you and labels it a fragment, you should still make certain that it is incomplete before revising it.

CORRECTING SENTENCE FRAGMENTS

How you correct a sentence fragment depends upon what is causing the fragment. Often, you have more than one option.

1. When the sentence subject is missing, you can correct the fragment two ways:
   a. Add the missing subject.
   b. Connect the fragment to a sentence.

Fragment:	I wanted to work full-time over the summer. *Yet could find only part-time employment.*
Add the missing subject:	I wanted to work full-time over the summer. Yet *I* could find only part-time employment.
Connect the fragment to a sentence:	I wanted to work full-time over the summer *yet* could find only part-time employment.

2. When all or part of the verb is missing, you may be able to correct the fragment two ways:
   a. Add the missing verb or verb part.
   b. Change the verb form.

Fragment:	Adrian ran for the bus. *However, it gone before he reached the bus stop.*
Add the missing verb or verb part:	Adrian ran for the bus. However, it *was* gone before he reached the bus stop.
Change the verb form:	Adrian ran for the bus. However, it *went* before he reached the bus stop.

3. When the subject and the complete verb are missing, you have two choices:
   a. Add the missing elements.
   b. Connect the fragment to a sentence.

Fragment:	The new Mexican restaurant was an instant hit. *Particularly with young people.*
Add the missing elements:	The new Mexican restaurant was an instant hit. *It was* particularly *popular* with young people.
Connect the fragment to a sentence:	The new Mexican restaurant was an instant hit, *particularly with young people.*

4. When a dependent clause is capitalized and punctuated as a sentence, you have two choices:
   a. Change the dependent clause to an independent clause.
   b. Connect the dependent clause to a sentence.

Fragment:	*When the curtain came down to signal intermission.* The audience stormed the concession stand.
Change the dependent clause to an independent clause:	The curtain came down to signal intermission. The audience stormed the concession stand.
Connect the dependent clause to a sentence:	When the curtain came down to signal intermission, the audience stormed the concession stand.

ESL NOTE

The Past Participle and Passive Voice

Regular verbs have the same form for the past tense and for the past participle. The past-tense form can stand alone.

Yes (past tense): The boy *walked his dog.*

When you are using the past-participle form for the passive voice, be sure to combine it with *am, is, are, was,* or *were.* Otherwise, you will have a sentence fragment. (In passive voice, explained on page 117, the subject *receives* the action of the verb.)

No (sentence fragment): The child's allowance *earned* with hard work.

Yes (correct passive voice): The child's allowance *was earned* with hard work.

EXERCISE Sentence Fragments

Directions: Where necessary, correct the following to eliminate the fragments. Some are correct as they are.

1. After returning from the beach. The children were exhausted.
2. The rain showed no signs of letting up, so flash flood warnings were issued.
3. After Howie had attended drama class several times and bought a subscription to *Variety.* He was sure he would become a big star.
4. Although Marie missed several training sessions. She learned to use the new computer.
5. By midnight the party was over.
6. John neglecting his assigned duties and spending time on independent research.
7. The reigning dictator, being an excellent administrator and former army officer.
8. Being the most indispensable part of the Channel 27 news team. Antonio got a raise.
9. Cal dropped calculus. Which he had dropped several times before.
10. When Sean went to his karate class. His home was burglarized.
11. After a while, the fog cleared.
12. How can you expect that of me?
13. Carlotta skipped breakfast. Although she needed the nourishment.
14. Working together to save our environment. We can leave the world a better place than we found it.
15. Dad cleaning the hull of the boat, helping to set the lobster traps, and still finding time to teach his younger daughter how to bait her own hook.

Directions: In the paragraphs that follow, correct the fragments.

16. [1]Virgil Trucks won a World Series game for the Detroit Tigers without ever winning a regular-season game. [2]Because he was in the Navy at the time. [3]Trucks missed most of the season in 1945. [4]Discharged after the war. [5]He returned in time to pitch five innings against the St. Louis Browns and help the Tigers win the pennant. [6]On the last day of the season. [7]He was not credited with the win, though, and finished the season with a record of 0–0. [8]The Tigers faced the Chicago Cubs in the World Series that year. [9]The Tigers triumphed in seven games. [10]Trucks, who had not won a game that year, went the distance in the second game. [11]Beating the Cubs 4–1. [12]As a result, Trucks being the only pitcher to win in the World Series without winning during the regular season.

17. [1]Much literature written for adolescents is of the highest quality. [2]For example, *IOU'S,* by Ouida Sebestyen, being a well-written story of adolescent conflict that both teens and adults would enjoy. [3]The main character is 13-year-old Stowe. [4]A boy who lives with his divorced mother. [5]The novel chronicles Stowe's efforts as he wrestles with an important decision, struggles with friendships, and makes peace with his family. [6]Like most adolescents, Stowe longs for the independence of adulthood at the same time he fears it. [7]Briskly paced, tightly narrated, and thought-provoking, *IOU'S* is a novel teens will see themselves in. [8]And a novel that will remind adults of the struggles inherent in adolescence. [9]It is poignant, funny, and subtle. [10]And above all realistic.

18. [1]In the late 1800s, Harry Stevens sold concessions at the New York Giants home baseball field. [2]Named the Polo Grounds. [3]One day it was rather cool, and Stevens was not selling very much. [4]At the time, the only food sold in ballparks being cold. [5]Not one to stand for poor sales, Stevens shopped for something warm to sell. [6]He found a butcher shop and bought warm sausages, but he needed a way to serve them. [7]When he came up with the idea of serving the sausages in a bun. [8]The hot dog was born. [9]However, the sausage in a bun was not yet named "hot dog." [10]A New York cartoonist, Tad Dorgan, is responsible for the name. [11]Dorgan drew a picture of the product. [12]Using a dachshund in the bun. [13]It was Dorgan who first used the name *hot dog.* ■

Run-On Sentences and Comma Splices (r/o, cs)

www.mhhe.com/tsw
For information and exercises on run-on sentences and comma splices, go to Catalyst 2.0 > Editing > Run-On Sentences and to Catalyst 2.0 > Editing > Comma Splices

A **run-on sentence** occurs when two or more independent clauses are written without correct separation. (**Independent clauses,** explained on page 118, are word groups that can stand as sentences.)

Independent clause: the power was out for two days

Independent clause: most of the food in my refrigerator spoiled

Run-on sentence: The power was out for two days most of the food in my refrigerator spoiled.

A **comma splice** occurs when two or more independent clauses are separated by nothing more than a comma. It can also occur when two or more independent clauses are separated by a comma and a conjunctive adverb such as *therefore* instead of by a coordinating conjunction. (For a list of conjunctive adverbs, see page 585. **Coordinating conjunctions,** explained on page 118, are *and, but, or, nor, for, so,* and *yet.*

Independent clause: Rocco studied hard for his final exams

Independent clause: he passed them all with high marks

Comma splice: Rocco studied hard for his final exams, he passed them all with high marks.

Comma splice: Rocco studied hard for his final exams, therefore he passed them all with high marks.

FINDING RUN-ON SENTENCES AND COMMA SPLICES

If you tend to write run-ons and comma splices, edit a separate time, checking just for these errors. Study each group of words you are calling a "sentence," and ask yourself how many independent clauses there are. If there is more than one, make sure the clauses are separated by either a semicolon or a comma and a coordinating conjunction. When you find a run-on or comma splice, make the correction according to the guidelines in the following section.

If you compose at the computer, use the search function to locate the conjunctive adverbs listed on page 585. Each time you locate one of these adverbs, check for independent clauses on both sides. Wherever you have independent clauses on both sides, make sure you have used a semicolon before the word. (Conjunctive adverbs may appear in the middle of a clause or at the end of the second clause.)

Another computer tip is to hit the tab key twice before each capital letter marking the beginning of a sentence. The visual separation will allow you to check the number of independent clauses more easily. After finding and eliminating run-ons and comma splices, reformat your text.

If your computer's grammar checker tells you that a sentence is a run-on or a comma splice, check to make sure that the sentence is, in fact, faulty before correcting it.

CORRECTING RUN-ON SENTENCES AND COMMA SPLICES

Run-ons and comma splices can be corrected five ways.

1. Separate the independent clauses with a period and capital letter to form two sentences.

   Run-on: The power was out for two days most of the food in my refrigerator spoiled.

   Correction: The power was out for two days. Most of the food in my refrigerator spoiled.

   Comma splice: Rocco studied hard for his final exams, he passed them all with high marks.

   Correction: Rocco studied hard for his final exams. He passed them all with high marks.

2. If the two independent clauses are closely related, you can separate them with a semicolon.

   Run-on: The personnel department was praised for its efficiency all the workers received a bonus.

   Correction: The personnel department was praised for its efficiency; all the workers received a bonus.

   Comma splice: I never like to wear wool, its coarseness irritates my skin.

   Correction: I never like to wear wool; its coarseness irritates my skin.

3. Separate the independent clauses with a comma and coordinating conjunction *(and, but, or, nor, for, so, yet).*

Run-on: The new computer's manual is very clear Enrico learned to use the machine in an hour.

Correction: The new computer's manual is very clear, so Enrico learned to use the machine in an hour.

Comma splice: The hospital laid off 100 workers, most of them will be called back in three months.

Correction: The hospital laid off 100 workers, but most of them will be called back in three months.

Note: Run-ons and comma splices frequently occur when writers confuse the following **conjunctive adverbs** for coordinating conjunctions:

also	hence	nevertheless
consequently	however	nonetheless
for example	indeed	therefore
furthermore	moreover	thus

Conjunctive adverbs cannot be used to join independent clauses with a comma; only the coordinating conjunctions can do this.

Run-on: I was certain my interview went well therefore I was surprised when I was not among the finalists for the job.

Correction: I was certain my interview went well; therefore, I was surprised when I was not among the finalists for the job.

Comma splice: The party was dull, consequently I left early.

Correction: The party was dull; consequently, I left early.

Notice that a conjunctive adverb can join independent clauses when a semicolon comes before the conjunctive adverb and a comma comes after.

4. Change one of the independent clauses to a dependent clause.

Run-on: My car stalls when I accelerate quickly the carburetor needs to be adjusted.

Correction: Because the carburetor needs to be adjusted, my car stalls when I accelerate quickly.

Comma splice: Spring is supposed to be a happy time, many people get depressed.

Correction: Although spring is supposed to be a happy time, many people get depressed.

5. Recast the sentence.

Run-on: The museum has a traveling exhibition that goes to local schools it is very popular with young children.

Correction: The museum's traveling exhibition, which goes to local schools, is very popular with young children.

Comma splice: The silver earrings are an heirloom, they have been in my family for four generations.

Correction: Having been in our family for four generations, the silver earrings are an heirloom.

ESL NOTE

Commas and Independent Clauses

In several languages, including Spanish and Vietnamese, commas can legitimately separate independent clauses. If you speak one of these languages, check your written English carefully to be sure you are separating independent clauses in the ways explained in this chapter.

EXERCISE Run-On Sentences and Comma Splices

Directions: Correct the following run-ons and comma splices using any of the methods discussed.

1. My first bike will always be special to me it was a yellow dirt bike named Thunderball.
2. Brad loves to gossip about others he becomes angry if he even thinks someone is gossiping about him.
3. Yesterday the fire trucks raced up our street three times it must be the summer brushfire season.
4. The large black ants marched upside down across the kitchen ceiling, I wonder where they came from.
5. The package of chicken fryer parts was obviously spoiled he returned it to the manager of the market demanding a refund.
6. My daughter's baseball pants are impossible to get clean, why does the league insist on purchasing white pants?
7. Randy is a terrible soccer coach, he cares more about winning than he does about the children he manages.
8. Stevie is so warm and open that it is hard to resist his charm, he seems to smile all the time.
9. Cotton material is all that they claim it is—lightweight, soft, and comfortable be careful when laundering it often shrinks.
10. My mother has often been my best friend, she is caring, supportive, and nonjudgmental.

Directions: In the paragraphs below, correct the run-ons and comma splices.

11. [1]My day off made me wish I was back at my job everything went wrong. [2]First I overslept and neglected to get my son to day camp on time. [3]Then there was no milk for breakfast my son ate pizza. [4]The dog had raided the wastebasket during the night half-chewed paper and bits of garbage

littered the living room carpeting. [5]I plugged in the sweeper, one of the prongs broke off in the outlet. [6]I drove to the local hardware store to purchase new plugs. [7]I returned home to discover the plug was the wrong size for the sweeper cord I drove back to the store to exchange the plug for the proper size. [8]Then I cut my finger when the screwdriver slipped while I was trying to attach the new plug. [9]In the middle of all this chaos, the phone rang, the neighbor was calling to tell me that my German shepherd had chased the letter carrier away from her house. [10] By the time I was finished listening to her, I started to itch I looked down to see the unmistakable red blotches of poison ivy rising on my arms and calves.

12. [1]Every object in the universe pulls on every other object, this is called gravitation. [2]Interestingly, the strength of the gravitational pull depends on two things: how much matter a body contains and the distance between the objects. [3]Objects with very little matter have very little gravitation, for example, the earth has more matter than the moon, so the earth's gravitational pull is stronger than the moon's. [4]Also, the closer together objects are, the greater their gravitational pull. [5]The earth has more matter than a human being, so its gravitation pulls the human to the earth. [6]However, the earth acts as if all matter were at its center thus the strength of gravity at a location depends on its distance from the earth's center. [7]This means that gravity is stronger at sea level than on a mountaintop.

13. [1]The Underground Railroad was a network that helped slaves escape from the South to freedom in the North, it was set up by Harriet Tubman (1826–1913). [2]Tubman was motivated to help others, including her family, find freedom after she escaped slavery. [3]For 10 years, Tubman was a "conductor" on the Railroad. [4]In that time, she made at least 15 trips into slave states. [5]She was able to guide her parents and siblings to freedom, in addition she helped more than 200 slaves to freedom in the North. [6]These journeys were demanding and dangerous. [7]Although Tubman was a small woman, she had exceptional leadership qualities. [8]For her efforts to emancipate slaves, Tubman was called "Moses" by many people author and reformer Thomas Wentworth Higginson called her "the greatest heroine of the age." ■

Verbs

www.mhhe.com/tsw
For information and exercises on verbs, go to Catalyst 2.0 > Editing > Verbs and Verbals

VERB FORMS (vb fm)

Except for *be,* English verbs have five basic forms: the base form, the present tense form, the past-tense form, the past-participle form, and the present-participle form.

Base Form: *love/hold*

The base form is used with *I, we, you, they,* or a plural noun to form the present tense (to show that something occurs *now*):

> I (we, you, they, the children) *love.*
> I (we, you, they, the children) *hold.*

Present-Tense Form: *loves/holds*

The *-s* or *-es* form is used with *it, he, she,* or a singular noun to form the present tense (to show that something occurs *now*):

> It (he, she, the child) *loves.*
> It (he, she, the child) *holds.*

Past-Tense Form: *loved/held*

The past-tense form shows that something occurred in the past:

> I (we, you, he, she, it, they, the child, the children) *loved.*
> I (we, you, he, she, it, they, the child, the children) *held.*

Past-Participle Form: *loved/held*

The past-participle form is used with *has, have, had, am, is, was,* and *were:*

I (we, you, they, the children) *have loved/have held.*
It (he, she, the child) *has loved/has held.*
I *am loved/am held.*
It (he, she, the child) *is loved/is held.*
We (you, they, the children) *are loved/are held.*
I (we, you, they, he, she, the child, the children) *had loved/had held.*
I (he, she, it, the child) *was loved/was held.*
We (you, they, the children) *were loved/were held.*

Present-Participle Form: *loving/holding*

The present-participle form adds an *-ing* to the base form. It is used with *am, is, are, was,* and *were:*

I *am loving/am holding.*
It (he, she, the child) *is loving/is holding.*
We (you, they, the children) *are loving/are holding.*
I (he, she, it, the child) *was loving/was holding.*
We (you, they, the children) *were loving/were holding.*

ESL NOTE

Use of *Am* with the Present Participle

Be sure to use *am* between *I* and the present participle.

No: I *working* 20 hours a week at Wal-Mart.

No: I *is working* 20 hours a week at Wal-Mart.

Yes: I *am working* 20 hours a week at Wal-Mart.

Regular Verb Forms

Regular verbs form their past-tense and past-participle forms by adding *-d* or *-ed* to the base form.

Base	Past Tense	Past Participle
work	worked	worked
talk	talked	talked

Irregular Verb Forms

The forms for **irregular verbs** vary. They are given in the dictionary entry for each verb. Following are the forms for some of them.

Some Common Irregular Verbs

Base	Past Tense	Past Participle	Present Participle	*-s/-es* Form
arise	arose	arisen	arising	arises
become	became	become	becoming	becomes
bring	brought	brought	bringing	brings
buy	bought	bought	buying	buys
do	did	done	doing	does
drink	drank	drunk	drinking	drinks
fly	flew	flown	flying	flies
get	got	gotten, got	getting	gets
go	went	gone	going	goes
grow	grew	grown	growing	grows
hang (a picture)	hung	hung	hanging	hangs
hang (execute)	hanged	hanged	hanging	hangs
have	had	had	having	has
hide	hid	hidden	hiding	hides
know	knew	known	knowing	knows
lay	laid	laid	laying	lays
leave	left	left	leaving	leaves
lose	lost	lost	losing	loses
prove	proved	proved, proven	proving	proves
ride	rode	ridden	riding	rides
rise	rose	risen	rising	rises
see	saw	seen	seeing	sees
sit	sat	sat	sitting	sits
spring	sprang, sprung	sprung	springing	springs
steal	stole	stolen	stealing	steals
take	took	taken	taking	takes
tear	tore	torn	tearing	tears
throw	threw	thrown	throwing	throws
wear	wore	worn	wearing	wears
write	wrote	written	writing	writes

Forms of *Be*

Unlike other verbs, *be* has eight forms.

Base Form: *be*

The base form of *be* is used in commands and with *to:*

Be careful or you will hurt yourself.
Jan is studying *to be* a court reporter.

ESL NOTE

Incorrect Use of *-d* and *-ed* Endings

Do not add a *-d* or *-ed* ending to the past-tense or past-participle forms of irregular verbs.

No: Hannah *wored* a new sweater today.

Yes: Hannah *wore* a new sweater today.

No: Stavros *has tored* his pants.

Yes: Stavros *tore* his pants.

Present-Tense Forms: *am/is/are*

I *am* the first person in my family to attend college.
Julio *is* sick with the flu.
The board members *are* interested in a fund-raiser.

Past-Tense Forms: *was/were*

The CD *was* scratched and unplayable.
We *were* uncertain about which way to go.

Past-Participle Form: *been*

Lanie *has been* my best friend for 15 years.
The window *had been broken.*
They *have been* here before.

Present-Participle Form: *being*

She *is being* rude to the salesclerk.
The children *are being* quiet right now.
You *were being* too sarcastic.

ESL NOTE

Use of *Has, Have,* or *Had* with *Been*

Be sure to use *has* or *have* with *been.*

No: He *been* anxious about the exam.

Yes: He *has been* anxious about the exam.

Yes: He *had been* anxious about the exam.

No: The children *been* good all day.

Yes: The children *have been* good all day.

Yes: The children *had been* good all day.

Present-Tense Forms of Regular and Irregular Verbs

For the present tense, remember to use *-s* or *-es* with the base form when the sentence subject is *it, he, she,* a singular noun, or a singular indefinite pronoun. (Indefinite pronouns, listed on page 605, are words like *anyone, somebody,* and *everything.*)

No: My uncle *eat* in a restaurant every night.

Yes: My uncle *eats* in a restaurant every night.

Yes: It/he/she *depends* upon you.

Yes: The soprano *sings* beautifully.

Yes: Everybody *confuses* the twins.

For more on this grammar point, see subject–verb agreement below.

SUBJECT–VERB AGREEMENT (s–v agr)

www.mhhe.com/tsw
For information and exercises on subject–verb agreement, go to Catalyst 2.0 > Editing > Subject/Verb Agreement

The rule for **subject–verb agreement** is straightforward: A present-tense verb should always agree with its subject *in number.* That is, a singular subject requires a singular verb, and a plural subject requires a plural verb.

Singular subject, singular verb: The green *ink looks* difficult to read.

Plural subject, plural verb: The *desks are* highly polished.

Most of the time, subject–verb agreement is easily achieved. However, some instances present special agreement problems, and these are discussed below. Also, if your computer's grammar checker highlights an agreement error, make certain the error does, in fact, exist before making changes.

Compound Subjects

A **compound subject** occurs when two or more words, phrases, or clauses are joined by *and, or, nor, either . . . or,* or *neither . . . nor.*

1. When the parts of a compound subject are linked by *and,* use a plural verb:

   The *lioness and her cub share* a close bond.

2. When subjects are preceded by *each* or *every,* use a singular verb:

   Each lioness and *each cub faces* starvation on the drought-stricken plain.

3. When singular subjects are linked by *or* or *nor* (or by *either . . . or* or *neither . . . nor*), use a singular verb:

   Drought or famine threatens all wildlife.

4. When plural subjects are linked by *or* or *nor* (or *either . . . or* or *neither . . . nor*), use a plural verb:

   Neither the children nor their parents are enjoying the play.

5. When a plural subject and a singular subject are joined, use a verb that agrees with the nearer subject:

   A couch or two chairs fit in the den.

   Neither the scouts nor their leader is willing to camp out on such a cold night.

   For a more pleasant-sounding sentence, place the plural form last:

   Neither the leader nor the scouts are willing to camp out on such a cold night.

Subject and Verb Separated

Words, phrases, or clauses that come between the subject and verb do not affect the subject–verb agreement rule:

> The *chipmunks,* burrowing under my flower bed, *raid* my vegetable garden.

The subject *chipmunks* is plural, so the plural verb *raid* must be used, even though the phrase *burrowing under my flower bed* separates subject and verb. Here is another example:

> *One* of the demonstrators *was* fined $100.

Although the phrase between the subject and verb contains the plural word *demonstrators,* the singular subject *one* still requires the singular verb *was.*

Inverted Order

When the verb appears before the subject, the word order of the sentence is **inverted.** Be sure the verb agrees with the subject and not some other word close to the verb:

> Floating on the water *were three lilies.*

Sentences that begin with *there* or *here* often have inverted order, as do sentences that ask a question:

> There *are* many *causes* of cancer.
>
> Here *sits* the *box* of records.
>
> Why *are* your *questions* so hard to answer?

Indefinite Pronouns

Indefinite pronouns refer to a nonspecific member or nonspecific members of a group of people, items, or ideas. The following indefinite pronouns are singular and require singular verbs:

anybody	everyone	nothing
anyone	everything	one
anything	neither	somebody
each	nobody	someone
either	none	something
everybody	no one	

Nobody ignores an insult all the time.

Everybody retaliates once in a while.

No one likes to be the butt of a joke.

Note: Although *everyone* and *everybody* clearly refer to more than one, they are still singular in a grammatical sense and take a singular verb:

Everyone is invited to the party after the show.

You may be tempted to use a plural verb with a singular indefinite pronoun followed by a phrase with a plural word. However, the singular verb is used in formal usage:

Each of the boys *is* willing to help rake the leaves.

Neither of us *plans* to contribute a week's salary to the Christmas fund.

The following indefinite pronouns are plural:

both few many several

Both hope to join us for dinner.

Several expect to compete for the prize.

The following indefinite pronouns may be singular or plural, depending on the meaning of the sentence:

all some most
any more

Most of the players *are* injured.

Most of the pie *has* been eaten.

All of the bills *are* paid.

All of the food *tastes* good.

Collective Nouns

Collective nouns have a singular form and refer to a group of people or things. The following are examples of collective nouns:

audience crew jury
class faculty majority
committee family team

Collective nouns take a singular verb when the noun refers to the group as a single unit:

The *number* of people attending the concert *poses* a fire hazard.

The women's basketball *team is* still in contention for the state championship.

Collective nouns take a plural verb when the members of the group are functioning individually:

A *number* of those in attendance *seem* over 30 years old.

The *faculty have* agreed among themselves to promote tougher admissions standards.

If you prefer to use a plural verb, you can often add a phrase like *members of:*

The *members of* the committee *have* agreed to a new set of membership guidelines.

Relative Pronouns

Who, whom, which, and *that* are **relative pronouns.** They refer to nouns in a sentence.

1. When the relative pronoun refers to a singular noun, use a singular verb:

   My roommate, *who is* on the cross-country team, runs at least 50 miles a week.

2. When the relative pronoun refers to a plural noun, use a plural verb:

   The advertisements, *which were* offensive to women, were pulled from the newspaper.

3. When the phrase *one of the* appears before a plural noun, use a plural verb:

   Kamie is one of the two scholarship winners *who hope* to be a veterinarian.

4. When the phrase *only one of the* appears before a noun, use a singular verb:

   Kamie is the only one of the two scholarship winners *who hopes* to be a veterinarian.

ESL NOTE

Singular Verbs and Noncount Nouns

Use a singular verb with nouns that name something that normally cannot be counted (**noncount nouns**). These are nouns like *air, baggage, hunger, honesty, water, sugar,* and *health.*

No: Her *wisdom surprise* me because she is so young.

Yes: Her *wisdom surprises* me because she is so young.

EXERCISE Subject–Verb Agreement

Directions: Choose the correct verb form in the following sentences.

1. Three wolves and a grizzly bear (stalk/stalks) the grazing caribou herd.
2. The hunter, not natural enemies, (is/are) responsible for the decline in the bald eagle population.
3. Only recently (has/have) we seen the rebirth of violent protest.
4. There (is/are) few American holidays more popular than Thanksgiving.
5. None of us really (know/knows) anyone else.
6. All of us often (disguise/disguises) our real feelings.
7. Neither of the cubs born to the huge female grizzly (appear/appears) undernourished.
8. The chief reasons for the country's high unemployment rate (has/have) been the attempts to bring inflation under control.
9. Each of the campers (is/are) responsible for bringing cooking utensils.
10. A majority of people (feel/feels) insecure about something.
11. There (is/are) few presidents more admired than Lincoln.
12. Neither time nor progress (has/have) diminished the affection most Americans feel for our sixteenth president.
13. One of my favorite poems (is/are) "The Rime of the Ancient Mariner."
14. Most of the beetles (is/are) trapped.
15. Either Shania Twain or Celine Dion (deserve/deserves) the Grammy for record of the year.
16. Your family often (demand/demands) to know your innermost secrets.
17. Each of us (decide/decides) whom we will trust.
18. Everyone (need/needs) someone to talk to.
19. Fifteen adult white-tailed deer and a single fawn (was/were) observed by the backpackers.
20. All the elements of nature (act/acts) to maintain the balance of the animal population.

Directions: In the following paragraphs, correct problems with subject–verb agreement.

21. [1]One of the islands in the Caribbean Sea is called Bonaire. [2]A number of tourists are attracted to Bonaire because it is a nesting site for pink flamingos. [3]However, the clear waters of the sea makes the area a perfect spot for diving. [4]There is numerous underwater attractions for either the experienced diver or the amateur who requires a guide. [5]On the coral reef is groupies and moray eels. [6]Also, there are small "cleaner fish," called hogfish, who eat the harmful parasites off the larger fish. [7]The colorful reef itself is a spectacular sight where one can observe a variety of coral.

[8]Throughout the reef is sea anemones, shrimp, and crabs for the diver to observe. [9]Although the underwater attractions of Bonaire is not commonly known, time and word of mouth will bring more vacationers to this island off the coast of northern South America.

22. [1]About 150 miles west of New Orleans sits the bayous of Cajun country. [2]This is one of the areas famous for crawfish and zydeco music. [3]However, it also happens to be famous for Tabasco, the original hot sauce. [4]This most famous of all hot sauces has been produced on Avery Island, Louisiana, for 134 years. [5]A rare pepper, the *Capsicum frutescens,* provides the heart of the sauce. [6]The pepper, which is the proud discovery of Edmund McIlhenny, was first planted on the island by McIlhenny in the 1860s. [7]Anyone of us who wants to make the sauce would have to follow McIlhenny's original recipe. [8]Each of the peppers used is picked when it is ripe. [9]Then workers mashes them and mixes them with ground salt. [10]The mixture of peppers and salt are stored in oak barrels for an amazing three years. [11]After that, it is strained, mixed with vinegar, and fermented another four weeks. [12]Not until then can this magic mix of aged ingredients be bottled. ■

TENSE SHIFTS (t shft)

Verb tense indicates past, present, and future time. Once you begin a sentence with a particular verb tense, maintain that tense as long as you are referring to the same period of time. Switching tense without a valid reason creates a problem called **tense shift.** The following paragraph contains unwarranted tense shifts (the verbs are italicized to help you recognize the shifts):

> Hockey player Bill Mosienko *dreamed* (past) of making his way into the record books, and on March 23, 1952, his dream *comes* (present) true. His team, the Blackhawks, *was playing* (past) the New York Rangers. Blackhawk Gus Bodnar *gets* (present) the puck and *passes* (present) it to Mosienko, who *scores* (present). At the following face-off, Bodnar *gains* (present) possession, *passes* (present) to Mosienko, who *scored* (past) again. Bodnar *won* (past) the face-off again and *passed* (past) to Gee. Gee *passed* (past) to Mosienko, who *scores* (present) again—for three goals in 21 seconds.

The verbs in this paragraph shift back and forth from present to past tense, interfering with an accurate representation of the action of the game. To prevent confusion about time sequence, once you use a verb tense, maintain that tense consistently and shift time only when the shift is justified.

A corrected version of the example paragraph reads like this:

> Hockey player Bill Mosienko dreamed of making his way into the record books, and on March 23, 1952, his dream came true. His team, the Blackhawks, was playing the New York Rangers. Blackhawk Gus Bodnar got the puck and passed it to Mosienko, who scored. At the following face-off, Bodnar gained possession and passed to Mosienko, who scored again. Bodnar won the face-off again and passed to Gee. Gee passed to Mosienko, who scored again—for three goals in 21 seconds.

A shift from one tense to another is appropriate when the time frame has changed:

> When I first *began* (past) working as a waiter, I *hated* (past) my work. Now I *am enjoying* (present) my job more than I *thought* (past) possible.

In the above example, each shift (from past to present to past) is justified because each verb accurately reflects the time period referred to.

EXERCISE Tense Shifts

Directions: Revise the following sentences to eliminate inappropriate tense shifts. One sentence is correct.

1. While you were turned around, a miracle happened. The line drive hits the base runner, so no runs were scored.
2. Just when Katya thought her homework was finished, she remembers she has history questions to answer.
3. Grandma Rodriguez seemed totally bored with the baseball game when suddenly she jumps up and screams, "Park it, Jimmy!"
4. Many educators in the United States believe in the principle of grouping students according to ability because as long as bright students were competing against other bright students, they performed better.
5. By the end of her essay exam, Jeanine had her facts all confused; she is positive, though, that she passes the multiple-choice section of the test.
6. The governor announced a new tax proposal and explained that he is confident it will solve the state's budget problems.
7. Young people in the 1960s demanded a religion that calls for a simple, clean, and serene life.
8. Marty asked Lynn if she wants to go out with him, but she brushed him off and left with Jerome.

9. As Sue collected her clubs and new golf balls, she thinks how difficult this tournament will be.

10. Consequently, we can see that the human race has progressed or at least seemed to have progressed.

Directions: In the following paragraph, correct unwarranted tense shifts.

11. [1]Theatre has a long history. [2]The Chinese first performed dramalike dances in temples; later a playhouse is used that is a platform without curtains and a roof like that of a temple. [3]The ancient Japanese developed a form of theatre called Kabuki that was also performed on a platform with a temple roof. [4]In ancient India, dramatic performances were given on raised platforms with drapes for background. [5]The ancient Greeks developed a form of drama performed to audiences seated on a hillside. [6]The play took place on a grassy circle, and a building called a skene is used for the entrances of actors, dressing, and scenic background. [7]In the Middle Ages, the Christian church condemns drama, but later religious drama becomes an important part of church life. [8]During the reign of Elizabeth I, the English theatre takes a leap forward and the first playhouse is built, known simply as "The Theatre." [9]Soon other theatres were built, including the Globe, where many of Shakespeare's plays were performed. [10]The audience stood in a pit, in front of and around the sides of the stage, or were seated in boxes around and above the stage. [11]Our modern theatre had its beginnings with these early English theatres. ■

VOICE SHIFTS (v shft)

www.mhhe.com/tsw
For information and exercises on voice shifts, go to Catalyst 2.0 > Editing > Verb and Voice Shifts

Active and passive voice are discussed on page 117. When a verb is in the **active voice,** the subject of the sentence *performs* the action. When a verb is in the **passive voice,** the subject of the sentence *receives* the action.

Active voice: The doctor *gave* the girl a shot.

Passive voice: The girl *was given* a shot by the doctor.

In general, avoid shifting from active to passive voice unnecessarily.

Shift: Cell phones *offer* convenience. However, other people *are* frequently *irritated* by thoughtless cell phone users.

Better: Cell phones *offer* convenience. However, thoughtless cell phone users frequently *irritate* other people.

Not all shifts from active to passive voice are inappropriate. Passive voice is useful when you do not know who performed the action or when you want to emphasize the receiver of the action.

Appropriate passive voice: The rear bumper of my car *was dented* in the parking lot.

EXERCISE Verb Forms and Voice Shifts

Directions: In the following paragraph, correct problems with verb forms and *inappropriate* shifts in voice.

[1]Perhaps you be in college because you have always want to earn your bachelor's degree. [2]You may not know that the more accurate name for a bachelor's degree is "baccalaureate degree." [3]Now, however, "bachelor's degree" is used more often by people. [4]*Bachelor's degree* is took from the Latin word for "farmland," *baccalarius,* which in turn is took from the Latin word for "shepherd's staff," *baculum.* [5]In the Middle Ages, people called knights who were too young and unskilled to have their own banners "knights bachelor." [6]Students who knowed some things but who were not yet masters of a body of knowledge thus became "bachelors of arts or sciences." [7]Only much later did "bachelor" come to mean an unmarried man. ■

Pronouns

www.mhhe.com/tsw
For information and exercises on pronouns, go to Catalyst 2.0 > Editing > Pronouns

A **pronoun** substitutes for a noun. Using pronouns helps writers and speakers avoid monotonous repetition, as the following example shows.

Repetition: The kitten licked the kitten's paw.

Pronoun used: The kitten licked *her* paw.

PRONOUN–ANTECEDENT AGREEMENT (p agr)

Pronouns must agree with the nouns to which they refer—with their **antecedents**—in **gender** (masculine, feminine, or neuter) and **number** (singular or plural). Many times this agreement is easily achieved, as in the following example:

Kurt lost *his* tennis *racket*, but *he* eventually found *it*.

The pronouns *he* and *his* are singular and masculine to agree with the number and gender of the antecedent *Kurt,* and the pronoun *it* is singular and neuter to agree with *racket*.

At times, pronoun–antecedent agreement is not as obvious as in the above sentence, and these instances are discussed next.

www.mhhe.com/tsw

For information and exercises on pronouns and antecedents, go to Catalyst 2.0 > Editing > Pronoun–Antecedent Agreement

Compound Subjects

A **compound subject** is formed by two or more words, phrases, or clauses joined by *and, or, nor, either . . . or,* or *neither . . . nor.*

1. When the parts of the antecedent are joined by *and,* use a plural pronoun:

   The shoes and baseball cap were left in *their* usual places.

   Linda, Michelle, and Audrey finished *their* group project early.

2. When the antecedent is preceded by *each* or *every,* use a singular pronoun:

   Every citizen and each group must do *its* part to elect responsible officials.

   Each school and athletic department must submit *its* budget to the superintendent.

3. For singular antecedents joined by *either . . . or* or *neither . . . nor,* use singular pronouns:

   Has *either Sean or Frank* taken *his* batting practice today?

   Neither Melissa nor Jennifer has finished packing her bag.

4. For plural antecedents joined by *either . . . or* or *neither . . . nor,* use plural pronouns:

   Neither the teachers nor the students have *their* coats.

5. If one singular and one plural antecedent are joined by *or, either . . . or,* or *neither . . . nor,* be sure the pronoun agrees with the antecedent closer to it:

   Either Clint Black or the Oak Ridge Boys will release *their* new album soon.

   Note: Placing the plural antecedent second makes a smoother sentence.

Collective Nouns

Collective nouns have a singular form and refer to a *group* of people or things. Words like these are collective nouns:

audience	committee	panel
band	group	society
class	jury	team

1. If the group is functioning as a single unit, the pronoun that refers to the collective noun is singular:

   A civilized *society* must protect *its* citizens from violence.

2. If the members of the group are functioning individually, use a plural pronoun:

Yesterday the *team* signed *their* contracts for next season.

Indefinite Pronouns

Indefinite pronouns refer to a nonspecific member or nonspecific members of a group of people, things, or ideas. Indefinite pronouns can be antecedents.

The following indefinite pronouns are singular, and in formal usage, the pronouns referring to them should also be singular:

anybody	everyone	no one
anyone	neither	one
each	nobody	somebody
either	none	someone
everybody		

Anyone who has finished *his or her* essay may leave.

Nobody on the football team should assume that *his* position is safe.

Neither of the young mothers forgot *her* exercise class.

Note: See the discussion on gender-neutral pronouns that follows.

In formal usage, a pronoun referring to a singular indefinite pronoun is singular, even when a phrase with a plural word follows the indefinite pronoun:

Each of the boys selected *his* favorite bat.

Few and *many* are plural, so pronouns referring to them are also plural:

Many of my friends have already bought *their* tickets.

The following indefinite pronouns are plural:

both	few	many	several

Few of the workers are willing to give up *their* annual wage hike.

Many of the campaign workers are passionate about *their* candidate.

The following indefinite pronouns may be singular or plural, depending on the meaning of the sentence:

all	more	some
any	most	

Some of the book is still attached to *its* binding.

Some of the band forgot *their* sheet music.

Gender-Neutral Pronouns

The pronoun agrees with its antecedent in this sentence, but the meaning excludes women:

> *Each* **contestant must bring** *his* **birth certificate.**

To avoid using pronouns that inappropriately exclude one gender, you have three options.

1. Use a masculine and a feminine pronoun:

   Each **contestant must bring** *his or her* **birth certificate.**

   This option can be cumbersome if you must use *his or her, he or she,* or *him or her* often. In that case, one of the following options may work better.

2. Rewrite the sentence to make the pronoun and antecedent plural:

   All **contestants must bring** *their* **birth certificates.**

3. Rewrite the sentence to eliminate the pronouns:

   Each contestant must bring a birth certificate.

EXERCISE Pronoun–Antecedent Agreement

Directions: For each sentence, choose the correct pronoun.

1. Neither Angelo nor Doug volunteered (his/their) services for the Downtown Cleanup Crusade.
2. Each teacher and principal agreed that (he or she/they) would contribute to the United Way.
3. The secretary of the Scuba Club urged everybody to pay (his or her/their) dues by the end of the month.
4. Anyone wanting a successful college experience must spend much of (his or her/their) time studying.
5. A dog and two cats could feed (itself/themselves) very nicely with just our family's table scraps.
6. The hostess asked that either Cara Smith or the Kanes move (her/their) car.
7. Both Matt and Joey lost (his/their) lunch money.
8. Few of these candlesticks are in (its/their) original boxes.
9. That tribe holds (its/their) sacred initiation rites each autumn.
10. When asked to make statements, the sheriff and his deputy insisted on (his/their) right to remain silent.
11. The company fired (its/their) inefficient workers.
12. The herd moves ever westward as (it/they) graze(s).
13. The Ski Club held (its/their) first meeting after the holiday season.

14. The squad of police antiterrorists took (its/their) positions around the abandoned warehouse.
15. The city council debated whether (it/they) should pass the new anti-smoking ordinance.
16. No one should force (his or her/their) vacation choice on other members of the family.
17. Questioned by the precinct worker, neither Annette nor DeShawn would reveal (her/their) party affiliation.
18. To prepare for hurricanes, each coastal town has (its/their) own special warning system.
19. Most of the Pep Club had (its/their) pictures taken for the yearbook.
20. Both Jeff and Greg took (his/their) lunch to work.

Directions: In the following paragraph, correct problems with pronoun–antecedent agreement.

21. [1]The kind of voice a person has depends on their vocal cords, which are composed of elastic fibers. [2]The bundle of cords is very flexible; in fact, they can become tense or slack to assume 170 different positions. [3]If slack, the cords vibrate at about 80 times per second, creating a deep tone. [4]If tense, they vibrate rapidly, perhaps 1,000 times a second, producing a high-pitched tone. [5]As a child grows, his vocal cords elongate, causing the voice to deepen. [6]The length of a man's and woman's vocal cords differs. [7]He will have longer cords than she, which explains his deeper voice. [8]A boy grows so quickly that they cannot control the pitch well, which is why young boys experience a "break" in their voices. [9]The quality of men's and women's voices, however, depends on other factors, especially the resonating spaces such as his or her windpipe, lungs, and nasal cavities. [10]Someone who has a beautiful voice has well-shaped resonating spaces, which they know how to control. ■

PRONOUN REFERENCE (p ref)

If you fail to provide a clear, stated antecedent for a pronoun, you create a problem with **pronoun reference.** The most common kinds of pronoun reference problems are described below.

www.mhhe.com/tsw

For information and exercises on pronoun reference, go to Catalyst 2.0 > Editing > Pronoun Reference

Ambiguous Reference

Ambiguous reference occurs when your reader cannot tell which of two possible antecedents a pronoun refers to.

Ambiguous reference: When I placed the heavy vase on the shelf, *it* broke. [What broke, the vase or the shelf? Because of the ambiguous reference, the reader cannot tell.]

To eliminate the ambiguous reference, replace the pronoun with a noun.

Correction: When I placed the heavy vase on the shelf, *the shelf* broke.

Unstated Reference

Unstated reference occurs when a pronoun has no antecedent to refer to.

1. Unstated reference occurs when a pronoun refers to an unstated form of a stated word.

   Unstated reference: Carla is very ambitious. *It* causes her to work 60 hours a week. [*It* is meant to refer to *ambition*, but that word does not appear; *ambitious* does.]

   To correct a problem with unstated reference, substitute a noun for the pronoun.

   Correction: Carla is very ambitious. *Her ambition* causes her to work 60 hours a week.

2. Unstated reference occurs when *this, that, which, it,* or *they* has no stated antecedent. To eliminate the problem, supply the missing word or words.

   Unstated reference: When I arrived at the office, *they* said my appointment was cancelled. [*They* has no antecedent to refer to.]

   Correction: When I arrived at the office, *the receptionist* said my appointment was cancelled.

   Unstated reference: At my last appointment with my advisor, I decided to major in marketing. *This* has made me feel better about school. [*This* has no word to refer to.]

   Correction: At my last appointment with my advisor, I decided to major in marketing. *This decision* has made me feel better about school.

   Unstated reference: In the newspaper, *it* says we're going to have a hot summer.

   Correction: *The newspaper* says we're going to have a hot summer.

3. Unstated reference occurs when *you* appears with no antecedent. To solve the problem, replace the pronoun with a noun.

   Unstated reference: A teacher becomes frustrated when *you* do not ask questions. [*You* has no antecedent to refer to.]

   Correction: A teacher becomes frustrated when *students* do not ask questions.

4. Unstated reference occurs when a subject pronoun refers to a possessive noun. To solve the problem, replace the noun with a pronoun and the pronoun with a noun.

   Unstated reference: In Barbara Kingsolver's novels, *she* writes about strong women.

   Correction: In her novels, *Barbara Kingsolver* writes about strong women.

EXERCISE Pronoun Reference

Directions: In the following sentences, correct problems with pronoun reference.

1. The song lyrics were particularly offensive to women. This caused many radio stations to refuse to play it.
2. Doris explained to Philomena that she had to help clean the apartment.
3. I left the spaghetti sauce and the milk on the counter, and when I answered the phone, my cat knocked it over.
4. I was nervous about today's midterm examination. It made sleep impossible last night.
5. Rodney's car is double-parked. He is certain to get a ticket.
6. Dale is a very insecure person. It is his most unattractive trait.
7. The personnel director explained that I am entitled to 12 vacation days a year, which is guaranteed by the union contract.
8. By the time I arrived at the Dean's office, they had left for lunch.
9. Julius was on the phone with Roberto when he realized that he forgot to go to the bank and cash a check.
10. Dr. Wang is known to be a patient math instructor. It is the reason so many students sign up for his course. ■

PERSON SHIFTS (p. shft)

When you refer to yourself, you use **first-person pronouns.** When you speak to other people directly, you use **second-person pronouns.** When you refer to other people and things, you use **third-person pronouns.**

First-Person Pronouns	Second-Person Pronouns	Third-Person Pronouns
I	you	he
we	your	she
me	yours	it
us		they
my		his
mine		him
our		her
ours		hers
		its
		their
		theirs
		them

When using the above pronouns, be consistent in person.

Shift from third to second person:	If a football player works hard, *he* has many chances for financial aid, and *you* might even be eligible for a full scholarship.

Shift eliminated:	If a football player works hard, *he* has many chances for financial aid, and *he* might even be eligible for a full scholarship.
Shift from second to first person:	An empathetic friend is one *you* can tell your most private thoughts to. This kind of friend also knows when *I* want to be alone and respects *my* wish.
Shift eliminated:	An empathetic friend is one *you* can tell your most private thoughts to. This kind of friend also knows when *you* want to be alone and respects *your* wish.

EXERCISE Person Shifts

Directions: Correct the errors in the following sentences to eliminate person shifts.

1. In high school, I liked geometry because it came easily to me, and you could progress at your own rate.
2. I enjoy riding to the top of the city's tallest building where you can see for miles in all directions.
3. After we received our boots and uniforms, you were shown how to polish and fold them according to army regulations.
4. We are all painfully aware that you can't depend on the boss for help.
5. While taking part in a marathon, a runner should never think about what you're doing.
6. When I ask Sybil to help with some typing, she never turns you down.
7. When a person drinks to excess, you should never attempt to drive a car.
8. In July, people welcome a cool evening, but you know that it is probably only a temporary relief from the heat.
9. By the end of a person's first term as committee secretary, you feel that you are finally beginning to understand the job.
10. I liked my research course better than any other this year. You were on your own searching the library for references.

Directions: Eliminate the unwarranted person shifts from the following paragraph.

11. [1]As soon as we entered the room, you could sense the tension in the atmosphere. [2]This was the day for the first exam to take place. [3]We were quietly taking his and her places. [4]Pencils were being sharpened; papers were being prepared. [5]Once the class was under way, the quiet tension spread. [6]The only sounds were of paper shuffling and pens scratching. [7]We all hoped that your first efforts would be successful. [8]Finally, the instructor announced that anybody who was finished could turn in your papers and leave. [9]Exhausted and relieved, we filed from the room leaving their papers on the teacher's desk. ■

REFLEXIVE AND INTENSIVE PRONOUNS (ref/int pn)

Reflexive pronouns and **intensive pronouns** end in *-self* in the singular and *-selves* in the plural. The reflexive and intensive pronouns are as follows:

Singular	**Plural**
myself	ourselves
yourself	yourselves
himself	themselves
herself	
itself	

Reflexive pronouns can show that the subject of the sentence did something to or for itself. They often express the idea of acting alone:

Shirley taught *herself* to play the guitar.
We solved the homework problems *ourselves.*

Intensive pronouns can emphasize the words they refer to:

I *myself* never believe politicians.
The teachers *themselves* are opposed to ability grouping.

1. Do not use a reflexive or intensive pronoun without an antecedent.

   No: Hector and *myself* drove 550 miles to Tucson.

   Yes: Hector and *I* drove 550 miles to Tucson.

2. Never use *hisself* or *theirselves.*

   No: Nick locked *hisself* out of his apartment.

   Yes: Nick locked *himself* out of his apartment.

   No: The children entertained *theirselves* for an hour.

   Yes: The children entertained *themselves* for an hour.

PRONOUN CASE (case)

A pronoun's **case** is the form the pronoun takes to indicate how it functions in a sentence. Pronouns that function as the subject of a sentence or as the subject complement are in the **subjective case.** These are the subjective case pronouns:

I	he	they
we	she	who
you	it	whoever

Subjective case pronoun as subject: *We* should ask for directions.

Because the pronoun is the sentence subject, it is in the subjective case.

Pronouns that function as the subject complement are also in the subjective case. A **subject complement** comes after a linking verb and describes or renames the subject. **Linking verbs** do not show action. They are verbs like these: *am, is, are, was, were, been, seem, appear, taste, feel, smell,* and *sound.*

Subjective case pronoun as subject complement: The person I trust is *he.*

The subjective case pronoun *he* is used because *is* is a linking verb and because *he* renames the subject, *person.*

Pronouns that function as the direct object, indirect object, or object of a preposition are in the **objective case.** These are the objective case pronouns:

me	him	them
us	her	whom
you	it	whomever

To be in the objective case, a pronoun can be one of three kinds of objects: the object of a preposition, the direct object, or the indirect object. Let's first discuss pronouns as the object of a preposition.

A **preposition** connects words by showing how a noun or pronoun relates to another word in a sentence. A pronoun is the **object of a preposition** when it follows the preposition and is one of the words connected. A pronoun that is the object of a preposition is in the objective case.

Objective case pronoun as object of preposition: The dog is near *me.*

The preposition *near* connects *dog* and *me* by showing how they are related to each other—they are *near* each other.

A pronoun is the **direct object** when it follows a verb and identifies who or what receives the verb's action. A pronoun that is a direct object is in the objective case.

Objective case pronoun as direct object: The angry child kicked *him.*

The pronoun is in the objective case because it follows the verb *kicked* and receives its action.

A pronoun is an **indirect object** when it answers the question "to or for whom?" after the verb. A pronoun that is an indirect object is in the objective case.

Objective case pronoun as indirect object: I gave *her* the ball.

The pronoun is in the objective case because when you ask the question "gave to whom?" the answer is *her.*

Most of the time, choosing the correct pronoun case is not a problem. However, a few special circumstances present special problems. These circumstances are described below.

Pronouns in Compounds

Use the subjective case for subjects and the objective case for objects.

Subject: *He and I* prefer to drive to Nashville. [sentence subject]

Subject: The ones I like are *she and he*. [subject complement]

Object: Police authorities gave *them and us* citations for bravery. [indirect object]

Object: Professor Whan asked *her and me* to help out after class. [direct object]

Object: Joyce sat down near *him and her*. [object of preposition]

When a pronoun is paired with a noun, you can often tell which pronoun is correct if you mentally cross out the noun and the conjunction, leaving the pronoun. For example, which is correct?

Ricardo asked Dale and *me* to leave.
Ricardo asked Dale and *I* to leave.

Cross out *Dale and* to find out:

Ricardo asked ~~Dale and~~ *me* to leave.
Ricardo asked ~~Dale and~~ *I* to leave.

Now you can tell that the correct form is:

Ricardo asked Dale and *me* to leave.

Pronouns after Forms of *to Be*

In strict formal usage, the subjective case is used after forms of *to be (am, is, are, was, were):*

It is *I*.
The stars of the play are Carlotta and *she*.

Pronouns in Comparisons

When *than* or *as* is used to compare, some words may go unstated. You can choose the correct pronoun by mentally adding the unstated words. For example, which is correct?

Jackson works longer hours than *I*.
Jackson works longer hours than *me*.

Add the unstated words to decide:

Jackson works longer hours than I do.
Jackson works longer hours than me do.

With the unstated words added, the correct choice is clear:

Jackson works longer hours than *I*.

Sometimes the pronoun chosen affects the meaning of the sentence:

I enjoy running as much as *she*. [This sentence means that I enjoy running as much as she does.]

I enjoy running as much as *her*. [This sentence means that I enjoy running as much as I enjoy her.]

Pronouns Followed by Nouns

When a pronoun is followed by a noun, you can choose the correct form by mentally crossing out the noun. For example, which is correct?

We students resent the tuition increase.
Us students resent the tuition increase.

Cross out the noun:

We ~~students~~ resent the tuition increase.
Us ~~students~~ resent the tuition increase.

Now the choice is clear:

We students resent the tuition increase.

Who, Whoever, Whom, and *Whomever*

Who and *whoever* are the subjective forms and are used as subjects:

Henry is the one *who* understands Phyllis. [*Who* is the subject of the verb *understands.*]

Whom and *whomever* are the objective forms and are used for direct objects, indirect objects, and objects of prepositions.

Direct object: *Whom* did you take with you? [Recast questions as statements: You did take *whom* with you.]

Indirect object: Give *whomever* you want the job.

Object of preposition: Seat yourself near *whomever* you wish.

Choosing between *who* and *whom,* or *whoever* and *whomever,* can be tricky when you are dealing with questions. The choice is easier if you recast the questions as statements and then decide whether the subjective or objective pronoun is needed. For example, which is correct?

Who did you see at the concert?
Whom did you see at the concert?

Recast the question as a statement, and you see that the object pronoun is needed to function as a direct object:

You did see *whom* at the concert.

Now it is clear that the correct sentence is:

Whom did you see at the concert?

When you recast questions as statements, use the subjective *who* and *whoever* after forms of *to be (am, is, are, was, were).* For example, which is correct?

Who was the top point scorer in the game?
Whom was the top point scorer in the game?

Recast the question as a statement:

The top point scorer in the game was *who*.

Now it is clear that the correct form is:

Who was the top point scorer in the game?

Pronoun Reference and *Who, Whom, Which,* or *That*

ESL NOTE

Do not use a pronoun to refer to a word that is already referred to by *who, whom, which,* or *that*.

No: I asked directions from the man who *he* was standing on the corner.

Yes: I asked directions from the man who was standing on the corner.

No: Jillian was not interested in the movie that we wanted to watch *it*.

Yes: Jillian was not interested in the movie that we wanted to watch.

EXERCISE Pronoun Case

Directions: Choose the correct pronoun form in the following sentences.

1. (She and I/Her and me/She and me) expect to graduate a year early because we attended summer school.
2. Gloria is a much better math student than (I/me).
3. The union plans to strike to win a 10 percent pay raise for (we/us) dock workers.
4. Ask Lionel (who/whom) he plans to train as his replacement.
5. (We/Us) adult learners add an important dimension to the classroom.
6. It is (he/him) who can tell you what you need to know.
7. Mario is the young man (who/whom) I was telling you about.
8. Give that box of tapes to Alice and (they/them) to store in the basement.
9. If I were as good at science as (he/him), I would major in chemistry or physics.
10. Because of our vision problems, all colors look similar to Lisa and (I/me).
11. Helen admitted that the tricksters were (she and he/her and him).
12. Juanita is a much better planner than (I/me), so she should chair the committee.

13. Professor Altman asked (they and we/them and us/they and us) to review three textbooks and give our opinions of them.
14. None of (we/us) new volunteers realized the training program was a week long.
15. The firefighters and police officers (who/whom) were cited for bravery will be the grand marshals of the Thanksgiving parade.
16. It is (we/us) homeowners who pay the highest taxes. ■

Modifiers

www.mhhe.com/tsw
For information and exercises on modifiers, go to Catalyst 2.0 > Editing > Misplaced Modifiers

A **modifier** is a word or word group that describes or "modifies" another word or word group. Two kinds of modifiers are adjectives and adverbs.

ADJECTIVES AND ADVERBS (ad)

Adjectives modify nouns and pronouns, and **adverbs** modify verbs, adjectives, and other adverbs.

Adjective modifying noun:	The *hungry* baby cried for her bottle.
Adjective modifying pronoun:	They are *foolish* to hike at night.
Adverb modifying verb:	The senator campaigned *vigorously* for tax cuts.
Adverb modifying adjective:	For July, the temperatures are *unusually* cool.
Adverb modifying another adverb:	Jan slept *very* soundly after final exams.

Many (but not all) adverbs end in *-ly.*

Adjective	**Adverb**
quiet	quietly
angry	angrily
clear	clearly
bright	brightly

1. Be sure to use adverbs to modify verbs, adjectives, and other adverbs.

   No: The audience shouted that the speaker was talking too *soft.* [An adjective modifies the verb *shouted.*]

   Yes: The audience shouted that the speaker was talking too *softly.* [An adverb modifies the verb *shouted.*]

2. Use *good* and *well* correctly. *Good* is an adjective; *well* is usually an adverb, but it is an adjective when it means "healthy."

   ***Good* as adjective:** Mother keeps the *good* dishes in the attic.

   ***Well* as adverb:** Julio plays the piano *well,* although he has never had a lesson.

   ***Well* as adjective:** Grandmother has not felt *well* since March.

   Use *good* after linking verbs and *well* (as an adverb) after action verbs. **Linking verbs** are forms of *to be (am, be, is, are, was, were, been, being)* and verbs such as *appear, become, feel, look, seem, smell, sound,* and *taste* when they express a state of being rather than action. **Action verbs** show movement, thought, or process. They are verbs such as *run, sit, consider, develop, organize,* and *whistle.*

   ***Good* after linking verb:** The weather forecast for our vacation is *good.*

   ***Good* after linking verb:** The brownies *smell good* even though they are burned.

   ***Well* after action verb:** Although it is 15 years old, the television *works well.*

3. Use *bad* as an adjective and *badly* as an adverb. Be sure to use *bad* as an adjective after linking verbs.

   ***Bad* as adjective:** The *bad* news is that I must cancel my trip.

   ***Bad* as adjective:** The teacher felt *bad* about the test results.

   ***Badly* as adverb:** Parents who dance *badly* often take lessons before their children's wedding receptions.

4. Use *real* and *really* correctly. *Real* is an adjective and should not be used as an adverb. *Really* is the adverb.

Real as adjective: The *real* problem is that the company is short of money.

Really as adverb: The menu for the dinner party is *really* [not *real*] interesting.

Comparative and Superlative Forms of Adjectives and Adverbs

Adjectives and adverbs have a **comparative form** for comparing two elements and a **superlative form** for comparing more than two elements.

Base form: This ice cream is *sweet.*

Comparative form: This ice cream is *sweeter* than my homemade ice cream. [compares two]

Superlative form: This is the *sweetest* ice cream I have ever tasted. [compares more than two]

Most comparative and superlative forms are made by adding *-er* and *-est* or by adding *more* and *most* or *less* and *least.*

Base	Comparative Form	Superlative Form
slow	slower	slowest
young	younger	youngest
lucky	luckier	luckiest
beautiful	more beautiful	most beautiful
slowly	more slowly	most slowly
quickly	more quickly	most quickly
brave	less brave	least brave

1. Use comparative forms for two elements, and superlative forms for three elements.

   No: The twins are excellent runners. Of the two, Joe is the *best* sprinter, but Jim is the *best* distance runner.

   Yes: The twins are excellent runners. Of the two, Joe is the *better* sprinter, but Jim is the *better* distance runner.

   Yes: Joe is the *best* sprinter on the team, but Jim is the *best* distance runner.

2. Do not use *more* or *most* with *-er* and *-est* forms.

   No: Hannah is *more friendlier* than Marcus.

   Yes: Hannah is *friendlier* than Marcus.

3. Be aware that some adjectives and adverbs have irregular comparative and superlative forms.

Base	Comparative Form	Superlative Form
bad	worse	worst
badly	worse	worst
good	better	best
little	less	least
many	more	most
much	more	most
some	more	most
well	better	best

4. Recognize that some adjectives and adverbs do not have comparative and superlative forms. For example, something cannot be "the most perfect" because "perfect" is as good as something gets. These modifiers do not have comparative and superlative forms:

dead	favorite	unanimous
empty	perfect	unique
endlessly	perfectly	

No: *Death of a Salesman* is my *most favorite* play.

Yes: *Death of a Salesman* is my *favorite* play.

ESL NOTE

A, *An*, and *The*

A, an, and *the* are special adjectives called **articles.** The following are some of the rules for using articles.

1. Use *a* before a word that begins with a consonant sound and *an* before a word that begins with a vowel sound:

a hat	an idea
a baby	an uncle
a big tree	an old movie

2. Be aware that the letter *u* sometimes has a vowel sound and sometimes has a consonant sound:

a union   an uncle

3. Use *a* when the letter *h* is pronounced and *an* when the letter *h* is silent.

a hairy beast   an honest politician

4. Use *a* or *an* with *singular* words that name items that can be counted *and* whose specific identity is unknown to the reader or listener. Use *the* with *singular* words that name items that can be counted *and* whose specific identity is known to the reader or listener:

André applied for *a* scholarship.

André applied for *the* Perlman Scholarship.

5. Do not use *a* or *an* with plural words or with singular words that name items that cannot be counted.

   No: The gardener planted *a* trees along the fence.

   Yes: The gardener planted trees along the fence.

   No: My advisor gives me *a* helpful information.

   Yes: My advisor gives me helpful information.

6. Use *the* to point out something specific:

   A sales tax discourages new business. [This sentence says that sales taxes *in general* discourage new business.]

   The sales tax discourages new business. [This sentence says that a specific sales tax in a specific location is discouraging new business.]

EXERCISE Adjectives and Adverbs

Directions: In the following sentences, choose the correct adjective or adverb.

1. The doctor explained why I should begin physical therapy, but I did not understand him very (good/well).
2. The car in front of us was going so (slow/slowly) that traffic was backed up for a mile.
3. For the best produce, shop at a farmer's market, where the fruits and vegetables are (real/really) fresh.
4. The stew tasted (bad/badly) because it needed more seasoning.
5. The (happier/happiest) employees are the ones who take pride in their work.
6. People tell me I look (good/well) with short hair, but I think they are being polite.
7. Enrico has been taking his sinus medication for a week, but he feels (worse/worst) than he did before he began taking it.
8. (More/Most) people questioned believed that the worsening economy is the country's biggest challenge.
9. Consumers pay (less/least) attention to a product's ingredients than to the product's cost.
10. Janine's biggest problem is that she makes important decisions too (quick/quickly).

Directions: Correct the errors in the paragraph to eliminate the problems with adjectives and adverbs.

11. [1]Mildred Hill was a teacher at the Louisville Experimental Kindergarten. [2]She was considered to be one of the most best experts on spirituals in

the region. [3]She was also known to play the organ extremely good. [4]Her sister was Dr. Patty Hill, principal of the kindergarten and later the head of the Department of Kindergarten Education at Columbia University's Teacher College. [5]Together, the sisters wrote a school song called "Good Morning to All." [6]The song was real popular and ultimately published in 1893. [7]Thirty-one years later, Robert H. Coleman published the song without permission and added a new second verse: "Happy Birthday to You." [8]It became one of the more famous birthday songs ever written. [9]The first verse was dropped very quick and the song became known as "Happy Birthday to You." [10]After Mildred died, Patty and another sister went to court to prove they owned the melody, and they won the lawsuit. [11]Now, every time the song is played commercially, a royalty must be paid. [12]Because of the song's popularity, the recipients of the royalties are among the most luckiest people. ■

DANGLING MODIFIERS (dm)

www.mhhe.com/tsw

For information and exercises on dangling modifiers, go to Catalyst 2.0 > Editing > Dangling Modifiers

A modifier that has no stated word in the sentence to describe sensibly is a **dangling modifier.** Dangling modifiers often create silly sentences, as this sentence illustrates:

While basting the turkey, the sweet potatoes burned.

While basting the turkey is a modifier, but there is no sensible word for the modifier to describe. As a result, it seems that the sweet potatoes basted the turkey.

You can correct a dangling modifier two ways. You can leave the modifier as it is and supply a word for the modifier to describe. *This word should be the sentence subject.*

Dangling modifier: *Listening for the telephone,* the doorbell rang.

Because there is no word for *listening for the telephone* to describe, the phrase is a dangling modifier. The sentence indicates that the doorbell listened for the telephone.

Correction: Listening for the telephone, I heard the doorbell ring.

I, as the subject, is a word the modifier can logically describe.

A second way to eliminate a dangling modifier is to rewrite the modifier as a dependent clause (see page 120).

Dangling modifier: *Jogging along the side of the road,* a car splashed me with mud.

Because there is no word for *jogging along the side of the road* to describe, the phrase is a dangling modifier. The sense of the sentence is that the car did the jogging.

Correction: While I was jogging along the side of the road, a car splashed me with mud.

The modifier has been rewritten as a dependent clause to eliminate the dangling modifier.

As the above examples illustrate, dangling modifiers often occur when sentences begin with an *-ing* verb form (present participle). However, a dangling modifier can also occur when a sentence begins with an *-ed, -en, -n,* or *-t* verb form (past participle) or when it begins with the present-tense verb form used with *to* (infinitive).

Dangling modifier (present participle):	*While rocking the baby,* the cat purred contentedly.
Correction:	While rocking the baby, I heard the cat purr contentedly.
Correction:	While I was rocking the baby, the cat purred contentedly.
Dangling modifier (past participle):	*Tired from the day's work,* weariness overcame me.
Correction:	Tired from the day's work, I was overcome with weariness.
Correction:	Because I was tired from the day's work, weariness overcame me.
Dangling modifier (infinitive):	*To excel in sports,* much practice is needed.
Correction:	To excel in sports, an aspiring athlete needs much practice.
Correction:	If an aspiring athlete wants to excel in sports, he or she needs much practice.

EXERCISE Dangling Modifiers

Directions: Rewrite the following sentences to eliminate the dangling modifiers.

1. Feeling it was too late to apologize, the disagreement was never resolved.
2. While sitting at the drive-in movie, shooting stars could be seen in the clear night sky.
3. Climbing across the pasture fence, Peter's pants were torn in two places.
4. To understand the latest computer technology, these courses should be taken.
5. Faced with the possibility of suspension, studying became attractive to me.
6. When listening to my iPod, cleaning the apartment does not seem so hard.
7. To get to class on time, my alarm is set for 6:00 A.M.
8. Struggling to earn enough money to pay next term's tuition, the job came along just in time.
9. To study in quiet surroundings, the library is the best place to go.
10. After ending the relationship with Joe, loneliness was Ann's biggest problem. ■

MISPLACED MODIFIERS (mm)

A **misplaced modifier** is positioned too far away from the word it describes. The result is an unclear, silly, or illogical sentence. (Do not rely on grammar checkers to find misplaced modifiers, as they do not identify these errors very well.)

Misplaced modifier: The strolling musicians played while we were eating dinner *softly*.

The modifier *softly* is intended to describe *played*. However, *softly* is too far removed from *played*, so it seems to describe *were eating*. To correct a sentence with a misplaced modifier, move the modifier as close as possible to the word it describes.

Correction: The strolling musicians played *softly* while we were eating dinner.

A misplaced modifier can be a word, a phrase, or a clause.

Misplaced modifier (word): There must be something wrong with this cookie recipe, for it *only* requires a half-cup of sugar. [Placement of *only* indicates that no other ingredients are needed.]

Correction: There must be something wrong with this cookie recipe, for it requires *only* a half-cup of sugar.

Misplaced modifier (phrase): Across the street, *playing far too wildly*, we saw the young children. [The phrase seems to describe *we*.]

Correction: Across the street, we saw the young children *playing far too wildly*.

Misplaced modifier: (clause) We brought the rubber tree into the house *which was at least eight feet tall*. [The clause seems to describe the house.]

Correction: We brought the rubber tree, *which was at least eight feet tall*, into the house.

EXERCISE Misplaced Modifiers

Directions: Rewrite the following sentences to eliminate the misplaced modifiers.

1. The mattress was built for people with bad backs with extra firmness.
2. Most viewers have misinterpreted the significance of the president's State of the Union address completely.
3. The Chevrolet's muffler fell off after we turned the corner with a loud bang.
4. Kathleen sold her bike to a neighbor with stripped gears for $25.
5. The little girl wore a flower in her hair that had pink petals.
6. We were fortunate to get a cabin by the lake with three bedrooms.
7. The child ran after the ball pulling the rusty wagon down the street.

8. The old car raced down the street with its muffler dragging.
9. The missing wallet was finally found by my aunt Norma under the couch.
10. Turning to go, Lee waved to the gang in the van listening to the stereo. ■

EXERCISE Dangling and Misplaced Modifiers

Directions: Eliminate the dangling and misplaced modifiers in the following paragraph.

[1]The Egyptian Pharaoh Ramses II had temples built at Abu Simbel about 3,200 years ago. [2]Carving stone out of the face of a cliff, the temples were built by workers beside the River Nile. [3]Carved 197 feet into the cliff, the Great Temple had 14 rooms. [4]Four huge stone figures of Ramses flanked the entrance seated on his throne. [5]In the 1960s, the new Aswan Dam blocked the Nile, causing its waters to rise. [6]To save the structures, huge blocks of the temples were cut by workmen weighing 20–30 tons each. [7]They raised these to the nearby hilltop and fitted them together again. [8]To help pay for this project, 50 nations gave money. ■

Punctuation

Punctuation marks aid communication because they signal where ideas end, how ideas relate to one another, which ideas are emphasized, which ideas are downplayed, and which ideas are expressed in someone's spoken words.

THE COMMA (,)

Writers who do not know the rules often place commas wherever they pause in speech, but listening for pauses is not a reliable way to place commas. If you have not yet learned the rules, study the next pages carefully.

Commas with Items in a Series

A **series** is formed by three or more words, phrases, or clauses. Use commas to separate each item in the series.

Words in series: The gardener sprayed the *grass, trees, and shrubs* with pesticide.

Phrases in series: George Washington was *first in war, first in peace, and first in the hearts of his countrymen.*

Clauses in series: Before the first day of school, *Shonda took her kindergartner on a tour of the school, she introduced him to the principal, and she bought him school supplies.*

If the items in the series are separated by *and* or *or,* do not use a comma:

The only vegetables Tom will eat are *carrots or peas or corn.*

Some writers omit the comma after the last item in the series, but you should get in the habit of using the comma to avoid misreading.

EXERCISE Commas with Items in a Series

Directions: Place commas where they are needed in the following sentences. One sentence is already correct.

1. The vacation brochure promised us fun relaxation and excitement.
2. The trouble with the mayor is that she does not delegate responsibility she does not manage city finances well and she does not work well with city council.
3. Before you go, clean your room and sweep the porch and take out the trash.
4. The instructor explained that the class could write a paper on a childhood memory on a decision recently made or on a favorite teacher.
5. When you edit, be sure to check spelling punctuation and capitalization. ■

www.mhhe.com/tsw
For information and exercises on commas, go to Catalyst 2.0 > Editing > Commas

Commas with Introductory Elements

Elements placed before the subject are usually followed by a comma.

1. Follow an introductory dependent clause with a comma (see page 120):

   Although she promised to meet me for lunch, Caroline never arrived at the restaurant.

2. Follow introductory phrases with a comma:

   By the end of the first half of the tournament, our team had won nine games.

3. Follow introductory adverbs with a comma. (See also page 122.)

   Quickly yet cautiously, the store detective moved in on the suspected shoplifter.

   Reluctantly, Mr. Simpson told his oldest employee that he was selling his business.

   Note: You may omit the comma after a very brief opener:

   Unfortunately the exam grades were lower than expected.

   or

   Unfortunately, the exam grades were lower than expected.

EXERCISE Commas with Introductory Elements

Directions: Insert commas in the following sentences where they are needed.

1. When Sherry arrived at the resort she was disappointed to find that there were no rooms available.
2. Before he was 20 he believed that everything would work out for the best.
3. Very slowly and silently the deer moved toward the water hole.
4. As a result of the devastating heat wave the death toll rose to 108.
5. Frequently we accuse others of the behavior we dislike most in ourselves.
6. After we checked to be sure all the doors were locked we left the beach house until next summer.
7. During the bleak evenings of winter a cozy fire in the fireplace is welcome.
8. At the time of the plane's arrival the crosswinds had finally died down.
9. Lovingly the young mother stroked her new daughter's chubby cheek.
10. Hastily the six-year-old wiped the telltale signs of strawberry jam from the corners of his mouth. ■

Commas to Set Off Nouns of Direct Address

The names of those directly addressed are set off with commas:

"*Dorrie,* you must get ready for school now."
"Get away from that hamburger, *you mangy dog.*"
"If you ask me, *Juan,* we should turn left."

EXERCISE Commas to Set Off Nouns of Direct Address

Directions: Insert commas to set off the nouns of address.

1. "Ben help me carry the groceries into the house."
2. "You know Son it's too cold to be outside without a jacket."
3. "Friends may I have your attention please?"
4. "Heidi make sure you give fresh seed and water to the bird."
5. "Can you help me with my math tonight Alice?" ■

Commas with Nonessential Elements

Nonessential elements are words, phrases, and clauses that are not necessary for the clear identification of what they refer to.

Nonessential element:	Uncle Ralph, *who has been on the police force 20 years,* believes handgun legislation is the key to reducing violent crime.

Who has been on the police force 20 years is nonessential because the person it refers to (Uncle Ralph) is already clearly identified.

Essential element:	The student *who wins the state finals in speech* will get $1,000.

Who wins the state finals in speech is necessary for identifying which student will win $1,000; therefore, it is an essential element.

1. Use commas to set off nonessential clauses:

   Sara Summers, *who is a senior,* was voted president of senior council.
   My roommate collects soda cans, *which she stacks against the wall.*

   but

   Dr. Kingsley is a person *whose opinion I respect.* [Clause is essential.]

2. Use commas to set off nonessential phrases:

   The sparrows, *hunting for food in the snow,* sensed the cat's approach and took off suddenly.

   but

   The child *playing in the sandbox* is my nephew. [Phrase is essential.]

3. Use commas to set off nonessential appositives. An **appositive** is a word or word group that renames the noun it follows.

   Nonessential appositive: My brother, an investment banker, makes $200,000 a year. [*An investment banker* renames *my brother,* so it is an appositive. Since it is not necessary for identification, commas are used.]

   Essential appositive: My son the doctor is not as happy as my son the actor. [*The doctor* is an appositive renaming *my son,* and *the actor* is an appositive renaming the second *my son.* In both cases, the appositives are essential for identifying which son is referred to, so no commas are used.]

EXERCISE Commas with Nonessential Elements

Directions: Insert commas where they are needed in the following sentences.

1. My father who worked for the Bell System for over 30 years has made many sacrifices for me.
2. A Democratic city councilperson who supports his party will try to support the policies of a Democratic mayor.
3. The Luray Caverns which I visited this year are a breathtaking sight.
4. A blue wool suit sporting brass buttons and a traditional cut is always in style.
5. The Empire State Building one of the tallest buildings in the world is a popular tourist attraction.
6. Dale Norris a brilliant teacher will retire next month. ■

Commas with Interrupters

Interrupters are words and phrases that "interrupt" the flow of a sentence; they function more as side remarks than as integral parts of sentences. Often transitions interrupt flow and are considered interrupters, which is why the following partial list of interrupters includes some transitions.

after all	in fact
as a matter of fact	in the first place
by all means	it seems to me
consequently	of course
for example	to say the least
in a manner of speaking	to tell the truth

Interrupters are usually set off with commas.

Interrupter at beginning: *Of course,* not everyone shares my concern about this issue.

Interrupter in middle: The students' behavior at the concert, *it seems to me,* was exemplary.

Interrupter at end: News broadcasts have become insubstantial, *to say the least.*

EXERCISE Commas with Interrupters

Directions: Set off the interrupters with commas in the following sentences.

1. The children it seems will always find something to complain about.
2. As a matter of fact the lamp needs a larger-watt bulb.
3. This report I feel is inadequately prepared.
4. The customer unfortunately insists that the bike was never properly assembled.
5. I am not convinced this is the right time to begin our fund-raising project however. ■

Commas with Independent Clauses

1. When two independent clauses are connected with a coordinating conjunction (*and, but, or, nor, for, so, yet*), place a comma before the conjunction (see page 118).

   The match was over, *but* the spectators refused to leave.

   The garden was heavily fertilized, *so* the yield of vegetables was even higher than expected.

2. Do not use a comma before a coordinating conjunction linking two elements that are not main clauses.

   No: Lee asked for forgiveness, and promised to try harder.

   Yes: Lee asked for forgiveness and promised to try harder.

EXERCISE Commas with Independent Clauses

Directions: Insert commas where needed in the following sentences.

1. Janice had been rejected many times yet she retained her sense of humor and her cheerful disposition.
2. The pipe to the house was broken and we would have to assume the cost of fixing it.
3. Jake wanted to fly to Maine but Jo had always wanted to drive across country.
4. The students were confused so the instructor assigned them extra pages to study.
5. Karen fastened red bows to the lampposts for the holiday season was fast approaching. ■

Commas between Coordinate Modifiers, Commas for Clarity, and Commas to Separate Contrasting Elements

Coordinate modifiers are two or more modifiers referring equally to the same word. Commas separate such modifiers when they are not already separated by *and* or *but.* (If the order of the modifiers can be reversed or if *and* can be used to join the modifiers, they are coordinate and should be separated with a comma.)

An *expensive, well-tailored* suit is a necessary investment for a young executive. [The order of the modifiers can be reversed: a well-tailored, expensive suit.]

They ate their picnic lunch under the *blossoming apple* tree. [*And* cannot be used between the modifiers, nor can the order be reversed.]

She is certainly a *happy and carefree* person. [No comma is needed because *and* is used.]

Sometimes a comma is necessary for clarity, to prevent the misreading of a sentence:

For Easter, lilies are the most popular flower. [Without the comma, the first three words might be read as a single phrase.]

Commas also set off an element that contrasts with what comes before it:

Dale is only lazy, not stupid.

EXERCISE Commas between Coordinate Modifiers, Commas for Clarity, and Commas to Separate Contrasting Elements

Directions: Insert commas where needed in the following sentences.

1. The muddy rough course was made even worse by the two-day downpour.
2. Ohio State's noisy enthusiastic Pep Club congregated in the middle section of the bleachers.

3. The twins were young not inexperienced.
4. Many new songwriters use concrete visual images to set a mood.
5. The rough manuscript is promising although rambling.
6. Of all spectator sports fans seem to enjoy football most. ■

When Not to Use a Comma

1. Do not use a comma to separate a subject and verb.

   No: The governor-elect, promised to work to change the way public education is funded in our state.

   Yes: The governor-elect promised to work to change the way public education is funded in our state.

2. Do not use a comma between a preposition and its object.

   No: The United States has a government of, the people.

   Yes: The United States has a government of the people.

3. Do not use a comma between a verb and its object.

   No: Carl smacked, the ball out of the park.

   Yes: Carl smacked the ball out of the park.

4. Do not use a comma between a verb and a subject complement.

   No: Louise will become, a concert pianist if she continues to practice.

   Yes: Louise will become a concert pianist if she continues to practice.

5. Do not use a comma after a coordinating conjunction linking independent clauses.

   No: I have tried to understand Juan but, his behavior continues to puzzle me.

   Yes: I have tried to understand Juan, but his behavior continues to puzzle me.

6. Do not use a comma before the first item or after the last item in a series.

   No: The math test covered, improper fractions, common denominators, and mixed fractions.

   Yes: The math test covered improper fractions, common denominators, and mixed fractions.

   No: Improper fractions, common denominators, and mixed fractions, were on the math test.

   Yes: Improper fractions, common denominators, and mixed fractions were on the math test.

7. Do not use a comma between a modifier and the word it modifies.

   No: The frayed, curtains must be replaced.

   Yes: The frayed curtains must be replaced.

8. Do not use a comma after *such as* or *like.*

   No: Kurt believes in some unusual ideas such as, reincarnation, transmigration, and mental telepathy.

   Yes: Kurt believes in some unusual ideas, such as reincarnation, transmigration, and mental telepathy.

   No: Medical technology students must take difficult courses like, physiology, biochemistry, and pharmacology.

   Yes: Medical technology students must take difficult courses like physiology, biochemistry, and pharmacology.

9. Do not use a comma between *that* and a direct quotation.

   No: The school board president said that, "we are considering a ten-month school year."

   Yes: The school board president said that "we are considering a ten-month school year."

EXERCISE Using Commas

Directions: In the following sentences, add commas where they are necessary and delete any that do not belong. (One sentence is correct.)

1. In business—as in most things—hard work, and ambition are rewarded.
2. Muttering under her breath Lola stormed out of the room and slammed the door.
3. When she got off the roller coaster Camilla had a stiff neck and she had a sore throat from screaming.
4. Senator Stone believe it or not is a big fan of soap operas.
5. Although corporate officials repeatedly denied the rumors of impending bankruptcy investors were worried, and began selling their stock.
6. The FBI's chief suspect who insists on defending himself may be declared incompetent to stand trial.
7. By early morning the storm clouds had gathered, and many residents were boarding up their homes.
8. A school board member who votes to change the academic calendar is likely to anger parents in my opinion.
9. The leafy, green, vegetables on the buffet were swimming in salad dressing.
10. A book sure to make the best-sellers list is both funny and poignant.

Directions: In the following paragraph, add commas that are needed and delete any that are not needed.

11. [1]Carry Nation achieved prominence at the end of the nineteenth century in the temperance movement the movement to ban liquor. [2]Born Carry Moore in Kentucky she experienced poverty her mother's mental instability and, frequent bouts of ill health. [3]Although, she held a teaching

certificate her education was intermittent. [4]In 1867, she married a young physician Charles Gloyd whom she left after a few months ironically because of his alcoholism. [5]Later she married David Nation a lawyer journalist and, minister who divorced her on the grounds of desertion. [6]She entered the temperance movement in 1890. [7]She believed saloons were illegal so she felt they could be destroyed by anyone. [8]Alone or accompanied by hymn-singing women Nation would march into a saloon and proceed to sing pray, and smash the bar fixtures and stock with a hatchet. [9]A formidable severely dressed woman, Nation became a figure of notoriety. [10]Her fervor, at one point, led her to invade the governor's chambers at Topeka. [11]Jailed many times she paid the fines from her own money not from donations. [12]She made $300 a week lecturing and selling souvenir hatchets. [13]Temperance was not Nation's only cause for she also supported women's suffrage and fought against fraternal orders tobacco foreign foods corsets and provocative art. [14]Nation died in Kansas after a period of hospitalization. ■

THE SEMICOLON (;)

A **semicolon** separates two independent clauses not linked by a coordinating conjunction:

The canvas raft floated near the edge of the pool; it was pushed by a gentle summer breeze.

The A team wore the old uniforms; the B team wore new ones.

A semicolon should appear before a conjunctive adverb that joins two independent clauses. Here is a list of conjunctive adverbs:

also	indeed	nonetheless
besides	instead	similarly
certainly	likewise	still
consequently	meanwhile	subsequently
finally	moreover	then
furthermore	nevertheless	therefore
however	next	thus

1. When you join two independent clauses with a semicolon and conjunctive adverb, place a comma after the conjunctive adverb:

   The car I want to buy is a real bargain; *furthermore,* the bank is offering me an excellent finance rate.

   The test grades were low; *consequently,* Dr. Barnes allowed us to retake the exam.

www.mhhe.com/tsw
For information and exercises on semicolons, go to Catalyst 2.0 > Editing > Semicolons

2. For clarity, use a semicolon to separate items in a series that already contains commas:

   The following Sun Belt cities have experienced phenomenal growth in the past five years: Las Vegas, Nevada; Phoenix, Arizona; and Orlando, Florida.

EXERCISE The Semicolon

Directions: Place semicolons where they are appropriate in the following sentences.

1. The ideal football player is dedicated, for he must work long, hard hours intelligent, for the game is very much one of strategy and physically tough, for he must endure a great deal of punishment.
2. The hand-tied rope hammock was made to hold the weight of two people it was the hook that broke, sending Christie and Jim crashing to the ground.
3. The quarterback hesitated for an instant then he passed the ball to the wide receiver, who waited in the end zone.
4. College can create anxiety because of the pressure for grades, which is constant the concern for future job opportunities, which is always present and the uncertainties of life away from home, which are the most unnerving of all.
5. We tried for two hours to start the car finally we gave up and started the long trek back to town.
6. The trip was canceled because of the snow storm however, it has been rescheduled for next weekend. ■

THE COLON (:)

A **colon** is used after an independent clause to introduce a word, phrase, or clause that indicates a particular example or examples or that explains.

Colon to introduce phrase that particularizes:	Four occupations were represented in the union membership: secretaries, maintenance workers, cafeteria workers, and bookkeepers.
Colon to introduce word that explains:	Rick writes soap opera scripts for one reason: money.
Colon to introduce clause that explains:	All of Terry's efforts were directed toward one goal: She wanted to be a dancer.

Do not use a colon between a verb and its object or the subject complement, or between a preposition and its object.

No: The students who will compete in the debate are: David Haynes, Lorenzo Ruiz, and Clara Jakes.

Yes: The students who will compete in the debate are David Haynes, Lorenzo Ruiz, and Clara Jakes.

Yes: The following students will compete in the debate: David Haynes, Lorenzo Ruiz, and Clara Jakes.

www.mhhe.com/tsw

For information and exercises on colons, go to Catalyst 2.0 > Editing > Colons

No: I am afraid of: heights, small rooms, and water.

Yes: I am afraid of heights, small rooms, and water.

Yes: I am afraid of these things: heights, small rooms, and water.

EXERCISE The Colon

Directions: Place colons where appropriate in the following sentences. One sentence does not require a colon.

1. My courses for next semester are these political science, algebra, biology, and Advanced Composition I.
2. The basket overflowed with fresh fruit peaches, grapes, apples, and bananas.
3. Mr. Grantley seems to have one mission in life making everyone around him miserable.
4. There are complicated reasons for our company's poor safety record we do not supply incentives for employees to exercise more care on the job, our safety equipment is obsolete and ineffective, and we do not require enough proper training for new employees.
5. I knew that success in my journalism class would require curiosity, energy, and writing skill.
6. Of all the distance runners, only one seems to run effortlessly Mark. ■

THE DASH (—)

A **dash** (formed on the keyboard lacking a dash key with two hyphens) indicates a pause for emphasis or dramatic effect. It should be used sparingly and thoughtfully so that its emphatic or dramatic quality is not weakened by overuse. Often dashes can be used in place of commas, semicolons, colons, or parentheses; the mark used depends on the effect you want to create.

www.mhhe.com/tsw
For information and exercises on dashes, go to Catalyst 2.0 > Editing > Dashes

Jake told me—I can't believe it—that he would rather stay home than go to Las Vegas. [Parentheses may be used instead.]

I know why Tony's bike disappeared—it was stolen from the backyard. [Semicolon or colon may be used instead.]

Vinnie is 35—although he won't admit it. [A comma may be used instead.]

EXERCISE The Dash

Directions: Place dashes where appropriate in the following sentences.

1. The new Corvette red, shiny, and powerful was just the thing to make her friends drool.
2. Certain members of this family I won't mention any names are going to lose their allowances if they don't start doing their chores.

3. My history professor at least he calls himself a professor is the most boring teacher on campus.
4. I have only one comment to make about your room yuk!
5. There is a very obvious solution to your school problems study! ■

PARENTHESES ( )

Parentheses enclose elements you want to downplay. Often parentheses signal a side comment or incidental remark:

> Louise Rodriguez (you remember her) has been elected president of the Women's Action Council.
>
> When I was in college (over 20 years ago), writing was taught very differently.

Commas or dashes often set off material that could also be enclosed in parentheses. However, commas and dashes will emphasize the material, whereas parentheses will deemphasize it.

Parentheses deemphasize:	This week's lottery prize (an incredible $12 million) will be split between two winners.
Dashes emphasize:	This week's lottery prize—an incredible $12 million—will be split between two winners.
Commas give more emphasis than parentheses but less than dashes:	This week's lottery prize, an incredible $12 million, will be split between two winners.

1. Do not place a comma before the element enclosed in parentheses.

   No: Most of the class, (easily 30 of us) felt the test was too long to complete in an hour.

   Yes: Most of the class (easily 30 of us) felt the test was too long to complete in an hour.

2. Use a period and capital letter with a complete sentence enclosed in parentheses when the sentence is not interrupting another sentence.

   No: After three days (Most of us wondered what took so long.), the winners were announced.

   Yes: After three days (most of us wondered what took so long), the winners were announced.

   Yes: After three days the winners were announced. (Most of us wondered what took so long.)

3. Place a comma or end mark of punctuation *outside* the closing parenthesis:

   The new parking deck is an imposing structure (it has 15 levels), but people have trouble finding their cars in it (a serious drawback).

4. Use parentheses to enclose numbers and letters in a list of items:

   The Citizens' Coalition has three reservations about endorsing Smith for mayor: (1) she is inexperienced, (2) she opposes increasing city taxes, and (3) she has no clear position on minority hiring practices.

EXERCISE Parentheses

Directions: Place parentheses where they are appropriate in the following sentences. If necessary, also add periods and capital letters.

1. The police officer gave David a ticket he was traveling 50 miles per hour in a school zone.
2. Recent reports indicate that fewer workers are smoking probably because of increased awareness of the health hazards.
3. Sales of trucks particularly those with luxury features are at an all-time high.
4. At Debby and Antonio's wedding what a fiasco Antonio forgot the ring, Debby tripped on the hem of her dress, the best man was late, and the caterer served undercooked chicken.
5. Jon's favorite meal scrambled eggs, spaghetti, and corn disgusts most people. ■

THE APOSTROPHE (')

The **apostrophe** is used most frequently to show possession. It is also used to form contractions and certain kinds of plurals.

www.mhhe.com/tsw
For information and exercises on apostrophes, go to Catalyst 2.0 > Editing > Apostrophes

The Apostrophe to Show Possession

The apostrophe is used with nouns and certain indefinite pronouns (see page 594 for an explanation of indefinite pronouns) to signal possession.

1. To form the possessive of a noun or indefinite pronoun that does not end in *-s,* add an apostrophe and an *-s:*

   The *apartment's* bedroom is much too small.
   Anybody's help would be appreciated.
   The university has agreed to fund a library for *women's* studies.

2. To form the possessive of a *singular* noun that ends in *-s,* add an apostrophe and an *-s:*

   Charles's stolen car was found across town.
   The *business's* stock climbed three points.

3. To form the possessive of a *plural* noun that ends in *-s,* add just the apostrophe:

   The *governors'* council on aging will examine the issue of adequate health care.

4. To show joint possession of one thing, use an apostrophe only with the last noun. To show individual ownership, use an apostrophe with every noun:

   Manuel and Louise's committee report was thorough and clear. [one report belonging to both Manuel and Louise]

   Jason's and Helen's financial problems can be solved with better money management. [Jason and Helen have separate financial problems.]

5. To show possession with a hyphenated word, use the apostrophe only with the last element of the word:

   The *editor-in-chief's* salary was cut in half after the magazine's circulation decreased dramatically.

   I have planned a surprise party to celebrate my *mother-in-law's* 60th birthday.

6. Do not use apostrophes with possessive pronouns *(its, whose, hers, his, ours, yours, theirs).*

   No: The expensive vase fell from *it's* shelf and shattered.
   Yes: The expensive vase fell from *its* shelf and shattered.

   No: The book that is missing is *her's.*
   Yes: The book that is missing is *hers.*

The Apostrophe to Indicate Missing Letters or Numbers and for Some Plurals

A **contraction** is formed when two words are joined and one or more letters are omitted. In a contraction, the apostrophe stands for the missing letter or letters.

isn't (is not)	we'll (we will)
hasn't (has not)	who's (who is or who has)
they're (they are)	that's (that is or that has)
we're (we are)	she'll (she will)
haven't (have not)	it's (it is or it has)
I'll (I will)	shouldn't (should not)

1. When you reproduce dialect or casual speech, use an apostrophe for missing letters in words that are not contractions:

   add 'em up (add them up)
   sugar 'n' spice (sugar and spice)
   ma'am (madam)

2. Use an apostrophe to stand for missing numbers:

ESL NOTE

Its and *It's*

Be sure to distinguish between *its* and *it's. Its* is a pronoun that shows ownership. Notice that it does *not* have an apostrophe:

The pen is missing *its* cap.

It's is a contraction that means "it is" or "it has":

It's difficult to predict how long the concert will last.
It's been three years since I had a cigarette.

Its' is not an English word.

The class of '67 will hold its annual reunion the day after Thanksgiving. [The apostrophe stands for the missing *19*.]

3. Use an apostrophe and an *-s* to form the plural of letters and words meant to be taken as terms. You do not need an apostrophe to form the plural of numbers.

   If I get any more *D*'s, I will lose my scholarship.
   How many *t*'s are in *omit*?
   Mark makes his 3s backwards.
   Janice is too polite; I am tired of all her *yes sir*'s and *no ma'am*'s.

   Note: Underline or italicize letters, numbers, and words used as terms. In printed copy, these words may be set in italics. Do not underline or italicize the apostrophe and added *-s*.

EXERCISE Apostrophes

Directions: Use apostrophes where they are needed in the following sentences. In some sentences, you will need to add an apostrophe and an *-s*.

1. The panel awarding the scholarships spoke to several instructors about the three finalists grades and motivation.
2. In 85, my sister-in-laws German shepherd saved the life of a five-year-old by dragging the sleeping child from her burning bedroom.
3. I can never read Harrys writing because his *o*s look like *a*s.
4. No one thought that Al and Janets business would do so well in its first three months of operation.
5. Todays women still dont earn equal pay for equal work, but in many ways womens situation has improved.
6. Charles older sister is encouraging him to major in computer science, but he isn't sure he wants to.

7. The hot dog vendor bellowed, "Get em while theyre hot."
8. Recent studies confirm that televisions effects on childrens attention spans should be a source of concern.
9. When I graduated in 70, students social awareness was at an all-time high.
10. Lois new car must be a lemon, because its engine is not running well, and its been in the shop three times in a month. ■

QUOTATION MARKS (" ")

www.mhhe.com/tsw
For information and exercises on quotation marks, go to Catalyst 2.0 > Editing > Quotation Marks

Quotation marks enclose the exact words somebody spoke or wrote. For information on this use of quotation marks, see pages 178 and 498.

The salesclerk explained, "For eighty dollars, you can buy a wireless mouse."
"For eighty dollars, you can buy a wireless mouse," the salesclerk explained.
"For eighty dollars," the salesclerk explained, "you can buy a wireless mouse."

1. Use quotation marks to enclose the titles of short published works (poems, short stories, essays, book chapters, and articles from periodicals). Titles of longer, full-length works (books, magazines, and newspapers) are underlined or italicized:

   "To His Coy Mistress" is my favorite poem, and *The Sun Also Rises* is my favorite novel.

   Do not use quotation marks, underlining, or italics for unpublished titles, including the titles of your own papers.

2. Use quotation marks around words used in a special sense:

   Your "humor" is not funny.

EXERCISE Quotation Marks

Directions: Add quotation marks where needed in the following sentences.

1. Be sure to read The Rime of the Ancient Mariner on page 99 of your poetry anthology.
2. Tell me the whole story, I said to Linda.
3. I always worry when someone tries to fix me an interesting meal.
4. Chapter 1, Idea Generation, is the most important chapter in the writing book.
5. Your frugal ways are costing me money. ■

THE ELLIPSIS MARK (. . .)

The **ellipsis mark,** which is three spaced periods, indicates that something has been purposely omitted from a quotation. Most often, writers use ellipsis marks to shorten quotations so they can use just the portion they want. The ellipsis mark indicates where the omission occurs. Ellipsis marks are often used in research papers according to specific conventions, which are explained on page 499.

When you omit part of a quotation, you must not change the meaning of the original.

Original Quotation

> There is also a tendency to somehow feel that "black" history is separate from "*American*" history. "Black" history *is* American history—they are not mutually exclusive. The struggles of black people in America strike at the core of our country's past and its development. One cannot, for instance, hope to thoroughly study the factors leading to the Civil War or Reconstruction without investigating the issue of slavery and the emancipation of those slaves. American music and dance has little significance without the recognition of black influences. Spirituals, jazz, and blues are a vital and important part of American culture. To speak of the experience of black people in America (as some are inclined to do during the month of February) as independent of the American social, political, and economic forces at work in our country is a misreading of history at best and a flagrant attempt to rewrite it at worst.
>
> —Wayne M. Joseph, "Why I Dread Black History Month"

No: "To speak of the experience of black people in America . . . is a misreading of history at best and a flagrant attempt to rewrite it at worst."

Yes: "To speak of the experience of black people in America . . . as independent of the American social, political, and economic forces at work in our country is a misreading of history at best and a flagrant attempt to rewrite it at worst."

Notice that the three periods are evenly spaced.

To Omit the End of a Sentence

If you are omitting words from the end of a sentence, use a period followed by the ellipsis mark. In the following example, also notice that single quotation marks are used where double quotation marks appear in the source (as explained on page 499) and that the italics in the source are reproduced:

"There is also a tendency to somehow feel that 'black' history is separate from '*American*' history. 'Black' history *is* American history. . . ."

To Omit the Opening of a Sentence

Do not use an ellipsis mark when you omit material from the beginning of a quotation. However, if you change the capitalization of the first word, place the letter in brackets.

"[D]ance has little significance without the recognition of black influences."

To Omit a Sentence or More in the Middle

Use a period followed by the ellipsis mark.

> "'Black' history *is* American history—they are not mutually exclusive. The struggles of black people in America strike at the core of our country's past and its development. . . . To speak of the experience of black people in America (as some are inclined to do during the month of February) as independent of the American social, political, and economic forces at work in our country is a misreading of history at best and a flagrant attempt to rewrite it at worst."

EXERCISE The Ellipsis Mark

Directions: Read the following passage and write quotations according to the directions that follow it. Disregard the superscripts when you write your quotations.

> [1]In the late 1940s, two pivotal events in engineering had a dramatic impact on the development of computers. [2]The first event was the development of the transistor by John Bardeen, Walter H. Brattain, and William B. Shockley in 1947. [3]The second event was the invention of the ferrite core memories by An Wang. [4]The transistor was important because it eventually replaced the vacuum tube and became the technology for building computers. [5]Ferrite core memories were significant because they led to random access memory (RAM), which allows quick and easy information retrieval.

1. Quote sentence 2, omitting all the people's names.
2. Quote sentences 2 and 4 in a single passage, omitting sentence 3.
3. Quote sentence 5, stopping at the comma.
4. Quote sentence 1, beginning after the comma. ■

BRACKETS ([ ])

Brackets indicate that you have added a word, phrase, clause, or sentence to a quotation that is otherwise reproduced exactly. Often brackets enclose explanatory material, as the following examples illustrate. Brackets are often used in research papers according to conventions explained on page 499.

> "Just after the Russian satellite Sputnik was launched, the president [Eisenhower] created the Advanced Research Projects Agency to advance technology in the United States."

The original sentence did not give Eisenhower's name. The writer added it in case the reader did now know who the president was when Sputnik was launched.

```
"In the 1960s [well before the Internet was devel-
oped], Arthur C. Clarke [the science fiction writer
who penned 2001: A Space Odyssey] predicted that
by 2000 a 'global library' would be developed."
```

The information in brackets, which did not appear in the original material, is explanation added to help the reader.

Brackets also enclose the Latin word *sic* to indicate that an error in the quotation appears in the original.

```
"The earliest digital machines were based on vaccum
[sic] tubes."
```

Sic indicates that *vacuum* was misspelled in the original sentence.

EXERCISE Brackets

1. Quote the following sentence and add the fact that 553.33 meters is the equivalent of 1,815 feet.

   Toronto's CN Tower, the city's most distinctive landmark, reaches 553.33 meters into the sky.

2. Quote the following sentence, adding the fact that the cost of building the castle was 3.5 million dollars.

   The only real castle in North America, Casa Loma, is located in Toronto. It was originally built for a surprisingly small amount by Sir Henry Mill Pellatt in 1914.

3. Quote the following, adding *sic* where it is needed.

   The creator of Superman, Joe Shuster, was born in Toronto. In fact, *The Daily Planet,* Clark Kents employer, was modeled after *The Toronto Star.* ■

ITALICS AND UNDERLINING (ul/ital)

Italics is slanted type. Word-processing programs allow you to use italics. If you are writing by hand or on a typewriter, use underlining.

1. Italicize or underline the titles of works that are published separately (books, magazines, newspapers, plays, television and radio programs, long poems, and movies). Do not italicize or underline unpublished titles, including the titles of your own works.

   Animal Dreams is the last novel I read, and *Phantom of the Opera* is the last play I saw.

   Shorter works, such as magazine articles, appear in quotation marks (see page 644).

www.mhhe.com/tsw
For information and exercises on italics, go to Catalyst 2.0 > Editing > Italics

2. Italicize or underline foreign words and phrases unless they have become an accepted part of the English language (laissez-faire, taco):

   Enrico graduated *magna cum laude.*

3. Italicize or underline words, letters, and numbers used as words:

   Your *3*s look like *B*'s to me.

4. Italicize or underline words or phrases that you want to emphasize:

   What do you mean, *we* have a problem?

EXERCISE Italics and Underlining

Directions: Add underlining where necessary in the following sentences.

1. On the first day of the Caribbean cruise, I attended a raucous bon voyage party.
2. As both a book and movie, Schindler's List is powerful.
3. You forgot to cross the t's in tattoo.
4. What does politically correct mean to you?
5. I Love Lucy and The Dick Van Dyke Show are classic television comedies. ■

Capitalization, Spelling, Abbreviations, and Numbers

CAPITALIZATION (cap)

Below are rules governing the most frequent uses of capital letters. If you are unsure whether to capitalize a word, you can consult a dictionary.

1. Capitalize proper names of people and animals:

Harry	Rover
Joe Popovich	Einstein

2. Capitalize names of nationalities, languages, and races:

American	Asian	Chinese art
Spanish	Italian architecture	French cooking

3. Capitalize names of specific countries, states, regions, places, bodies of water, and so on.

Minnesota	Crandall Park	North Pole
Zimbabwe	Trumbull County	Fourth Avenue
Lake Huron	Europe	Brooklyn

Do not capitalize *the park, the beach, a large city,* or *the town hall.*

4. Capitalize proper names and titles that precede them, but not general terms:

www.mhhe.com/tsw

For information and exercises on capitalization, go to Catalyst 2.0 > Editing > Capitalization

Judge Walters	Chairman Mao
Prime Minister Gandhi	Mayor Johnson
Professor Kline	President Obama

Do not capitalize *the judge, the president,* or *the chairman.*

5. Capitalize words designating family relationships only when these are not preceded by a possessive pronoun or article:

Grandma Moses	Mom (as in I asked *Mom* to come along)
Aunt Donna	Cousin Ralph

Do not capitalize *my uncle, his aunt,* or *her mom.*

6. Capitalize specific brand names but not the type of product:

Coca-Cola	Colgate
Crisco	Nike

Do not capitalize *soda pop, toothpaste, oil,* or *athletic shoes.*

7. Capitalize directions when they refer to specific geographic regions:

the Midwest	the Middle East	the South
the East Coast	the Pacific Northwest	the North

Do not capitalize *east on I-680, three miles south,* or *the northern part of the state.*

8. Capitalize specific course titles and all language courses:

History 101	Intermediate Calculus II
French	English

Do not capitalize studies that do not name specific courses: *math class, chemistry, drama.*

9. Capitalize the names of ships, planes, and spacecraft:

the *Enterprise*	the *Challenger*
the *Queen Elizabeth*	the *Titanic*

10. Capitalize the names of specific buildings, institutions, and businesses:

the Empire State Building	South Bend Water Department
Chrysler Corporation	Harvard University

11. Capitalize names of religions, sacred books, and words that refer to God:

the Almighty	Jewish	the Qu'ran
Islam	the Holy Bible	Buddha
Jesus Christ	Catholic	Jehovah
the Old Testament	the Scriptures	Mohammed
Christianity	Protestantism	the Trinity

12. Capitalize modifiers derived from proper nouns:

French accent	Renaissance art
Georgian hospitality	Shakespearean comedy

13. Capitalize the first and the last word of a title and the first word of a subtitle after a colon. In between, capitalize everything except articles (*a, an, the*), short prepositions (*of, as, to, in, near*), and short conjunctions (*and, but, for*). You can consider "short" to be fewer than five letters.

Star Wars	*Of Mice and Men*
The Grapes of Wrath	*The Last of the Mohicans*
The Sun Also Rises	*Graffiti World: Street Art from Five Continents*

Note: For discussion of capitalization rules for direct quotation, see page 179.

Capitalization

Capitalization rules in your native language may differ markedly from English rules for capitalization. If you speak Arabic, Chinese, or Japanese, you may not readily see the significance of the size difference between capital and lowercase letters. If you speak a Romance language, you may not be accustomed to capitalizing the names of languages, religions, nationalities, and days of the week. Be patient with yourself and focus on capital letters in your reading to become more familiar with the rules.

ESL NOTE

EXERCISE Capitalization

Directions: Capitalize where necessary in the following sentences.

1. Jessica lived in the east all her life.
2. When Mrs. Torres read *Gone with the wind,* she became fascinated with the old south.
3. One of our most unpopular presidents was president Nixon.
4. After my mother died, my aunt raised my sister and me.
5. As professor Wu entered the room, his history 505 class became quiet.
6. The Monongahela river and the Allegheny river flow into the Ohio river.
7. The Republican party's presidential nominee is the incumbent president.
8. Most people believe that the first day of spring is march 21st.
9. Davy Crockett, a confirmed westerner, spent several years as a congressman living in washington.
10. Learning french was very difficult for harry.
11. Of all the fast-food restaurants, burger king is aunt Mandy's favorite.
12. The national centers for disease control, at its Atlanta headquarters, announced its findings on Legionnaire's disease.

13. Many lovers of jazz think miles davis was the world's finest jazz trumpeter.
14. Designed by frank lloyd wright, fallingwater has been acclaimed for its unique structure and its harmonious coexistence with the natural beauty that surrounds it.
15. The Golden Gate bridge is a modern architectural wonder. ■

SPELLING (sp)

A paper with frequent misspellings makes the writer seem careless, so whenever you have the slightest inkling that a word might be misspelled, check your dictionary. If you have a serious, persistent spelling problem, study the rules in this chapter, as well as the frequently confused words beginning on page 568. In addition, try these tips:

1. Check spellings *after* revising your content.
2. Buy and use a collegiate dictionary, or use an online dictionary.
3. Use your computer's spell checker—but use it with the understanding that it will not catch everything. A spell checker will not flag soundalike words that are used incorrectly—for example, *its* for *it's* or *here* for *hear.*
4. Keep a personal spelling list. Include misspelled words your instructor marks, important terms you must use in your classes, and words you frequently misspell. Study the list often.
5. Spell by syllables or parts—for example, *leth ar gy* or *un bear able.*
6. Pronounce words correctly to spell them correctly. If you mispronounce "athlete" as "ath-e-lete," you will likely include an extra *-e.*
7. Use memory tricks. For example, if you misspell *instrument* as *insturment,* think of the fact that you *strum* a guitar, which is an instrument.

www.mhhe.com/tsw
For information and exercises on spelling, go to Catalyst 2.0 > Editing > Spelling

Adding a Prefix

A **prefix** is one or more letters added to the beginning of a word to form a new word. Adding a prefix does not change the spelling of the base word.

un + nerved = unnerved	dis + satisfied = dissatisfied
de + emphasize = deemphasize	im + mobile = immobile

Choosing *-ie* and *-ei*

Use *-i* before *-e* except after *-c,* or when sounded like *a* as in *neighbor* and *weigh:*

achieve priest ceiling sleigh

The rule applies when the *-ie* or *-ei* are pronounced as one syllable, but not when the letters are divided between two syllables:

deity diet science

Memorize these exceptions:

ancient	height	protein
caffeine	leisure	seize
either	neither	weird

Adding Endings to Words with a Final *-y*

Change *-y* to *-i* when there is a consonant before the *-y*. Keep the *-y* when there is a vowel before it or when adding *-ing:*

cry + ed = cried	enjoy + ment = enjoyment
kindly + ness = kindliness	play + ed = played
marry + ing = marrying	try + ing = trying

Memorize these exceptions:

daily	laid
drily	paid
gaily	said

Adding Endings to Words with a Final *-e*

Drop the silent *-e* if the ending begins with a vowel (*a, e, i, o, u*). Keep the silent *-e* if the ending begins with a consonant.

drive + ing = driving	care + ful = careful
love + able = lovable	encourage + ment = encouragement

Memorize these exceptions:

acknowledgment	judgment
argument	mileage
awful	ninth
courageous	truly

Adding *-s* or *-es*

Add an *-s* to form the plural of most nouns.

Singular	**Plural**
ship	ships
hat	hats
umbrella	umbrellas

Add an *-s* to most verbs to form the present tense used with *he, she, it,* or a singular noun:

He sings.	It works.
She understands.	The child sleeps.

If the word ends in *-s, -x, -z, -ch,* or *-sh,* add *-es:*

address + es = addresses	sandwich + es = sandwiches
fix + es = fixes	dish + es = dishes
waltz + es = waltzes	

If the word ends in a consonant and *-y,* change the *-y* to *-i* and add *-es.* If the word ends in a vowel and *-y,* just add *-s.*

Consonant and *-y*		**Vowel and *-y***	
fly	flies	toy	toys
lady	ladies	key	keys

If a word ends in a consonant and *-o,* add *-es.* If it ends in a vowel and *-o,* just add *-s.*

Consonant and *-o*		**Vowel and *-o***	
hero	heroes	zoo	zoos
tornado	tornadoes	ratio	ratios

Doubling the Final Consonant

When you add an ending to a one-syllable word, double the final consonant if the ending begins with a vowel *and* the last three letters of the word are consonant-vowel-consonant:

hop	hopped	run	runner
grab	grabbing	slim	slimmer

Do not double the final consonant when the one-syllable word does *not* end in a consonant-vowel-consonant:

clear clearest peel peeled fear fearing

Here are some exceptions to memorize:

boxing busing (*Bussing* means "kissing.") sawed

When a word has more than one syllable, double the final consonant if the ending begins with a vowel *and* the last three letters of the word are consonant-vowel-consonant *and* the accent (emphasis) is on the last syllable:

begin beginner refer referral regret regretted

Do not double the final consonant if one of the conditions is not met:

commit commitment visit visitor

Here are some exceptions to memorize:

cancellation	excellence
equipped	excellent

Frequently Misspelled Words

absence	definitely	leisure	receive
accessible	disastrous	license	recommend
accommodate	discipline	lightning	reference
achievement	efficient	maintenance	relieve
amateur	eighth	mathematics	restaurant
apologize	environment	mischievous	ridiculous
apparent	especially	necessary	roommate
argument	exaggerate	ninety	secretary
athlete	existence	noticeable	separate
beginning	familiar	occurrence	several
believe	February	omission	sophomore
bureaucracy	foreign	particularly	succeed
business	forty	personnel	surprise
cemetery	grammar	picnicking	thorough
column	guarantee	precede	tragedy
committee	humorous	prejudice	truly
conceive	immediately	privilege	usually
conscience	intelligence	proceed	vacuum
convenience	irresistible	pronunciation	Wednesday
criticize	judgment	psychology	weird
deceive	knowledge	quantity	villain

ESL NOTE

Spelling

If your native language does not have the same sounds that English does, mastering spelling can be more complicated for you. Spanish, for example, does not have the *-wh* sound, so Spanish speakers may spell *whether* as *wether.* Be sure to keep a personal spelling list and study it daily.

EXERCISE Spelling

Directions: Find and correct the spelling errors in the following passage. Be sure to consult a dictionary whenever you are in doubt.

[1]Perhaps you have heard of three famous women associated with World War II: Rosie the Riveter, Tokyo Rose, and Axis Sally. [2]"Rosie the Riveter" refered to American women who worked factory jobs as part of the war effort. [3]Automobile plants and other industrial facilaties were converted into defence plants to manufacture airplanes, ships, and weapones. [4]As World War II wore on, an increasing number of men went overseas to fight, which resulted in a shorttage of civilain men. [5]The women pitched in, however, and

took over the jobs previously held by men. [6]Many of these women were diss-placed when the men returned to their jobs and civilian life. [7]Nonetheless, the contributions of Rosie the Riveter were instrumental to the war effort.

[8]"Tokyo Rose" was the name given to a woman who broadcast propoganda and demoralizing messages from Japan that were intended to weaken the resolve of the American and Allied troops. [9]Heard by soldiers and sail-ores in the Pacific, the messages were usually disregarded or laughed at.

[10]"Axis Sally" was the name given to the woman who broadcast demoralizing messages from Germany, which were heard all over Europe. [11]Of course, the Allied powers also engaged in their own psychalogical warfare: American planes droped pamphletts over Germany, telling of Nazi defeates. ■

The Hyphen (-)

1. If a word is too long to fit at the end of a line, use a hyphen to divide the word between syllables. If you are unsure of the correct syllable break, check your dictionary. (Never divide a one-syllable word.)

   Note: Most word-processing programs automatically space text so that hyphens are not required.

2. Use a hyphen between two or more words used to form an adjective that precedes a noun or to form a noun:

   high-interest loan　　state-of-the-art computer
   low-cost mortgage　　sister-in-law

   If the adjective follows the noun, the hyphen is usually not needed:

   The computer was *state of the art.*

   Do not use a hyphen with an *-ly* adverb:

   eagerly devoured meal　　badly reviewed play

3. Use a hyphen with the prefixes *all-, ex-,* and *self-:*

   all-inclusive　　ex-husband　　self-starter

www.mhhe.com/tsw
For information and exercises on hyphens, go to Catalyst 2.0 > Editing > Hyphens

4. Use a hyphen to separate the numerator and denominator of a fraction:

   one-half　　two-thirds　　three-fourths

5. Use a hyphen with whole numbers from twenty-one to ninety-nine, and when a number is combined with a word:

   twenty-one thousand　　thirty-three　　a nine-page letter

EXERCISE The Hyphen

Directions: Use each of the following in a sentence, adding hyphens where they are needed.

1. High stress occupation
2. Mother in law

3. Ex football player
4. A five hundred word paper
5. Eagerly awaited novel ■

ABBREVIATIONS AND NUMBERS (ab/num)

www.mhhe.com/tsw
For information and exercises on abbreviations, go to Catalyst 2.0 > Editing > Abbreviations

1. Use A.M. (a.m.) and P.M. (p.m.) for exact times of day. Either uppercase or lowercase is acceptable; just be consistent.

   We left home at 6:30 A.M. and arrived at 7:00 P.M.

2. Use A.D. before the year and B.C. after the year. A.D. is the abbreviation for the Latin *anno Domini*. B.C. stands for "before Christ." Use both B.C.E. and C.E. after the date. B.C.E. (before the common era) and C.E. (common era) are increasingly seen as alternatives to B.C. and A.D.

   The artifact is dated 50 B.C., but it is similar to items dated A.D. 500.

   The artifact is dated 50 B.C.E., but it is similar to items dated 500 C.E.

3. Do not use periods with familiar abbreviations:

FBI	CIA	NATO
AT&T	UFO	MTV

4. Recognize that some titles come before a person's name, and some come after:

Ms. Jenkins	Mr. Hank DuBos
Dr. Louise Garcia	Louise Garcia, MD
Tony Minelli, CPA	Mrs. Atwood

   Ordinarily, do not use titles both before and after a person's name.

   No: Professor Lee Morrison, Ph.D.

   Yes: Professor Lee Morrison

   Yes: Lee Morrison, Ph.D.

5. Use *U.S.* as a modifier and *United States* all other times:

   The U.S. ski team did well in the Olympics.

   The United States has a huge national debt.

6. Do not abbreviate place names, except in addresses.

   No: The Metropolitan Museum of Art in N.Y. has more than a million exhibits.

   Yes: The Metropolitan Museum of Art in New York has more than a million exhibits.

7. Most often, use words rather than numbers for anything that can be written in one or two words. Hyphenate two-word numbers between 21 and 99,

www.mhhe.com/tsw

For information and exercises on numbers, go to Catalyst 2.0 > Editing > Numbers

and write out in numerals numbers that require three or more words. (A hyphenated number is one word.) Finally, spell out any number that opens a sentence.

eighteen fourth twenty-five 1,503 one-third

8. Use numerals for time, addresses, measurements, percentages, page numbers, and decimals:

5 A.M.	2' 3"	page 3
100 Oak Street	15 percent	1.5 ounces

EXERCISE Abbreviations and Numbers

Directions: Correct any problems with abbreviations and numbers.

1. 3 of my best friends have job interviews with I.B.M.
2. At 8:00 pm, we left for Cooks Forest with Dr. Joshua Schwartz, MD.
3. The Centers for Disease Control in Atlanta, GA, is aggressively researching the origin of a new strain of virus.
4. Here in the U.S., 1/4 of all women are victims of abuse.
5. People between 30 and 45 make up one-third of our student body. ■

Parts of Speech

Understanding the parts of speech will help you better understand the grammar and usage explanations in Part 4, which, in turn, will help you find and correct sentence errors. The eight parts of speech are:

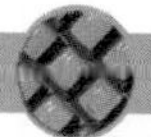

www.mhhe.com/tsw

For information and exercises on parts of speech, go to Catalyst 2.0 > Editing > Parts of Speech

- Nouns
- Pronouns
- Verbs
- Adjectives
- Adverbs
- Conjunctions
- Prepositions
- Interjections

NOUNS

A **noun** names a person or other living entity, place, object, emotion, or idea.

Nouns naming persons or other living entities:	tree, doctor, Henri, Professor Marx, brothers, ducks
Nouns naming places:	New York, town, river, Brazil, cities, countries
Nouns naming objects:	car, boot, Chevrolet, hats, buildings, toys
Nouns naming emotions:	love, jealousy, fear, depression, joy
Nouns naming ideas:	wisdom, thought, democracy, concepts, beliefs

Kinds of Nouns

Common nouns are general persons and other living entities, places, objects, emotions, and ideas:

child park street automobile happiness cowardice

Proper nouns are specific persons and other living entities, places, or objects. Proper nouns are always capitalized:

Charles Orlando Central Park Tenth Avenue Buick

Concrete nouns are persons and other living entities, places, and objects that can be experienced with one or more of the five senses (sight, sound, taste, smell, touch):

cake music painting odor sweetness velvet

Abstract nouns cannot be experienced through one of the five senses:

democracy bravery thoughtfulness freedom

Collective nouns name groups:

committee jury family team band

Count nouns name persons and other living entities, places, objects, ideas, and emotions that can be counted:

one toe/five toes one flower/a dozen flowers one hour/six hours

Noncount nouns name persons and other living entities, places, objects, ideas, and emotions that cannot be counted:

water luggage furniture honesty pride

PRONOUNS

www.mhhe.com/tsw
For information and exercises on pronouns, go to Catalyst 2.0 > Editing > Pronouns

A **pronoun** substitutes for a noun. The noun a pronoun substitutes for is the **antecedent.**

antecedent *pronoun*
Enrico gave *his* credit card to the clerk.

Kinds of Pronouns

Personal pronouns refer to people or animals, places, objects, ideas, or emotions. They can be sentence subjects (*I, you, he, she, it, we, they*), direct and indirect objects, objects of prepositions (*me, you, him, her, it, us, them*), and possessives (*my, mine, your, yours, his, her, hers, its, our, ours, their, theirs*):

I asked *her* for *it*.

Indefinite pronouns refer to nonspecific persons, places, objects, emotions, or ideas. Some common indefinite pronouns are *anyone, anybody, anything, both,* *few, each, either, everybody, everyone, everything, many, neither, nobody, none, no one, nothing, one, several, somebody, someone,* and *something:*

Someone is coming.

Relative pronouns (*who, whom, whose, which, that*) introduce certain kinds of subordinate clauses:

She is the woman *who* won the award.

Demonstrative pronouns (*this, that, these, those*) point out the antecedent:

Those towels are clean.

Reflexive pronouns (*myself, yourself, himself, herself, itself, ourselves, yourselves, themselves*) indicate that the subject of the sentence did something to or for itself:

Antonio taught *himself* the guitar.

Intensive pronouns (*myself, yourself, himself, herself, itself, ourselves, yourselves, themselves*) emphasize the antecedent:

The judge *herself* was not sure whether the defendant was guilty or innocent.

Reciprocal pronouns (*each other, one another*) refer to an exchange between parts of a plural antecedent:

The union and management negotiators finally understand *each other*.

Interrogative pronouns (*who, whose, what, which,* etc.) introduce a question:

Who do you think will win the Oscar for best actor?

VERBS

A **verb** can show action (*run, eat, dance*), occurrence (*become, seem*), or state of being (*am, is, were*).

www.mhhe.com/tsw

For information and exercises on verbs, go to Catalyst 2.0 > Editing > Verbs and Verbals

Kinds of Verbs

Action verbs express an action, a process, or a thought:

consider	enjoy	go	leave	think
do	fall	hit	love	try

The dry cleaner *ruined* my coat.
Cassandra *believes* in reincarnation.

Linking verbs indicate a state of being or a condition. They "link" the subject to a **subject complement** (a word or words that rename or describe the subject). These are common linking verbs:

am	was	appear	taste
be	were	feel	smell
is	been	seem	look
are	being	sound	become

The garden *is* full of weeds.

Helping verbs, which are sometimes called **auxiliary verbs,** are used with action or linking verbs to form a verb phrase. These are the helping verbs:

am	were	must	do	had
be	been	might	did	shall
is	being	could	does	will
are	may	would	have	
was	can	should	has	

The baby *should* feel better soon.
The chef *has* prepared a special meal.

www.mhhe.com/tsw
For information and exercises on adjectives, go to Catalyst 2.0 > Editing > Adjectives and Adverbs

ADJECTIVES

An **adjective** describes or limits a noun or pronoun.

Kinds of Adjectives

Descriptive adjectives give a quality, characteristic, or condition of the noun or pronoun:

The *red* dress is on sale.

I need a *basic, inexpensive* computer for the office.

Limiting adjectives specify or point out the noun:

Turn right at the *first* street after the light.

I'll lend you *my* car for the weekend.

Some audience members talked during the play.

This problem is easily solved.

Proper adjectives are derived from proper nouns, and they are usually capitalized:

Chinese food	Aztec culture	Spanish art	Shakespearean actor
Exceptions:	french fries	cesarean section	

Articles, which appear immediately before nouns, are *a, an,* and *the. The* points out a specific person or other living entity, place, object, emotion, or idea; *a* and *an* do not. Use *a* before words beginning with consonant sounds; use *an* before words beginning with vowel sounds:

The reason I quit my job is personal.
The doctor described *an* exercise to reduce my back pain.
A kind word can help more than you know.

ADVERBS

www.mhhe.com/tsw
For information and exercises on adverbs, go to Catalyst 2.0 > Editing > Adjectives and Adverbs

An **adverb** describes or limits verbs, adjectives, other adverbs, or clauses.

Verb described or limited:	The play should close *soon.*
Adjective described or limited:	The weather is *unusually* cold for this time of year.
Adverb described or limited:	The speaker talked *too* softly.
Clause described or limited:	*Fortunately,* the sales tax will not be raised.

Adverbs describe or limit by answering *how, when, where, how often,* and *to what extent.*

How:	The teacher answered my question *patiently.*
When:	Maria will arrive *soon* to visit.
Where:	I moved the vase *back,* so it would not fall.
How often:	The football team practices *daily* beginning in July.
To what extent:	After his dog died, Julio became *very* depressed.

Adverbs are often formed by adding *-ly* to adjectives.

Adjective	Adverb
careful	carefully
loud	loudly
soft	softly

CONJUNCTIONS

A **conjunction** connects words, phrases, and clauses.

In the fall, we buy apples *and* chestnuts at the farmer's market.
Dwayne looked for his keys everywhere; *however,* he did not find them.

Kinds of Conjunctions

Coordinating conjunctions join words, phrases, and clauses of the same kind or of equal importance. These are the coordinating conjunctions:

and	for	or	yet
but	nor	so	

Both the movie *and* the book are long *yet* fast-paced.

Subordinating conjunctions begin dependent clauses and join the dependent clauses to independent clauses. These are some of the common subordinating conjunctions:

after	before	so	when
although	if	so that	whenever
as	in order that	that	where
as if	once	unless	wherever
because	since	until	whether

When Jeremy graduated, he joined Americorps.
The town was evacuated *since* the river was rising fast.

Conjunctive adverbs both connect and describe. Like conjunctions, they link sentence elements. Like adverbs, they describe by showing such aspects as similarity, contrast, result, addition, time, emphasis, and example. These are common conjunctive adverbs:

also	hence	nevertheless
consequently	however	nonetheless
for example	indeed	therefore
furthermore	moreover	thus

People should begin saving for retirement in their twenties or thirties; *however,* young people often fail to do so.

Correlative conjunctions are used in pairs. These are the common correlative conjunctions:

both . . . and	neither . . . nor
either . . . or	not only . . . but [also]

Both the mayor *and* the governor support tax reform.

PREPOSITIONS

A **preposition** shows relationship by signaling direction, placement, or connection. These are some of the common prepositions:

about	among	between	from	of	over	under
above	around	by	in	off	through	with
across	before	during	inside	on	to	within
along	behind	for	into	out	toward	without

Some prepositions are made up of more than one word:

according to	in spite of	instead of
as well as	in addition to	out of
contrary to	in regard to	with respect to

A preposition is used with a noun or pronoun, which is the **object of the preposition.** A preposition shows the relationship between its object and something else in the sentence. For example, the preposition in this sentence shows the relationship between *dust* and *bed:* one is under the other:

The dust *under the bed* is causing an allergic reaction.

Preposition:	under
Prepositional phrase:	under the bed

INTERJECTIONS

Interjections express strong emotions. These are common interjections:

good grief	oh	whew
hey	oh my	wow
hooray	ouch	yikes

When an interjection appears alone, it is followed by an exclamation point. When it is part of a sentence, it is followed by a comma:

Yikes! I didn't realize we were having an exam today.
Goodness, are you here again?

Document Design

Whether you are writing for the classroom, on the job, or in your private life, you should understand the visual component of various types of documents. Just as you would never turn in a paper written in an impossibly small font and with no margins, you should follow other principles of document design. This appendix introduces you to some of the more important ones.

VISUALS FOR ESSAYS

Often, you will want to supplement the content of your classroom essays with visuals. Visuals such as tables, charts, and graphs can present large amounts of information clearly and concisely. They can also reinforce points graphically. For instance, if you are writing a comparison-contrast essay examining two plans for your school's recycling program, you might use a bar graph to show how one plan will reduce significantly more waste per month than the other.

All the visuals you include in your essays should be easily comprehensible, and they should all have a purpose—do not add visuals purely to give your paper color or to meet a length requirement. Also, keep in mind that different types of visuals are better suited to presenting different types of information.

Tables

A **table,** which presents information in columns and rows, is best used to organize data for readers so they can scan and understand the information quickly. Tables function less to show relationships and more to keep large amounts of data clear. For instance, consider this table showing response times by a university's security patrol for various locations around campus.

Campus Patrol Response Time, Fall 2005 (in minutes)					
LOCATION	SEPTEMBER	OCTOBER	NOVEMBER	DECEMBER	**AVERAGE**
Morrison Hall	6.2	5.8	5.2	6.8	**6.0**
Hassenger Stadium	9.8	10.1	9.4	11.3	**10.2**
Snyder Auditorium	3.4	3.8	2.9	4.2	**3.6**

Note that this table contains a great deal of information—response times during four separate months for three different locations. Yet all of it is easy to grasp. Note also that the table includes a prominent title, clear column labels, and a highlighting of key information (the average response time). These are all elements of a well-executed table.

Pie Charts

To illustrate graphically how something is divided—the various parts of a whole, in other words—you can use a **pie chart.** Pie charts give visual emphasis to how much the various elements make up of a total—the amount of time per day spent on different activities, for instance, or the amount of pollution that comes from various sources. An effective pie chart has only a few divisions with some stark contrasts among them. A pie divided into 30 almost identical slices does not communicate much to anyone. Combine categories in your pie chart to highlight key differences, as the student who made the pie chart below does. By limiting the pie chart divisions to only four categories, the student makes the relationships among the various spending categories clear and striking.

University Spending on Campus Staff, 2005

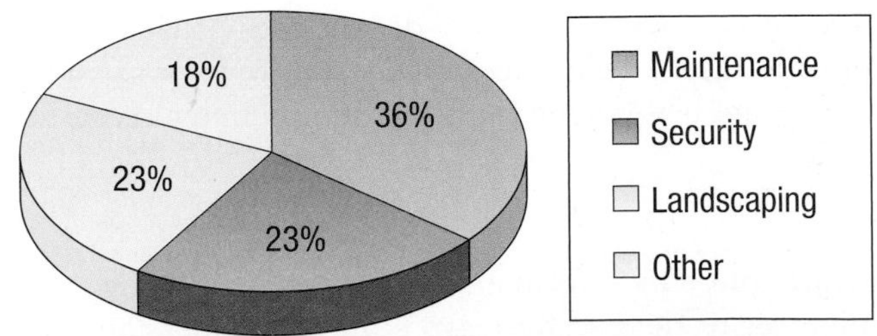

Bar and Line Graphs

Bar graphs and **line graphs** are most effective in showing comparisons between two or more variables, especially over time. Pie charts, for example, show the divisions of a whole at one particular time—in a single academic year, as in the preceding chart, for instance. Bar and line graphs can show how variables, and the relationships between them, change.

Consider the following bar graph, which compares the number of university employees in landscaping and security over four years.

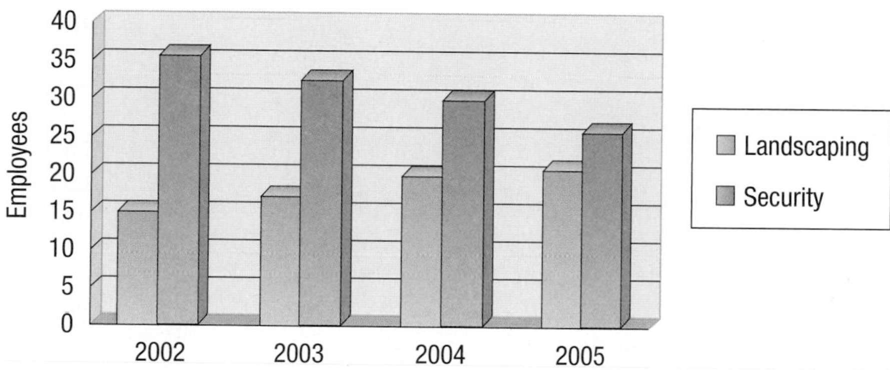

The bar graph clearly shows a decline in security personnel and, over the same period, a rise in employees working in landscaping. A table could present this same information, but the effect would not be as striking. The bars give the numbers a notable visual impact.

The information might be even more strongly communicated, though, in a line graph. While bar graphs are useful in showing and comparing total amounts, line graphs are more effective in showing trends over time—how things rise and fall. Following is a line graph created using the same data as in the bar graph. Notice how the rise in the number of landscaping employees and the fall in the number of security employees receive greater emphasis in the line graph than in the bar graph. In choosing which visuals to use, keep your thesis in mind: What point will best support your thesis, and what type of visual will best communicate that point to your reader?

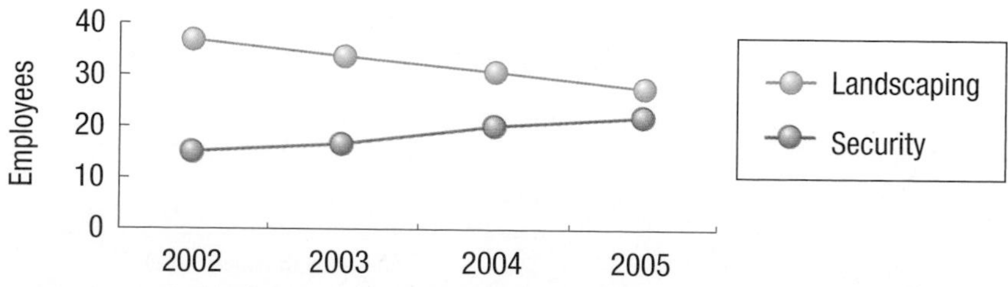

Regardless of whether you are using a bar graph or a line graph, be sure to include a prominent title and to label your *x*- and *y*-axes. If you include a key, as our bar and line graphs do, make sure it is straightforward and includes all the information a reader will need to interpret the graph.

E-MAIL DESIGN

You probably don't think of an e-mail as something you "design." Most e-mails are written quickly and without much attention to spelling or grammar, much less to their overall appearance. Still, there will be times in your academic or professional career when you need to communicate significant information via e-mail. When this occurs, you'll want to organize your e-mail so that it is easy to understand. Keep in mind that most people read e-mails the way they write them—quickly and imprecisely. Just because you are writing an important e-mail does not mean the recipients will read it that way. So you'll want to ensure that key points jump out at the reader, that the most important information comes first, that you are concise and do not include information not relevant to your reason for writing, and that you use a clear, specific subject line. Also, the significance of your e-mail should be reflected in the quality of your writing: In an important e-mail, follow all the rules of punctuation, capitalization, spelling, and so on.

Following is an example of a poorly designed e-mail and a more effectively designed one. Notice how in the second e-mail, Adam demonstrates all the features of effective e-mail design: He includes a specific subject line; he places his most important point early and puts his key ideas in boldface; he

From: az99@nku.edu
To: rj88@nku.edu; sp36@nku.edu
Subject: Work

hey guys – how was your weekend? i have been feeling sick all morning. anyway. i was thinking we shld get going on our group project. email me and we can set something up. how's everyone's thursday? maybe we can do it on the new student union, since that is something we're all interested in. Oh, also, I ran into Prof. Caldwell & he said we need to have an outline done by next class. So def. email me.

-Adam

Poorly Designed E-mail

From: az99@nku.edu
To: rj88@nku.edu; sp36@nku.edu
Subject: ENG 111 Group Presentation – Meet on Thursday?

Hi Sol and Roger,

I'm emailing because we need to start working on our **group project for English 111**. I ran into Professor Caldwell, and he reminded me that we need our outline done by next class. Can we plan to **meet Thursday, around noon?**

Please email me back to let me know.

Thanks,
Adam

Effectively Designed E-mail

uses concise, focused language; and he follows all the rules of spelling, grammar, and punctuation. The e-mail on the left contains essentially the same content, but its sloppy construction and extraneous information make it less likely to elicit an immediate or relevant response.

EFFECTIVE POWERPOINT SLIDES

www.mhhe.com/tsw
For further help using PowerPoint, go to Catalyst 2.0 > Writing > PowerPoint Tutorial

One of the most popular tools for creating visual supplements, especially for oral presentations, is **PowerPoint.** This powerful, intuitive software lets you design a slide show featuring text, graphics, and animations to support a classroom or workplace presentation. Because PowerPoint slides are often viewed from a distance (e.g., from the back of a classroom), be sure the text on your slides is large and legible. Don't crowd your slides with too much clip art or other graphics—include an image only when it supports your discussion or contributes to a slide. A good general tip is that with PowerPoint, less is more: Keep your text and images to a minimum. Remember, the slides are the *support* for your presentation. Keep them general and brief, and give the specifics yourself.

Following are two examples of effectively designed PowerPoint slides. Note that both slides have large type, lots of white space, and a minimum of graphics. They offer the highlights of a discussion clearly and cleanly, and do not overwhelm the viewer with excessive information.

Campus Security Issues

- Too many unlit pathways
- Campus security is slow to respond to complaints
- No late-night shuttle bus from fraternity row back to campus
- Chancellor Street security booth is often unattended

Making Fullard Hall Safer

- Keep the skyway open after midnight
- Add keycard access to the dining hall
- Have all non-student guests sign in with security

WEBSITE DESIGN

It is now easier than ever to design and post a website on the Internet. Companies like Yahoo! allow you to make a site without any computer programming skills—and for free, too! If you decide to create a website, whether for personal use or as part of a business endeavor, you want to be sure it represents you well.

One of the keys to building an impressive, easy-to-use website is navigation. Every page on your site should include a list of links to the major parts of your site. This way, no matter where a user is on the site, he or she can always get to other parts without repeated clicking and searching. Another key is to limit the number of graphics you use. Websites with numerous pictures on every page do not look sophisticated or high-tech—they look crowded, and they often load slowly. Build your site around a few high-impact images, and group any other images you want to include under a *Pictures* link. Finally, be aware of who your users are. What will they be looking for when they visit your site? Make the answer to this question the centerpiece of your design.

Consider this website, the home page of the Edgar Allan Poe Museum in Richmond, VA. The design of this page is simple and effective. It is immediately clear what the site represents and what it offers. The single, central picture of Poe draws the viewer's interest. And the navigation bar across the top of the screen provides access to all the major sections of the site.

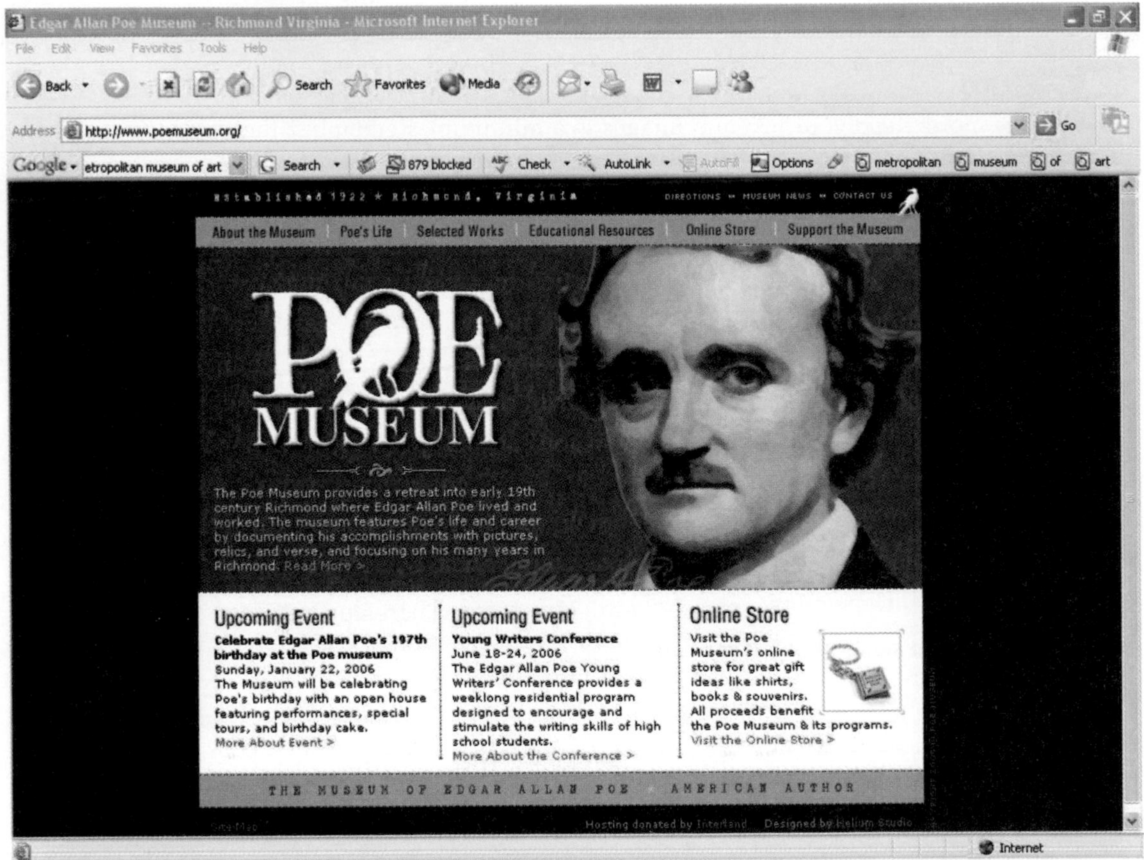

Reprinted with permission from PoeMuseum.org.

CREDITS

Photo Credits

Page 22: Image courtesy of The Advertising Archives; **23:** © AP Photo/Eric Gay; **26:** Courtesy, Lance Armstrong Foundation, LIVESTRONG.ORG; **28:** © 2004 Thinkstock, LLC; **60:** © Robert Garvey/Corbis; **96:** © Royalty-Free/Corbis; **116:** Courtesy, Obama for America/www.barackobama.com; **142:** © Vincent Dolman/Getty Images; **162:** © Michael St. Maur Sheil/Corbis; **169:** Courtesy, Colorado Tourism Office; Agency: MMG Worldwide; Photographer: Glenn Oakley; **195:** © Bettmann/Corbis; **208:** Courtesy of Russell Stover Candies; **236:** Collection of the Norman Rockwell Museum at Stockbridge, Norman Rockwell Art Collection Trust, Printed by permission of the Norman Rockwell Family Agency © 1961 the Norman Rockwell Family Entities; **273:** © Marvel Entertainment, Inc.; **297:** Reprinted with permission of State Farm Mutual Automobile Insurance Company; **302:** © Stefan Puetz/zefa/Corbis; **304:** © Najlah Feanny/Corbis Saba; **327:** © Sonda Dawes/The Image Works; **332:** © Glyn Kirk/Getty Images; **352:** © Fred Lyons/Cole Group/Getty Images; **355:** © 2001 Princeton University Press; **384:** © Seattle Post-Intelligencer Collection; Museum of History and Industry/Corbis; **392:** © James Chiang/Proof Photographic Agents; **396:** © Royalty-Free/Corbis; **409:** © Don Murray/Corbis; **416:** Courtesy, American Indian College Fund; **420:** (left) © ADBUSTERS/Image courtesy of The Advertising Archives, (right) © Image courtesy of The Advertising Archives; **463:** © Dan Guravich/Corbis; **465:** © Image courtesy of The Advertising Archives; **466:** © Paramount Classics/Photofest © Paramount Classics; **514:** © James Estrin/The New York Times/Redux Pictures; **550:** © BananaStock/JupiterImages

Text Credits

"School is Bad for Children" by John Holt is reprinted with permission from *The Saturday Evening Post* magazine, © 1969 Saturday Evening Post Society.

"The Environmental Issue from Hell" by Bill McKibben from *In These Times*, April 30, 2001. Reprinted by permission of *In These Times*, www.inthesetimes.com.

Graph, Opinions on Taxing and Spending:
Reprinted by permission of the National Opinion Research Council, University of Chicago.

"Prairie Vertigo" by Verlyn Klinkenborg from "The Rural Life" column in *The New York Times*, December 10, 2000. Copyright © 2000 New York Times. Reprinted with permission of the author.

"Anguished Cries in a Place of Silence" by Lynn Sherr from *The New York Times*, August 18, 2002. Copyright © 2002 New York Times. All rights reserved. Used by permission.

"Where Nothing Says Everything" by Suzanne Berne from *The New York Times*, April 21, 2002. Copyright © 2002 New York Times. All rights reserved. Used by permission.

Excerpt from "Metropolitan Diary" by Deborah Hautzig from *The New York Times*, April 15, 2002. Copyright © 2002 New York Times. All rights reserved. Used by permission.

"In Line at the Post Office" by Steven Doloff from the "City Commentary" column of *The Epoch Times*, November 1–7, 2007. Reprinted by permission of the author. Steven Doloff is a Professor of English at Pratt Institute. His writing has appeared in *The New York Times, The Washington Post, The Boston Globe, The Philadelphia Inquirer* and *The Chronicle of Higher Education.*

"The Boys" from *I Know Why the Caged Bird Sings* by Maya Angelou. Copyright © 1969 and renewed 1997 by Maya Angelou. Used by permission of Random House, Inc, and Virago, an imprint of Little, Brown Book Group.

"The Telephone" from *The Boy from the Tower of the Moon* by Anwar Accawi. Copyright © 1999 by Anwar Accawi. Reprinted by permission of the author.

"Fox's Flapdoodle" by Michael Shermer from *Scientific American*, June 2001. Courtesy of Michael Shermer and *Scientific American*.

"Shoddy Service Sows the Seeds of Discontent" by Dawn Turner Trice from *The Chicago Tribune*, February 1, 2002. Copyright © 2002 Tribune Media Services, Inc. All rights reserved. Reprinted with permission.

"Speech Codes: Alive and Well at Colleges" by Harvey A. Silverglate and Greg Lukianoff. First appeared in *The Chronicle of Higher Education*, August 1, 2003. Reprinted by permission of the authors.

Drawing of cellular respiration:
From *Human Biology* by Sylvia S. Mader. Copyright © 2004 The McGraw-Hill Companies, Inc. Reprinted with permission of The McGraw-Hill Companies, Inc.

"Round Comfort" by Leah Eskin (sidebar from "The Tao of Dough") in *Chicago Tribune Magazine*, October 21, 2001. Copyright © Tribune Media Services, Inc. All rights reserved. Reprinted with permission.

"How to E-Mail a Professor" by Michael Leddy. Blog posting on Orange Crate Art, January 10, 2005. Reprinted by permission of Michael Leddy.

"The Wicked Wind" by Ben McGarth. Copyright © 2003 Condé Nast Publications. All rights reserved. Originally published in *The New Yorker,* October 20, 2003. Reprinted by permission.

Figure of cactus & sail (in "Wicked Wind"article): Copyright © 2003 by Michael Kupperman. All rights reserved. Used by permission of Michael Kupperman.

"Annie Smith Swept Here" by Eric L. Wee in *The Washington Post,* March 3, 2002. Copyright © 2002 The Washington Post. Reprinted with permission.

Excerpt from "Comics Off to Save Mumbai" by Jason Overdorf from *Newsweek,* August 2, 2004. Reprinted by permission of the author.

"Fable for Tomorrow" from *Silent Spring* by Rachel Carson. Copyright © 1962 by Rachel L. Carson, renewed 1990 by Roger Christie. Reprinted by permission of Houghton Mifflin Harcourt Publishing Company and Gerald Pollinger, Ltd. All rights reserved.

"That Lean and Hungry Look" by Suzanne Britt in *Newsweek on Campus,* October 9, 1978. Copyright © 1978 by Suzanne Britt. Reprinted by permission of the author.

"The Army's Killer App" by Lev Grossman from *Time,* February 21, 2005. Copyright © 2005, Time Inc. All rights reserved. Reprinted by permission.

"Smoke 'Em If You Got 'Em" from *The Atlantic,* May 2008. Copyright © 2008 by The Atlantic Monthly. Reproduced with permission of The Atlantic Monthly via the Copyright Clearance Center.

"Eight Reasons Plagiarism Sucks" by Jack Shafer from *Slate,* March 7, 2008. Copyright © 2008, Slate. Reprinted by permission.

"It's Not Just How We Play That Matters" by Suzanne Sievert in *Newsweek,* October 14, 2002. Copyright © 2002 Newsweek, Inc.

"Our Schedules, Ourselves" by Jay Walljasper is reprinted with permission from *The Utne Reader,* January/February 2003, a digest of the alternative press, www.utne.com. Copyright © 2003 Ogden Publications, Inc.

"Hero Inflation" by Nicholas Thompson in *The Boston Globe,* January 13, 2002. Copyright © 2002 The Boston Globe. Reprinted by permission of the author.

"My Way!" originally appeared as "Who's The Boss?" from *1-800-AM-I-NUTS?* by Margo Kaufman. Copyright © 1992 by Margo Kaufman. Used by permission of Random House, Inc.

"I Remember Masa" from *Weedee Peepo* by Jose Antonio Burciaga. Copyright © 1988 Pan American University Press. Reprinted by permission of the publisher.

"Volcanoes" excerpt from *The Handy Science Answer Book, Centennial Ed.,* by The Carnegie Library of Pittsburgh. Copyright © 2003 The Carnegie Library of Pittsburgh. Reprinted by permission of Visible Ink Press.

"The Dog Ate My Disk, and Other Tales of Woe" by Carolyn Foster Segal from *The Chronicle of Higher Education,* August 11, 2000. Reprinted by permission of the author.

"The Truth about Lying" by Judith Viorst. Copyright © 1981 by Judith Viorst. Originally appeared in *Redbook.* Reprinted by permission of Lescher & Lescher, Ltd. All rights reserved.

"Growing Up Asian in America" by Kesaya E. Noda from *Making Waves* by Asian Women United. Copyright © 1989 by Kesaya E. Noda. Reprinted by permission of the author.

"The Ways of Meeting Oppression" by Martin Luther King, Jr. Reprinted by arrangement with The Heirs to the Estate of Martin Luther King, Jr., c/o Writer's House as agent for the proprietor, New York, NY. Copyright © 1958 Dr. Martin Luther King, Jr.; copyright renewed 1986 Coretta Scott King.

"Wired's Geekster Handbook: A Field Guide to the Nerd Underground" by Troy Brownfield. Copyright © 2008 Condé Nast Publications. All rights reserved. Originally published in *Wired.* Reprinted by permission.

Excerpt from "No Sea, Plenty of Sand" by Paul Tolme in *Newsweek,* November 21, 2005. Copyright © 2005 Newsweek, Inc. Reprinted by permission of Paul Tolme, www.paultolme.com.

"Hold the Mayonnaise" by Julia Alvarez. Copyright © 1992 by Julia Alvarez. First published in *The New York Times Magazine,* January 12, 1992. Reprinted by permission of Susan Bergholz Literary Services, New York, NY and Lamy, NM. All rights reserved.

"Juvenile Injustice" by Angie Cannon from *U.S. News and World Report,* August 9, 2004. Copyright © 2004 U.S. News and World Report, L. P. Reprinted with permission.

"Boy Brains, Girl Brains" by Peg Tyre in *Newsweek,* September 19, 2005. Copyright © 2005 Newsweek, Inc. All rights reserved. Used by permission.

"Letter to the Editor" by Renee Salinger Audette in *Dallas Morning News,* July 23, 2002. Reprinted by permission of the author.

"Why I Dread Black History Month" by Wayne M. Joseph in *Newsweek,* February, 1994. Reprinted by permission of the author.

"The Case for Torture Warrants" by Alan M. Dershowitz. Copyright © Alan Dershowitz. Reprinted by permission of the author.

"Torture Warrants?" by Harvey A. Silverglate from *The Boston Phoenix,* December 6–13, 2001. Reprinted by permission of the author.

Excerpt from "Smart Moms, Hard Choices" by Peg Tyre from *Newsweek,* March 6, 2006. Copyright © 2006 Newsweek, Inc. All rights reserved. Used by permission.

Copyright page and title page from *The Conscience of a Liberal* by Senator Paul Wellstone. Copyright © 2001 by Paul David Wellstone. Used by permission of Random House, Inc.

TOC and first page of article, "My Learning Disability: A (Digressive) Essay" by Andrea Freud Lowenstein, in *College English,* vol. 66 (6), July 2004. Copyright © 2004 by the National Council of Teachers of English. Reprinted by permission of National Council of Teachers of English.

Front page of *The New York Times,* March 7, 2006. Copyright © 2006 The New York Times. All rights reserved. Used by permission.

"Coca-Cola and Coco Frio" from *City of Coughing and Dead Radiators* by Martin Espada. Copyright © 1993 by Martin Espada. Used by permission of W. W. Norton & Company, Inc.

"A Gathering of Deafs" by John Heaviside in *Olive Tree Review, 8,* Fall 1989. Published by *Olive Tree Review,* Hunter College, City University of New York. Reprinted by permission of the author.

INDEX